EARLY GREEK POETRY AND PHILOSOPHY

HERMANN FRÄNKEL

Early Greek Poetry
and Philosophy

A history of Greek epic, lyric, and prose
to the middle of the fifth century

Translated by Moses Hadas and James Willis

A HELEN AND KURT WOLFF BOOK
HARCOURT BRACE JOVANOVICH
NEW YORK AND LONDON

880.9
F

Library of Congress Cataloging in Publication Data

Fränkel, Hermann Ferdinand, 1888-
Early Greek poetry and philosophy.

"A Helen and Kurt Wolff book."
Translation of Dichtung und Philosophie des frühen Griechentums.
1. Greek literature—History and criticism.
1. Title
PA3079. F713   1975   880'. 9'001   74–10724
ISBN 0-15-127190-9

First American edition 1975

B C D E

Contents

Translator's Preface

The translation of *Dichtung und Philosophie des frühen Griechentums* was first undertaken by the late Professor Moses Hadas, and all will regret that his untimely death prevented him from completing the task. He left behind him a typescript translation of the first 273 pages—up to the end of the chapter on Solon. I have carried on the rendering from there to the end, and have revised the first part, which had not received the *secundae curae* which Professor Hadas would have given to it if he had lived.

I have generally rendered into verse the translations from the Greek poets, since Professor Fränkel's lively renderings into German seemed too striking and characteristic a feature to be neglected in presenting the book to an English-speaking public. The exceptions to this practice have been the lyric poets, since I did not believe that English Sapphics or Alcaics could be recognized as a verse form. To avoid the danger that successive translations might move too far from the original text, I have consulted in almost all cases the Greek from which Professor Fränkel was translating. A debt to Diels' *Vorsokratiker* and to Farnell's translation of Pindar will be obvious to the reader.

JAMES WILLIS

PUBLISHER'S NOTE

The publisher's thanks are due to Dr.
Sabine MacCormack for editorial
supervision of this book at all stages,
and for preparing the index

Preface

The present work is addressed to laymen as well as to specialists. It attempts to present in readable form the history of Greek literature from Homer to Pindar. Less important authors are disregarded, as are those beyond our interpretative grasp because too little of their works have survived. Another consideration led me to exclude the drama of Epicharmus, Phrynichus, and Aeschylus: a satisfactory treatment would have overreached the intended compass of the book.

Numerous original texts will be presented here in translation and discussed in detail. What we are studying is their content and climate of ideas, their artistic form, and the function of a given work in contemporary life. At the same time, we are also trying to exploit the texts as documents of their age. To ascertain in its essential features the frame of mind peculiar to the epoch, and to follow up the changes it underwent in the course of time, has been one of my principal concerns, and the procedure I adopted was designed for this purpose. The rather general and abstract notions used to describe the spirit of the era will be less likely to melt into vague ambiguities if they stand before the reader's eyes side by side with the concrete material from which these notions are extracted, while their light in turn clarifies the deeper import of what the texts happen to say. By this method, in and through the literary products of the period, it ought to be possible to delineate with some degree of accuracy the important initial phase of our western civilization.

On the historical perspective basic to this book some remarks will be found in its opening and concluding chapters. Its aim is not to examine the early period of the Greeks as observed by one who holds the classical period in mind and expects to witness the nation's first faltering steps on its way to that ultimate goal. In such a view (which may be legitimate in a framework with a different orientation) Greek man of the early period must appear as a person who is not quite sure who he is and how he is supposed to act, but nevertheless dutifully prepares the ground for the higher ends of history. Actually, the Greeks of that epoch had an uncommonly clear vision of their own situation and a strong will to translate those ideas into real life. Our aim, then, is to interpret the age, in its entirety as well as in each of its various stages, just as it presented itself in its own eyes; its values will be sought where it placed them itself, regardless of whether later successors continued to cultivate them or allowed them to languish and die. With such an approach, the shifting panorama of history, while losing some of its attractive orderliness of progression, will acquire, it is hoped, a richer diversity and a sharper realism. Among other things it will be shown how after the 'epic' age, the 'archaic' came forward in violent and deliberate opposition to its predecessor; even so, the classical period in its turn did not spontaneously arise out of a logical development of archaic thought, but was set on its course by protesting reformers.

The continuity of literary genres, whose autonomy has sometimes been overemphasized, is here subordinated to the flow of historical currents. I have tried to make clear, for instance, how the contemporaries Simonides and Xenophanes struck out in a similar direction in their different literary media, or how the philosopher Heraclitus with his doctrine of opposites gave a new theoretical foundation to a mode of thinking and feeling which had played a dominant role in poetry for generations.

Evenness of treatment has not been pursued any more than completeness of any sort. I have rather wished, in discussing each author, to offer whatever appeared most appropriate and useful. Thus few passages of Homer are quoted because the Iliad and Odyssey are available for every one to read and appreciate on his own; on the other hand much of Pindar is translated and commented upon in detail. All translations are meant to serve only as props; I am well aware that their quality is uneven. Preference was given throughout to the closest possible rendering of the immediate textual meaning. Key words which have no equivalent in a modern tongue are occasionally represented by varying circumlocutions. Harsh turns of phrase were not avoided if a smoother rendering would have entailed a deceptive anachronism.

Phrases however which sound anachronistic when put into the mouth of an early Greek writer, may be admissible, or even necessary, when we are no longer translating the text but analyzing its underlying ideas for our own benefit. It seems obvious to me, for instance, that in order to understand certain passages from Hesiod, we cannot help speaking of Being and Not-Being, as Parmenides did centuries after Hesiod, or of Actuality and Potentiality, as Aristotle did in a still more advanced period and frame of mind. I do not adhere to the doctrine that we have no right to ascribe to a thinker a notion for the unequivocal expression of which he possessed and used no specific tool. Quite to the contrary: it is perfectly normal for this or that concept to have existed in a person's mind, in a less definitive form, long before someone else couched it in dry and set philosophical phraseology. Hesiod's creative thought operated in the medium of myth; he did not just play with mythical tales and mythical descriptions that held no ulterior meaning for him. Thus we are prepared to find in his writings views waiting for us to translate them into our own medium. A realization that it is easy to mistranslate, foisting upon the ancient thinker concepts alien to him, must not prevent us from following up clues where we see them clearly pointed in a definite direction. I should only wish that the reader, after any such digression into the province of a later age, revert to the text from which we started, reading suitably back into it whatever he has gained on his excursion, and leaving the final word to no other than the original author.

Many more controversial points are involved in the material with which we are dealing. Yet, for the sake of brevity and a clearer organization, much of what this book proposes is rather suggested than argued out in full, or tacitly implied by mere arrangement and grouping. Since the texts have all been worked over by me time after time, I believe I can for a number of passages offer novel interpretations, without always explaining the reasons why I have adopted them; the scholar, I hope, will nevertheless see what was in my mind.

I have made fuller use of scholarly literature than the express citations would indicate; these name only a selection of the writings to which I am indebted. Moreover, ideas cannot be neatly catalogued and labelled, and at any given time certain views are afloat that one seems to inhale from the surrounding atmosphere. But I have doubtless overlooked or neglected to consult many publications by which my book might have profited greatly; there is more specialist literature afoot than the individual would be able to absorb in a multiple lifetime. My own publications are cited without their author's name. To my *Wege und Formen frühgriechischen Denkens* (second edition, Munich 1960; here abbreviated *Frühgriech. Denken*) I have had to refer more frequently than I should have liked. The articles collected in that volume have largely served as preliminaries for this present book, and thus much of what is given a fleeting mention here was more adequately exposed there.

Finally, I should like to call attention to 'Index A', which will be found near the end of the volume. From its basic function as a repertory of page numbers, this Index has eventually been elaborated to the point where it is more or less readable, in the hope that the brief survey can now stand as a semi-independent adjunct; it will however be understood that the summary condensation cannot but oversimplify the complex facts. The purpose of such an appendix is self-explanatory. While in the body of the book, with its consecutive account of authors and works, our individual observations are isolated and widely scattered, the Index brings together certain results of our diverse inquiries under practicable rubrics, and in a systematic order. If some of them in their changed environment exhibit a different complexion and reveal a novel facet, they will thereby not lose their identity but rather be more fully defined.

Preparation of the book has occupied me, with interruptions, for a great number of years. It was first published, under the title *Dichtung und Philosophie des frühen Griechentums*, at New York in 1951 by the American Philological Association, with the generous, and by no means merely financial, assistance of that Association. Eleven years later a new edition, extensively revised, was brought out by C. H. Becksche Verlagsbuchhandlung in Munich, Germany. The present English rendering of the Munich edition is due to the initiative and persistent endeavors of the late Kurt Wolff and of Mrs. Helen Wolff, and to the labors of two translators, the late Professor Moses Hadas of New York, who worked on the initial sections, and Professor James Willis of Nedlands, Australia, who also revised what had been done by Professor Hadas. The author is delighted to see his work made accessible to the English-speaking public.

PALO ALTO, CALIFORNIA   APRIL 1968

I

Early Greek Literature: Survival and Ostensible Origin

For us Greek literature begins with the Homeric *Iliad* and *Odyssey*. Why, unlike the literatures of other peoples, does it start at once with such brilliant and mature creations? Why does it not crawl painfully into view out of murky depths, gradually gaining sureness of form and clarity of content? Why are the cruder and duller early stages, which must have existed in Greece as in other lands, not known to us and not preserved?

Of the writings of ancient times we today possess some which have never been lost, and some which had been forgotten and lost to sight and then recovered. Our knowledge of ancient Babylonian, ancient Egyptian, or Old High German literature is based exclusively upon documents of the second category. Here blind chance determined what it would deny us or what it would yield into our hands. The intrinsic value of the work is not a factor. With Greek literature it is different. The Greek tradition has never been wholly severed in our western world, and hence many of its writings have found readers— and consequently copyists and later printers—in uninterrupted succession down to our own day. Our possession of such writings is due not to the accident of physical preservation of materials or to the finder's luck of researchers, but rather to the lively interest which the book has been able to arouse in a long succession of generations, from the day it was first published until the present. Only books of some real worth can be preserved in this way. Of the literature with which our book is concerned there have reached us in this fashion only the Homeric *Iliad* and *Odyssey* (each in twenty-four 'books,' that is sections of up to a thousand lines or so), three books of Hesiod, one book of Homeric Hymns, two books of Theognis, and four books of the lyrics of Pindar. All else perished because at some point in antiquity or the Middle Ages interest waned. All that was able

I

to maintain itself until the Renaissance was saved permanently.

To sketch even an outline of the history of early Greek literature would be impossible if fragments at least of the lost works had not come down to us. Many later authors of antiquity whose writings we do possess cite pieces of ancient texts more or less verbatim, with or without telling us the context of the quotation. These fragments are indeed mostly very short; but the early literature is so compact, and its form is in such close harmony with its thought, that much may often be deduced from a few words. The choice of fragments is determined by the personal interests of the author citing them. Athenaeus' voluminous *Deipnosophistae* deals with usages at dinner parties in earlier centuries, and so it comes about that our fragments concerned with eating and drinking are particularly numerous. A book of the grammarian Apollonius Dyscolus deals with pronouns in the ancient tongue and the dialects, and cites lines of verse in which pronominal forms occur. Systematic citations and references in which the content of works lost to us is faithfully represented are available only for the philosophical writings of our period. In the school of Aristotle works of the older philosophers were systematically excerpted, but only from the point of view of their relationship to Aristotelian problems. In modern times all this widely scattered fragmentary material has been carefully brought together, and no increment of new material from this source is to be expected.

In recompense a new mine of Greek tradition has been opened up during the past century. Excavations in Egypt have brought Greek papyri[1] to light in such abundance that scholarship cannot keep pace. The majority of the texts are nonliterary—litigation, accounts, letters, and the like; but some part of the papyri derives from manuscripts of books, and of these some contain early Greek texts. Among others the papyri have vouchsafed us fragments of Sappho and Alcaeus, a large piece of Alcman, paeans of Pindar, and a generous quantity of the poems of Bacchylides. Since papyrus is brittle and apt to crumble, completely preserved poems are a rare exception; most of the shreds which are recovered contain only fragments and parts of lines, and to complete and interpret and identify them requires patient labor. The results are nevertheless invaluable, and we may be confident that a constant increment of

---

[1] Writing 'paper' was manufactured out of the stalks of papyrus plants; because of the dry climate of Egypt this material resists decay. After the foundation of Alexandria by Alexander the Great, Egypt was extensively hellenized; the older Greek literature was widely read and circulated in books or, more precisely, papyrus rolls.

new material in the future will enrich our knowledge, widen our horizons, and clarify our views.

The Greek papyri found in Egypt were written, at the earliest, toward the end of the fourth century B.C., for it was at this time that the hellenization of Egypt began. Hence all older literature which was not preserved and transmitted down to that period by the Greeks themselves is definitely lost. It was the Greeks who exercised the first choice of what was not to perish at day's end. The sifting was oriented otherwise than among other civilizations. Other nations have preserved sacred books out of gray antiquity verbatim because they believed the text was a revelation which might not be altered. Or they preserved cultsongs, prayers, magic formulae, or laws in their precise formulations because they believed that to change the form would disrupt the magic or render the law ineffective. But the Greeks were no worshipers of the letter in their creeds, their rituals, or their laws. Always and in all areas they expected to devise the appropriate expression anew while preserving the desired meaning. Everything therefore remained fluid: and since in the early period to which we now address ourselves value was placed not on the individual style of the particular artist but rather on the quality of the work, there was no occasion for preserving texts unaltered, except in a single situation—where a particular artistic form approached the end of its career. Only if nothing but progressive degeneration was to be expected did it make sense to halt historical change and transmit works of literature to succeeding generations in their actual state. So it comes about that the Greeks did not preserve the antique and primitive; for example, they abandoned their earliest lyric poetry. Instead they made their national literature begin where their first leading genre, epic, had just left its last and greatest height behind and had begun its descent.

That is why for posterity Homer alone stands at the beginning of Greek literature. Since the gaze of a man looking backward is prone to perceive a teleological order in what he sees, the Greeks themselves constructed a theory according to which all Greek literature, indeed Greek education and civilization as a whole, had its origin in Homer and only in Homer; and modern scholarship is similarly inclined to follow such views. The very great influence of Homer on all succeeding generations of Greeks is beyond question; but it is nevertheless wrong to believe that a straight line leads from Homer across early Greek culture to the classical age of the Greeks.

Such a picture is basically unhistorical. Straight-line development may in fact occur at best in narrowly defined areas of human activity, but never for a true historical whole. No generation is content merely to supply the preliminaries for its descendants and to leave to them the ends for which they wish to employ them. Insofar as an age aims at permanence, it desires to perpetuate its own tendencies; and insofar as these tendencies prevail, they are changed by their victory. Mainly, however, every period seeks its own perfection and its own system. This system must be demolished by its successors in order to build their own, for every essential alteration brings others in its train. What the successors can use they do not employ in the sense of their fathers, but do violence to their legacy in order to adapt it to their own ends. The historian of an epoch must therefore not regard it as a preparation for what is to come. How an epoch influenced the future, and how it was constituted and understood itself, are very different things.

The early Greek period, as we know it from its writings from Homer to the middle of the fifth century, lived its own self-sufficient life and thought its own independent thoughts. It brought to maturity many high values, which perished with it because classical Greece could no longer cope with them. In the following pages we shall lay special stress upon those spiritual and artistic values which are characteristic of the early Greek period and have never attained equal beauty and strength elsewhere.

In the span before us—we may style it the heroic age of Greece— things were often stormy and violent. Positions won through hard struggle were soon surrendered because development suddenly changed direction. Even within the stretch from Homer to Pindar the principle that the line of historical progress never coincides with the shortest distance between beginning and end is applicable. Immediately after Homer there follows so sharp a break that we are compelled to divide the early Greek period into two ages, the 'epic' and the 'archaic.' Here literary history is in step with art history, in which similarly the geometric period is followed by the 'orientalizing' style and the new archaic period of plastic art.

In the Homeric epics we can see for ourselves that the position they occupy signifies not a beginning or middle but an end. Instead of continuing Homeric poetry and attitudes with slight deviations, the archaic period which followed rebelled against them and began almost wholly anew. This revolution was one of the most dramatic turns in the entire history of the Greek spirit. One who ignores this phenomenon and instead sees Hellenism marching armed and steadfast upon a once determined path, closes his eyes to a singular feature of Greek courage, which was capable of searching out and attaining a clear new path in the midst of dark confusion.

The archaic age is robbed of its proper character if we harmonize it unduly with the two ages which preceded and followed it. But even Homeric poetry itself is inadequately understood if we derive all later Hellensim from it. It then becomes a junction for all the lines that diverge from it. But Homeric epic never deliberately chose its position as a center of gravity for all the forces and potentialities of early Hellensim. Rather, at the ostensible inception of Greek literature there stands a poem which gives extreme and one-sided expression to certain peculiarities of Greek character and suppresses others with partisan bias. For example, there is virtually nothing in Homer of Greek philosophy and its preliminaries; and Homeric religion expresses only one side of Greek piety, but that one with overwhelming emphasis. During the entire span of their national existence the Greeks suffered from this state of affairs. The Homeric images of the gods were always current coin for them, but accepted always with misgivings.

II

Homer

(a) *The Singers and their Epics*

Of the many early Greek heroic epics only two, the *Iliad* and the *Odyssey*, have come down to us. Despite their great length—15,000 and 12,000 hexameters respectively—both poems are only parts of a larger whole, the Trojan cycle. The complete cycle consisted of eight epics, which went together without gap or overlap. Five epics, of which the *Iliad* was the second, recounted the Trojan War from its beginning until the capture of the city; the sixth, *Nostoi*, reported the homecomings of those who sailed to Troy, with the exception of Odysseus; the seventh was the *Odyssey*; and the eighth dealt with the further travels of Odysseus and his death. The *Iliad* and *Odyssey* were obviously the principal pieces in the series. The *Iliad* alone with its twenty-four books was larger than the other four Trojan War epics together (twenty-two books), and the *Odyssey*, also in twenty-four books, was five times as long as the poem which dealt with the home-coming of all the other heroes (five books). Along with the Trojan there were other cycles, notably a Theban one.

According to tradition the *Iliad* and *Odyssey* were composed by a wayfaring singer named Homer who came from the Ionian East. Other epics were ascribed to other poets; often the ascription varies. Homer's name appears more often than any other, and is also used collectively for all epic poets.

This is all that the earliest tradition can tell us of Homer. There are no external data to determine how far the person and authorship of Homer are historical. It is possible that tradition, simplifying matters as the Greeks often did, used the name of Homer to embrace a whole literary age.

'Homer' looks like a genuine personal name, not an artificially invented symbol. Probably, therefore, a man called Homer was concerned with the composing of epics in some way which gave occasion

6

for linking his name with the works forever. Nonetheless Homer cannot be the author of both principal epics because the *Iliad* and the *Odyssey* differ too widely in language, style, and thought to be ascribed to one and the same author; here the tradition is mere legend. Furthermore, the Homeric epics arose under conditions in which one cannot speak of literary property in our sense. Every epic singer freely took over the work of his predecessors and used it as he wished. Hence the question of Homer's authorship comes down to asking what part he took in the composition. Two possibilities are open. Either a singer of this name laid hold of the fluid tradition with particular energy and impressed it so strongly with the stamp of his individual art that later poets, in abiding memory of his contribution, designated and transmitted as Homer's the work which they recited and eventually wrote down. Or, secondly, the *Iliad* and *Odyssey* entered history under Homer's name because Homer gave one or both of the poems its final form and its definitive version. The further question must remain open for all time: Did Homer change much or little in the epics when he put the last touch upon them? Was he a creative spirit, a skillful reviser, a virtuoso performer, a busy copyist, or perhaps only the latest editor whom no successor deprived of his title of honor?

Since we have so little information, sober criticism cries halt when it comes to questions concerning the person of Homer and his share in the *Iliad* and the *Odyssey*. Of no single line in the epics of 'Homer' can we say that it is surely Homer's. We know nothing of the idiosyncrasies of the man, and if we use his name here it signifies nothing more than the notion of epic composition in general as it presents itself to us in the *Iliad* and *Odyssey*.

But this does not imply that no individuality can still be seen in the epics. Not only does early Greek epic as such have a pronounced character, but within the epics portions stand out by reason of their peculiarities, so that we have grounds for ascribing certain complexes (as for example the Telemachy) to individual poets. There is no doubt that epic poetry profited from the participation of numerous individuals. This resulted, however, in various kinds of unevenness in execution, for it is practically impossible for a new piece to fit with hair's breadth precision into older matter: singers were not bound by a rule of strict consistency, which would have fettered their creative spirit. On the other hand, the incongruities provide us with occasional insights into the complicated prehistory of both epics, for close examination reveals clear signs of additions, omissions, or alterations in a piece. On this basis scholars have often tried to work out the prehistory of either of the epics stratum by stratum. Some of these reconstructions—those that are tasteful, free from pedantry, and rich in ideas—help us to understand the genre and the particular texts because they show by specific example how our epics might have taken shape stage by stage; but in no case can we believe that the development was precisely as assumed. For probability sinks rapidly when one conjecture hangs upon another and the number of equal possibilities becomes legion.

It is only rarely given us, therefore, to see behind the individual epics; but a glance into them reveals multiplicity and movement. Many parts are obviously more modern than others and hence presumably younger. Thus the *Odyssey*, taken as a whole, is decidedly more modern than the *Iliad*, taken as a whole. The striking difference in attitudes between the older epic and the younger takes us at once into a world of sweeping historical changes. Even if the prehistory of the epics is shut off from us in detail, the contradictory forces within the poems compel us to consider a broad vista of historical events.

Even the artistic practice from which our epics are distilled is one of which change and movement are characteristic. Whereas literature is normally fashioned with a view to completion and permanent retention of form, epic poetry remained fluid and transient by the intention of its creators. This is a kind of poetry which is poised, phrase by phrase, verse by verse, between enduring tradition and momentary improvisation. This lends it a particularly fascinating charm, which continues fresh and effective even when the book is eventually reduced to writing. To appreciate the special quality of Homeric epic we must therefore picture for ourselves the peculiar artistic practice out of which it sprang and for which it was adopted. Secondly, we must ask what changes were produced by the reduction of a fluid tradition to a rigid book-text. Carrying the art over into an alien medium was bound to have consequences.

The general conditions under which the ancient epics came into being can be illuminated from three angles. First, the epics themselves contain certain information concerning singers and epic recitations; second, later Greek tradition has much to tell of ancient epic poets; and third, so-called folk epic among other peoples provides analogies. What the Homeric epic itself tells us is especially valuable because it is authentic; but it leaves very many gaps. A much richer picture is sketched by the late biographies of Homer and the lively *Contest of Homer and Hesoid*; but these writings are romance rather than history. The fullest picture is that provided by comparative studies in folklore, but we cannot know how much of this may be applied to Homeric art. In any case it is better to confine ourselves to a single analogy than to mix individual traits out of various cultures. Best suited to our purpose is the Serbo-Croatian epic, for it is nearest our cultural milieu, it reaches down into the present, and it has been thoroughly investigated by a scholar who was himself a Slav, Mathias Murko.[1] Naturally, we shall not overlook the great differences. In literary quality the South Slavic epics are far inferior to the Greek, both in content and in form. Nevertheless the analogy is of great value. Confronting a tangible reality affords a more accurate picture than theorizing at a desk.

Whereas the written book must seek its readers individually and privately, ancient Greek epic addressed itself to wide circles which hailed it with passionate interest. It developed among the upper social classes and flourished predominantly, if not exclusively, among them (cf. Murko 173, 25). It was poetry for entertainment, hence 'pure' art; it had neither ritual function nor any other objective. Its place in life was leisure. At meals and particularly after meals, with drink and dessert, men sat together and listened to the recital hour-long and night-long. It was always a single person who recited, and the audience heard him spell-bound, enchanted, wholly absorbed in listening—thus the singers of our *Odyssey* (17, 518–21)[2] describe it. The song of the Sirens who enticed voyagers and ensnared them to their destruction—this song is an epic recitation, an account of the Trojan War and of all else that takes place on 'the earth that nourishes many' (*Od.* 12, 189ff.); such power does epic song wield over the hearts of its hearers. The modern witness can report the same of South Slavic recitations.[3] Words are dominant in

[1] Murko's work is published in *Sitzungsberichte der Wiener Akademie, phil.-hist. Klasse*, 173, No. 3 (1913); 176, No. 2 (1915); 179, No. 1 (1915) (hereafter cited only by volume); summary in *Neue Jahrbücher* 1919, 273ff. Murko's work was carried forward by H. Geseman, Milman Parry, and A. B. Lord (*Trans. Amer. Philol. Assn.*, 67, 69, 70), and research is still in progress. Likewise the modern Greek folk epic has been studied and compared with the Homeric. So, for example, the chant of a Cretan bard has been recorded on tape; it tells of the attack of German parachute troops on Crete in 1941 and celebrates the defenders who met their death. To our unschooled ears the recital sounds monotonous and spiritless, but the singer is so moved by thoughts of his fallen friends that his voice fails him and he falls silent in the midst of his song. Parallel phenomena the world over are traced by C. M. Bowra, *Heroic Poetry* (New York and London, 1952). This instructive book sets forth the typical traits of the genre which recur in many places, and also the variability of this type of poetry among different nations. See now also A. B. Lord, *The Singer of Tales* (Cambridge, Mass., 1960).

[2] During the singing a man could discuss confidential matters because general attention was focused on the singer (*Od.* 8, 83–95; 17, 358; 1, 156–327).

[3] The hearers are singularly attentive ('quiet as in a mosque') and follow the course of the action with a feeling of participation. The serious, respectable, and restrained *begs* sit silently, gradually a certain excitement is perceptible in their expressions, eyes light up, one and another smiles . . .' (Murko 173, 27).

this 'song,' which is rather a *recitativo parlante*. The singer accompanies
himself on a stringed instrument. All verses have the same structure—
ten syllables among the South Slavs, six units of either two or three
syllables among the Greeks. There are professional singers, but many
members of the company are familiar with the art. Later the
professional element was strengthened, and social and other differences developed between the singer who lived by his art and the
public that received the entertainment he offered. In the earlier
period, however, there was only a homogeneous circle which provided its own entertainment through the voice of its specially gifted
members. Epic singers are never mentioned in the *Iliad*; only once
are heroic lays sung, and that by Achilles. He sings to dispel his
long ennui while he is resentful and refuses to participate in battle.
He sings for his own amusement[4] and his sole auditor is his friend
and comrade Patroclus, who will take his turn when Achilles grows
weary. Though there is no singing elsewhere in the *Iliad*, the heroes
do occasionally tell stories of their own and their kinsmen's lives; to
some degree these are preliminary stages of heroic song. In those
days the heroes themselves recounted their deeds. So the poets of the
Iliad saw the picture of the olden days, when their own class had not
yet come into being.

Things are different in the *Odyssey*, which is younger and more
inclined to reflect the life of its own times than to sketch a picture of
the remote past. Men at their drink are entertained by professional
singers. And whereas in the *Iliad* a man like the aged Nestor or the
aged Phoenix may occasionally speak of earlier times, in the *Odyssey*
the principal hero is himself a great storyteller and makes ample use of
his skill within the epic, whether in the court of the Phaeacian king,
where he enchants the gentry, or in the bare hut of the swineherd.
When the epic singer delivered such passages and rendered the long
narrative of Odysseus in epic verse and style, the situation reported
fused with the present. The singer became Odysseus, whose role he
enacted, and his audience felt themselves to be Phaeacians or 'divine
swineherds'—humble and needy, to be sure, but of noble temper.
Many might even dream that, like Eumaeus, they were truly and
rightfully of royal birth and that only a contrary fate was responsible
for the poverty and dependence of their hard lives.

But the similarity goes much further. Odysseus is not only skillful
in telling tales, 'knowledgeable as a singer' (11, 368; cf. also 17, 518);
as a needy wayfarer he must depend, as the singers themselves do,
upon the charity of those who receive him. Small wonder, then, that

---

[4] This too is often reported of the South Slavs; for example, a man may recite
epic songs to himself while riding or to shorten the tediousness of a long journey.

the singers of the *Odyssey* were especially sympathetic toward their hero and identified themselves with him, and that they even transferred to him and his tale items of their own experience which are wholly inappropriate to the story. In this way we receive indirectly an intimate insight into the life and character of the wayfaring singers, particularly of its darker side. For when the singers describe their own class directly, they bring the bright side forward and depict the ideal. Demodocus and Phemius alike are described as permanent court singers; it must have been the dream of every wayfarer to be able to remain permanently at the same royal court and to be treated as respectfully as those two were.

But surely the reality was very different. The singer moved from place to place. He stood before many strangers' doors, never knowing whether they would open to him.[5] If he were admitted, he probably had to remain at the threshold at first, the place of beggars, and wait till he was invited to sit in the room. So far most of the time we see the table of the lords in the king's house at Ithaca through the eyes of Odysseus, from the perspective of the threshold. In gratitude for hospitality the wayfarer had to accommodate himself to every whim of the master and his guests in order to amuse the company.[6]

This irksome humiliating treatment must have been experienced by the singers with all the greater bitterness because they considered themselves superior to their temporary employers in education and manners. Being much traveled, they had, like Odysseus, 'learned the minds of many men' (1, 3); every page of the *Odyssey* shows their subtle distinctions. In particular they had occasion to study and form moral judgments upon the attitudes of various individuals toward wayfarers. This interest they projected into the action of the *Odyssey* to such a degree as to produce contradictions.

According to the story of the *Odyssey* the suitors were all slain, without exception, because they wooed a woman whose husband might still be alive and because they took forcible possession of a stranger's house, wasted its wealth, and played the master in it. That is the simple sense of the story, and Penelope, if anyone, should have so understood it. But when she receives word of the destruction of the suitors and cannot yet believe that her husband has returned, she thinks that some god must have slain the suitors because in their arrogance they showed no honor to strangers who came to them

---

[5] It is indicative that people in the *Odyssey* very often listen to what is going on behind a wall (1, 328; 10, 221; 17, 492–506, 541f.; 20, 92, 105, 387–89; 23, 148); once new arrivals on the outside hear and smell that a large meal is in progress inside (17, 269–71).

[6] Cf. Odysseus' boxing match with Irus for the amusement of the suitors.

(23, 62). Once even Odysseus expresses himself in the same sense
(22, 413). In the preceding episode we are told: 'Athene aroused
Odysseus to beg bread of every man so that he could ascertain which
were decent and which lawless' (17, 360); but the poet continues:
'But even so none was spared destruction'—admitting that the
separation of suitors into good and bad runs counter to the sense of the
story (similarly in 18, 155). The wayfaring singers felt themselves to
be inspectors of the many people they came to know in the practice
of their profession. Once an understanding suitor makes a significant
remark about Odysseus: 'Who knows whether the stranger is not a
god who goes through the world in this guise in order to inspect men's
misdeeds and their righteousness?' (17, 483).[7]

How the performances of the singers took place we can deduce
from what the *Odyssey* reports concerning the singing of songs and the
telling of tales. For what we read in the epic concerning the relationship of narrators and their auditors we may reasonably transfer to
the singers of epic and their audience.[8]

The singer's performance did not follow a fixed program but, until
the epic became a rigid book-text, it preserved the social character
of a free conversation. It is conjectured that rather less than corresponds to a single book of the epic was delivered continuously and
without pause.[9] After a short piece[10] the singer broke off, and during
the interruption the listeners poured and drank their wine (*Od.* 8, 89)
and spoke with one another and with the singer.[11] During the
interruption the singer received friendly words of thanks and praise,
or perhaps a tidbit of food, a garment, or the promise of a present
(cf. *Od.* 11, 384ff.), together with a request to sing on (*Od.* 8, 87–91):[12]

[7] According to 3, 265, Agamemnon engaged a singer as a sort of chaplain for
his wife when he went off to war.

[8] Two grounds justify the transfer. The epic poet depicts ideal narrators and
hearers, and for him the ideal modes are naturally those he himself practices.
Secondly, he delivers the stories told by his personages in epic form so that they
coincide with his own chant. Actually, the form is identical in both cases.

[9] The division of the epics into 24 books each was made later.

[10] *Od.* 8, 87–91 shows that during a recitation which included a single battle
scene (cf. 75–82) several pauses intervened. In *Iliad* 11 there are two pauses, only
80 verses apart (217/18 and 298/99), which are noted in the text. In general the
breaks and resumptions are not expressed in the text: they were improvised by
the singer.

[11] Cf. the interlude in the midst of a long narrative, *Od.* 3, 201–52 and 11,
333–84. The same is reported of the South Slavs: 'In the pauses the *begs* praised
their singer as the best of the Krajina, admired the heroes who left such fame as
to be glorified in song—a thing the greatest men of today do not attain. . . . In the
popular coffee-houses also men speak about the song and things connected with
it. (Murko 173, 27f.)

[12] Occasionally the hungry singer trades his poetry for food, passage by passage.

'Please tell us also this and that' (*Od.* 11, 370). Or the listeners might put questions like these: 'Say, how did Agamemnon die? Where was Menelaus, that he did not help him? Did Aegisthus behave dishonorably? Had Menelaus not yet returned home?' (*Od.* 3, 247). At the beginning of a new recital the singer might put a transitional question[13] himself (e.g., *Il.* 16, 692f.); or he might direct it to the Muse, that is, the tradition from which he received his knowledge. So the story proceeded by fits and starts, as long as the hearers were pleased (*Od.* 8, 90). If the hour grew too late for continuation it could be postponed for the next evening (cf. *Od.* 11, 328ff). In this way the same fabric could be spun out for weeks. When Odysseus was Aeolus' guest he told him all through a month 'of Troy, the ships of the Argives, and the return of the Achaeans' (10, 14). That is to say, he delivered the Trojan epic, out of which the catalogue of ships (*Il.* 2) was specially selected, and also the *Nostoi* (only a small part of the contents of which ought to have been familiar to Odysseus)—in a word, the entire Trojan cycle up to his own situation at the moment. This recital was kept in its channel by questions and materially supported by hospitable entertainment: 'And he [Aeolus] entertained me and asked me about each thing.' At Eumaeus' house Odysseus recounted his tale for three days 'without telling his sorrows to the end,' which is to say, exhausting his repertoire (*Od.* 17, 513).

When his audience's interest in the narrative of the professional singer began to lag, he had to leave his host and eke out a precarious existence until he could find a new refuge. It was therefore of great importance not to allow interest to slacken. At interludes in his delivery or when he stopped for the evening he managed the interruption so that it constituted no real conclusion. On the contrary, from the end of one section he glided quickly and unobtrusively to the interesting beginning of a new section and broke off after the new beginning.[14] One seeks in vain for an artistically satisfying conclusion

In *Od.* 7, 213–31 Odysseus interrupts the narrative of his woes (213f.) with a remark: his suffering belly leaves him no rest to think of his woes; he must first have his supper. The passage does not fit into the context in which it now stands, but it throws light on a standard situation with a frankness elsewhere avoided. Cf. also the hint in *Od.* 14, 457ff.

[13] If desired, the singer could naturally skip (μεταβῆναι): cf. *Od.* 8, 492.

[14] Cf. passages cited in notes 10 and 11. The same applies to professional storytelling the world over. The framework narrative of *The Thousand and One Nights* reflects the anxiety of the Arabic storyteller over the flagging interest of his auditors. Scheherazade saves her life night after night by leaving her auditor intensely curious about the continuation. Similarly the framework narratives of the Turkish *Parrot-book* and of the Indian *Vetālapañcaviṃshatikā* pause at the moment of highest tension.

at the end of a large body of material in the epic or at the end of the whole. For practical reasons, and also in keeping with its own deliberate style, the artform is always calculated for continuation; it does not aim at formal conclusions in which its movement comes to a stop.

But there is a developed art of beginning, or of beginning anew after an interruption. Thus the poet's recital of the evening began, after a prayer or hymn (see p. 246, below), with a set proem. From many examples in both epics we can abstract the scheme basic to these proems. The singer (a) begins with a formal address to the host and others present, and (b) praises the hospitable board and the pleasures it provides. Such words include thanks for hospitality (though direct expression is tactfully avoided)—thanks indeed in the name of the entire company. From this point the singer makes his transition to his own designs; (b) 'How agreeable it is to sit at this richly spread table and listen to the singer, (c) as he reports the numerous afflictions and deeds of prowess which he knows how to describe skillfully, (d) how they all came about by divine dispensation. (e) Of the many deeds of Odysseus in the Trojan War, (f) I will recount that in which he . . .'[15]

The theme of the recitation (e) may also be announced by praying the Muse to sing of it (e.g., *Il.* 2, 484ff.), then a definite question is addressed to her (f), by means of which the narrative begins to move (e.g., *Il.* 1, 8; 2, 761f.; 11, 218ff.). The proems to both *Iliad* and *Odyssey* are constituted according to this plan, except that in the written book the address to the listeners and the reference to the hospitable board had to be omitted.

In its third member (c) the schema of the proems contains a commendatory indication of the beauty of the stories to come. Details vary, but the commendation always concludes with the thought that the narrative will deal with 'many afflictions.' In the first place, notice is given that the material will be abundant; so the opening of the *Iliad* speaks of a *thousand* woes and *many* souls; and the proem of the *Odyssey* speaks of the man *much* driven about, the cities

---

[15] The schema is especially obvious in the dry introduction of *Od.* 4, 235ff. Elsewhere we find (a) address—*Od.* 9, 2 and 15, 390; (b) praise of the occasion—*Od.* 9, 3–11; 15, 391–400 (cf. also 11, 373f. and 379 with anaphora like 15, 392f.), a twist to suit the present conditions, 14, 193–95; (c) will be dealt with shortly in the text; (d) 'according to the will of the gods'—*Il.* 1, 5; *Od.* 12, 190 (cf. 17, 119; 8, 82), 14, 198; 9, 15; 7, 242; 9, 38; 1, 327; 4, 236; (e) general statement of theme—*Od.* 4, 243; 3, 100/103ff. For 'Trojan War' there is a slight periphrasis— δήμῳ ἔνι Τρώων, ὅθι πήματα πάσχον Ἀχαιοί. (f) Narrowing to a specific theme—*Od.* 4, 242; 7, 243; 19, 171. In the first fragment of the rhapsode Xenophanes (see p. 326, below) (b) is particularly elaborated.

and minds of *many* men, and *many* woes upon the sea. Secondly, in the opening and elsewhere, the singer and narrator rarely gives his material a neutral name like information, story, or deeds; as a rule he designates them as afflictions, sorrowful woes, and the like. Of the war at Troy, the matter of the four war epics, Nestor in the *Odyssey* uses expressions like *miserable, woeful*, and continues, indicating the abundance of events, 'what mortal man could tell it all? Even if you stayed with me for many years and inquired in detail what misfortunes we suffered there, you would return to your home sated before you heard all' (*Od* 3, 103–19). Similarly, the content of the *Odyssey* is so described (*Od.* 23, 306):

> Then did Zeus-born Odysseus recount the pains and the sorrows
> Which he inflicted on men and those which he suffered in anguish.
> She took pleasure in hearing his tale, nor ever did slumber
> Fall on her eyelids till the whole long tale was related.

And before Odysseus tells his life story Eumaeus says to him (15, 398):

> We will take pleasure in recalling the past woes that beset us
> While eating and drinking at home, for a grief remembered gives pleasure
> When one has suffered much and seen many lands in one's travels.

What the Homeric singer aimed at was to arouse feelings of fear and of pity through imagined participation in tragic events[16]—fear more prominently in the older pieces and in the *Iliad*, and pity in the later parts and in the *Odyssey*. In the younger epic there is a general tendency toward sentimentality; people weep even in the greatest gladness (*Od.* 10, 415; 16, 213–19) and they 'enjoy' even laments for the dead (*Il.* 23, 10, 98; *Od.* 11, 212). When Odysseus hears the singer celebrate his own glory his face does not light up in happy pride, but he weeps—as a woman weeps whose husband is slain before her eyes and an enemy lays hands upon her shoulder to take her to slavery (*Od.* 8, 521; cf. also 8, 83ff. and 577–80). Hence only what is sorrowful is worth preservation in song (*Od.* 8, 579). In the *Iliad* Helen says of herself and Paris (6, 357): '—upon whom Zeus has imposed a heavy fate, so that we may become matter for song for men in the future.'

The most important characteristic of the unwritten bookless epic is the fluidity of tradition. At every performance the singer was at liberty to alter the text in any way; he could even recite a quite new text. In the written texts of the *Iliad* and the *Odyssey* this characteristic

---

[16] 'Even more interesting' (than what preceded) means, accordingly, 'more apt to arouse compassion'—*Od.* 11, 381; see also 12, 258. Cf. Murko 176, 21: 'Tears came sooner into the eyes of the old Muslims; they wept over their heroes.'

cannot find direct expression. All the more valuable for us, then, are
the observations which have been made in living epic. According to
Murko's testimony singers are able to improvise a new song in the
traditional style; for them song is, so to say, a language, in which
they are able to speak freely. As a rule, however, they recite existing
and familiar songs or materials (cf. *Od.* 1, 337ff.; 8, 74). Even so they
move about freely in their individual structures. 'The singers have
no fixed text; they always fashion their chants anew, though they
maintain they are always the same or that they delivered them as they
had "taken them up" or "heard them" . . . Huseinbeg Staroselać
demanded of his singer: "Praise the hero and praise his horse;
you're not going to buy it from him! . . .". The recording commission
prescribed that every text was to be written down before the sound
recording was made. Thereby I discovered that even the same singer
dictated quite small fragments of an epic chant (some twenty verses)
in one way, and after a few minutes differently in practising with the
gramophone horn, and again sung it differently at the recording.
Since I had stenographers available in my second journey I was able
to submit three, in one case even four, parallel texts. Deviations were
not limited to changing words or altering word order. Rather, whole
verses appeared in a wholly altered form or were omitted, so that,
for example, fifteen dictated verses yielded only eight in the phono-
graphic recording. A good singer from northwest Bosnia turned out
to give even the first verse quite differently three times. He dictated
"*Beg Osmanbeg rano podranio*" (Beg Osmanbeg arose early); in practicing with the horn: "*Beg Osmanbeg na bedjem izigje*" (B. O. walked out
on the wall); and at the recording "*Beg Osmanbeg gleda niz Posavlje*"
(B. O. looked down on the land of the Sava).[17] It was directly from
my experience with the recording that I drew the unqualified conclusion that all Serbo-Croatian epic songs as presented in books were
so sung or dictated only one single time' (Murko 1919, 285ff.). So
the compass of the 'same' song may vary greatly in size, because the
singer 'curtailed or lengthened it at will. He simply guided himself
by his listeners. Art goes in pursuit of bread, and may actually be
dependent upon the moods of such artists' (173, 18). 'So the Matica
Hrvatska [the Croatian Archive] had the song of a twenty-five-year
old convict recorded; it ran to more than 4,400 verses, whereas his
teacher's ran to about 1,500' (1919, 285).[18]

[17] Is it mere accident that the three versions represent three succeeding stages
of time (arose, walked on the wall, looked down in the valley) and that the opening
of the poem moved further in time during these repetitions?

[18] Obviously the prisoner did his best to lengthen the interruption of the
monotony of prison routine. In the area of Russian *bylina* two versions of the same

In the South Slav epic, therefore, every new recitation signifies a
new fashioning of the material, and we have no grounds to assume
that it was otherwise with the Homeric singers.[19] Nothing was
repeated verbatim, for the mind of the reciter did not repeat a text
mechanically, but reconstructed the story afresh.[20] Every epic
recitation was an active reinterpretation of traditional material.

In the process of this continuing transformation the poems gained
in length as well as depth. The tendency to length is inherent in the
character of epic art. The same events are constantly set forth with
increased precision and adorned with richer detail.[21] Apart from the
heroes of his tale each poet could introduce new minor personages or
develop more fully the minor personages already in the tradition.[22]
Similarly, new episodes could enter the general framework, for epic
has a natural tendency to forming additional episodes. The parts and
the whole to which they belonged were elaborated simultaneously
and with mutual influence.[23] As in all Greek creations so here too the
forces of strict organization beautifully balanced the tendency
toward expansion. Each of the Greek cycles has a simple basic idea

poem from the lips of the same singer are extant. In 1871 this very peasant
dictated to Hilferding (*Onĕshkija byliny*, Vol. 1, No. 63, zbornik 59) the song of
Suchman's heroism, captivity, and death which he had recited in 1860 to Rybnikov
(2nd ed., Moscow, 1910, Vol. 2, No. 148). The variations are greater than could
be expected. As a whole the second version is much worse. It is full of gaps, is
obscured by the insertion of an alien episode, and is more monotonous and lifeless
in presentation as in speech. But in details it is better and fuller.

[19] The word 'rhapsode' signifies 'inventor of songs', rather than 'stitcher of songs'.
Later reciters must have inherited this honorable title from their predecessors the
poets (cf. 'Hesiod,' fr. 265: ἐν νεαροῖς (!) ὕμνοις ῥάψαντες ἀοιδήν of the original composition of Homer and Hesiod). Cf. *Glotta* 14, 3; Marx, *Rhein. Mus.* 74, 399.

[20] Remembering the tradition and composing afresh thus coincided as an
inseparable operation for the singer. The 'Muse' represented both in common.
On the same ground the singers could believe in the truth of their poems.

[21] The epics grew in compass also from the circumstance that alien and hitherto
independent material was included in them. So, for example, the wandering
adventurer Odysseus was drawn into the circle of the heroes at Troy in early epic
times, though he had nothing to do with Troy originally.

[22] *Od.* 1, 95 could be rephrased, with some overemphasis, to say, 'And so that a
song might be sung of Telemachus' experiences also.'

[23] There is no ground for assuming that individual singers carried only portions
of the tale of Odysseus in their heads, without being able to recite the whole tale of
Odysseus in sequence. This disposes of the theory according to which Homer
created one or both of his epics from little epics or disconnected individual bits.
Our *Odyssey* was preceded by another *Odyssey* (cf. P. von der Mühll, *RE* Suppl. 7,
1939, p. 699); and our *Iliad* arranges various episodes from the Trojan cycle
anew, but not for the first time, within a general framework. According to W.
Schadewaldt, the treatment of Achilles in our *Iliad* was largely conceived after the
model of that part of the Trojan cycle which told of Achilles' victory over
Memnon and his death (*Von Homers Welt und Werk* 2 1951, pp. 155ff.).

which permeates every part. None is planless and amorphous, like
the *Mahābhārata*, and never is a series of unconnected stories forcibly
held together by a contrivance of purely external framework as in
The Thousand and One Nights.

Side by side with lengthening came deepening. The stage in which
heroes were differentiated only by their names and deeds did not
last long; soon each was endowed with special character which
corresponded with this special achievements. Similarly, causes and
motives were subsequently attributed to events and actions, where
previously the bare statement of facts had sufficed.[24] Such alterations gave the story a firmer bond; but it could also easily happen
that the superimposed motive did not agree with the existing material
at all points. Hence, as in any fluid production, the epics are in-
consistent at many points. New inconsistencies emerged from changes
in beliefs and customs and from developments in men's notions of
human nature. Hence much that had previously seemed simple
and right became improbable and objectionable. In order to accommodate the new beliefs, efforts were made to revise characters
and motives so far as possible. But however much the stories changed
in course of time, the singers themselves surely conceived of their
innovations not as wilful inventions but as intuitive interpretations of
tradition.

In the end the latest stage of formulation was followed by phenomena of weariness and reaction. The powerful forward march of
narrative began to halt, and space was found for treatments of mood
in which the substance of the story is sampled at leisure for its most
delicate nuances.[25] In this later stage there is nothing left for the
pictorial imagination to do for the principal personages and so it
occupies itself with the subsidiary figures. It sketches scenes in which
the center of the stage is occupied by the son of the hero or his aged
father, the household staff, the suitors, or the people of Ithaca helplessly torn between conflicting anxieties and inclinations.

Furthermore we now come to retroactive reactions. After the basic
line of the story has been followed through without additions, it seems
too matter-of-fact to yield further illumination and too familiar to
arouse excitement. There comes a time to relieve the inflexible mono-
lith of its rigidity and to restore to it at least a momentary motion.

[24] An obvious addition to the story of Odysseus' many sufferings by sea and of
the wrath of that element against the hero is the identification of Polyphemus,
whom Odysseus blinded, as Poseidon's son, thus providing a personal motive.

[25] For example, the charming idyl of Odysseus' sojourn with Eumaeus; or the
Telemachy with its abundance of interesting situations—which do not advance
the action of the *Odyssey* in the least. Aside from this consideration, the Telemachy
is meant to offer an edifying model of refined behavior.

Achilles fell before Ilium as a gallant warrior in the bloom of his youth: so much legend knows and tells, the listeners know it as well as the singer, even Achilles himself knows it, for his mother had told him so. How effective the shock, how liberating amidst a conviction of doom, when the hero cries out in anger that he will no longer risk his only and irretrievable life for the sake of the Atridae, no more spend nights without sleep and days in bloody battle! Early on the morrow he will be at sea, on his voyage home; he desires a long and peaceful life, not an early death . . . (*Il.* 9, 307ff.). Actually he will do nothing of the kind, and the poet need waste no word over the possibility. But the truth has acquired fresh strength by the circumstance that it has been for once exposed to real doubt.

Of the two factors in epic recitation we have sought to form a clearer notion of one, namely remodeling. But what of the preservation of traditional form? Did the memory of any man suffice to retain whole epics, indeed whole cycles? The investigator of South Slav epic has remarkable accounts of the retentive memories of unlettered men. One would be tempted to doubt if the trustworthiness of the reports were not above suspicion. We shall let sober figures speak.

Murko established that the singers of the Bosnian Mohammedans as a rule have at their command more than 30 or 40 chants, some more than 80 or 100, some even more than 140. Some of the chants are two to three hours long, but most are much longer. Many last seven to eight hours, with pauses, and require one or more nights until daybreak for their performance (173, 18; 176, 18f.; 1919, 284). Forty three-hour chants means a repertory of 120 hours of recitation (including pauses). At Agram, from January 10 to February 17, 1887, Salko Voinikovič dictated 90 chants with more than 80,000 ten-syllable lines. This filled seven folio notebooks, the equivalent of more than 2,000 pages of print, and represented 80 hours of recitation, not counting pauses. In bulk 80,000 ten-syllable lines correspond to some 52,000 Homeric hexameters, that is, almost twice the *Iliad* and the *Odyssey* together, or some 15 books more than the entire Trojan cycle with its 77 books. 'Jure Jurič of Gromiljak sang to a Pasha in Banja-Luka for three months, from evening to midnight, and was certainly not permitted to repeat much' (176, 19).

The modern analogy can also serve in the question of how the transmission of the art and the material to the next generation was managed.[26]

[26] The only passage in the *Odyssey* which speaks of learning songs is 22, 347f. Here the singer Phemius boasts that he is self-taught; a god implanted songs of all sorts in his spirit. This means that he could not only repeat songs he learned (that

When Murko inquired at what age the instruction began, he found
to his astonishment that it began in childhood. Further questioning
elicited even earlier ages. 'The age at which singers begin to "take up"
their songs was lowered to eight years in 1913; indeed many begin to
play the *gusle*[27] and to sing while they are on the knees of their
father or another relative. Earlier, *gusle* playing and singing were
generally "like a school." . . . A member of the Orthodox Church
remarked that at the age of eight he knew his *gusle* better than his
Paternoster. Next to a Muslim singer in the coffeehouse at Konjič
there sat his nine- and ten-year-old sons, of whom the first was
reputed to know all his songs. Even in 1913 the usual age was ten to
twelve up to fifteen—the golden years "when one has not begun to
think." Many limit the capacity to remember at twenty-four or
twenty-five years. . . . In youth a single hearing is sufficient to retain
any song. . . . One "took songs up even while asleep." All speak of an
irresistible pressure (*volja, merak, srce zaiskalo, krv mi steže za pjesmom*)[28]
to let the songs "penetrate"' (176, 12f.). 'If the singers detect a gifted
pupil, they fill him with zeal for song. Many are themselves driven
to it by an irresistible urge. So Muharem Hošič explained it to me in
Bihač: "From the age of ten to twelve I went along with the people in
the Čaršija (market, bazaar) and in coffeehouses and would gladly
have listened to songs all night long. At home I could not fall asleep
until I had myself sung the song, and when I fell asleep the song
was written down in my brain." For most singers a single hearing of a
chant was enough; one only had to hear a song twice, because of
noise; another learned a song imperfectly from a singer he was

is, heard) from others, but could also 'produce by himself' (that is, compose) songs
of any desired content. An illustration is offered by the first book of the Odyssey
(325–27, 350–52): there Phemius sings a 'very new' song, which deals with the
events of the last decade. Obviously the epic singers constructed a theory, which
may be schematized somewhat as follows: (1) The artistic form of the epic chant
is poetic creation, but the content is historical. (2) The epic chant is the only and
natural form of historical tradition. (3) Every historical tradition derives finally
from the period in which the events took place. From these three premises it
follows that the epic tradition finally derives from men who first reduced the
history of their own time to epic form; in the time of Odysseus there must have
been singers like Phemius who did not learn their songs from others but made
them up themselves. This same theory is the basis of *Il.* 2, 485: the Muses (i.e., in
this context, original poets) themselves experienced the events and as 'eye-
witnesses' (ἴστε, cf. Bruno Snell, *Philol. Unters.* 29, 25) transmitted 'knowledge'
(κλέος=hearsay) of them to later men. In *Od.* 12, 189–91 the Sirens boast that
they can sing all the events of the Trojan War and all that happens in the world
generally.

27 The *gusle* is the string instrument on which the singer accompanied himself,
corresponding to the *phorminx* of the Greek singer.

28 'Desire, being enamored, my heart demands it, my blood yearns for the song.'

driving, because he was too drunk and therefore listened half asleep' (173, 17).[29]

The surprisingly early age at which prospective professional and amateur singers were introduced into their art makes possible a trait which ancient Greek epic shares with modern Slavic. The epics tell of events out of a long-submerged past, and in many respects they reproduce the conditions of the olden time with astonishing fidelity. For example, Greek like Slavic singers describe objects of a kind and shape which have not been in use for centuries, and in both cases archaeological examination confirms the accuracy of the descriptions. The epic poets could preserve memories of an older civilization because from early childhood each new generation grew up in a double world, that of the reality of their own time and that of poetry. So it comes about that as soon as they begin, singers speak the language of poetry instead of the ordinary vernacular, automatically submerge themselves in remote antiquity, and move about with complete confidence in an environment known to them only out of poetry (see pp. 34f. and 45f., below).

Even when the Slavic singer has long been master of his art he does not scorn to learn new material from his fellow craftsmen. 'Singers often travel distances of many hours to hear a famous comrade and do not merely compare his work to see if it is "better," but even take "good" songs from him' (176, 14). They also exchange songs with one another (173, 17; 176, 14). Greek singers probably did the same. Through exchange they kept themselves abreast and they regularly compared their reworkings and new compositions with one another. Only in details might the *Iliads* and *Odysseys* of different singers vary, because the rhapsodes were convinced that in essentials their accounts told true history.

Such a social art required no special appurtenances for its cultivation. Whenever there was time, or when time could be taken, epic songs were delivered and heard. If no professional singer was available, more than one man in a gathering would be able to entertain the company.[30] On special occasions, as for example weddings or other festivities, singers came of their own accord or were invited (173, 48). We hear the same in the *Odyssey*; singers as well as

[29] Of a region in which there is already much recitation from books Murko remarks an interesting fact: 'There are also some who cannot "learn" a chant when it is read to them. All are at one in believing that it is much easier (one said seven times easier) to learn a poem from hearing it recited than from hearing it read or reading it.'

[30] A friend once told me that in the First World War Croatian soldiers passed the long hours of anxious waiting, while they sat at their posts, by reciting epic chants.

physicians, seers, or carpenters were summoned at need (17, 385). Princes like the king of the Phaeacians or the lords in Odysseus' palace, kept singers in their regular service. 'As late as 1913 a *beg* took his singer with him to Bad Rohitsch-Sauerbrunn' (1919, 270). 'Dedaga Cengić was one of the last great lovers of heroic song, which he had to have, literally, with his coffee every evening after the table had been removed; and any other listeners might be present only out of special grace. Of entertainment other than the singing or storytelling of a singer he knew nothing; it was as necessary to him, before retiring, as the rubbing of his feet by a servant' (176, 46 and 1919, 295). Court singers were also drawn into many other duties, and so it must have been among the Greeks also.[31]

The reasons why many made a profession of the singer's art may have been various. One may have been motivated by his superior talent and overpowering passion for the art; others may have been constrained by necessity. Demodocus in the *Odyssey* and the singer of the Hymn to Apollo were blind; among the South Slavs also there are blind singers (173, 6f.). Many may have become wandering singers because they had lost their property, or they had had to leave home because of a murder, or for political reasons, as later happened to Xenophanes of Colophon.

From the post-Homeric period we hear of contests of singers at religious festivals or funeral games. After the epic had ceased to be produced, good society in Greece continued to take pleasure in song, but the new age favored lyric song rather than epic chants. The Homeric rhapsodes turned into mere reciters who declaimed and interpreted the fixed text, and eventually into schoolmasters and grammarians.

Spoken epics turned into written books when the desire for constant transformation was weakened; and in return, writing fettered the creative energies which had long enjoyed scope in free composition.[32] On the other hand, a written work offers the possibility of careful and eventual improvement. The first written copies were perhaps not intended for the general public but only served as a help for the singer, who no longer wished to rely on memory and improvization. In any case, the *Iliad* and the *Odyssey* as we read them today reached posterity through a regular book edition, not in the form of singer's texts.[33]

---

[31] Cf. *Od.* 23, 133; *Il.* 24, 720; *Od.* 3, 265ff.; and Telemachus' remark, *Od.* 19, 27f.

[32] It is not easy for us to imagine the specific process of fixing the text. Here the analogy of the South Slav songs fails us because these were first written down and printed under alien, western-European influence.

[33] A comparison with the transmission of the *Nibelungenlied* makes the difference plain. The old manuscripts of the *Nibelungenlied* differ by hundreds of strophes,

Even so, the written texts still show traces of the old fluidity. Books transmitted the beginning of the *Iliad* in two forms—as the start of a new poem, and as a continuation of the preceding epic.[34] The singer might choose one form or the other according as he performed the *Iliad* alone or as part of a larger whole. The first books of the *Odyssey* present a compromise: they provide material either for an independent *Odyssey*, or for one to be recited in connection with the preceding epic. The first scene of the *Odyssey* is so attached to the last book of the *Nostoi*, which depicts Orestes' vengeance upon Aegisthus, that it is hardly intelligible unless a recitation of the *Nostoi* preceded;[35] all through the opening books parallels are drawn between Telemachus and Orestes. On the other hand, the composer of the Telemachy plundered the *Nostoi* and incorporated central sections of it into the third and fourth books of the *Odyssey*. For an independent *Odyssey* this is a gain, but after the *Nostoi* the repetitions would he hard to tolerate, and in such a case the singer did well to omit the doublets. It was only natural that the singers should transpose their material this way or that as occasion demanded. Odysseus' narrative of his wanderings did not necessarily require the Phaeacians as an audience. Actually our *Odyssey* tells how Odysseus again presented the same report, enriched by later experiences, to Penelope. In this passage the text provides only a dry summary of contents (*Od.* 23, 310–41) as a surrogate, so to speak, for a complete account by a singer who began his performance with the hero's landing in Ithaca.[36]

Freedom of choice explains a structural weakness in the second part of the *Odyssey*. Several times the situation is constructed with the conscious objective that the slaying of the suitors must follow at once, but this end is postponed by the intervention of further and further material. Preparations remain unused, crises are not resolved, and the heaping up of similar episodes spoils the effect. These troubles

for each represents the individual version of its writer. Of the *Iliad* and the *Odyssey*, by contrast, only a single version was passed down; uncertainties in the tradition, though numerous, are always confined to single phrases, single verses, or at most a short succession of verses. Expansion through insertion of formulaic verses appears to be more frequent than curtailment.

[34] There was yet a third opening, when a hymn (see p. 246, below) to Apollo and the Muses preceded the epic narrative.

[35] *Od.* 1, 29–47. Cf. especially 'now' in 43 (the 'now' in 35 does not properly fit with it). Compromise is obvious in the inadequate recapitulation at 29f. and 35–43.

[36] In this case further alterations were naturally required; but even singers with book-texts were initially still capable of improvizing the necessary adaptations. After *Od.* 1, 93 an ancient manuscript contains two additional verses, according to which Telemachus was still to journey to Idomeneus in Crete—which implies a considerable expansion of the Telemachy.

disappeared if the singer did not use all the episodes each time.[37]

The *Iliad* yields insights even more valuable. Every singer was naturally concerned to include as many attractive pieces as he could in the framework he chose. Within the framework of 'the wrath of Achilles' our *Iliad* includes portions that belong to the beginning of the war (like the great march to battle and the catalogue in the second book and all the events in the third and fourth books) and events from the end of the war (like the death of Hector). Similarly, some books are filled with fresh memories of the prehistory of the war, while others lie under the shadow of Ilium's imminent fall. This procedure is not correct realistically, but it is artistically appropriate so long as the *Iliad* is heard or read by itself. Within the segment it offers, the whole long war is reflected. But for the cycle as a whole there are drawbacks. In the epic preceding the *Iliad* pieces which properly belong there are wanting because they had already found a place in the *Iliad*. Obviously the *Iliad* became a book before the other epics of the Trojan War,[38] so that the later authors could consult it. We may explain similarly the disproportion in size of the epics (the *Iliad* had claimed most of the material), and the fact that the *Iliad* bears a title to which it has no better right than any of the other four epics on the fall of Ilium. The competition of authors for the best pieces to put in their books is part of the reason why the ancients thought that the poetic worth of the other cyclic epics was slighter than that of the *Iliad* and the *Odyssey*. The other authors came too late. Only subjects which had an unalterable place in the story, as for example the sack of Troy, were safe from covetous hands. Natural selection had cumulative effects. With sure judgment the best singers chose the best frame and packed it with the best scenes and episodes; they gave their material the most finished poetic form; they met with the greatest applause; and so their works established themselves as norms, for the public wished to have the stories recited as they recited them. With the help of selection, and thanks to the skill of their arranger, our *Iliad* and our *Odyssey* are reasonably if not perfectly planned in their general structure.[39] How similar previous *Iliads* and *Odysseys*

[37] It can be shown that our *Odyssey* presents a series of alternative preparations for the slaying of the suitors, of which many are designed for a different version of the slaying.

[38] The period at which the *Iliad* and the *Odyssey* became books cannot be determined precisely. It may have been the eighth or the seventh century.

[39] Individual sections would indeed be seen against the background of the whole action, but this is present only in approximate outline. Specific relations between verses from widely separated parts of the epic can indeed be established by the modern scholar, but surely the original audience valued only what it heard in its immediate context.

were to our two epics, and how original the final arrangement was, can at best be surmised in scattered details.[40]

And finally we can understand why transitions from one episode to another in both epics are frequently unable to withstand pragmatic criticism. Since the episodes often had to change place, connections here and there were very loose or were left, with a splendid insouciance, to be guessed at. The epics thus have only a general unity. Strata of various ages lie one upon the other, in the midst of one another, with some missing, and the special qualities of individuals who contributed to the wonderful work are entangled together. Not even classical Greek tragedies are uniform, though each was written by one man within a short space of time. In all comprehensive compositions each portion has its own tendencies—every scene, every motif, every character. A pedantic consistency which carefully eliminated every possible conflict would have destroyed or impoverished its own creation. Hence the epics are not free of partial or complete contradiction in details. But over the whole there is a dominant unity, for each poem and each section has a simple basic thought.

Moreover, beside the approximate unity of action there stands a firm, traditional unity of form, in language, and verse, and style.

(b) *Language, Verse, Style*

All Greek creations carry not only the general hallmark of Greek character, but each after its own kind maintains its appropriate style. In addition to its own characteristic style Homeric epic has its own language, an artificial language which never existed outside epic, and which belongs only to epic. From epic this special language was inherited by elegy; lyric also often uses epic words and forms in order to give its language an epic coloring and to conjure up epic associations. Besides the internal laws of its art, the accident of history also had a share in forming epic speech.

In Greece itself, in the mother country, epic passed only through its initial stages. The testimony of epic language shows that the actual bloom and development of this poetry took place in the colonial area of the East, on the west coast of Asia Minor and its offshore islands. Greek tribes settled there toward the end of the second millennium, Aeolians to the north, south of them Ioians, and farther south Dorians. The epic dialect is basically Aeolic; accordingly epic was first cultivated in the north, not far from the ruins of ancient

[40] Confident assertions concerning 'Homer's' contributions cannot be proved, but they often help us to understand better what lies before us.

Troy. Epic was taken over from the Aeolians by the Ionians; Homer himself was regarded as an Ionian. Now Ionian linguistic features were channeled into the epic dialect, but without displacing Aeolic words and forms completely. The Ionian singers had no thought of systematically translating the songs which they first heard and learned from the Aeolians into their own dialect. To do so they would have had to surrender and destroy many useful coinages because Ionian had nothing to correspond to them or because the corresponding Ionian would not fit into the verse. Thus a mixed language came into being. In the course of time the Ionic ingredient was strengthened, but until the end Ionian singers never scorned to use Aeolic words, forms, phrases along with Ionic even for their own compositions. A radical break with tradition was alien to the Greeks; and there was a practical advantage in having a choice of possibilities.

Greek epic reached maturity, therefore, not in the limited area of the self-sufficient motherland, but abroad, in the colonial area of the East. Of all the Greek tribes the Ionians were furthest advanced at the time; and during the whole archaic period Ionia was regularly a stage ahead of the rest of the Hellenic world. Alert, receptive, and enterprising, the descendants of the old emigrants developed more quickly than those who stayed at home. In the new country they were in daily intercourse with several foreign races, and the Phoenician merchants who touched at the harbors on the seacoast and islands made them acquainted with wares, people, and ideas from all the Mediterranean lands. Trade routes between the Asiatic continent in the East and all regions of the West, between Egypt in the South and the countries to the North, all crossed in Ionia. Toward the end of the epic age the eastern Greeks themselves took an increasingly active part in navigation, so that agriculture was reduced to second place. Soon the Greeks of Asia Minor succeeded in wresting primacy in sea trade from the Phoenicians. From the eighth century on a new wave of Greek colonization was in motion; a single Ionian city, Miletus, settled the coast of the Black Sea with a whole chain of trading stations. It is believed that an echo of these new interests may occasionally be heard in the *Odyssey*.[1] An abundance of fresh impulses must have streamed over the eastern Greeks. But the Greek character was in itself strong enough not to succumb to the alien influences. What came from without was either rejected or adapted and assimilated.[2] Cultural development followed its

[1] Odysseus examines the land of the Cyclopes with the eye of a man accustomed to estimating the economic possibilities of a new country (*Od.* 9, 106–41).

[2] Greek culture was able to maintain itself on the coasts of Asia Minor for three millennia, until it came to an abrupt and horrible end in the catastrophe of 1922.

own laws, promoted but not cramped by incursions from without.

Although it came into being at the outposts of Hellenism, during constant interchange, peaceful and warlike, with many alien cultures and much alien crudeness and barbarism, epic became unmistakably, firmly, and purely Hellenic and remained so in character and language; to a large degree, indeed, it helped form and create Greek life and culture. For the Ionians epic art signified a kind of self-awareness: men came quietly together to turn their glance away from the surrounding world and the present and to find refuge in the old traditions of remote antiquity, before the migrations.

The epic poetry thus produced was then carried by traveling singers everywhere Greeks lived. Perhaps in the eighth, and at latest in the seventh century, the epics began their victorious march through Greek lands, a march visible to our senses in the painted vases with their endless abundance of pictures out of the epics.[3] So the epic, whose earliest seed sprouted in the motherland, became in its Ionian maturity and perfection the enduring possession of the Greek nation. After the recitations turned into books, Homeric epic became a universal item of education for the nation at large and an educational force for one generation of Greeks after another.

Effects so enduring can be exerted only by creations which themselves resulted from constant development, by means of which they became treasure chambers of slowly amassed riches. Only when the wisdom and art of many men, working simultaneously or in succession, is concentrated upon the same enterprise can a final result as humanly perfect as Homeric epic be attained. Next we shall examine the style and verse of the Homeric epics.

The linguistic stock of epic verse is shot through with obstinately surviving archaisms and with foreign-sounding Aeolisms. The solemn-antique and the unaffected-modern are either mixed in equal proportions, or else distributed in varying concentrations according to the content and mood of a scene. Sections and passages of somber grandeur, like the appearance of the vengeful god in the first book of the *Iliad*, maintain more rigidly the dignity of the old traditional speech, while lively and vigorous pieces, like the recriminations in the same first book of the *Iliad*, are a closer approach to the current vernacular.[4] On the whole the epic language always remained easily intelligible to anyone who had once listened to it attentively. But

---

[3] Cf. Zschietzschmann *Arch. Jahrbuch*, 1931, 45. In Attica the visible effect of epic begins later and quite abruptly about 570–560, that is to say, at the time of the new institution of the Panathenaea (566) and the introduction of recitations of Homer at this festival.

[4] *Il.* 1, 88 with two contractions is more modern in form than *Od.* 16, 489.

in details many an archaic word or expression became mere sound, and many an epithet of a god became a name or title which was used without being associated with a precise meaning. There was also transfer of meanings, which amounted to productive misunderstanding, and new words were constructed in what was believed to be the old style on the model of existing old forms.[5]

Use of formulae is another element of epic style. Portions of verses, verses, or groups of verses appear again and again in identical form. To have at hand a permanent reservoir of coinages made improvisation easier for the singer. But its practical advantages can only superficially excuse, not explain, the existence of formulae; and excuses are out of place, for it is only a later stage of art that finds fault with repetition. The ancient epic poet saw no reason to be original where change would only worsen the expression, or to put the same goods into different wrappings every time. On the contrary, along with the transitory and individual he wished to give expression to the permanent and typical in form just as in matter.

In the formal verses the essence of the act which is their subject is stamped in a convenient form once and for all. They are so delicately and perfectly worked out that it is worth while to analyze an example in detail—the couplet on eating one's dinner. First there are preparations by the host and his household, and then, literally (e.g., *Od.* 17, 98f.):

> The guests put forth their hands to the pleasures that lay ready;
> Then, when they had set aside their desire for drink and food
> Spoke . . .[6]

First, it is striking that nothing is said of the actual eating; it took place, unsung, between the two verses. The animal activity of chewing and swallowing is decently passed over.[7] Nothing is said of the substance which passes from table to gullet, only of the hands that might freely take it and of the desire which might be freely gratified.[8]

---

[5] Cf., for example, 'Antidoron,' *Festschrift für J. Wackernagel* (1924), 274ff. The assumption of productive misunderstanding is overworked by Manu Leumann, *Homerische Wörter*, Basel, 1950.

[6] οἱ δ' ἐπ' ὀνείαθ' ἑτοῖμα προκείμενα χεῖρας ἴαλλον.

αὐτὰρ ἐπεὶ πόσιος καὶ ἐδητύος ἐξ ἔρον ἔντο.

[7] Similarly the food is not named directly but by a circumvention—'pleasures'— and then for 'drink and food' the nouns of action 'drinking' and 'eating' are substituted. On the choice of the art word ποτῆτος elsewhere, cf. J. Wackernagel, *Kl. Schr.*, p. 1137.

[8] In the second verse (which recurs 20 times in the *Iliad* and the *Odyssey*) ἐξ (ἔρον) ἔντο does not mean 'drove away.' This translation is objectionable, for it not merely ignores the pleasures of the feast but denies them. When the heroes sat at table with good food and good wine they were not concerned solely with

The meal is described from the viewpoint of the pleasure which the host prepares for his guests. In this respect too the epic is social poetry. Each of the formulae performs its special function most aptly. Those which introduce a speech provide, by their easy uniformity, a convenient neutral foil for the dramatic speech which follows.

Most of the formulae do not make up a complete verse but only part of one; and there are hexameters composed of two, three, or four formulae put together; for the formulae are so arranged that they fit each other precisely.⁹ They obey the general laws for the internal structure of the hexameter, to which we now turn.

Epic verse is one of the greatest achievements of Greek artistic genius. And though it is generally impossible to attain a full appreciation of an artistic form through intellectual analysis, the formal system of the hexameter can be completely mastered by rational means. It is therefore worth while to enter into technical detail, since style and content are inextricably bound up with the structure of the verse.¹⁰

As in all ancient Greek verse forms, so in the hexameter rhythm is produced by a regular pattern of long and short syllables.¹¹ In this respect ancient verse is more mechanical than modern, which rests upon the rhythm of stressed and unstressed syllables. For whereas the stress laid on a word bears a certain relationship to the content of a text, the length or shortness of syllables has nothing to do with the meaning of words or sentences. But in the hexameter¹² this dis-

---

'driving out' unpleasant feelings. Rather the phrase means 'they let the desire out, they allowed it free course' (a positive pleasure), in contrast to 'they held it back in their breast' (unpleasant). Cf., e.g., *Od.* 11, 105, θυμὸν (here='tormenting hunger') ἐρυκακέειν or *Il.* 4, 430, ἔχοντ' ('holding back') ἐν στήθεσιν αὐδήν as opposed to 3, 321, ἀλλ' ὅτε δὴ ὅπα τε μεγάλην ἐκ στήθεος εἴη. Our expression 'to release his anger' offers a good analogy. The sense of ἐξ ἔρον εἶναι in *Il.* 13, 638 is simple: 'Of everything one eventually has enough, even of things where the wish 'to indulge an urge' is even stronger than in war.' The thought would be absurd if the wish was originally directed to 'become free of the urge,' for in this case it would not be worth noticing that after a time one is rid of the urge and 'has enough.'

⁹ Once the poet plays with the epic formulae. In *Il.* 1, 229f., Achilles says to Agamemnon ('You are no warrior'): ἦ πολὺ λώϊόν ἐστι κατὰ στρατὸν εὐρὺν Ἀχαιῶν δῶρ' ἀποαιρεῖσθαι ὅστις σέθεν ἀντίον εἴπῃ. This is like a parody of the standard description of a true hero who steps before the broad front of the hostile army (and not, like Agamemnon here, before his own Achaeans) in order κατὰ στρατὸν εὐρὺν Ἀχαιῶν (1, 484; 2, 439; 19, 196) θυμὸν ἀφαιρεῖσθαι (cf. 20, 436) ὅστις τοῦ ἀντίον ἔλθῃ (5, 301; 17, 8).

¹⁰ Cf. *Frühgriech. Denken*, 100–56.

¹¹ The Greeks pronounced and heard longs and shorts precisely. Our usage, in reading ancient verse, is to stress the longs, thus falsifying the nature of the verse.

¹² A hexameter is a succession of six measures (or feet); each measure is either a dactyl (i.e., 'finger'—long, short, short, like the articulation of fingers), or a spondee (long-long). The last foot in the line always consists of two syllables: long-short or long-long.

advantage is outweighed through a peculiar management of the
relationships between the sense of the words and the rhythm of the
verse. In order to clarify the basic principles of this management we
shall begin by formulating the problem which it resolves.

In the natural language of daily life successions of words flow in an
articulated course. Periods are separated from one another, and
within periods individual word groups, long or short, are set apart
from one another; in the division and subdivision of the whole, under
certain circumstances, a single word may constitute a member in
itself. Articulation is expressed audibly, especially in slow and
emphatic speech, through stronger or weaker interruptions of the
vocal tenor[13] of the speech at the boundaries between members. At
the sharpest divisions (but only there) there is also a pause in the
flow. The problem in the art of hexameter composition[14] was therefore this: whether and how the natural sense articulation of the text
should come to terms with the prescribed succession of longs and
shorts in the versification. The verse runs rhythmically in six short
elements (metra) of three or two syllables each, whereas the meaning
contained in the verses (of some fifteen to seventeen syllables each)
has divisions here or there, whose distance apart from one another
is not rhythmically determined. This produces a conflict which calls
for compromise. Otherwise, either the verses would follow one
another in a uniform sequence of sound with no consideration of
meaning, or else individual verses would be recited with marked
separations according to sense and so be broken into unrhythmical
sections now at this point and now at that.[15]

Now Greek hexameter takes account of the requirement for
sense articulation within a verse by the fact that each verse is divided
into four segments (cola) which are calculated to articulate the text in
accordance with its meaning. The first colon begins as the verse
begins, and the three succeeding cola start with a perceptible interruption (caesura).[16] The conditions for placing the caesura are such

[13] By 'vocal tenor' I mean the whole complex of modulation in respect to pitch,
volume, timbre, tempo, etc.

[14] The problem presents itself in all so-called speaking verse. The Greek
trimeter was regulated in a manner similar to that described here for the hexameter.

[15] A third possibility would be that the sense divisions should always be placed
where one verse ends and the next begins, as is very frequent in South Slav and
modern Greek folk epic. This is primitive and unsatisfactory. The sequence of
verses becomes a monotonous jingle, and the verbal expression must often be
artificially inflated to fill the whole space to the end of the line. South Slavic epic
verse is only ten syllables long, probably for this reason.

[16] If we designate the three caesuras A, B, and C, and the points at which they
are admissible as A1, A2, and so forth, the scheme is as follows:

that its verse is subdivided according to harmonious relationships; for the first interruption there are four choices (A1 to A4), for both others two each (B1, B2 and C1, C2).[17] Thanks to this freedom of choice the poet is not unduly constricted in shaping his text, and there is also no monotony, as there would be if all the verses followed an identical pattern. On the other hand, though the verse structure can be varied in many ways[18] the system remains simple and uniform. As soon as several verses are delivered in their well-articulated flow, according to the caesuras the hearer at once senses the regularity and the harmony between the rhythm of the verse and the rhythm of the meaning. No theoretical clarification of the applicable rules is necessary: that is why the old singers did not elaborate theoretical subtleties and pass on to their posterity a parcel of abstract rules. Rather, the system was implicit in the traditional recitation of verse: violations became noticeable by the fact that no faulty verse could be recited in the traditional manner. In the medium of recitation the articulation of the hexameter was maintained by the Greeks for two thousand years; it was refined, in the course of time, but never overthrown.

Every hexameter is therefore a miniature strophe, and the over-laying of the mechanical rhythm of long and short by an audible sense rhythm harmonizing with the mechanical, gave the Greek hexameter more than one additional element of aesthetic satisfaction. The art, in fact, received a new dimension. Verse and content no

[17] Provision is made for legitimate exceptions also. Especially long and important words ('heavy words') can suppress a caesura which should come at the end of a word and allow it to come later than the rules require. These will here be noted as A! and C!. An example of A! is *Il.* 1, 356: '(Agamemnon)/has-offended-me (A!); he took and keeps my own prize.' In Greek 'has-offended-me' is a single word, and here its weight is the heaviest imaginable, for the whole action of the *Iliad* is based on the affront to Achilles. An example of C! is *Il.* 1, 1: 'Sing, Muse, the anger of son-of-Peleus (C!) Achilles.' In such cases the harmony of the articulation is disturbed, but in a meaningful way: the verse yields under the pressure of the content. Epic versification makes rich and impressive use of this device. A second legitimate but less frequent exception is the possibility of filling two cola with a single word, so that the verse has only three cola instead of four. For example the B-caesura is bridged over ('Bx') in the verse 'Seed-of-the-gods/ son-of-Laertes/ ingenious Odysseus' (A4 Bx C1).

[18] The freedom of choice for each of the three caesuras (with 4, 2, and 2 possibilities) in itself results in 16 possible arrangements. The number is enlarged by the admissibility of postponed caesuras. The absolute and relative strength of the division may also vary at will for each passage.

longer ran parallel, like two bands, but were combined with complete plasticity, and the result was the formation of a new and flexible power to express what was to be communicated. The fusion of verse and sense took place naturally, with no compulsion or artifice, for in its essence the articulation is no different from the compelling rhythm of the things which lie enchained in word and verse. How much the hexameter poetry of the Greeks gains by learning to recite it correctly as it was meant to be recited cannot be described in words but only experienced by intimacy with the original text.[19]

The three internal divisions between the four cola of the hexameter do not come at equal intervals. The first may (but need not) come very soon after the beginning of the verse; the second comes at one of two places immediately before the middle of the verse (an exact halving would break the verse into two); and both places open to choice for the third break are so situated that after the interruption a relatively long stretch of at least five syllables remains safe from division by a caesura.[20] Restless as the verse may be at its beginning, in its fourth colon, at least, it has an uninterrupted and even course, with a third or more of the total length of the verse available.

It is precisely the final portion of the verse, and especially its last third, which is the favored place for the epic formulae; and the uniform recurrence of the formulae lends epic style consistency and dignity. For example, in the 32 verses at *Il.* 6, 254–85 we find 15 instances of the verse concluding with a phrase found one or more times elsewhere in the *Iliad* and the *Odyssey*. Of these 15 formulae 11 fill the last third of the line; they read, approximately, 'sons of Achaea,' 'moved thee thy spirit,' 'all the immortals,' 'the lady his mother,' 'red-glowing winebowl,' 'with beautiful tresses,' 'innocent

[19] To make the system concrete I subjoin a very inadequate attempt to render several verses of the *Iliad* in the original articulation. Caesuras are indicated by punctuation or a diagonal stroke. (Context: Agamemnon has taken a girl to keep as a concubine; the girl's father, clothed with the insignia of priesthood, approaches the king to ransom his daughter with rich gifts; Agamemnon speaks to him as follows:)

26   'Look to thyself, old man: I will/ that thou bidest no longer
      Tarrying/ here by the ships/ nor venturest/ hither hereafter.

28   Else shall thee/ nothing avail/ thy staff/ and the bands of Apollo.
      Her will I/ never set free; but old/ shall she grow in my service

30   Under my roof,/ in my palace/ of Argos, far from her homeland,
      Weaving/ day in and day out,/ and my bed/ shall she deck for the nightime.
      Go you then,/ vex me no longer:/ so mayst thou yet/ go from me scathelses.'

The caesuras are: 26– A4 B2 C1; 27– A3 B1 C2; 28– A3 B1 C1; 29– A3 B1 C1; 30– A4 B2 C2; 31– A2 B1 C1; 32– A3 B2 C2.

[20] Cf. Notes 16 and 18 above.

children,' 'Troy's holy city,' 'rouser of terror,' 'that I command him,' 'down into Hades.' The four others begin a little earlier in the line: 'to pray to the highest,' 'bright-helmeted Hector,' 'dark-clouded Cronian,' 'Athene the giver of booty.' The concluding word of the verse is frequently the name of a god or hero, to give the verse a weighty conclusion. But since most names are too short to fill the last third of the line by themselves, the name is frequently preceded by a traditional epithet. For example, 'swift-moving Iris,' 'fleet-footed Achilles,' 'lord of the storm Zeus.' This prevents a break in the final portion of the verse. For in the course of the narrative the appearance of a god or hero is a definite mark of a new beginning; by means of the epithet the new personage is announced in advance, as it were, and the verse concludes without a disturbing surprise. The assured completeness of the final third of its verse gives the epic hexameter a sober and solemn character and differentiates it from the hexameter in Hellenistic poetry. Callimachus, the Hellenistic poet who lived half a millennium later, was more concerned with the flexibility and point of his verses than with spacious dignity and so did not hesitate to introduce new ideas at the conclusion of a line.

In this and similar ways verse and word alike profited by their alliance with one another. As a variable miniature strophe the hexameter did not run a neutral and uniform course to carry desired matter in a form desired; its four members could develop a life of their own: a powerful beginning to initiate the line; a factual second colon, a frequently emphatic third; and a rolling, resounding fourth—such is the usual pattern. There are many others, but in all cases the verse is animated and planned as a whole.[21]

Since the cola differ from one another, and since each of them possesses or can easily assume a character of its own, the location of a word or phrase in a line is not a matter of indifference; a certain uniformity arises of itself. So, for example, the third member of the verse, which may be as short as two syllables and is partial to marked stress, is a favorite place for the name of the highest god (Διός or the like)[22] or for the word 'god' or 'gods' (θεός, θεοί, and the like). Fixed formulations which recur frequently have their regular place within the line into which they are fitted bodily according to their size. And since the expressions are adjusted to the general laws of the verse, no member interferes with another; they are fitted together

[21] Verses may also have a significant correspondence with one another through parallel divisions or similar sound, as e.g. *Il.* 1, 13 and 95 (with a long interval); or in a sequence of verses the organization may suddenly shift, as in the A1 caesura at *Il.* 1, 52, with great effect.

[22] In the nominative Ζεύς is often found at the beginning or end of the verse.

like building blocks which bind and complement one another.[23] The adjustment takes place with no constraint nor any absolutely binding rule, but in good taste and with effortless assurance. The whole style is permeated with typical elements, and all these elements have their mutual affinities and relationships.

The fixity of types[24] is shown, among other examples, by the fact that the same epithets are repeatedly applied to persons and things regardless of their particular situation. So the poet speaks of 'sea-faring' ships when they are drawn up on shore and of 'swift-footed Achilles' when he is sitting still. This may be questionable to modern taste, and it has been inferred that the practice was followed to facilitate improvisation. But this explanation is inadequate because all Greek art at all times exhibits similar traits. Rather, the epic singers employed standing epithets regularly and consistently to signify the unalterable nature of things and the outstanding traits of persons. Essentially ships are vessels for travel over the pathless sea,[25] and by his nature Achilles was swift and stormy. Epic narrative style aims to express the permanent beside the momentary and to temper the accidental with the essential.

From the properties of epic style in language and versification we now turn to style in its wider sense: the tendencies which governed the presentation of the narrative.

A specific and conscious style so rigorously prevails in Homeric epic that we may properly speak not merely of style but of stylization. In the older portions of the epics stylization is especially powerful and exclusive: in the younger strata counter-tendencies have begun to relax the older rigidity. This is only what we should expect in a kind of poetry which we know only in its last stage, when corruption has already set in. If we wish to trace the strict and pure outlines of ancient epic stylization, therefore, we must rely mainly on the *Iliad* which by and large represents the older stages.

A feature characteristic of Homeric stylization is the deliberate antiquity of the events narrated and the conditions described (see p. 21, above). The song which carries the speaker and his listeners

[23] So the formulae which mark the close of a speech are adapted to the four positions of the 'A' caesura. For A1, ἦ serves; for A2, ἦ ῥα, or before a vowel, ὣς φάτ'; for A3 ὣς φάτο or ὣς ἔφατ'; and for A4, ὣς ἄρ' ἔφη.

[24] Color of hair, for example, conforms to type. All women are blonde (as in vase painting); so are young men like Achilles and Apollo and also the handsome Menelaus; mature men like Odysseus and Zeus have black hair. This disposes of all inferences concerning the racial derivation of epic personages (cf. *Deutsche Literaturzeitung*, 1924, 2369).

[25] Another standing epithet for ships, 'hollow,' signifies their function as receptacles for men and goods.

back to ages long past is careful to observe the distinction between
then and now. This applies particularly to the externals of civilization
(pp. 45f., below). The heroes of the Trojan War lived in the Bronze
Age, and the singer therefore has them fight one another with
weapons of bronze, though in his own daily life he had long been
using implements of iron.[26] Before an audience which was used to
riding and fighting on horseback, the singer has the heroes go out to
battle in war chariots. Furthermore, though these poems had behind
them a long period of maturity in the Greek East, they ignore the
overseas migration and the colonization of the East. The epic knows
only the Greek world of the motherland with its old capital cities
before the migration.[27]

The singers retained the picture of the old forms of life with such
fidelity because they believed that the age of which they told was,
despite its technical backwardness, greater than their own. Again and
again, when the prowess of heroes is reported, we are told that 'men
such as live today' could not perform such feats. The historical
perspective is one of steady degeneration. And just as the epic
figures transcend modern men, so, according to the first book of the
Iliad, were they themselves inferior to their predecessors. At the same
time this passage (1, 247ff.) shows wherein the higher worth of
earlier generations was thought to consist. There the aged Nestor
says to the quarreling kings, neither of whom will yield: 'Once I had
to do with men who were better than you, with Lapiths, against
whom none of today's men would be able to fight. They respected me
and listened to me; so may you two listen to me. You, Achilles, are
good, and yet you should accept my advice.'[28] What do 'good' and
'better' mean here? The saga depicts the Lapiths as vigorous, unyielding, and overbearing, and here Nestor says of them, 'these were the
mightiest our earth has nourished; they were the mightiest and fought
against the mightiest, against the half-beasts of the wilderness, and slew
in their rage.'[29] Brutality, hardness, joy in conflict and battle—obviously
this comprises the greatness of earlier humanity. In this sense the
proem of the *Iliad* advertises as its great subject the baneful (οὐλομένην)
anger and strife, to which an untold number of Greek lives fell victim.

[26] Hence, e.g., the remarkable contrast that whereas Achilles gives Hector his
death blow with a bronze-pointed spear, he is reproached by his dying foe as a
'man with a heart of iron' (*Il.* 22, 328; 557). For the metal purely as a symbol the
rule of archaizing does not apply.
[27] Even *Il.* 4, 51–56 with its intimation of a future fall of Mycenae is kept
within the chronological framework, for Mycenae fell in the early twelfth century.
(It is otherwise, perhaps, in *Il.* 20, 302–8.)   [28] On 1, 275 cf. *Glotta* 14, 8.
[29] ἔκπαγλος (268) does not mean 'what arouses terror' (active), but rather (passive)
'demented, raving'.

Admiration for animal savagery, obsessive pride, wholesale slaughter, is no longer naïve in the *Iliad* but is now romantic, for the singers and in general 'the men who live today' are of a different cut. Nestor with his advice for a friendly reconciliation represents modern reasonableness; but if the quarreling princes had indeed listened to the voice of reason, as even the Lapiths allegedly did, there would have been no anger of Achilles and no *Iliad*. The mature and late epic art of the *Iliad*, which owes its perfection to humanization and spiritual purification, glorifies the wilder and cruder type of humanity which it had transcended; and yet it could not but lend to its personages many of its own traits. Here the cleavage characteristic of all romanticism is revealed. Then in the *Odyssey*, as we shall see (Ch. IIg), the modern spirit gains the upper hand, and thereafter the epic age as a whole comes to its end.

The world in which the events of the *Iliad* take place is also idealized, and its laws are different from those of ordinary reality. Gods and great heroes live in a sphere of their own, which they share only with their equals. All that impinges upon their sovereignty is, as it were, erased and extinguished. Their actions are not subject to limitations of space or time, and nature does not gainsay them. There is no summer or winter, no bad weather, no cold. The Trojan field is only an arena for the Trojan War, not a countryside. Always present is the shore with the camp of the Achaeans, and the lofty city of Ilium. Occasionally there is a landmark at need, a hill, a fig tree or tomb, and if a hero has need of it a boulder lies ready for him to throw. In the first book of the *Iliad* a plague befalls the host, and it is assumed as obvious that only the common soldiery will be visited by it. No one imagines that one of the princes might be afflicted; the god punishes the king by making his subjects die. Once the rivers of the Trojan landscape, here conceived of as gods, enter into the fight, and Achilles is in danger of drowning. He complains that he must end like a boy who keeps pigs, and immediately two gods from Olympus stand beside him to assure him: 'It is not fated that the stream overwhelm you' (*Il.* 21, 279ff.). Only respectable and worthy forces can exercise their effects upon great personages, for we move in a poetic world in which nothing is mechanical and coarse and casual. In a duel between two warriors the decision regularly follows the relative worth of the opponents, and in the hand of a great hero the weapon itself carries instant destruction if it only touches its victim superficially.[30] A further rule for battle scenes is

[30] One of the epic heroes himself enunciates this principle. Diomedes is struck by Paris' arrow and calls to him: 'You have only scratched my heel and are boasting in vain. I take no thought of it, as if a woman had hit me, or a child

that there are no slow deaths and no serious wounds. The principal heroes do occasionally suffer slight injuries, which take them out of the battle only temporarily if at all; in general they are either unhurt or killed on the spot. This latter simple alternative applies to the lesser figures only. The poet who wishes to use the figure of a warrior once only, decides his fate simply and finally. Half measures would make the battle scene less monumental.

That the compulsion to extreme solutions is a matter of style and not unfeeling savagery is indicated by the *Iliad's* consistent attitude to battle 'rich in tears.' The fearful seriousness of war is always present, and over every warrior who falls the terrible grandeur of death overshadows the clattering arms that encase his dying body. Even to the undistinguished warriors who are included only to succumb to their betters, the poet often gives words which endow the victim with a personality and make his tragedy felt. 'He was a great hunter and a disciple of Artemis, but the goddess and his archery did not help him' (*Il.* 5, 51–54). 'His father begot him outside wedlock, but his stepmother treated him like her own children, to please her husband' (*Il.* 5, 70f). 'He was rich, hospitable, and had many friends, but none was now there to save him from destruction' (6, 14–17). All these comments are calm and factual in expression; but though they are not emotional in language they are so in effect.

This takes us to a further hallmark of Homeric style: restrained objectivity and aloof detachment. The singer reports but he does not reflect. As a person he retires behind his subject completely. He passes no judgment upon his figures,[31] and does not indicate his own opinions of their character; he allows us to understand them only through their actions and speeches. Problematic questions are never raised in the narrative. The epic gives very few descriptions of inner states.

Nevertheless the poetry is replete with differentiated characters, stirring problems, and tense situations. For the epic developed its own art of indicating by other means matter which, by the rules of its style, might not be uttered directly. Much of its detail is invented not so much to illustrate the action as to illuminate its background by means of indirect lighting.

In the passage of the *Iliad* where Helen is first introduced in person (3, 125) the poet wishes to set the theme which is to dominate the

without understanding. For dull is the weapon of an unwarlike, worthless man. But sharp is the weapon in my hand, and even if it touch you but lightly it brings instant destruction' (*Il.* 11, 388–92).

[31] At most the poet calls a man 'foolish,' but the folly is an objective quality, for it is identical with the lack of success of his action (cf., e.g., *Il.* 12, 113).

scenes that follow (130–38, 156–60, 164–65): this is the woman for whose possession nations struggle in bloody war, and she is aware of her great and terrible, though passive, role. But instead of pointing at her with his finger and analyzing her situation he tells us: 'Iris found her in the hall, seated at the loom, working on a purple web many pictures of the sufferings of war which the hand of Ares imposed upon the horse-guiding Trojans and bronze-clad Achaeans for her sake.' As an example from the *Odyssey* (2, 15–23) we may take the manner in which the complicated and confused situation in Ithaca is represented indirectly. Anxiety and bitterness had spread among the people from the time when no more had been heard of the men who sailed to Troy. Some Ithacans sued for Penelope's hand; others attended to their affairs; many persisted in faithful loyalty to their king. All this the poet is able to make plain briefly by creating a man who is personally involved in all the contradictory interests: 'At the assembly the hero Aegyptius, bent by age and knowing many things, began to speak. One of his sons had sailed with godlike Odysseus to horse-taming Ilium. . . . Three sons more he had, of whom one, Eurynomus, was one of the suitors; the two others steadily cared for the paternal possessions. But Aegyptius was not forgetful of Odysseus, but mourned and grieved for him.'

Like actions and persons, so too things are used for indirect communication. The discreet but intelligible language which lifeless things speak in Homer must be learned and understood. If the poet lingers over objects he does so with design. If the weapons of a hero are described in detail, the significance is that they will soon achieve great deeds. At the beginning of the eleventh book of the *Iliad* Agamemnon arms himself for his forthcoming *aristeia*. The thought that this time it is the great king of the host in person who will distinguish himself by prowess in arms, the leader of the most glorious campaign in history, a man whose enterprises the whole wide world follows with interest—this thought the singer incorporated in the following form of the description of the arming. Agamemnon, he says, put upon his breast the armor which Cinyras (ruler of Cyprus) had sent him as a guest present; for the great tidings had reached Cyprus that the Achaeans with their ships would voyage to Troy: therefore Cinyras sent the armor to the king to give him joy (*Il.* 11, 19ff.). Then the display of colors of the various materials of the armor is described as follows: 'Upon it were ten bands of black enamel, twelve of gold, and twenty of tin; snakes of enamel stretched to the neck, three on each side, like the rainbows which the son of Cronus raises in the clouds as a marvelous sign for speaking men.' The conventional progression of numerals, 10–12–20, renders reconstruction of the armor, which has often been attempted, impossible. But the poet is not concerned with literal representation: it is the word which teaches understanding. Snakes are symbols of uncanny blood lust and lurking death in Homer (cf. *Il.* 3, 33–37), and the rainbow is not a bridge of peace for Homer's people but an awful presentiment of approaching horror (cf. *Il.* 17, 544–52). Translated into speech, the description of the armor means: Agamemnon clothed himself with a savage urge to kill, and dreadful deeds of war were in preparation.[32]

Such traits, among many others, stamp Homeric narrative with its characteristic impress. But do they entitle us to speak of stylization instead of merely style? Did they actually impose constraint upon the ancient poet? Perhaps the singers saw the events of the past in all simplicity and only from a distance and saw them as objectively and ingenuously as they reported them; perhaps it was impossible for them to represent life in any other way and perhaps their language was incapable of speaking of other things.

These doubts can be resolved. The late form of the epic which we possess is anything but naïve, even in its art; it archaizes not only in language but also in thought. For within the epic there are certain passages in which rules that apply elsewhere are transgressed. The singers *could* do otherwise.

The restraint which the epic poet imposes upon himself is set aside in the numerous speeches which he weaves into his work.[33] Only so long as the singer is reporting events does he remain a mere shadow, discreet and neutral. But as soon as he impersonates one of his figures and utters that figure's words with his own lips, he absorbs his blood and himself becomes a person. In the role of an epic personage the singer may and does reflect, he can scan and comment on what is taking place, he can describe and expound a situation, and he can even supply masterly characterizations and evaluations.[34] In

[32] The epic of the shield of Heracles (see Ch. IIIc, below) carries the symbolism of weapons considerably further. Actual shields were often decorated with symbols of this sort; Mycenaean daggers with lion battles and beasts of prey falling upon their victims are analogous to the Homeric similes. Odysseus' buckle (*Od.* 19, 226–31) which holds his fluttering garment together carries the picture of a dog at the throat of a quivering hind (Ovid, *Metamorphoses* 8, 318 and 14, 394 has *mordebat fibula vestem*). In words as in pictures the Greeks symbolized function.

[33] In this respect the history of Thucydides is a parallel.

[34] Compare the delicacy of characterization in *Il.* 3, 210–23 (speech) with the coarse caricature in 2, 212–23 (narrative). In *Il.* 3, 60–66 Paris says to Hector, in effect: 'You have courage and I have charm; both are distinctions given by gods; I did not seek my gift, but I cannot dismiss it. (Nevertheless, I will now try to be a warrior like you if you like . . .' 67ff.) More precisely, Hector's energy is described as follows, with the help of a simile: (In contrast to natures like that of Paris,

general the speeches are freer and richer; their style and their mode
and course of thought are more modern than is narrative. In the
speeches we find quite often ideas, reflections, relationships, in
contradiction to those upon which the narrative and action rest.
It is as if forces held in check had here broken out with elemental
strength.

Just as the speeches of the *Iliad*, in contrast to the narrative, show
the difference between relative freedom and traditional stylization,
so, in the next place, the numerous similes supply insights into the
natural world picture of the poet which deviates sharply from the
artificial one of the narrative. Alongside the heroic subject we have
here a complementary pendant in the everyday world; alongside the
peculiar and unusual event, its foil in the customary and familiar.
For the similes the rule of selection which governs the narrative does
not apply. Here the writer does not archaize or stand on his dignity,
and he does not ignore the forces of his environment. Here there are
simple people of humble station with their work and care; there are
petty and rancorous squabbles over a tiny field; there are animals
which are complete living beings and act and feel as a man or a god
does; there is a tree in the glory of its blossoms broken down by a
cruel storm; there are storms and seasons and sickness. As the similes
do not merely clothe facts of the past in words but rather illuminate
and illustrate the events, so the speaker is no longer a mere reporter.
He adds something of his own and places himself in a man-to-man
relationship with the hearer. He enters the domain of his own time
and ordinary experience, in order to set the ancient things forth with
greater clarity and fullness.

The numerous similes constitute one of the most striking elements
of style in the epics, especially in the *Iliad*. Their nature and function
have often been misconceived; we shall conclude our examination of
epic style with some remarks on Homeric similes.

In the midst of a narrative, abruptly interrupting its steady
advance at an exciting moment, an 'as when' will introduce a
simile. A scene is built up, frequently with numerous details, so that
many a simile requires a whole series of verses, until at the end, when
the picture has been rounded out, the narrative resumes its advance
with 'so.'

which, after an initial effort, give up at first difficulty, *Il.* 3, 30ff.), Hector's is a
'temper unterrified' (63) and his heart can never be worn down, like the ax (of a
shipwright) which, guided by the man's hand (the heart is regarded as a tool, an
implement which Hector uses), cleaves through the timber when he skilfully
trims a ship's beam (i.e., hardness and keenness and strength do not simply hew
away, but shape the material deftly and expertly and cleverly), whereby it (the
ax, the heart) promotes the force of the man.

Ancient epic knew only linear representation, and the simile provides a second, parallel line alongside the narrative. Doubling gives the matter greater weight, and the reader who is required to combine disparate pictures is stimulated to think the situation out thoroughly. The similarity of the two pictures is not limited to single traits; rather, there is resemblance in the structure of the scene or course of the action as an entirety.[35] The stereoscopic double view produces a new plasticity. The more a simile is elaborated, the brighter the light it throws on the total situation for all the participants alike. In the interplay of the two pictures, the mood and temper of the actors are brought into the foreground with greater force than in bare and reticent narrative. Hope, greed, determination, anxiety, yearning, fear, disillusionment, despair: scarcely ever do these spring more directly from the persons of the story to the sympathetic hearer than by the indirect working of this 'artistic device', the simile.

The similes only suggest the parallelism, without stressing it point for point. What is missing in one of the pictures is supplied by reflection from its counterpart. And beyond what is expressed in words on this side and that, much more is adumbrated in the background of the simile. For most of the similes are typical, and the hearer is familiar with the types. Just as each portion of a narrative tells us more in its context than it could in isolation, so the individual simile gains in content from the fact that the hearers recall the family connections of the picture.

A large family of similes has the shepherd and his typical experiences as its theme. In its shortest form the comparison between hero and shepherd is suggested when, as often happens, the hero is called 'shepherd of the people' (ποιμὴν λαῶν) because he protects his men from the enemy as the shepherd does the cattle entrusted to him from beasts of prey.[36] In the wars of the Homeric period the roles of leader and of his men were apportioned very differently from what they are today. Only the leader, a wealthy nobleman, was fully equipped with costly offensive and defensive arms and had at his disposal a war chariot to give him mobility. In close battle the ordinary man was virtually defenseless before the champions of the enemy—like sheep before lions. The masses therefore mostly kept in the background, at a long space from the enemy, while between the

[35] Individual traits often become transitions from the narrative to the simile or the reverse, e.g., 'Just as speedily . . .' This does not mean that the simile is intended to illustrate the single trait (speed) exclusively or even principally. Cf. H. Fränkel, *Die homerischen Gleichnisse* (Göttingen, 1921), pp. 3ff.

[36] 'And he who is no warrior should also be no shepherd.' Only later, under the influence of pastoral poetry and the New Testament, did the shepherd become a symbol of peaceful gentleness.

battle-lines the champions fought their peers. Often a champion
would try to break into the enemy line with a leap and create
carnage. The opposing champion had to try to protect his people—
as the shepherd his flock from the lion. If he failed to do so they were
lost.

Now a simile. Diomedes son of Tydeus is slightly wounded by an
arrow; a comrade removes it and Diomedes is again hale and
vigorous (*Il.* 5, 134):

> Now Diomedes again went forward to the front of the battle.
> Long had his heart been afire with rage to slaughter the Trojans;
> Now was that wrath threefold. As when in the pastures a lion,
> Leaping the sheepfold wall, is struck by the spear of a shepherd;
> Pained by the wound, not quelled, his furious anger arises;
> Nor does the shepherd resist, but crawls in fear to his refuge,
> Scattered and slain his sheep lie slaughtered one on another.
> Then leaps the lion in fury away high over the hurdles:
> So on his foes with wrath came raging great Diomedes.[37]

The triumph of victorious pursuit and the horror of helpless
flight are described in the following simile (*Il.* 11, 172):

> Across the midst of the plain the Trojans escaped like cattle
> When a grim lion pursues: in the middle of the night he attacks them
> All, but for one of them is no flight from headlong destruction:[38]
> First he seizes the neck in his crushing jaws and he breaks it;
> Next he will lap up its blood and feast on the flesh and the offal:
> So drove Atreus' son, the ruler of men Agamemnon,
> Killing whoever ran last: they scattered in terror before him.

Often the massed line of commoners succeeds in fending an enemy
champion off and pressing him back. So Ajax was once forced to
retire (*Il.* 11, 546):

> While he drew back he glared like a beast on the ranks of his foemen,
> Turning and turning again, while step by step he retreated.
> As when a crowd of farmers and dogs are driving a lion
> Back from the high-walled pen and will not yield and allow him
> Freely to eat of the fat of their cattle; thus they remain there
> Watching throughout the night; but he in the greed of his hunger
> Crouches to spring, yet stays where he is, for so many lances
> Thrown by undaunted hands are everywhere flying about him,
> Many a firebrand too, which he fears in spite of his anger.
> As the day dawns, he retires cast down and troubled in spirit.

[37] The simile carries the action through up to the withdrawal of the lion; the
parallel thus runs far ahead of the narrative. Consequently, the transition from
the close of the simile to the narrative is not very smooth.

[38] αἰπύς means 'steep,' and the phrase likens death not to a drop from a cliff
but to running against a wall. Cf. *Il.* 13, 317.

So did Ajax retreat with sorrowing heart from the Trojans
Slowly, consumed with care for the threatened ships of the Argives.

Shepherd and beast-of-prey similes are all similar, and the beast
similes are in turn related to images of the chase. For every situation
in Homeric battle the large family of similes has a picture that will
fit or can be made to fit. So, for example, warriors fighting in a band
are likened to a pack of wolves or to hounds that the huntsman
(leader) urges on against the beast of prey or the game, and so on. In
pictures from this familiar circle a few hints are enough to build up a
complete situation. This remedies a weakness of the linear style,
which can ordinarily thrust only a small segment of a total event into
its picture. Similes broaden the horizon by bringing the headlong
action to a momentary halt in order to introduce a detailed reflection
of the situation.

A second system of similes draws its images from the play of natural
forces. Wind and wave, cliff and peak and cloud, serve as symbols of
determination, thrust and counter-shock, resistance or compliance.
The champion is the towering 'cliff' against which the 'storm' of
attackers breaks. Or the streaming horde is seen as 'waves,' which
protected by the 'helmet' of foaming whitecaps (κορύσσεται, *Il.* 4,
424) break furiously against the 'cliffs.' The 'wind' which drives
the breakers against the shore becomes the driving will, either of the
masses themselves or of the leader who sweeps them along. From the
massed soldiery the picture can be transferred to the massed folk in
the assembly. Agamemnon had made a suggestion to the assembled
army, and the masses accepted it joyfully, 'aroused like the great
waves of the sea which the stormy Southeast wind has set in motion'
(*Il.* 2, 144). Shortly thereafter the mood is reversed; Agamemnon
makes a contrary proposal, and this too is accepted with enthusiasm
(*Il.* 2, 394):

So he spoke, and the Argives shouted aloud, like the surf
Crashing on a rocky shore when the south winds blows, which impels it
Raging against some cliff; the breakers never leave it
Driven by all the winds which are blowing from every direction.

Here the visible link between simile and narrative is the roar of the
waves and of the masses. The 'cliff' is now the leader himself. This
time the simile closes with a remarkable sentence. In view of the
radical change in the popular will the language of the image explains:
However the wind may blow,[39] always the masterful leader (the
towering cliff) is surrounded by acclamation (the roaring surf). Once

[39] The image of the *popularis aura* (Horace, *Odes* 3, 2, 30) survives through all
antiquity. Cf. J. M. Linforth, *Solon the Athenian* (Berkeley, 1919), p. 215.

an appropriate image has been found, such as 'storm at sea,' to symbolize will power driving in a definite direction, it can be given many new applications. So at one time (*Il.* 14, 16) the uncertainty of a man waiting for an impulse to move him in one direction or the other is likened to the silent ground swell which rolls about uncertainly, waiting for the storm to give it a decisive direction.

The *Odyssey* is not nearly so rich in similes. It uses fewer of them because its action itself in larger part moves over the free and open world on which the similes of the *Iliad* cast only a momentary ray of light. On the other hand, many of the similes in the *Odyssey* are original and not constrained by a system.

An example. Odysseus, lodging in his own house as an unknown beggar, has lain down to sleep in the anteroom. There he witnesses deeds that deeply offend his dignity as master. But he represses his rising anger. If he took action at this time all would be lost. First some clever counter-measure must be planned (*Od.* 20, 25):

'As when a man at a bright blazing fire turns a pudding full of fat and blood this way and that, eager to roast it quickly, so he turned this way and that scheming how to lay hands upon the shameless suitors, he one and they many.'

Here the sensible link between simile and narrative is the restless tossing in bed, which is like the turning of the sausage over the fire. But what is intended is the turning of possibilities this way and that in Odysseus' thoughts and the impatience with which he awaits the proper moment for his vengeance, as a hungry man does the preparation of his food. The picture is expressive but peculiar, and constitutes an extreme example of the occasional decadence of Homeric style in the *Odyssey*. As the similes of the *Iliad* descend from the heroic level to the commonplace, so the sausage simile of Odysseus' unheroic situation descends to the vulgar.

(c) *The Material*

Whence do the materials which make up the subject matter of our epics ultimately derive? As early as the sixth century B.C. there were in Greece skeptics who held that the content of the epics was pure fiction; and in the nineteenth century scholars were unanimous in thinking that the Trojan War and everything connected with it could be nothing more than poetic fable. The question was reopened thanks to the salutary fanaticism of a layman. Ridiculed by specialists, yet unshakably believing in the literal truth of the poetic words,

Heinrich Schliemann took up the spade in the year 1870 and found Troy and the age-old city of Mycenae. He found more indeed than he sought: not one Troy, but the remains of seven or nine or more cities, one over the other. But he and his successors also found less than they expected: the Homeric Ithaca, for example, as the *Odyssey* describes it, never existed. The question in its simplest form— Is Homer's narrative true?—cannot be answered simply.

First a distinction must be made between the truth of the general conditions and that of the particular events and persons. The action of the epics takes place in the remote epoch before Greek settlement of the East, where the epics were created. Is the picture of the age and its civilization as the poets described and supposed it correct? Or was it only free invention, based on a dream of a good olden time which in hard fact had never existed?

In general, so far as history can be illuminated without written records,[1] researches following up those of Schliemann have to a large extent confirmed the accuracy of the Homeric picture. Approximately from 1570 until after 1200 B.C.[2] there flourished in Greece a unified, advanced, and highly individual culture. It is this bronze-age culture which is reflected in Homeric epic; in the poems bronze takes the place occupied by iron in the poet's lifetime. The center of that early Greek civilization was Mycenae, 'rich in gold.' When Schliemann opened the six shaft graves at the ancient royal citadel of Mycenae in 1876, the yield of golden ornaments and vessels from the sixteenth century amounted to fourteen kilograms. Such were the treasures which the historic soil guarded for three and a half millennia and preserved for the man whose naïve trust in his Homer, as he understood him, gave him the courage to search for and bring back confirmation of his faith in the form of heavy masses of solid gold out of the earth.

Schlieman was convinced that Homer was contemporary with the events he narrates. This idea we cannot share. For us the epics are not verse chronicles which fix recent experience for all future time,

[1] I am no judge of how far written evidence of the second millennium B.C. from Mesopotamia, Egypt, and the land of the Hittites can throw light upon the Greek world. But since 1953, thanks above all to the extraordinary achievement of Michael Ventris, numerous inscribed clay tablets of the 15th to the 11th century from sites of Cretan-Mycenaean culture have been read and understood. These are by far the oldest written records in Greek. Much work on these texts has been done and is going on, though there are still those who hold that their decipherment and interpretation as Greek is illusory. The material consists exclusively of written lists of physical objects, assignment of work, and the like, from princely households.

[2] Following Karo, *RE* Suppl. 6, 584ff.

but the end product of centuries of development. In the early twelfth century Mycenaean culture was destroyed; its fall was due to the irruption of new and as yet uncivilized Greek tribes—the so-called Dorian invasion. Under the pressure of these immigrants who poured out of the north over the Greek mainland and the Peloponnese in several waves during a considerable space of time, many Greeks for their part abandoned their mother country and settled the islands of the Aegean as well as the Asiatic coastland. They took their native traditions with them, and from these formed the cycle of epic poems. In the epics the picture of the Mycenaean epoch is preserved with great fidelity in many details (see pp. 21 and 34f., above). Excavation of Mycenaean sites and tombs has yielded new objects and remains of buildings whose pictures can serve to illustrate the Homeric poems.

On the other hand the epic tradition has utterly erased an important historical fact. Mycenaean culture was not indigenous and not native Greek but only an offshoot of the Cretan. Developed on Cretan soil, it was taken over by Greek immigrants and from Crete carried to the palaces of the mainland.[3] About this the epic is silent, so that the excavations of Evans in Crete (beginning in 1900) created a new sensation, this time in an opposite sense. Now the results of spadework provided undreamed-of correction of the picture of antiquity sketched in the epics. Epic tradition gave no intimation that the heroic age was so strongly influenced from abroad. It had effaced all alien traits in the ancient culture and retained only those which were in keeping with Greek ways of life.[4] In retrospect the national past was cleansed of un-Greek elements, precisely as the epic in the colonial lands, where it attained its full bloom and maturity, kept itself pure of everything Asiatic, except what had become wholly Greek through assimilation.

If we ask, secondly, about the historical truth of events and persons, the kernel of the Trojan epics is probably historical. Shortly after 1200 one of the cities at Troy[5] was burned and destroyed by foreign invaders. This is precisely the period at which the Trojan War was alleged to have taken place, according to Greek chronology. There are no sufficient grounds to doubt that a Greek raiding expedition

[3] But these views are still not fully established.

[4] Cf. G. Karo, *RE* Suppl. 6, 601f.

[5] Troy VII, according to Blegen, *Amer. Journ. Arch.* 39 (1935), 550f.; 43 (1939), 204f. Investigation and discussion of the site are still in progress. For a summary account see now Blegen in A. J. B. Wace and F. H. Stubbings, *A Companion to Homer* (London and New York, 1962), 362–86; and for the historical elements in the *Iliad* see D. L. Page, *History and the Homeric Iliad* (Berkeley and Los Angeles, 1959).

conquered, plundered, and destroyed the flourishing city on the west coast of Asia and, after heavy losses, returned to its mother country.[6] This happened late in the Mycenaean age, before the whole culture collapsed. Thus it is easy to understand that, as the last great deed of the Mycenaean age, the expedition against Troy was fixed most impressively in the memory of generations following and that the brilliance of high heroism in epic was flavored with the gloom of approaching destruction which gives the poetry of Troy its somber grandeur. How far individual personages in the epics are historical is questionable, and the probability of conjectures varies from case to case. Certainly some pure inventions were added to the historical core, and in general the picture of the expedition became more all-embracing and more magnificent in the course of time. Much is half-true. According to the *Iliad* (5, 627ff.), Tlepolemus and Sarpedon, leaders of the Rhodians and the Lycians, fought one another before Troy. Lycia is the mainland region opposite the island of Rhodes, and Tlepolemus is in Greek legend the leader of the Greek settlers who occupied Rhodes. So the duel between the two in the *Iliad* may reflect a historical battle of the Greeks of Rhodes against the inhabitants of Asia Minor; only later was the battle transposed to the north and to an earlier period, through the magnetic power of the epic which attracted all possible material to the great expedition against Troy.

Third and last, the question of historicity does not have the same significance for the *Odyssey* as for the *Iliad*. The stories of the two epics are wholly different in their nature. Even if everything the *Odyssey* narrates were true the events are irrelevant to history. History is little concerned whether Odysseus reached home or not, or whether Telemachus or one of the suitors was his successor. On the other hand, a historical atmosphere breathes through every episode of the *Iliad*; everything that is done or said is of immediate significance for the fate of nations. Here the personages deal with one another as princes, generals, and allies communicate and treat with one another. In the *Odyssey* the relations are as father and son, man and wife, guest and host, wanderer and shepherd, master and slave, beggar and beggar; one man is related to another according to private and accidental circumstances. Even where occasions for political formulations offer themselves they are not exploited.[7] Obviously the authors had no wish to leave the sphere of private life.

[6] Cf. M. P. Nilsson, *Homer and Mycenae* (London, 1933), pp. 249ff., and J. A. Caskey, *Amer. Journ. Arch.* 52 (1948), 121f.

[7] Between the suitors we would expect jealousy and intrigue, influenced by political considerations, especially since some are at home in Ithaca and others

The plot of the *Odyssey* is essentially the plot of a novel or romance; but many traits derive from the realms of myth and fairy tale. The fascinating romance of the prince who travels far afield as a young man and returns as an aged beggar, all alone, and with strength and cunning regains his proper station; of the unrecognized husband who finds his wife on the point of celebrating a new marriage; of the faithful but despairing wife and of the son who wishes to help but does not know how, of loyal and disloyal servants and maids—such themes do not require comment or analysis. But myth and fairy tale do demand a word of explanation.

Unlike historically based saga, the romance is not by its nature tied to a given spot. Hence it is no wonder that excavators could not find Odysseus' palace at Ithaca, as they could the citadel of 'Agamemnon' and the fortress of King 'Priam.'[8] The Odysseus story is localized on an insignificant island, remote from the centers of Mycenaean culture. The reason is presumably that the story has adopted elements from the sun myth.[9] The far west is considered the abode of the sun, and according to the *Odyssey* (9, 25) Ithaca is situated 'at the extremity toward the West.'[10]

There is a series of touches in the *Odyssey* which point to the original solar nature of the hero,[11] and there are not a few passages in it which can be understood better from these relationships. But in the epic that we read, the religious elements of the fable, except for slight vestiges, are secularized and humanized.

come from abroad; instead, they are in agreement, like ideal business partners. Between the allies before Troy there is much livelier conflict than between the rivals in Ithaca. Telemachus rejects the thought that he wishes to win the kingship (which is his by right) for himself; he is only concerned for mastery of his own house. He summons an assembly, and the people expect that public business will be discussed; but he explains that he wishes to speak only of his own private cares (2, 30–45). The poets do depict in detail the lively partisanship of the people in the affairs of the royal home, but they invent no attempt at active intervention (except for the feeble postlude—24, 413ff.).

[8] Cf. M. P. Nilsson in *Einleitung in die Altertumswissenschaft* II, 3d ed. (Leipzig, 1922), 279.

[9] For a long while so much misuse was made of alleged sun and star myths that this species of explanation has been suspected and condemned. It is time the ban were broken.

[10] This does not fit the facts, but the Ionians of the East knew little of the far West of Greece. The topography of the island in the *Odyssey* does not fit the facts either.

[11] In the *Odyssey* Helios is not angry with Odysseus but with the other Ithacans who devoured his kine, just as Odysseus is angry with the suitors (who were originally all Ithacans) because they slaughtered his kine. The miracle scenes (12, 394–96 and 20, 345ff.) are very similar. But analysis of these and other passages would carry us beyond our present scope.

There is much wider scope for the miraculous and for the fairy-tale element as compared with the *Iliad*, which admits the former only rarely and the latter not at all. In his adventurous voyages, which carry him to the back of beyond, Odysseus experiences fairy-tale wonders which are not only unhistorical but which have little to do with geography or ethnography. The poet has no interest in telling the reader where to look on the map, or even in pretending to do so,[12] he wishes only to entertain, surprise, and astonish. These stories are only loosely connected even with the romance material in the *Odyssey*.

Almost all travel adventures derive from the free fancy of a seafaring population. Anxiety dreams play a part, in which the fisher plays the part of the fish. Just as the fisher hauls his prey out of the sea, so the monster Scylla seizes the seaman sailing by in order to swallow him up. On the coast of the Laestrygonians the comrades of Odysseus are caught in an enclosed bay with a narrow opening as in a trap; the giants shatter their boat and hunt the swimming men down with spears 'like fish' (*Od.* 10, 124) in order to devour them.

Another group of motifs derives from the sphere of men who sail the seas themselves but from their kinsfolk. Many a sailor goes to sea and nothing more is ever seen or heard of him. He may have perished, or be held captive far away, or have remained there voluntarily. To those who vainly await his return all that is left is to brood over the loss. Their imagination fills the grim and shapeless void of the disappearance with concrete images which, in part at least, are drawn in friendly colors. 'He has not returned' was expressed in early Greek as 'He has forgotten his homecoming'. It is in part a metaphor but in part also a fairy tale when his kin say of a man long absent that he had eaten of the plant 'forget-your-home.' Odysseus and his comrades arrive at a country where such a plant grows, the land of the lotus-eaters. The *Odyssey* ascribes no magic powers to the lotus and no evil purposes to the lotus-eaters (9, 92). The flowery honey-sweet food was so delicious that for its sake the comrades 'wished to forget their homecoming' (9, 97). In the story of the Sirens (12, 39ff., 158ff.) the enticing charm which holds voyagers forever on a foreign strand is the song of women, originally, in all probability, choral lyric, but in the epic, naturally, epic recitation (see p. 9, above). The effect of the song of the Sirens is that 'neither wife nor children surround the returned voyager and rejoice'—which is the viewpoint of those left at home. The eventual fate of the victims is

[12] With few exceptions, like the difficult story of the Laestrygonians, 10, 82ff. On the other hand, the story of the Argonauts is intended to give a straight travel report, however fanciful it may be in detail.

here sketched in gloomier colors (12, 45f.).[13] Circe possesses actual
magic power; she is evil, and transforms the men who are in her
power into beasts. But as soon as Odysseus breaks her magic Circe
becomes his mistress. Calypso is only a mistress, and she wishes to
make Odysseus immortal in order to live with him forever. Nymphs
are spirits of a locality; they represent the living nature of a countryside, the freshness of its brooks and meadows, the growth of its
forests, the solitude of its hills. The landscape of Calypso's island is
described most attractively in the *Odyssey* (5, 63–74): 'even an
immortal could be astonished and take pleasure in it.' In the Calypso
legend the unknown faraway place which keeps the missing wanderer
forever is embodied as the amorous nymph of an earthly paradise,
who will vouchsafe the seafarer everlasting bliss at her side. And in
this legend the divine power itself is called simply 'disappearance,'
for the name 'Calypso' is obviously derived from καλύπτειν, 'to swathe,
hide away.'[14]

From the fields of the lotus-eaters and from the islands of Circe and
Calypso, according to this notion, no one was ever to return. And yet
at least one must have succeeded in coming back, for otherwise we
should have no knowledge of all these matters. He must have been,
like Odysseus, bolder and more determined than ordinary men, so
that he could even wrench himself away from a Calypso; he must
have been cleverer than others and have enjoyed divine assistance
not to succumb even to the magic of a Circe. Such a man can even
descend to the realm of the dead and get back. It is very natural
that many adventures were heaped upon one and the same person.
Thus Odysseus appropriated material which previously belonged in
the saga of the Argonauts.[15] Since the hero of the *Odyssey* was
intended as a model of Ionian cunning and boldness and since he
too was long absent, it was natural enough that travel adventures
also should be attributed to him. Furthermore, it is typical of reports
of wonderful journeys, ancient and modern, that the traveler is
imagined as reporting his own journeys in the first person; so it
happens also in the apologues of the *Odyssey*.

Apart from material gradually developed out of a historical kernel,

[13] Other written and pictorial tradition presents the Sirens as half woman, half
bird, for in the Greek imagination the singing of women was associated with the
song of birds. The *Odyssey* suppresses this primitive feature.

[14] Hermann Güntert's book *Calypso* (Halle a.S., 1921) identifies Calypso and
the other fairyland figures with death. The thesis has been quite generally
accepted; but this interpretation spoils the point. For Calypso and kindred
figures were invented by people who wished to think of the absent not as dead but
as living.

[15] Cf. K. Meuli, *Odysee und Argonautika* (Berlin, 1921).

or out of themes of romance or fairy tale, the epics also include material which accrued to them in their latest stage out of fresh invention. A new age gave currency to its new ideas and tendencies, for example in the travel books of the Telemachy (*Od.* 3 and 4), in the Eumaeus idyl (*Od.* 14 and 15), and at the conclusion of the *Iliad* (Book 24), which can be compared with a passage from the next-to-last book of the *Odyssey*.

The Telemachy as well as the Eumaeus idyl belongs to those portions in which the stream of epic action is halted and dammed up into a quiet lake (see pp. 18f., above). The Telemachy has a young man go on a journey to gain information, to be educated, and to visit heroes of the Trojan War. If Telemachus' modest heroism is still in the future, Nestor, Menelaus, and Helen have their great deeds behind them: through the fortunate eyes of the youth we observe the domestic life of the princes who reside in their royal seats and enjoy high dignity, the one with prudence and piety and the other pair with wealth and brilliance.[16] We look upon the great heroes from a humble level: the poet of the Telemachy may well have looked upon the glorious figures of the *Iliad* with the same awe as did Telemachus himself. On the other hand, we enter the hut of Eumaeus with firm and confident step. Even in its presentation the wholly different milieu, with its simple warmth and unadorned humanity, touches us much more nearly than the stateliness of the grandees. And when Eumaeus and the wanderer speak to each other of their past, their stories are indeed enthralling, but neither pathetic nor heroic; the lives of both men have been ruined by the treachery of others. Just as the Telemachy looks back upon the proud kings of the *Iliad* from the level of the *Odyssey*, so the Eumaeus scenes look into the everyday life which was opened up for epic by the Odyssey.[17]

The mood has changed. The romantic attitude of shuddering admiration for awe-inspiring men and events is also on the wane. A gentler mode of feeling asserts itself, and in the end affects both epics, transforming and reshaping them: bitter hatred is quieted before the corpse of a slain enemy, and a chivalrous code has the last word.

In the *Iliad*, the old and the new stand side by side in contradiction. There is no suppression of the horrible abuse of Hector's body by which Achilles avenges the death of his dearest comrade even on a dead enemy,[18] avenges it the more savagely and cruelly because he

---

[16] Cf. P. Von der Mühll, *RE* Suppl. 7, 707.

[17] For this and the following cf. pp. 85f., below.

[18] Except that the singer alleviates the horror by a divine intervention and expresses his own revulsion at such barbarity through the lips of a god (*Il.* 23, 284ff.; 24, 18–54).

was himself in part to blame. There follows then the journey of the aged father to the slayer of his son and the gripping encounter of the two. The closing notes of the war poem resound with gentle sorrow, but without abating the heroic temper of the great figures or lessening the fateful seriousness of the events.

To demonstrate the corresponding transformation toward the close of the *Odyssey* we must deal with it at somewhat greater length. On the day upon which the long wooing of many men for the hand of Penelope was to reach its goal, and with the weapon whose mastery was to determine the choice of husband, Odysseus slaughtered the entire company of suitors, good and bad, in the men's hall. Now he has a three-fold claim to possess his wife: as her husband, as her avenger, and as a victor in the contest for the high prize. A bitter irony is involved, in that until the moment when he grasped his bow and entered the contest, Odysseus was a beggar, regarded seriously by no one. This touch should logically point to a concluding picture of equally powerful irony. Such a scene is in fact present. After the corpses are stowed in the courtyard (22, 448–51) Odysseus and Penelope celebrate their second marriage together in the freshly cleansed hall. Music and the tread of dancers echo in the royal hall, while in the nearby courtyard the best youth of the land lie in their blood. Outside, people pass whose brothers and sons had had to pay for the festivities with their lives (23, 148ff.):

> Those who could hear the rejoicing spoke then one to another:
> 'So now someone has won her, the queen with so many suitors.
> Strange, that she had not the strength to guard the house of her husband
> Faithfully up to the end, till he came again home to his people.'
> Thus they murmured in passing, but knew not what had befallen.

This is an impressive conclusion for the great drama, but in our *Odyssey* it is masked by being painted over and deprived of its effect. The festivity is no longer a real festivity[19] but only a cunning trick to deceive the kinsmen of the slain men and to detain them long enough for Odysseus to prepare his campaign of vengeance. In our *Odyssey* the aged Euryclea is not permitted, when she sees the slaughter, to utter the loud cry which women emitted on joyous occasions (ὀλολυγή). Odysseus restrains her with words of warning (22, 411ff.):

> Only rejoice in your heart, old woman; cease your exulting:
> Impious rises the victory song by the corpse of the vanquished.
> These found death by the will of the gods and by their own passions.

[19] That it was originally genuine is confirmed by 21, 428–30, which points forward to 23, 143–45.

In the *Iliad* boastful cries of victory are constantly uttered over the body of an enemy, and no one takes exception to them. The later singers felt otherwise. Their new piety spoiled the fine old scene of the bloody marriage feast in the *Odyssey*, and in the *Iliad* it created the fine new scene of ransoming Hector.

(d) *Gods and Powers*

'Deeds of men and of gods' constitute the themes of epic recitations (*Od.* 1, 338). Thanks to the divine Muse who inspires him, the poet knows how to sing and tell even of those higher powers whose doings are hidden to the ordinary man.[1] The inclusion of gods in our *Odyssey* is sufficiently motivated by the fable itself, for here the gods direct every phase of the action for long stretches, and Athene vouchsafes the hero and his son a series of services, both great and small. In the *Iliad*, however, the numerous scenes involving gods are not to be understood in this way. Here the gods do not appear merely to intervene in the events of the Trojan War, but what happens in the world of gods is for the poet obviously a second, independent theme alongside the human. The action takes place on two levels basically, in heaven and on earth, and one of the two may occasionally retreat into the background. Secondly, the divine scenes often contain no action, properly speaking, but are descriptive in nature, like the late descriptions of the human milieu in the *Odyssey*. And thirdly, among the divine scenes are some of unattractive coarseness, spiced with vulgar jokes and raucous laughter. Gods quarrel with and deceive one another, gods come to blows or fall full length—and what gigantic length it is!—on to the ground.[2] Such behavior of the gods among themselves must have been offensive to pious sensibilities, beginning with Xenophanes, a rhapsode of the sixth century (pp. 330f., below). If to Homeric man religion was nothing but the transcendental basis of morality, the religion of the *Iliad* would have been absurd and highly objectionable; and if the gods meant nothing to him but the highest powers which impinged forcefully upon the life of man, these descriptions of the gods in the *Iliad* would still be frivolous sport with the loftiest of figures, and the

---

[1] This happens consistently only in the narrative; the speeches of epic personages keep within the sphere of ordinary mortals (cf. O. Jörgensen, *Hermes*, 1904, pp. 357–82). In this respect also, therefore, the narrative is differentiated from the speeches (pp. 39f., above), but here it is the narrative that enjoys greater liberty.

[2] *Il.* 1, 533ff.; 14, 153ff.; 21, 385ff. The *Odyssey*, too, contains some Olympian buffoonery, but only indirectly, in a reported song of a bard (*Od.* 8, 266ff.).

more reprehensible in that they are unnecessary for the action of the poem.[3] But no religion develops consistently out of one sole idea of the divine. The three difficulties can be cleared up together if we can understand the peculiar conception which the Homeric world of gods helped to fashion.

In this conception of the divine we encounter for the first time a form of thought which was to become dominant in the archaic age of the Greeks, after Homer—the mode of polar opposites. Qualities could be conceived only if opposites were conceived at the same time. The narrow limitations of human existence accordingly requires the counter-image of unlimited but otherwise manlike divine existence.[4] In this conception the god is not more ethical than man, for strict ethics is a burdensome constraint; but he enjoys a superhuman abundance of vital existence. Hence the gods are sharply individualized, not abstract; hence they constitute a numerous divine society, with Zeus as their paternal[5] head, like human families and society. A further consequence is that there cannot be much historical action for them, but rather only existence, milieu, and episode. Nothing needs to be taken seriously. When the gods are by themselves they laugh, as no human can, their Homeric laughter, unrestrained and untroubled. They laugh while men struggle with one another in dust and pain and blood. And when men fight for life and death, the gods join in as a joke and Zeus' heart laughs for joy at their strife (*Il.* 21, 389). Strife is the theme of the *Iliad* and of much other epic composition (*Od.* 8, 75). If man is savage and quarrelsome the god must be so likewise. Hence the gods combat one another, taunt one another, and then caress and comfort one another. Tragic happenings on earth demand similar, but untragic, happenings on Olympus. Paradoxical as it may seem, the fact that the gods engage in absurd pranks with one another is inherent in their godliness.

The gods can be unthinking because they are certain.[6] When man enters upon war he causes his fellow men countless woes and casts many brave souls to death as his trophy, only himself to suffer woe

---

[3] A man to whom religion signifies pious regard for the sublime can be properly satisfied with only two Homeric scenes: when Zeus nodding assent causes Olympus to shake, and when punishing Apollo makes himself 'grin as the dark of night' (*Il.* 1, 528 and 44ff.).

[4] The opposition is precise even in details. The gods 'who dwell in Olympus', eat immortality (ambrosia) in exact contrast to the earth dwellers who 'eat the fruit of the earth' (*Il.* 6, 142) and are therefore subject to earth and death (*Il.* 13, 322; 21, 465).

[5] Cf. G. M. Calhoun, 'Zeus the Father in Homer,' *Trans. Am. Phil. Ass.*, 1935, p. 1.

[6] Cf. *Il.* 22, 19.

and death in the end. But the gods intervene in human fate with a light hand, like a child playing in the sand, building and destroying (*Il.* 15, 361). It is precisely the wantonness which we sense in the coarse play of the gods with one another and with mankind that contributes to their uncanny greatness; for the ancient epic looks with admiration upon these lordly figures, living their untroubled and unconstrained lives. When the god has had enough, he needs only to stop. Wounded Ares ascends to heaven; he is healed in an instant by the physician-god; Hebe, the resplendent essence of youthful bloom, washes his earthly dirt away; he dresses in attractive clothing and takes his seat near Father Zeus 'joyful because of his [recovered] dignity [κῦδος]' (*Il.* 5, 906; cf. *Frühgriech. Denken*, p. 314). The god can return to his lordliness at any time (*Od.* 8, 362–66), but man must bear to the bitter end all that men and gods and he himself do to him. He is tied to his earth; the gods come and go. They can participate in the great drama or enjoy it as spectators; and they can 'sit serenely in their chambers, where the house of each is built on the slopes of Olympus' (*Il.* 11, 75). What for men is the first and the last, the one and the all, is for the gods an entertaining play from which they can look away if they choose, and have no personal concern. For them the great war, as one of them remarks upon occasion, is 'the lesser thing,' lesser, that is, than the joys of a feast in jolly company (*Il.* 1, 576).[7] The divine capacity for turning away from the frightful things on earth and looking ahead rules an horizon and appoints boundaries for the Trojan War and all human existence. Human suffering takes place only in the one half of a two-sided world. In an epic poem the other side must not be wanting. For only by means of the divine foil, as the logic of the age postulates, can humanity be shown in its appropriate place.

Gods who could shut themselves away from all else and remain self-sufficient in their own heaven did not have to deal with affairs of the world except according to desire and inclination.[8] Thus this concep-

---

[7] Cf. P. Friedländer, 'Lachende Götter,' *Die Antike* 10, 209. The auditors of an epic recitation must also have felt like the gods when with food and drink they enjoyed the spectacle which the poet's song spread before their minds. Like the gods in the *Iliad*, they too would have discussed the events with passionate partisanship during the entr'actes, and have argued about how it would turn out. Cf. p. 12 n. 11, above.

[8] In *Il.* 1, 423–27, Thetis informs her son Achilles that 'all the gods' (i.e., the Olympians, of whom Thetis herself, as a lowly sea goddess, was not one) had gone to the edge of the world for twelve days to enjoy a long holiday among the Ethiopians. During this time battles went on before Troy without divine surveillance. Only after the gods returned to Olympus could Thetis speak with Zeus privately and bring the human situation to his attention (493ff.).

tion of the gods stands in irreconcilable opposition to that in which the gods are the effective and decisive powers in all earthly happenings. Both views occur in Homer side by side. There is no effort to harmonize them, for epic poetry has no desire to go into theology or formulate a consistent world picture. It takes what it is able and willing to use.

In their quality as regents of the world the gods of Homer fuse into a unity in which individuals no longer need be differentiated. Mention is made simply of 'the gods,' or also in the singular, without essential distinction, of 'God' or 'Zeus.' It is a firm belief that all that happens takes its course 'according to the counsel of the gods.' But all expressions of this sort are limited to generalities, as the epic generally is reticent and indefinite as soon as a personal element ceases to appear in tangible form.

The *Iliad* becomes articulate and specific at once when the gods separate into parties, and favor or persecute one or the other of the human parties. Individual heroes also may have their special friends among the gods. This situation then gives rise to many conflicts within the divine company.

A residual and collective notion of all that is assumed to be determined, without troubling over how and why it is so regulated, goes by the name of 'order' or 'fate.' 'Order' (θέμις) designates the unalterable rule which governs or should govern the relations of man to man. It embraces the norms and the facts of laws, ethics, and social institutions; even sexual intercourse is 'order' (*Il.* 9, 134). Out of this total aggregation of order, *one* institution is emphasized in manifold ways and put into close relationship with the gods, and that is the dignity of the king; his prerogatives and his claims upon the community are repeatedly derived from Zeus. There is no particular conception of natural law.[9]

For fate Homeric language has several names of which the most common, literally translated, means something like 'portion' (μοῖρα, αἶσα). The choice of such words indicates that it was not the rule, the universal law, that was to be designated, but the adaptation of the special fate to an individual, his personal 'portion.' So also fate is always spoken of in the sense of producing an important individual event. However, the whole, of which individual fates are a 'portion,' is not named. The gods are occasionally designated as givers of the 'portion'; but as a rule, fate, in contrast to the original meaning of 'portion,' is understood as an active force which 'over-

[9] But in the speeches of the *Odyssey* δίκη is used to designate a thing as natural; cf. *Frühgriech. Denken*, pp. 172f.; and further, K. Latte, *Antike und Abendland* II (1946), 64ff. (on θέμις and δίκη).

takes,' 'fetters,' 'seizes,' 'casts down,' 'constrains,' or 'slays' its victim.[10] For fate is predominantly active in catastrophes, defeat and destruction. When it brings deliverance or success, it is used mostly in the negative ('it was not yet his fate to fall'), seldom in a positive form. Very often 'fate' signifies 'death.' There is no special god called 'Death.'

In Homer fate is sometimes called 'the dispensation of the gods,' and is thus in some fashion attributed to the gods. In other places, however, the epic allows us to understand, contrary to the frequently expressed belief in a divine government of the world, that the course of the epic action is predestined by a fate to which even the gods must bend themselves. Before Hector's death Zeus consults the golden scales and puts the lot of death on both balances, one for Achilles and one for Hector. Hector's 'fated day' sinks to the depths and disappears in Hades. The god who had hitherto protected him deserts the victim, and Athene comes to support Achilles (*Il.* 22, 209ff.).

The idea of predestination is so alien and unconnected in the spiritual world of Homer that it must have a separate origin of its own, and this is not hard to find.

In the moving account of Hector's death the singer is convinced that the actual outcome was natural and logical: Hector's sense of honor (22, 99–110) and his discernment (111–30) leave him no other choice but battle to a final decision, and Achilles was the better fighter (40 and 158). On the other hand, the poet openly sympa-thizes with the underdog; Zeus himself wishes that Hector would escape death this time (168–81); and it is always possible for the gods to make even the improbable come about (cf. 202–04). But here they did not do so: Hector did in fact fall. Hence another power which stands even higher than the gods must be involved.

This conclusion drawn from a single example can be generalized. To the Homeric singer the events which he reported were not saga but reality. The main outlines of the course of events were fixed, and in particular the catastrophes; but within the framework which limited him the rhapsode might be guided by his own inspiration. The freer his scope inside the frame, the more tangible was the rigidity of its outer limitations. Again and again conflict must have arisen between the outcome of an episode as the tradition laid it down and the outcome the poet wished—out of preference for one party, out of sympathy for a man condemned to die, or because in

[10] Cf. E. Leitzke, *Moira und Gottheit im alten homer. Epos* (Göttingen, 1930), pp. 18f.; W. Greene, *Moira* (Cambridge, Mass., 1944), treats Homer on pp. 13ff. and *passim*.

his view, only his own outcome commended itself as right, natural, and artistic. The actual outcome, he felt, was other than it might have been or should have been; and so for him the tradition which had predetermined the outcome took on the form of a predestined fate.[11] As a rule he could regard this power as 'the fate of the gods,' for his intuitive interpretation of history could so manipulate the gods that they wished and caused what eventually happened. But many times, as he knew, the gods were split into warring parties; often they were not pleased with the turn events actually took; hence fate had eventually to be understood as a power to which even the gods must bow. It is inherent in this conception that fate is absolute, that is to say, it stands in no organic relationship to other powers in the world, and that its decisions are wilful, that is to say, not based on logic or capable of being understood. For this reason any attempt on our part to rationalize the power of fate in Homer, and fit it meaningfully into the Homeric world system, is doomed in advance. It represents the hard residue of fact which is insoluble by analysis of history and to which everything else must somehow accommodate itself. It is a strange and self-willed *must* which the poet can only accept as a datum and which his gods like his heroes[12] must accept as premises.

Thus for the epic poets to be driven back on fate was a simple necessity, and they could not do much about it; but the actual portrayal of the gods aroused their active interest. We have spoken above of the Olympian gods as rulers of the world who determine the course of events either by ordaining it from above or by taking a hand in it. But the conception of gods as bearers of power can be developed in another direction also. The gods may each be allotted a special function by virtue of which they operate in the world from within—as the goddess Earth and the god Sea, as sky and weather gods, or as love or war. But what does the *Iliad* think of the gods as separate partial powers in the life of the whole?

The narrative of the *Iliad* is concerned not with the normal course of natural things but with the unusual; and it is more interested in persons than in things. Where the greater Olympians are concerned, therefore, it pushes their practical functions into the background. According to his epithets, to be sure, Zeus is the god of the storm; but

---

[11] Cf. p. 75, below. The same applies to Attic tragedy, and hence the operation of fate is more marked than it probably was in living belief. In general, a man looking back on history is always tempted to become determinist and to think that all that went before necessarily led up to what in fact happened.

[12] 'The day will come when holy Ilium shall fall,' says Hector (*Il.* 6, 448). Cf. also p. 19, above.

his actions are almost exclusively those of the highest lord of the whole world. He needs to create no storms because clear sunlight always shines on the hosts; he is master of the storm only when he hurls lightning or causes bloody dew to rain down to rouse terror or announce coming woe or to swathe the warriors in clouds and dust. Just as Zeus has his seat 'in the bright heaven and the clouds,' so Poseidon dwells 'in the gray sea' (*Il.* 15, 190). But the sea is hardly more than his residence and realm; he is not identical with the element. When his chariot speeds over the waves, cleaving the water like a ship, and with dolphins sporting about it, the sea can do no better than recede and make way for him (*Il.* 13, 21ff.).[13] Similarly Thetis lives in the sea and sea nymphs accompany her (*Il.* 18, 35; 24, 83), but otherwise she is only Achilles' mother.[14] The goddess Earth appears in the narrative as little as Demeter. Things are different in the similes, for there the other, unstylized world appears, in which nature and life are filled with divine presences. In a simile 'fair-haired Demeter separates wheat and chaff in the stirring wind' (*Il.* 5, 500). This Demeter has nothing personal about her except her fair hair; she is, in fact, identical with the activity of winnowing.

For the lesser nature gods the rule does not apply. Scamander is at once river and person (*Il.* 21, 212ff.). Hypnos is both sleep and a person (*Il.* 14, 231ff.), and the winds are storms and persons in one (*Il.* 23, 198). When they are summoned from a feast by prayer and divine bidding and hasten to their task, they charm the clouds and the sea on the way into movement; for where the wind is, there the storm rages. It is otherwise with them than with Poseidon, for whom his element makes way.

The greater a god is the more he is a person for the epic poets, and the less a thing. This in no way corresponds to general Greek belief: Homeric poetry stylizes its gods one-sidedly in a particular direction. The great divinities Athene and Apollo appear here only as free and independent personalities. When Athene operates as a counter-weight to the god of war on the opposite side (*Il.* 4, 439), or is named with him as expert in warfare (13, 128), that does not make her war itself; she is only a warlike goddess who is active in war. According to general belief Apollo, in addition to other specific functions, was a god of death for men, as Artemis was a goddess of death for women; but the grand scene of his shooting arrows of pestilence in the first

---

[13] Only once is a kind of sympathy between the god and the element indicated. While Poseidon is leading the Achaeans to battle the sea rumbles against the shore (*Il.* 14, 392). Also the first of the similes adjoining, but only one of three, points to the murmuring sea.

[14] Thetis can even be contrasted with the sea (*Il.* 16, 34).

book of the *Iliad* can be understood and appreciated without knowledge of this fact. On the other hand, those of the Olympians who
cannot be dissociated from a specific function come to be treated as
gods of lesser rank (cf. *Il.* 5, 898). It is no accident that in the
burlesque scenes it is always Hephaestus the artisan, Ares who is
war, and Aphrodite who is love, who make themselves ridiculous and
despised.[15] On Hephaestus and his late acceptance in Olympus there
were special legends. As a smith he is obviously a person.[16] But
Aphrodite and Ares are only half person, half thing,[17] and yet the
epic poets admit them into their Olympus and their narratives as
living figures, themselves and their suite of related powers with them.
Out of the infinite company of such beings who play so significant a
role in Greek thought, those two emotional powers were chosen
which compel human beings to fall in love with one another, like
Helen and Paris, or to rage against one another in war, like Achaeans
and Trojans.[18]

Since Ares belongs to the Olympians in Homer, he can be regarded
as fully a person; he can have a love affair with Aphrodite, and although he is the god of war he can be wounded in battle. Wounded
Ares roars 'as nine or ten thousand men roar in war when they begin
the strife of Ares,' and both armies are frightened by the cry (*Il.* 5,
859–63). The description shows a transition from the person Ares to
the thing war. For the god's cry of pain is explained as the battle cry
of attacking armies, and it affects the armies as a terrifying battle
cry.[19]

[15] Artemis does indeed cut a very poor figure in the scenes in Olympus of Book
21. But the exception confirms the rule, for here Artemis' specific functions are
emphasized. Hera admonishes her that she should not have gone beyond her
functions as huntress and goddess of death ('lioness of women'; *Il.* 21, 481ff.).

[16] Hephaestus can also represent fire, and the epic once uses his name in the
sense of 'fire' (*Il.* 2, 426). But when Hephaestus appears in the narrative as a god,
he is not identical with fire but is 'he who produces fire' (*Il.* 21, 342).

[17] Aphrodite and Ares are on a level of equality only for the epic, and they are
not wholly equal even there (cf. Kurt Latte, *Gött. Gel. Anz.*, 1953, 33). Whereas
Ares represents only war in Greek religion outside the epic, Aphrodite 'was a great
nature goddess in the regions of Asia Minor where the epic took shape'; and
whereas the word 'Ares' is used in epic indifferently for the person of the god and
for the thing war, the name 'Aphrodite' is used only once (*Od.* 22, 444) for the
act of love.

[18] Still, there is a long way from this position to Empedocles' doctrine of love
and hate as world forces. The old heroic epic takes a basically unphilosophic
stance; these things are taken unquestioningly as they presented themselves for
epic treatment. But this does not prevent philosophic premises, conscious or
unconscious, from being formed already. Philosophy keeps breaking in.

[19] So in 863 Ares is called 'insatiable in battle', though as a person he leaves the
scene of battle at once.

It is because 'Ares' is used indifferently of the god and the thing that Ares' function can never be forgotten. Ares has no proper name; he is not 'the god of war' but 'the god war.' He is thought of as operative in every warlike action, and the energy let loose in the hurling and thrusting of weapons may be designated simply as 'Ares.' So it is said of the spear still quivering in the body of the man struck, 'here raging Ares released his unleashed fury' (*Il.* 13, 444; similarly 16, 613; 17, 529).[20] Just as Ares is the action of the actor so he is also the suffering of the victim (*Il.* 13, 567): 'struck between navel and genitals where beyond all places Ares comes painfully to pitiful mortals.' Ares is transferred here from the weapon to the wound.[21]

Along with Ares other related forces are at work in the battles of the *Iliad*. There is one description of how both armies advanced to battle (*Il.* 4, 439):

> Ares drove these on, and gray-eyed Athene drove the others,
> Terror drove them, and Fear, and Discord that never lies idle:
> She the sister and friend of Ares, man-slaying warfare,
> Small she is first when she dons her helmet; then very swiftly
> Grows till with her head she strikes heaven, while striking the earth with her feet.
> She then threw down strife in the midst, between the two armies,
> Striding along the ranks, enjoying the groans of the wounded.

'Discord,' the armies' will to battle, is slight enough when they are arming themselves in comparison with the extremity of fury in the heat of battle itself. Terror and Fear (δεῖμος and φόβος) are intended in an active rather than passive sense; they are the terrifying horror that accompanies a charging army against its frightened opponents.

Powers such as these are neither allegories nor the creations of fancy. War, battle lust, and the terror of an approaching enemy are realities. It is only that we are no longer capable of speaking of them so simply.[22] But the early Greeks liked to think in terms of powers and qualities, and it is out of powers and qualities that early Greek philosophy built its pictures of the world. Even epic narrative, which purposely suppressed everything which was not person or

---

[20] The spear can also almost be personified as a warrior, for it receives such epithets as 'capable of war,' 'helmeted with bronze' (εἵλετο δ' ἄλκιμα δοῦρε δύω, κεκορυθμένα χαλκῷ, *Il.* 11, 43 and *passim*), as it is said of a spear that missed that it was hungry to wound (*Il.* 21, 168). This sounds like primitive animism, but it only symbolizes function (see p. 39, n. 32, above).

[21] In the dynamic aspect both sides fuse into a single notion; so do fear-inspiring and fear in the next section of the text.

[22] In an expression like 'war broke out' war is regarded as a wild animal breaking out of its cage. But the original notion has been long forgotten.

personal effects, was forced to make some concession to this mode of thought. Hence it adopted Terror and Fear as powers in description of battles. But occasionally it endowed both with the character of persons who could sometime do something other than inspire fear; once it is said of them (*Il.* 15, 119) that as servants of Ares they harnessed his war chariot.

The basically tragic posture of the *Iliad* allows only dark powers to appear in the train of war; we look in vain for Hesiod's 'Nikê [victory] of the delicate foot.' And aside from the few powers that we have named, no others occur, except for slight allusions,[23] in contrast not only with Hesiod but with the entire body of other early Greek writings and works of art.

This restraint in epic narrative also rests upon stylization and not on the supposed circumstance that the 'personifying' mode of thought was not current among the epic poets. Epic speeches, on the contrary, develop ideas of this sort freely and with great skill. After Agamemnon has realized that it was folly to affront Achilles, he describes in detail (in the manner of the description of Discord which we have just read) the character and power of Zeus' unruly daughter Atê (*Il.* 19, 90ff.). The untranslatable word *atê* signifies a complex of blindness and error and the mischief that this fault brings with it. The same Atê, with reference to Agamemnon's fateful overreaching against Achilles, recurs in a speech of the aged Phoenix, and here there appear with Atê the 'Prayers,' the kindly admonition to understanding and yielding. Agamemnon has now offered Achilles abundant recompense, and the envoys of the commander in chief urge Achilles to accept the atonement and give up his obstinate resentment (*Il.* 9, 502):

> Prayers are also daughters of Zeus, the father almighty.
> They are lame and wrinkled, and cast their eyes sidelong;
> Slowly they toil on their way, and are left far behind Atê;
> For she is strong and sound on her feet, and hence she can always
> Far outrun all Prayers, and win into every country
> To force men astray; and the Prayers follow as healers after her.
> If then a man shall respect these daughters of Zeus at their coming,
> They will greatly benefit him and hear his words of entreaty;
> But if a man shall deny them, and harshly turn from their presence,
> Straightway they go to Zeus, son of Cronus, and pray him that Atê
> May soon overtake the man, that he suffer and pay for his madness.

Phoenix does not simply cite facts, as the archaizing narrative does,

---

[23] *Themis* (order) once summons the gods to assembly (*Il.* 20, 4), for as an institution the assembly of the gods is 'order.' Once she is even permitted to speak two lines, for considerate tact, which Themis here observes, is 'order.'

but in a modern spirit deduces from the experience a theory from which Achilles is to draw the practical application.[24] Atê must be swift and strong because her victim acts vigorously and rashly and causes great damage (Agamemnon's violence had caused Achilles to withdraw from battle, and hence heavy losses and defeat for the army). But the placating Prayers are by contrast lame, for they always arrive too late, and they are wrinkled like old women, for mild and perceptive reason is appropriate to old people like Phoenix. They look sideways, because their goal is aslant: they wish to steer the stubborn man away from his unbending path.[25] Atê and 'Prayers' explain each other mutually by the polar opposition between folly and wisdom, haste and prudence, headstrong self-will and yielding change of heart; such polarizations are typical of the following period (see p. 54, above), and therefore modern for the epic poets.[26] In Agamemnon' speech Atê is designated daughter of Zeus, obviously because she is one of the great powers in the world. Without Agamemnon's Atê in the first book there could have been no *Iliad*. In Phoenix' speech the Prayers in their turn are called daughters of Zeus. They are not, indeed, as proud and imposing as the lordly Atê but like wrinkled old women; they are however, understanding, gentle and benevolent. The last book of the *Iliad* stands under their ensign (pp. 51f., above).

'Atê' and the 'Prayers' as developed in the speeches are simply a particular force in life; aside from their special function they have no existence. On the other hand, the great gods as they appear in epic narrative are first and foremost free personalities who are not in the universe to discharge duties; they exist primarily for their own sake. Only secondarily and occasionally do they help the world on its way. Their interventions in earthly affairs therefore do not need any profound motivation. If the course of events is not plotted out by nebulous fate, the gods behave all too humanly according to their own whims. If Poseidon opposes the Trojans it is because an early

[24] οὕνεκα ('because') in 505 means 'this I conclude from the fact that ...' (*Frühgriech. Denken*, pp. 191f.).

[25] This follows from the rhymelike correspondence in both spondaic endings: παρατρωπῶσ' ἄνθρωποι—λισσόμενοι (500) and παραβλῶπές τ' ὀφθαλμώ (503). The symbolism has been misunderstood in antiquity and by moderns. The notion of litai must be understood to cover λίσσεσθαι (to beseech) of 574, 581, 585, and 591 also. The picture of a contrite sinner who is wrinkled by his cares and does not dare to look straight forward does not fit. The daughters of Zeus are not shy and embarrassed; they speak (with Phoenix) the language of reason, not of penitence.

[26] The threats implied in the three concluding verses are proved true in the sequel. Achilles is obdurate to the pleas of the envoys, and is then himself smitten by Atê, for instead of helping the Achaeans out of their great crisis he sends his best friend into the battle, where he is killed.

Trojan king deceived him (*Il.* 21, 441ff.). Troy must fall, not because
justice is on the side of the Achaeans, but because Hera wishes it so,
out of hatred for Priam and his children and the other Trojans (*Il.* 4,
31ff.); one of Priam's sons had affronted her (*Il.* 24, 31f.). In order
that Troy may be destroyed a peace which could have been just is
purposely obviated by the gods (*Il.* 4, 1ff.). It is love and hate which
call the tune; love and hate against whole peoples as much as against
individual men.

(e) *Gods and Men*

It is not only as the events of the great war were experienced by
Achaeans and Trojans that the poets of the *Iliad* describe them. They
know more about these things than any one of the actors on the earthly
stage below. The gift of the Muses enables them to include the other
side also, and not only what the gods did but how they did it. In
what manner and in what form does the divine will operate in
human reality according to the epic account?

The opening of the eleventh book of the *Iliad* narrates the beginning of a day of battle as follows:

> Dawn now rose from her bed where she lay with noble Tithonus,
> Bringing the light of day to the deathless gods and to mortals.
> Then Zeus sent down Strife to the speedy ships of the Argives,
> Baneful Strife, who bears in her hand the dread image of warfare.
> Straightway taking her place she stood by the ship of Odysseus
> Beached in the midst of the line, that all might hear when she shouted.
> ....
> There she stood, the goddess, and cried her terrible war cry,
> Shrieking, and into the heart of each and every Achaean
> Came great fury and hatred and eager desire to be fighting.
> Atreus' son cried out that all should arm for the battle.

The beginning and the close of this passage yield the simple
information that a new day dawned and Agamemnon alerted his
army for a new battle. But the poet has more to tell. Dawn brought
the new day to men and gods, and it is with the gods that the narrative
begins. According to Homeric belief all initiative is reserved for the
gods.[1] If, instead of reacting to an existing situation a man sets boldly
about something new and different, he receives it as an inspiration

---

[1] Hence the opening of the *Iliad*, after posing the quarrel of the princes as the
first theme, asks which god caused the strife, and answers, Apollo. But the
explanation does not quite fit the facts, for the chain of causes and effects begins
before Apollo's intervention.

from above. It 'comes over him.' In this case the will to armed
conflict which comes over the Achaeans has been sent by Zeus. The
word 'eris' denotes any kind of discord or strife; the quarrel of the
kings in the first book is 'eris.' Since it is war that is now the issue,
Eris carries the 'dread portent of war' in her hand, which defines her
more precisely as lust for battle. How the emblem looked we need
not ask, for it is no more corporeal than Eris herself.[2] Eris is called
'baneful' or 'perilous' (ἀργαλέη) because she would soon grow far
beyond mortal stature (Il. 4, 442f.; p. 61, above). A battle, even
when we begin it as 'our' battle, soon goes its own way and appears
to us mortals as an independent force. Hence Eris is a divine power;
hence she is on hand, sent from heaven, when an army is alerted.
Humanly considered, only Agamemnon issues the order to arms; but
metaphysically, and indeed in very truth, the call is more than any
human cry. The physical sounds are human, but what they signify is
in fact from the gods.

In the example just analyzed human will is identical with divine,
as far as that is possible. The divine power which impels to deeds of
blood speaks with the voice of a man calling to battle, and both mean
the same thing. But how does it look when in his action man pursues
aims other than those of the gods who caused him to act? How does
the epic deal with the working together of unequal partners, man and
god?

The fourth book of the *Iliad* presents a scene of this sort at its
opening. Achaeans and Trojans have met and solemnly sworn a
sacred pact. Instead of waging a general battle and so incurring heavy
losses, the decision would be reached by a duel between Menelaus,
the offended husband, and Paris, the seducer. The duel is fought and
Menelaus clearly wins. Here a meteor scattering sparks passes
between the encamped armies. Trojans and Achaeans see the
miraculous sign and ask whether it signifies new battle. Or is Zeus,
the lord of battles, giving friendship and peace? Now Laodocus,
Antenor's son, approaches Pandarus, one of the Trojan leaders. He
proposes that he shoot Menelaus; by doing so he could perform a
great service to all the Trojans and especially to Paris. The 'reckless'
Pandarus follows the advice. He shoots, but Menelaus is only slightly
wounded. The oath, however, is now broken, the battle begins anew,
and Troy will fall.

Antenor is a familiar figure, but his son Laodocus is never mentioned elsewhere in the *Iliad*, and tradition knows nothing of the

---

[2] In the *Shield of Heracles* (339), Athene, who had just promised the two heroes
Heracles and Iolaus victory over the robber Cycnus (p. 109, below), held 'victory
and glory in her immortal hands.'

man who suggested the fateful step to Pandarus. Someone or other makes a suggestion; one of the heroes recklessly translates it into action; but the issue turns out otherwise than the actor thought, and the fate of Troy is sealed. This is the physical aspect of the matter, but it half reveals, and half conceals, what actually happened. If we ponder over the real significance of the shot and the power implicit in the words of this Laodocus from nowhere, we sense the presence of a god's voice. The poet does not merely sense it; he knows it. He recounts the events differently and more fully. The gods held a council after the duel and resolved that Troy should nevertheless fall; the Trojans had to violate their king's oath. Athene was sent down to earth, and her path was like the fall of a meteor. She stepped among the Trojan companies in the form of Laodocus; it was she who enticed Pandarus to his fateful act, and she gave the flying arrow only enough force to accomplish the breach of the truce.

In the artistic structure of the *Iliad* the episode of the pact and its breach has a solvent effect. The goal to which the action is directed is put into question before it receives a further accentuation.[3] The agreement between the two armies is reasonable, and had reason continued to prevail, it would have brought about a conclusion gratifying to bourgeois notions. But a happy ending is impossible. It is not feasible because tradition knows that Troy fell; furthermore, the older epic is not bourgeois but tragic. The poet whose theme was the portion of man reflected that it was right practically, but wrong artistically, that a bloodless duel should bring comfortable peace to both parties after the gigantic effort of mustering a Panhellenic host across the sea. At the council of the gods Zeus stirs thoughts of peace; but Hera, who is hostile to Troy, refutes him with this argument (*Il.* 4, 26):

> How can you wish to make wasted and fruitless all this endeavor,
> All this sweat that I sweated in toil, and my horses exhausted
> Gathering my people, to bring destruction to Priam and his children?

Zeus reproaches her with senseless cruelty, but he accommodates himself to a compromise and yields Troy. This time, then, the poet does not have recourse to fate, but makes Zeus yield anyway. Thus, after the action has been diverted from its prescribed course by the pact, the second breach brings matters back into their old course. The gods effect what is necessary for history. Human reasons formed the pact, and it was wrong in the higher sense; the gods infatuate men so that they foolishly break the pact, and in the higher sense that is right. Understanding and error, gods and men, play a confusing

[3] See p. 18, above.

game, but the gods are always the winners. The poets believed that the saga was historically true; they believed that gods were wilful and so it is natural that they clarify matters in this fashion, both for themselves and for their auditors. What tradition and art dictated was sufficiently explained for them in the decree of the gods.

In the general framework of the Trojan cycle it is unnecessary and disturbing that the Trojans incur guilt for the war a second time. But for the *Iliad* itself the repetition is advantageous. After the part of the Trojan tale which the *Iliad* tells had grown to a full epic, the outbreak of the war was lost to it. By means of this repetition we learn, within the *Iliad*, that the war began because of Trojan guilt. In strict consistency the new story of the outbreak of war should be preceded by a new *casus belli*. Likewise, Helen's amour with Paris should begin again as guiltily as before. Accordingly, such a story is told, and here too divine power intervenes forcibly to bring it about.

We refer back to the end of the third book (*Il.* 3, 380ff.). In the duel with Menelaus Paris is disarmed, but Aphrodite has spirited him away and taken him to his 'fragrant chamber.' Now the goddess goes to summon Helen and to bind her anew to Paris in love and desire. In the guise of an old slave woman she tells the lady of the charms of the lover who is awaiting her. But the disguise is penetrated, for Helen senses the stirring of love within her; she recognizes 'the goddess' wondrously beautiful neck and enticing bosom and sparkling eyes.' She refuses to go, for she yearns for her parents, her home, and her husband (cf. 3, 139f.), to whom, according to the poet and the outcome of the duel, she again belongs. But Aphrodite threatens her so harshly with her annihilating anger that Helen is frightened and starts on her way: 'before her went the demon,' the goddess Love.

Here, unlike in the scene of the shooting, the human aspect cannot be dissociated from the divine, for Aphrodite is recognized as a goddess. Helen knows what she is doing. No false promises are necessary and no divine counsel needs to explain what is bound to happen. In her threatening words Aphrodite points out why Helen must be seduced a second time. One blessed with such love-charm by Aphrodite's grace must play the role of lover and beloved to the end.[4] It is unthinkable that an epic character should prove untrue to

---

[4] 'Otherwise,' says Aphrodite (3, 414–17), 'I will withdraw my grace [i.e., if Helen turns modest she will lose her fascination for men] and will cause the general respect, for which you have me to thank, to turn into general hatred of both partners [i.e., hatred of the woman responsible for the war will flare up, when she loses the beauty which seemed to make any sacrifice worth while; cf. 3, 156–58] and you will be ruined.'

itself, or rather to the god who has singled it out. Shortly before, Helen's paramour, like her a favorite of Aphrodite, had said as much (3, 65f):

> He acts wrongly who spurns those gifts with which gods honor mortals:
> Of their own will they give them: a man cannot gain them by his own trying.

As these two examples have shown, in their epiphanies of the gods the poets have no interest in ghostly or monstrous apparitions. On the contrary: on the rare occasions when a god's voice speaks to a mortal, it does so in the unpretentious covering of the commonplace. The higher power is revealed through the more than human range of the words.[5] Difficulties and uncertainties appear only if the idea of transformation is pursued realistically in all its implications. In this respect the *Iliad* is discreet and restrained. The god takes on human shape only long enough to communicate the impulse, and the personality he borrows is so indifferent that we do not ask about its usual owner. But in the *Odyssey* Athene-Mentor accompanies her protégé in a long journey; matters reach a point where someone is puzzled at having two Mentors and draws the conclusion that one of them must have been a god (*Od.* 4, 653–56).

Divine prompting can occur even without transformation. The gods of the *Iliad* associate with their favorites in their own form. In the first book (188ff.) Achilles is on the point of killing Agamemnon, who has affronted him before the whole people. Should he summon his men to protect him while he plunges his sword in Agamemnon's breast[6] or should he control himself? Athene comes from heaven, steps behind him, grasps his fair hair, and pulls him back. He looks

[5] In *Iliad* 2 the Achaean army moves forward to battle, and the approach of the enemy is reported to the Trojans in the voice of the swift-footed scout Polites, who had been sent to reconnoiter (*Il.* 2, 786ff.). Actually, however, it is not the man who speaks, but wind-swift Iris, who comes from aegis-bearing Zeus with the painful news. Aristarchus took exception to the apparently unnecessary substitution of the goddess. The reason is probably that originally the impending battle was the first of the Trojan War and that it kept a similar function within the *Iliad*. (Only on this premise can the entire section from 2, 442 to 4, 456, as it is conceived and stylized, be fully understood; p. 24 above.) So the report of the change from 'former peace' to 'unwearied war which has now begun' (797) is too important for the Trojan Polites, and the divine messenger is substituted for him. Contrariwise, a human being can take over the task of a god if he is capable of it. In *Il.* 2, 155ff. Hera sends Athene to the Achaean army to restrain the masses streaming to their ships. Athene finds Odysseus 'whose wisdom was like Zeus', and gives him the message in the same words in which she had received it. Transformation is here unnecessary.

[6] Τοὺς μὲν (191) refers to Achilles' own followers; cf. *Frühgriech. Denken*, p. 80, n. 2.

around, astonished, and recognizes the goddess. As if he knew nothing of what she wanted of him he asks: 'You have probably come as a witness of his affront. Surely he will soon pay for it with his death.' But Athene admonishes him: for the present he must do no more than answer with harsh words; even so he will surely receive satisfaction. 'The gods must be heeded,' answers Achilles, and acts accordingly. All this takes place after Achilles has already begun to draw his sword and before he thrusts it back into its scabbard, that is to say, in a brief moment; and Athene, it is said, is visible to him alone. Athene is the divine power which alters his purpose. But at the same time she is present actively and in person; she actually grasps his hair; he turns his head to her and converses with her. The believing poet felt no occasion here to keep apart the physical and metaphysical aspects of the one event.

The power of the gods operates in life, and the one way in which it accomplishes this is by working upon the will and spirit of men. Words are necessary if some communication is to be made and some new direction prescribed. But in the battles of the *Iliad* a god can encourage a warrior to be brave and arouse energies which will be released in vigorous attack, without the use of an epiphany or speech. According to Homeric belief, every initiative must come from the gods, and Homeric tactics demand great initiative of the leaders. While the masses stand in the background for the most part without much to do (*Il.* 17. 370–75), the leaders observe each other closely, awaiting an opening, or keep each other engaged so that some favorable opportunity may present itself in the light skirmishing. Suddenly it occurs to a champion to charge his opponent. He is driven on by a force that makes him irresistible. The flicker of an unearthly radiance clings to the shining bronze of his weapons and glows over his head and shoulders like a baleful star, and it drives him where the enemy throngs crowd thickest (*Il.* 5, 1–8). Not 'it' but rather a god impels him. Athene bestowed upon Diomedes raging power (μένος) and boldness, so that he was noticed by all men and achieved noble glory. It was Athene who kindled the fire which gleamed in his weapons. Whether it was actual fire and whether it was miraculous is an idle question for the poet. This same untiring power, as of a devouring fire, will be associated with the hero's shimmering armor in his warlike achievements. The Homeric poet does not describe armor and fire as physical entities. He speaks of the force which is awake in the armed Diomedes and which manifests itself to the senses and directly to the mind, like a baleful star terrifying the enemy. The same something which manifests itself in Diomedes' armor as flame shows itself upon Agamemnon's shield as the likeness of poisonous serpents rearing up, like a rainbow which bodes impending catastrophe (p. 38, above).

Varying images and varying expressions for the same thing are a sure sign that the image is not to be understood too realistically and the expression too literally. Once Hector says (*Il.* 15, 725): 'Zeus is arousing us and summoning us forth.' The same event the poet himself describes as follows: 'Zeus thrust Hector forward with his mighty arm and commanded the soldiers to follow him' (694). There are many different expressions for a god bestowing courage, superiority (κῦδος), or victory upon a warrior, for giving him energy (μένος), or for 'inspiriting' or arousing (ὦρσε) him. Often it is said that a god is physically present among the fighters; the epic singer as well as his public were convinced that a god is present at the crises of our lives, if he chooses to be.[7] But even then he applies the same indirect methods to the course of events. The god comes and stands beside a favorite to bestow ideas and energy upon him, he confronts an enemy in order to hamper him. Or he fires a whole army with zeal, he impels it to the attack, and he shouts the battle cry. The poet has an unobstructed view into this background of earthly happenings; not infrequently the great heroes have similar insight, in varying degrees of clarity and fullness. But never is the distinction of the orders of being to which man and god belong forgotten. Even when a god steps between men who are fighting, he nevertheless dwells in a dimension of his own. He remains invisible (*Il.* 15, 308), or fear holds men back, for it is contrary to order for a man to touch a god in grim battle (*Il.* 14, 386).[8]

The gods do more than merely arouse a man's will; they also give him strength and skill in execution, and in addition success or the reverse. In all three phases of a human action, the irrational and the uncertain are under divine guidance, for the Homeric poet: the inexplicable element in the spontaneous decision which gives us a goal, as well as the imponderable element in successful or unsuccessful execution and the incalculable element in accidents which promote or frustrate. Athene 'guides' the weapon of Diomedes, so that it finds its mark and kills (*Il.* 5, 290). Athene, who had just instigated Pandarus to shoot at the unsuspecting Menelaus, so guides the bolt

[7] A fact which has lately come into view is of fundamental significance for our understanding of such epic expressions. Archilochus, a poet who ushered in a revolt against the epic cult of the past and against the romantic glorification of existence (p. 137f., below), felt the effective presence of the gods in his own battles in precisely the same way (fr. 51 I A 54f. and IV A 4–5; see p. 147 below). These expressions in the *Iliad* are not artistic devices of the epic poet or literary fictions or conventions, but derive from genuine belief.

[8] On exceptions in *Il.* 5 and 16 see pp. 74f., and n. 14, below.

as to make it harmless, as a mother brushes away a fly from her sleeping child (*Il.* 4, 127ff.). Precisely how the gods manage such matters is always left in the dark in the *Iliad*.[9] Was the hand of the archer not as sure as at other times? Did the arrow have a flaw? Did a gust of wind spoil the aim? Or was it simply a miracle? The poet scorns such questions. The one thing he knows and tells is that a god was involved and that he intervened between the human effort and its outcome. The god may intervene even at the start and 'maim the battle-readiness' of one party (*Il.* 15, 467). Teucer has newly fitted a well-twisted bowstring on his flawless bow, which should have lasted for many shots; but when he aims at Hector Zeus makes the bowstring break. Teucer is depressed when he recognizes the divinely ordained mishap. Hector equally understands the sign and calls to his people that the god is manifestly on their side (*Il.* 15, 458–93).

It now becomes clear why the Homeric gods often help or hurt human beings by petty and cunning devices and why eventually, in the *Odyssey*, they play the role almost of servants. Since they cannot step out of their own realm, they are debarred from direct contacts and must resort to crooked byways—through the will and energy of men or through management of the seemingly accidental.

But this is not all. The gods exert themselves only where nature itself offers free access. If one driver loses his whip in a race, so that he tearfully despairs of victory, the mishap can equally well be interpreted either as accident or as the doing of a god; but the mishap transcends ordinary experience when the whip wrested from the charioteer by Apollo is restored to him by Athene (*Il.* 23, 382ff.).

No sharp line can be drawn in the *Iliad* between out-and-out miracle and that which is almost or possibly miraculous. Many divine interventions are on the boundary, neither wholly on one side nor on the other. And if the boundary is crossed we do not thereby go at once into a wholly strange world. For one who believes that a god frequently appears to us in human shape and speaks to us, it is only consistent that the god should be recognized for what he is, and that after he has completed his task, by virtue of his divine power he disappears.

It is inherent in the notion of miracle that no limitations are imposed upon it, and the Indian epics of gods and heroes therefore make the freest possible use of miracles. But Greek epic shows great restraint in this respect. No fire falls from heaven to destroy Ilium by

---

[9] In *Il.* 14, 459–64, on the other hand, the procedure is clarified. To avenge the death of a comrade, Ajax hurls his spear against the Trojan who had slain him; but the Trojan evades the spear by springing aside, and the weapon struck another Trojan, 'for the gods had decreed destruction for him.'

the will of the gods; no dead man is brought back to life. Rather, the conduct of the Homeric gods is regularly such that things which seem to us supernatural or contrary to nature are contrived by them in a relatively obscure place within the causal nexus; they take a detour, even in their miracles, by way of human personages or earthly things. They deceive a man and mislead his will: at the final battle between Achilles and Hector, Athene comes to Hector in the guise of Deiphobus, and the support of his supposed brother gives Hector courage to desist from flight and face his superior opponent (*Il.* 22, 226–47). Sometimes the gods supply or withdraw from a man the things he needs: Athene, who stands by Hector in the guise of Deiphobus, hands back to Achilles the spear which had missed its mark (22, 276f.); but when Hector, whose spear had similarly been hurled in vain, asks it back of Deiphobus, Athene-Deiphobus has vanished. Sometimes the gods remove hindrances; Apollo 'smooths the whole way' for the battle chariots, and he tramples down the escarpments of the defense works, as easily as a child at play builds and destroys fortresses of sand (*Il.* 15, 355ff.). Hermes does not steal the body of Hector (cf. *Il.* 24, 23–30), but in the guise of a young Myrmidon he escorts the aged Priam by night to Achilles' quarters, puts the sentries to sleep, and opens the heavily barred doors from without (*Il.* 24, 440–57). Hindrances of other kinds also can be removed by the gods. Glaucus, wounded in his arm so that he cannot wield his spear, prays to the healing god Apollo: he is obliged to defend the corpse of his fallen friend. Soon the flow of blood dries up, the pain passes away, and fresh energy flows into his spirit (θυμός, *Il.* 16, 508–31). Hector is hurt in battle, but is aroused out of a deep swoon; Apollo comes and gives him fresh energy, so that he stirs vigorously like a horse at his crib, who then breaks his halter and bounds out prancing over the meadow (*Il.* 15, 243ff.).

Divine intervention may also take the form of a propitious or an unfavorable atmosphere. The Achaeans are advancing, but the storm god Zeus grasped the aegis (*Il.* 17, 593ff.):

> Seized his glittering shield, and wrapped tall Ida in storm clouds,
> Lightened and thundered[10] aloud and shook the hills with the earth-
>   quake,
> Gave the day to the Trojans and filled the Achaeans with fear.

The luck of the battle, that indefinite but very real entity which determines the outcome, is in Homer's language 'light'[11] or 'heavenly

[10] Lightning and thunder are the only language in which the lord of heaven speaks to mortals; he is too lofty to communicate with them in words, as the other gods do.

[11] 'Light' (φάος) can serve as metaphor for a turn to the better and deliverance; here there is no need to think of physical light.

lightness' (αἰθήρ, αἴθρη), and its opposite is 'night,' 'cloud,' and 'darkness.' Athene goes before Achilles in battle, gives him light, and arouses him to slay (*Il.* 20, 95). On the other hand, Hera envelops the fleeing Trojans in thick mist and holds them fast (*Il.* 21, 6). When a son of Zeus has fallen, his divine father envelops the battlefield in 'baneful' night, so that 'baneful' fighting may take place over the body of his son (*Il.* 16, 567); here darkness is obviously thought of as connected with toil and death. In another passage (*Il.* 17, 366–77) 'heavenly brightness' is associated with desultory fighting without losses, whereas a 'cloud' which seemed to extinguish sun and moon signifies at the same time a physical cloud and the weariness and dangers of battle.[12]

When the gods rule over light and darkness in this fashion, they give the action a certain atmosphere and lend it a particular character, and nothing more. It is quite a different thing when Hephaestus wraps his priest, who was in imminent danger, in night, and so saves him from his attackers (*Il.* 5, 23). During a battle between Achilles and Aeneas, Poseidon pours night over Achilles' eyes and draws Aeneas off (*Il.* 20, 321ff.). Here 'night' has the property of a material, which is thrust as a protective shield between the man endangered and his pursuer; and this kind of interposition is carried to the point of physical removal. Warriors in the most desperate danger are often saved in the *Iliad* through being enveloped and spirited away (*Il.* 3, 380, 5, 311, 344, 445; 20, 443; 21, 597; cf. also 16, 436, 666ff.). The miracle may even be further developed: a phantom takes the place of the man spirited away (*Il.* 5, 449), or the supporting deity himself takes on the form of his protégé to mislead his pursuer (*Il.* 21, 599–22, 20). But the removals are never employed to move men to a place where they take an active part.[13] And it is always Trojans, the weaker party, who are so saved from the death which is not destined for them. In the case of Aeneas it is expressly stated that his deliverance is necessary because he is destined to continue in life (*Il.* 20, 302ff.). The miraculous removals forcibly bend the action to enable it to follow the course prescribed by tradition (cf. p. 57, above). It was inevitable, in the long war for Troy, that Achilles and Aeneas must sooner or later confront one

[12] Cf. also 17, 268–73. Physical and metaphysical light and darkness are indistinguishable in the *narrative*; in the speech of prayer, 645–47, the two aspects are differentiated so sharply that physical brightness (clear air) can be associated with metaphysical darkness (destruction). In the *narrative* following (648ff.) the physical and metaphysical are again combined so that light comes in and at the same time the situation is improved.

[13] A partial exception to this rule is Paris when he is removed from the battlefield and awaits Helen in his bedchamber, to converse with her in love (*Il.* 3, 382ff.).

another—and the poet does in fact have such a meeting. Now according to the logic of epic Aeneas would have to succumb to his far greater
opponent; but he did not, for he and his children and his children's
children continued to rule in the Troad. Something extraordinary
must have happened—and so the poet makes something extraordinary happen. To the unreflecting poet, who accepted his tale at face
value, the Muse offered the tangled knot and its miraculous solution
simultaneously and in the same manner. In the *Iliad* the miracles are
obviously conceived with devout reverence. In the *Odyssey*, on the
other hand, the poet often seems to handle his gods with careless disrespect, and he looks into their miracles with an inquisitive stare.

If we ask what divine intervention meant to one of the poets of the
Iliad, clear and magnificent testimony is offered by the deeds of
Patroclus (Book 16). Patroclus goes into battle with a strictly defined
purpose. Achilles, who is still wrathful, forbids him to do more than
merely relieve the pressing need of the Achaeans. But the flame of his
courage cannot be quenched, and he does more than he should have
done (*Il.* 16, 685):

> So was he stricken with blindness—
> Fool!—for had he remembered what Peleus' son had told him,
> He might have escaped from the evil snare of death and destruction,
> Yet the will of Zeus is stronger than the counsel of mortals;
> Even the bravest of men he destroys and deprives him of conquest,
> Easily, or he inspires him and makes him mighty in battle,
> Just as he kindled the fury of war in the heart of Patroclus.
> Who was the first, Patroclus, and who the last that you slaughtered
> When the immortals called you and led you to die in the battle?

In this fine passage the poet first expounds the tradition. It condemned
Patroclus to death in gallant fighting, and the poet explains this
outcome to himself and his hearers as the will of Zeus and of the
gods generally. But the tragedy of the situation so arouses him that,
contrary to rule, he indulges in a reflection: more obedience and
less gallantry might have saved Patroclus. Patroclus now passes
victoriously on to the walls of Troy, and the Achaeans would have
taken Troy that day if Phoebus Apollo had not mounted the tower.
Thrice Patroclus set his foot upon the rampart, and thrice the god
thrust the man's shield back with his arms. Here, exceptionally,
matters came to a physical conflict between god and man.[14] At the

---

[14] In the remarkable and extremely primitive fifth book of the *Iliad*, a man
breaks through the barrier which separates gods and men. Athene removes the
darkness from Diomedes' eyes so that he can perceive the gods (127). Diomedes
wounds Aphrodite (335). He is bodily thrust back by Apollo (437). Athene
mounts his chariot and the axle bends under her weight (837). He thrusts a spear
into the body of Ares, and Athene supports him (856). But he will have to atone

fourth attempt Apollo calls out to Patroclus: 'Retire! It is not fated that Troy should fall to your spear, or to the spear of Achilles, who is much greater than you' (698ff.). Here the poet has so magnified the heroism of Patroclus that a god must physically take a hand in order to help destiny back to its rightful place; 'destiny' here, of course, is the outcome dictated by tradition. Further on, the Achaeans under Patroclus' leadership gain the upper hand 'beyond fate' (780). Never again in epic does anything happen 'beyond fate.'[15] The poet knows that he is transgressing against tradition, but his view of Patroclus is so great that he has no other choice. Patroclus is allowed a final triple course of victory; then Apollo intervenes. Wrapped in a cloud, he steps behind Patroclus and strikes him with the flat of his hand on shoulders and back; the hero's eyes roll helplessly. The god tears Patroclus' helmet from his head, breaks his spear, causes his shield to fall, and loosens his armor. Now the Trojan Euphorbus thrusts his spear into the back of the disarmed man, where the god had laid his hand upon him. Only now does Hector run his lower body through with his spear. Patroclus does not end as a man defeated but as a victor misdirected by the supreme deity, physically thrust back by Apollo and physically disarmed. The verses which describe his death breathe profound piety. No outward necessity demanded the miracle here. Nothing stood in the way of Hector's proving the better man in regular human combat—nothing but the heroic stature to which this poet exalted 'beyond fate' a Patroclus doomed to death.[16] The unexampled miracle reconciles the conflict between two equally sovereign entities for this poet: heroism, and the will of the gods.

(f) Homeric Man

Each of the figures in the epics has its own identifying stamp, though its peculiarities never harden into a rigid character mask; the

for his daring by his death (406): thus the ancient goddess Dione comforts wounded Aphrodite. This leads Dione to tell of other cases in which mortal men approached the gods too nearly (383ff.). The legends which she reports are apocryphal. Nothing of this nature occurs elsewhere.

[15] But the phrase is used to show what would have happened if a god had not intervened (Il. 2, 155; 17, 321; 20, 30 and 336; 21, 517). Walter Leaf (in his commentary on the Iliad) seeks to interpret ὑπὲρ αἶσαν in 16, 780 as 'beyond the expected'; but this solution is not feasible.

[16] Apparently vv. 644–55 mark the place where the poet deviated from tradition. Here Zeus (i.e., the poet) considers whether Patroclus should fall beside the body of Sarpedon at once, or first throw the Trojans back to the city and slay many enemies; and the second alternative seemed right. There follow the charge against the city and the physical intervention of Apollo in vv. 700ff. and 788ff.

changing play of vigorous action constantly brings new traits to the fore. But all are related to one another, like the members of a large family, the figures of the *Iliad* as if they belonged to an older, and those of the *Odyssey* to a younger, generation.

What are the distinguishing marks which differentiate Homeric man from all others? Is he 'naïve' and 'natural'? And if so, in what sense?[1] At all events Homeric man is not confused or dull, but clear and alert; he is master of refined forms of social intercourse; he speaks with astonishing skill; he is indeed passionate but on the other hand so objective that he often describes as 'knowledge' what we should call 'feeling.' An attempt to describe the nature of Homeric man by predicating his qualities cannot be very promising, because all expressions of this kind must suffer from confusing ambiguities. It is better to sketch the structure of Homeric man as far as we may— which must involve excessive sharpness of outline and oversimplification to make it more intelligible. The premise must be that Homeric man in fact has a structure different from what we know today. Man is by no means essentially the same in all ages and all regions. Human nature too has its history, and its vicissitudes are perhaps the most momentous and the most interesting of all historical happenings.

In this sense our inquiry has to do with the way in which the soul of Homeric man is made up, and the first answer which our texts give us is that the question in this form is un-Homeric. Homer's language has no word for the soul of a living man, and consequently none for his body either. The word ψυχή (*psyche*) is used only of the soul of the dead, and the word σῶμα, which denotes 'body' in post-Homeric Greek, means 'corpse' in Homer. Not in his lifetime, but only in death (and in a lifeless swoon), was Homeric man divided into body and soul. He felt himself not as a cloven duality but as a unitary being. And because he felt himself such, such he was in fact. It was not imperfect observation or undeveloped power of discrimination[2] that was to blame for the absence of the notion of a living soul, for in actuality Homeric man had no 'soul' in our sense of the word.

Homeric man is not the sum of body and soul, but a whole. But of this whole, specific portions, or better, organs, can sometimes occupy

---

[1] Homer was regarded as naïve and natural even by an age which considered a pastoral drama as the appropriate expression of naïveté and naturalness.

[2] On the contrary, epic is astonishingly rich in mature and discriminating insights into the structure of personality; they are so consistent that the latent theory can be reconstructed out of them. This will be attempted in what follows, and in some detail, since the subject is so difficult. The principal work is Joachim Böhme, *Die Seele und das Ich im homerischen Epos* (Leipzig, 1929).

the foreground. All individual organs appertain directly to the person.[3] Arms are as much an organ of the man himself, rather than of his body, as *thymos* (the organ of excitement) is an organ of the man, himself, rather than of his soul. The whole man is equally alive in all his parts; activity which we would term 'spiritual' can be attributed to each of his members. The *Iliad* tells (13, 59ff.) how Poseidon, in the guise of a seer, touched two Achaean warriors with his staff; thereby he filled them with victorious energy (κρατερὸν μένος) and made their members agile, both their legs and their arms. The men so favored express their feelings concerning what a god in human form had bestowed upon them. The one says: 'The *thymos* in my breast stirs more mightily to war and battle; my legs rage below and my arms above.' The other reaffirms the sentiment in like terms: 'Even so do my arms too rage in grasping the spear, my energy has been stirred up, and with both legs below I press forwards.' Every individual organ of Homeric man can deploy an energy of its own, but at the same time each represents the person as a whole. Physical and spiritual organs appear alongside one another at the same level and are alike referred to the self when the second speaker in our passage says 'My arms—my energy (will: μένος)—I with my two legs.'[4] So Homeric man often uses 'my arms' to denote the notion 'I' if action is in question (*Il.* 1, 166); or he will use 'my μένος' (energy, will) when a clash with an opponent is in question (*Il.* 6, 127).[5] Such circumscriptions (and periphrases like ἱερὴ ἲς Τηλεμάχοιο, the sacred strength of Telemachus)[6] illustrate by the choice of the concepts used in them how Homer understood man essentially in dynamic terms. Man is seen as what he does rather than as what he is.

Homeric language differentiates several organs of feeling and

[3] The Homeric word for person is 'head.' Similarly in the language of Roman law *caput* and *capitalis* are used for 'person' and 'relating to the person,' as distinguished from *res*, which is used for property. *Poena capitalis* and *deminutio capitis* are to be understood in this sense.

[4] In *Od.* 6, 140 we read 'Athene put boldness in Nausicaa's *spirit* [φρένες] and fear from her *limbs* [γυῖα].'

[5] As late as the sophist Antiphon we find a similar conception of the structure of men. He says (*Vorsokr.* 87 B 44 A 2–3: details p. 252 n. 1): 'There are laws established for the eyes, what they may and may not look upon [i.e., there are rules for modest downcasting of eyes; cf. Theognis 85f.]; and for the tongue, what it may and may not say; and for the arms, what they may and may not do; and for the legs, whither they may and may not go; and for the mind [νοῦς], what it may and may not desire.' Such a conception of man was surely long antiquated in Antiphon's day; but the sophist wished to appeal from artificial law to elemental nature and hence speaks of the natural functions of the individual organs.

[6] The occasion for the periphrase was the desire to conclude the verse with a proper name (p. 32f., above). The nominative could not be used for this purpose.

thinking. Each has a specific function, but naturally the spheres of action which belong to the various organs cut across one another.[7] These centers are called θυμός, φρήν, and νόος (*thymos*, *phrên*, and *noos*). *Thymos* is approximately 'temper,' the organ of moods and emotions such as vexation, rage, courage; desire, satisfaction, hope; pain; astonishment; timidity; pride and cruelty. Also included under *thymos* are intimations which have no rational certainty and deliberations which have an emotional element. And finally *thymos* is the seat for eager enterprise,[8] weary distaste, or indifference. More intellectual is *phrên* (φρήν or in the plural φρένες). *Phrên* works over things and ideas, it determines a person's attitude and conviction, it is the thinking, reflecting, and knowing reason.[9] Rational like *phrên*, but even more firmly determined by objective content, is *noos*, that is, insight, understanding, thought, and even plan. As 'thought' and 'plan' *noos* can detach itself from the person and in itself designate the content of thought.[10]

Since in man's every action and reaction the appropriate organ was dominant, no conflict between the various organs need arise. But once—significantly, not in the narrative but in a simile placed alongside the narrative—there is a picture of a man who, in our language, constrains his weary body to a difficult task through his soul's power of will. The epic poet does not, however, speak of body and soul, but of *thymos* (the organ of fresh vitality) which was suffering from weariness and sweat, and of the 'conquering energy' (κρατερὸν μένος) which was 'put on' like armor (*Il.* 17, 742–46).

Soliloquies are represented in Homer as addresses to the *thymos*; of all organs of this class the *thymos* is the most comprehensive and at the same time the most spontaneous. Soliloquies take place only when a man wishes to clarify a situation and the action needed to meet it. This is not a real splitting of the ego but only discursive thinking.

[7] Similarly such notions as soul, mind, feeling, heart, understanding, reason, etc., are separable in principle, but not at every point where they are applicable.

[8] On the other hand μένος (*menos*), i.e., will and purposeful energy, is not an organ but a power which stirs in men. *Menos* and *thymos* are extinguished at death (*Il.* 4, 294).

[9] *Phrên* is at the same time a physical organ, the diaphragm.

[10] This explains the later significance of *noos* in philosophy. Thinking detaches itself from ties with the thinking person and becomes pure 'spirit.' The Homeric phrase Διὸς νόος amounts to the first step on the way to the purely spiritual god of Xenophanes (see pp. 331f., below). It is worth noting that among the Greeks it was not the soul but thought that was first constituted an independent power to stand in opposition to the material world (fully developed in Anaxagoras). Cf. K. von Fritz, *Class. Phil.* 38 (1943), 79; 40 (1945), 223; 41 (1946), 12; B. Snell, *Die Entdeckung des Geistes* (3rd ed., Hamburg, 1955; English translation, *The Discovery of the Mind*, Cambridge, Mass., 1953).

Hence the notion of two partners talking with one another is not firmly fixed in Homer.[11]

Even if the organs do not vie with one another, the ego can nevertheless prevent one from achieving what it wants. Homeric man can 'master' (δαμάσαι) his impulse (θυμός or μένος) or 'hold it back' (ἐρητύειν). Here also the unity of the person is preserved.

Seen with modern eyes, Homeric man seems marvelously simple and closed. Whatever portion of his being acts or suffers, it is always the whole man acting or suffering. There are no boundaries, there is no cleavage between feeling and the corporal situation; the same word denotes fear and flight (φόβος) and the same word is used for 'trembling' and 'falling back' (τρέω). If a hero meets with suffering his tears flow freely. Hence for the Homeric man there is no threshold to separate will to action from carrying that will out, a threshold before which a man can stand hesitant, like Hamlet. When he recognizes what must happen he does not require a resolution of his own to proceed to the deed.[12] The plan itself obviously implies the impulse toward its execution. So Homeric language regularly employs words like 'designing, planning' (μήδομαι) in such a way that the execution of the plan is tacitly implied.

If what man wills and is, is straightway and without hindrance transformed into action, then every human trait and every character passes unchecked into outward expression and achievement; and the society of the *Iliad* is so organized that it affords broad scope for the noble character. So a man and his actions become identical, and he makes himself completely and adequately comprehended in them; he has no hidden depths. This situation justifies the epic in its traditional form. In its factual report of what men do and say everything that men are is expressed, because they are no more than what they do and say and suffer. They are not insulated from the outside world but their nature pours forth into the world with their deeds and their fortunes.

That is why the qualities displayed in human actions play a special role in the Homeric picture of human values. The verbal expressions are hard to translate, and are often flattened out or falsified in traditional renderings. Upon a hero a god bestows κράτος, which is not absolute 'strength' but transcendent 'power' and 'force'; the corresponding adjective κρατερός can be rendered by 'victorious,

[11] Cf. *Il.* 11, 403–11. What was first brought in as an address to the *thymos* is later designated a 'dialogue of the *thymos*,' and third and last a 'pondering in *phren* and *thymos*.'

[12] Cf. Bruno Snell, *Aischylos und das Handeln in Drama* (Leipzig, 1928), and *Philologus* 85, 141ff.; Christian Voigt, *Überlegung und Entscheidung* (Berlin, 1933).

violent, compelling.'[13] Another important word is κῦδος. It designates the property of having success and going forth as victor; but it also designates the 'glory' of success, prestige, authority, dignity, high rank.[14]

If man is, as it were, a field of energy, whose lines extend into space and time without limit or restraint, then external forces, for their part, operate in him without hindrance, and it is meaningless to ask where his own force begins and that from outside ends. In what they receive and suffer also, there men are wholly open to the outside world, so wide that our own basic antithesis between self and not-self does not yet exist in Homeric consciousness. Even what seems to us a highly personal achievement, a thought, say, or an impulse, is thought of in the *Iliad* as a gift received. A bold advance in battles is vouchsafed to the warrior by a god, who channels initiative (μένος) into him and 'impels' (ὦρσε) him. Similarly a god may 'thrust' a warrior 'into fear' (*Il.* 11, 544; 16, 689–91). The decisive question was not whether man is a free agent or compelled from without,[15] but whether his path led him to the heights or the depths. The power of the gods over life was premised from the beginning, and there was no part of the realm of spirit which a man could wish to retain for himself alone. The unsuccessful and cowardly man is 'bad,' and the man the gods assist is 'good' and bold (*Od.* 3, 373f; *Il.* 4, 390 and 408). The tacit assumption here is that the god helps only the man worth helping.

In the *Iliad*, then, man is completely a part of his world. He does not confront an outside world with a different inner selfhood, but is interpenetrated by the whole, just as he on his part by his action and indeed by his suffering penetrates the total event. Proud and straightforward, he gives himself forth without restraint in action and speech, even if the forms in which he expresses himself are regulated by the

[13] E.g., κρατερὸς δεσμός of the shackle or prison that forcibly holds a man against his will.

[14] Anthropologists have failed to notice that no Homeric word comes as close to the widely discussed *mana* and *orenda* as κῦδος does. The traditional rendering 'Fame' is false. κῦδος never signifies the fame which spreads itself abroad. Fame (κλέος) is applicable even to the dead, but κῦδος belongs only to the living (*Il.* 22, 435ff.). From Homer to late antiquity derivations of κῦδος serve to designate the feeling of a man sure of himself and confident of the future. Cf. Georg Finsler *Homer* I[2] (Leipzig, 1924), 142, and Gerhard Steinkopf, *Unters. zur Geschichte des Ruhms bei den Griechen* (Halle, 1937), pp. 23ff. (esp. p. 25, bottom).

[15] The question of attribution is occasionally discussed in speeches in order to assign to higher power blame for failure (e.g., *Il.* 3, 164; 19, 90ff.) or merit for an enemy's success (e.g., *Il.* 20, 94–98). The narrative of the *Iliad* constantly reports the direction or misdirection of the heroes by the gods. For the *Odyssey* see p. 90f., below.

norms of aristocratic decorum. Holding nothing back, he accepts all
that life brings him, even death. The warrior does indeed fight hard
and bitterly in battle and in his anger against other men; he does
suffer agony under our general human necessity; but he does not
attempt to ward necessity off or to strive against it.[16] He accepts it
sorrowfully as what is fated for him.

> He spoke, and while he spoke came death and closed all about him;
> Fluttering free from his limbs his soul went down into Hades
> Mourning over her fate, leaving youth and manhood behind her.

So Patroclus dies (*Il.* 16, 855). And Lycaon, still half a boy, tearfully
beseeches the fearsome Achilles for his young life, grasping his
opponent's murderous spear; but when he hears these words—

> So, friend, you die also. Why all this outcry about it?
> Is not Patroclus dead, who was far, far better than you are?
> Do you not see what a man I am, how tall and how splendid?
> Son of a noble father, the mother who bore me immortal?
> Even for me waits death and the fate that is stronger than I am.
> One hour shall come, in the dawn or the afternoon or the noontide,
> When some foe in the fighting will take the life from me also,
> Either with the spear or an arrow flown from the bowstring.

—when Lycaon hears this answer his knees and heart are loosened,
he lets go his enemy's spear, he crouches down with arms outspread
to receive the death-stroke (*Il.* 21, 106). With the same conscious
readiness as the boy Lycaon, Achilles too goes to meet his approaching death. 'I will receive death as soon as the gods ordain it' (*Il.* 18,
115; 22, 365).

All this takes place not under the pressure of a dull submission or in
a fury or primitive savagery, but with a radiant freshness and an
aristocratic clarity which lends even the gloomiest scenes a glow of
serene grace. Homeric man understands the good and the evil that
confront him. Just as he is accessible to the operation of the forces
that seize upon him and to the fate that befalls him, so too is he open
to a free view of actuality and its existing order, and he draws the
consequences of his actions without shuddering or wincing. The
organ of insight is blocked by no timidity and no brutality. These
volatile men are at once and to an astonishing degree intelligent and
experienced. They are accessible to the word and masters of the
word. In the midst of difficult situations the circumstances are clearly
laid out in a conversation going into details without regard to the
shortness of time, and the right course of action is hit upon. And as
soon as a plan has been conceived it is carried out. The path to

[16] Cf. Snell, *Aischylos* (see n. 12, above), pp. 82f.

action leads unfalteringly through the spirit; the short cut of unconscious reactions is disdained. To intervene in a critical situation
with lightning speed is in Homeric language 'sharp understanding'
(ὀξὺ νόησε).

Knowledge offered Homeric men broad avenues to many kinds of
things. It leads into an objective world, into the world of what is, as
well as the world of what should be. Even what we call 'duty' or
'morality' is attained through knowledge. When Odysseus in great
danger in battle hesitates whether to escape or stand fast, it is
sufficient for him to reflect how bad men act and, on the other hand,
how men who excel in battle behave; an 'I know' is enough to
resolve his doubt and to take the only course possible for a brave
man (*Il.* 11, 403ff.). Not dim instincts but clear capacities rule.
Hector refuses to withdraw from battle for a space: 'My mind
[inclination, desire, *thymos*] does not consent, for I have learned[17] to
be noble without cease and to fight among the foremost' (*Il.* 6, 444).
Much that we call 'character' or 'giftedness' is for Homer knowledge of
the matters in question and of their proper disposition. 'He was a good
man' is expressed by 'he knew how to be friendly to all' (*Il.* 17, 671).
The word 'knowing' (εἰδώς) in Homer also covers the area which
we assign to temper rather than knowledge. Homeric men 'know'
friendliness, gentleness, rules of conduct (θέμιστας); or lawlessness,
wickedness (λυγρά), irregular and unsocial conduct (ἀθεμίστια); a
man 'knows' love for his neighbor, and so forth. It is convenient but
wrong to maintain that in such passages the word 'to know' changed
its meaning and is to be understood as 'was minded.' One passage
speaks of a man who 'is hard in himself [i.e., in character] and knows
hardness' (*Od.* 19, 329). For the author of the passage, being hard
and knowing hardness are two different things, even when they are
attributed to the same person. The presence of 'knowing' in a
function which we attribute to character or feeling provides an
insight into the practicality of Homeric man; he looks at what
objectively can be done and is done.

A regard for what is actually done may be seen also in the fact
that the word 'love' can be used for hospitality. 'A whole month he
loved [φίλει] me' (*Od.* 10, 14). So community of interest is at once
taken as evidence of a friendly attitude. 'I know well,' Agamemnon
says amicably to angry Odysseus, 'that the temper in your dear

---

[17] ἔμαθον, i.e., 'I have learned through word and example, I have resolved to
be noble.' The aorist indicates the act of turning toward, the setting out on a
particular path. In general, cf. B. Snell, *Die Ausdrücke für den Begriff des Wissens* ...
(Berlin, 1924), pp. 72f. The life of a hanger-on can also be 'learned' in Homer (*Od.*
17, 226).

breast knows friendly intentions, for you think the same things as
I' (*Il.* 4, 360f.);[18] the content of the thought, in this case, is a firm
resolution to defeat the enemy. A decision to do something can also
be expressed with the help of the word 'love': 'since it is "beloved"
to you gods to destroy Troy' (*Il.* 7, 31); 'let it be "beloved" to you to
ward off the enemy' (*Il.* 16, 556). In general the adjective 'beloved,'
'friendly' (φίλος) has a wide range in Homer. It can be applied to
anything connected with a person, not only to his 'dear comrades'
but also to his own organs. For the organs are helpers and agents of
the self, when a man reaches for what he desires with his 'dear hands'
or raises his 'dear arms' in prayer to the gods, since he cannot ascend
to them himself, or lays upon his 'dear knees' a thing he would like
to retain but must soon part with (*Od.* 21, 55). On the other hand, the
self participates in the experiences of its organs, whether it is that his
'dear arm' is pierced by an enemy spear, or that food and drink
happily enter his 'dear throat' (*Il.* 19, 209), or that his 'dear heart' is
aroused. The organs are 'friendly' to the self; in general all the
elements in a person—limbs, intellect, feeling, will—cooperate
sympathetically for practical ends, without conflict or complications.

Man in the *Iliad* remains always himself; he is not shattered by the
hardest blows, nor is he capable of development. He reacts to
situations sharply, and the mood he then takes on passes with the
situation without leaving a trace.[19] He has indeed very developed
forms of social intercourse: he obviously feels that he is not constricted
but uplifted by the social rules, for they lend him nobility. He manages
the forms, moreover, with a virtuosity which proves him their
master, not their slave. This appears most plainly in the elegance of
his speeches and the diplomatic finesse of which he is capable.[20] But
in anger he can also become coarse or sarcastic.

[18] The attitude of one man to another does not rest on an encounter of souls in
sympathy or antipathy (there is as yet no soul), but men find themselves at one
in the same thinking, knowing, and acting. Cf. B. Snell, *Gnomon* 7 (1931), 84f.

[19] The principal example is Achilles' behavior in *Iliad* 9, and especially his
announcement that he will give up his heroic career and live out his life in peace
at home (see p. 19, above). His final word is that he would reflect on the morrow
what he will do (618f.), and there the matter stands; what actually happens on the
morrow is never told. How the poet intends us to understand this he tells us in vv.
677–703. According to Odysseus' report, Achilles' hesitation regarding the reconciliation is intended to be taken seriously, but his proposal to return home was
only a threat. Diomedes explains that Achilles' pride has been only enhanced by
the excessive offers; he should be left to himself and not be entreated to give up
his plan to return home; he will join the fighting again as soon as his inner feeling
(*thymos*) and a god arouse him to do so.

[20] An investigation of Homeric social forms is an urgent desideratum. It could
be expected to produce rich and surprising conclusions, especially with reference

Homer's people have an elemental vitality. They make no secret of their joy in physical pleasures like food and drink, in the sweet gift of sleep, in love, though they speak of it in discreet language. They love festivities and joyful dance; even lamentation is for them a 'joy.'[21] The life they lead is worldly; of a world beyond, they expect nothing. Death destroys men, in their view, when the soul's breath of life departs from what remains behind as a corpse. The soul then journeys down to the dark underworld as a shadow, there to continue a darkling and unreal existence which is worse than the hardest life in the sunlight. The shade of Achilles says very bitterly (*Od.* 11, 489):

> Far rather would I live upon earth[22] as the slave of another,
> Landless and poor, than lord it here over bodiless shadows.

As long as a man remains on earth he lives his life manfully. Only when something happens is he aware of himself. It is in conflict above all that a man confirms his own existence, to himself and to others, whether it be in armed battle or in dissensions and quarrels. Sufferings are involved, and these are taken as part of the bargain. Conflict and pain are the themes of the epics, and suffering is the law of humanity (*Il.* 24, 525):

> Such is the way the gods spin life for unfortunate mortals;
> We live in pain: but they are as strangers to care and to sorrow.

For the suffering that he must bear in life and for the ineffable horror of annihilation in death, Homeric man knows only one compensation—glory. Only in this medium can a valid image of his essence and his worth be imprinted; for there is not yet a conscience in which a man can see his own reflection. The heroes of the *Iliad* lead a public life and their conduct is determined by consideration of contemporaries and posterity (*Il.* 6, 441–43; 9, 459–61). Public opinion speaks clearly (νεμεσσάω), when any base action is taken, and there is never a notion that this instrument might operate wrongly and unjustly. There are no hidden motives and dark backgrounds in the *Iliad*; a man is as he behaves.

The epic which perpetuated the glory of the heroes shows them as they actually were in the poet's eyes. But it shows only what is essential in them. The accidental and insignificant idiosyncrasies which

to the speeches. But the speeches must not be approached with the narrow and superficial categories of formal rhetoric, as has often been attempted with no substantial gain.

21 *Il.* 13, 636–9; *Od.* 4, 102–05.

22 The nonce word ἐπάρουρος is to be understood as 'upon the earth'. cf. *Il.* 18, 104.

merely distinguish one individual from all others are omitted in poetry. Poetry shapes not likenesses but prototypes, each of whom embodies one of the general potentialities of recognizable humanity. Just as Nestor is the prototype of a noble old man, so is Achilles the prototype of a noble young man. Furthermore, the personages are stylized consistently; each peculiarity pervades its bearer uniformly and is proportionately visible in every part of his being. The commander in chief Agamemnon not only has a princely bearing: he is also handsome as few others are (*Il.* 3, 169). Thersites is as ugly in form as he is shameful in behaviour (*Il.* 2, 212–19). The consistency makes the figures monumental, and at the same time simplifies the presentation. When it is said of Nestor that he is a 'clear-sounding speaker,' the connotation is that he is also a skilful and clever orator and statesman; and when Achilles is called 'swift-footed,' his temperament as quick to anger is also implied. From one trait the others are to be deduced, for the lines of each character are never broken or obscured in this poetry; they traverse the entire personage in steady course, and from his person thrust out into the open field of his environment. Even what a man does to others is part of himself.

(g) *The New Mood of the* Odyssey *and the End of Epic*

If we want to learn the structure of human nature in ancient epic, we must adhere mainly to the *Iliad,* for the picture begins to change markedly in the *Odyssey.* The contrast between the epics can be inferred at once from the programmatic verses with which they begin.[1] As the proems indicate, the hero of the *Iliad* is great because he is wrathful and stubborn; that of the *Odyssey,* not because he is self-willed but because he is 'versatile.' Achilles shows his worth by sacrificing to his resentment 'the souls of many heroes' out of his own camp (and soon he will sacrifice his own soul also: cf. *Il.* 9, 104–16); Odysseus, by contrast, preserves himself because he understands how to save 'his own soul and the homecoming of his comrades'— although the comrades perish in the end, through no fault of his. The *Iliad* depicts horrible things which (like everything on earth) came about according to 'god's will'; the *Odyssey* does indeed tell (among many other things) of the terrible death of the comrades, but they invited divine punishment 'on their part through lack of understanding.' Inflexible resentment here, pliable accommodation there;

[1] The differences in content between the two poems are the more marked in that their form follows the same plan: cf. pp. 13f., above.

destruction of others and self here, preservation of self and others there; the will of the gods here, and man's own success or failure there. The *Odyssey* is no longer romantically lamenting a submerged world which was fatefully ruined by its own stormy nature; instead it celebrates the manful realist of a new present who cleverly and resolutely takes his destiny into his own hands to rise superior to all opposition.

The greater realism and contemporaneity in the *Odyssey* give the entire poem a different character. The distance between the narrator and his subject which is so strictly maintained in the *Iliad* is here perceptibly slackened, and the rigour of the stylization is modified. The Phaeacians are idealized Ionians of the present. Nature is largely restored to its rights. Winter and bad weather afflict Odysseus (*Od.* 14, 457ff.); he is afraid of the cold of night and the wind on the riverbank, and of savage beasts by sea and land (*Od.* 5, 465–73; 421). There are now beggars and humble folk, even a dog, who is the only creature to recognize his homecoming master. The graybeard is no longer above all the bearer of accumulated sagacity, but a fragile man in need of help (*Od.* 17, 195f.). The use of similes is much reduced, for the real world, not a stylized one, enters freely into the narrative itself and does not have to lurk in little digressions.

The people of the *Odyssey* no longer live in an almost empty space; they take pleasure in the abundant variety of things to be seen and heard and experienced. The world is wide and full of wonders, which a man may visit to try his powers against them. The joy of discovery and the love of adventure form the background for a large part of the epic. Odysseus ventures into the cave of the Cyclops out of curiosity and because he hopes to receive gifts of hospitality (*Od.* 9, 224–30), and some of his comrades have to pay for his rashness with a horrible death. Life for these people is full of interest, but also of difficulty. The outside world, which is no longer shadowy but now surrounds and oppresses the individual with its massive presence, constantly thrusts him into situations with which it is hard to cope. So man begins to put a distance between himself and the world. Men are no longer freely receptive and freely outgoing; they are now reserved and calculating. Aloofness and distrust become necessary, indeed a virtue which is glorified in the epic. Even deception and falsehood are now legitimate weapons in the struggle for existence. The modern ideal of the clever and experienced man who makes his way by all means, straight or crooked, displaces the heroic ideal, and antagonism to the outmoded view leads the poets to exaggerate and overvalue the traits which now occupy the foreground. Odysseus the 'rogue'

(*Od.* 5, 182) is the master of the new art of living, recognized and admired by men and by gods.[2] The proud reserve of unbending rectitude has been given up. For a long while Odysseus plays the role of beggar, and plays it almost too realistically.[3] On occasion his character appears to become quite uncertain.

And yet Odysseus is by no means an actor without a character of his own, or an adventurer ignorant of what he is really seeking; nor is the *Odyssey* a poem of roguery. With all his ingratiating amiability, its hero is a serious, mature, and energetic man, and with all his cunning, he pursues a high goal and, thanks to his toughness with himself, attains it. The iron strength with which he masters feelings, resists seduction, and breaks attachments is a new kind of heroism. This 'iron heart' (*Od.* 4, 293) the epic celebrates by regularly attaching the epithet πολύτλας to his name; 'much enduring' is only a vague rendering. What πολύτλας really means is shown by a scene at the beginning of Book 20. Odysseus lays himself down to sleep as a beggar in the vestibule of his own house, on the eve of the vengeance through which he will regain his place as master and king. There he hears certain of the maids going, with laughter and jests, to meet their lovers among the suitors. Odysseus' heart begins to rage and to 'bark,' for as master of the house the maids belong to him, and it is a form of unfaithfulness for them to give themselves to the suitors of their own will. Natural pride would impel him to strike them all down at once, and his heart bays like a hound over what has been tossed to it, irritable and determined to protect its treasure. But he chides his heart and admonishes it to 'endure' (τλῆναι): 'Even dealings more doglike did you endure when the Cyclops devoured my comrades. You endured until wit brought you out of the cave, which would otherwise have been my death.' In Homer the dog is an image of bold audacity and unflinching determination.[4] In the cave the Cyclops had killed and devoured two of Odysseus' comrades. 'In my proud temper,' so Odysseus tells the story to the Phaeacians (*Od.* 9, 299), 'I seized upon the thought of approaching and slaying him. But another purpose restrained me, for then we too would have been irretrievably lost, for we could not have rolled the heavy stone from the high doorway with our arms.' So Odysseus controlled himself then, and had to look on while two more of his companions met the same gruesome end before the proper moment came for the appropriate action. Then, as now, something in his heart raged

---

[2] Penelope too is once praised for similar qualities in contrast to 'the women of olden times' (*Od.* 2, 118ff.).

[3] The *Odyssey* invents a similar exploit in the Trojan War (*Od.* 4, 240ff.).

[4] Not a symbol of the acceptance of humiliations.

doglike and wished to assert itself in righteous indignation, and now, as then, he constrains his proud temper to 'endure.' 'So he spoke, admonishing his dear heart, and it abode in obedience, without yielding.' So too Odysseus 'endured' (*Od.* 13, 307) when after twenty years he finally entered his own house as a beggar, to suffer many affronts, and revealed his identity to no one until he had obtained exact information and had matured his plan of vengeance. He sits opposite his own wife and plays a subtle game of hide-and-seek with her,[5] because the time has not yet come for an open declaration. In the patience of the 'much enduring' Odysseus, in the suppression of his pride and other natural impulses, there is much forceful activity, and this is carried on not for its own sake but to promote an objective. Odysseus is the man who pursues his objectives against all opposition. This quality the epic expresses in other standing epithets which adorn the name of Odysseus: πολύμητις, 'rich in ingenious ideas,' and πολυμήχανος, 'rich in devices to gain an end.' With such attributes does the new age, which graded its values very differently from the old, bedeck its idol.

In the younger epic Odysseus enters upon the heritage of Achilles, who was the most brilliant figure in the *Iliad*. Odysseus as heir of Achilles: this formulation we do not conceive in retrospect, for it is in this conception that the epic itself at once perpetuated the changed ideal of human excellence as soon as it appeared. This time saga, which reflects so many events of political history after its own fashion, has concentrated a historical evolution in values into a profoundly meaningful legend.[6] One of the epics of Troy, the *Little Iliad*, relates that after the death of Achilles an argument arose as to who was now the best man in the army and so entitled to the armor of Achilles. The candidates were Ajax, the doughty but slow-thinking champion, and Odysseus, the clever but less powerful warrior. The decision was sought from the enemy camp, because the opposition knew best whom they had most to fear. A spy overheard a conversation between Trojan maidens (at the spring); the decisive words were spoken by a Trojan woman who pointed out that Ajax was like a tough and reliable workman, whereas Odysseus was a man of

[5] Bk. 19. At the same time the clever Penelope (n. 2, above) for her part plays a dangerous game with her guest, who is apparently her husband but might be a deceiver. In this way both advance their own, converging plans. (On this see the important article of P. W. Harsh, *Amer. Journ. of Philol.* 71 [1950], 1–21.)

[6] One of the many things which give early Greek literature its peculiar value is that poets and thinkers themselves were clear about their historical position. Each new generation not only produced its own ideas but also explained the transition which led them from the old to the new, and so provided an authentic interpretation of the course of history.

initiative and adroitness.[7] After the armor was awarded to Odysseus, Ajax took his own life in chagrin and shame.

Our *Odyssey* has another confrontation between the two. Odysseus reports to the Phaeacians (11, 543ff.) that he saw the shade of Ajax in the realm of the dead and that Ajax kept his distance in anger at his defeat. And the narrator remarks:

> Would I had never been victor and won so fatal a contest!
> It is for this that the grave now holds so mighty a hero—
> Ajax, in looks and in actions the greatest of all the Achaeans
> Saving only Achilles, the peerless offspring of Peleus.

Nothing could be more significant of the amiable side of the new humanity (see p. 52, above) than these words of Odysseus. They breathe a generous and understanding kindliness—one of the new virtues. There speaks here an insight which recognizes the superiority of a defeated opponent and which would willingly forego the proudest honor if it had to be purchased by the death of such a man. With such feelings Odysseus addresses conciliatory words to the shade of Ajax in the underworld. But this is not the sort of language to prevail over the intransigent pride of the olden days (11, 563):

> So I spoke, but he gave no reply, and turned himself from me,
> Joining the other ghosts of the dead who dwell in the shadows.

On aesthetic grounds we could wish that the scene ended here. But our text contains an after-word which softens the bluntness:

> Yet he might still have spoken for all his angry resentment.
> I might have spoken again; but the heart in my bosom was eager
> Still to see more and to talk with others among the departed.

It is quite possible that these three transitional verses to what follows come from another hand than the scene itself. In any case, they are significant of the optimism with which the new age trusted its new men. Its cleverness and warmth would be able to thaw the rigidity of the old heroism and to reconcile an angry Ajax with an Odysseus. Only the curiosity of Odysseus, wishing to converse with other souls, prevented the continuation of the dialogue.

The hero of the *Odyssey* displays his manifold abilities in having to deal with beings of all kinds, one after the other, and in being involved in difficulties of all kinds. Always he comes to the fore as master, and by his unique greatness leaves all others, friend and foe alike, far behind him; his role is not, like that of Achilles in the *Iliad*, *primus inter pares*. But if the lesser figures of the *Odyssey* are not of the same

[7] This is probably the meaning of Fr. 3 (E. Bethe, *Homer* II [Leipzig, 1922], 170).

calibre as Odysseus, they are nevertheless of similar style. They too derive from the new age: the hero's wife holds the suitors off by her ingenuity;[8] Circe is cunning, and Calypso is warm-hearted and kindly—or pretends to be; the suitors, for their part, intrigue against Telemachus, but their attempt on his life miscarries. The few open and forthright characters fall into special types because of those traits; so, for example, the faithful and amiable swineherd, or the savage and detestable Cyclops, a naïve and conceited blusterer, whose deception is almost tragic (9, 447–60). The lesser like the principal figures move largely among peculiar and precarious circumstances. This makes the action of the *Odyssey* more complicated but also more unified. For every element of the action there are precisely ascribed conditions, and these are all interrelated. The *Iliad*, by contrast, is more loosely jointed, for its theme is simply strife and contention in the war at Troy.

Hence the persons of the *Odyssey* require a different kind of divine assistance for discharging their tasks. Divine providence now takes on the character of a constant surveillance which watches over its protégés with great punctiliousness and intervenes to support them according to a precise plan with either natural or miraculous means. At the same time the people of the *Odyssey*, in their detachment and shrewdness, begin to insulate themselves against the outer world. The individual is no longer an open field of action, but self and not-self are differentiated, so that even divine influence on their conduct is externalized. When Odysseus lands in Ithaca he receives from Athene not inspiration, but detailed information and instructions (*Od.* 13, 372–428), like the information and instructions for his journey given him by the goddess Circe (*Od.* 10, 490–540; 12, 37–141). So in the *Odyssey* a distinction is occasionally drawn which would not have occurred to the older age: '. . . whether it was that a god implanted this thought, or whether he himself devised it' (4, 712).[9] Divine direction and individual action can now be separated from one another, so that man becomes responsible for his acts in a new sense.[10]

Man is not transparent in the *Odyssey*, even when he is not actually

[8] In contrast to Helen of the *Iliad*, who could have played a double game between her two husbands and peoples, but does not. The Helen of the *Odyssey* did so: *Od.* 4, 250–64, 270–89.

[9] Naturally this passage occurs in a speech, for the narrator, who is well aware of the divine aspect of the thing, does not need to leave the question open (see p. 53, n. 1, above). In general, nevertheless, the *Odyssey* still speaks as if every attitude and intention was inspired by the gods (2, 124; 3, 215, 269).

[10] 1, 32–43; cf. W. Jaeger, *Sitzungsber. Preuss. Akad.*, 1926, 73f.=*Scripta minora* (Rome 1960) I, 321f.=*Five Essays*, transl. A. Fiske (Montreal 1966) 83f.

lying; he is variable and reserved and sometimes not too certain of
himself—like Telemachus and some of the suitors, and probably
Penelope also. Not infrequently, then, the representation in poetry
must be content without complete clarity and openness. Neither the
report of the narrator, who still discreetly restricts himself to externals, nor the speeches of the epic personages, who are far from
expressing themselves frankly, can set forth everything the poet has
in mind. Instead of the bright footlights before which the heroes of the
Iliad performed, a softened and shifting half-light plays over the
personages of the younger epic, sometimes flaring up only to be
dimmed again. For such a presentation traditional epic style was not
suited. An astonishing example can show how, in a very late part of
the *Odyssey*, the poet drew the utmost refinements from a style not
well suited to them.

In the guise of Mentes, a man from a family of friends, Athene
comes to the palace at Ithaca, where the suitors have made themselves at home (*Od.* 1, 103ff.). In the midst of the general turmoil
Telemachus receives the visitor and does the honors of the house.
Between the two a conversation takes place which becomes intimate
at once. Telemachus is oppressed by his embarrassing impotence in
his own house. He no longer dares hope for the return of his father,
which would change everything. The stranger, for his part, is full of
friendly reassurances; in his view, he remarks comfortingly, such a
man as Odysseus will somehow overcome all hindrances. Homeric
etiquette now requires that after a stranger has been received inquiry
should be made concerning name (τίς), father (πόθεν), home (πόλις),
and other personal details. The visitor had already supplied the information, and now he puts the corresponding questions to his host,
in order to satisfy the formal requirements, for in fact he had already
treated Telemachus as the man he was (187). He therefore phrases
his question to become a compliment on Telemachus' resemblance
to his famous father (206): 'Tell me this and relate it truly, if you
are indeed the son of Odysseus himself. You are marvelously like him
in head and handsome eyes. . . .' Whereupon the visitor receives an
extraordinary answer (214):

> Friend, I will speak to you as clearly as I am able.
> My mother tells me that I am his son: yet truly for my part
> I cannot say: what man can know for sure his conception?
> Wish that I were a happy man's son—one favored by fortune,
> Sitting among his kin, with a tranquil old age to await him!
> But they tell me that he, instead, the most luckless of all men,
> He was my father: I tell you, for that was the question you asked me.

Telemachus' reply begins with an ordinary epic formula which

elsewhere (cf. 179) says nothing more than that one is ready to give
the desired information accurately and truly. But this time Telemachus carries accuracy and truth very far, and in a singular
direction. Obviously Telemachus had often worried over the
misfortune bequeathed to him by an absent man whom he scarcely
knew, of whom he was told that his name was Odysseus and that he
was his father. His worry now rises to acute doubt: all of this may
not be true,[11] and it would be better if it were not. Naturally the
doubt is not real, nor was the stranger's question motivated by real
doubt; and it is unreasonable, for Penelope is the proverbially
faithful wife. But the keen desire of the young man to dissociate
himself from his fate and his identity suggest such fancies,[12] for which
he eventually apologizes: '[Excuse my outbreak, but you evoked it]
because you asked me whether I was my father's son.' The response of
the stranger tactfully veers back to the normal (222):

The gods have not given you a nameless ancestry, since Penelope bore you
to a man such as Odysseus.

Mentes will not deny that no man has personal knowledge of his
origin, but in this case the later development of the child banishes
every doubt, for Telemachus, as was already noted, has grown up to
be a true image of Odysseus.[13] The implications are two-fold: the
young man can be proud of his descent, and has no reason to struggle
against it.

The section just examined appears so strange and un-Homeric
that one is tempted to evade the interpretation here sketched; but
the text admits no other explanation. This astonishingly modern
piece shows how far Greek epic in its latest stage has travelled from its
starting point. It is minded to overstep the boundaries set for this
genre.[14] No further advance was possible along this road. Only
followers and imitators could be expected.

[11] For the significance of (αὐτὸς) οἶδα—'I can testify by my own knowledge'—
cf. p. 19, n. 26, above, and p. 335, n. 19, below.

[12] Wish-fantasies crop up frequently in this section: 163–65; 196–99; 203–05;
237–40; 255–66.

[13] The interpretation of 1, 222f. given above (cf. Amer. Journ. Philol. 60, 1939,
477, n. 8) is confirmed by the exact parallel 4, 62–64. The τοι ('your') γενεήν in 1,
222 takes up the τοῦ μ' ἔκ φασι γενέσθαι of 220; and οὐ νώνυμνον (222) establishes the
exception to what the young man, in 216, had said about the anonymity of father-
hood in general. The aorist ἔθηκαν cannot refer to anything future; hence ὀπίσσω,
'afterwards' (as in Od. 14, 232), applies to what has appeared in the interval,
after the procreation (similarly ἔπειτα in Il. 19, 113: 'But afterwards the oath
showed itself to be a great mistake').

[14] 'Epic poetry mainly presents man working outside himself: battles, journeys,
enterprises of every kind which provide some sensible breadth; tragedy presents
the man turned inward upon himself.' Goethe, Über epische und dramatische Dichtung.

The new humanity which asserts itself in the *Odyssey* takes away from epic the basis of its existence. The epic form was created in order to give a complete and definitive account of unquestioned actuality either directly or by transparent symbols, not to beat to and fro in a misty environment of hazy possibilities and everyday attitudes. The grandiose language and the powerful verse are not suited to the subtle or the commonplace[15] which they are now used to express. Where previously all that was named or told of was glorified, and only what was praiseworthy had the entrée to epic, now the gates are flung wide to persons and things of every description, and the singer's performance is no longer, as it had been, devotion to and celebration of gods and great men. The poetry is no longer stylized, as it formerly was, but depicts the world more realistically and in a more modern spirit.

The figure of the principal hero embodies the modern spirit at its purest and fullest. From Odysseus contemporary audiences could learn to master life. Why then the roundabout way via an art originally intended for looking backward into a different past? The inherited epic form would have to be alienated from its nature or surrendered entirely, for literature to be able to fulfill the tasks now set before it: to know the world as it is constituted, to confront situations in the way that is most advantageous, and to come to grips with one's life, each with his own.

Into such a situation there now enters the singular figure of Hesiod, and then, with a very different function, lyric poetry: Hesiod to master and encompass the outer world instructively, still in the language and versification of epic; lyric to seize upon the inwardness of personal life in poetry of a new form. The two have now parted. The old unity is broken.

---

[15] The epithet 'leader of men' (ὄρχαμος ἀνδρῶν), distinctively used for kings of hosts, is now applied to a swineherd who has a few slaves under him.

III

Hesiod

(a) *The Poet*

In the more rigorous stylization of epic, such as prevails in the *Iliad*, the singer narrated selected stories of individual human and divine personages in a factual narrative. The persons occupied a space related only to themselves; the natural environment in which human beings exist was as far as possible suppressed. Hesiod, by contrast, in a first great poem, the *Theogony*, presents systematically and comprehensively man's total environment, how it came into being and how it is, all things in the world, all gods and powers and all nature, excepting only man himself and animals and plants. The narratives of the *Iliad* ignore the ordinary existence of ordinary people and deal only with the extraordinary deeds and sufferings of proud heroes at war. Hesiod, by contrast, presents in a second epic, the *Works and Days*, a picture of the daily life of men and the rules which govern it, and imparts good lessons for right and decent conduct. In a third poem, which is not preserved, he told of the connections of gods with human women; from these unions the ancestors of all contemporary noble houses were believed to have issued. The literary form is that of epic, but vocabulary, versification, and style go far astray in Hesiod. The content is highly individual. In number of verses, each of the two surviving epics is approximately equal to a book of the *Iliad*; but to the reader they seem considerably longer, because the subjects are various, the mutual connections complicated, and the understanding of the words is often difficult.

From what he himself says we know a little about this singular man who, about the year 700 (the date is uncertain)[1] and in Boeotia, wrote these poems—oddly provincial poems, strange and awkward, but with depth and power and appealing to our most basic

[1] For a recent discussion see M. L. West's edition of the *Theogony* (Oxford, 1966) 40ff.

feelings. All Greek posterity admired Hesiod and recognized him as a unique poetical phenomenon.

How did the gift of song ever reach Boetia and the 'Boeotian porkers,' as they were nicknamed? Hesiod's father was an eastern Greek, an Aeolian from Cyme in Asia Minor, who found a new home in the back-of-beyond mountain village of Ascra (*WD* 637ff.):

> He did not flee from riches and blessings of cheerful abundance.
> No, but from hunger and want, the burden that Zeus lays on mortals.
> Near mount Helicon made he his home, in a beggarly village,
> Ascra, freezing in winter, parching in summer, good never.

So his son Hesiod tells us with his characteristically acid humor. From the East the father brought a knowledge of things of which the peasants of Ascra were ignorant. Ascra is inland while Cyme is on the sea, and the peasants there used the seasons when there was no work in the fields for small trading voyages by sea. In their boats they fetched and carried goods to dispose of at a profit. Hesiod himself was never on the water, except once when he crossed a small sound, now bridged over, to Euboea and back. But his father gave him such detailed advice on seafaring that the son could set it forth in his *Works and Days*. Whence he got his knowledge of seafaring Hesiod tells us indirectly (*WD* 633–38, 646–51) and then continues (661): 'Nevertheless [i.e., though I lack personal experience] I will set forth the will of aegis-wielding Zeus [i.e., the rules of seafaring], for the Muses have instructed me to sing my song without restriction.'[1a] Hesiod knows that he is master of a power which permits him to ignore the narrow limitations of direct physical experience. From the mere words of his father he is able to derive a divinely established reality which he never saw with his own eyes; he can hear, think, and speak. This art he owes to the Muses. Hesiod must have been familiar with the Muses' art of verse discourse from the recitals of epic singers, who were even then plying their craft in backwoods Boeotia and seeking a livelihood. As a young man (pp. 20f., above) Hesiod acquired the ability to emulate those travelling singers and himself to compose and recite in the language, verse, and style he learned from them. He too became a singer, if only as a sideline: his principal occupation was as shepherd and as peasant. As a rhapsode he once travelled as far as Euboea and received a prize at funeral games there: this was the journey that gave him occasion to step on board ship.

Hesiod himself describes in his first poem the decisive event of his call by the Muses. The passage is usually called his poetic dedication,

---

[1a] For ἀθέσφατος cf. *Antidoron*, Festschrift für J. Wackernagel (Göttingen, 1923), pp. 281f.

but the words are anything but dedicatory. At the opening of the
Theogony (22ff.) the poet praises the Muses:

> Once they taught Hesiod the wonderful gift of the singer
> While he guarded his sheep on cloudy [?] Helicon's pastures.
> These were the words which they, the divine ones, first uttered to me,
> They who dwell on Olympus, the Thunderer's children, the Muses:
> 'Shepherds who live in the backwoods, you pitiful creatures, mere bellies,
> We have the art of speaking in lies which are true in all seeming;
> Truth can we also impart if ever we chance to desire it.'
> So said the children of Zeus, his daughters skilful in speaking,
> Gave to me too a staff for my hand, of the evergreen laurel,
> Which they had plucked, a beautiful branch, and gave me resounding
> Speech as their gift, to sing of the past and to sing of the future.

This, then, is how Hesiod experienced his awakening. To the young
shepherd who with his companions led a half-animal and coarsely
material life in the summer pasturages in desolate mountain loneli-
ness, sleeping on the bare ground with his father's sheep, it became
clear that a spiritual realm high above the basic bodily existence was
accessible to him—a heavenly, airy, dangerous region of words and
thoughts, where essence and appearance were harder to distinguish
than in the lowly regions where things dwelt.[2] He realized that he
himself was competent in the arts of the Muses and hence forward
might carry the staff of the rhapsodes. But his intention was not to
recite fanciful stories, as he had so often heard the travelling singers
do: it was to communicate reality. He took his art very seriously.

(b) *Theogony*

In later times, Hesiod's first epic came to be called *Theogony*, that is,
'Genesis of the Gods.' If we wish to make the title correspond with
the actual contents, we must understand each of its component parts

---

[2] In true archaic fashion (see p. 54, above) the special quality of a singer's
spiritual world is marked by contrasting it with the world of a wretched and
awkward shepherd who, like his charges, knows no higher good than to fill his
belly. In this sphere, at least, there is no danger of deception: a 'mere belly' always
knows whether it is full or empty. If we may take it literally that the Muses called
Hesiod when he was tending sheep, we can imagine him as practicing his art among
the shepherds until he mastered it. But of pastoral sentimentality Hesiod knows
nothing; the shepherd's life seemed to him that of an animal. Of the South Slavs,
Murko (p. 9, n. 1, above), 176, 10, reports: 'Especially numerous [among the
singers] are shepherds who "have nothing to do in their pasturages but watch the
cattle, pray, and sing to the gusle." ' On the whole passage cf. K. Latte, *Antike
und Abendland* 2 (1946), 152, now in *Kleine Schriften* 1968, 60–75.

in a special sense. The gods whom Hesiod deals with include not only the personalized gods like Zeus and Apollo, but also the basic elements of nature, like earth, sky, stars, and wind, and forces of life like victory, strife, falsehood; hence 'genesis of the gods' is also 'genesis of the world.' And to express this 'genesis,' or 'birth,' Hesiod uses the framework of a family tree of gods and the world for two further purposes. He follows the history of the universe to its present stage and reports how three generations of gods can be distinguished in the world order; and secondly, he specifies the nature and function of the powers with which man must daily come to grips. On the other hand, he never speaks of forms of cult and worship.[1] He is rather concerned to clarify the essence of the powers whose sphere of activity is likewise the sphere of our existence.

The content of Hesiod's *Theogony* was derived from three sources. One portion came from the living, native belief of Boeotia and from tradition otherwise apocryphal, but accessible to Hesiod.[2] Here belong the primitive myths, like that of the emasculation of the sky or of the three creatures with a hundred arms, and other obscure and gloomy legends of gruesome battles of the gods and deeds of violence. These legends had remained untouched by the humanization and refinement which took place in the colonial East. The second is the Homeric world of the gods. Hesiod knew it well from the heroic epics, to which he was indebted for a language and form in which he could think and sing. But there is nothing drier and more lifeless in the *Theogony* than the passage where Hesiod refers, very briefly, to the Homeric system of gods (912–42). The personified gods of Homer and their capricious behaviour offered no opening for his kind of speculation. Hesiod believed in these figures also, but he has little to say about them. The third element Hesiod himself contributes out of his own resources. No doubt he changed, to a greater or lesser degree, the traditional stories which he retells. Over and above this he contributes much that no one before him had seen and said. Externally, what is original cannot be distinguished from

[1] Gods who receive service and sacrifice are not differentiated in Hesiod from beings who never had any place of worship. Only once (*Theog.* 535ff.) is a cult usage mentioned and explained. Cf. further p. 130, nn. 27 and 28, below.

[2] A continuing tradition of myths of gods and the world, with a metaphysical ingredient, must have existed before and after Hesiod, but we know almost nothing of it. As far as the tradition was literary, it was clothed predominantly in the form of epics and hymns. In a few passages the *Iliad* refers to this mass of tradition. That Near Eastern myths and legends also gained entry into the tradition is becoming clearer from year to year: see M. L. West's edition of the *Theogony*, especially pp. 19ff. and his bibliography, p. 106; also P. Walcot, *Hesiod and the Near East* (Cardiff, 1966).

what is traditional, for Hesiod virtually never introduces any reflections leading to a new conviction, but brusquely declares what he believes he knows through his intuition. The early Greek cosmologists assert; they do not argue.

The narrative framework of the *Theogony* includes many pictures and references in which Hesiod is not reporting what happened once upon a time but is describing present and continuing conditions. Even the stories out of antiquity, the myths of the gods and the world, serve him largely to make present existence intelligible by the mirror of coming-to-be and being. Among all peoples the earliest specula-tion, as yet incapable of abstract thought, clothed its ideas in the form of mythical narratives; Plato still spoke in myths when he wished to give form to what could not be spoken. Such myths were not to be taken too literally; it is rather a matter of the thoughts which they express.[3] To what degree did Hesiod regard his meaningful legends as literally true? In such matters, as we know, there is not only outright belief and disbelief, but various shades between them; and in details we cannot discern how literally he would have us understand his tales. In any case he too has myths which can hardly be more than a cover for something the poet could not formulate directly. A garment can be changed at need, and Hesiod, like Plato, often expresses the same truth through several myths which if taken literally would be mutually exclusive.

Here is an example. Zeus and his party purposed to wrest sovereignty from the Titans by force. Now Hesiod tells us that before he began the battle Zeus released three Cyclopes from the imprison-ment into which their father Uranus (sky), the first ruler of the world, had cast them. The names of the three Cyclopes are derived from the words for lightning, thunder, and glare; 'they had strength and violence and skill in their handicraft,' and they were the makers of thunder and lightning. In gratitude for their liberation, they supplied Zeus with thunder and lightning. With these Zeus fought the Titans, and 'because of these weapons' (or 'these helpers') he ruled over mortals and immortals (139–146, 501–06, 690ff.). The simple sense of the legend is that it shows how Zeus acquired the strongest means of power, with which he won world dominion and with which he now makes good his will against all resistance.

[3] But the early creator of myth could scarcely have been aware of what part of his creation was literally true and what he intended merely as a covering; in the only language of thought available to him the two flowed into one another. In the subsequent transmission, the proper meaning of the myth might be completely lost; it could be taken at face value or a new and productive meaning might be read into it.

With this myth another similar one is associated in the *Theogony*. Between Zeus' party and the Titans there raged frightful war for ten years, without decision. Then Zeus liberated three hundred-armed giants out of the depths of the earth where their father Uranus had thrust them. To these liberated giants the gods granted nectar and ambrosia, that is, divine status; in return the three joined in the battle against the Titans and procured victory in favor of Zeus (147–53; 617–63, 713–17). In this version lightning and thunder are replaced by hundreds of arms which are put at Zeus' disposal, and it becomes clear that the myths are not so much concerned with Zeus' specific instruments as with brute strength and constraining power in itself, through which he won supreme mastery over the world and by which he maintains it.[4] Zeus and his companions are indeed cleverer than the older powers (655ff.), but less strong and violent. Hence Zeus had to win over to his side some of the older Titanic powers, powers of brute strength. So a civilized people wishing to subdue savage barbarians draws a part of them over to its side and by their help overcomes the rest. And just as the tribes which fought for the victor receive a reward and a privileged status to ensure loyalty, so the hundred-armed were raised by Zeus to divine status, in recompense for having entered the god's service.

If we follow the line of this myth with the help of our more abstract conceptions, we observe that the brute power by which the god rules cannot be a quality proper to the god himself, but only an instrument which he uses. The forces at his disposal are, so to speak, his obedient servants, and they are themselves divine only because they impose the god's will upon the world. To this and other notions Hesiod has given shape in a third legend. No other ancient text mentions or alludes to the legend, and for this reason it is probable that Hesiod invented it. Here the mythical cover is thinner and more transparent than in the two others. Zeus' helpers in this legend are no primitive monsters but actual factors in life which operate always and everywhere that god or men exercise power. These are the entities Envy, Victory (*nike*), Strength, and Force. Hesiod's narrative, which begins at a point dictated by the genealogical framework, reads as follows (383ff.):

> Styx now, daughter of Ocean and bound to Pallas in wedlock,
> Bore in his halls Contention and Victory, the light-footed goddess,
> And she bore likewise Power and Force, her wonderful children.

[4] According to the *Iliad* (1, 401ff.), one of the hundred-armed giants later helped Zeus suppress a revolt of the other gods. According to Hesiod the hundred-armed giant kept Zeus in power by maintaining a sure watch over the vanquished Titans (734f.; 815–19).

These have no house or abode but with Zeus, and dwell with him always,
Nor do they go from his side, but follow his going or coming:
Only with thundering Zeus is their home and place of abiding.
Such was the plan she made, the eternal daughter of Ocean,
Styx, on the day when the Lord of Olympus, wielder of lightning,
Summoned all the immortal gods to the heights of Olympus.
These were his words: whoever confronts the Titans in warfare,
In league with himself, to him he would not grudge a reward;
Honor should always be his and glory among the immortals.
They who had had no honor or rank in the kingdom of Cronus,
Now should have honour and rank, the rewards which justly became
them.
Then it was, that eternal Styx came as the first to Olympus,
She together with her children as her dear father had willed it.
Zeus gave her honor and rank; and an abundance of gifts he gave her,
Making her name the holiest oath that is sworn by immortals,
Taking her children too to dwell in his household for ever.
Likewise for the others he abode by his word and faithfully gave them
All he had vowed; he now is the ruler, great and commanding.

The kinship of the third narrative with the two others[5] is obvious, but here the thought has grown more mature and more general. Hesiod had reflected upon the nature of dominion, the sovereignty of the supreme god over the world as well as the lordship of a prince over his subjects and of a victor over the vanquished.[6] All dominion is based on a will to power ('Contention') and actual 'Power,' which exercises physical and moral 'Force' and achieves 'Victory' (Nike with delicate foot) over recalcitrants. Should we then conclude that legitimate sovereignty is to be derived from the power with which it asserts itself and that whatever profits the stronger is right? Hesiod's answer is that on the contrary the four—Will-to-power, Power, Force, and Victory—are servants and henchmen of the highest, hence of right; for the *Works and Days* shows that for Hesiod Zeus is the divine bearer of right. The four, he says, are at home only with Zeus and always do only his will; they come only to the man to whom Zeus leads them. In itself brute strength is as lowly[7] as it is stupid and lacking in independence,[8] but their position as servants

[5] Cf. in particular 403 ('Zeus is master' [thanks to his alliance with the four]) with 506.

[6] The extension of the theme was natural, for according to Greek belief, which Hesiod shared (*Theog.* 96), all dominion on earth is of Zeus.

[7] Similar thoughts on the subordinate position of Force and Might in the service of Zeus are suggested by Aeschylus in the prologue of the *Prometheus*. An interesting passage in the *Iliad* (5, 897f.) notes that the savage and war-loving Ares is 'lower than the heaven-dwellers.'

[8] This appears to be indicated by the fact that the four children can make no decision of their own but are brought to Zeus by their mother.

gives them 'dignity and honor' (396). These are very interesting thoughts.[9]

The legend of the four children was obviously invented by Hesiod in order to express in the pictorial language of myth the truths he himself had discovered. Side by side with his invention, and without regard for strict consistency, he reproduces the more primitive parallel stories of the Cyclopes and the hundred-armed which had come down to him out of old tradition. Stolid ancestral credulity and forward-looking speculations flourished side by side in his head, as indeed might be expected at this stage.[10] The picture of the genesis and nature of the world which Hesiod sketches is especially rich in seminal thoughts which later philosophers were to take up and develop.

First, according to Hesiod, came chaos (116), yawning emptiness.[11] Before there was anything, only a void existed in which things would enter and which encompasses all things. Next was formed 'Earth with its broad bosom, sure ground of all things.' For Hesiod the peasant the whole world of objects and beings is based on earth and issues out of earth. Third is the moving energy for future productions—'Eros, handsomest of gods and men.' Out of chaos (the void) darkness and night arise. These two mate, and through the power of creative love (Eros) positive forces issue out of the negative potencies: day and the brightness of heaven (Aether). Day is thus a daughter of night and the bright blue sky a son of darkness; here non-being precedes being.[12]

Earth, for her part, brings forth sky (Uranus) to envelop herself (126) and the high mountains. Without the agency of sexual union she brings forth Pontus, the raging sea, which in Greek poetry is the

[9] To the objection that wrong often has the upper hand Hesiod would counter with his conviction that all unrighteousness is punished sooner or later (*WD* 213–24 and *passim*). For the whole legend cf. *Frühgriech. Denken²* 324–29; F. Schwenn, *Die Theogonie des Hesiodos* (Heidelberg, 1934), pp. 99f. (on Styx).

[10] The myths of the Cyclopes and the hundred-armed lose credibility by their competing with the myth of the four children and with one another. Nevertheless, as Hesiod tells them they are too solid and palpable to serve as mere imagery; to a considerable degree Hesiod must have believed in their literal truth. In general, we can neither overlook the rich stock of ideas in Hesiod nor interpret the primitive beliefs away for the sake of the ideas. Violent excisions are no help. Though the Hesiodic texts are surely much interpolated, it is better to be too tolerant than too strict with this author. Any attempt to reduce Hesiod to formulae of any sort must mistake the man and his position in history. The formula which states that the object of the *Theogony* is to reduce the gods of Homer to a system is also misleading (see p. 97, above).

[11] Our notion of chaos as a state of disorder rests upon a confusion with the primal state of the world later postulated by Anaxagoras. Cf. *Ovid* (Berkeley, 1945), 209, n. 6.

[12] Primitive notions made day follow night, not the other way around.

primal image of lovelessness and cold cruelty. Now earth couples
with sky and earth with sea, and the offspring couple in turn: the
world is completed and filled with beings. Sky (Uranus) is the first
lord of the world. Against his cruelty his children the Titans rise,
under the leadership of Cronus. Cronus castrates his father, and the
Titans attain power over the universe. But then they in turn are
overthrown by the following generation. Zeus, son of Cronus, with
his children and kin, overcomes the Titans and imprisons them in the
depths under the earth. Thus there comes to power the generation of
gods which now guides the destinies of men.

Of the battles between the generations of gods Hesiod tells gruesome and violent stories whose meaning is obscure and hard to
grasp. But in the genealogies which he constructs much is perfectly
clear. To the descendants of sky and earth there belongs, predominantly, whatever is powerful and clever; to those of the sea, the
changeable and unformed. From one, Ceto (the name is formed
from the word for monster), monstrosities derive; the stars have
Astraeus for their father; all rivers are sons of the primal river
Oceanus,[13] and all springs and brooks are daughters of Oceanus.[14]
In such fashion it is made plain that individual entities derive
from certain basic qualities and types and are so to be understood.
The confusing variety of phenomena are reduced to a few principles,
so that they can be grasped by the mind.[15]

Alongside the system of things positive which stem from primal
mother earth, Hesiod sets up a second, negative system. Out of
Chaos, the void, darkness and night were born. United in love, the
two produced day and the brightness of heaven; but alone, without
the productive power of love, night becomes primal mother of all

[13] Oceanus was conceived of as a river which flows around the world (only later
did it become the ocean); for the land masses of the earth had to be separated and
enclosed by the other element, water. Bordering the sky also, the stream flowed
in the same direction as the stars orbited, and it provided the road upon which the
sun and other stars moved from setting to rising (cf. Mimnermus frs. 11 and 110;
pp. 212f.; 284f., below). According to Homer the stars 'bathe' in Oceanus.

[14] The thought that Oceanus is the father and primal image of all rivers was
common property before Hesiod. The type is embodied in a definite exemplar as
prototype: Oceanus 'the perfect river' (242) is not an empirical but a postulated
river (see preceding note). On the other hand, Hesiod probably invented Astraeus
and Ceto, and here abstraction moved a step further. For Astraeus is not himself
a star but the potentiality of starhood; and similarly Ceto is shapelessness, not a
shapeless something.

[15] Linnaeus' lifework was the result of a similar tendency. His system of three
kingdoms—animal, vegetable, and mineral—was not intended as a genealogical
doctrine but as a reconstruction of the plan followed by God in creation. Among
other writings Linnaeus also produced a treatise on *Genera Morborum*.

negative things (211ff.).[16] She bore the powers of death and death itself, that is to say, destruction-of-life and no-more-living; sleep and dreams, that is to say, unconscious living and experience of the unreal. What is involved are not things having no existence at all, but things whose conception premises the existence of a something; the something is, however, of a negative nature.[17] Other children of night are 'Mockery' (μῶμος, degradation, obscuring of values); 'distress'; 'punishment'; *Nemesis* (disapproval), 'Old Age' (decay); 'Deception'; 'Eris' (conflict); and other destructive potencies. But the Hesperides ('evening' nymphs) are also introduced as daughters of night (215), apparently because they have their dwelling 'at the extremity of night' (275). In the construction of family trees various arrangements clash in Hesiod. As mother of the Hesperides Night is here the physical phenomenon, whereas as mother of Distress, Deception, and the rest she is the metaphysical principal of negation. Both are presumably intended when 'Enjoyment of Love' is inserted (224): he is as well a child of physical Night, under whose protection lovers unite, as of the negative principle, because of the association of love with deception (cf. 205f., 224, and the Pandora story, p. 117, below): the love-urge deprives the lover of his understanding (see *Frühgriech. Denken*² 320, n.1.). Corresponding to the changing viewpoint of his classifying arrangements, Hesiod's use of the figurative expression 'she bore' also includes its literal meaning.

In the continuation of the family tree the word 'bore' at once receives a new meaning. Eris (conflict, hostility), daughter of night, gives birth to children, and it now appears that descent no longer means a relationship of being subsumed under a general notion (every individual negative derives from the concept of negation); the children of Eris are actual consequences of conflict and to that degree born out of hostility. They too are of a negative nature—anxiety, forgetfulness,[18] hunger, and pain; further, battles and wars and murder; quarrels and falsehood and deception; unlawfulness and blindness; and oath (a consequence of litigious strife), 'which causes most harm to men when it is a knowingly false oath.'[19]

[16] In Parmenides' world of appearances the negative potency is also named 'night.'

[17] In Greek not οὐκ ὄντα but μὴ ὄντα. Later Greek philosophy wrestled mightily with the problematical nature of the μὴ ὄν.

[18] In the heat of conflict the peasant 'forgets' his work and so must suffer hunger.

[19] In the posterity of night all conflict, including litigiousness, is shown in its destructive aspect. Constructive strife, which establishes order, is represented among the four children of Styx, the oath-mother (p. 100, above). Similarly the beneficial winds, which have a heavenly origin (378–80), are distinguished from the destructive ones, whose grandfather is Tartarus (869–80).

If the family relationships in these genealogies are only symbolic of various kinds of natural kinship, similar things could be expressed through other images also. Just as in the genealogical part everything negative constitutes a single branch of the tree, so in a later passage (744–806) some of these negative things[20] are relegated to a particular region of the world or rather an underworld beneath the physical world. That underworld (Tartarus) is a monstrous abyss, a 'great yawning void' (*chasma*, 740f. =*chaos*, 814, also 720–25), hence a piece of the void which came into being before the earth and the positive world came into being (116ff.). Into this new context of the description of the underworld new notions enter, concerning, for example, the relationship of night and day; in the former passage night, which was previously styled daughter of 'void' and mother of day (see p. 102, above), dwells with her child. The description of the denizens of Tartarus begins as follows (744):

> And here stand the terrible houses of gloomy Night,
> And the buildings are sheathed in clouds and encompassing darkness.
> Atlas, son of Iapetus stands there, staunchly sustaining
> Spacious heaven on his head, and with arms unwearying bears it,
> There in the realm where Night and Day come close to each other,
> Speaking a word of greeting, as each crosses over the brazen
> Threshold, the one going out from the hall and the other returning
> Back from abroad; for the house never holds them both in the same hour,
> But at all times, while one is abroad and wandering widely
> Over the length of the earth, the other, still abiding indoors,
> Waits for the time to go forth, when the other returns from her journey.
> One brings light and the fullness of vision to earth-dwelling mortals;
> Slumber, the brother of Death, is borne in the arms of the other,
> And she is Night, the destructive, with darkling clouds to shroud her.

In the image of the threshold where day and night meet, the connection of opposites, which at once exclude and reinforce one another, is given vivid expression. It is always day *or* night, and the threshold is represented by the *or*, in a rather metaphysical than a spatial sense.[21] The passage continues (758ff.):

> There too the children of darkling Night have their dwelling.
> Sleep and Death they are, mighty gods. The star of the day
> Never shines on them with the light of his eye-beams,
> When he climbs up the sky and descends in the evening.[22]

[20] Their names, again, are: the yawning void, night, death and sleep, and oath (this time Styx, by which the gods swear) as a result of dissension.

[21] Otherwise it would have to be in West and East simultaneously. Hesiod's description of the underworld is not intended to be topographical.

[22] This too is intended metaphysically; physically Helios does indeed look upon the sleeping and the dead, but Darkness itself in whose power they are is not penetrated and illuminated by sunlight.

One of these wanders abroad on the expanse of the sea
And on the earth, peacefully, and is kind and gentle to mortals,
But the other has a heart of iron, and hard as bronze is his bosom.
No pity dwells in his breast; when he seizes a man, then he holds him
Fast for all time: detested is he even by the immortals.
Here also the god of the depths abides in his echoing palace,
Hades, masterful lord, with his queen, great Persephone.
There stands a terrible hound and keeps his watch without pity,
Guarding their door, and cruel sport does he have, ever fawning
On those who come, with his wagging tail and his ears bidding welcome;
But if they wish to return, and pass again out through the portals,
Then he lurks and springs out and seizes and wholly devours them.
Likewise is there a house of a goddess whom the other gods loathe:[23]
Styx the abhorred, the first-born daughter of back-flowing Ocean.
Far withdrawn from the gods she dwells and abides in her palace
Overarched with high towering rocks: a circuit of silver
Columns girds it about, which rear themselves upwards to heaven. . . .

The beautiful and rich language of such images speaks for itself.
Energy and vividness of presentation were more important to Hesiod
than meticulous consistency. Here too the same things appear in several
distinct pictures: death as death, as the realm of Hades, and as a dog.
The archaic mode of thought does not deal with an object once and
for all, thereafter simply discarding it; rather, its habit is to circle
around its object, in order to inspect it ever afresh from changing view-
points. This applies to Hesiod's *Theogony* in details and as a whole.

The description of the underworld begins with verses of apocalyptic
power (736):

There, for the dark-hued earth, and for Tartarus' realm of the twilight,
And for the restless sea and the sky which supports the stars,
For all these, are found the springs and the limits in their order.
Gloomy the place and threatening: even the gods feel its horror;
Empty, immense and gaping: if once a man were within it,
He would sink down for a whole year's space, and not come to the bottom;
Stormblast on stormblast would buffet him restlessly this way and that
    way.
Even the gods themselves shrink back from the place and its horrors.

Profound ontological speculations are embodied in these verses.
In the beginning we heard that before *being* there was void, into which
being entered (p. 101, above); here it is not the genesis of the world
that is spoken of but its structure, and Hesiod says that the
'boundaries' and 'sources' (or 'roots,' 728) of all objects in being
overlie the 'empty gulf.' Formulated in our language, this means that
everything in being exists by the fact that it is opposed (spatially,

[23] The name 'Styx' is etymologically associated with loathing.

temporally, and logically) by an empty non-being; what it is, is determined by its boundary with what it is not, to wit, the void. Hence the universe and everything in the world 'in its order' has boundaries at which it comes up against the 'void'; and just as boundaries are not only ends but also beginnings, so the boundaries of things are also their 'sources' and 'roots,' for it is to the delimitation against non-being that things owe their being and their being what they are.[24] At a parallel passage (811ff.) Hesiod, extending older ideas (cf. *Il.* 8, 15), postulates for the entry to the lower world a 'stone gate with a brazen threshold, indestructible, strengthened with roots passing through it, self-created.' When Hesiod thus describes the threshold between things and void as immovable, rooted, and self-generated, he is expressing, after his own fashion, the thought that the boundary is not a secondary product of the clash of being and non-being but, on the contrary, the primary and autonomous premise of all beings.[25] Again the threshold of a gate marks the *or* of an alternative (p. 104, above): being or non-being.[26] Such thoughts Hesiod could not have grasped and expressed

[24] In vv. 736f. four realms are distinguished. On one side is Tartarus, 'cloudily dark'; on the other are the solidly dark earth, the sea which is ἀτρύγετος, whatever that means, and the sky fraught with stars (=light). The 'boundaries' are called 'springs' with the sea in mind, and 'roots' with the earth in mind (728, cf. *WD* 19 and Pind. *Pyth.* 9, 8). Atlas, unwearying under his burden, provides the foundation of the firmly fixed sky (for the epithet cf. Pind. *Nem.* 6, 3ff.) at the ends of the earth (518), just before the beginning of Tartarus (746). This beginning is defended by a brazen wall (726), and the entrance is further guarded by a threefold belt of night (726ff.) and by raging storms (742f.). The want of consistency in the representation comes mainly from the various elements' being intended symbolically rather than literally. The idea of unifying 'roots' for earth, air, and sky was maintained until Lucretius (5, 554–63), but he saw in them only half-mechanical and half-organic groupings. Pytheas wrote (according to Strabo 2, 4, 1 =fr. 7 a 1 Mette) that on a journey to the far north he saw a place 'where there was no longer earth alone or water or air but a mixture of these [three things],' and he was told that there 'the earth and the sea and the universe in general were kept hovering, and that this was also the bond [δεσμός] of the universe.' When Pytheas went on his journey he probably already had in his head a theory concerning the bond of the universe at the north pole and its hovering in space and, as was natural, interpolated this theory into what he actually saw and what was told him. Where Strabo, following Pytheas, reports that the point of juncture is μήτε πορευτὸς μήτε πλωτός, the words recall Ovid's description of the primal mixture (*Metam.* 1, 16): *instabilis tellus, innabilis unda.*

[25] Therefore 'self-generated' (αὐτοφυής) cannot mean a contrast to artificial production, because the notion that one of the primal elements of world structure was made instead of coming into being could not arise. The contrast could be only that between primary and secondary.

[26] The connection with all later speculation concerning πέρας and concerning negativity as a condition of all qualified being (Parmenides) is obvious.

in open, uncoded, conceptual language. The path which his thought
must tread is deep and dark, and we are not surprised that he calls
those sources and boundaries 'difficult and inarticulate' and 'unapproachable to the gods themselves.' The metaphysician is troubled
when his speculation leaves the familiar world of heaven and earth,
of gods and all being, behind, in order to thrust forward beyond their
boundaries. It is as if storms, the mysterious forces of the void, barred
his approach.[27]

The picture of the underworld is fitted into the narrative of the
battle of the gods and Titans under the leadership of Zeus; the
vanquished Titans are banished from the positive world (813) and
imprisoned in the underworld. As later in Herodotus, the broad span
of the historical framework is adapted to accept material of all sorts.
One can hardly give a complete account of the matter of this un-
organized poem, especially since much of it is only partly intelligible
and we must always reckon with the possibility of textual corruption
and interpolations by other hands. Artistically the poem is very uneven; in general it is far inferior to the Homeric epics and wholly
lacking in their brilliant elegance. The poet manipulates the alien
language of epic only imperfectly.

What Hesiod himself thought of the art he practiced we can deduce
from the proem of the *Theogony*. Every rhapsode began his recital
with a prayer and with praise of god, and Hesiod opens the *Theogony*
with a long hymn to the Muses who released him from a lowly
animal existence and blessed him with their wonderful gift (pp. 95f.,
above). Hesiod depicts the loveliness of the goddesses in attractive
images, and exalts the power of their art in lofty tones. When a poet
sings the glory of men of old or celebrates the gods, even a deeply
troubled hearer forgets his sorrows at once (98–103). As guardians of
the remote past the Muses are daughters of Memory (*Mnemosyne*),
yet they also cause forgetfulness (*lesmosyne*, 54f.); old stories drive out
new sorrows (98–100). But the power of the Muses prevails not only
in the song which resounds in festal hours; it asserts itself in the
market place also, if the king who pronounces justice has received the
gift of the Muses at his birth. Contrary to tradition, therefore, Hesiod
has so far expanded the sphere of the Muses as to embrace the power
which governs the words of a wise king who issues just decisions. The
speech of such a king quiets great strife (85f.), just as the song of the
singer assuages recent sorrow (98–103). If injustice has afflicted a

[27] According to Pherecydes (*Vorsokr.* 7 B 5, detailed reference p. 252, n. 1)
'Tartarus is guarded by the daughters of the North Wind, the *Harpies* and *Thyella*
("Stormwind"), and thither Zeus banishes gods when they have transgressed
through uprising.' Cf. also the δεινοὶ ἄνεμοι of the underworld in Plato, *Phaedo* 112 b.

citizen the judgment of such a king can set the matter right with ease (μετάτροπα τελεῦσι, 89) just as the singer 'turns away' a sorrowful mood (παρέτραπε, 103).[28] Lightly uttered words (ἔπεα, 90) of the king bring about actual facts (ἔργα, 89); this amounts to more (cf. προφερεστάτη, 79) than the singer who causes actuality to be forgotten, but the power is of the same kind and origin. By the side of the kingly function, which comes from Zeus, stands the singer's function, which comes from Apollo and the Muses; both are distinguished by the gift of attractive and persuasive speech.[29] Many have felt that the singer should rank with the king, and the Greeks of the early period assigned a high position to the poet. For Hesiod there is the further consideration that he lived among Boeotian peasants, to whom his own awakening made him feel superior. His isolation, which he makes only too explicit in contrasting himself with the brutish shepherds, reinforced the poet's conviction of a prophetic mission and gave his speculative genius an unhampered and unrestricted drive.[30]

(c) The Ehoiai and the Post-Hesiodic Shield

The epic rhapsodes from whom Hesiod learned his craft had developed to perfection the art of beginning a recital, but they had no pattern for conclusions, only for transitions (p. 13, above). Hesiod's *Theogony*, as it has come down to us, does not end when all the 'births of the gods' have been recounted. After a dry catalogue of the wives and children of Zeus and other gods, the author does indeed take leave of his theme (963), but in the same breath he proposes a new, related theme and recounts unions between goddesses and mortals from which 'godlike offspring' issued. There then follows (1019ff.)

---

[28] Cf. also παραιφάμενοι, 90. The parallelism of expressions for the action of the king and the singer is obviously intentional.

[29] Cf. P. Friedländer, *Gött. Gel. Anzeigen*, 1931, p. 249. In the *Works and Days* the relation of king and singer is blurred for Hesiod. Where he had previously glorified the ideal king, he now has objections to actual 'kings' or noblemen in power; since these had proved corrupt he himself undertakes to 'settle the great issue capably'—a task which belongs to the king according to *Theog.* 87.

[30] The preceding section on the *Theogony* has shown, I hope, that although the epic deals in myth, it can find room for what amounts to speculations on basic questions of metaphysics, and that it is not correct to make Greek philosophy begin simply with Thales and Anaximander. If Aristotle's view was (*Metaph.* 4, 1000 a 18) περὶ τῶν μυθικῶς σοφιζομένων οὐκ ἄξιον μετὰ σπουδῆς σκοπεῖν ('it is not worth while to examine carefully the opinions of those who exercise their cleverness in the form of myths'), this view need not be binding for us. On cosmogony in the lyrist Alcman, see pp. 163–65 and 252f., below.

the transition to an inventory of the much more numerous unions between gods and mortal women, from which arose the mythical founders of princely Greek families (*Fragmenta Hesiodea*, ed. R. Merkelbach and M. L. West [Oxford, 1967], fr. 1 = Pap. Ox. 2354:

Sing now with lovely voices, you chaste Olympian Muses, daughters of thundering Zeus, sing now and tell of those women, loveliest far of their time, who ... loosed the girdle ... to consort with gods ... in those days there was sitting together and dining together; then the immortal gods sat down at the table of mortals.

The epic of the birth of heroes which was once attached to the *Theogony* is lost as an entirety, but from fragments and from its wide influence in antiquity we can form some idea of it.

In antiquity the work was called 'Catalogue of Women,' or, after the stereotyped formula with which individual sections began, Ehoiai (ê hoiê: 'or such as she').[1] Whether Hesiod himself intended his register of nobility to be complete[2] we do not know, but the tendency to completeness is implicit in the theme. It is not to be wondered at, therefore, if the catalogue received many additions and expansions in later days. The current epic language readily lent itself to such a task. Of one of the *Ehoiai* we possess a substantial part and a long addition, *The Shield of Heracles*, though this poem in the form in which we have it is not Hesiod's.[3] It deals with Alcmene and her son Heracles, the greatest of all heroes. With an easygoing and somewhat banal fluency, very different from the manner of the *Theogony*, the author depicts Alcmene as outstanding among all other mortal women in beauty and virtue and tells the story of her begetting of Heracles by Zeus. To the account of the birth of the 'defender against destruction for men and gods' (20) there is attached a continuation of more than 400 verses in which Heracles' conflict with Cycnus is narrated. Cycnus, we are told, was a robber who plundered pilgrims going to Delphi (479f.), and Apollo therefore

---

[1] Grammatically ἢ οἵη is related to the οἷον which introduces an example or a reference; for οἷος to introduce a narrative cf., e.g., *Od.* 4, 242; Pindar, *Py.* 9, 105. Some scholars doubt that Hesiod himself is the author of the *Catalogue* or indeed of the end of the *Theogony*; for this complicated question see M. L. West's edition of the *Theogony*, pp. 49ff., 397ff. and references there.

[2] In the *Theogony* (337–70) Hesiod names as children of Oceanus 25 rivers and 40 + 1 brooks and springs; then he says he has mentioned only the most important, for there are in fact 3,000 springs and as many rivers; for a mortal it is difficult to know all their names, but people who lived near them did know them. There certainly Hesiod did not intend to be complete.

[3] The begetting of the Boeotian Heracles must certainly have been included in Hesiod's original *Ehoiai*. Perhaps some authentic material lurks in the first 56 verses.

sent Heracles against him (69). The father of Cycnus is Ares, War himself, and he seeks to avenge the death of his son upon Heracles. But with Athene's help Heracles overcomes even the god. This religious and moral background is indicated very briefly, but the whole account is a peculiar treatment of the theme of war against war.

The defeat of a violent robber, who is a son of 'War' (Ares),[4] by the greater warrior Heracles, who achieves peace and security for men and gods, serves as a framework within which the full horror of war and mortal combat is represented. This is the real theme. For this purpose the poet employs a form which he borrowed from Homeric epic. When the ancient epic had warlike deeds to report of a hero, it started with a description of his armor. Piece by piece the singer names the weapons with which the warrior clothes himself and describes them as instruments of force and destruction. The outer appearance of this deadly equipment is interpreted as an image of the terrible forces which will be unleashed in the imminent battle.[5] Similarly and with similar images the armor of Heracles is described here, but the poet goes much further in this direction than did Homeric epic. Heracles puts on the quiver (130ff.):

> And in it were arrows in plenty,
> Chilling, dispensers of death which makes speech forgotten;
> They bore death on their points and they trickled with teardrops;
> Smooth and very long were the shafts; at the ends
> Feathers bedecked them from the wing of the darkling fire-flashing eagle.

The parts of the arrow are described in such a way that they arouse thoughts of their three-fold function: the violent leap forward, the smooth stretch of the flight, the deadly hit. To bring 'tears' into the picture is wholly un-Homeric.

The climax of the account of the weapons is the description of the shield, whose 130 verses make up more than a third of the whole. This is what has given the poem its title, *Shield of Heracles*. Like the shield of Achilles in the *Iliad*, that of Heracles was made by Hephaestus and decorated with an impossible medley of designs. But whereas the pictures on the shield of Achilles represent the whole world and the life of man, the shield here described is focused on the theme of war. Two pendants are added, but only as foils, in order to make the nature of war more striking by the archaic polarizing technique. After the image of a city under attack there follows one of a city enjoying the blessings of peace in festivity, work, sport, and play (270–313); and as a contrast to the image of the war gods Ares

---

[4] An earlier victory by Heracles over Ares: 359–67.

[5] See p. 38f., above.

and Athene, there is Apollo playing his lyre, to rejoice the gods with his harmonies (201–06); and the passage ends with a description of swans, Apollo's birds.[6] Apollo is the god in whose service Heracles undertook the battle.

The inexhaustible theme of war is diversified on this wonderful shield by a host of weird and supernatural monstrosities. A magical vitality makes the snakes on the shield grind their teeth audibly when Heracles is fighting (165, cf. 235), and the hollow shield echoes to the tread of the Gorgons depicted on it (231–33). The figure of Perseus is in actual flight, not attached to the shield at any point, yet inseparable from it (217–22). The whole description is out of proportion and grotesque; there is none of that wise restraint which normally distinguishes things Greek. The shield has many pictures of the animals to which warriors in Homer are customarily likened, and elaborate scenes extend the war of men to the animal kingdom. An army of wild boars fights with an army of lions (168–77); and predatory dolphins pursue fish (207–43)—this at any rate is true to life. Room has also been found for the story of Perseus, rather than forgo Medusa's head and the Gorgons. The demonic powers which exercise their infernal qualities in warfare recur again and again. The poet wallows in horror and does not shrink from the repulsive and the vulgar; his symbols are calculated to show war as it really is. Of the Keres, the demons of death, he says (249ff.):

Keres with white gnashing fangs and blue-black horrible faces,
Fearful of look and gloomy of mien, insatiable, bloody,
Struggled and fought over the slain, for they all were hotly desiring
Dark warm blood for their drink. As soon as they found a man fallen
Or new-wounded and sinking to earth, straightway they grasped him
Striking home with their claws in his body: his spirit sank downwards
Into the frozen realm of Tartarus. When they were sated,
Glutted with human blood, they cast the carcass behind them.
Hastening back for their share in the bloody battle and slaughter. . . .
Now they began to fight and glare on each other in fury,
Quarreling over the next who should fall their victim, and ever
Clawing and striking each other with hands and pitiless talons.

With the next demonic figure, 'Darkness of Night,' it is no longer the battlefield which is in view but the home of the fallen. When the terrible news comes, the eyes of his kin are darkened with night, there is no desire for food, there is loud lamentation, tearing of cheeks until the blood runs, and rolling in the dust. This is represented by the following image (264ff.):

[6] The swans are swimming in Oceanus, whose image surrounds the shield as it does that of Achilles in the *Iliad* (18, 607).

There stood Darkness of Night, in lamentation and madness, withered and deathly pale, shrunken and shrivelled with hunger, standing with swollen knees, with fingernails uncut and hanging; mucus runs from her nose; from her cheeks blood is always dripping down to the ground; on her face is the leer of undying affliction. Dust lies thick on her shoulders, muddied and sodden with teardrops.

With such repellent scenes, reminiscent of Goya, the horrors of war are illustrated; and at the same time by means of them, Heracles, the bearer of the shield, is celebrated as the person destined to scourge war by his own powers. The gloomy symbolism of this successor to Hesiod recalls Hesiod in many respects, but the speculative element is wanting. There is no hint of the relationships in which war and battle stand to other things in life, except for the opposition to peace and to Apollo's harmony in the two contrasts. The account of the actual fighting is brief, but here too a foil has been inserted. The bitter strife of arms, so we are told, took place in high summer, when cicadas begin to sing to men from early morning to evening, in the searing heat, 'when the beard grows upon the millet, and the grapes which Dionysus gave as a joy and sorrow to men begin to color' (393–401). This description of the serene and drowsy summer, the time of quiet growth and ripening, again recalls the genuine Hesiod— not the Hesiod of the *Theogony* but the Hesiod of *Works and Days* (582–96; see p. 125, below).

(d) *Works and Days*

The *Theogony* explained the structure of the world and gave speculative information about the gods who rule it and the powers that are at work in it. In the *Works and Days* Hesiod sketches a general picture of the daily life of the peasant and gives practical prescriptions for the 'works' (382) which must be performed. A concluding section, from the hand of another author,[1a] deals with the importance of particular days of the month: hence the double title.

If the *Theogony* was un-Homeric in its theme and in Hesiod's speaking of himself and mentioning his own name, now the break with the old epic tradition is complete. The singer no longer tells tales of long ago but instructs his hearers on their immediate tasks. It is no longer the Muse speaking through the lips of a nameless

[1a] However, the genuineness of this section has recently been defended by W. J. Verdenius in *Hésiode et son Influence* (Entretiens sur l'antiquité classique VII, Geneva, 1962), pp. 154ff. Cf. S. Benardete, *Agon* 1 (1967), pp. 150ff.

man who narrates his subject objectively from a suitable distance: it is one particular man speaking to other men, and what he wishes to expound and prove he illustrates by examples from his own private life. All the general truths which Hesiod has to set forth in this epic he develops out of his own situation at the time of writing, when he had a quarrel with his brother Perses over a legacy. First he addresses Perses, and then the kings who are to decide the suit. But the special case is speedily made a matter of principle, and from it inferences are drawn which have universal relevance. But conversely conclusions, applicable to the present issue are occasionally drawn from the general truths. Such oscillations between the particular and the general, the present and the eternal, henceforth become almost a trademark of archaic composition.

As far as we can tell from the text, the situation in the lawsuit, as Hesiod sees it, is somewhat as follows: At the death of their father the brothers divided the inheritance. The division was to be final, but Perses later appropriated additional portions which belonged to Hesiod's share. While he was carrying out this 'thieving' aggression he courted the 'kings,' the noble judges, and presented them with gifts so that they would confirm his possession. Thus the kings have a question of justice between the brothers to settle. What the issue is we are not told; apparently Perses is again claiming objects or rights out of the total inheritance.[1] In the poem, Hesiod hopes and urges that the conflict may find a speedy and just decision which will put an end to all doubts. He bases this hope on two grounds. On the one hand, thanks to his aggressions the brother has already received more than his rightful share. On the other hand, his quarrelsomeness and litigiousness has caused him to neglect his work, to squander his property, and to exhaust his provisions: Perses has even come to Hesiod to beg grain of him (396).

Out of this situation the poet draws a two-fold program for his didactic work. One theme is justice and its value; the other is success through hard work. Both stand in opposition to amoral and unproductive strife.

The special concern of the *Works and Days* with the concrete details of workaday life remains without successor in Greek poetry; but the two-fold theme of justice and success is symptomatic of the age at whose threshold Hesiod stands. The epoch is filled with an incessant struggle for justice, human justice and the postulated

---

[1] The issue might concern a few head of cattle, vessels, pasturage rights, or the like. Whether the present litigation is considerable or trifling is irrelevant. Hesiod was a sturdy peasant and fought for his rights for the sake of principle. Cf. *Frühgriech. Denken*, p. 89, n. 2.

divine justice, and with a continuous wrestling over the outward and the inward in human life.[2]

Politically and socially the age was filled with ceaseless battle and confusion. The old order had collapsed, and neither states nor individuals could attain peace and development until new forms were invented and new values recognized. The *Works and Days* presents a picture of utter moral corruption. Even the bond of blood, upon which the old dominion of the nobility was based, no longer held fast; every man is ruthlessly centered upon his own advantage, and might has precedence over right and loyalty. At such a time the hard work of the clever peasant who wrests his own living from his own land receives new meaning and dignity. Dependent upon himself alone, he can still maintain himself when all else fails.

It is with this change in conditions that the new ideals in Hesiod's *Works and Days* are connected. But despite the absorption in what is nearest, no sense of pettiness or narrow-heartedness is to be felt in the epic; the decay of human morality did not avail to shake the poet's belief in divine justice. This time the proem of the epic is not a dedication to the Muses but to their father, the supreme deity himself. In hymnlike tones Hesiod praises Zeus as the almighty refuge of justice:

> Come, Pierian Muses, whose strains give honor and glory,
> Come now and sing of Zeus, who is your own father
> Him by whose will we mortals are famed or for ever unspoken;
> For to be known or nameless rests all in his sovereign power.
> Easily he bestows strength, and easily brings strength to confusion,
> Easily he puts down the great, or raises to power the humble,
> Easily makes straight what is crooked, and crumples the pride of the
>   mighty,
> Zeus, who dwells with the lightning and has his mansion over the world.
> Hear me, Zeus, see me, and harken: let righteousness dwell in thy
>   judgment,
> Mine let it be to declare thy truth and wisdom to Perses.

In the concluding words the poet sets himself, as spokesman of truth, beside Zeus, as lord of reality, in the sense of what he had said concerning the servants of Apollo and of Zeus in the opening of the *Theogony*.

Now Hesiod begins to speak of Strife, not of the special case in hand but of strife, Eris, in general. He looks back to the genealogy of Eris in the *Theogony* (225ff., pp. 103f., above) and says (11ff.):

---

[2] In a certain sense the *Odyssey* too may serve as an example of this double theme.

The words which I spoke of one Strife were false; here among mortals there are two kinds, if a man is acquainted with one, he respects her, but he detests the other, for their natures are very unlike.

Hesiod corrects himself in a surprising fashion, which does honor to his intellect and breadth of mind. Instead of saying 'How right I was when I wrote that Eris is the mother of Hunger, and Disorder,' he puts himself on a common footing with his brother on the ground of strife, and discovers a new and good Eris alongside the bad. First he describes the bad:

One deals only in hateful war and goads us to battle: she is hard and forbidding; no one loves her, but under compulsion by the design of the gods we serve this burdensome Eris.

The Eris of war comes upon men from time to time; so in the *Iliad* Zeus sends Eris down from heaven to begin the battle (pp. 64f., above), and so Bacchylides says (fr. 24): 'As little as blessings come to men of their own free choice, so it is with war also; all-disposing destiny veils now one land with the cloud of this misfortune, now another.' But this Eris, according to Hesiod, has an elder, that is, a worthier, sister of the same name (17):

But the other is an elder daughter of gloomy Night. Cronus' son, who dwells high above in the ether, has set her deep in the roots of the earth and made her a blessing to mortals; she drives to his work even the most unskilled.

This Eris, then, is not an event which sometimes breaks in upon us from above, like a storm, but is a permanent institution implanted in our earth in order to arouse us (21ff.):

For, when the poor man looks at the work of the rich man, his neighbor, sees how he works with the plough and toils with his planting, and still labors to improve his farm, then, one neighbour vying with the other, he too pushes ahead: this strife is good among mortals. Thus there is strife between potter and potter, joiner and joiner; so beggar feuds with beggar, and likewise singer with singer. Think about this then, Perses, and treasure it up in your heart.

Language has not yet coined a word for 'competition,' but Hesiod makes his meaning clear by means of examples, and with humorous self-irony places the singer alongside the tramp.[3] Perses should stick to honest competition in order to make himself the richer, and give up his wicked strife with his brother.

---

[3] Actually the wandering singer was often not much better regarded than a beggar (p. 11, above). Jealousy between beggars is illustrated in *Odyssey* 18.

The differentiation of strife, as Hesiod presents it here, derives its
chief importance by distinguishing not only between a bad and a
good power,[4] but also between a destiny occasionally imposed by
heaven and a permanent force inhabiting earth, of which we may
make use according to our desire. In the *Iliad* every human initiative
is referred to a divine inspiration; in the *Odyssey* divine will and
human action begin to be separated (p. 90, above). But Hesiod
writes the *Works and Days* to supply a methodical answer to the
question, What can we do to improve our lot? What is the condition
of the world about us, and how must we comport ourselves to cope
with this condition as satisfactorily as possible? The heroes of the
Iliad needed only to be brave and great and devoted; all else lay in
the lap of the gods. As Zeus-nurtured (διοτρεφέες) kings they lived
from the labor of their slaves and the tribute of their subjects (*Il.* 9,
154–56)—which were among the special privileges bestowed by
Zeus (*Il.* 9, 98f.). But the men of Hesiod must above all prove practical and industrious; as peasants they knew well that a man must go
hungry if he is negligent and unskillful in his work.[5]

That human existence is laborious and wretched is the premise of
Hesiod's teachings and admonitions; but he does not simply accept
the fact. It might have been, he says at the beginning of this work
(42ff.), that we could gain a livelihood without working the land in
the sweat of our brow and without going on trading voyages; but it is
not so. The cause he finds in the jealousy which prevails between men
and gods. Men wish to have things better than they deserve, and to
punish them the gods make their lives hard. The contrast between
human and divine existence, upon which the traditional image of the
gods rests insofar as they are regarded as 'blessed' (pp. 54–56, above),
must therefore be maintained; if men succeed in improving their lot
the gods restore the balance by imposing new pains upon them.
Building on an ancient tradition, Hesiod clothes the idea in a story
in which the Titan Prometheus appears as the champion of mankind.
Prometheus had sought to deceive the gods at a sacrifice (48; cf.
Theog. 533 ff.), and in requital the gods 'hid the means of sustenance'

---

[4] For destructive and constructive forces of a similar sort in Hesiod, see p. 103,
n. 19, above. To be consistent Hesiod should not have derived creative Eris from
'Night'; but he probably did not wish to carry his correction so far.

[5] Naturally, Hesiod has no illusions about human effort and intelligence being
able to command success. Upon occasion he indicates that Zeus as lord of the
weather holds the prosperity or failure of a harvest in his hands and that his will
(future weather) is hard to divine (474; 483ff.). So Zeus or Poseidon may destroy
a ship even in the season Hesiod recommends for sailing, if he is set upon it
(πρόφρων, 667). But since we are powerless against such eventualities Hesiod sees
no occasion to say much on the subject.

so that man must now seek them out laboriously. Zeus also hid fire,[6] but Prometheus stole it and brought it down to earth, and thereby afforded men a higher civilization. As a penalty[7] Zeus sent woman to man, in the shape of the shameless, cunning, beautiful, and bejewelled Pandora, together with all other evils.[8] Hesiod regarded women as evil, among other reasons, because like drones they consume without working (*Theog.* 591–612).[9] According to him Zeus shrewdly made woman so attractive in order that 'all might be glad of heart when they embraced their own destruction' (*WD* 58).

So far Hesiod has told the story almost exactly as in the *Theogony*. But now he gives it a new and peculiar turn (90ff.):

Heretofore the races of men on earth had been living free from all pain and unoppressed by the burden of labor, knowing nothing of disease which brings man down to his deathbed. Then came the woman and lifted the lid: out of the vessel every plague came forth: it was she who founded our sorrows. Only Hope remained in the jar, imprisoned for ever: before she could attain the rim and flutter away to freedom, Pandora brought down the lid on the vessel. This had been willed by Zeus, the thunderer, shaking the aegis: all those other disorders and plagues beset us in thousands; the earth is full of evil, and full are the waters. Sicknesses come to a man by day, and others at night-time; they come of themselves, uncaused, and bring great anguish to mortals, stealing in silently, for provident Zeus has struck them with dumbness.

In true archaic manner, actual human misery is highlighted by the

[6] The clear connection in *Theog.* 562–70 is disturbed in *WD* 47–50 by the dragging in of this 'hiding of means of livelihood' to suit the new theme.

[7] The story of the theft of fire as a punishable offence reflects the primitive feeling that appropriation of fire was a transgression, because fire properly belonged to the god who hurled it in his lightning bolt.

[8] The story of Pandora, as Hesiod twice tells it, presents difficult problems of many sorts (Otto Lendle, *Die 'Pandorasage' bei Hesiod*, Würzburg, 1957). Some very interesting information concerning the survival of the figure of Pandora in literature and art down to the present time is given in Dora and Erwin Panofsky, *Pandora's Box: The Changing Aspects of a Mythical Symbol*, New York, 1956.

[9] In the social level to which Hesiod belonged wives and daughters obviously did no heavy labor; they were well-tended creatures of luxury (*WD* 519–23) whose charms invited matrimony, but then (89) they proved too extravagant and demanding for the frugal household of a Boeotian peasant (*Theog.* 593). The female type Hesiod has in mind may be illustrated by Semonides 7, 57–70 (type of the proud mare; p. 203, below); cf. in details Sem. 63f. with *WD* 519–23; Sem. 68f. with *Theog.* 593 *et al.* Much of the text sounds as if Pandora was the first woman of any kind, but apparently only woman as a creature of luxury is intended; for the Pandora fable is wholly inappropriate to the maids of *WD* 303f., and Hesiod would not have assumed that mankind had hitherto reproduced without sex. Just as there were gods and goddesses from the beginning, so there were men and women also.

postulated counter-image of a blessed past. Zeus puts a period to the state of paradise by sending woman and releasing all other woes upon mankind through her agency.[10] The *Iliad* once mentions (24, 527) two vessels in the house of Zeus, from which he apportions pains and joys. From the store of possible events, the god takes a single blessing or disaster on occasion and brings it to pass in a specific man.[11] In Hesiod it is different. Misfortune is not caused by the god upon occasion, with the consequence that man must simply accept it, but seizes upon us of itself. For all evils are given liberty once and for all,[12] and they are empowered to seek their victims 'of their own accord' (*automatoi*). If that is the case, we may investigate the nature of evil to defend ourselves against it, sometimes with success. From the god-sent sufferings of the *Iliad* and the arrows of pestilence shot by Apollo there is no line of development to medical science; but from Hesiod's realization that diseases and other pains afflict mankind according to their own impulse and nature, a straight line leads to the theory and empirical methods of a Hippocrates.

And what is meant in this story by the imprisonment of Hope? In the Homeric picture emergence out of a vessel was identical with passing into actuality; and by Hope, which Hesiod sees as 'vain' illusion (498), wishes and longings that are never fulfilled are intended. Whereas all evils can swarm out freely to realize themselves, Hope is deprived of this gift. When she is on the point of stepping over the threshold into reality (the lip of the vessel), the door of her prison closes before her and she cannot break out of it (ἄρρηκτοι δόμοι). The imprisonment of Hope and the release of the plagues are complementary acts. Hitherto there was only unwished-for blessing, now there are powerless wishes, and full authority to afflict us is given to disaster of every kind. Woe comes 'in silence, for Zeus has taken care to deprive it of its voice.' When it enters it is simply there, in brutal, senseless, reality: it needs no language to report its presence and explain itself. But Hope—so we may infer by contrast—is only feeling

[10] For Hesiod Pandora was only an instrument of divine will, to which her own will (ἐμήσατο, 95) automatically conforms.

[11] The idea of a pre-existent store of possible events is automatically implied in the collective experience of life and its precipitate in language, which for every event has a name ready to hand which can be applied to it at once and at its first appearance. The image of the vessel in the house of the father of men and gods was formed by analogy with the vessels of a father of a household, out of which he distributes corn and oil and wine to his family and dependents, and so it represents latent or potential nurture. The symbolism is extended in the *Iliad* by the fact that a vessel of afflictions is added to that of blessings. In Hesiod, on the other hand, there is only a vessel of disasters; according to him the good things of life are not gifts of the gods but on the contrary are 'hidden' (42; cf. p. 116, above).

[12] Just as good Strife is implanted in the world once and for all.

and thought, only speech (cf. λόγος), only the announcing and explaining of wishes, without the ability to become fact (cf. ἔργον).[13]

After the conclusion of the story of Pandora Hesiod announces 'another story' (106). What follows is a second myth on the same theme, namely, the decline of humanity from an original godlike existence to its present wretched state. Again, then, Hesiod does not hesitate to illustrate the same fact through several myths which would exclude one another if we chose to take them literally. This time the descent of humanity is not a sudden fall but proceeds by degrees, in a succession of ages. Hesiod's point of departure is that gods and men 'sprang from the same stock,' and hence are basically alike in nature. The first age of the world was the 'golden' (109ff.):[14]

The earliest race of articulate mortals was golden, made by the great immortals who dwell on lofty Olympus. They lived in olden times when Cronus was ruler in heaven.[15] Like the gods they lived: no suffering dwelt in their hearts. Strangers to toil and pain, they knew no old age and its sorrows; rather, a constant strength informed their limbs and their bodies; they were happy, rejoicing in festival, and free from misfortune. Death came to them like falling asleep: there was in their possession all that is good. The generous earth gave bountiful riches all of her own, unasked. In ease, with tranquil enjoyment they did all things, and enjoyed many blessings. After they were called by fate to die and lie down in darkness. Purely spirit are they: they dwell upon earth and are active workers of good; they watch over men and guard them from evil. Lawsuits too do they see and the wrongs wrought by the ungodly wandering ever abroad, concealed in a garment of twilight, givers of wealth: for to them this kingly task is commended.

[13] For the notion of the 'imprisoned' wish-dream cf. Shakespeare, *All's Well*, Act I, Sc. i (Helena):

> 'Tis pity ...
> That wishing well had not a body in't
> Which might be felt; that we, the poorer born,
> Whose baser stars *do shut us up in wishes*,
> Might with effects of them follow our friends
> And show [ἔργοις] what we alone must think [λόγους], which never
> Returns us thanks.

The collocation of plagues and vain hopes recurs in Semonides, fr. 1 (see below, pp. 201f.). On the whole section cf. *Frühgriech. Denken*, ed. 2, pp. 329–34.

[14] It is possible that the notion of ages characterized by metals came from the Near East and reached the poet via the Hellenism of Asia Minor, from which Hesiod's father derived. Cf. R. Reitzenstein, *Alt.-Griech. Theologie und ihre Quellen* (*Vortr. der Bibl. Warburg*, IV, Leipzig, 1929). On the ages of the world in Hesiod cf. T. G. Rosenmeyer, *Hermes* 85 (1957), 257–85.

[15] Here, then, Cronus' realm has a paradisal character which it lacked in the *Theogony*.

The next generation, that of silver, did not live longer than a helpless childhood and a foolish and brief young manhood; for a hundred years the child remained at home with his dear mother, an utter simpleton. And when they were full-grown they lived only a short span, and that in sorrow, because of their folly. For they could not refrain from violence, nor would they serve the gods and offer customary sacrifices. So Zeus grew angry and hid them underground, where they live a blessed existence.

The third generation that Zeus created was of bronze, sprung from ash trees.[16] They were a terrible race, and their work was war. Their armor was of bronze, their houses of bronze, and of bronze their implements; there was no black iron. Here is their end (152f.):

These too, brought to the dust by the violent hands of each other, sank down into the gloomy halls of shivering Hades, leaving no name; and death, for all their roughness and valor, seized them and took them away from the cheerful light and the sunshine.

The brazen race which wrought its own destruction belonged, according to Hesiod, to the Bronze Age, which is also the background of Homeric poetry. We cannot, however, equate Hesiod's brazen generation with the heroes of the epics, but with an earlier and more primitive generation of the breed of Caeneus and his Lapiths, who represented a savage and cruel past even to the heroes of the *Iliad* (pp. 35f., above). Hesiod's brazen men died 'nameless'; they are told of in no poetry but only by dim report, because cultivated Homeric epic had long ceased to celebrate such 'formless' inflexible figures (148) and dealt instead with clearer and more human heroes with sensitive spirits.

Hesiod places 'the divine race of heroes' after the age of bronze. These heroes too were destroyed by fighting, in the wars at Thebes and Troy. They are the heroes of whom the two cycles of epic in the Homeric style tell. They were, as Hesiod says, a better and juster race than the brazen, and after their death they were granted a state of blessedness. This generation obviously does not fit into the framework of the myth. The line of progressive degeneration from the divine is broken and the basic idea of the myth is injured. There was no new metal that could be assigned to this generation. The explanation is simple. Hesiod could not ignore the Homeric age, but the figures developed by the remote colonial region in the East did not fit into the general picture as he saw it. His perspectives were those of the mother country, and from such a point of view Homeric man was an intruder who could find no proper place in the system.

[16] Spear shafts are made of ash wood, and among early Greeks the spear is the symbol of war, like the sword among ourselves.

The final member of the series starts differently from the others. The narrative is pushed aside and interrupted by a passionate wish (174): 'Would that I were not among the men of the fifth generation, but either had died before or been born afterwards. For now is a race of iron, and men never rest from labor and sorrow by day or by night, wearing themselves out; and the gods shall lay sore trouble upon them. But, notwithstanding, even these shall have some good mingled with their evils.' Thus the picture of the present is transformed into one of the future and subjected to the anxious query, How will it be then? 'Only more pain and torment,' is the answer, 'and a little good in between.' But the remoter outlook is gruesome: 'Zeus will destroy this race of mortal men also, when they come to have gray hair on the temples at their birth (the contrast to the childish silver age, is one of hoariness), and when no order will be kept, when no bonds between parents and children will subsist, rights of hospitality will have no validity, there will be no respect for age and no piety, when there will be no esteem for oath-keeping; but violence will bring honor; when foul-mouthed Envy will accompany all wretched men, delighting in evil, with scowling face.' Then (197f.):

Then, forsaking mankind, Aidos and Nemesis will go up to Olympus, from the earth of the wide ways, shrouding their goodly forms in garments of white, to their tribe of the immortals. And bitter sorrows will be left for mortal men, and there will be no defence against evil.

Aidôs is reverence for that which deserves it, and *Nemesis* is the reaction of displeasure at offenses against justice, morality, and decency. Positively and negatively, the two conceptions describe the feeling for moral values and for the sanctity of justice. This feeling is prerequisite for any kind of order, and when it is gone there is no hope left.

The myth of the ages of the world gave expression to the conception of step-by-step deterioration of ethics and justice. Justice is the theme of the whole following section. It begins with a little fable, with which Hesiod addresses himself to the kings, the judges in his lawsuit (202): 'A hawk seized a nightingale in his talons.' Among the Greeks the hawk is a symbol of tyranny, predatoriness, and violation of justice,[17] and the nightingale, whose Greek name means songstress, represents the poet. The victim complains, but the bird of prey answers with an assertion of power: 'I am higher and mightier than you. I can drag you whithersoever I will, and can devour you if I will. He is a fool who tries to withstand the stronger; he suffers pain

[17] Cf. Plato, *Phaedo* 82a, 3.

besides his shame.' Here the fable ends. Its function will become clear at once if we imagine the hawk and the nightingale as a drawing and the rest as caption. Hesiod says in words what would be a political cartoon with us.[18] Now Hesiod preaches, to his brother and the kings, a sermon on the blessedness of justice and the accursedness of ruthless power. That the god knows what happens on earth and is aware of breaches of justice is then conveyed in a mythical picture. Zeus has invisible observers everywhere on earth, immortal watchers who report to him on all things. Then the same thought is expressed in a more imaginative picture. Dikê, or Justice, sits down by Zeus and complains to him when she is abused by mankind. And finally we are told a third time, with a directness almost totally free of imagery (267): 'The eye and the mind of Zeus are all-seeing and all-understanding.' Again and again it appears that myth is for Hesiod often only a cloak which can be changed at will. The following verse points a moral applying to the lawsuit in hand: 'These things too he beholds if he wishes, and does not fail to notice what sort of justice it is that is practiced here in the city.' Previously Hesiod had said that thanks to the God's blessing the righteous city flourished physically also: oaks bear fruit on their boughs and bees in the trunk, sheep produce thick fleeces and women children that resemble their fathers; to the city in which violence prevails, on the other hand, god sends hunger and pestilence and smites women with sterility (225–47). Now a small doubt appears: Zeus will reckon with this case 'if he wishes.' And now there follows a confession that hovers between conviction and doubt (270ff.):

Now as things are, I would not myself be righteous to others—[19] neither I nor my son, for righteousness has not much to commend it, if the unrighteous man has greater rights: but I hope that Zeus the Planner and Guide lets no such thing be accomplished.

The next verses are addressed to Perses: 'Fishes and beasts and winged fowl devour one another (as the hawk devours the nightingale) for right is not in them; but to mankind Zeus gave right.' Now there follows a serious call to 'Goodness' (aretê), with a new opening. Goodness is understood as diligence, and the notion includes the successful conclusions at which diligence aims and the respect which the diligent man enjoys (κῦδος, 313). 'The path that leads to goodness

---

18 Hesiod's caricature (and v. 278) shows plainly how the words δημοβόρος βασιλεύς ('folk-devouring king') in *Il.* 1, 231 are meant. Agamemnon too 'devours' his subjects when he takes their private possessions (not δήμια; cf. 123f.). Cf. also δημοφάγον τύραννον, Theognis 1181, and p. 192, nn. 6 and 7, below.

19 The expression ἐν ἀνθρώποισιν is dictated by its contrast with ἐν αὐτοῖς ('animals') in 278.

is long and steep,' says Hesiod, 'but when a man has scaled the height
by the sweat of his brow his way grows easy thereafter. But to
badness the way is short and smooth; it is to be had easily and in
abundance. That man is best who considers all things himself and
marks how the end will be; and he who accepts good counsel is also
not to be despised. So listen to me, work without pause, so that
Hunger may hate you and crowned Demeter love you and fill your
barns with food. Both gods and men are vexed with the man who
will only consume, like a drone. Let it be your care to attend to your
work properly. Work is no disgrace; it is idleness which is a disgrace.'[20]

There follow reflections on *aidôs*, that is, pious restraint which
forbids us to exploit accidental superiority (317–35). We should not
seize advantages over others either by violence or 'tongue robbery,'
not injure helpless strangers, not corrupt a brother's marriage (after
their marriages sons often remained together in their father's household), not maltreat or rob orphans, not use harsh language to a father
grown old and feeble. With the admonition to respect for parents the
Greeks often associated reverence for gods. Gods should be rendered
well-disposed through service and sacrifice; then they will assist you
so that (341) 'you may buy another's holding and not another
your's.' Here the language becomes more down-to-earth and more
concrete, and it remains so in the following section in which rules for
daily intercourse with other peasants are given (342ff.):

Always invite your friend, and never your foe, to your table; that man
invite, above all, who lives not far from your dwelling. When there is
anything wrong in the village, your neighbors come at the run unbidden:
your kinsmen will come when they have dressed.

Mutual support of kinsmen, practiced by the gentry, is here opposed to mutual support based on neighborhood.[21] The whole
series of proverbs in vv. 342–72 deals with friend and neighbor,
lending and giving, contracts and trust, expenditure and thrift.
Dominant throughout is a spirit of shrewd prudence which departs
markedly from the magnanimity of Homeric heroes. On the other
hand, Hesiod is free of the calculating miserliness and pedantic
penny-saving which is so repellent in the elder Cato's book on
agriculture. One must not be stingy and petty, says Hesiod, with

[20] A sharp contrast to Homeric epic, where δρηστήρ, i.e., a man who works and
does something, signifies a slave.

[21] In many regions the duties of neighborly assistance were regarded as legal
obligations, e.g., in Aeolian Cyme, from which Hesiod's father came. Cf. K. Latte,
Hermes 66 (1931), 36.

grain in the storage vessel (*pithos*, 368): 'Take you your fill from the top of the jar and from near to the bottom; but in between go slow; you can't save at the last spoonful.'

Some further maxims lead to the core of the epic. The poet lays out the peasant's year before the hearer, with all that it produces and demands (381–617). In contrast to the empty and uniform timelessness of the Homeric poems we hear now of the regular rhythms of nature and of the corresponding tasks of the farmer. Hesiod is convinced that the order of labor also, like the order of nature, is established by the gods (398).

Hesiod does not treat his subject with a uniform thoroughness. At the beginning he goes into the construction of wagon and plough with precise technical details and measurements (420–36), and proudly boasts of his expertise (455), but soon he grows weary of details. The further the account proceeds the more relaxed is the tempo. Housekeeping arrangements seem more primitive than those we know from Homer: grain is not ground in a hand mill (*Od.* 20, 106–11) but pounded in a mortar with a pestle (423). For marking the seasons there are no names of months (except 504), but the rising and setting of stars, the migration of birds (448; cf. also 486), and the change in the life of plants. Weather, naturally, is often mentioned.[22]

The whole treatment is unsentimental; there is no pastoral atmosphere. The heavy work of the peasant is not idealized but regarded as hard necessity. Amidst the practical counsel, time and again the terrifying spectre of hunger and bitter hardship, which will overtake the incompetent and negligent, is conjured up. Nor must we entertain exaggerated notions of the 'wealth' which Hesiod himself apparently possesses and to the acquisition of which he urges his brother and his listeners. 'Wealth' probably signifies no more than having enough to eat once a day the year through.

The treatment is adequate but not tedious. Hesiod gives more than merely technical information; he encourages and admonishes and draws lively pictures of what happens if one heeds or neglects his prescriptions (472):

[In this way you will get a fine harvest]: then you will happily brush the cobwebs from your grain bin; then you will be glad to feast on your garnered plenty, living content the whole year through, with never a hungry glance at your neighbors' barn, but yourself much envied by others.

---

[22] 548–60 is an astonishingly rational and detailed description of the formation of moist masses of air and their rise and fall in the wind (like the later theories of the philosophers). The cold moisture helps crops (549) but injures cattle and men (558); ears are particularly susceptible (546).

The pendant is the sorry harvest with short stalks and dried-up fields (480):

You will kneel down to reap it, scarcely filling your hand with the cornstalks, you will bind it crosswise, all dusty: you go home, carrying sadly all your crop in a basket: there will be few to respect you.[23]

Hesiod sketches the resulting situation dramatically,[24] and weaves general adages into the text. So he reminds us that workers and implements must be prepared and put in order in advance, and then continues (408):

Or else you will ask another, and he will deny you, and you go short, and the season escapes you and then your work has to suffer. Do not put off till tomorrow or till the day after tomorrow; you cannot fill your barn if you leave your jobs only half done, or if you put them off: it is perseverance that does it; once a man puts things off, he has opened himself to disaster.

Again he says (448):

Take good note when you first hear the cranes flying over, coming each year without fail and crying high in the heavens. They will give you the sign for ploughing and tell when the winter's rains are at hand: at their call the man without oxen trembles. Then give your oxen plenty of fodder— if you have oxen. It is easy to say, 'Please lend me your oxen and waggon,' easy also to answer, 'I'm sorry, I've work for my oxen.'

For the winter season Hesiod warns against the seductive attraction of warm places (493):

Walk straight on past the blacksmith's shop with its crowds and its gossip, when the winter is on you, and frost prevents you from working. If you are active, a thousand things can be done in the winter, greatly improving the house and making sure that you want not during the winter and rub your swollen legs with hands all shrunken.[25] Hope is a poor support for a man fallen into poverty, when he sits there in the sun and has no food for his belly. Tell your workmen as well, while summer still glares in the meadow: it will not always be summer. The barns had better be building.

But on the whole, the account of the year's course is not comprehensive and not well ordered. Hesiod is here as little master of the abundant material and of the thoughts that stream in upon him as in the *Theogony*. Only three times does he describe moments in the life of the farmer in detailed and unitary pictures. He depicts summer and

[23] For the interpretation of 481 cf. P. Mazon's edition (Paris, 1914), pp. 115f.— 'look' in 478 and 482 also implies respect (cf. 21) and desire for assistance.

[24] Small illustrative scenes like this do not recur until Hellenistic literature, except that tragedy occasionally admits them in speeches of peasant messengers.

[25] More than any other early Greek work, this poem invites illustration by small pictures in the margin.

eating and drinking in the open air which may be indulged in when
the weather is hottest (582–96). In even greater detail he describes
the worst cold of winter, from which all creation suffers. The icy
blast penetrates the thickest animal skin; only the sheep are im-
mune—and the tender skin of the delicate maiden, for she abides
indoors and bathes and beautifies herself (504–60). And he sketches
this picture of the start of ploughing, with which the years' cycle of
work and rest, hope and anxiety, takes its beginning (465):

Make your prayers to Zeus of the deep and to holy Demeter, so that the
sacred crop may grow to fullness and ripeness, when in the year's first
ploughing you lay your hand to the ploughtail and with the pricking
goad belabor the backs of the oxen, so that the yoke-straps pull hard on
the pin. Have a small boy behind you drawing the earth with a hoe to
cover the seeds and to make life hard for the birds.

Only on this one occasion does Hesiod prescribe a prayer for the
task, and in the Greek fashion it is natural and matter-of-fact,
without rigid formula or ritual. The beginning of ploughing Hesiod
describes with much detail in a sentence of three members ('when —,
and —, and —'). The fullness has no practical purpose: Hesiod
makes the subject concrete and lingers over it so long because he
wishes to stress it as a significant act. In Hesiod factual detail can be
used for a kind of dry emotive effect, in keeping with his dry
temperament.

There is a fourth time where Hesiod at least approaches a finished
and rounded picture. He has spoken of the preparation of implements and now offers suggestions for the choice of animal and
human helpers, with reference to the special service to be expected
of each (436–47). For the plough Hesiod recommends oxen of nine
years. They are still in the prime of strength, but will not fight with
one another under the yoke and so break the plough. They should be
followed by a forty-year old slave who has eaten the four quarters of
a loaf of bread. Such a man will keep his mind on his work, and not,
like a younger man, on his fellows. It is clear that Hesiod's thoughts
follow the same track whether they are directed to the oxen or to the
slave (cf. 608). He shows the same practical understanding of the
behavior of animals as of men. This applies not only to domestic
animals; in his picture of winter he speaks of the 'boneless one'
(octopus or cuttle?) who 'gnaws his foot in his fireless house and
wretched home, for no sun shows him where to look for his living;
the sun lingers over the people and city of dusky men and shines
more sluggishly on the Hellenes.' The beasts of the forest also have
only the one thought of seeking shelter from the cold (524–33).
Here too Hesiod the Greek stands in contrast to Cato the Roman,

whose book on agriculture is solely concerned with the economic interests of the owner of a farm. Hesiod does not let his objective tie him down to one single theme, but takes in its whole natural setting as well. At the beginning of his picture of winter he speaks of the north wind which blows across horse-breeding Thrace, stirs up the sea, makes earth and forest howl, and fells many trees; the beasts shiver.

After the farmer's year Hesiod deals with the calendar for sailing. This section too is formally addressed to Perses, although his property lay inland; but the poem means to offer instruction to those farmers who wish to include a trading voyage in the height of summer—the season of rest in Greek agriculture. Hesiod begins with practical prescriptions for the care of a ship and its equipment during the time when it is not in use (624–29); he had obviously seen how all this was managed at some seaside place (651, 655). Otherwise, for want of personal experience (p. 95, above), he is able to give no directions for seafaring. But concerning the enterprise as such he had been instructed by his father, and what he lacked in concrete experience he supplied by thoughts on basic principles. This section is based more than any other upon one controlling idea—the notion of order (cf. εὐκόσμως, 628, εὐκρινέες, 670), that is to say, the right time (ὥρη, 630, 642, 665), the right measure (μέτρον, 648, 694; cf. 689f.), and the right choice (καιρός, 694). Like order in general, the ordering of trade voyages (which here implies special conditions to which the merchant must prudently accommodate himself) is, for Hesiod, god-given; he calls it the 'mind of Zeus' (661). Zeus makes the weather on which seafaring depends. More specifically, the poet defines his theme as the 'measure of the sea' (648), that is, the temporal limits within which it is advisable to sail the sea. He warns against setting sail in spring, for the sea is dangerous at that season; yet even this is often done, 'for possessions mean as much as life to poor mortals' (686). One should also be moderate in not venturing all he owns on one ship, but only the lesser part, just as one should not overload a waggon (689–94). One should not undertake too great a risk in the expectation of greater gain. That is all Hesiod has to say about trading as such. He concludes the section with a formulation of the leading idea (694):

'Observe due measure; in all things proper choice is best.'

As long as Hesiod was speaking of the farmer's work he could not urge strenuous effort too strongly, for without it the farmer must starve or beg. But here where the subject is the profit of trading and the hope of wealth he advises prudence and, above all, observance of divinely ordained measure. In the dominant idea of this passage we encounter for the first time a categorical demand for moderation (cf. also 715)—a bourgeois requirement which could not be emphasized in the romantic and heroic world of epic. Even in the *Odyssey* the new ideal of clever adaptation and self-control does not show that men had become more modest and gave less scope to their own desires; rather, adaptation and self-control were new weapons in their struggle to reach the highest goal. Moreover, for all his prudence and restraint Odysseus was a gambler for high stakes; he entered the cave of the Cyclops out of curiosity and because he hoped for a gift of hospitality. Hesiod is not curious, and he finds it lamentable that a man should risk his life for the sake of gain. He believes that everything in our world has its own order, and to wish to be emancipated from that order seems to him not only impractical but also improper.

In the continuation of the poem the notion of right time and choice forms a transition to directions for matrimony (695–705). The man should marry at thirty, the woman four years after puberty. She should be a maiden, who learns love from her husband, and a maiden from nearby, who is known to him, so that 'his marriage shall not be a joke to his neighbors.' A man wins nothing better than a good wife, and nothing worse than a bad one.

There follow further suggestions on maintaining proper measure in relations with other people. All of these admonitions and warnings are put in the form of prohibitions and injunctions and usually begin with 'Do not.' The first injunctions read as follows (707):

Never admit your friend to an equal place with your brother yet be never the first to harm the friend you have chosen, and do not be a flattering tongue-friend only.[26] But if ever either in word or deed he does that which your heart cannot favor, do not forgive the offence, but pay back

[26] The passage is generally misunderstood. Χάριν does not appear here 'for the first time as a mere preposition'; γλώσσης χάρις is 'a grace consisting of mere words,' 'lip service' (cf. Matthew 15, 8). The closest parallel to our passage is Aeschylus, *Prom.* 295ff.; μάτην χαριτογλωσσεῖν in opposition to the συμπράσσειν of a βέβαιος φίλος. For the meaning or construction of ψεύδεσθαι γλώσσης χάριν cf. further *Od.* 14, 387 μήτε τί μοι ψεύδεσσι χαρίζεο; Theognis 63 and 979; Aeschylus, *Choeph.* 265: γλώσσης χάριν δὲ πάντ' ἀπαγγείλῃ τάδε πρὸς τοὺς κρατοῦντας ('as a service rendered with mere words, but which those in power will reward greatly'); (Theocritus) 25, 188 γλώσσης μαψιδίοιο (genitive!) χαριζόμενον παρεοῦσιν (dative!); Euripides, *Orestes* 1514: δειλίᾳ γλώσσῃ (instrumental) χάριζῃ (sc. ἐμοί, cf. 1516: λέγειν ἑμ ἣν χάριν), τἄνδον οὐχ οὕτω φρονῶν; the opposite in Bacchylides 5, 187: ἀλαθείας χάριν αἰνεῖν (instead of suppressing merited praise out of envy). The same Greek turn of expression may stand behind the words of Terence (*Heaut.* 702f.): *ne falsam gratiam studeas inire*. In *WD* 720 recurs, half ironically, without pejorative significance: (according to sense) 'the best courtesy of the tongue is often keeping silent'.

double. But if he wants to repair the friendship and give you due satisfaction, then take him back. A poor wretch is he who is constantly
changing friend for friend. Make your inner worth no less than your
outer [?].

Several of the maxims in this series have to do with the question of
how we should speak to and of others and what others say about us.
In this respect too measure must be maintained (719):

It is the best of all treasures if your tongue is never unruly: you will be
most beloved if it keeps due measure and season. Give other men a bad
name, and you get back worse than you gave them.

A neatly phrased proverb forms the conclusion (760):

Be on guard against gossip: a perilous power dwells with it. Slander is
easy and light: you pick it up without trouble; then you can't lay it down,
and it is very awkward to carry. Gossip never quite dies, when once two or
three of your neighbors say the same thing about you. She too must be
reckoned a goddess.

Into this chain of proverbs a series of prohibitions of another sort
is inserted (724-59). Most are instructions to perform physical
actions in a prescribed way, and the rules are not of a rational but of
a superstitious character. Such gross superstition as appears here is
not consonant with the picture of Hesiod's mode of thought which
we receive elsewhere, and there is an additional consideration which
makes us doubt whether Hesiod wrote these maxims. Often the
author appends to his prohibitions such remarks as 'For this is not
good,' 'For this entails punishment.' If Hesiod had indeed written
these prescriptions he would have known how to justify them better
than by meaningless or mystifying tags. There follow (765ff.) further
superstitious teachings concerning the various days of the month,
which set forth the kind of work for which each is favorable or unfavorable. The accepted text concludes by promising to deal with the
flight of birds and its use for predictions. Hesiod did not write any of
this. Expanders and continuators completed his epic according to
their lights.

This then is Hesiod's poem of peasant life. It deals with justice,
with the work of farmer and merchant, with intercourse with friends
and neighbors, and with many other things. It is a work full of
character, but not very systematic. The many different subjects touched
upon sometimes fail to meet and sometimes overlap. It is not easy
to view the work as a whole because of Hesiod's relaxed and personal
mode of expression and a peculiarity of style which we shall encounter
in archaic poetry henceforward. This style sets less value upon clearly
distinguishing the sections of a work than on forging steadily ahead:

the end of one section fades into the beginning of the next. The transitions, often surprising but never abrupt, give Hesiod's narrative a peculiar and odd charm of their own.

Of the various themes, that of the peasant's working life is covered most thoroughly, both on the theoretical and on the practical side. The second principal theme, 'justice, right conduct, and decency,' is often dealt with impressively but not really systematically. Hesiod is less concerned with factual instruction on what is right and proper (everyone knows that anyhow), than with urgent admonitions to embody moral teachings in our lives. Of religion Hesiod speaks only in general terms, of cult scarcely at all.[27] He could not give details if only because his poem was apparently meant to apply to all Greece, and festivals, sacrifices, and rituals were everywhere different.[28]

There are two other, more interesting, omissions. Though Hesiod has many shrewd things to say about relations with people, he limits himself to intercourse between the head of the family and those outside it and says nothing about the life of the household and the treatment of slaves and maidservants; he never speaks even of the relations between a father and his son.[29] Apparently he felt it inappropriate to meddle with the intimacies of domestic life in a public poem. The second and more remarkable omission is the lack of any allusion to the state and communal life; this applies not only to *Works and Days* but to the *Theogony* also. The institution of public assemblies is not mentioned at all.[30] Communal ties are mentioned in the sermon on justice and injustice, where Hesiod says that justice causes a community to flourish and that the entire community is penalized for injustice. Here, however, reward and punishment do not come by way of pragmatic political consequences, but rather as divine visitations, in the form of such things as peace or war, good or

[27] 336–41 enjoins sacrifice to the gods, according to ability, and propitiation with libations and incense evening and morning, 'so you may buy another's holding and not another yours.'

[28] Hesiod himself alludes to the variety in sacrificial requirements at 137.

[29] Hesiod does indeed speak of the constitution of a household: choice of a wife (695–705); choice of a maid (602f.); limitation to a single heir (376–78); frequent mention of slaves (441, 459, 469f., etc.): but there are no directions for behavior among the members of the household except for the verses deprecating adultery with a sister-in-law and harsh words to an aged father (328–32). Against the wantonness and wickedness of women Hesiod does speak out vigorously (67, 373–75, and *Theogony* 570–612), but the only practical suggestion he has to make is to keep them at arm's length: 'The man who trusts womankind trusts deceivers' (375).

[30] In the Hecate passage of the *Theogony* assemblies and war are mentioned as occasions when a man could distinguish himself (430–33), as often in Homer; but I believe that the whole passage is not genuine Hesiod.

bad crops, fertility or sterility of women (225–47, 260–62; p. 122, above). For Hesiod the state exists only in its juridical procedure, and the 'kings' are only judges and arbiters.[31] The frightful picture of the corruption of the iron age (p. 121, above) wastes no words on the decline of the sense of community and the abdication of state agencies; it shows only the immoral attitudes of individual to individual: guest to host, comrade to friend, brother to brother, son to father. If Hesiod, who has so much to say of divine order, is so utterly silent on political order,[32] we may infer that in his world the state functioned hardly at all. The struggle for existence must therefore have been all the harder, and such help as Hesiod afforded all the more welcome: enlightenment on the nature and interrelations of gods, things, and forces of life, and good counsel for the man who seeks to forge his own modest fortune in a decent manner. Peasants have less need of the state than any other class.

[31] Cf. the law sections of *WD* and *Theogony* 80–90. An exception is the consideration of the legitimacy of power as such, pp. 98–101, above.

[32] 'Order' (θέμις, δίκη, νόμος, etc.) is for early Greece an encompassing reality, within which no distinction need be drawn between natural order, social order, moral order. In this sense Hesiod speaks of πεδίων νόμος (*WD* 388), i.e. the natural order for agriculture; and his Eunomia, together with her sisters Dike and Eirene, daughters of Themis and Zeus, are Ὧραι who ὡρεύουσι (*Theogony* 901–3) men's agricultural tasks. This is how the passage cited above (*WD* 225–47) is to be explained: if order (in this case justice) is injured by a man, the consequence is cessation of natural order (in this case fertility of fields and wives, weather for seafaring, peace, etc.).

IV

Ancient Lyric[1]

(a) The Founder: Archilochus[1a]

As our path through the history of early Greek literature leaves the narrative epic of Homer and the didactic epic of Hesiod behind and enters into the archaic age there are long stretches ahead (to Ch. VI, inclusive) in which we shall have to make do with very scanty materials. From the period down to roughly 500 B.C. no single complete book of a poet (except for the special case of Theognis) or philosopher has survived, and even complete poems or verbatim quotations in prose writers are rarities. In general we must have recourse to short, sometimes quite tiny, fragments (p. 1f.); our undertaking would be hopeless if the early authors had not composed with such attention to every detail that even their slightest remnants carry a recognizable stamp. Hardly a line is irrelevant or characterless, and hence it is possible to infer essentials from even slight remains. From about 500 to the end of the archaic age at about 450 (Chs. VII and VIII) the material becomes more plentiful though it still shows considerable gaps.[2]

[1] Numbers in the citations of the fragments of Archilochus, Callinus, Tyrtaeus, Semonides, Mimnermus, Hipponax and Solon refer to *Anthologia Lyrica*, ed. Ernst Diehl (Leipzig, 1922 et seq.). For the remaining lyric poets, unless otherwise noted, numbers refer to the fragments in *Poetae Melici Graecae*, ed. D. L. Page (Oxford, 1962). There is a convenient concordance of the various fragment numbers of the lyric poets used by the principal editors (Bergk, Diehl, and Page) in G. Fatourgos, *Index Verborum zur Frühgriechischen Lyrik* (Heidelberg, 1966). In recent years our store has been greatly increased by the publication of fragments from papyri, and there are now also separate editions of individual lyric poets, like those of Archilochus by François Lasserre (1958) and Max Treu (1959)—another by Werner Peek is in prospect; Sappho and Alcaeus by Edgar Lobel and Denys Page (1955), and by Max Treu (1952 and ²1958); Anacreon by Bruno Gentili (1958).

[1a] For a collection of substantial new work on Archilochus see *Archiloque* (Entretiens sur L'antiquité classique X, Geneva, 1964).

[2] The clearness of our account will be hampered by the fact that we cannot make a representative selection out of a full store but must exploit such various materials as accident has provided.

The literature of the archaic period is rich in works of art, large and small, in vivid personalities and significant thoughts; its historical life was changeable and on occasion stormy. Even within the epic a basic change is unmistakable, but its rigid artificial style and its fixed themes obstructed the new tendencies and dulled their effects.[3] Hesiod, again, went his own way. He was too versatile and original to be classified, labelled, and put in his place in the changing picture of history. But now the powerful, even grandiose, drama of historical progress enters fully into its rights. First the sudden swing from epic to lyric, then the succession of various lyrists, and later, along with the lyrists the succession of philosophers—all these phenomena following one another illustrate the sway of historical forces and historical accidents which ran their course freely according to their own laws.

In the archaic age of Greece, before philosophical works entered the arena, lyric[4] was the characteristic literary form, as heroic epic was for the earlier, and to an even greater degree than tragedy was for the beginning of the classical age.

How did it come about that the short song came to be cultivated instead of the long epic, and what does it signify? Apart from mere difference in length, the lyric poem does not, like the recitation of a nameless singer, resort to the past in order to fill leisure hours agreeably with traditional tales of the olden times, but centers on the personality of the speaker, the time of delivery, and the particular circumstances of its origin. In a certain sense lyric stands in the service of the 'day' and is 'ephemeral.' It is from the archaic Greek conception of 'day' and of the 'ephemeral' that the transition from epic to lyric may be understood.

We must go back to Homeric epic to see how the new view of 'day' developed. In Homer the day is the only measure whose rhythm punctuates the continuous flow of epic events, and also it is that notion of time which can take on a positive and definite content (the time at which . . .):[5] 'The day will come when sacred Ilios shall fall'; 'If I were as young and strong as on the day when . . .'; 'the day of destiny'; 'the day of homecoming'; 'the day of enslavement'; 'the

[3] The illusion of unity in the two Homeric epics is so strong that they were long considered to be the free and original creations of one poet, and many still believe in a Homer who 'wrote' the *Iliad* and the *Odyssey* in the same sense that Tolstoy wrote *War and Peace* and *Anna Karenina*.

[4] Here, deviating from the ancient usage, by 'lyric' we mean short poems of various sorts and in various meters, including elegiac.

[5] 'Time' (χρόνος), on the other hand, has only a negative character in Homer. The word occurs only when someone must wait, exerts himself to no effect, and the like. Cf. *Frühgriech. Denken* 1–22.

pitiless day' (αἴσιμον, νόστιμον, δούλιον, νηλεὲς ἦμαρ). 'Day' so conceived
receives its character from the event that takes place on it, indeed
becomes identical with the event it brings. So an epic expression like
'to avoid the evil day' (*Od.* 10, 269) is equivalent to 'escape destruction.' The new turn which leads into lyric is bound up with men's no
longer believing in the possibility of avoiding the day (i.e., events and
circumstances) but rather feeling themselves controlled by it in every
respect. The new conception of 'day' finds expression in a younger
portion of the epic, and in fact where one is least surprised at
modernity of thought, in a speech from the *Odyssey*.

An old beggar sits at the threshold of the hall in which the gentry
are at table and receives small gifts from them in return for the
delightful entertainment which he has afforded them by boxing with
another beggar. On the morrow he will slay them all and again
become master in his own house. One of the suitors hands him food
with a friendly wish: 'May it go well with you again hereafter, old
man, who are now oppressed by misfortune.' Odysseus thanks the
donor for his kindly thought, and then continues (*Od.* 18, 129):

> In return I will tell you, and you mark closely and listen:
> Out of the many creatures that breathe and live under the heavens,
> Nourished on earth's broad bosom, man is the weakest and frailest.
> While the gods give him wealth and success and strength of the body,
> He never supposes that hardship may come upon him.
> And when the blessed gods send sorrow and pain as his portion,
> This too he bears perforce and makes his heart to be patient.
> For the mind of each whom Earth produces is ever
> Such as the day he receives from the father of gods and of mortals.

Whereas animals all remain what they are, the lion a lion and the
sheep a sheep, man is always what the particular day makes him:
a creature proud and lordly or humble and patient. God's 'day'
even alters our 'mind' (*noos*), the core of our self. Man is wholly
'ephemeral,' that is, subject to day and liable to its vicissitudes.[6]
Odysseus was once a powerful prince and is now a humble beggar;
his nature has changed with his situation.

The sentiments which the epic singer assigns to Odysseus, Archilochus, the founder of Greek lyric, seized upon and made his own. A
poem of his (68) begins this way:

> This our human heart is ever molded, O Leptines' son[7]

[6] This, and not 'lasting one day, short-lived,' is the meaning of ἐφήμερος. Cf.
Frühgriech. Denken 23–39.

[7] The addressee is known to us as a historical person through the discovery of a
large stone in Thasos bearing this inscription: 'I am the monument of Glaucus son
of Leptines, erected by the sons of Brentes' (J. Pouilloux, *Bull. Corresp. Hellen.* 79,

Glaucus, as the day is fashioned which the son of Cronus sends.
What we feel is always such as are the things confronting us.

Our world of thought and feeling is radically moulded for us by the
events which befall us; we are the echo, so to speak, of the conditions
in which we find ourselves at a given time.[8] With no refuge and no
respite we are subject to the will of the gods (58):

For the gods all things are easy. Often they raise
From misfortune him who lay low and humbled in the dust.
Often too they throw us down: the man who walked with speedy step
Suddenly is tripped, falls prostrate: many sorrows bear him down.
Hunger makes him wander homeless; all his thinking is destroyed.

The simple and straightforward language of the verse with its
elementally simple thoughts and elementally powerful images defies
translation. The new realism is very far from the steady and dignified
movement of the elaborate epic style. And in contrast to Hesiod, the
form here is one of immaculate perfection. A characteristic feature of
Archilochus' style is the gradual pointing of thought and sharpening
of tone. The high point of the fragment is the assertion that poverty
and degradation overthrow man's thought and manner of feeling
(both are implied in *noos*) and so disrupt the self.[9] Nothing is really
ours (8): 'Everything, Pericles, we receive from success [τύχη] and
destiny.'[10]

Archilochus goes further than the epic poet whom he cites could
go. In the still romantic *Odyssey*, even as a beggar the hero remained
an unbroken man, rescued by his own spirit from hunger and
poverty. According to Archilochus, however, hunger drives man
astray and suffering destroys his spirit. The poet takes seriously the
notion that human nature is plastic, is remolded by some new day
and thenceforward bears its stamp; and he urges that the outside
world must be reckoned with. Repeatedly, even in the few remnants
of his work that we possess, Archilochus vigorously combats exaggerated ideals and stands up for sturdy common sense without cant.

1955, 75–81 and 348–51). On the Parian colonists on the island of Thasos in the
north, see p. 147, below.
  [8] On the influence of Archilochus fr. 68 see p. 363, n. 37, below (Parmenides fr.
16) and p. 372 (Heraclitus fr. 17).
  [9] The gods are not even partially justified by making the destruction of our
mental powers the cause of misfortune; rather this destruction is an additional
misfortune that is yet (ἔπειτα) to befall the victim. What Archilochus suggests
here is made more explicit in an elegy in the Theognis collection (373–92: see pp.
312f., below).
  [10] Cf. Diagoras of Melos in Sextus Empiricus, *Adv. Math.* 9, 53: κατὰ δαίμονα καὶ
τύχην πάντα τελεῖται. Cf. further p. 163 and n. 9 below.

If man's spirit is so completely changeable, and if the instant which alters our nature radically changes our picture of the world also, the momentary state of the individual ego assumes supreme importance. The current situation of the individual finds artistic expression in short lyric poems which speak a direct, open, and natural language corresponding to the new realism. In a single poem the reaction of the speaker to what is at that moment happening is given an objective existence. Epic is now an anachronism. Its solemn and ceremonial language is no longer suitable for what men have to say. There is no longer any belief in fixed characters such as epic employs. With neutrality and detachment epic tells us of men long dead; but now the fates of other men long ago do not interest the poet—life can now be understood only by living it.

This is roughly the attitude of lyric poetry at the time when its founder Archilochus broke with traditional ideologies in order to put something totally new in their place. We shall now look into the poems and personality of Archilochus.

Archilochus was an Ionian from the marble island of Paros in the midst of the Cyclades—or he was at any rate half Ionian. On his father's side he sprang from one of the first families of the country. His grandfather (or father) had led a Parian colony to the island of Thasos, which was particularly valuable for its gold mines. Thasos lay to the north, near the Thracian coast, and from the island the Parian settlers crossed to the Thracian mainland in order to acquire still more land. In the incessant fighting with the natives, slaves too were taken. Archilochus came into the world as the bastard son of a noble father and a Thracian slave woman. He led an adventurous life as a soldier and mercenary. His life span falls roughly in the years 680–40.[11]

Archilochus had no property but lived by fighting (2):

In my spear is my kneaded bread, in my spear is my wine of Ismarus; when I drink I lean on my spear.

He was warrior and singer in one, the servant of the two deities who

[11] According to F. Jacoby, *Classical Quarterly* 35 (1941), 97–109. Our bases for the chronology of Archilochus and the historical background of his work are uncertain and ambiguous. According to F. Hiller von Gaertringen (*RE* s.v. Thasos, col. 1312, and *Göttinger Nachr.* 1934, 51), fr. 51 IV A 22f. refers to the Parian colonists of Thasos and the native women they took into their houses. The number 'thousand' would fit this well because this was the conventional number (not to be taken literally) for the full body of citizens of a community; cf. Xenophanes (*Vorsokr.* 21, full reference p. 252 n. 1) 3, 4 and Heraclides, *Politeiai* 11, 6. That Archilochus' mother was of non-Greek and indeed of Thracian descent is in any case very probable.

on the shield of Herakles appear as representatives of two opposite forms of existence (1):

I am both, the follower of the god Enyalios (Ares), and I understand the art which is the gift of the Muses.

In the fighting with the Thracian natives, called Saii, it once happened that he had the choice of dying behind his shield or running away to survive without it. The traditional code of honor, as the Spartans long maintained it, prescribed death in such a case. 'With it or on it,' the Spartan mother adjured her son when she handed him his shield as he went forth to battle: come back a corpse rather than shieldless! But Archilochus says in an elegy (6):

So my shield, which I left unwillingly—it was a good one—somewhere behind a bush, now is a Thracian's delight. Still, I came off with my skin: the shield is not so important. Well, let it go. Very soon I'll buy another as good.

Probably this passage was followed by the contrast expressed in two lines from the *Iliad* (9, 408):

But you cannot recover the life of a man, cannot buy it or win it back by force once it has crossed the teeth's barrier.

So speaks Achilles to declare his rejection of a hero's death, in a scene which gives expression to opposite and mutually destructive modes of feeling (p. 19, above). Again we see Archilochus taking over from epic a thought to which the normal attitude of epic is opposed. The Achilles of the *Iliad* is only toying with the pretence that life could be dearer to him than honor; Archilochus seriously balances the value of life against an exaggerated notion of honor, draws a realistic conclusion, and acts accordingly; and at once, in a tone of aggressive challenge, he proclaims to all the world what he has done.[12] He boldly ridicules the convention which esteems something that is bought and sold more highly than a unique and irreplaceable life. He was certainly no coward, and eventually, like Achilles, we may assume, he met a warrior's death. But precisely because he was a professional soldier, the iconoclast rejects a self-sacrifice that seems to him pointless.

Opposing romantic ideologies, Archilochus grasps vigorously at basic realities and places values where they really belong. He will not let himself be blinded by false glitter. In Homer the heroic personage was of course a stately figure, handsome and magnificent, with long,

[12] I cannot believe that Archilochus is in any way laughing at himself in these verses: one of his essential features is that he takes himself seriously, as we shall see in the following pages.

waving hair (cf. p. 85, above). Even the *Odyssey* in its present form makes a regrettable concession to this ideal by having Odysseus magically rejuvenated and beautified. But the bastard of Paros says (60):

How I hate the tall and handsome, tiptoe-strutting officer, proud with fashionable hair-style, smoothly shaven underneath! Give me one who's short of stature, mean to look at, bandy-legged, sure and steady on his feet, with guts and backbone—give me him.

The same applies to the style of Archilochus' poetry; in his songs we find no adornment, no striking of poses, but a firm and steady tread; and his way of expression is certainly not lacking in backbone.

A similar contrast between exaggerated and realistic aspirations is the basis of the following fragment (22):

For Gyges' golden riches I care not at all: I feel no envy of him. How the gods behave leaves me unmoved; a tyrant's throne I do not want since I see none of that before my eyes . . .

So far the text is preserved verbatim. It proceeded something like this:[13]

But when I see So-and-So pass me in the pride and power of his dirtily gained money, then all I want is to throw my axe at his head. So spake Charon, a carpenter of Thasos.

Gyges, 'lord of sheep-nurturing Asia' (fr. 23), ruled over the Lydian kingdom in Archilochus' time; he possessed unheard-of riches and gave offerings of solid gold to the Greek god at Delphi. The words 'What the gods do [i.e., the fabulous good fortune which the gods sometime allow a man] does not trouble me' reproduce a proverb which declares 'What the gods grant a man we do not begrudge but rather praise his fortune.'[14] Tyranny was craved by proud men ambitious for power in the archaic age and was enjoyed as the highest fortune on earth.[15] Even in the *Iliad* (3, 60f.) the carpenter was a stock example of an industrious man; hence he was ready to hand for Archilochus as a contrast to the upstart who became rich by roguery. In the guise of the carpenter Charon, Archilochus hurls at his adversary reproaches whose coarseness[16] we can only surmise. But after his manner, Archilochus starts with a purposeful prepara-

---

[13] For the continuation cf. *Frühgriech. Denken* 57.

[14] Bacchylides 5, 187–93 cites the thought from Hesiod; cf. further Pindar, *Isthm.* 5, 22–25; Petronius, *Sat.* 38, 9: *ego nemini invideo siquid deus dedit.* On Theognis 169 see p. 408, n. 17, below.

[15] Cf. Solon 23, 5–7.

[16] ἀγροικία, according to Aristotle, *Rhet.* 3. 17. 16.

tion and speaks of men whose good fortune he does not begrudge. His reason is that he does not have to see it with his own eyes. He turns from the faraway, of which he has only heard, to the present, which he has himself experienced. Here again we can see the upheaval in thought which produced the transition from epic to lyric. Archilochus decisively seizes upon the first and nearest data of the individual: the now, the here, the I. The glitter of the highest, the greatest, the most powerful, before which all the world stands in longing and admiration, means little to him in comparison with the relatively modest success of a man in Thasos who kindles his personal and as it were intimate hate.[17] World history pales in the face of what goes on in our own street. At that time the rich Greek city of Magnesia in Asia Minor was overrun and plundered by the savage Cimmerians. The catastrophe must have made a deep impression in the Greek world; but Archilochus, who fought and suffered on Thasos, declared (19): 'I pity Thasos' suffering, not Magnesia's.' Archilochus falls back upon his own life and abandons all forward positions. He cares not what others may think of him (9):

If, Aesimides, you will attend to the gossip of others, then you will find in life not very much to enjoy.

The distich is only the first half of an antithesis (the μέν clause) which Archilochus would obviously conclude by saying that only a man who freely strives for what pleases him attains satisfaction. In these challenging verses the poet turns smartly against the general conviction that the opinion of our contemporaries holds before us a mirror in which alone we can recognize our essential character and our own worth or lack of it (see p. 84f., above). Even the ideal of posthumous glory he found refuted by his experiences (64):

No one, once he has died, is held in honor and renown by his city; we, the living, court more keenly the good will of the living. It's the dead who always have the worst of luck.[18]

So it is small wonder that Archilochus refuses to sacrifice his life for the imaginary honor of saving his shield (fr. 6, p. 137, above). As a

---

[17] The contrast is complicated by the change from admiration to hatred. Without the complication the upshot of the new turn is that the things which merit a crown are not generally and publicly admired for their proud splendor, but those by which our own personal and intimate inclination is inflamed. In this form we shall encounter the thought in Sappho 16.

[18] The conventional ideas against which frs. 9 and 64 are directed are to be found, e.g., in Pseudo-Tyrtaeus 9 (p. 338, below): the brave warrior is honored after his death (vv. 29f.), and during life has 'much that makes him fortunate' (v. 38).

soldier he had personal knowledge of how little gratitude the warrior might expect (13):

Glaucus, the soldier is loved as long as he fights, and no longer.

Archilochus believes in only one reality, that of direct action. A man who wishes to be respected must show the world that he cannot be affronted with impunity. Hence the poet rolls himself into a ball like a hedgehog and presents his quills in all directions (103; 66):

The fox knows many things, the hedgehog one big one.

. . . one big thing I know how to do—terribly repay with sorrow sorrow that is done to me.[19]

Under the strange but vivid image of the hedgehog, for the first time in European literature the ego becomes a polar opposite to the non-ego. The self whose existence is threatened with dissolution and destruction by recognition of the 'ephemeral' nature of man, affirms its own being by conflict and defence against others.

Fighting is for Archilochus a necessity, comparable to physical compulsions (69):

I would rather fight with you than drink a flagon when I'm dry.

When he prays it is usually to call destruction down upon his enemies (30):

Great lord Apollo, strike,[20] oh strike the guilty down; O god of plagues, with plagues afflict my enemies.

Here is a wordplay on Apollo and ἀπόλλυμι = 'destroy.' Similarly the god of fire is besought for help (75):

Hear me, ruler, hear, Hephaestus; on my knees I pray to you. Fight, I beg you, at my side, and give me that which is your gift.

Another time Archilochus calls the searing heat of the Dog Star down upon his adversaries (63):

Many of them, as I hope, will burn and shrivel in the heat of the Dog Star: others . . .

For meekness Archilochus has no understanding; he taunts a man (96):

You have no gall in your liver.[21]

The greatest document of Archilochus' hate and scorn has been

[19] A new but more conventional parallel is supplied by *Oxyrh. Pap.* 2310, fr. 1, col. II.

[20] πήμαινε according to *Oxyrh. Pap.* 2310, 14–16; σήμαινε, Macrobius.

[21] Cf. Thersites' taunts in *Il.* 2, 241f. and Alcaeus 348, p. 192, below.

vouchsafed us by a papyrus discovery. The poet sends his curse upon someone and wishes him shipwreck on the dangerous coast of Salmydessus on the Black Sea, whose inhabitants lived largely by the wreckage which the storms brought them. Archilochus imagines his victim washed ashore (79):

> ... carried far off by the waves; in Salmydessus Thracians with their shaggy hair lovingly [?] seize him all nude. Then will he feel a thousand different pangs eating the bread of slavery; his body stiff with cold and covered half with kelp left by the surf of the sea.[22] There may he lie with chattering teeth, at his last gasp, flat on his face, like a dog, cast up by currents on the very farthest shore [?]: how I should love to see him, the man who wronged me, trampled our oath with his feet, who once was a friend!

The situation may be reconstructed as follows. The poet and other fortune hunters banded together to fight the natives and despoil them. When the company got into difficulties one of the 'friends' (ἑταῖρος, v. 14) stole away and made off for new shores.

The language is as simple as it is fluent, as always in Archilochus. Except for one conventional epithet of epic origin (Θρήικες ἀκρόκομοι. literally, 'Thracians with topknots') it resembles ordinary speech, Without deviating from normal word order in the least, the text naturally falls into perfectly pure and strongly built verse.[23] In the true archaic mode and with true Ionian clarity the thought is conveyed in clear, lively, and objective pictures. A different art and a different age would have discussed the misdeed of the faithless comrade in great detail, would have declaimed ponderously on the sanctity of oaths, or would have depicted the painful disillusionment of the speaker with much emotion; instead, Archilochus sketches the concrete picture he has imagined in concrete words, in order to conclude with the impossible wish: Would that I had seen it with my own eyes! Only with the final couplet does the whole receive its meaning and its justification retrospectively. The speech moves toward its goal surely but slowly, to reach it at the very end. Only a consummate master of his art can bring such greatness into being with modest means and in limited space.

[22] The text is very doubtful here. Re-examination of the papyrus by J. Schwartz has led to the reading χν⟨ό⟩ου at the end of v. 7 (formerly [ρό]θου) and to the reading ἐπιχ⟨έ⟩οι at the end of v. 8 (formerly ἐπ [έ] χοι); see Olivier Masson, *Revue Et. Gr.* 64 (1951), 427–42. This makes the ἐκ wholly unintelligible; ἐπιχέοι lacks a subject (in *Il.* 9, 7 κῦμα is the subject); and the stranded man would be 'covered' with seaweed, not 'buried' (cf. also *Od.* 23, 236f.; Plato, *Republic* 10, 611d).

[23] For fr. 79, at all events, this can be said only with reservations since the text has become doubtful, but it applies unconditionally to all other fragments with very few exceptions.

A newly found piece might (with strong reservations) be reconstructed in part as follows (*Oxyrh. Pap.* 2310, fr. 1B 22ff.):

That was a lengthy voyage in your little ship: you sailed from here to Gortyn and came safely back.

[*lacuna of eight verses*]

I never would again have found a friend like you if you had perished in a storm, or by the hand of enemies and so had lost your prime of life. Now, since a god has shielded you and you are back, . . . left me alone . . . I lay [before this on the ground] and in the dark now I [again stand up and] walk into the light.[24]

Archilochus could not have been a man with whom friendship was easy. He felt himself neglected by his friends (67b):

My heart is strangled by my friends.

A projected marriage ended in bitter resentment. Lycambes betrothed his daughter Neobule to the poet (71):

If it could only be vouchsafed that I might touch the hand of Neobule.

But Lycambes withdrew his promise (88; 95);

What is this, old Lycambes, what is this you have done? What god has robbed you of your wits? You used to be a clever man, but now, look you are the butt of every joke in town. You have defiled the greatest bond of all, the fellowship of bread and salt.

The merciless pasquinades of Archilochus were calculated to make Lycambes ludicrous and him and his daughter a byword. One such poem began as follows (74):

Nothing can be unexpected, nothing can be disbelieved, nothing wondered at since Zeus, our father in the heaven above, brought us midnight out of midday; took the sunlight clean away. Everyone was filled with terror; all who saw it blanched with fear. Since that day we may believe in anything; we may expect anything: no man should be surprised at what he sees you do. When the creatures of the woods and fishes swimming in the sea change their places with each other, when our cattle choose the waves rather than the solid land, and fish prefer to climb the hills—

Here our fragment breaks off, but we know at least the substance of the conclusion:

So I am not surprised at the abominations which my daughter Neobule has committed. So spake Lycambes.[25]

---

[24] The restoration is still quite doubtful. Line 23, perhaps πόντον περή]σας; line 32f., φίλον δ' ἂν ἀλ]λ[ον?] and τοσοῦτον, εἴ σ]ε; line 36, νῦν δ' ὡς ἀνῆλ]θες; line 38f. τὸ πρὶν χαμαὶ μὲ]ν and . . . ὀρθὸς]ἐς:cf. fr. 58.

[25] Now a few more verse endings have been added by *Oxyrh. Pap.* 2313(a) which make the reference to Lycambes doubtful. W. Peek, *Philologus* 100 (1956), 2, but cf. M. Taen, *Archilochus* 162, 223).

The poem was obviously constructed like that on Gyges' wealth (22; pp. 138f., above), but the edge is even sharper. A more spacious proem precedes the declaration proper, very lively and calculated to arouse the listener's interest, though he cannot yet surmise what the upshot will be. Only then does the moderate burden of the preparatory thought shift to the victim. 'All nature is turned topsy-turvy—in Neobule. So spoke her own father.' The effect of the poem on the persons so pilloried is depicted in a legend which declares that Lycambes or his three daughters committed suicide out of chagrin. Certainly the 'hedgehog' made effective use of his quills.

With such a temperament the poet must have made more enemies than friends, and in his fighting career triumphs alternated with defeats. Situations arose for which he could see no solution. Where he sought stability is shown by this fragment (67):

Heart, my heart, by countless sorrows much bewildered and perplexed,[26] pluck up courage and encounter those who hate you face to face. Though your enemies come running forward to attack you, still stand fast; confront them boldly. If you conquer, do not brag before the world: if you lose, do not lie prostrate, or go running home to cry. When your luck is good, enjoy it: in misfortune do not grieve past all measure. Understand the rhythm of man's rise and fall.

Nothing helped the Greek to come to terms with suffering and misfortune so much as the clear recognition of a universal rule of law. Such a temperament as that ascribed to Odysseus might help somewhat. But the fairy dream of epic is done with. For Archilochus' self-control is no longer a means of winning an imaginary final victory over all enemies; it could only lend stability and power to resist and moderate excessive fluctuations of sentiment.

Alternating success and disaster are the rule of our existence according to Archilochus. Hence sorrow can be overcome only by joy. With this in mind the poet makes a lamentation for the dead end in exultation. Of this we are informed by the remains of a very remarkable elegy[27] on the death of gallant men drowned in a shipwreck; among them was Archilochus' brother-in-law (7):

Not to belittle our painful sorrows would one of our townsmen, Pericles, or our town delight in festivities, since such excellent men were just now lost in the raging waves of the sea, and our hearts are swollen with pain and grief. And yet, dear friend, for evils beyond curing, calm resolution

[26] As in Homeric conversations with one's self, it is the *thymos*, the organ of moods and feelings, which is addressed.

[27] Even the fragments derive from different elegies; the structure of fr. 7 requires some such conclusion as fr. 10.

comes from the gods as a remedy. Ills move among men variously. Now we are afflicted; now it is we who groan over a bloody wound: next time it is somebody else. Come, at once, be firm, and banish womanish wailing.

Let us sink the painful gift of lord Poseidon in the deep. (11)[28]

[Pain for my brother-in-laws' death would be lighter] had the funeral fire taken his head and the fair frame of his limbs, wrapped in robes of white, as is seemly. [In spite of this I will now drink and be cheerful.] Nothing is made any better by tears; nor, if I seek pleasure, company, friendship, and joy, do I make anything worse. (10)[29]

Not to dishonor the dead (7, 1–2), but for the sake of manly self-control Archilochus bids the survivors celebrate and drink and be cheerful (10). Temper or control (τλημοσύνη) does not signify for him, as it does for Odysseus, balanced tranquility, but a swing to the opposite direction. Hence self-control can be paradoxically called a remedy ordained by the gods[30] for the irremediable; for a misfortune which cannot be redressed it supplies a joy which expels sorrow perforce. The pendulum of feelings cannot hang still. First comes the violent expression of grief, and then follows joy.

Love poetry in the modern fashion is not to be expected in the archaic period; women eligible for matrimony were not serenaded.[31] If Archilochus praises girls they are always presumably hetaerae:

In her hand a myrtle sprig delighted her and a lovely rose. . . . And her hair came down dark on her shoulders and back. (25)

. . .her hair perfumed with myrrh and her breast, so that even an old man would be passionate. (26)

Or the poet speaks of his own condition (112):

Such a desire for her love, rolled up under my heart, poured a great darkness on my eyes, and robbed from my breast its tender wits.

. . . Miserable I lie under desire, lifeless, with harsh pains because of the gods, pierced to the very bones. (104)[32]

Archilochus describes the workings of sexual passion with the same directness as he does everything else. He speaks quite unashamedly of the heat of his passion (fr. 72) or of his subsequent exhaustion (fr. 34). One poem jibed at an aging woman, and so set a regrettable

[28] The meaning was perhaps: 'We could not bury the dead, but even so we will bury the misfortune with which the sea god visited us and relegate it to oblivion.'

[29] Little is to be made of the scraps added by *Oxyrh. Pap.* 2356 before and after the text of fr. 10 as hitherto known.

[30] ἐπὶ κακοῖσιν ἔθεσαν φάρμακον (7, 6f.) happens to sound like ἐπιθήσει φάρμακα in *Il.* 4, 190; but here there is no tmesis: ἔθεσαν is 'established,' 'created.'

[31] But the tone of fr. 71 is an exception from the norm as we otherwise know it. We cannot be sure that Archilochus always observed convention.

[32] The interlocked word order in the second verse is quite unusual in Archilochus.

literary precedent (followed in e.g., Horace, *Epode* 8); it begins this way (113):

No longer does your skin bloom as it once did; now it is already wrinkled.

One epigram good-naturedly mocks a harlot nicknamed Pasiphile, 'every man's friend' (15):

Figs that grow on a rock have crows ever feeding upon them: so are all comers received by the fair 'every-man's friend.'

A mocking tone is also present in the following fragments:

The cross-grained babbler walked into the house—(32)

The voluble man is so tedious that there is only one way to be rid of him:

A pair of legs is then the finest thing a man can have. (132, Bergk).

Nor does Archilochus spare the comrades to whom he addresses serious and friendly poems elsewhere:

Sing of Glaucus—Glaucus of the horn-shaped haircut. (59)

You drank your fill of wine, and drank it neat, but you never paid a penny toward the cost, dear Pericles,[33] and you did not come invited as a friend to grace our board. No: your belly took command, and made your brains say 'fare-you-well' to self respect. (78)

The fragment last cited obviously belongs to a class of banqueting poems, as do probably most of the erotic poems. At the beginning of the banquet and in the course of it hymns were sung to the gods, including some to the giver of the wine (77):

I can lead the dithyramb, Lord Dionysus' lovely song, when the wine with summer lightning rolls and thunders in my head.

There were also occasions for companionable drinking on campaigns and raids. On a voyage the ship usually beached at nightfall and a meal was taken on shore (5, 4):

Quick now, get a jug to draw with, and off with you; Over the well-framed deck haste to the corpulent keg. Bring us the rough red wine from the grapeskins: how can a sailor sit up and watch all night sober and dry as a bone?

The style of this fragment is remarkable. Only the concluding verse shows the vigorous languages found elsewhere in Archilochus; the first three verses with their descriptive epithets and details recall the pomp and circumstance of epic. The reason is probably that

[33] This line is not preserved complete in the original.

banqueting poetry took a genial delight in dwelling on the details of those pleasures which the festive hour promised.[34]

On the constant peril of the seafarer's existence Archilochus framed this beautiful expression (21):

When our life [literally, our soul] lies in the arms of the waves—

The following verses were taken by ancient commentators as a simile for the threat of the dangers of war (56):

Glaucus, see, the ocean depths are swelling into angry waves, and upon the cliff of Gyrae [?] clouds are quickly gathering, signs of tempest: fear and tension gather in the tranquil sky.

Some fragments show that Archilochus also used animal fables. As a genre the animal fable rests on the assumption that animal nature, as it is known or believed to be, provides a fixed system of types for similes. In contrast to the infinite variety of human characters and modes of relationship, each animal has its own fixed and familiar characteristic,[35] and fixed and familiar relationships among themselves. Hence animal creation provides guidelines for orienting us in the human world and ready symbols for the quick apprehension of the characters and actions of persons, assuming that we are more interested in types than in individuals. It is in this sense that Homeric epic employs animal similes and Hesiod the illustration of the hawk and the nightingale. Of the fables of Archilochus one can be reconstructed in its context:

There is a well-known story told how once the fox and eagle made a solemn pact and bond of friendship. (89). [When on one occasion the eagle had no food for its young, he enticed the children of the fox], killed them and set this cursed meal upon his board. (90) [The fox was furious, but someone admonished him:[36]] you see that rocky wall of cliff, that over there stands hostile and unclimbable? On that he sits: your war cries only make him laugh. [Now the fox prayed:][37] Zeus, Father Zeus, yours is the power in heaven above, you see the works of godless men, their lawless crimes, and likewise among beasts and birds you punish those who break your laws. (94)[38]

[34] Cf. *Od.* 9, 5–11; Xenophanes fr. 1, and others.

[35] Cf. Philemon fr. 89 (Kock II 1, p. 504). One passage of the *Odyssey* (p. 134, above) goes so far as to say that all animals have a fixed character, which human beings lack.

[36] A new papyrus (*Oxyrh.* 2316) appears to show that the admonition was quite extensive.

[37] It is not certain that this fragment belongs to the same fable.

[38] In Archilochus' fable the animals are so humanized that even moral imperatives are applicable to them and the gods watch over their rectitude. It was different in Hesiod, where the fable of the hawk and the nightingale is followed by

In the continuation of the fable the eagle snatches sacrificial meat from the altar and carries it to his eyrie, and so commits a new trespass; a glowing spark which still clung to the meat sets the eyrie afire and the two eaglets, still unfledged, tumble to the ground and are devoured by the fox. This fable again deals with broken faith between friends; perhaps it reflects a personal experience of the poet, and threatens the betrayer, overt or concealed, with such a punishment as that visited upon the eagle.

A number of fragments are concerned with Thasos, the island inhabited by Thracians upon which a community of Parian colonists had settled. On Thasos Archilochus fought with the natives and suffered a reverse.[39] Into the newly won colonial area broken men thronged from everywhere (54):

Thasos has become the home for all the woes of all the Greeks.

Archilochus could not warm to the stony country (18):

. . . There the island lies just like a donkey's backbone, maned with shaggy woods . . . this is no place a man can love, no place of charm or beauty, as the land beside the Siris is.

One Greek tried political negotiations with the natives on his own account. An imperfectly understood fragment (51 IA 46) says:

'The son of Pisistratus' came with musicians 'to Thasos and brought pure gold as a present to the Thracian dogs. For the sake of their own gain they brought about general misfortune.'

Of war, which was his other calling, Archilochus speaks often. He tells how his troop was cut off and how Hermes saved him (51 IV A 4–5). Hermes is the guide of wanderers, the god of thieves and of windfalls; apparently Archilochus slunk through the enemy lines unnoticed. A battle in which the Parians defeated the inhabitants of the neighboring island of Naxos is reported by Archilochus in a manner reminiscent of epic, because here the same belief in the gods was still alive[40] (51 IA 54):

. . . Graciously Pallas, child of Zeus the Thunderer, stood beside them in the fight; she, in that dejected army, raised up every soldier's heart.

New papyrus finds have shown how accurately Archilochus told of battles of many sorts and in general how much contemporary history entered into his poetry. Of course we are able to infer only a

the observation that beasts know only crude power, whereas Zeus has given man justice (WD 202–12, 276–80).
[39] Cf. frs. 6 and 19, pp. 137 and 139, above.
[40] See p. 70, n. 7, above.

fraction of the events and circumstances from the terribly mutilated texts.

Two fragments are concerned immediately with fighting:

Bid the youngsters keep their hearts high: victory is with the gods. (57)

Erxies, how is the luckless army mustering again? (62)

Here is a taunt after an engagement (61):

Seven enemies have fallen, whom we overtook in flight; count the names of those who killed them; you will find a thousand men.

One elegy praises the Euboeans as chivalrous fighters (3):

Not many bows will be drawn and not many slings will be whirling once the great Ares shall give sign for the fray to begin. Deeds that make women weep will all be done at the sword's point. That is the kind of fight where they are truly at home, those great lords of Euboea, the Abantes, famous as spearmen.

Archilochus' fiery career ended on the battlefield. 'The war god is impartial; before now he has killed the killer': so says Hector in the *Iliad* (18, 309) after he has declared his resolution to fight with Achilles for victory or death. Archilochus appropriated the sentiment (38):

I will do so [?]—for Ares is in fact impartial.

When Paros was again at war with Naxos, Archilochus fell. An interesting legend declares that the Naxian who killed him was barred by the Pythia from Apollo's Delphian shrine because he had slain a minister of the Muses. He justified himself on the ground that the deed was done in hand-to-hand combat: 'war is impartial.'

We do not possess much of Archilochus' poetry, and no single poem is preserved complete. Nevertheless even the scantiest scraps bear the unmistakable stamp of genius. Genius cannot be explained; but the particular nature of the phenomenon may be partly indicated and defined.

In the personality of Archilochus everything that fitted him for his place in history conspired together; the circumstances of his life, his character, his thoughts, and his art combine to form a sharply defined picture. As the illegitimate son of a distinguished house, the earliest author we know of personal lyric had to stand on his own feet and pioneer a path of his own for his individual personality. He led the active, hard, and unbridled life of a soldier of fortune on the frontier between civilization and barbarism. As a half-breed he was equally familiar with both; he was at home in two languages and two basically different modes of life. He was therefore able to take an objectively critical view of every opinion and every habit, and was forced to do so. For him there was no comfortable seclusion, and in addition to other gifts nature granted him the touchy self-conscious-ness which his irregular position required. The maternal legacy of primitive force enabled him to tear down the antiquated ideologies of his paternal tradition and to pioneer the way to a fresh and un-burdened naturalness. With barbaric abruptness he completed the transformation from the epic to the lyric age, and he formulated a revolutionary programme with Greek clarity.

So the pronounced realism with which Greek lyric begins came into being. In his verses Archilochus is unqualifiedly frank, to the point of coarseness, and he avows himself free to do or not to do what he chooses.[41] He took into his poetry the things of life as they came, without distinction of decent or indecent.[42] Even the little that has come down gives us a notion of the unlimited span of his material.[43]

The meters which Archilochus employs are varied, but all are constructed on simple principles, and the recurrent unit embraces only one or two verses.[44] His language is consistently realistic and un-

[41] Cf. also Critias in Aelian 10, 13.

[42] Even lice are mentioned (fr. 137, Bergk).

[43] To illustrate the variety of subjects and the spectrum of tones at Archilochus' disposal several additional characteristic fragments are subjoined. From a pasquinade on an upstart (70):

Lophilos is now the first; it's Lophilos who has the power, Lophilos decides on all things; all look up to Lophilos.

From an address to the people (52):

Citizens betrayed and cheated, hear and listen to my words.

Easy narrative (107):

Erasmon's son, my Charilaos, I am going to tell a funny story. You, old friend, will be amused at it.

A confession (73):

I have erred; this very blindness fell on many men before.

Two pictures:

An ox is standing in our barn, a working beast with curling horns and clever at his tasks. (48)

The cunning woman bears in one hand water, in the other fire. (86)

Material from legend also occurs in Archilochus (147, Bergk; cf. also 150 and 190, Bergk).

[44] In stichic arrangement (i.e., verses repeated in uninterrupted succession) Archilochus uses iambic trimeter and trochaic tetrameter; the latter is also used for narrative poetry (fr. 51) as substitute for the stichic hexameter of epic, which he disdains. In addition there is a considerable number of two-line strophes, namely, the elegiac distich and the 'epode'; and finally there are the asynartetics.

sentimental;[45] its powerful and gripping effect rests, in true archaic fashion, not upon the use of big and emotive words, but on things and thoughts, his expression of them being sober, simple, and strikingly specific. No word is empty or ornate. With the exception of the elegiac fragments, which here and there show an epic tinge, the language of his poetry is indistinguishable from prose. The poet is so consummate a master of his art that he needs to take no poetic licence, not even in word order. The impeccable purity of his meter and language[46] lends his poetry, regardless of its subject, an exquisite refinement of its own and implies a rigorous artistic discipline.

.The monumental grandeur of his poetry requires no analysis. Humanity steps forward as it is, in heroic nakedness; with virile resolution it strips itself of all restricting conventions and all meretricious adornment.

Archilochus' world of thought and feeling is subject to the archaic law of polarity. The vigorous movement which permeates his poetry is sometimes evoked by the tension of diametric opposites, of which the one repels and the other attracts.[47] But the discourse never wavers this way and that between the two,[48] as elsewhere in archaic poetry: the poem takes its one single course from here to there; from the beginning it drives steadily toward its goal. In the poems of personal attack the discourse first creeps in toward its victim slowly and surreptitiously, without revealing its intentions, in order to swoop upon him with a fierce leap and destroy him in the end. Deceptive, too, is the dramatic masquerade behind which the poet sometimes conceals himself.

But aside from this the expression is unsparingly straightforward. There is no discreet courtesy, no delicate shading, no play of half-lights, and depths of background are lacking. Everything takes place under the same bright light, upon one and the same level.[49] Hence the direction which epic took in its last phase (pp. 90–93, above) is reversed. The primary data of 'now,' 'here,' and 'I' are for Archilochus also the final data, without qualification and without doubt.

---

[45] With the exception of frs. 104 and 112 (p. 144, above).

[46] Archilochus also disdains to give his poetry local color by un-Greek words, unlike Hipponax later.

[47] Often in the form 'not . . . but.'

[48] Unless the brevity of our fragments misleads us in this respect.

[49] For the expression of intensification there appears in Archilochus not the perpendicular dimension of intensity but the horizontal dimension of quantity (cf. B. Snell, *Gnomon* 7, 81f.). Just as in epic one begs not 'urgently' but 'much' (*Il.* 5, 358, etc.), so in Archilochus we read not of 'bright' but of 'much' laughter (88); 'much,' not 'disgusting,' seaweed sticks to the body of the castaway; and 'much,' not 'heavy,' misfortune threatens him in slavery (79).

The lyric of Archilochus proceeds wholly out of the personality of the poet or leads to it; but it is not subjective in the sense that it wishes to give a picture of life individually shaped and colored. What Archilochus communicates is in its essence typical. His experiences are uncomplicated and his emotions are exhaustively described by the simple words hate and love, contempt and esteem, pain and joy. Greek lyric poets did not aim to make themselves interesting by their peculiar sensibilities, but sought rather to demonstrate the general and the basic by the example of themselves.[50] Sharply as the individualities of the poets differ from one another for us, what they wish to set forth is not their own natures but objective human reality.

But the archaic age saw human reality under the aspect of the omnipotence of the 'day' sent by the gods,[51] a horrifying image. Man feels himself helpless.[52] There is nothing further to do than live each day fully, whether it be good or bad, and seek one's footing in the recognition that human life is subject to the law of vicissitude (67, 7). Lyric offers scope both for releasing feeling and for reflection. It renders objective typical alterations of personal life in enduring patterns, with effects salutary both for the creator of the poems and for anyone who repeats them in similar circumstances. The artistic form refines and clarifies experience. It stamps it into acceptable currency of full weight which passes from hand to hand and thus establishes a communion among people similarly blessed or afflicted. And just as the common ownership of literary property releases the individual from his isolation, so, in view of an ever-consistent pattern, it shows him that what happened to him was only human.

(b) *Military and Political Elegy: Callinus and Tyrtaeus*

In the poetry of Archilochus the change over from epic to lyric is shown in its most abrupt form. Other poets did not break so radically with the epic stock of ideas and forms of expression, but rather modernized the traditional art and outlooks. The first to be mentioned in this connection are the elegists. Elegy has an affinity to epic in

[50] When Archilochus says 'I do not love such an officer' (60), or 'I am not troubled by the wealth of Gyges' (22), he wishes not to express his own taste but to lend real values their proper recognition. The 'I' who passes judgments in archaic lyric is always intended as a representative.

[51] As Archilochus does at the beginning of the archaic age so Pindar at its end speaks with heavy emphasis of the 'ephemeral' nature of man (*Py.* 8, 95; see pp. 499f., below).

[52] On lyric ἀμηχανία, cf. B. Snell, *The Discovery of the Mind*, pp. 51ff.

meter, but elegiac poems differ from traditional epic in their brevity, in their structure of two-line strophes instead of continuous hexameters, and in their different content; occasionally they too are narrative, but their proper purpose is admonition, instruction, reflection. The predominant character of archaic elegy is that of a public or half-public address. Even when the poet happens to be addressing an individual he is speaking to the generality of people in the same situation, and even when he is speaking of himself his own person serves only as example.[1]

The earliest elegiac poet of whom we can form some notion is the Ionian Callinus of Ephesus in Asia Minor. Callinus certainly lived in the seventh century and was probably a contemporary of Archilochus. At the time the Ephesians had many wars to fight; they warred with other Greeks and they had to defend themselves against the Lydians and the barbarous Cimmerians. The following portion of a war elegy does not indicate the particular occasion; probably it is purposely kept general so that it might be used for any battle (1):

How long will you sit down? When will you be active and warlike,
    Young men? Have you no shame, seen by your neighbors around,
Thus to be idle and slack as if there were peace all about us,
    Sitting at ease, while war ravages all that we own?
[*lacuna*]
Let him cast one last spear, who is sinking in death.
Honor it brings to a man and renown, if he fights with his foemen
    In the defence of his child, his virtuous wife, and his land.
Only once can death come to a man, on the day that the Moirai
    Spun for him when he was born. Up then and into the fray!
Hold your spearpoints before as we meet our foe in the battle,
    Keeping a steadfast heart under the covering shield.
No man can always escape and keep black death at a distance;
    No man, not even he who has a god as his sire.
Often, surviving the fray and the splintering crash of the lances,
    Home he returns and death comes to him there in the house.
Yet such a man is admired by none: there is no-one to miss him;
    But for the brave all weep, humble and great, if he falls
Every soul in our city laments a great-hearted fighter
    If he is slain: if he lives, he is held a peer of the gods.
On him they gaze with their eyes as a tower; for what is accomplished
    By many brave men combined, that he performs on his own.

----

[1] For the first person as representative cf. p. 151, n. 50, above. Of Archilochus' elegiac pieces two conclude with an exhortation (the group 7, 11, 10 and fr. 5, p. 143f. and 145, above), both with an exhortation to drink. This is no accident: the gathering of men to drink was the normal occasion for poetic instruction and reflection (cf. p. 372 and 401, below).

Much as the verses echo Homer, they are harder and more angular in their content and development. The opening reproaches the young men, at random and apparently without cause, with sluggish indifference, in order to spur them on to intense exertions by the goading contrast.[2] And in order to combat the natural fear of death a series of arguments are woven into the poem; these are not very consistent but all are at one in the conclusion to be drawn from them. The impression of a hammering staccato is strengthened by the play and counter-play of manifold contrasts. As a moral motive protection of home and family is mentioned briefly only once; but again and again stress is laid on the choice between glory and honor or indifference and shame, and on the reactions of their own community and of neighboring peoples to the behavior of the men. The fragment culminates in the ideal portrait of a man who is recognized by his people as a living embodiment of the old Homeric heroism.[3]

There is an even closer connection with epic in several of the war-songs of Tyrtaeus. Tyrtaeus sang his songs not to the Ionians but to the most war-like race of the mainland, the Spartans. On his origin and person most diverse beliefs were current: among others it was alleged that he was an Athenian. Apparently it could not be admitted that the Spartans had produced a poet. But in his songs he presents himself as a Spartan citizen. He wrote probably towards the end of the seventh century when the Spartans were for the second time engaged in a difficult war with their sometime subjects, the Messenians. It is to the first conquest of Messenia that these verses look back (4):

> . . . to him who was once our king, the friend of the gods, Theopompos,
>> Under whose rule our race captured Messenia fair—
> Rich Messenia good for the ploughing and good for the seeding.
>> Nineteen years for its sake desperate battle was waged
> By stout spearmen, our fathers' fathers, never once flinching
>> Back from the heat of the fray, stubborn and steadfast of heart.
> But in the twentieth year the enemy fled from his ploughlands
>> Fled from Ithome's heights, granting the victory to us.

'and they appropriated the land'—so it probably went on—'Shall we now prove inferior to the achievements of our ancestors and let

---

[2] Cf. the baseless charge of inferiority in *Il.* 4, 371ff. and the charge of bandying words as in time of peace in *Il.* 2, 796f.

[3] 'Demigods' signify the heroes of epic; 'tower' in Homer is an image of the steadfast warrior (especially for Ajax); the quantitative definition of an outstanding warrior at the close recalls passages of the *Iliad* where an epic hero handling heavy objects surpasses many times over what men 'such as live today' can do.

go what they won?' The conquered Messenians had to work as serfs on the land which was formerly their property (5):

Just as a donkey sweats under the burdening pack so they bear our loads: of all that comes from their tillage, harvest, flock and field, half they pay to their lords.

At the death of their hard master they had to stand about the corpse and raise the traditional cry of lamentation:

They themselves and their wives must sing the dirge of their masters, every time that death comes for a lord of the land.

As we can see, Tyrtaeus does not gloss over the hardness of Spartan domination, against which the Messenians had now revolted. Tyrtaeus also wrote a political elegy when, under the pressure of war, one party (perhaps those who had lost their Messenian property) demanded that the distribution of land to individual citizens should be revised. In this poem, apparently, he reproduced the oracle in which the Delphian Apollo had sanctioned their new constitution for the Spartans; but between the hexameters of the original Tyrtaeus must have inserted supplementary pentameters, as the elegiac form demanded.[4]

The war songs of Tyrtaeus fall into two very distinct classes. One portion of the poems is addressed to the elders, among whom the poet counted himself; naturally the speaker who admonishes and instructs is an older man. Accordingly the songs speak in the nominative plural, and the exhortations are couched in the polite subjunctive ('let us . . .') or future ('we shall . . .') (fr. 6 and 1, see n.20 below). In other poems 'the young men' are addressed as 'you,' and the poet employs the more direct imperative of the second or third person ('fight!' or 'one must . . .;' fr. 7 and 8).[5]

First a song intended for the elders, the fathers of families. It pictures to the Spartan possessors of Messenian property the consequences which would be entailed for them personally if the conquered territory should revert to the Messenians. Each of the landlords would lose his land; not only would his economic status be lost but his status as citizen would be forfeited, for in Sparta only an owner of land could be a citizen (6):[6]

[4] Cf. K. Latte, *RE* sv. *Orakel* col. 843.

[5] Callinus does not distinguish between the young men (1, 2) and the fathers of families (1, 7). Archilochus fr. 3 is in the future but not in the first person; the context may have been similar to that of Tyrtaeus 1, 19–24.

[6] The notion of a formal judicial degradation for cowardice is excluded by v. 11: not cowardice but loss of house and land deprives a man and his family of public esteem. The 'forfeiture of fields' in v. 3 is paralleled in 4, 7: a man who allows himself to be beaten in battle thereby surrenders the contested land. For those

Splendid is death if one dies in the foremost ranks of the fighters
  Like a courageous man, fighting for country and kin.
But to go out from one's fellows, to leave one's generous farmland,
  Begging one's daily bread—that is the bitterest grief,
When with his much-loved mother, his aged father, his helpless
  Children, his own dear wife sadly he wanders abroad.
Then is his company hateful to those among whom he may wander
  Under compulsion of need, driven by poverty's law.
And he disgraces his house, destroys his pride of appearance,
  On his degraded steps shame and dishonor attend.
If then a man who has lost his land has no share of honor,
  None for himself nor yet any for children or wife,
Let us all fight and die for our native land and our children—
  Not cling fast to a life clasped in a shivering hand.

This clear and simple piece deals with a single thought positively and negatively, in order to draw a practical conclusion in the end. A man who falls in battle thereby proved himself 'good'; to one who loses his property in unsuccessful war, 'badness' of every sort attaches, namely disrespect and misery.[7]
Now a poem addressed to 'the young' (7):

Now, young men, stand firm and fight close flanking each other;
  Spare not a thought for fear or for the shame of retreat,
Make your courage strong, have soldierly strength in your bosom;
  Hold not your life too dear when you join battle with men.
Do not retreat and leave your elders bearing the burden,
  Old men graying with age, stiffening now in the knees.
Shameful it is if an old man lies in front of the young ones
  Slain in the foremost ranks during the wavering fight
Someone with whitening hair on his head, with beard all of silver
  Breathing his brave soul out as he lies low in the dust
Clutching in anguished hands his genitals injured and bloody
  —That is an ugly sight, sickening him who beholds—
All his body exposed. For the young man all things are seemly

who had no landed property in Messenia, πόλιν is added (v. 3); upon defeat they do not indeed forfeit 'their own fields', but probably the vital interest of 'their own commonwealth.'

7 The mention of the 'appearance' which must not be belied (v. 9) is interesting. The word εἶδος means 'appearance, form, beauty'; later it is used for 'type, classification', and Plato uses it to designate the 'idea' or the 'ideal.' Here obviously, the 'image' of Spartan man is intended, which the individual has hitherto represented outwardly; through the appearance that he keeps up, his dress, his presence, and his mode of life, he has made a claim upon a dignity which he must now justify by his readiness to die. Cf. further εἶδος-νόος WD 714 (with ἐλέγχω, unclear) and Od. 8, 176f.; εἶδος-φρένες Il. 3, 45 and Od. 17, 454; ἐξαπατῶσ' ἰδέαι Theognis 128; ὅσσον ἴδην Sappho 50; εἴδωλα-καρδίη Democritus B 195 (the concluding words show that Democritus has Archilochus fr. 60 in mind), and several others.

> While the fresh bloom of youth decks him with radiant charm
>   Men will admire his beauty of form and women will love him
>   While he yet lives: if he die boldly then too is he fair.
>   So to the fray; now firmly advance, stand fast in the battle
>   Both feet firm on the ground, biting your lip in your teeth.

The first three distichs are made up of alternate commandments and prohibitions; the central section is argument; and the last distich returns to exhortation. Lively sketches demonstrate what is 'ugly' and what 'beautiful'. Ugliness and beauty are the leading ideal of the piece, and moral and aesthetic values are absorbed in these concepts (cf. esp. v.12). Apparently there is not yet for Tyrtaeus a special sphere of morality; his thought works with concrete, sensual images, which are either desirable or repulsive.[8] Young and old form a second opposition; the contrast is emphasized to the degree that the old are now white-haired ancients. According to Spartan usage the elders stood in the rear ranks and the younger men belonged in front.[9] Hence it is doubly 'ugly and vexatious' when the young men retire too quickly and abandon to death an old man not as agile as they. The picture of the old man dying[10] is painted with brutal realism.[11]

The concluding distich of this elegy returns 'to the young', in the midst of another poem which was apparently written in a critical period (8):

> Make your hearts strong, for you are the race of the never-defeated
>   Heracles, neither does Zeus stand with his neck held awry.
> Be not afraid of the enemy numbers; flinch not before them;
>   Upright carry your shields into the front of the fight.
> Have no love for your life; let death's dark powers delight you;
>   Love death as you would love day and the light of the sun.
> Well do you know the baneful works of grief-bringing Ares
>   Much have you seen of war, suffered its tricks and its turns,
> Oft have you fled with the fliers, pursued with pursuers;
>   Aye, from each of these cups, lads, you have drunken your fill.
> And you have learned that men who stand fast, supporting each other,

[8] Hence fr. 9, which sorts out and evaluates the individual components of a complex picture with a rigorous analysis, cannot come from Tyrtaeus (see p. 386 below).

[9] Cf. U. Kahrstedt *Griech. Staatsrecht* (Göttingen 1922) I 308, with reference to Thucyd. 5. 72, 3.

[10] A passage in the *Iliad* (22, 71–76) is very similar and one half-verse is nearly identical. There too it is pointed out that in the case of a young man even death is beautiful. But the thought for which the contrast is exploited in the *Iliad* is less illuminating than in Tyrtaeus.

[11] Warriors wore only a short tunic (and no trousers), and the armor protected only the upper body; the lower body and hips were left free to move.

Men who hold the front line, coming to grips with the foe,
Fewer of them are slain, and they save their comrades behind them.
Those who turn and retreat lose all their manhood and worth (*aretê*).
No-one can reckon in full the tale of the sorrows and evils
Which crowd in on a man guilty of cowardly flight.
Keenly the enemy grasps at the chance: in turning and fleeing
Men are struck down from behind: bitter and ruthless is war (?).
Ugly it is when a man lies dead in the dust and the trampling,
Smitten through from behind by the point of the spear.
So to the fray; now boldly advance; stand fast in the battle,
Both feet firm on the ground, biting your lip in your teeth,
Guarding your thighs and your shins, protecting your breast and your shoulders
Under the broad and deep curve of the covering shield
Balance the heavy spear in your good right hand: let your helmet
Toss its unconquered plumes threatening over your head.
Warfare is only learnt by a man's own valorous actions;
Never should warrior skulk out of the reach of the shafts.
Close with the foe, each man, with the spear slay him who confronts you,
Or with the thrusting sword each lay an enemy low.
Setting foot against foot, with target pressed against target,
Haughty crest against crest, helm still clashing on helm,
Chest thrust hard against chest: this is how a man meets his opponents
Grasping the sword in his hand or the far-injuring spear.
You too, skirmishers, crouching behind the shields of the others
Keep up a hail of stones into the enemy mass;
Hurl your sharpened darts at the foe, and keep yourselves ever
Close to the shields of those who are full-armed for the fray.

At the beginning of this elegy Tyrtaeus appeals to the self-conscious-
ness of the Spartan nation, which could take pride in descent from
Heracles, the son of Zeus,[12] and to their confidence in Zeus, lord of
battles, who would keep loyal faith with the people of his descendants.[13] With this hope Tyrtaeus seeks to invigorate the spirit of the
army anew after serious reverses (v. 9f.) and to arouse each individual to gallantry in battle. With challenging exaggeration he
enjoins youth to despise life and to wait for death eagerly as (under
ordinary circumstances) they love life. In the sequel this paradox is
resolved rationally: the man who ventures his life has the greatest
prospect of preserving it, and the man who flees in order to save it

[12] The two royal houses of Sparta were descended from Heracles, and the whole
nation could be regarded as one great family.
[13] The 'neck awry' is a mark of the slave, who has forgotten how to hold his head
erect because he must bear burdens, and the crookedness is also applied to his
character (Theognis 535ff.). It is said of the slave that he is untrustworthy and
abandons his friends (Theognis 529f.).

will soonest lose it (vv. 5–20). Into the conclusion of this thought Tyrtaeus inserts the warning that cowardice utterly destroys *areté* or virile worth, that death from a wound in the back is ugly, and that a man who suffers himself to be branded with cowardice[14] will have to undergo countless afflictions.[15]

As elsewhere in Tyrtaeus, practical and moral considerations are interwoven; any argument is welcome that can be used for the only objectives that concerns him: be brave in battle! And again the argumentation culminates in vivid action-pictures. Three distichs (21–26) portray the firm stand of the defenders by naming all the parts of the body and weapons from foot to crest of helmet in order. Three other pairs of verses (29–34) follow the same principle in depicting the attacker who charges his adversary with vigor. Tyrtaeus carries exaggeration so far that the weapons and bodies of the opponents touch each other at every point.[16] The two pictures are separated by a distich with a hint to the inexperienced soldier (27f.); in an earlier section (7–10), on the other hand, Tyrtaeus appeals to the experience which his hearers had had of the vicissitudes of war. From the experience of these and the inexperience of the others Tyrtaeus draws the same conclusions; and hence it matters little, practically, if in one place he seizes upon one group and in another upon the other, and elsewhere addresses all without distinction. The elegy as a whole is addressed to the younger men among the heavy armed full-citizens equipped with the large shield (28) who constituted the core of the Spartan army. An after-word of two distichs applies to the conduct of the light-armed soldiery.

The content and structure of Tyrtaeus' war poems are determined rather by will than by thought. Not infrequently the thought proceeds by leaps and the argumentation is vulnerable. In the instructions references to practical advantage are bound up with moral admonitions in a manner which offends our feeling for logical accuracy. But for Tyrtaeus what is good and right must be good and right in every respect. In the concrete images, which Tyrtaeus weaves into his poem in proper archaic fashion, physical and spiritual considerations coincide; body and soul are not yet separated, just as no cleavage has as yet opened up between will and action or

---

[14] This is probably the meaning of ἢν αἰσχρὰ πάθη v. 16 (literally: 'if things shameful befall him').

[15] V. 15 seems to point to the disadvantages which will befall the coward during the rest of his life if he survives the battle. Tyrtaeus does not go into details because in this elegy he wishes to concentrate exclusively on the bearing of men in battle.

[16] The model for this was a passage in the *Iliad* (13, 130–133); but the *Iliad* speaks of the close contact of men with their comrades in the front line.

emotion and reason.[17] Moreover, the portraits have a pictorial completeness, so that the models are not only instructive but also artistically satisfying.[18] Correspondingly, the deterrent counter-images are carried into such detail that they arouse revulsion. Everywhere what should be and what should not be are sharply and decisively opposed to one another. Carefully drawn antitheses help to push the hearer in exactly the direction required. The emotional impact of this poetry is very great; that is why it lacks the ease, the richness, the spaciousness, the mobility, and the polished elegance which Homeric epic possesses even in battle scenes. Though Tyrtaeus takes his language and phraseology for the most part from epic, the difference in the stylistic character is considerable. Furthermore Tyrtaeus' imagery (7, 7–13; 8, 21–38; also 6, 4–10) stands still as if it were painted: there is no movement in time.[19]

(c) *Alcman's Choral Lyric*

The Sparta of the later seventh century in which Tyrtaeus sounded the serious and hard notes of his military and political elegies, also witnessed the first performances of Alcman's choral odes. The Sparta of that century was still receptive to the arts conceived as entertainment, as they were practised in the Greek and barbarian East; and yet it was already about to clothe itself in that narrow self-sufficiency, like rigid, suffocating armor, for which it would soon become famous or notorious. The poems of Alcman, and the many specimens of art on a small scale which recent digging has brought to light, bear witness to these two conflicting elements in contemporary Sparta— the pre-occupation with its own separate life and a ready response to stimuli from outside.

Alcman's compositions were intended to be sung and danced by a complete chorus with instrumental accompaniment. To perform such a song, a company of men, boys, or young women in festal attire stepped forward led by a chorus-master draped in a long robe and carrying a cithara; a flautist also participated. As soon as the leader sounded the first notes on his instrument, the company began to sing and to move in rhythmic dance, to accompany the melody of the

---

[17] If necessary, feelings are to be reversed by the will: life is to be hated and death loved.

[18] To enliven the instructive with the pictorial is characteristic of ancient didactic poetry as a whole.

[19] The Berlin papyrus (fr. 1) contains remains of war songs in the 'we' form, with frequent use of the future, in which several similes of the Homeric kind occur.

sounds in continuously changing figures and to give visible expression
to the meaning of the words by significant movements.[1] The melody
and rhythm were invented anew for each new song, but within the
song they were repeated from strophe to strophe.[2] The singing was
monophonic. The style of the songs was elegant and artistic; the
contents consisted of prayers, narratives out of mythical antiquity,
and personal self-expression. The leader might be a paid professional
artist who possessed the gift of writing and composing new songs—
a man like Alcman. But the choristers were members of the community, and when they performed a song they did so in the name of
the community to which they belonged. The chorus represented the
community collectively, and choral lyric was a communal art—the
most solemn and representative art Hellenism knew before tragedy
was invented. All members of society were trained in singing and
dancing choral lyric from youth onward,[3] just as in an earlier period
everyone was capable of reciting heroic epics. So a wandering chorus-
leader might everywhere find a tradition that he could use: trained
choristers were at his disposal, and an audience capable of appreciating the subtleties even of the more difficult performances. At
the rehearsals the members of the chorus had opportunities to ask the
poet himself about the meaning of his text, and anyone interested
could make himself familiar with the songs in advance.[4] Alcman
wrote many of his songs for choruses of girls. In Sparta young girls
appeared in public more than in other Greek lands.

Alcman himself was perhaps no Spartan, though he was fully
acclimatized in Sparta, and at home in her dialect. He was probably
a Greek from the East and came, not from one of the rather isolated
Greek immigrant settlements on the coast, but from Sardis in the
interior of Asia Minor, the highly civilized capital of the mighty
Lydian realm. One of his maiden-songs began as follows (16):

[1] The ancient Greeks like those of today had a developed language of gesture.
Dancing involved not only the feet but the whole body and in particular arms and
hands. (cf. *RE* s.v. *Tanzkunst*, col. 2243 and 2246.)

[2] In later choral lyric (e.g. in Pindar) the strophes are expanded into triads, see
p. 437, n. 2 below.

[3] And they practised it only too gladly. Singing and dancing (μολπή τε γλυκερή
καὶ ἀμύμων ὀρχηθμός) was a delight for which they felt an 'urge' (ἔρος) comparable
to that for the pleasures of sleep and love. This emerges from a passage in the *Iliad*
(13, 636–39)—which is also testimony that choral lyric in itself was as old as
the *Iliad* (hence there is more than one epic Muse), but at that time it was not so
highly developed a literary genre, for otherwise the Greeks would have preserved
choral lyrics of the age before Alcman and continued to copy and perform them.

[4] Later this applies to the profound choral lyrics of tragedy which were rehearsed by the poet himself and of which many private homes possessed written
texts before the performance; for the chorus consisted of citizens of Athens.

He was no peasant and no boor, nor . . . nor a Thessalian by origin, nor an Erysichaean (a tribe in the wild uplands of Acarnania), nor a shepherd: from lofty Sardis came he (who made this song).

It was usual for the poet to name his home in his song, as a seal of authorship; sometimes he put the information in the mouth of his public, so that praise of the poet could be attached to it.[5] But no other self-praise is like this of Alcman's; no other poet points, as he does, to all that he is not and to places from which he does not come before he proudly reveals his origin. It also happens elsewhere in early Greek poetry that the poet promises the man of whom he sings that his fame will spread over all lands and seas upon the wings of his song;[6] but it is, so far as we know, unparalleled that Alcman should name people after people to whom his songs, as he hopes, will make their way (148 and 150–53 Bergk). Among them were the most insignificant tribes and the remotest people of fable, and the philologists of antiquity had very great trouble identifying them. The abundant use of proper names in poetry makes its statements seem particularly real, for names identify their objects precisely and unequivocally as no other designation can do. On the other hand, names carry no content for one not already familiar with the bearer of the name. Alcman's poetry, as will appear, is full of references and allusions which could have meaning only to the initiated.

The bombast with which Alcman praises himself is naturally intended as a joke; but if we subtract the exaggeration there still remains a strong conviction of his own worth. All the Greek poets of the age exhibited a proud self-consciousness; the professional artist found it useful to tell the public frequently how important his achievements were, and the genuine poet was steeped in the belief that he had a high mission to fulfil. Alcman has his chorus sing the words (38):

Many maidens as we are, all praise the lyre-player.

He was not, like Archilochus (fr. 1), warrior and poet in one; but still he equates what he has to give Sparta with the warlike deeds of Spartan armies (41):

The steel is balanced by the lyre's beautiful playing.

The lyre (*cithara*, or *magadis* in fr. 101) symbolizes musical art as a whole, for with it the chorus leader gave the performers melody and rhythm; for the audience, however, its thin and transient tones would have been drowned by the voices of the ten or eleven maidens of one

[5] So the singer of the *Hymn to Apollo* and Theognis 22f.
[6] For example, Theognis 237ff., Pindar, *Nem.* 5, 1ff.

of Alcman's choruses. The accompaniment proper was the clear, swelling tone of the 'flute' (more precisely, double oboe). This instrument was native in Asiatic Phrygia and was always regarded as oriental by the Greeks. From Phrygia too came the flautists themselves whom Alcman employed; they may have been slaves. Their names are mentioned in Alcman's songs with praise, names of exotic sound like Sambas (fr. 109; cf. 126). The Muse's art of the lyre-player had to invent a new 'tone' for every song (14):

Muse, clear-voiced Muse of many tones, begin a new tone for the maidens to sing.

For melodic motives the song of birds was imitated (40):

I know the tunes of all the birds.

Alcman invented words and tune by which he put into words of melody the voice of the kakkabis bird. (39)

In Greek poetry the sound of women's voices was frequently likened to the singing of birds; and contrariwise, singing birds were conceived of as transformed women in Greek myths, and their conduct and song interpreted by the fortunes which befell the woman before her transformation. The kingfisher (*halcyon*) too was woven about with sentimental legends; it was thought that the male bird, grown old, was carried by the female on her wings. Alcman alludes to this when it became difficult for him, in old age, to lead the dance (26):

Maidens of sweet-flowing song, with enchanting voices, no longer will my limbs bear me in age: would I were a king-fisher, flying on the kind wings of my mate, at rest from fear and from trouble, over the crests of the waves, in purple hue, a sacred bird.

Since choral lyric was a social art, the girls were encouraged by Alcman to contribute their own inventions to the writing, composition, and choreography (59b):

This gift of the chaste Muses blond Megalostrata, blessed among the maidens, has shown.

Perhaps we are thinking too much in modern terms if we suppose that the songs were reduced to their final form before they were rehearsed. Perhaps they were worked out and brought to their final form in trial runs. It is a feature of choral lyric that it breaks the illusion and speaks of its genesis and performance within the song itself. The festal occasion can very fitly be reflected in the art-form, and thus becomes at once the object and the medium of the presentation. So the song can praise its maker and those who trained for it;

the girls compliment the chorus leader, and Alcman on his part hails the charm and skill of the girls.[7]

Thanks to a papyrus find of a century ago, we possess the greater part of one of Alcman's maiden-songs.[8] The beginning of the part preserved celebrates a native band of heroic brothers who had fallen in battle with Heracles and the Dioscuri (?) in mythical times. Alcman does not recount the course of the battle but gives a list of all those heroes whom 'he does not wish to pass over'. Again we hear name after name: there are eleven names in eleven quite short lines. Subjoined are considerations of a general nature on the limits of what is human. They begin (1.13) with a reference to

Aisa and Poros, most worthy of honor among gods.

Aisa designates ordained lot and destiny; *Poros* is something like access and solution, remedy. Whereas *Aisa* imposes a compulsion from which we cannot withdraw, *Poros* offers open possibilities to the inventive or favorably situated man.[9] When *Aisa* and *Poros* are called most worthy of honor (or eldest) of the gods, the implication is that absolute compulsion and relative freedom are the basic principles of the world.

Alcman illustrates *Aisa* as well as *Poros* in the following. *Aisa* establishes our human limitations firmly and places us far below the gods:

Let no man's striving spirit soar up to heaven,[10] nor seek to wed Aphrodite, queen of Paphos, or any beautiful child of the sea-god Porkos.

Defiant struggle[11] cannot win for man the utopia of the divine and the perfect, it does not open the heights of heaven to him or the depths of the sea—

—but the Graces with lovely eyelashes come to the house of Zeus.

[7] Naturally no value is to be assigned to Chamaileon's anecdotal interpretation of fr. 59b.

[8] Now we have the remains of a commentary in *Oxyrh. Pap.* 2389 (vol. 24, 1957) fr. 6 and 7 (also in Page, *Poetae Melici*, after fr. 1).

[9] On πόρος in this sense cf. e.g. Eurip *Medea* 1418. The contrast between *Poros* and *Aisa* seems to recur in fr. 102: 'Narrow (thin, hard to recognize and pass) is the straight path, pitiless the compulsion (necessity).' See also M. L. West, *CQ* n.s. 13 (1963) 154. Cf. the similar pair *Tyche* (luck, success, windfall) and *Moira* in Archilochus fr. 8 (p. 135 above) and Wilamowitz, *Hermes* 64, (1929), 486.

[10] I supply: Ἀπέδιλος ἀλκὰ μή ποκ᾽ ἀνθρώπων ἐς ὡρανὸν ποτήσθω. The word ἀπέδιλος recurs in Aeschylus, *Prom.* 135; it can be no accident that both contexts involve flying (as an expression of excited haste ἀπέδιλος would fit better in Hellenistic poetry than in Aeschylus). Accordingly I take ἀπέδιλος as a circumlocution for 'in flight'; cf. Euripides, *Helen* 1516: πτεροῖσιν ἀρθεῖσ᾽ ἢ πεδοστιβεῖ ποδί (so now also Denys Page, *Alcman, The Partheneion* (1951) 34f.).

[11] ἀλκή does not mean 'force' but 'defense, struggle, valor'.

Not contentious violence but *Charis* ('charm, amiability, complaisance, grace' and the like) leads man to the house and throne of god, which he must approach as a guest, not as a presumptuous claimant. After all, the Charites themselves live together with the Muses on Olympus (Hesiod, *Theog.* 64) and so the poet's charming art gains access: 'May my song be pleasing to the house of Zeus' (fr. 45). Even if *Aisa*, destiny, separates man and god forever, *Poros*, the possession and graceful use of good gifts, builds a bridge over the abyss.[12]

To match this astonishing example of highly abstract philosophical speculation in a choral ode of Alcman, we now (since 1957) have another. In the fragment of a commentary on a text of Alcman not preserved (*Oxyrh. Pap.* 2390 fr. 2 = fr. 5 Page) we read: 'In this ode Alcman speculates upon nature (φυσιολογεῖ)'; and we learn further that the poet deduces the genesis of our world from the basic principles at work in it. The one principle is again the 'ancient revered' (πρέσγυς) *Poros*; but its partner this time is not *Aisa* but *Tekmôr* (τέκμωρ), of which, as a variant of 'destiny', '(binding) establishment'[13] must be the meaning.[14]

Alcman appears to have applied the pair of conceptions 'open possibility and binding establishment' to the ordering of the world as it comes into being, in the sense that the two together separate 'day' from 'darkness' by creating a separate existence for (sun and) moon, and by establishing their orbits, phases, and seasons upon which all earthly existence depends. We shall later come to speak of the new fragment somewhat more fully (p. 253f.): for the present we shall turn back to the song of the maidens.

The verses following are badly mutilated. All that we can see is that the subject is again battle and the death of heroes or giants who opposed the gods. Attached to the end of this myth are more *sententiae* (1, 34):

Dreadfully they suffered who plotted evil. There exists a retribution of the gods. Happy is he who cheerfully weaves the day to its end without tears.

[12] For the bridging of a gulf established by *Aisa* (= *Moira*) by means of χάριτες cf. also Aesch. *Choe.* 319f.: σκότῳ φάος ἀντίμοιρον, χάριτες δέ ... (of the song of prayer); Pindar, Pyth. 5, 96–107 (of the prize song); also Plut. *Mor.* 745 G: ἄμουσον γὰρ ἡ Ἀνάγκη, μουσικὸν δ' ἡ Πειθώ. Further, cf. Aesch. *Ag.* 182f.: βία of the gods and χάρις. Cf. on this further p. 314 n. 25, below.

[13] So *Iliad* 1, 526f.; this corresponds to the use of the related verb τεκμαίρεσθαι which always means 'establish, ordain' in Homer. Once (*Il.* 13,20) τέκμωρ means 'goal (of a course)' in Homer, and four times it is used very remarkably, in the sense of μῆχος, of a thing (τί *Od.* 4, 373 cf. *Il.* 2, 343) which one must 'find' before one can bring what is desired to pass.

[14] The new text thus supplies welcome confirmation of our interpretation of this section of the song of the maidens.

With all the uncertainty of our conditions, which might be transformed from one day to the next by the intervention of superior powers, a day of happiness concluded without tears, is the sum of human happiness, and we should enjoy it as such.[15] This again is an application of the doctrine of the ephemeral nature of man.

With the words 'But I praise the light of Agido' the song takes a new turn. 'I' is each individual songstress, and Agido is one of the girls. All that follows, perhaps half of the original whole, is devoted to the glorification of the chorus. All ten of its members are called by name (again a catalogue of names), and of each some word of praise is said. The break between the first portion and the second is explained by the juncture of themes: after the admonition to enjoy what the moment decrees, the chorus itself turns to the moment which it is experiencing in order to take pleasure in its own glory.

The second half of the song is well preserved but hard to understand. Alcman has tailored his poem so accurately to the single occasion and the circumstances of the day that the uninitiated are confronted with an enigma. Properly the song should have perished after it had fulfilled its immediate purpose and a new song would have to take its place on each subsequent occasion. That this did not happen is probably due to Spartan conservatism, which kept forever what it had once possessed.

'There exists vengeance of the gods' begins a strophe. It proceeds as follows (v. 39):

But I sing the light of Agido. I see her like the sun—[unintelligible]—but I can neither praise nor blame her; I am forbidden by the famous leader, who is outstanding as if among the cattle one should place a steed, swift, prize-winning, with thundering hoofs, in dreams that dwell under the rock.

The mood of the concluding words is not easy to interpret, but the animal similes are simple. In Sparta groups of young people were called 'herds' (ἀγέλαι); and from Homer onwards the horse symbolized proud and self-conscious beauty. In Aristophanes too (*Lys.* 1308–15) Spartan women liken themselves to horses. The picture is developed in the next strophe (v. 49):

Do you not see? The racer is of Venetic breed. The mane of my cousin Hagesichora shines like pure gold, and her silver face glows brilliantly.[16]

---

[15] Similarly Pindar, *Isthm.* 7, 40: Ὅτι τερπνὸν ἐφάμερον διώκων ἕκαλος. On what precedes in Alcman (ἄλαστα-τίσις 34–36) cf. in the same Pindaric poem v. 47f.; and on Alcman's 'not flying to heaven' (v. 16) cf. Pindar v. 44–47. The whole complex of thought recurs in the Pindaric passage (see p. 474f., below).

[16] I take διαφάδαν with what precedes. It is too bold to introduce an interruption: if attached to λέγω, διαφάδαν spoils and confuses the simple thought; Theocritus 18, 26 writes: Ἀὼς ἀντέλλοισα καλὸν διέφανε πρόσωπον.

Why need I speak? There she stands, Hagesichora. As second in beauty she
comes after Agido, a Colaxaean steed behind an Ibenian. For the Pleiades
fight with us who bring a robe for Orthia, like Sirius rising through the
ambrosial night.

The most likely interpretation is that our chorus is offering Artemis
Orthia, the tutelary goddess of Spartan youth, a robe as an annual
offering;[17] and that it had to compete in a contest of beauty and
song with another chorus, 'The Pleiades.' Sirius (the dog-star) was
regarded as evil and dangerous because it brings the scorching summer
heat. Again the strophe closes with a poetic image as the former does
with that of the dream-horses and an earlier one with the Charites
in the house of Zeus.

From this point onwards (v. 64ff.) the meaning becomes quite
obscure. It appears that the special advantages of this chorus over
the other are praised, and first of all the rich ornaments which the
girls wear: much purple; a colourful snake of gold (or bracelet); and
a Lydian hair-band, the pride of the girls with lovely eyebrows. Then
the girls themselves are named: 'the hair of Nanno,' 'the divinely
beautiful Areta,' and so on. Finally, there are suggestions of rivalry
between the groups and passionate attachments among the girls.
This strophe concludes with the words, 'But Hagesichora holds me
fast (?).'[18] A new strophe begins (v. 78) with Hagesichora and
Agido and soon turns to a prayer to the gods: 'Come, you gods,
receive their supplication. With you (?) are success and consummation.' At the end reference is made to an earlier victory in a competition,[19] credited to Hagesichora. The last strophe compares the
girl leading the chorus to the lead-horse of a chariot and to the
helmsman of a ship; in the art of song she almost equals the Sirens.
The chorus (?) 'sends forth its voice like the swan on the bank of the
Xanthus; and the girl with charming hair—.' Here the text of the
manuscript breaks off, but we know that only four concluding lines
are missing.

Like the spirited frolic of young horses at pasture, the second half of
the song offers the spectator an attractive spectacle with no special
relevance or profundity. The girls converse with one another in
sprightly and intimate banter about their own concerns,[20] and the
kindly spectator is ready to share their confident joy in themselves

---

[17] On 'Orthia' and 'robe' cf. J. A. Davison, *Hermes* 73 (1938), 446–50.

[18] According to D. Page (p. 163 n. 10, above) the papyrus reading is not τηρεῖ
('holds fast') but τείρει. The meaning is not clear.

[19] On πόνων ἰάτωρ (88) cf. Pindar *Nem.* 4, 1 εὐφροσύνα (the victory celebration)
πόνων κεκριμένων ἰατρός.

[20] It is easy to imagine that the girls participated in working this portion out.

and one another. These light occasional verses make no effort to become independent of the fleeting day for which it was directly intended. It expressly points back to the actuality which it serves: 'What shall I say? There she stands, Hagesichora.' The form is surprisingly forceful in the compact and beautiful similes; for the rest it crumbles into small-talk or over-expands into catalogues.

The characteristics of the large-scale song of the maidens recur in the small fragments we possess of Alcman's other work, for example, the waggish tone in which the speaker addresses himself and the other members of the close-knit group, the details of ordinary life, even the most trivial, into which the speaker enters. He enumerates six kinds of wine, one after the other (fr. 92), or various kinds of pastry (fr. 19 and 94), and he writes verses like these (17):

And I shall give you a cauldron for the tripod in which you can put— [lacuna]—together. Heretofore it has been without fire, but soon it will be full of the pottage which the glutton Alcman loves after the summer solstice. He eats no delicate viands, but seeks what is common, like the people.

Along with the down-to-earth names of two dishes Alcman once puts as a third the high-flown expression 'waxen harvest' (πηρίναν ὀπώραν fr. 96), that is, 'honey-comb crop,' as a circumlocution for honey; prose and poetry here rub shoulders. The goddess Artemis, of whom it was believed that she participated in the nocturnal orgies of Dionysus[21] with a team of lions, is addressed as follows (56):

Often on the mountain tops when gods take pleasure in torch-lit festival, into a golden vessel, a big bowl such as shepherds use, you put the milk of lions with your hands, and make a big cheese, unbroken, shining white (?).

On the procession of the seasons he speculates as follows (20):

Of seasons he created three, summer and winter and the third autumn; fourth is spring, when things grow, but there is not enough to eat.[22]

Passages which have to do with eating and drinking are specially plentiful, thanks to Athenaeus. Other themes in Alcman are little known because our material is too scanty. Of this treatment of legend we know only that he often leans heavily on Homer for matter and expression, for example in fr. 80:

Circe once plastered with wax the ears of the comrades of clever Odysseus.

[21] The significance of Artemis is suggested by Wilamowitz, *Glaube der Hellenen* II, 80, with reference to Pindar, fr. 70b, 19ff. (Snell). On this and on the other fragments of this group see Peter von der Mühll, *Kultische und andere Mahlzeiten bei Alcman*, in *Schweiz. Archiv. f. Volkskunde* 47 (1951) 208–14.

[22] In Spring the stores of the preceding year's crop are low.

or (120):

The goddess seized the hair of his head in a firm grasp—

which recalls a scene in the first book of the *Iliad* (197ff.). A fragment shows the opening inherited from the earliest days of man, 'Once upon a time'—(74):

There was once a man Cepheus, who ruled over . . .

Didactic *sententiae* scarcely occur among the individual fragments, and apparently only by accident, for the disquisitions in the long song of the maidens had to do with life in general, as was usual in choral lyric. In this portion there occurred the remarkable doctrine that life can be explained by the opposition of Aisa and Poros. The style of such thinking is the same as in Hesiod's *Theogony*. Hesiod's mode of thought is also suggested by an expression of Alcman's concerning Tyche (fr. 64), that is, 'accident, luck, success or failure,' which is here understood as political success.[23] *Tyche* is said to be a daughter of Prometheia (foresight) and her sisters are Eunomia (good public order) and Peitho (persuasion). The expression 'daughter' in fragment 57 refers to connections in the world of living nature:

(Flowers) such as are nurtured by Herse (dew), daughter of Zeus and Selene.

Zeus is here the god of sky and weather: in moonlight nights abundant dew falls from heaven. A quite different and very deep feeling for nature gave rise to the fragment on the half-mythical mountains in the midnight portion of the world, which hide the sun at night (90):

Rhipaean mountains, thick with forest, bosom of black night.

These words, meaningful and powerful beyond translation,[24] in which nature is understood organically and at the same time piously revered, recall the beautiful images at the end of several strophes in the song of the maidens.[25]

---

[23] Cf. the *Tyche* in Pindar, *Ol.* 12, 1 and fr. 39, and later in the Hellenistic Age the *Tyche* of cities.

[24] For the Greeks, who did not practise forestry, 'forest' was a natural, desolate growth. The verb (ἐπ)ανθέω signifies that something like a fluff or bloom or glow enveloped the object.

[25] The genuineness of fr. 89, which passes under Alcman's name, is dubious. It has a quite modern sound:

Asleep are peaks and gorges, cliffs and ravines, the forests (?ῦλα θ᾽ Pfeiffer) and all creeping things nourished by black earth, the mountain-dwelling beasts and the race of bees and the creatures in the depths of the purple sea; asleep are the tribes of wing-spreading birds.

Alcman invited the Muse to come to him in Sparta (27):

Come, Muse Calliope, daughter of Zeus, begin a lovely poem, make bright our song with winning charm, our dance with grace.

Even today we see the charm and attraction of the dramatic, fresh, and warmly human passages of his poetry; but we can also see the dry prosiness of other pieces. The Eastern Greek, transplanted from the refined cultural atmosphere of Lydia to a Sparta which already inclined to fossilization, practised disparate modes in rapid alternation: poetry to endure and poetry for the occasion, world poetry and local poetry. A fusion of the conflicting elements, such as the genius of Aristophanes achieved in Athens of the fifth century, is not to be expected in Sparta of the seventh. There the prime requirement was to be Spartan, and everyone was expected to praise and approve of people and usages and things as they were. Alcman was naturalized into the community and struck precisely the courageous cheerful, loyal, humorous tone of a man who knows and accepts the society about him. He glorified things great and small without distinction; he attached his poetry to the most elementary data: this group of girls, this wine, this pease pudding, and—not least—this Alcman. The numerous proper names he mentions demonstrate a direct equation of name and thing in a degree not to be surpassed. And then in the midst of his sure grasp of solid earth he has poetic images flutter up like winged birds: dreams rise soaring from their cave under the rock;[26] an evil star rises in high heaven; the Charites

We must remember that centuries had to elapse after Alcman before anyone could feel that mountain and valley, cliff and gorge could lie in nocturnal slumber like animals—the things themselves, and not nymphs representing living nature. When Danae prays in Simonides, 'May the sea sleep, may our measureless woe sleep' (fr. 543; see p. 315, below), sleep is rather a vivid expression for a real change in the conditions by which the speaker is afflicted at the time than an exaggerated 'pathetic fallacy.' But for a valid judgment we should need to have much more plentiful remains of early Greek poetry at our disposal than the wretched crumbs which accident has allotted us (cf. also following note); we should not have expected such philosophical utterances as we now know Alcman made (p. 163–65, above). The genuineness of fr. 58 has lately been defended by Max Treu (*Gnomon* 26, 1954, 172) and Rudolf Pfeiffer (*Hermes* 87, 1959, 1–6).

[26] In 1957 the publication of a new papyrus find gave us fragmentary verses of Alcman in a style like that of 'Dreams under the rock' (fr. 1, 49, p. 165, above) but so far only individual poetic elements can be recognized while the context remains enigmatic; for example (*Oxyrh. Pap.* 2387, 3, col. 2=fr. 3 Page): '. . . limb-loosening yearning, and as melting as sleep and death she glances hither . . . Astymeleia answers me nothing . . . with a garland (in her hair), like a star which glides (?) through (?) the shining firmament or a golden shoot, or delicate bloom (?) . . . she walks through with delicate foot.' The much mutilated text allows us less to see than to guess at some very remarkable things.

soar aloft to the house of Zeus—which means, art and grace liberate themselves from the heaviness of earth.

Alcman served two masters, and Sparta gratefully requited him for the service he rendered her. A monument was erected to him at the *dromos*, the young man's athletic field, near the *heroon* of the sons of Hippocoon whose heroic death he celebrated in an extant poem. In another sense his deliberately provincial art is realistic and true to life like Archilochus'. To the question of what real life is there are many answers.

(d) *The Lyric of Lesbos*

I. SAPPHO[1]

In turning from Alcman to Sappho we leave the realm of choral lyric for a while[2] and enter that of 'monodic' poetry, that is, poetry recited by a single voice, to which the work of Archilochus belongs. Monody employed different meters, music, and style from those of choral lyric, so that we have not only variation of poetic personalities but also variation of their genres. Nevertheless the circles circumscribed by genres intersect, for each poet used the forms familiar to him for more than one purpose.[3]

Sappho's time is around 590. She was born in the neighborhood of Mytilene, the capital of the island of Lesbos, which was settled by Aeolians. Only a narrow strait separates Lesbos from the coast of Asia Minor, and the Lesbians were therefore immediate neighbors of the Lydian kingdom from whose capital Alcman had gone to Sparta. For Sappho, as for contemporary Greeks generally, Lydia was the land of the strongest military power, the greatest wealth, and the most exquisite elegance in their range of vision.

She came of one of the best families in Lesbos. At the age of six she lost her father. A brother was appointed, as a boy, to serve as cupbearer at official entertainments of the municipality, because of his noble descent and his beauty; Sappho was so proud of this that she

[1] For Sappho and Alcaeus the fragments are numbered according to 'LP,' i.e., *Poetarum Lesbiorum Fragmenta* ed. Edgar Lobel and Denys Page, Oxford, 1955.

[2] For the later history of choral lyric, from Stesichorus to Pindar and Bacchylides, see Chs. VI and VIIIc. below.

[3] Thus Sappho also wrote marriage songs for choruses; the style in the second half of Alcman's maiden song is as simple as that in the monodies of Sappho; in content choral lyric is frequently as personal as monody, and Alcman speaks of himself not only in the third but also in the first person; Archilochus claims to have sung dithyrambs while drunk (fr. 77); and so forth.

spoke of it more than once in her songs. She herself, by her own account, was small and dark and not very pretty. Another brother, Charaxus by name, carried Lesbian wine on a trading voyage to Naucratis in Egypt and fell in love there with a Greek *hetaera* named Doricha; this passion, which cost him his property, brought disgrace upon the family. We possess remains of two poems of prayer which relate to Charaxus. The one (15 LP) wishes him fair weather for a new voyage to Egypt and that '(he arrive at the roadstead) of the proud harbor (?) happily.' The last strophe contains a plea to Aphrodite to deny the girl her sway over Charaxus this time:

Be not so gracious[4] to her as then, goddess Cypris, do not let Doricha boast that now for the second time he came to yearning love.

The other prayer (5 LP) begins as follows:

Cypris and you Nereids, grant that my brother return safe to us, that he accomplish whatever is in his heart, that he amend his former errors and become a joy to his friends, and to his enemies a bane.

In what follows Sappho spoke of the 'former trouble' and how the 'talk of people would cut her heart,' and in the end again prayed to Cypris for her divine assistance.

Sappho was married, and her husband was said to be a wealthy citizen of the island of Andros. She had a daughter (132 LP):

I have a beautiful daughter, in form like to golden flowers, darling Cleïs, for whom I would not give all Lydia nor lovely . . .

About the year 600 Sappho had to leave her native country for some time and seek refuge in Sicily.[5] Possibly from the period of her exile comes a poem to her daughter Cleïs, of which some portions have come down—but so fragmentary that much must remain very uncertain (98 LP):

My own mother [often said] that in her youth if a girl wore a purple ribbon about her head it was thought that she was finely dressed. But for a girl with hair blond as torchlight a wreath woven of fresh flowers is more becoming. Lately [I saw?] a colorful band made in Sardis[6] . . .
  [*lacuna*]
But where I might get a colorful band for you, Cleïs, I do not know . . .

Sappho's poems can be divided into three groups, according to their content and tone: songs for a chorus of girls which sing what the

---

[4] Read πικροτεραν.

[5] Denys Page (*Sappho and Alcaeus*, Oxford 1955, 244f.) dates Sappho's exile between the years 604/3 and 596/5.

[6] Sardis was the capital of the luxurious Lydian realm; from Sardis too came the 'colorful shoes' (cf. Anacreon fr. 358, 3) cf. fr. 39 LP (p. 181, below).

hour demands at festive occasions; songs in which Sappho herself
speaks to men or gods of whatever moves her at the moment; and
third, a poem (16 LP) which meditates and argues like choral lyric.
The second group is represented most abundantly by far.

To the first group belong the marriage songs. In antiquity they
were the most famous of Sappho's poems, and to us too they speak
the most easily. The simplicity of their theme gives purest expression
to a particular side of Sappho's character: her fresh and radiant
warmth, her sweet charm, and her unconstricted naturalness and
straightforwardness.

At the first glow of the evening star, according to ancient usage, the
bride was brought to her groom. Therefore the boys in the chorus
sang (104 b LP):

Evening star, most beautiful of all.

The girls greeted its appearance with different feelings (104 a LP):

Evening star, you bring all that shining dawn scatters; you bring the sheep,
you bring the goat, you bring the child to its mother.

'Why then (as it must have continued) do you now take an innocent
girl from her mother?'[7]

The immaculate purity of the bride is praised in a simile (105 a LP):

Like the sweet apple that reddens on the topmost twig, of the topmost
branches; the apple-pickers have forgotten it—not forgotten it: they
could not reach it.

The charming correction obviates a misapprehension. The girl was
not overlooked, as if she were not pretty enough to arouse the
desires of men, but was too carefully watched to fall victim to their
dishonorable desires. In another song the bride is likened to a
garden flower, and when she shines forth in clear light on her
wedding day it is as if she had not been reared by human beings but
by divine nature itself: the hedged and guarded garden belongs to
the nymphs, and it is by them that the young shoot was watered and
tended with loving care.[8]

The counter-image of an untended girl who has lost her purity is
set up as a foil to the virgin who is now entering matrimony (105 c
LP):[9]

[7] Cf. the parallels Catullus 61, 56ff.; 62, 20ff.; Sophocles *Trach.* 529.

[8] Cf. *Frühgriech Denken*, 44f.

[9] The commentators believe that Sappho fr. 105c LP and Catullus 62, 46f.
allude to the loss of virginity on marriage; but, aside from other considerations,
the new home into which the bride moves would hardly be likened to an untended
hill nor the groom to heedless shepherds (in the plural!). Cf. also Himerius 1, 16
(Sappho fr. 93 Test. Bergk) who contrasts loss of virginity πρὸ ὥρας and καθ' ὥραν.

Like the hyacinth in the mountains trodden down by shepherds' feet, its purple bloom on the ground.

So, after the archaic mode, the value of the gift which the groom is now receiving is emphasized by the contrast with an imaginary counter-image.

The comparison belongs to the style of marriage songs generally.[10] The groom too is celebrated by images of all kinds (115 LP):

To what shall I liken you, dear bridegroom? I could best liken you to a slender sapling.

He is praised (106 LP) as 'towering over all, as Lesbian song over all other songs,' or as a second Achilles (fr. 93 Test. Bergk), indeed as an image of Ares, the god of war himself (111 LP):

Raise the ceiling—Hymenaon—
Raise it, you carpenters—Hymenaon—
The groom is coming like Ares,
And far taller than a tall man.

Today the groom feels himself a hero, a god, a giant, and the others sympathize with him and see him so also; the house must expand in order to contain him.

When the pair sit side by side, the chorus sings (112 LP):

Happy groom, for you the wedding is set in order, as you desired: you have the maiden whom you desired.

And to the bride[11] the chorus says:

Lovely is your form; your eyes are honey-soft, and an alluring charm plays over your beautiful face.

Finally the pair are escorted into the bridal chamber, and the moment has come for the husband to make his youthful wife his own. Before the chamber the bride's girl-friends gather, as if to save the poor child from base violence (Pollux 3, 42). But a friend of the groom stands stoutly at the door and bars their entry. With mock indignation the girls scold the coarse and crude (ἄγροικος fr. 98 Test. Bergk) behavior of the man inside, and tease the doorkeeper. In this case too, his office is reflected in his person; with his firm stance he seems like an uncouth giant (110 LP):

The doorkeeper's feet are seven fathoms long, his shoes of five ox-hides; ten cobblers toiled on them.

From inside the chamber a dialogue seems to be overheard (114 LP):

[10] Cf. B. Snell, *Hermes* 66 (1931), 72.
[11] Choricius states expressly that σοι χαριεν ειδος refers to the bride.

Maidenhood, maidenhood, where are you going, away from me? 'I shall never come back to you, never come back.'

In these marriage songs, and only in them, Sappho develops a kind of popular art, in which words and thoughts correspond as in a rhyme-scheme and are repeated like an echo; the conceptions are of an unpretentious and homely simplicity, and as in a dream, the mood creates its own world according to its own logic.

A narrative poem of which two papyri have restored the final portion to us is probably also to be considered a marriage song. Here the fetching of Hector's bride Andromache, who came to Troy from abroad by sea, is vividly described in much detail. Presumably the song was intended to be sung at a Lesbian marriage and to glorify a celebration of a bride's arrival from abroad, with the glamor of heroic antiquity. [12] The herald Idaeus, familiar from the *Iliad*, comes as a 'speedy messenger' and announces the arrival of the ship which has brought the bride from her country (44 LP):

'Hector and his comrades bring the beautiful-eyed one from sacred Thebe and the ever-flowing waters of Placia, the delicate Andromache, on ships, over the briny sea, and many golden bracelets, and fragrant (?) purple gowns, varied trinkets, countless silver cups, and ivory.' So spoke the herald. Her dear father sprang up nimbly; the report went over the wide-wayed city to friends. Immediately the Trojans harnessed mules to carts with handsome wheels; the whole crowd of women mounted, and of fair-ankled girls. The daughters of Priam rode apart. The men hitched horses to chariots, all the unmarried . . .

After a gap we hear how the young couple, 'like to the gods,' entered Ilion:

Sweet-toned flutes and the lyre mingled, and crashing cymbals; clear-voiced maidens chanted a pure song, the divine sound ascended and the Olympians smiled . . . Everywhere in the streets . . . Mixing bowls and cups . . . Myrrh and cassia and incense mingled. The women shouted out, all the older ones, and all the men sang out a lovely song summoning Paean (Apollo) the far-darter, him of the lovely lyre, and sang of Hector and Andromache, like unto the gods.

Here the poem closes. The song of Hector and Andromache ends with an account of a song on Hector and Andromache; it leads into itself in a circle. [13] The poem is not divided into strophes, but repeats

[12] From the island of Lesbos it was not far to the site of ancient Troy, so that places and heroes of Trojan legend had a neighborly familiarity for the Lesbians.

[13] The song could therefore be repeated *ad libitum*, for at the close which announces, so to speak, a song on Hector and Andromache, this very song of Sappho's on the couple was attached anew. In this way all the spectators whom the escorting processional passed were able to hear the whole. A song of Pindar's (*Nem.* 2) is demonstrably arranged for such a cyclic repetition (see p. 429 n. 6, below).

a single simple verse rather like the epic hexameter. In language too it resembles the epic, from which, indeed, the subject is taken, but in character it is basically different. The epic in its restrained and dignified manner would have called Priam by name and attached some proud epithet; Sappho styles him, out of intimate proximity, from the viewpoint of the bridal couple, as 'dear father.'[14] The broad sweep of Homeric narrative art is here replaced by an artless series of simple statements. All sentences are main clauses, and where the bride's dower is enumerated, even sentence-structure is sacrificed (a 10). As directly as possible, facts are reported in words with a minimum of qualifying periphrasis. The treatment is simple but rich. Many people are mentioned and many things listed. A gay and stirring profusion of events passes rapidly before our eyes; each small action is at once dissolved in another. Everything is enlivened by excitement, illuminated by beauty, and inspirited by sympathetic joy at the happiness of the couple.

The poems of the second group, in which Sappho speaks in her own person, are quieter, soberer, and more powerful than the marriage songs for choruses; they are less naive and radiant, never high-spirited and unrestrained. Most of them are concerned with the young girls whom Sappho gathered about herself. In Lesbos, as also elsewhere, young women of the upper stratum were associated in cult organizations (*thiasoi*);[15] and since religion was not severed from other aspects of life, the Lesbian *thiasoi* were to a large extent institutions for living in which girls under the supervision of a woman were trained for a happy and decorous life for themselves, their future husbands, and the community. For a girl of good family, requirements in manners and education were not slight; this was catered for by the Lesbians' own tradition with its cultivation of poetry and music and its many contacts with the aristocratic and elegant Lydia. In the *thiasoi* the girls enjoyed company and friendship; they worshipped the gods together in song and dance, not only in times of festival but whenever an occasion could be found; the life of the group was under Aphrodite's special grace. The girls showed passionate affection for each other and the woman at their head, and Sappho on her part felt warm attachment to one or another of the growing girls. Such inclinations were not condemned, but acknowledged and considered desirable. Since the early sixth century or thereabouts the Greeks in general regarded homosexual love as more dignified and uplifting than love between the sexes. The untamed craving of that urge which finds fulfilment and satisfaction in the

[14] For this cf. p. 282 and n. 4, below.
[15] See Kurt Latte, *Gött. Gel. Anz.* 207 (1953), 36f.

union of man and woman was not so celebrated in poetry as was homosexual love which feeds unquenchably on the sight, on the physical proximity and spiritual presence of another, and together with him seeks, by common action and united striving, the path to parallel self-fulfilment. Love between a man and boy or youth, between woman and girl, was regarded as the most important educative force, provided it impelled its partners to provide and imitate a model of ideal existence by passionate emulation.

For the marriage of one of the girls of her group Sappho dedicated a personal poem which has a tone very different from that of the choral songs which adorned a festival. It too begins with praise of the groom as equal to the gods, and then turns to the bride (31 LP):

He seems equal to the gods, the man who sits opposite you and hears your sweetly sounding voice nearby and your lovely laughter which has troubled my heart in my breast. For when I look toward you my voice fails, my tongue is broken, a subtle fire runs through my body, with my eyes I see nothing, my ears pound, sweat pours over me, trembling seizes the whole of me, I am as green as meadow-grass, almost I am dead. But everything may be endured,[16] for—

This is Sappho's own felicitation. In keeping with the objective mode of thought of that age, nothing intangible, like the beauty of the festivity or the happiness of the marriage, is named and praised; for Sappho all that is divine and magnificent is contained in the three persons present. The man looks to her like a god; the marriage-pact which has been concluded is made manifest in the intimate conversation between the two (otherwise, according to prevalent custom a girl might not sit next to a man); the charm of the bride comes to life in her voice; her loveliness transforms itself into love— into the reality of Sappho's ardent love for her.[17] Sappho's passion too is seen as event, not emotion. Sappho does not wallow in emotion but reports events. After the ultimate effect, the swoon into almost death, has been mentioned, there is no summing-up formula like 'So much do I love you.' Everything is contained in the facts.

Everything stands upon one and the same level. No depths of the soul are opened up; the thing itself is discovered in its phenomena. The tremblings by which Sappho was permeated were not, for her,

---

[16] The text has τολματον 'can be endured', and not τολματεον 'must be endured' (as it is generally translated). Cf. E.-M. Hamm, *Grammatik zu S. und Alkaios* (Berlin, 1957), 142, 5.

[17] Such charm and such susceptibility to it were regarded as an honorable gift from Aphrodite to those distinguished by them. For power to inspire love cf. Sappho 112, 5 LP (to the bride), and for the power to feel it Pindar fr. 123, 4 (p. 504f. below).

'symptoms' of something, to wit love, but they *are* love, they are the effect that the presence of the girl works in Sappho, especially in the hour of festivity and parting; body and soul are still one. If we apply to this poem our own modern perspectives, we misunderstand it. It may even appear to us that Sappho is expressing jealousy of the husband. In fact the words conceal nothing: Sappho does not mean more than she says. The description moves on one level plane: without divisions or gradations it glides from one person to the next and lists one after the other all the things that she underwent. Our text breaks off at the point where the speaker has begun to reflect upon the event with a certain objectivity.[18]

Another song shows Sappho suing for love. It is not to the girl that she speaks, however, but to Love itself, Aphrodite; Aphrodite is to help her win the girl's favor. As was customary in songs of prayer, Sappho reminds the goddess how she had graciously fulfilled a similar prayer on an earlier occasion; she pictures the past benevolence in detail in the hope that with the renewal in words a repetition of the fact also could be conjured up (1 LP):

Immortal Aphrodite of the manycolored throne, cunning daughter of Zeus, I beseech you, lady, break not my heart with pain and grief.

But come now as once you hearkened to my supplication and left your father's house and yoked your golden chariot. Beautiful sparrows brought you

Swiftly over the dark earth, wings whirring through the air of heaven. Speedily they came. And you smiled, with countenance immortal, and asked

What had befallen and why had I summoned you? What would I most desire to take place, in the madness of my heart? 'Whom should I now sway to your love?

Who, Sappho, has wronged you? Even if she shuns you now, soon she will pursue; even if she refuses your gifts she will give them; if she does not love you,

Soon she will love you, even if she does not wish to.' Come now too, relieve me of my grievous woe. Bring about what my heart craves, fight on my side!

Again a spiritual thing is seen in concrete form. But whereas the preceding poem could address its statements to physically existing persons, this time the appearance of the goddess is, as far as we can make out, nothing but a creation of the fancy. Had Sappho perhaps actually seen an embodiment of Aphrodite in a vision and thought

[18] Reflection from a distance will be encountered also in fr. 16 (p. 186, below).

she heard her voice?[19] But a vision would be limited to what was visible and audible to Sappho. Instead, the descent of the goddess is dramatized, as in epic: her departure from her father's golden house, the long journey; moreover, the smile on the immortal face responding to the need of the mortal woman, and the speech which is no reflection of Sappho's wish, but conceived and felt in the person of Aphrodite. Sappho experienced what we should call an inward event, a transition from pangs of torment to confident hope, which was later realized, which she understood and rendered in words appropriate to her belief in the divine power of love. Like the epic poets (p. 64–69, above) she reads into the event its metaphysical meaning.[20] But unlike the epics, nowhere in Sappho do the physical and metaphysical event diverge; there is only a single view of the event, and it reveals everything. This is involved in the flat character of the archaic mode of viewing, a mode which might be styled one of absolute presentness. Just as in respect to content the spiritual event coincides with the (imagined) physical event, so in the manner of presentation there is only room for one view, but that an all-embracing one. In continuous discourse everything is placed in one line and in the foreground.[21] The dimension of depth that is given by intensification is also lacking; it is supplied by massed quantity. The goddess does not ask 'urgently' or promise 'expressly,' but she asks the same thing and promises the same thing repeatedly.[22] Sappho on her part is not now addressing a prayer of this kind to Aphrodite for the first time; again and again the goddess must help her in like need. Each time the passion dominates her whole being, but its object changes; for her emotion is not attached to the accidental and the

[19] See C. M. Bowra, *Greek Lyric Poetry* (2nd ed., Oxford, 1961) 202ff.

[20] Cf. fr. 2 and 95, p. 179 and 184f. below. But apart from the deviation from the epic mode now to be mentioned, there is another difference. When a god in the *Iliad* comes in person (e.g. 13, 59ff.) to give a man special powers, this happens at the time and place that the powers are used. We would then expect that Aphrodite's epiphany, so vividly seen, would take place at the instant when Sappho approached the beloved girl anew, and now successfully, in order to overcome the hesitation of the shy young thing; at that moment Sappho felt the power of successful wooing awakening in her, and that the mighty goddess 'herself was campaigning at her side.' Instead, the epiphany took place in a solitary hour of prayer; and it was not the fulfilment of her desire that was then granted Sappho, but the promise of early fulfilment. Anything further remains outside the circle in which the account of the epiphany moves. Framed by the new and now actual plea for help, the scene is 'lyrically' enclosed in itself.

[21] Cf. *Frühgriech Denken* 47–50.

[22] See p. 150 n. 49 and 153 n. 3, above. Similarly in the marriage songs the importance of the groom (111) and the doorkeeper (110) are seen under the quantitative image of gigantic size (p. 173, above).

peculiar in the individual girl, but is applicable to the delicate loveliness of noble youth which always renews and repeats itself. So too,
by virtue of Sappho's inexhaustible gift, her love is constantly
renewed; wave upon wave comes and goes.

Every separation, however, brings bitter pain (94 LP):

In good faith, I wish I were dead. She left me, crying bitterly, and said
to me: 'How terrible it is for us, Sappho; truly I go unwilling.' I answered:
'Go and think of me, happily. You know how I worshipped you. If not
I wish to remind you what fair and lovely things we enjoyed. With many
garlands of violets and sweet roses on your tresses you sat by me, on your
soft neck many necklaces woven of flowers. Your hair you drenched with
myrrh, with *brentheion* (your face and body) and with royal Lydian spices,
laid upon soft coverlets . . .

to still your longing . . . No sacred grove nor shrine was there which we
did not fill with the sound of our songs and music of the lyre.[23]

The distress of parting from a beloved girl is bound up in the song
with the sweet pleasure of memory. The two emotions do not fuse
into a gentle melancholy, but each is savoured in turn. In both
women the sorrow of parting speaks a language that could not be
simpler—the language of absolute reality which requires no veil.
Protestations like 'in good faith' and 'truly' are frequent in Sappho.
In the midst of sadness there sounds the Greek valediction, 'Be happy,'
that is, I wish you joy.

It was not merely things of the spirit that brought light and joy
to Sappho's circle. In addition to singing together at holy places and
to the pleasure which the girls took in each other's company, there
are refinements of sensuous pleasure. All the senses participate, even
the tactile sense of physical contact. Limbs are stretched out on soft
coverlets, the body is drenched in perfume, and flowers are wreathed
about head and neck. The girls also enjoy the quiet beauty of a
hallowed precinct in the still hour of evening (2 LP):

(Worshipful Cyprian goddess Aphrodite—descend to our festal band)
down from heavenly heights,

Here to the pure temple where stands a grove of apple-trees and altars
smoking with frankincense. Here cool water rustles through the apple
branches.

The whole place is shaded with rose bushes, and sleep flows down from
the shimmering leaves.

Here blooms a meadow where horses pasture, (?) rich with blooms of
spring, and the wind breathes sweet fragrance—

[23] The last two lines of the translation render the remains of two strophes in the
original. The end is missing.

Come here, Cyprian lady: pour us nectar, flavored with high festive joy, in golden cups. Be our cupbearer![24]

Apple trees were planted in Aphrodite's grove because the apple was regarded as a symbol of love;[25] in the marriage song too the bride is likened to an apple. In her shrine the Cyprian goddess would entertain the girls with gifts appropriate to her. In companies of men cheerful songs praised the altar smoking with incense in the midst of the revellers, the viands with which the table before them was richly furnished, and the abundance of good wine ready to hand. Men called upon the god of wine and other gods in hymns to bless the festival and its participants with grace;[26] and attractive boys, alluring as Eros himself, filled the office of pouring. Sappho does not speak of eating, but of the loveliness of nature about them, and the drink which is poured is for them not mere wine but Aphrodite's nectar, because nectar released the pleasing sensibilities whose giver is the goddess.[27] Thus the girl who serves the wine becomes an embodiment of Aphrodite: 'Be thou our cup-bearer!'

Nature in its gentler manifestations, as meadow and garden, as babbling brook and grove, was inwardly enjoyed by Sappho and her maidens. Sappho tells how 'she watched a tender girl picking flowers' (122 LP). Her poems are wont to show people in action, at work, in graceful movement. Just as, in keeping with the rules of archaic style, her songs never pause in their course but constantly hurry forward, so in what they depict everything is event and happening. On the power which dwells in flowers as an adornment Sappho instructs one of her girls as follows: (81 LP)

Dika, put wreathes on your pretty hair, weaving shoots of dill with your tender hands. For the blessed Charites look only on her who wears flowers, but from the ungarlanded they turn away.

Dika may have been proposing to make herself ready for some religious observance, at which she would pray the gods for grace (*charis*). And grace is imparted by the *Charites*.

[24] Almost throughout much remains uncertain. In general I follow W. Theiler and P. Von der Mühll (*Mus. Helvet.* 3 [1946] 22ff)—The anaphora of εν (also in v. 7 ενι, cf. Xenophanes 1, 7) recurs in the description of festivity in Pindar's *Cerberus* (fr. 70b, 10ff.); the wild noises in the dithyramb are here replaced by the charms of tranquility. V. 11f. shows why Sleep lies in wait for Zeus in the branches of a tree in *Il.* 14, 286–91.

[25] Cf. M. Fränkel, *Archäolog. Zeitung* 31 (1874), 36ff. and B. O. Foster, *Harvard Studies in Class. Philol.* 10 (1899) 39ff.

[26] Cf. e.g. Xenophanes, fr. 1 (p. 326f., below).

[27] A drinking-song of Bacchylides (fr. 20b 8) says 'a presentiment of Cypris flavors the gifts of Dionysus.'—By cups of 'gold' Sappho does not mean the physical material; all divine appurtenances are called 'golden' in Greek poetry.

One song shows flower-studded fields by the light of the moon (96, 11 LP, p. 184, below). Unlike Pindar, Sappho does not praise the overpowering sunlight of the day, but the moon and the nocturnal company of stars (34 LP):

As the stars round about Selene's beauty again hide her bright form when at her full she shines silver bright on earth—28

Birds are the only members of the animal kingdom to appear in the fragments. Sappho hails 'Spring's herald, nightingale of lovely voice' (136 LP)—speaks of the 'swallow, Pandion's daughter' (135 LP)—the swallow was regarded as a transformed woman—and says of frightened doves, 'Their heart grew cold, and their wings drooped' (42 LP).

Sappho, like Alcman, calls by name the objects and accessories which her carefully groomed girls wore and tells us where they came from, but she never mentions food. She speaks of various kinds of scent, flowers, wreathes, garments. One girl 'clothed her feet in colorful purple shoes, beautiful Lydian work' (39 LP); a friend from Phocaea had 'sent as a fine gift perfumed (?) purple towels' (101 LP).29

Among the beautiful things of which Sappho reminds her friend at the hour of parting (94, 25ff. LP) is the service of the heavenly beings. These young people were not called upon in dull credulity to observe rigid, mysterious, even dangerous rites. But rather the maidens gladly went to the holy places in order to worship there, and in festive attire to sing a new and pious song to their mistress, which would please gods and men.

In a holy precinct which contained altars of the three gods, Hera, Zeus, and Dionysus,30 the chorus (or perhaps Sappho alone) sang a song of four strophes which appear to have concluded with a plea that a certain voyage might prosper; and the prayer appealed to a precedent from the time of the Trojan War. The first three strophes (with free conjectural supplements) read somewhat as follows (17 LP):

At my supplication, goddess Hera, may your gracious favor be present to help me as it once prospered the proud Atreid kings

When they finally vanquished Troy; and when their fleet sailed from

---

28 μεν and οππστα show that a simile was presented in paratactic form. Fr. 94 Diehl is hardly Sappho's [but cf. now Benedetto Marzullo *Studi di poesia eolica*, Florence, 1958, 1–60, who thinks the poem geniune; on this see Max Treu, *Gnomon* (1960), 745f.].

29 Catullus 12, 12–17 is apparently an echo of this passage. The thought that the affection is more to be prized than the material recalls Sappho.

30 Alcaeus speaks of the establishment of the sanctuary in 129 LP; see p. 191f., below.

Asia's coast they landed here, but no wind vouchsafed them homeward
voyage
   Until they invoked you and Zeus in prayer and the son of Thyone,
handsome Bacchus. So now . . . as once of old.[31]

The following fragment points to the legendary origin of a cult usage
(*Inc.* 16, p. 294 LP)

So once Cretan women rhythmically danced with delicate feet about the
fair altar and trod upon meadow flowers softly sprouting.[32]

Such activity took place at night also (154 LP; *cf.* 43 LP?):

The moon shone full, and the girls took their places to dance around the
altar.

The annual celebration of Adonis' death and resurrection was the
occasion for a dramatic lament for the beloved of Cytherea (i.e.
Aphrodite), of which the opening is preserved (140 LP):

He is dying, Cytherea, this tender Adonis. What shall we do? Beat your
breasts, girls, and tear your tunics.

So far as we can judge from the remains, Aphrodite was the goddess
to whom Sappho's circle showed the greatest devotion. In a dream
Sappho conversed with the goddess of Cyprus (134 LP). Eros too
'clad in a purple mantle descended' to the poetess (54 LP). In her
own name or in that of the chorus she invokes the 'rosy-armed, pure
Charites, daughters of Zeus, hither' (53 LP), so that they may bless
the song then beginning (cf. 128 LP).
   Sappho's relations with the girls were changeful and dramatic,
but without the biting hardness of Archilochus. The polar opposite
of affection is not enmity, but indifference and oblivion (129 LP) or
shifting to another. 'I am not one to bear a grudge, but my temperament is easy-going,' says Sappho herself (120 LP). And yet something
like Archilochus' experience (67b) befell her also (26 LP):

Those whom I treated kindly do me, (Atthis), gravest injury.

On her part she assures the group of her loyalty (41 LP):

To you, the beautiful, my temper shall never change.

   The old image of the tree assailed by storm is given a different

---

   [31] The emphatic πλασιον which begins the song indicates that Sappho is praying
for the assistance of the goddess (cf. Euripides, *Or.* 1159, and παρίσταμαι *Od.* 13,
301); to supply οναρ (v. 1) is wrong in every respect. In v. 2, e.g., σα χ[αρις ηδ᾽
αρωγα], cf. C. Theander, *Eranos* 41 (1943) 144ff.
   [32] It is not certain that Sappho is the author of this poem or that the third verse
belongs to it.

turn in Sappho. In the *Iliad* it is used of steadfastness against attack (12, 132ff.), or for the fall of a warrior brought down by his enemy (17, 53ff,); now it is applied to the spiritual experience of an overwhelming passion (47 LP):

Eros has shattered my spirit like a storm in the mountains which assails the oaks.

To the divine compulsion which assails her she surrenders with that knowledge of helplessness which is characteristic of Greek lyric[33] (130f. LP):

Again limb-loosening Eros overwhelms me, the bitter-sweet, before whom we are helpless, Atthis; loathing of me has come over your mind: you fly to Andromeda.

A violent oscillation between bitter emotions and sweet was a basic element of lyric of this kind from the beginning: what is new here is that the opposing qualities are experienced in the same act. The tension is contained in one and the same emotion. The notion of love evokes its opposite 'hate,' but hate is moderated: Atthis does not hate Sappho, but she hates taking interest in Sappho, for she has turned to Andromeda. Andromeda was a rival of Sappho and also headed a group of girls.[34] Sappho alludes to Andromeda when she addresses a girl, perhaps Atthis, as follows (57 LP):

What a vulgar woman has infatuated your wits? She does not know how to draw her dress over her ankles.

Painting shows us what is meant. The long undergarment was gathered with the left hand so that pleated folds were formed on the left side of the body; but propriety demanded that the legs remain covered down to the ankles.

Sappho addressed many another song to Atthis. One began (49 LP):

I loved you, Atthis, long ago—

and it must have continued 'and now my love burns hotter than ever.' Then Sappho's memory slips back to the time when Atthis first came to her:

When you appeared to me, a small and unattractive child.

A poem of which a considerable piece is preserved makes Atthis form part of a new constellation. It appears that Sappho is speaking of

[33] See p. 151, above.

[34] Another time Sappho greets Andromeda politely and with punctilio (155 LP); we are told that the tone is ironic.

a common friend[35] who has left the group to move to Sardis (96 LP):

—from Sardis turning her thoughts hither often, how we clung (?) to one another. She thought you equal to the goddesses
And took greatest pleasure in your song. But now she shines among Lydian women, as when the sun sinks,
The rosy-fingered moon, outshining the stars, pours her light over the salt sea and equally on flowery fields;
Lovely dew pours forth, roses bloom, and soft thyme and flower-like honey-lotus. Often in her roaming she thinks of lovely Atthis,
Longing in her fine spirit, and in sorrow her heart is consumed that we should come to her—
It is not easy for us to be like the goddesses in lovely form but (?) you have—
[after 3 lines:] Aphrodite poured nectar from a golden vessel.[36]

The simile of the moon whose bright glow extinguishes the light of the stars is here expanded to a whole landscape-painting. From Lesbos we see the moon, still ruddy from the mist of the horizon, ascending above the Lydian coast. Its light pours over the strait and over the flowery fields and gardens of Lesbos—now it is no longer a simile but a picture of the light in which the woman over there thinks of her friend here. It was a pretty custom of the ancients, upon viewing a handsome landscape, to think of those who were far away in body but near to one's heart.[37]

It was in Sappho's nature to react passionately and to be driven to extremity by crisis. Parted from a friend, she wishes for death (94 LP, p. 179, above). In another song she spoke to one Gongyla of something which had embittered her life, for so the text seems to carry on (95 LP):

Would you (hear) proof (comprehensible) to anyone? Hermes (just now came to fetch me and) I said, (I go willingly where you lead me) for truly, by the blessed goddess, I have no more joy (in life). I long to die and see the dewy lotus-banks of Acheron—[38]

Sappho had swooned in pain and half died, and her heart had consented to death. She sees and describes the event in the form familiar to her mode of thought. The divine guide who leads people down to the realm of death had come to her, and she had told him

[35] The word αριγνωτα remains puzzling in the incomplete (v. 3) and corrupt (v. 4f.) context. On τὴν ἀρίγνωτον γυναῖκα in a new fragment of Anacreon see p. 301f., below.
[36] On this see the closing strophe of fr. 2 (p. 180, above); here we cannot even guess at the connection.
[37] Cf. B. Snell, Athen. Mitteil. 51, 159ff.
[38] For the interpretation of this shattered text cf. Gött. Gel. Anz. 1928, 269ff.

that she was ready to follow him.[39] Even the annihilation she desires becomes a tangible picture; it appears to her as an invitingly beautiful landscape, as a river with lotus-blossoms and dewy green banks. Even the regions of darkness are illuminated by the vital force of the woman who is weary of life.

That the god visited her and that she spoke such words to him is for Sappho undoubted reality; she can adduce the fact as binding proof, to confirm the greatness of her trouble. She associates with the gods of her world as did the epic heroes. But for her the gods do not stand in another, separate space behind human existence; in her own life she encounters the powers to whose operation she stands so wholly open. This is how she addresses a dream that visited her (63 LP):

O dream, who wander through black night—when sleep (holds us fast), sweet god, powerfully from sorrow (you have released me).

Sappho does not feel herself a solitary soul, in exile in an alien, opaque, and predominantly hostile world, but as a natural being in the midst of the rest of nature, accessible to all that befalls her. 'Harmony with nature': Stoicism sought it by way of knowledge and discipline, with cold energy and brilliant dialectic when Hellenism had begun to dissolve; in Sappho it is simply accepted as true. She converses familiarly, speaking and being spoken to, with powers as with human beings. That is why her lyric is so natural; for early lyric is entirely, or almost entirely, talking to someone.

We are led a step further by a single poem of a different kind. Short as it is, its content includes all the elements of spacious choral lyric; meditation takes pride of place over the expression of momentary emotion. The form is no different from the others; the poem is written in the strophes called 'Sapphic' (16 LP):

Some say a chariot host is the fairest sight on the black earth, and some say infantry, some a fleet; but I say—what one loves.

It is very easy to make this clear to everyone. Helen, fairest of all mortal women, deserted the best husband, and embarked

For the voyage to Troy, and forgot her child and thought no more of her dear parents. (Through love Cypris) seduced her.

[39] An Attic artist has represented the death of a maiden in the same spirit on a beautiful lekythos with white background. Hermes sits waiting on the rock of the base, and raises his hand in a gesture; the girl stands before him and presses a diadem into her hair to make ready for her last journey. Cf. *Münchner Jahrb. der bild. Kunst*, N.F. II (1925) Heft 3/4 Plate 1ff. and Buschor's text; P. E. Arias and M. Hirmer, *A History of Greek Vase Painting* (London and New York, 1962), plates XLI, XLII.

(In the goddess' hand every man's heart is pliable, our thought tractable.) So she has recalled to my mind the faraway Anactoria

Whose lovely step I should rather see and the play of light upon her shining face than Lydian chariots and warring soldiers under arms.

The question of what is fairest on earth is answered twice in this poem, in general terms at the end of the first strophe, and with reference to the speaker in the last. Sappho finds the highest beauty not in the imposing parade of vaunting power,[40] but in the intimate charm of a beloved person;[41] and not in qualities which all men alike admire, but in what everyone loves and wishes for himself. All Sappho's poetry is based on this premise;[42] and Archilochus too had spoken to the effect that he cared more for subjective and personal value (or lack of it) than for the objective and general.[43] It was just such a position that underlay the separation of lyric from epic.

For us whatever we love and desire is beautiful, says Sappho, but what we wish to love is not in our power. The nature of man is ephemeral, and our thinking is wax in the hands of destiny and the gods. Helen possessed what any woman might wish for, and yet she gave everything up to follow a foreign lover because passion forced her to do so. The same Aphrodite who constrained Helen to seek happiness far away, reminded Sappho of Anactoria far away and thrilled her with ardent longing for the sight of the beloved girl.

Without doubt the experience was the occasion of the poem. Sappho was overcome by a wave of yearning; then she reflected on what had oppressed her and reduced it to its underlying principle. After the manner of choral lyric she begins her song by proposing a general thought (gnomê),[44] and then illustrates the opinion with a mythical example; later, as a second confirmation, comes Sappho's own experience. Intermediate between the myth and the present event, again as in choral lyric, are new gnomic utterances, expressing piety towards the gods.[45] Unlike the other poems, this song keeps

---

[40] Horses and ships as types of pride and ostentation recur in Pindar fr. 221 and *Isthm.* 5, 4f. (see p. 486, n. 11, below).

[41] Her own child is more precious than all rich Lydia (132 LP, p. 172, above).

[42] The thought recurs in Aristotle in a simplified form (*De Part. Anim.* I 644b 33: ὥσπερ καὶ τῶν ἐρωμένων τὸ τυχὸν καὶ μικρὸν μόριον κατιδεῖν ἥδιόν ἐστιν ἢ πολλὰ ἕτερα καὶ μεγάλα δι' ἀκριβείας ἰδεῖν κ.τ.λ.).

[43] See pp. 137–40, above.

[44] On the form 'Others say . . . I say' cf. Simonides fr. 4 and 48; Timocreon fr. I and Horace, *Carm.* I, 7. On this and on this fragment generally, cf. *Frühgriech Denken* 90–94.

[45] Among the Lesbians too, then, there were songs fairly close to choral lyric. This helps us to understand historically Horace's Roman odes and their Pindaric

its distance from the experience, and speaks of it only at the end.

The implications of Sappho's astonishing thesis are very far-ranging; it contains the potentiality of overthrowing any absolute value. For all values which are to be attained are subsumed under the conception of the beautiful, so that 'the beautiful' becomes the yardstick for practical activity.[46] According to Sappho, Helen, herself the most beautiful and most desired of all women, found life with Paris more beautiful than the life she had previously led; and she thought and behaved as she did because she was seized by love. We do not desire what is in itself beautiful, but we find what we desire beautiful. This anticipates half of the dictum of the sophist Protagoras, according to which man is the measure of all things. Not infrequently, in this age, poetry precedes philosophy and prepares the way for it.

This is the only poem of Sappho's that we know in which there is more than one level of feeling. All others bear the stamp of absolute and direct contemporaneity. Hence for her poetry as for that of Archilochus (n. 43, above) the category of the present, with its opposite the distant, takes on a special importance. Again and again we hear of touch[47] and sight, of calling and coming, of intimate association and conversation; of seeking and avoiding, of parting and separation, of longing, remembering, and forgetting. Within one and the same stratum poetry and actuality form a perfect union—a vintage in which there is neither scum nor lees.

This poetry is infused by the life of the group and its members as it is lived, and in turn guides and refines their lives. Their artistic efforts contributed to the victory of sense, consistency, order and propriety,[48] over dullness, disorder, accident, and coarseness. In such a spirit Sappho wrote and lived in the midst of the girls whom she shaped and loved, in whom she rejoiced and suffered. Her art was a sacred office. When her daughter burst into tears upon a death in her own house, the poetess bade Cleïs be silent (150 LP):

for in a house that serves the Muses it is not right for mourning to be heard; such is not seemly for us.

element (cf. Ed. Fraenkel, 'Das Pindargedicht des Horaz', *Heidelberger Sitzungsber.* 1933, p. 22f.)

[46] Cf. p. 155–8, above on Tyrtaeus.

[47] The tactile sense has been mentioned above (p. 179). Perhaps we should add *Inc.* 16 p. 294 LP (p. 182, above): the soles of the girls' feet feel the soft freshness of the meadow flowers, and its counterpart fr. 105c, crude unfeeling feet trample the wild hyacinths.

[48] If the first and last strophes of fr. 16 are taken together it appears that even when the poetess is speaking professedly about beauty, actually she is rather concerned with charm, with what is revealed as attractive and lovely in movement (p. 180, above) and in the play of light.

Though Sappho's lifework was devoted to the passing day, her poetry survived her. Sappho herself did not expect otherwise. Aware of her own worth, she addressed the following words to a rich woman (55 LP):[49]

When you are dead you will lie forgotten; there will be no memory of you, for you have no share in the roses of Pieria. You will wander unrecognized among the bodiless shades, far from the light of day.

But to the poetess graced by the Muses of Pieria Aphrodite has appeared and announced (65 +60(c) +87 (16) LP):[50]

A great gift you possess: remembrance among all men on whom the shining sun looks down. Everywhere your fame will . . . even beside Acheron you will . . .[51]

Like Archilochus Sappho too is one of the timeless figures of early Greek literature. But whereas Archilochus as man and warrior assailed respectable tradition at the turn of the age, in turn victor and vanquished, dejected and triumphant, Sappho's feminine nature knows only devotion to grace, the pain of spiritual passion, and perceptive intelligence. In the course of the two generations which separated Sappho from Archilochus, the new attitude for which Archilochus joined battle had become a secure and self-evident possession.

In Sappho's enchanting poetry the historical movement comes to rest for an instant; but it is not deliberately blocked, as it is in Homer; it stops because all forces are poised. The topical is allied with the eternal in perfect balance. Such reconcilement without struggle is little short of a miracle. There is nothing like it even among Sappho's contemporaries.

2. ALCAEUS

At the same time as Sappho, and also on the island of Lesbos, Alcaeus wrote his songs in metrical forms identical with or similar to hers. But Alcaeus made very different use of the same art and tradition, and not only because his life, in complete contrast to Sappho's, was directed to activities and objectives alien to poetry.

Alcaeus grew up in the midst of political agitation and battles in which his brothers had leading roles, and he himself was devoted to

[49] Cf. Aristides XXVIII, 51 Keil, vol. 2 p. 508 Dindorf.
[50] Cf. *Gött. Gel. Anz.* 1928, 269.
[51] Cf. preceding note.

the 'work' of war. His house[1] was full of weapons for his own use and for equipping other members of his political group (357 LP), and he depicts the spectacle with pleasure in these eloquent verses:

With bronze my broad house glitters: the hall is wholly decked with war, with shining helmets: from their tops wave white horse-hair plumes, the proud ornaments of a warrior's head. The hooks in the wall are hung with greaves of glittering bronze, protection against the sharp javelin; quilted coats of new linen and hollow shields lie ready to hand. Here are swords from Chalcis: here is many a belt and tunic. All this cannot be neglected, when we have once set our hand to the work.

In keeping with the archaic mode, Alcaeus identifies the way of life, which he celebrates by naming the concrete implements he employs —just as Sappho does. But where in Sappho can we find anything comparable to this detailed inventory and the practical spirit which informs it![2] And where would she vaunt her possessions with such satisfaction as our young nobleman does here![3]

The tranquil manner in which Alcaeus here catalogues his stock of weapons does not recur in other fragments; on the contrary, many have a vigorous and excited tone. Horace once characterizes the poetry of Alcaeus as singing in fuller tones than Sappho's the hardships of sea, or exile, and of war (*Carm.* 2. 13, 27). These are very different things from those which received Sappho's attention. Of the multitude of subjects with which Alcaeus' poetry dealt and of the elemental strength with which they were put into words, recent papyrus finds give a more impressive picture than was previously possible. The strong light in which everything is seen and sketched simplifies the pictures of persons and events; simple too are the

[1] That Alcaeus fr. 357 speaks of his own house is clear from the words of Athenaeus. For explanation cf. *Frühgriech. Denken* 52 and 82. The form αρη (v. 1) is difficult, but παισα κεκοσμηται στεγα requires an instrumental case of general content, and εργον τοδε at the end, i.e. ἔργον Ἄρηος (cf. *Il.* 11, 734) would have nothing to refer to if αρη is deleted. Perhaps we should write αρευι κοσμηται (for the tense cf. κοσμεῖσθαι, Plato, *Laws* 7, 796c; κοσμούμενον Dionys. Hal., *Antiq. Rom.* 11, 4, 7).

[2] With this fragment we might compare Sappho's enumeration of gifts at the joyous wedding celebration (44, 8–10 LP, p. 174, above); or also the verses in which Archilochus speaks of his soldiering and his spear (fr. 2 and 1, p. 152f., above); or Homeric scenes of arming with their symbolism of war (p. 38f., above).

[3] An ancient writer on music, Heraclides Ponticus, characterizes the Aeolians, in order to explain their music, as follows: 'Their nature is marked by a proud and strutting bearing and a touch of braggadocio; with this is connected their predilection for racing-stables and magnificent entertainments. They are not crafty but proud and straightforward. They have an inclination to drink, sensuality, and wanton living' (Athen. 14, 624d). Our fragments of the Aeolian Alcaeus present a similar picture; but we hear nothing of racing and hospitality.

feelings of the speakers. In contrast to Sappho's absorption in her own experience, in contrast to her subtlety and patient discipline in composition, here there prevails an uncontrolled wilfulness of spontaneous sensibility and unrestrained communication. But the definiteness and concreteness of all that is said is similar in both.

The battles in which Alcaeus took part were in large part internal dissensions. The noble families, to which Alcaeus himself belonged, fought against one another and against tyrants; various individuals and factions allied themselves with one another or opposed one another in constant alternation. In one poem Alcaeus pictures, under the image of a voyage, the confused and critical situation when a man named Myrsilus attempted to win sole rule for himself; the ship here means the ship of state[4] (326 and 208 col. 11 LP):

I do not understand the conflict of the winds: on this side a great wave comes rolling up, on that side another, and we in the middle, are borne along in our black ship, struggling with the tempest in utmost need. In the ship the water is over the mast-step, the sail is worn threadbare, with long rents ripping it to shreds the shrouds are hanging loose.

The perilous situation is pictured with many short, separate statements of detail; all the damage which the ship has suffered is described in sequence, just as Sappho describes her feelings. In another piece which may belong to the same poem a solution to the difficulty is found; here too the ship is symbolic, and Alcaeus appears to have suggested that it had grown old and weary after many voyages (73+306 (14) and (16) LP, much restored):

The freight is all jettisoned, the vessel heels far over as it scuds along, the breakers beat against the gunwales. To struggle longer against storm and surge—our ship (?) is no longer able: it must split on the lurking reefs. So it stands with the ship and the play of the waves. Be that forgotten, friends, and dismissed; I will seek pleasure with you, and drink together with Bycchis. Other things we shall leave for another day though someone . . .

Wine and the company of the handsome lad Bycchis will dispel care.

The same simile recurs in another poem; after two strophes it is tacitly abandoned, and instead of the language of images we hear tones which recall Tyrtaeus (6 LP):

Now the sea rises higher than ever before (?). I fear it will keep us busy

[4] The later so frequent image of the 'ship' of state first appears in Alcaeus. It serves the purpose of emphasizing a truth easily forgotten in the antagonism of interests and desires: that all members of the political community are subject to the same fate if intestine quarrel causes catastrophe to the state.

bailing, for into the ship rush (waves upon waves, driven by the wind).
       [two lines wanting]
We must strengthen our craft quickly and make for safe harborage.

Let no one now be struck with timorous wavering. Before our eyes there
stands a great (reward). Remember your former (deeds)! Now a man can
prove his worth.

We will not stain with base reproach our noble ancestors who rest in the
earth. (They have freely given us) our city—

In what follows Alcaeus speaks of the 'monarchy' of Myrsilus, which
must not be yielded to. Myrsilus died, and Alcaeus exulted (332 LP):

Now must a man get drunk, drink more than you can and want: Myrsilus
is dead.

But the strife continued. The most important opponent of Alcaeus
was Pittacus, who is counted among the seven sages. First, in alliance
with Alcaeus' brothers, Pittacus overthrew a tyrant: later he led the
army of the Mytileneans in a war with the Athenians for the possession of Sigeum, a coastal town on the Asiatic shore, valuable for its
position at the entry to the Sea of Marmora. Alcaeus also served in
this war, and sent a poem back to a friend at home in which he
reports that he lost his weapons in a defeat, but had saved himself by
flight; his shield the victorious Athenians had hung up in the temple
of their goddess Athene at Sigeum (428 LP). It would be interesting
if we possessed the text of this poem and could compare it with the
corresponding poem of Archilochus (fr. 6, p. 137, above).

After the war internal dissensions began anew. Alcaeus and
Pittacus were now on different sides: the poet lost and had to
withdraw to the country, far from the capital. A papyrus find has
restored to us the remains of the verses in which he described his
'exile' (130 LP):

. . . unhappy I live a peasant existence and yearn to hear the assembly
when the herald convokes it, Agesilaidas,

and the council. What my father and my father's father . . . possessed
as members of this citizen-body, who do each other ill, from this I have
been ejected

afar as an exile; like Onymacles I have settled here alone . . .

Three lines later Alcaeus' mood undergoes an astonishing change,
and the poet depicts his present refuge as a delightful resort:

. . . to the precinct of the blessed gods . . . I trod the black earth . . .
now I dwell stepping clear of all misfortune,

there where the Lesbian women move about in trailing robes for the judgment of their beauty⁵ and round about echoes the resounding cry of women which they utter loud for the sacred annual festival . . .

There follows a badly mutilated concluding strophe, apparently on the question when the Olympian gods would put a period to the poet's many afflictions.

If he could no longer fight with weapons at this time, he could do so with his verses and his imprecations, as in this petition to the same trinity to which Sappho (fr. 17 LP, p. 181, above) appealed (129, 9ff. LP):

> With gracious mind hearken to our prayer, release us from our present pain, let this bitter exile end!

> But that son of Hyrras (Pittacus) let the Erinys overtake, by whom we then took sacred oath that we would never betray (?) any of our friends

> But rather lie dead on the ground smitten by enemy hand (?), or else slay them and wrest our people from slavery.

> But this that fat-guts (Pittacus) took not to heart; frivolously he trod the oath underfoot in order now to do himself well at the people's expense.⁶

In his invectives, then, Alcaeus used no refined language; ancient philology amused itself by collecting seven coarse epithets which he applied to Pittacus: 'fat-guts' here, and 'cloven-hoofed' and the like elsewhere (429 LP).

Eventually the people of Lesbos grew weary of strife and elected Pittacus as arbiter (αἰσυμνάτας) with full powers to organize the disrupted state at his discretion. The poet was beside himself at the appointment of his adversary as director of the state (348 LP):

> That base-born scoundrel, Pittacus, they have chosen with one accord to be tyrant over the city that lacks gall, that is oppressed by an evil daemon.

In Alcaeus' opinion the citizens yoked themselves to great misfortune when 'without gall' they forgot the evils which Pittacus had done them instead of requiting evil with evil as just men should.⁷ The

⁵ Beauty-contests of Lesbian women are mentioned elsewhere also.

⁶ Literally, 'he devours the city.' Nothing murderous is implied; the meaning is indicated on p. 122, n. 18. In Alcaeus 70, 7 LP δαπτετω πολιν, is preceded by a strophe which depicts luxurious living. Perhaps Pittacus had already been elected sole ruler when Alcaeus wrote 129 LP.

⁷ On ἄχολος as a reproach cf. Il. 2, 241f.; Archilochus fr. 96. Since the Lesbians were so complaisant Pittacus could 'devour' them with impunity (cf. previous note and the beginning of the next quotation, 70, 7). Both reproaches are paralleled in Il. 1, 231: δημοβόρος (cf. δαπτει την πολιν) βασιλεύς, ἐπεὶ οὐτιδανοῖσιν (cf. πολεως τας αχολω) ἀνάσσεις.

poet found fresh ground for bitterness when the man 'of vile descent' took unto himself a wife of the ancient nobility, in order, as Alcaeus thought, to exploit the city in league with his new relatives as he had previously done in alliance with Myrsilus (70, 6 LP):

> But now intermarried with the Atridae he may devour the city as he did with Myrsilus until war again vouchsafes us victory (?).

> Then we would forget our anger, relax heart-devouring strife and intestine battles which some Olympian has roused, leading the folk to confusion; but to Pittacus he now gives pleasant glory.

For ten years Pittacus retained the dignity of supreme ruler with unlimited power; no less time was required to restrain the restless party-chiefs, of whom Alcaeus was one, and to restore effective order. Then, after he had performed the task entrusted to him by the people, he dutifully laid his office down.

The neighboring realm of Lydia sought to exploit the divisions of Lesbos. One poem (69 LP) begins as follows:

> Father Zeus, the Lydians indignant at our misfortunes (?) have given us two thousand staters so that we might be able to come to the city Ira (or: to the holy city),

> Although we never did them service previously . . . he, however, sly as a fox, hoped it would be easy for him unnoticed . . .

The poem is in Sapphic strophes, but there is nothing of poetry in it. Without introduction or other proprieties the agitated poet presents his case to the world-ruler to make him see the right. Nor is there any word to tell the reader what had gone before.[8] But Zeus and the citizens of Lesbos were well up with current affairs, and they knew who the unnamed 'he' was. In this example we can see how the new realism found expression in the writing of the day. Nor does Alcaeus hesitate (here and in 63, 7 LP) to specify the exact sum of money involved. The sum was very considerable; careful calculation shows that it was sufficient to maintain 500 mercenaries for several months.[9]

Alcaeus employs figures also in praising the heroic deed which his brother Antimenidas performed in the service of King Nebuchadnezzar. Apparently a set-back in partisan strife was the occasion for Antimenidas' going abroad and hiring himself out as a mercenary

---

[8] Moreover there are linguistic difficulties: the precise meaning of the subordinate clause in the first strophe is doubtful, and in the second the sense of γινωσκοντες and προλεξαις is obscure. There is something similar in Archilochus 51 I A 46 (see p. 147).

[9] According to Denys Page, *Sappho and Alcaeus* (Oxford, 1955), 232.

to the lord of 'holy Babylon' (48, 10 LP). In his service he went as far as Ascalon in the land of the Philistines. Upon his return Alcaeus greeted him with the following words (350 LP):

You have come from the end of the earth. Of ivory studded with gold is the hilt of your sword. (In the pay of the Babylonians you fought) a mighty battle and delivered them for their woes by killing a warrior who was only a span short of five cubits by the royal measure.

The magnitude of the deed is designated by the size of the opponent in a purely quantitative sense. Antimenidas apparently received the sword as a reward for the deed, and so again the value of the service is measured by the value of the weapon.

By contrast to these dry and dragging verses we have the vigorous and flowing language of a prayer to the Dioscuri—the divine pair of brothers who were thought to deliver ships from peril by sea and to make their saving presence known by the radiance now called St. Elmo's fire. The Dioscuri were at home in the Peloponnese, and it is from there that the poem summons them (34 LP):

Leave the isle of Pelops, you brothers, Zeus' and Leda's mighty twins, appear to us gracious and comforting, Castor and Polydeuces

Who ride over the broad earth and over all the sea on swift horses, and easily deliver the sailor from the fear of death,

Leaping up high on stout ships, gleaming afar (from mast and yards) and bringing the light of heaven to the black ship in fearful night.

Of Alcaeus' war songs proper we have no remains worth mentioning.[10] But the fragments do give us a notion of his banquet-poetry. Any occasion served Alcaeus as an excuse for drinking; the good news of Myrsilus' death must be celebrated with wine, and the cares for the ship of state must be dispelled with wine.[11] By his presence the boy Bycchis helped to gladden the poet's hours of care. So also in this fragment (335 LP):

We ought not to deliver our heart to woes, for sorrow gains us nothing, the best of medicines, Bycchis, is to fetch some wine and get drunk.

We drink in winter because it is cold (338 LP):

Zeus sends rain; from heaven a great storm descends, the water channels freeze stiff . . .
To thrust the storm away build up the fire, and pour strong wine in the bowl with generous hand, and about my temples place a soft cushion (?).

[10] The sentiment that death in battle is 'beautiful' (i.e., *decorum*, not *dulce* (fr. 400)) generalizes a thought of Tyrtaeus' (fr. 7, 16).
[11] Fr. 332 and 73 LP, p. 190f., above.

But in summer we drink because it is hot (347 LP):

Moisten my lungs with wine for the dog-star is raging, the season is hard, everything is thirsty with heat, from the leaves the sweet cicada sounds forth, the artichoke blooms; now women are wanton but men feeble, for Sirius scorches head and knees.

This description of summer does not contain a single stroke that Alcaeus did not draw from the section of Hesiod's *Works and Days* (582ff.) of similar content. Hesiod too recommended a genial draught at the hottest time of the year—only at that season, to be sure, which is the only one he describes in detail. Alcaeus follows this description step by step, and so clothes his invitation to drink and be merry with the authority of the Boeotian epic poet; but in his own fashion he breaks up Hesiod's long periods ('when the artichoke blooms . . . then . . . at that time you may . . .') into a loose sequence of individual statements. Like winter and summer, so the advent of spring also supplies Alcaeus with an excuse for revelry (367 LP).

Occasionally the tone becomes stronger. One banqueting song (50 LP) began:

Upon my head which has suffered so much pour myrrh, and upon my gray-haired breast—

Here is an antithesis to the picture of Sappho's girl anointing her delicate skin with perfume. A life which spent itself in tempestuous violence for decades, wishes to submerge itself for a few hours in comfortable ease: this desire is expressed in the vivid imagery of the much-afflicted head and graying breast being anointed with myrrh by a favorite lad. The poetry of Alcaeus shows a genial alternation between the large and monumental and the fugitive, careless and prosaic.

In one poem (38 LP) the invitation to drink is based on general arguments with reference to the legend of Sisyphus:[12]

Drink with me, Melanippus. What (do you suppose?) once you have crossed eddying Acheron you will never again see the pure sunlight. Then do not aspire too high; even Sisyphus, mighty king of the Aeolidae and cleverest of men (did not escape his fate); shifty as he was, twice the force of destiny carried him across eddying Acheron, and the son of Cronus, king of black earth, decreed heavy labor for him.

The conclusion, to judge by the remains, was somewhat as follows:

[12] According to Theognis 702ff. Sisyphus was so astute that his cleverness did not forsake him even in death as it does other people. Thus he was able to talk Persephone into allowing him to return to life. After his second death he was compelled to roll uphill a heavy stone which always slipped away from him at the last moment (*Od.* 11, 593–600).

'Therefore we shall not hope for what is impossible, but be glad, if ever, in this hour of our youth, and enjoy what it affords us. Outdoors the north wind blows, and the city . . .; but we fill the room in which we sit and drink with the sound of the lyre. . . .'[13] Greek lyric is almost never a soliloquy; as a rule the poet addresses a definite person or god. So the thought: 'I will drink and make merry because—' implies an admonition to a comrade: 'Do not suppose that you can snap your fingers at death; Sisyphus did succeed in returning from the underworld, but in the end came off not better but worse than ordinary people.' The object of the *memento mori*, according to the law of polarity, is to strengthen the will to enjoy life.

Elsewhere too Alcaeus has general *sententiae*. They are neither profound nor original; rather, some brief statement of general experience is brought in, when corroboration of some view is needed, like the common currency of our own proverbs, with no further claim than that they are true and applicable. Some of the *sententiae* are concerned with the relative importance of persons and things. So in one of the political poems (112, 10 LP) we have the epigram 'Men are the bastions of a city.' Just as Alcaeus here signifies that walls and towers win no war, so he concludes in another passage that weapons alone and the designs with which they are decorated remain ineffectual if their bearer is not a brave warrior (427 LP).[14] In a third passage Alcaeus deplores the fact that people value a man not according to his person but according to his possessions (360 LP):

For so did Aristodamus once very sensibly remark in Sparta, 'Money is man'; no needy man is ever distinguished or respected.

Archaic poets liked to cite the sayings of famous men: in this case the words of Alcaeus frame the dictum of a Spartan sage, a model of Laconic terseness, for the whole is said in Greek in two words. On the other hand poverty, according to Alcaeus is akin to helplessness (364 LP):

Poverty is a wretched and miserable evil; together with its sister helplessness, it masters even a great people.

By 'people' or 'following' (λαός) Alcaeus evidently means the group to which he himself belonged; his party, which had been 'great', that is, influential and proud, is now powerless, ruined economically and degraded morally. We can easily imagine that Lydian subsidies were accepted willingly.

[13] At the end of v. 5 and 6 something like μεγας and μορον ου φυγεν are to be supplied. The sense of παθην in v. 12 is probably as in Solon fr. 14, 4.

[14] The inventory of weapons in 357 LP (p. 189f., above) supplies the complement: courage alone is also not enough.

We should not seek behind these generalities a consistent philosophy of life: one adapts oneself to the most divergent principles according to need and wish. Generally Alcaeus is by no means resigned and philosophical, but in one passage he enjoins pious submission to the fate which is allotted each of us at birth (39. 7 LP): 'Whoso is wise and of clear understanding knows that[15] against the destiny of Zeus not even the hair . . .'; one is reminded of a saying in the New Testament (Luke 12, 7): 'Even the very hairs of your head are all numbered (before God).'

Again in a poem about a voyage (which is probably to be understood symbolically) we read (249 LP):

A man should plan his voyage on land, so far as he is able and understands how: but once he is at sea, he must accommodate himself to the winds that blow.

The following adage (341 LP) strikes strangely on our ears (its context may have been equally strange):

You can choose what you say, but not what others say to you.

This comes oddly from Alcaeus, who never seems to have cared what he said about anyone.

Recent papyrus finds have brought us expressions of a refined sensitivity to nature, and this seems astonishing in the Alcaeus we thought we knew. In any case it is not certain that all of the scraps (without context for us) were actually written by Alcaeus and that one or another is not Sappho's:

. . . birds from the sea to this city . . . hither from the peaks, from the fragrant . . . near the blue-green grapevines of the green marsh . . . springlike . . . visible afar . . . (115a, 6 LP)
. . . many-flowered . . . icy-cold . . . beneath Tartaros . . . calm rests upon the back (of the sea) . . . may you be unhurt . . . (286 LP)
. . . when the gates of spring are opened then . . . wafting ambrosia . . . (296b, 3 LP).

More than once Alcaeus takes his material from heroic legend, and specifically from the Trojan cycle. Like Sappho in 16 LP (p. 185f., above) but more harshly and sharply, Alcaeus[16] speaks in 283 LP of the affliction and madness which Aphrodite visited upon Helen 'so that she eloped with the Trojan betrayer of his host leaving her child and the soft bed of her husband' and of the bloody war

---

[15] Line 10 perhaps οιδεν]ως; nevertheless the course of thought in the whole fragment is doubtful.
[16] But we cannot be sure that the poem is not in fact hers.

which was the consequence. Another poem, preserved virtually complete, contrasts Helen's amour with the marriage of Thetis, which is celebrated in warm and friendly tones. Helen brought destruction to Troy, but Thetis bore Achilles, the greatest warrior on the battlefield of Troy (42 LP):

As the story goes, through evil (deeds) a bitter lot befell Priam and his children because of you, (and fire devoured) sacred Troy.

Not such was she whom the Aeacid, when he invited all the blessed gods to his marriage, fetched from Nereus' realm, a lovely maiden

Into the house of Chiron, and loosed her virgin's girdle. Love united them, Peleus and the best of the Nereids; at year's end

She bore a son, the greatest of the demigods the fortunate driver of bay horses. But those others perished because of Helen, and their city also.

Another poem also spoke of Achilles and his mother. It concludes as follows (44 LP):

He called his mother—the sea-nymph and she (embracing Zeus') knees pleaded—that he might (respect and assist) her child's wrath.

In these three lines two great scenes from the first book of the *Iliad* are clearly alluded to. The preceding part of the poem contained only five lines. The object of this bare allusion to individual scenes out of the Trojan legend is a puzzle. A fourth fragment recounts an episode from the end of the Trojan war and its sequel. When Troy fell and was plundered by the victors, Cassandra took refuge in the shrine of Athene. The 'lesser' Ajax, son of Oïleus burst in, and the prophetess clung to the image of the goddess; Ajax tore them both down, the maiden and the image. In requital he suffered shipwreck on his homeward voyage and was drowned (298 LP):[17]

(Sanctuary) of Pallas, who of all the blessed gods is angry with violators of temples. With both hands the Locrian seized the maiden who stood by the image (and dragged her away), without fear of the daughter of Zeus, giver of war. The goddess paled fearfully beneath her brows; over the wine-dark (waves she hastened and) roused up the winds which bring darkness.[18]

The conclusion of the section shows the rapid tempo of the lyric account, very different from epic: the crime and its punishment

---

[17] See now Hugh Lloyd-Jones, *Greek, Roman and Byzantine Studies* 9, 1968, p. 125–39 with new readings.

[18] αφαντοις θυελλαις in Alcaeus corresponds to δνοφώδη αἰθέρος φυσήματα in Euripides, *Troades* (79).

which were widely separated in time and place come in immediate succession.[19] One poem in which Alcaeus, like a dramatist, has another person speak without introduction[20] stands by itself. A woman laments her fate; if Horace's imitation (*Carm.* 3, 12) reflects the essence of the original, she was a girl in love, unable to yield to her passion. The poem begins as follows (10 LP):

Wretched am I, victim of every woe . . . hateful destiny . . . a wound irremediable smites me . . . and the cry of the terror-stricken doe takes shape in my bosom . . . raging . . . blindness . . .

Even the mutilated remains show how much more powerful the language and thought are than in Horace's imitation.

Alcaeus (327 LP) calls the god of love:

the mightiest of the gods, whom Iris of the lovely feet bore to golden-tressed Zephyrus.

The genealogy is original. Eros is made the son of a wind; Zephyrus can be wild and dangerous (Sappho described love as a storm) but also soft and gentle. What the mother Iris signifies it is hard to imagine. Alcaeus also wrote hymns to the gods; not only unpremeditated prayers in need like the poem on the Dioscuri or the complaints to Zeus, but also formal songs of praise to Apollo, Hermes, and other gods. But the remains of Alcaeus' hymns that have come down to us are to slight that we can form no proper notion of them. We can know him best in his personal poetry.

It is in the nature of early Greek lyric that poetry is concerned with personal experience, and therefore the quality of the poetry depends largely on what the poet did and underwent and what he himself made of his experiences. Alcaeus led an eventful life, and his powerful nature spoke passionately of all that he encountered, although from a narrowly selfish viewpoint.

Sometimes his poetry does not rise above the facts; sometimes his temperament prevents perfection of style; sometimes he rises above the moment and turns his raw material into genuine poetry which speaks directly to the heart even of one who has nothing in common with this limited world. In contrast to Archilochus and Sappho he is patchy and uneven. But in his poetry the old vitality lives freely, for the last time in our historical picture, impetuous and flaring aloft with a smoky flame.

[19] Hitherto such a rapid order of scenes from saga was known to us only from choral lyric; now we learn that the practise of monodic lyric was no different.

[20] Archilochus 22 also began with another person speaking, but was followed by an afterword, 'So spoke Charon, the carpenter of Thasos' (p. 138, above).

(e) *The Ionian Middle Classes*

I. SEMONIDES

If the Greeks of the colonies far outstripped those of the mother country and created literary forms perfect in their kind far sooner, one of the causes for their rapid development was probably close contact with the ancient cultures of the East. The literary works themselves give eloquent evidence of the close and multifarious relations of the colonial Greeks with oriental lands and peoples. Alcman, who led the dances of the noble maidens of exclusive Sparta and wrote songs for them, boasts of having come from Lydian Sardis, and a friend of Sappho moved to Sardis when she left the poetess' circle. Sappho's brother traveled to Egypt more than once, and Alcaeus wrote a poem describing the Nile from his personal experience. His brother took service under Nebuchadnezzar and in his army went as far as the 'boundaries of earth'; perhaps he assisted at the conquest of Jerusalem in 597 and in carrying the most prominent of the Jews into their Babylonian exile. In 590 some Greek mercenaries who came from the Asiatic coast and the islands near by went up the Nile in the service of the Egyptian King Psammetichus as far as Abu Simbel in Nubia, where they immortalized their memory on a colossal statue of Rameses in one of the oldest of all Greek inscriptions. With such lively intercourse there can be no doubt that ideas as well as goods and services were exchanged.

But the same forces which caused the early ripening of Greek culture in the East also exerted a disintegrating effect. After Alcaeus and Sappho the Lesbian Muse fell silent, as if she had spent her last strength in endowing these two poets with their gifts. Ionia continued productive, and it fathered great thinkers and considerable poets in the sixth century; but even at that early date there also arose in Ionia a literature which shows an unmistakable ingredient of bourgeois philistinism. Vitality declines and sentimentality makes its appearance for the first time; tragic feeling is supplanted by emotional lamentation, passionate commitment by the desire for an undisturbed and easy life. Poetry can no longer grip and stir as it had done, and in the end it is content to amuse. In their various degrees and modes the fragments of Semonides, Mimnermus, and Hipponax bear evidence of this weakening of the creative spirit.

Semonides was a native of Samos and leader of a colony that went to the small island of Amorgos; he was therefore of good family. His date is very uncertain; the end of the seventh century seems most probable. The metrical form of his poetry is predominantly iambic trimeter, the verse which was to become the medium for dialogue in drama. This verse was easy to manipulate and best suited to accommodate the ordinary language of daily speech; Greek theory therefore regarded it as the most relaxed and prosaic. Nevertheless it could also serve as vehicle for lofty poetry, as the example of Archilochus and tragedy shows; it demanded no specific style but was amenable to any that might be assigned it.

Of Semonides (and similarly of Mimnermus) we possess relatively abundant fragments of moralizing content, in keeping with the interests of an ancient *littérateur* who excerpted pieces of this kind from authors of all ages and transmitted them to posterity. In one of the fragments Semonides addresses an unnamed 'boy'; this gives his discourse the character of a communication of the experience of life to the next generation; thus he says in another passage that a young man should learn lessons necessary for life from an elder 'as a nursing foal runs by its mother's side.'(5)

The instruction which the young man receives this time is the following (1):

My boy, the end of all that happens in the world is in the hand of Zeus, who sways things as he will. We men do not know the truth, but like the beasts, whose life is of the day ('ephemeral'), so we too live in ignorance, not knowing how the gods will bring each thing about. Hope feeds us all, and confidence, which makes us work for that which does not come. 'Tomorrow,' this one says, 'next spring,' another thinks that all he hopes will come. No man has ever doubted that the coming year will see him crowned with riches and with happiness. But yet old age, with all its sorrows, comes on one before his wish is granted: on another falls a dread disease and slays him: one meets bloody death in war, and goes below to Hades' gloomy realm. The merchant in his vessel, striving with the storm and with the many billows of the purple sea, sinks, dies—it was to make a living that he sailed. And many knot the fatal noose about their neck, and by their own contriving quit the cheerful day. From evil fortune nothing is exempt: defeat and death and many thousand unexpected woes and griefs crowd on mankind. If you would listen to me, we should not long for what is evil, yield to pain, and by our yielding do harm to our mind and spirit . . .

The last lines clearly steer towards a positive and useful application; the *not this* must be followed by *but rather this*. But the counsel which concluded the discussion was sliced off by the excerptor because only the lamentations suited his purposes. Hence the precise meaning of the text, which is not very clear in any case, is made even more difficult.

The beginning of the fragment is spacious and forceful, but as it

proceeds the poem is increasingly dispersed into the lower reaches of
banality. The beginning contrasts god, who exercises full control
over reality, with men, who feed on agreeable illusions and lack insight into approaching actuality. Loosely connected with this is the
brief incidental remark that man is 'ephemeral'[1] and lives like cattle.
Then the counter-play of flattering hope and ugly reality is demonstrated by examples. The underlying idea is very close to Hesiod's
profound myth of captive hope and the woes which swarm abroad.[2]
But unlike Hesiod, Semonides makes it his main point that death
frustrates our hope for a better future. This would seem to indicate
that the portion preserved was followed by an injunction to enjoy
life and the present moment, that is to say, an invitation to festive
drinking. The penultimate verse of our excerpt appears to mean 'We
should not think of things that lead us into unhappiness.'[3] This
thought too may derive from Hesiod's story of Pandora (*WD* 58ff.,
p. 117, above). But compared with Hesiod's vigorous and incisive
analysis of the human situation Semonides' outpouring seems feeble
and erratic. Apparently the Ionian seeks nothing more than to
create a mood for banqueting. Of the spiritual pride in high en-
deavor, which is part of even the ephemeral nature of man, he knows
nothing. He advises against dangerous pleasures and instead
recommends the few comforts within our reach. Elsewhere he bases
the same admonition as follows (3):

The time hereafter, when we shall be dead, is long; our life is but a
span in length and full of woe.

In his treatment of disappointed hopes Semonides first established
the situation in general terms and then illustrated and defined it by
a number of typical cases. By the same method, but in reverse order,
he deals with the other half of the Pandora legend. That god associated woman with man for his destruction Semonides demonstrates by first describing a long series of female types (7):

Zeus when he began first made the soul of woman in many kinds. The
first was from the bristly sow, and in her household all is crusted over with
filth and lies in wild confusion on the littered floor. Herself unwashed,

---

[1] On the notion of the 'ephemeral' see p. 133–36, above.

[2] Individual parallels between Semonides fr. 1 and Hesiod's *Works and Days* are
numerous: Semon. 1–3 (*WD* 105); 1–2 (669); 11–12 (92–93); 15–17 (686–87);
15 θάλασσα (101); 20 (100–101), and for the expression κακῶν ἀπ' (91 νόσφιν ἄτερ
κακῶν; 23 (58). But none of these compels us to assume direct borrowing, as we
must in fr. 6 and 7, 110f. (p. 204 with n. 8, below).

[3] So the words are explained by von Sybel, *Hermes* 7 (1873), 361–62. This
meaning of ἐρῷμεν is confirmed by the parallels *Od.* 10, 431, Pindar, *Nem.* 11,
43–48, and Sophocles, *Antigone* 615–19.

and in the dirtiest of clothes, she sits and swills and guzzles all amid the mess.

Another kind great Zeus created from the fox, that crafty villain: she is up to every trick, she knows of every art, the better and the worse; and when she talks, sometimes the things she says are bad (?), and sometimes good. Her temper never stays the same.

Another from the dog, contentious (?), motherly (?):[4] She loves to hear all things and know all things that pass, to peer in every corner, scamper all about and raise an uproar, even when there's no-one there. She won't stop yapping even for her husband's threats, not even if he takes a stone and dashes out some of her teeth, or if he speaks in gentle tones; not even when she sits with strangers newly met: not for one moment will she shut her noisy mouth.

Another type the great gods sent to mortal man moulded of earth, a mental cripple; such a wife knows nothing—nothing bad and nothing good. Apart from eating there is nothing she can do. Why, if the winter weather blows and howls outside, she hasn't sense to move up closer to the fire.

Another from the sea; her nature has two sides. One day she laughs and sings, as jolly as can be: a stranger coming to the house is full of praise: 'In all the world you would not find another such—no wife so clever or so fair of face as she.' The next she's insupportable: you cannot bear to hear her or be near her: she will snap and snarl as touchy as a nursing bitch with seven pups to everyone, her friends and enemies alike, she shows herself ungracious, snappish and perverse, just as the sea stands sometimes smooth and calm and harmless, giving sailors joy to look at it on summer days, but also sometimes roars with rage heaving and tossing in the thunder of the surf. That is the closest thing a man can see to such a wife, her change-ful nature[5] and her shifting whims and moods.

Another from the donkey—ash-grey, stubborn brute . . .

Another from the weasel . . .

Another from the horse of pride and pedigree: she pushes onto others all the dirty work; she could not bear to turn a mill or shake a sieve, or clean the house and throw the rubbish out of doors, or sit too near the fire, for soot she can't endure. But yet she keeps her husband in the toils of love.[6] On every day she takes a bath, or two, or three, to wash her dainty skin; and then she steeps herself in perfumes, keeps her long, thick hair adorned with combs, and sets her beauty off with blooms of every hue. A lovely toy and showpiece such a wife may be to show to others, but to live with, not so good, unless her husband is a king or nobleman, who may afford to feed his pride with costly goods.

---

[4] λιτοργός is perhaps 'roused to anger by trifles'; on αὐτομήτωρ vv. 33–34 and *Od.* 20, 14 may throw light.

[5] πόντος is corrupt; πάντοτ' would fit the sense, but it is not attested until much later.

[6] For περιτρέπω 'to shift to others', cf. Liddell and Scott. In v. 62 ποιεῖται (middle) φίλον is 'makes him her friend.' On ἀνάγκη sc. ἐρωτική cf. Plato, *Republic* 458 d, Pindar, *Nem.* 8, 3.

Another from the ape . . .

Another from the bee: who weds her, weds good luck, for she alone of wives is free from all reproach, and in her hands his household grows in wealth and peace. Beloved and loving she grows old along with him, bearing him many children, fair of face and fame. This kind stands out among all others of her sex: the gods bestow a special, holy grace on her. She takes no pleasure in the company of wives whose talk is all about two subjects—men and bed. In character and understanding these are best of all that Zeus in kindly mood vouchsafes to men.

All other kinds, by art and malice of the gods, are sent to be a lasting torment to their men.[7] This is the greatest evil Zeus has ever made, women. For though they may appear to have their use, each to her husband shews herself the greatest curse. A man can never pass a day in happiness from dawn to evening, once he takes himself a wife. He finds it harder to keep hunger from his door, that worst of house-mates and most ill-disposed of gods; and if a man thinks he has reason to rejoice, when fortune or another man has stood his friend, she finds some ground for grumbling or starting a fight. For where a woman is, a man cannot receive his friend and fitly welcome him within the house. The one who seems most virtuous and best of all is usually the one who brings home most disgrace if not kept under eye: and then the neighbors laugh and make a joke of it to see him cuckolded. But yet each man, when speaking of his own dear wife, will praise her and condemn the rest. We do not see that we are all subjected to the self-same lot. For Zeus has made this first and foremost of our woes and shackled it upon us like a ball and chain, since Hades first received so many brave men's souls, who died when nations quarrelled for a woman's sake. Their very leader, when he came in triumph home, was murdered by the treason of his faithless wife.

The moral of the whole Semonides is elsewhere compressed into two verses (6):

A good wife is the finest thing a mortal man can have: a bad one is the greatest source of grief.

This couplet is virtually identical, word for word, with two hexameters from Hesiod's *Works and Days* (702f.); but Hesiod and Semonides alike seem to regard the good woman as so rare an exception that the possibility remains mainly theoretical and is hardly to be considered practically. The preceding verse in Hesiod (701) Semonides also used (7, 110f.), so that literary dependence is beyond question.[8]

A comparison between Hesiod and Semonides is to the disadvantage of the Ionian. Both address the same stratum of society,

[7] V. 94f. are essential as transition. On cf. W. Marg, *Der Charakter in der Sprache der frühgr. Dichtung* (Würzburg, 1938) 30.

[8] Hence the echoes cited p. 202 n. 2, above also rest on direct borrowing. See also p. 117 n. 9.

but Hesiod was, in his own way, elevated and large-minded; Semonides is not. Hesiod sought to penetrate the externals of things to their essence, and all that he says is strictly relevant; if he inserts sharply etched miniatures they are striking illustrations of precise injunctions and admonitions. In Semonides, on the other hand, the thoughts are superficial, the narrative disjointed, and the power of presentation extends only to detail. That the fault is not inherent in the literary genre is proven by the *iambi* of Archilochus with their combination of strength and beautiful form.

Of the types which Semonides sets up our translation has omitted three, for a complete translation would serve little purpose. A number of character-traits are repeated from one type to another because the author could not differentiate his thought sufficiently to create ten different female figures. And many of his pictures fail to illuminate because Semonides constructed his species of women on the model of species of animals instead of drawing them from experience. In him the comparison with animals is no longer merely a help towards initial understanding:[9] it now controls and falsifies the classification of human beings according to their types. The slatternly and un-washed woman must also be gluttonous because the swine combines these traits; and the cross-grained woman must also be gluttonous and libidinous because that is what the donkey is.[10] A rather different explanation is needed when the woman who resembles the bee (83ff.) is not only diligent and industrious but also chaste; here the one ideal figure must combine all desirable qualities.

The literary merit of Semonides' pedestrian satire on women is slight; and yet the poem has considerable significance for us, strange as this may at first sound, because of the modes of thought in which it moves. In the first place, an idea fundamental in early Greek philosophy makes its appearance—the idea of materials or quasi-materials as representatives of qualities (see p. 260f., below). For according to Semonides' actual language women are not only similar to various animals but were made 'out of' them by god. A second point is more interesting. In addition to the one good and seven bad animal-types[11] there is a pair of types of an essentially different sort: the two women whom god created out of 'earth' and out of 'sea' (21ff. and 27ff.). According to Hesiod the gods fashioned Pandora, the primal pattern of women, out of a mixture of earth and water (*WD* 61; but earth alone in 70 and *Theog.* 570). In Semonides this touch is given a

[9] See p. 146f., above.

[10] For gluttony ascribed to the donkey cf. e.g., Plato, *Phaedo* 81e.

[11] Phocylides, who probably lived later than Semonides, names only four types: horse, swine, dog, and bee (fr. 2).

surprising turn. According as the element of earth or sea pre-
dominates in the clay, the woman possesses an excessively dull and
inert or an excessively mobile and active nature. If we substitute our
own notions, rigid 'earth' here represents the principle of inert
material (the earthy woman knows no activity other than eating,
which is taking in of material), while the changeable 'sea' is made
to represent spontaneous energy. If earth and sea are understood
in this way their mixture and interplay will explain very much more
than merely two female types. Later, but still in the sixth century,
Xenophanes was to promulgate the doctrine that 'Everything that is
and grows is earth and water' (*Vorsokr.* 21, B 29); his greater disciple
Parmenides would deduce the entire phenomenal world from the
interaction of an inert and more material and active and more
spiritual element, and was to explain individual differences among
men by the changing proportions of the two elements. Semonides'
theory of women fashioned out of earth or sea probably reflects the
ideas of his countryman Thales of Miletus,[12] for we can hardly
consider Semonides as an original thinker.[13]

The other fragments are very short. We may infer from them that
Semonides wrote all sorts of trivial narrative poems, as for example
(14):

I put some myrrh and baccaris upon myself, and other scents: we had a
merchant in the house.

The recurrent 'I' (fr. 14, 15, 20, 21) is not necessarily Semonides, for
the poet speaks under assumed persons also, as Archilochus had done.
A cook boasts (31):

I singed the pig and jointed it as art demands in sacrifice, for I am master
of my craft.

A group of citations derives from the sphere of kitchen and dining-
room (fr. 10 (?), 20–24, 25 (?), 28). A man praises a 'wonderful'
Tromilean cheese which he had himself imported (fr. 20). There is
also an animal fable (8):

[12] The dates of Semonides as of Thales are uncertain, so that chronologically
such an influence is possible. On Thales see p. 260f., below; on Xenophanes, p.
334; p. 385, n. 36.

[13] Even the idea of female types called after animals must be older than
Semonides and Phocylides, perhaps older than Hesiod. Hesiod does not indeed
speak of women who resemble the industrious bee, but he does compare women as
a whole with drones (*Theog.* 594–601); he says that Hermes endowed Pandora with
a 'dog-like' spirit (*WD* 67); and he has her decked with a golden head-band upon
which many animals of land and sea are pictured (*Theog.* 578–84). Is this elaborately described ornament intended to symbolize the inventory of qualities which
may reside in a woman?

A hawk in the Maeander caught an eel; began to eat it, when a heron came and bore it off.

Of a dung-beetle a man says, in a clever double-entendre (11):

See what a creature this is, that goes flying past. His diet is the worst of any living thing.

Occasionally the tone rises (12):

Less terrified would he be who in the wooded hills, tracing a faint and solitary path, beheld at once a lion or a panther face to face.

The emotional content lifts the language to a different and higher level, as in the description of the raging sea in the two longer fragments (1, 15–17 and 7.40). Elsewhere the tone is one of light and lively chat.[14]

The *iambi* of Semonides satisfied the tastes of an audience which did not wish to be uplifted or enlightened by the poet but rather to be understood and reassured, touched and comforted, admonished and guided, and above all entertained and amused. In the world of this poetry every middle class citizen can recognize his own world. He is comforted by the assurance that everyone else fares as badly as he or even worse and that 'no single man is without mishap and without pain' (fr. 4). He takes comfort, for himself and others, when the wretchedness of humanity, by which many are driven to suicide, is set before his eyes. He is all the more receptive to the amusing sketches of life with which Semonides distracts his worries (cf. fr. 2) and his resentment. He could chuckle at the caricature of women in general and in particular; but he could also, if he wished, make a mental reservation in favour of his own wife.[15] And he accepts advice readily when the poet encourages and confirms his penchant towards the minor pleasures of drink and similar indulgences.

2. MIMNERMUS

While the poetry of Semonides, so far as we can see, was firmly associated with one single attitude of mind, the poetry of Mimnermus was more versatile and richer; moreover, the poetical powers of Mimnermus were considerably greater than those of Semonides. Our

[14] I have disregarded fr. 29. This elegiac 'Simonides' fragment is too modern in its language for Semonides. The poem may be a funerary epigram (cf. v. 12), just as many other elegies copied from stone were later ascribed to Simonides (of Ceos).

[15] According to 7, 83 and 92f. women of the bee type are indeed exceptional but they do exist; on the other hand, 110–114 suggests that a husband deludes himself in thinking that he has one.

historical sketch would therefore be more instructive if we could begin with Mimnermus as representing the transition to the bourgeois outlook and could start the sequence with him instead of with Semonides.[1]

Mimnermus came from the Ionian city of Colophon[1a] in Asia Minor and lived around 600. He wrote his poems as Callinus had done, in elegiac verse, which Archilochus too had used, along with many other meters; and like Callinus, Mimnermus too, as it appears, wrote a battle song for the Ionians, of which we possess a portion. In keeping with military usage, Callinus had opened his song with taunts and insults, so that his hearers would feel obliged to refute his accusations by deeds (p. 152, above). The reproach had a special sting when it took the form 'You are not worthy of your fathers' (cf. *Il.* 4, 370ff.). The context was probably the same in a poem of Mimnermus (13 Bergk) in which a certain warrior of the older generation is contrasted with one of the present:[2]

Not such was he: his manly heart, his impetuous courage come to my ears from the old—those who had known him themselves: how he had driven in flight the close-packed Lydian horsemen by the banks of Hermus, dauntlessly plying his spear. Never would Pallas Athene find anything to reproach in his manhood, when he with dauntless breast, foremost of all in the fray, stormed in the bloody strife of war, nor feared for the foemen's weapons, but undismayed faced the javelin hail. There was no better man in all the ranks of our army, none who could better achieve victory's work in the field while he yet lived and breathed and looked on the hastening sunlight.[3]

Colophon, like Smyrna which was not far distant, warred with the Lydians, and both cities were subject to Lydian rule for a time. On the battles of the Smyrnaeans against Gyges of Lydia, the contemporary of Archilochus, Mimnermus wrote an elegy (fr. 12A) which may have been identical with a *Smyrneis*. The *Smyrneis* was of a narrative nature, for one distich (12A) reads as follows:

[1] Perhaps our chronology should be corrected; Semonides may actually belong to the sixth century (cf. p. 206 n. 12, above); or iambic poetry was receptive to the new outlooks sooner than elegy; or the accidental course of real events did not exactly reflect the logic of the historical development.

[1a] Or else he was from Smyrna and descended from Colophonians. Cf. J. M. Cook, 'Old Smyrna, 1948–51,' *Annual of the British School at Athens* 53–54 (1958–9) 1–34.

[2] κείνου γε in line 1 (cf. Τυδέι γε *Il.* 4, 372) and τοῦ μὲν ἄρα in line 5 show that the emphasis is on 'he,' and not, as Wilamowitz, *Sappho und Simonides* (Berlin 1913) interpreted it, on οὐ τοῖον. Cf. further lines 2 and 9 with *Il.* 4, 374f.

[3] In excerpting the quotation something like θαλπόμενος has fallen out at the beginning of the pentameter (cf. Pindar *Nem.* 4, 13f.); and perhaps e.g. δέμας (then θάλπετο) took the place of φέρετ'.

So from beside the king, performing what he had bidden, they went forward at the run, guarding themselves with their shields.

Another elegiac fragment looks further into the past and recalls the time when 'we,' that is, the ancestors of the present Colophonians, migrated from the Peloponnese, settled lovely Colophon, and 'by the counsel of the gods' wrested the possession of Smyrna from the Aeolians (fr. 12). What is remarkable in these verses is that Mimnermus describes the occupation and settlement of Colophon by the forefathers as an act of violence and unprovoked aggression.

But the clamor of war and historical memories are not the most important element in the poetry of Mimnermus. In later antiquity Mimnermus was regarded as the creator of love-elegy. A series of fragments celebrate youth and the gifts of Aphrodite (1):

What then is life or its joys without golden Aphrodite? Better to die when the thought of these is lost from my heart. Love in a secret bower and sweet surrender to longing, all the bloom of delight plucked by a man and a girl in their summer of life. But when painful old age comes upon a man and makes him ugly, even though before he was lovely,[4] anguish and anxious thoughts are ever awake in his bosom, and he does not take, as once, joy in the light of the sun. Boys cannot bear his sight and women start to despise him: such is the burden of age laid by the gods upon man.

The easy unaffectedness with which Mimnermus bestows praise upon the joys of natural impulses excludes any prurience; the language possesses not only sweep but even a kind of dignity. Homer in his objective fashion called the intercourse of the sexes 'an order (*themis*) which obtains for men and women' (*Il.* 9, 134); Mimnermus gives the Homeric expression fragrance and color and speaks (literally) of the 'welcome flowers of life's ripeness which are the portion of men and women.'

A similar fragment also attaches to a saying of Homer. In Homer (*Il.* 6, 146) we read:

As is the generation of leaves, so is that of humanity.
The wind scatters the leaves on the ground, but the live timber
Flowers with leaves again in the season of spring returning.
So one generation of men will grow while another dies.

Mimnermus, probably after speaking of the eternity of the gods in the preceding verses, continues as follows (2):

We, like leaves that appear in the blooming hours of the springtime, when in the warmth of the sun nature is flourishing, we, like them, for a few

---

[4] Literally: 'which makes the handsome man as ugly (as the ugly man always was).' For the expression cf. Theognis 497f.: 'Wine in excess makes the spirit of fool and clever man equally empty.'

brief hours take joy in the sunny pleasures of youth, knowing nothing either of evil or good, by the command of the gods. But the fates are standing beside us; one holds hateful old age, sorrows so soon to be ours, one holds death. We reap but a slender harvest of pleasure, as long as the sunshine of youth glows on the meadow of life. But when once this springtime of life is gone by it is better to die than to continue alive. Numberless sorrows vex a man's heart: the stores of his household vanish away; then comes Want with her desolate train. One yearns most to have sons: they come not: he must go childless down from the friendly light into the caverns of death. Still to another's lot falls painful sickness. There is not one among men whom Zeus visits not sorely with grief.

The theme of these verses is similar to that of the first fragment of Semonides (p. 201, above), and yet everything is seen in a different spirit. Unsuspecting man is here likened not to cattle but to sprouting leaves; for whereas Semonides speaks of the short-sightedness of all humans, Mimnermus has the glad and burgeoning freshness of youth in mind. For Semonides actuality (τέλος) was only bad, and good was only an illusion ('hope'); Mimnermus contrasts desirable youth and undesirable old age as two (literally) 'actualities' (τέλος, lines 6 and 9) and deplores the fact that young men do not value properly what they possess,[5] for, in keeping with the principle of polarity, good by itself cannot be understood. In order, then, to lead youth to deeper enjoyment through awareness of its opposite, Minmermus shows the pains which it is inevitably approaching. They are pains, as he says, which affect the *thymos*, the organ of vitality, and we expect that Mimnermus will now speak of the joyless gloom of old age. Instead the poet adduces three objective instances of unhappiness: loss of property (because the old man can no longer supervise his economy or his business properly); death without heirs; and sickness. In the preceding fragment there were a different three: ugliness; cares which destroy the pleasures of life; and the contempt of boys and women. Things which we separate as 'external' and 'internal' are debited to old age one after the other without distinction. The thought which is introduced by his remark on the simple-mindedness of youth is stopped short; otherwise we should find some suggestion that the old man knows too much of good and evil to be happy.

Minmermus speaks of youth and old age repeatedly:

Would that without any sickness, without any trouble or sorrow, I could at three-score years come to the end of my days. (6)

Though he were handsome before, as soon as his youth is behind him, even a father forgoes love and respect from his sons. (3)

[5] 'Youth is a wonderful thing. What a shame to waste it on children' (G. B. Shaw).

Brief, too brief in its flight, goes like a transient dream youth with its store of joy. Old age, misshapen and troubled, hangs over each man's head, fatally swift to approach. Burdened with pain and contempt, it weakens the mind and the senses, stealthily binds one about, darkens the eyes and the heart. (5)

The fragments sound more pessimistic than the complete poems would probably have done. A positive admonition to cheerful enjoyment must surely have followed each of them, as we see in the following couplet (7):

Then let your heart take its pleasure. For out of your chattering neighbors some will be prompt to condemn, some will say nothing but good.

Archilochus had already said that a man should follow his own pleasures regardless of people's talk (fr. 9, p. 139, above). Mimnermus adds the argument that the opinion of people is not consistent and hence cannot be binding.

Archilochus, Sappho, and Mimnermus, each with significant variation, show the new way of basing personality on the individual existence. Archilochus is concerned with a life full of action, enjoyment, achievement, whose triumphant realization in fact and in poetry becomes an example to the world. Sappho ennobles her life through beauty and clarity, and she frees herself from the solitude of an existence based solely on self by pure surrender to the divine forces in life and by the sharing of joy and sorrow. The power of memory is her succor against the fleetingness of life; friends recall the beauty that was granted them, old age recalls the joys of youth,[6] and future generations will remember Sappho long after her death. Mimnermus, by contrast, looks not to what is lasting but to the moment; precisely because pleasure is so fleeting it should be enjoyed to the full while it is present. And whereas Sappho in her profound utterance on love and longing declares that they alone establish values, for Mimnermus sexual love and its joys are themselves the value. He is not primarily interested in the object to which our emotions sweep us, but in desire and its fulfilment.

The fragments of Mimnermus which we possess celebrate love in general and not any individual woman. Nevertheless, with a girl called Nanno, he must have practised what he preached for when booksellers and librarians later gave every literary work a title, they called a volume of Mimnermus' elegies *Nanno*.[7] Nanno was a flute-

[6] Fr. 24 and 29 (25) *a* LP combined by Eva-Maria Geiss: εμνασεσθ' α[—] και γαρ αμμες εν νεο [τατι-] ταυτ' εποημμεν.

[7] A *Nanno* collection was the source of fragments 4, 5, 8, 10, and oddly enough for 12 also.

girl (Athen. 13, 597a); beside her Mimnermus appears to have mentioned a musician with the Asiatic name Examyes in his poems also (Hermesianax fr. 7, Powell). Perhaps Mimnermus with Examyes and a 'Nanno' (it need not have been the same girl that he sings of under this name) formed a troupe which performed his poems and provided musical entertainment at social gatherings. It was expected of a flute-girl that she provide more than merely musical pleasure on festive occasions, and so 'Nanno' might have become the paradigm of the joyful love which Mimnermus never tired of praising; for in that age love for the opposite sex was relegated to the lighter kind of poetry aimed at pleasure and enjoyment.

Mimnermus illustrated the significance of the love of women in human life out of heroic legend as well. He spoke of the power of Aphrodite who was able to punish her adversary Diomedes (fr. 22 Bergk), and of Aphrodite's effective support with which she favored her protégé (11):

Never would Jason alone have returned in triumph from Aea, bearing the golden fleece, safe from the perilous seas; he would not safely have wrought those tasks which tyranneous Pelias set him; their vessel would not have burst into great Ocean's fair stream, (if Aphrodite had not availed them of Medea's love).[8]

The example concluded with these lines:

Forth to Aeëtes' beautiful town, where the hastening sun-god, Helius, stores his beams safe in a chamber of gold. Close by the margin of Ocean, where godlike Jason went.

Of the sun-god's course by day and journey by night Mimnermus speaks in detail in the following fragment from the Nanno-collection (10):

One day just as another Helius must suffer his labor; neither respite nor rest he knows, nor freedom from toil, not for his steeds, nor yet for himself, when Dawn, rosy-handed, rising from Ocean's deep, climbs to the lightening sky. During the night his longed-for couch still gently conveys him— hollow the couch and winged, wrought of the costliest gold by the immortal hands of Hephaestus—over the ocean, peacefully lapped in sleep from the Hesperides' isles back to the Ethiopians' land, where his speedy car and its horses stand at his call when Dawn, morning-begotten, appears. There Hyperion's son takes daily the reins of his horses.

By 'hollow bed' Mimnermus means the golden bowl in which, according to current belief, the sun was carried at night from the point of its setting to the place of its rising. The bowl floats upon the

---

[8] Cf. R. Pfeiffer, *Philologus* 84, (1940) 143.

stream of ocean which encircles the earth.⁹ So far Mimnermus only follows prevailing opinion. What is original is his friendly sympathy with the god who must ride his chariot every day from early to late and who longs for the sleep which he can enjoy during his return journey to the East. The poet's lucid mythological imagination conceives the career of Helios in such way as Ovid would do six centuries later (*Metam.* 2.385ff.); attractively and effortlessly the naturalness of the phenomenon is combined with the marvellous and the human with the divine. We would gladly know the context in which these verses stood in the original. Perhaps the poet's sympathy for the unresting labor of Helius issued from thoughts of the steady, incessant flight of days in which youth and life escape us; the same inexorable sovereign order by which the sun is impelled over its course, never suffers us to stand still on the path of our lives. Mimnermus is sympathetic too for the lot of Tithonus who, by an error, was granted eternal life instead of eternal youth (4):

Zeus bestowed on Tithonus an insurmountable evil—everlasting old age, worse in its horror than death.

Youth and the repulsive opposite to youth, the power of love and its raptures—these were obviously themes of which Mimnermus never tired.¹⁰ Hence vitality itself, its possession and loss in the natural course of the life of ordinary people, becomes a principal subject of poetry. In the texts before us Mimnermus treats it merely by setting it forth, with no great depth of ideas. Nevertheless his verses are not sunken in bourgeois banality and sentimentality but even in such a theme possess power and a certain dignity. In the poems of warlike or historical content his view is directed to other objects and values; and in the end there is a surprisingly serious fragment from the Nanno book (8):

Let truthfulness ever dwell in your heart and in mine—truth, that is noblest of all.

⁹ See p. 102 n. 13; p. 281f. On the other hand, the notion of the sun as a fire that burns in a hollow hemisphere rests on observation of solar eclipses (cf. pp. 384f., below); this is not consistent with the idea of the sun-chariot. The contradiction between the two competing theories is here reconciled by having one apply to the sun's course day by day and the other by night; but then the question remains how the horses and chariot got from West to East. According to this premise the Rhipaean Mountains in the north concealed the sun during the night journey, so that earth lay in the shadow of darkness (cf. Alcman fr. 90, p. 168, above, and p. 269 below on Anaximenes).

¹⁰ In this kind of poetry one expects praise of conviviality and wine, but this is wanting in the segments which have reached us in quotations.

Here uprightness is proclaimed as the core of righteousness, and thus of morality in general.

3. HIPPONAX[1]

How far Mimnermus wrote about his own experiences in the *Nanno* or elsewhere we do not know, and we cannot guess in what spirit he did so. But Archilochus, Sappho, and Alcaeus spoke out on personal matters continuously, with an uninhibited candor which has its outward counterpart in the sharpness and clearness of outline with which every statement in their poetry is expressed. Alcman also speaks of himself often enough in his choral lyrics; even so he poses a little, and lets us see that he is posing. Because his self-praise is tinctured with irony at his own expense, the effect is not unpleasing.

Hipponax' representation of himself goes a good deal farther, and in quite another direction. He was likewise an Ionian, from Miletus. Exiled by the tyrants there, he migrated to Clazomenae. His date falls in a later period (about 510)?; but the character of his art makes a short account of him appropriate at this point.

Hipponax speaks of his personal concerns and abuses his personal enemies as Archilochus does; but he presents his outpourings to an audience and entertains it like Semonides. The passionate eruptions of Archilochus become nonsense if they are not taken seriously; with the full-blooded stories in which Hipponax is at his best the situation is reversed. Here the intended effect is missing if one does not enjoy the play of riotous fancy which is involved with it. Hipponax is always playing a part, which is to be understood as such; he caricatures himself in order to amuse his auditors. As from the boards of a stage he carried the audience into his own situation dramatically (70):

Hold my jacket while I hit Bupalus in the eye. Yes, God gave me two right hands, and every uppercut hurts him.

Hipponax' verse is mostly the 'limping' trimeter or tetrameter. In the final foot, where every kind of verse is most sensitive to distortion, the limping iambus reverses the normal rhythm by ending the last dipody not with the regular short-long but with long-short (or long-long). This rude interruption of regularity gives the verse a special stamp, and the peculiarity is especially striking because Hipponax constructs his verses with absolute strictness and accuracy and permits himself no liberties.

[1] See now O. Masson, *Les fragments du poète Hipponax* (Paris, 1962).

To posterity Hipponax was known as a poet of invective. His insults were aimed most frequently against a respected sculptor named Bupalus.[1a] In this quarrel a woman named Aréte, who had to do with both men, appears to have been involved (21, cf. fr. 15):

I came as it was getting dark to Aréte; the auspices were good: I spent the whole night there.

The entertainment was not the most elegant:

We used a jug to drink from, since her one wine-cup was broken by her servant when he fell over. (16)

... and from the big milk-jug we took our turn to drink, myself and Aréte. (17)

Hipponax gives his verses local coloring appropriate to Asia Minor by inserting Lydian words, even for purely Greek things like the tutelary guardianship of the god Hermes over Cyllene in the Peloponnese (4):

He (Bupalus) called on Maia's son, the Cyllenian rajah. Lord Hermes, watchdog-strangler, friend to all burglars, Maeonian Candaules, help my skaparding.

To invoke a god under several names is common enough in prayers, but here the profusion and translation and explanation sound more literary than natural. The Lydian god Candaules is equated with the Greek Hermes. 'Candaules' is literally 'dog-strangler'; the god is so called because as companion to thieves he makes dogs harmless.[2] What is meant by 'skapard' is quite uncertain. In content too Hipponax cultivates local character (3):

... take the highway to Smyrna through Lydia, by Attalus' their king's tombstone, by the monuments of old Megastrys and Gyges, and by the grave of Atys el kebir Sultan, your belly always pointed to the sun's setting.

The squabble between Hipponax and Bupalus may be compared to that between Odysseus and Irus in the *Odyssey*, at which the suitors were amused spectators. Hipponax presents other scenes of

[1a] A tradition reports that Bupalus carved a portrait statue of Hipponax, who was remarkably ugly, so as to make him ridiculous, whereupon Hipponax revenged himself with his insulting poems (Plin. *Nat. Hist.* 36, 12). The poetic justice of the story renders it suspect, for it makes the poet's caricatures a reaction to those of the sculptor. From Semonides (fr. 48) and Pindar (*Nem.* 5, 1) we know of professional jealousy between sculptors and poets: but this was in an area which is irrelevant so far as Hipponax is concerned.

[2] So E. Lobel, *Oxyrh. Pap.* 18 (1941), 74.

low life: for example, he has a man and a woman curse each other (36):

Apollo take you!—Artemis take you likewise.

He bewails his own poverty (29):

The god of wealth is far too blind to see my house. He never steps inside and whispers, 'Hipponax, I bring you thirty marks of silver: please take them.'

He prays for winter clothing, along with much money (24):

Dear Hermes of Cyllene, son of great Maia, I pray to you with teeth a-chatter, half freezing: a coat I beg and fleecy cloak for Hipponax; a pair of stout boots and some gold staters, some sixty of them, from the inner wall, Hermes.

Since Hermes is the god of lucky finds and of thieves, the prayer is suspicious. How is the sixty staters from the 'inner wall' to get into Hipponax' hands? Naturally the picaresque prayer finds no fulfil-ment (25):

You never gave me any cloak with fleece lining to keep me warm in winter when I was freezing. Nor yet those thick warm boots to put my poor feet in to save me on the frosty days from all chilblains.

Another time his request is much more modest. Hipponax, or one of his figures, asks someone to send him a bushel of barley soon to quiet his hunger; otherwise he will sink into total misery (fr. 42).

New papyrus finds have produced, among other things, remains of an account in the first person; whether the "I" is Hipponax him-self or a person he is miming cannot be determined. Unfortunately, not enough of any single line is preserved to enable us to supply the remainder with certainty. So, for example, we read (fr. IX):

he broke . . . twisting fingers . . . abundantly . . . I rubbed him off while he winced (?) . . . I sprang at him with my heel in his guts . . . I pulled his coat off . . . I locked the doors . . . covered the fire . . . I smeared his nose with baccaris [a perfume], which was as good as that which Croesus . . . In Daskyleion . . .

Such scraps do at least give an inkling of the subject and the style in which it was treated. Some are so filthy they cannot be reproduced. Even heroic legend is represented; one poem bore the title *Odysseus* (*Oxyrh. Pap.* 2174 fr. 5) and one fragment deals with the Trojan War (41):

With chariot of war and speedy white horses of Thracian breed, to conquer Ilium's towers, came pasha Rhesus forth from Aenus and died there.

Verses which taunt a painter are interesting for their factual information (45):

Mimnes, you idiot, leave off! You've now painted along the many-jointed side of that trireme the serpent back to front, with head and jaws sternward. This is a very curse, the worst of all omens, you donkey, for the helmsman when he stands steering to have a viper snapping at his right ankle.

Decorations on vessels were not without meaning: the snake would symbolize the deadly 'bite' of the beak into an enemy ship.[3] Another fragment is remarkable for its mockery of a gluttonous woman in epic hexameters and in pseudo-Homeric style (fr. 77). Parody is not a 'popular' but a literary genre.

So far as we can see[4] the poems of Hipponax constituted a coarse and grotesque literature of entertainment.

(f) *Solon the Athenian*

Our study of Ionian poetry of entertainment has taken us down to the close of the sixth century. We now revert to the turn of the seventh to the sixth century. At that time Mimnermus in Colophon in Asia Minor composed this couplet (fr. 6, p. 210, above):

Would that, without any sickness, without any trouble or sorrow I could at three-score years come to the end of my days.

From the other side of the broad Aegean Sea, from the Greek motherland, came a polite criticism during Mimnermus' own lifetime (Solon fr. 22):

If you will heed my advice, though late, please alter the couplet; please do not take it amiss if I propose to emend. Alter the phrase, most gifted of poets, write it as follows: 'I could at four-score years come to the end of my days.'

This sounds as if only a single word required revision; actually the ground is cut from under one of Mimnermus' principal theses. If the limit of life worth living is so far postponed, the contrast of youth and old age of which Mimnermus makes so much (see p. 209–211, above) is pointless. Moreover the critic continues:

Nor let my death be unwept, unnoticed: may my old comrades shed for me many a tear when I have left them behind.

[3] See p. 39 n. 32, above.

[4] We have no piece of any length with unbroken context, and even if we had, we could understand it only imperfectly. Even in the specimens which we have offered many a detail is uncertain.

Where Mimnermus had thought that an old man was only an object of annoyance and general disdain (fr. 1 and 3), here there is hope that the death even of an eighty-year-old would be a grave loss to his friends. If Mimnermus complained that mental powers failed in old age (fr. 5), here the same elegy continues:

As I grow old I learn many new things on the way.

Nor will the critic admit that no willing partner for the game of love can be found in old age. On the contrary; after an active career which raised him to absolute dominion over his country, in his later years he undertook a program of devoting himself henceforward to the joys of love, wine, and poetry (20):

The works of the Cyprian goddess, of Bacchus and of the Muses too, which make men joyous at heart are dear to me now.

The man who, conscious of his own powerful vitality, entered the lists with the soft Lydian was Solon of Athens. For the first time the voice of Attica is heard in literature,[1] the land which later, in the fifth century, was to assume leadership. And for the first time we can hear, across an interval of millennia, the voice of one who played a great part in world history, and can be affected by the words he then spoke, in their authentic form.

Solon was born about 640 of one of the best families in the land.[2] He was thus a contemporary of Pittacus and of Alcaeus of Lesbos. At that time Attica began to give up its land-locked exclusiveness and to cultivate foreign trade on a large scale; these were the first steps on the path to power and grandeur. With Pittacus and the men of Lesbos Athens waged a war for the possession of Sigeum, which was an important station for trade with coasts of the Black Sea; it was in that war that Alcaeus lost his shield. But more urgent for Athens was the acquisition of the island of Salamis, which flanked the sea-lane out of the harbor of Athens; Salamis was held by the neighboring city of Megara. Solon advocated war to secure this island, which was essential for the rise of Athens, and made propaganda for his idea in an original fashion. Like Tyrtaeus, he puts his admonition in the form of an elegy. The first of its fifty couplets reads as follows (2):

Coming myself as herald from Salamis' beautiful island I bring you verses and song taking the place of a speech.

The poem is therefore a substitute for a speech in the popular as-

[1] From approximately the same time, the close (?) of the seventh century, comes the beautiful Attic *Hymn to Demeter* (p. 251f., below).

[2] Cf. I. M. Linforth, *Solon the Athenian* (Berkeley, 1919), 27ff.

sembly. Instead of delivering a discourse and arguing for it in the usual way, Solon appears in a dramatic pose with a song in which he plays the part of a supposed envoy from Salamis and in the name of the island pleads for its liberation.[3] The second fragment from the same elegy is also dramatic, if in a different way; now the fiction is abandoned and Solon speaks as an Athenian.

(If Athens abandoned Salamis) then would I fain change countries— Athenian call me no longer; name me Sicinnian then or Pholegandrian boor. All too soon would the saying arise, when men met together: 'These are Athenians—look!—those who let Salamis go.'

A warning that one's own nation must not become a laughing-stock to its neighbors was a traditional theme in a patriotic harangue;[4] here it is given effective point. Pholegandrus and Sicinnus, two tiny rock-islands in the Aegean, exemplify the state to which Athens might be degraded. The taunt at the end coins a new slogan, Σαλαμιναφέται ('forfeitors of Salamis') with which those like-minded with Solon could castigate their opponents. Still a third fragment of the elegy is preserved:

Let us go to Salamis then, to fight for the beautiful island, clearing away from our fair name shame and dishonor.

The enterprise was undertaken; it was successful; Salamis fell to Athens and was settled by Athenians.

The four distichs of the Salamis elegy show a noble inspiration and a vigorous political temperament; they also show the skill of a successful agitator. Whereas Solon's contemporary Alcaeus in his poems speaks out of his own heart again and again—he laments his sorrows or exults in his luck, he reproaches bitterly or brags stoutly, he complains indignantly or submits with resignation—Solon speaks to the hearts of his hearers in order to convince them by logic, vividly, to be sure, but above all rationally. The songs of Alcaeus are on the whole more poetic because they are more impulsive and lively in swiftly-changing emotions and in sharp and clear pictures of momentary conditions. Multiplicity of moods, so strikingly expressed in Alcaeus, is wanting in Solon's verses, for here the person of the speaker is wholly taken up in his subject, while the contrary is true of the Lesbian. Solon's purpose, for the most part, is to demonstrate or counsel; his poetry is predominantly didactic, like that of Hesiod, the other poet of the mainland. From the Ionian East Solon adopted

[3] We can easily imagine that Solon actually delivered his elegy first in the popular assembly before he circulated it as a broadside.
[4] Cf. Callinus 1, 2 (p. 152, above).

for his purposes the two forms of current poetic discourse, iambic and elegiac.

Solon's political capacity proved itself above all in the intestine quarrels which at that time divided and weakened Athens no less than other Greek communities. Here too he set to work with his poems. The subject was more difficult and complex than that of the Salamis elegy, if it was to be approached reasonably and not with blind fanaticism. Unlike Alcaeus, Solon tried to place himself above the contending parties. His poems reflect the contemporary state of affairs and of thought with all the problems which they raised. Each problem is thoughtfully examined from basic principles, and brought to a firm conclusion. The dark intensity of his thoughts combines with the bright intensity of his purpose to achieve an unostentatious emotive power which is characteristic of his poetry and his attitude to life. The Ionian translucency is wanting; often the verses are unclear. Wanting too is the flatness without depth which developed in the East out of the reaction against late epic and then became a natural attitude. Indeed, the firmly contoured style in general is absent. Solon of Athens does not carry forward what the masters of the art before him had begun. He does not take his place in a line of development, but borrows from tradition only what he is able and willing to use in order to help Athens in its need.

In an elegy of which we have considerable remains Solon offers the following diagnosis for ailments from which his fatherland was suffering (3):

> Never will Athens vanish away by immortal commandment,
>   By the Olympians' wish or by the will of Zeus,
> Since the daughter of Zeus, our guardian Pallas Athene,
>   Goddess proud and sublime, shelters us under her hand.
> Athens' own citizens, rather, astray and blinded by folly,
>   Mad with the lust for gain, threaten their state with its end.
> Unjust too are the thoughts of her leaders: looming before us
>   Countless sorrows appear, born of their arrogant pride.
> Nor have they wit to hold back from surfeit, nor to taste fitly
>   Pleasures that lie to their hand, joys that the banquet provides.

Solon is warning the thoughtless Athenians that catastrophe threatens the city if it continues as before. And indeed it is not divine fate[5] that desires the destruction of Athens; for his piety tells the poet that the city's tutelary deity will not allow it to fall of itself. Rather it is the citizens themselves who are responsible for the present situation. Thus, very strikingly, responsibility is removed from the gods and

[5] Solon has no occasion to differentiate between fate and the gods as epic sometimes does (p. 57, above).

imposed upon men.[6] The statesman demands that the community take its fate into its own hands. For it is not yet too late for reform, according to Solon, as the whole tenor of the poem shows; the first need is clearly to recognize the critical situation. So Solon informs the public that the citizens' selfish greed for money is on the point of ruining the state. The rich and noble gentry in whose hands lies the direction of public affairs bend and break the law; in their 'surfeit' they affront and humiliate the masses entrusted to their leadership; they do not understand the art of enjoying their happy circumstances decently, in a social and companionable way and of living their lives without harm to the community.[7]

After a gap there follows a single verse (3.11):

Having amassed their wealth by their unrighteous deeds.

then another gap and then the following (3.12):

Neither the city's store nor the possessions of gods
Do they hold in awe, but plunder and steal all things from all quarters:
    Dike's exalted law they rashly hold in contempt.
Yet she knows[8] in her silence the deeds that were done or are doing;
    And in time she comes always, to avenge.
Now this comes on the whole city, an inescapable wound:
    Quickly it falls into enslavement and shame
If it awakes intestine strife and slumbering discord,
    Cruelly cutting short many a life in its prime.
Soon at the hands of its foes will a lovely city be ruined
    . . . (unintelligible) . . .
Such are the evils that dwell in our midst, while many a poor man,
    Leaves his own country behind, sold into serfdom abroad,
Dragging out weary days in the shameful bondage of fetters.

In this section Solon attacks the faults of the ruling classes and

[6] Similarly at the beginning of the *Odyssey* Zeus says (1, 32ff.): 'Men blame the gods for what they must suffer, and thus they have pains (aside from the sufferings sent by the gods) which they draw upon themselves by their own wickedness over and above their fate . . . .' Cf. W. Jaeger, *Sitzungsber. Preuss. Akad.*, 1926, 69ff.= *Scripta Minora* I, 315ff.=*Five Essays*, 77ff.

[7] Cf. the beautiful description of such innocent pleasures in Pindar, *Py.* 4, 294: (Damophilos wishes) συμποσίας ἐφέπων θυμὸν ἐκδόσθαι πρὸς ἥβαν πολλάκις, ἔν τε σοφοῖς δαιδαλέαν φόρμιγγα βαστάζων πολίταις ἡσυχίᾳ θιγέμεν (cf. ἐν ἡσυχίῃ Solon), μήτ' ὤν τινι πῆμα πορών, ἀπαθὴς δ' αὐτὸς πρὸς ἀστῶν.

[8] Literally: 'who silent shares knowledge': a superhuman power takes cognizance of and remembers guilt in order for punishment to take place at a given time. Only at a considerably later period was a 'shared knowledge' ('with-knowledge'— συνείδησις, *conscientia*, 'conscience') transferred to the agent himself, so that he was split inwardly; beside the person who is tempted by transgression and may succumb to it, there resides within him a second person whose moral judgment cannot be bribed, his 'conscience'.

threatens the sinners with the punishment which *Dikê* (justice) would
surely exact at some time, though it might be later. He is not content
with citing the axiom that every sin will some day find its requital, but
seeks to describe in concrete form the mechanism by which political
transgressions consistently bring their own punishment.[9] Still, the
deduction is not quite clear. Solon points out that things are already
going badly for Athens; many citizens have fallen into slavery because
of debt, and by the harsh legal principles of the time were sold by their
creditors into slavery abroad. But an even worse fate is inevitable for
the entire community in the near future (v.17). After a gap there
follows a warning that no individual will be able to escape the
general disaster (3.26):

> Thus will the city's fate come home to every man's hearthstone:
>   Locking the gates of the yard serves not to keep it at bay.
> Over the highest fence does it leap, and comes at its victim
>   Straight, without fail, though he lie hid in the innermost room.
> By my soul I am bidden to teach the Athenian people:
>   What great evils and pains lawlessness brings to the state,
> Just as the well-lawed state makes all things fitting and even;
>   It fetters those who would trample on justice and right;
> Smooths what is rough, puts reins on extravagance, bridles presumption,
>   Nips in the earliest bud ruin that threatens to bloom.
> It straightens the twisted judgment and humbles all overweening;
>   Strictly suppresses wrongs bidden by faction and strife,
> Softens the anger bred by contention. Where there is good law,
>   There are all human affairs ordered with justice and sense.

The conclusion echoes the hymn which Hesiod had sung to Zeus
as guardian of right at the opening of the *Works and Days*. But now the
same praise is applied not to the god but to good social and moral
order (εὐνομία). As Solon says, order evens out all difficulties, and in
checking opposing forces preserves itself. For under order everything
is made 'even and reasonable' (39). 'Even' (ἄρτιος) is a favorite word
in Solon; it designates what is proper and right. Another word that
is noticeably recurrent is 'surely,' 'by all means' (πάντως). Just as it
is an established fact for Solon that the gods are well disposed to
Athens, so he believes that the natural chain of causes and effects will
'surely' satisfy the metaphysical postulate of guilt and requital (fr.
3.16 and 28; 1.8; 28; 31; 55). And just as he trusts his ideas, so he
does the zeal which inspires him. He relies not on a higher mission
assigned to him, but justifies his admonition by saying that it was
assigned to him by his heart (*thymos*).

In the confusion of contemporary political strife Solon felt like a

[9] Cf. G. Vlastos, *Class. Philol.* 41 (1946), 65ff.

man with sight among the blind. When the lower stratum, which was wholly in the power of the ruling families, rose against their conscienceless oppressors and the struggle for power between the two groups for a long while crippled the life of the state, Solon admonished both parties to use their reason. The elegy begins with these words (4):

Yes, I know, and my heart is filled with sorrow within me, when I behold our state, first of Ionian lands, now sinking to decay . . .

The vigorous opening which is not followed by a regular grammatical construction, arises out of the sense of responsibility of the counsellor who sees Attica, the ancestral home of the Ionian race, in collapse. Then to the powerful and wealthy he says:

. . . I am frightened seeing your greed for gold, seeing your actions of pride.

and then advises them to reform:

Bring under control the imperious heart in your bosom, you who enjoy to the full all that existence affords. Moderate your ambitions now, for we will not be the yielders, and you will not find all things easy and tractable.

The 'we' is to be explained as another dramatic element in Solon's admonition. In the elegy, as we are told, he battles 'for both parties against both parties.' Here where he is accusing the rich he identifies himself with the opposition. Then he again assumes his own person to urge all the contenders in common to a reconciliation.

The agitation was effective. Solon received plenary powers from his fellow-citizens to reform the Attic state. He administered this high office in the year 594 (?) and gave Athens a new constitution and new laws; moreover he enacted revolutionary emergency measures such as the cancellation of all public and private debts. After the expiration of his term he dutifully withdrew to private life. To confer absolute power for reorganization of the state was at that time nothing unusual; at about the same period Pittacus was entrusted with such a task in Lesbos. Alcaeus reacted with an expression of utter astonishment, for he could not imagine a selfless use of power; rather he expected that Pittacus would use the office that fell to him to plunder the city completely (fr. 129, 348, and 70, p. 192f., above). Solon too found that many could not understand his loyalty to the state; they explained his restraint as a sign of weakness and timidity. In a poem written not in elegiacs but in trochaic tetrameters Solon has these mockers themselves appear and express their opinions (23):

Solon is no clever thinker nor a sharp and prudent man. When the gods held out their greatest gift, he would not take it up; when his prey lay fast entangled, stupidly he failed to draw the net tight: he lacked the courage even as he lacked the wit. Now if I could win power and riches without end, and could be tyrant here in Athens for one single fleeting day, flay me into wineskins after, and blot out my family.[10]

To such unchecked avidity for power and enjoyment Solon does not oppose a 'conscience' which reminded him of his duty to his country; for there was no 'conscience' as yet.[11] But there was reputation and the expectation that he would hit upon a correct decision, and Solon hoped that a better reputation would follow upon his superior mode of action (23.8):

If I have spared my fatherland, if I have not turned my hand to tyranny and brutal force, if I have not soiled and stained the character I had before I am not ashamed, but rather think, by acting as I have, I rise above all other men.

What others call 'the best,'[12] the ruthless exploitation of power, seems to Solon a disgrace that would stain his reputation.

The purity with which Solon conducted his office appears in the fact that he sought his own path between the parties and in the end disappointed them all. We know a common saying on the tactics of political and personal rivalry: 'Be complaisant to your enemy, but when he is in your power forget the pretty words and be revenged on him' (Theognis 363f.). Many expected such behavior from Solon, and regarded his mild admonitions and warnings to both parties only as a cunning opening move; but then when things became serious, Solon would have to expropriate the rich for the benefits of the poor. On such presumptions Solon subsequently expressed himself in the following verses (23.13):

Many came with hopes of plunder: their expectations soared high, for they thought that wealth and riches were to drop into their hands, that after smooth complaisance I would bare a ruthless heart. All those hopes were vain and baseless: so they now with angry hearts look at men with a sidelong glance, as if I were their enemy. Wrongly so; for, thanks to god, I did exactly what I said. I would be false had I done more: to govern with a tyrant's sway became me ill, and I could not approve that here, on Attic soil, good and bad should share alike in this our rich inheritance.

It was not Solon's intention to create a democracy in the modern

---

10 That these verses refer to Solon's position as arbiter, as is assumed in the text above, is probable but not entirely certain.

11 See p. 221 n. 8, above.

12 On ἐσθλά (2) cf. *Frühgriech. Denken*, p. 67 n. 3.

sense; he makes a distinction between the classes of 'good' and 'bad.' In an elegy which he wrote after holding office he prides himself on having found a correct balance between the upper and lower strata (5):

> Power as much as sufficed I placed in the hands of the people
>   Nothing I took from their rights: nothing I added to them
> Likewise for those who were mighty, whom men esteemed for their riches,
>   I contrived that they should have nothing but that which was seemly.
> There I stood with my shield protecting the one and the other.
>   Neither this party nor that did I allow to win wrongly.

The lower stratum he sought to deal with in such a way that they remained content but did not kick over the traces (5.7):

> This way will best assure that the people go with their leaders,
>   Not too freely released, neither too sternly repressed,
> Outrage is Surfeit's child when men not balanced in judgment
>   Find in sudden excess riches and wealth in their hand.

Again and again Solon had to defend himself against accusations of both parties, for both thought they had received less than their due: 'in great actions it is hard to please all' (5,11). In happy contrast to Alcaeus, it is only with diffidence that he utters an 'open reproach' —which does not seem to us a reproach at all but rather a calm and objective statement of fact (25):

If I may openly reproach the citizens: What they now have, they never would have seen before, in their wildest dreams, (had it not been for me). The greater men, indeed, the mighty in the land, would praise me and would call me friend (if they only knew how another would have carried out this task, if it had fallen to his lot instead of mine): he never would have held the people back, or stopped his churning till he drew the cream off for himself. But I took up my station in the ground between the warring factions.[13]

The meter of this piece is iambic trimeter, which was later to become the principal meter of Attic drama.

The most important of all the fragments of Solon we possess, from a literary point of view, is another iambic piece in which he defends himself anew against the charge that he had abused the confidence of those who had commissioned his task and had broken his promises. Here he points with pride to the results he had effected by his cancellation of debts: he had abolished hypothecation of real estate and thereby liberated Attic land, indeed Mother Earth herself, from

[13] On the last verse cf. E. Römisch, *Studien zur älteren griechischen Elegie* (Frankfurt, 1933), 77ff. The supplements in the translation are intended only to complete the sense.

bondage;[14] he had freed Attic citizens who had been reduced to slavery by the debts guaranteed by their persons, and had abolished the institution of enslavement for debt. Such measures were acts of 'violence,' for they disrupted existing law; and yet they were 'righteous,' for the 'power' to effect them was placed in Solon's legally. The rest of what Solon has to say in this remarkable piece can be understood from the text itself without difficulty (24):

> But all those purposes for which I first drew together
> The people, I have now accomplished and fulfilled.[15]
> To be my witness at the judgment seat of Time
> First I call her who is of all the Olympian gods
> The common mother—dark Earth, from whom I drew
> The stones of debt that everywhere were driven in.
> She dwelt before in servitude: now she is free.
> And many I brought back from far to their own home,
> Divinely founded Athens—some who had been sold
> By form of law, some by no law, while some had fled
> Through burden of their debts, and now no longer spoke
> Their native Attic, wandering so long abroad;
> And others still, who in this land endured the stain
> Of slavery, and trembled at their master's whim,
> Through me regained their freedom. This is what I did
> By power of the law, combining force and right
> In one, and so encompassed all my promises.
> My laws I wrote for all, for high and low alike,
> And dealt an evenhanded justice out to each.
> If someone else had held the reins of power, a man
> Of evil will and greatly covetous of gold,
> He had not held the people back. If I had done
> At one time what my present enemies desire
> And at another what the rival party bade,
> Then would our state be poorer by full many lives;
> And therefore did I fight my fight on every side,
> Most like a wolf when many dogs encompass him.

The flow of these verses is wholly different from anything we have read before. It rolls onward like a great speech in classical tragedy. It is as if a dam were removed, as if Solon the liberator had unfettered the torrent of speech as well. Here is pendulum beat swinging to and fro in rhythmic alternation like waves on the sea-shore; no themes spreading out in ripples that move in circles and gradually ebb away; no rapid succession of individual statements busily floating

---

[14] Even Roman law designates certain obligations on land not indeed as hypothecation but as *servitutes*. In Greece a stone upon which the debt was inscribed was erected on the land subject to the obligation.

[15] τυγχάνω can be connected with neuter pronouns in the accusative.

new material to the same site.[16] Even the grammatical structure is different; the sentences are long and carry one subject after another to completion in a lucid arrangement without, at the end, slipping back to the beginning. Surely and steadily, the discourse presses forward without pause in a consistent and solid stream. There is nothing archaic in the style of this portion.

After his reorganization of the Attic state Solon took up his travels; allegedly, he removed himself from his country for ten years in order that the system he had created might go into operation independently of his person. In any case, he resumed his old calling of merchant and visited foreign countries. He sailed to the mouth of the Nile (fr. 6) and to Cyprus. There he was hospitably received by Philocyprus, the king of the island. At his departure he dedicated an elegy to Philocyprus in which he wrote the following (7):

> Many more years may you live and rule the people of Soloi
> Dwelling here in the state, you and your sons to succeed.
> Then may Cypris,[17] violet crowned, convey me in safety
> In my swift-sailing ship home from this island of fame.
> May she spread grace and renown and dignity over your people;
> May she safely bring me home to my own native land.

Here again we have the archaic beat of the pendulum: 'you-I-you-I.' Only occasionally and rarely in the flowing measure of the iambus, which had so bright a future before it, did Solon break the bonds of the antique mode of speech and expression.

Solon had disdained to draw in the wide-spread net and make himself tyrant of Athens; Pisistratus was otherwise minded. Twice he subjected the state to this rule, and was exiled twice. When he set about a third attempt he received this oracle from a knowledgeable seer (Herodotus 1.62):

Now the cast has been made and the net spread wide in the ocean; under the moonlit night soon will the tunnies abound.

The coup was successful; this time Pisistratus was able to retain his rule and bequeath his dominion to his sons.

Of Pisistratus' three periods of rule, Solon was still alive during the beginning of the first, in 561/60. More than thirty years had passed since he had renewed the Attic state, and he had become an old man. Pisistratus is said to have treated him with respect and to have sought his advice often, for his policy of favoring the people carried forward the democratic trend which Solon had begun. Although Solon

[16] For the characteristics of the archaic course of thought see Index A 3, 3 and *Frühgriech. Denken*, 40–96.

[17] *Cypris* designates Aphrodite as principal goddess of Cyprus.

approved much that Pisistratus did, he remained a sharp opponent
of monarchical government. He had seen the tyranny approaching
before it arrived and had warned his fellow citizens of the impending
danger in vain (10):

Out of the cloud comes the heavy snow and the hailstorm: hard on the
lightning flash follows the thunder's report. So through her greatest men
is a city ruined; the many by their foolishness pass under dominion of one.
He whom one lifts too high is not pulled down again lightly: all such
things should be weighed carefully before one begins.[18]

This parallel shows Solon as having found that just as nature possesses
an inner logic and regularity, so does political life also. If the
consequences do not please us, we must not let the causes come about.[19]
Again, this establishes human responsibility for human fate (see
p. 220, above); consistently with this, there is no god Zeus in the
simile to cause the tempest and hurl lightning.

Here the simile does not merely illustrate a situation, as in Homer,
but it argues and demonstrates a thesis.[20] Solon applies the same
method another time (11):

When the sea is in anger, its waves are raised by the tempest:
Nothing can be more just were it but left to itself.

Again the logic of nature is transposed to political events. Following
the precedent of Homer (p. 43, above) the sea serves as an image of
the people, its movement as a symbol for popular moods or movements, and the wind which stirs the waves corresponds to the will of
the popular leader. In his image Solon shows that the people in itself
is the 'justest of all things';[21] responsibility for unrest lies not with the
people but with its leaders.

[18] Perhaps ἀλλ' ἤδη χρὴ πρὶν ἅπαντα νοεῖν.
[19] Cf. also the chain of cause and effect in fr. 3, 17ff. (p. 221, above).
[20] Cf. O. Regenbogen, *Quellen und Forsch. zur Gesch. der Mathem.* B 1 (1930),
131ff. (=*Kleine Schriften* [Munich, 1961] 141ff.), and B. Snell, *The Discovery of the
Mind* (Cambridge, Mass., 1953) 191–226.
[21] According to Semonides fr. 7, 27ff. (p. 203 and 205f., above) the inconstant
and moody sea has two natures, one friendly and one raging, and in the general
ancient outlook the sea was 'associated with injustice' (A. S. Pease, *Harvard
Studies in Class. Phil.* 54 [1943], 71; other examples: Propertius 1, 15, 12, Ovid,
Am. 2, 11, 12). Solon corrects two errors at once by analogy: neither sea nor
people is unjust; rather the sea (people) becomes violent, unpredictable, and
mischievous only under the influence of winds (leaders): but when the sea is left
at rest (so that it can exhibit its own nature), it shows itself 'the justest of all things,'
i.e., there is nothing smoother, more innocent, and peaceable than the even
surface of the quiet sea, and the same is true of the broad masses of the people. The
comparison recurs frequently in ancient literature; so in Polybius 11, 29, 9–11:
καθάπερ κἀκείνης (sc. τῆς θαλάττης) ἡ μὲν ἰδία φύσις ἐστὶν ἀβλαβὴς τοῖς χρωμένοις καὶ στάσιμος

Solon's warning of threatening tyranny only resulted in his being considered crazy. To this accusation he replies with an expression of unshakable certainty (9):

Soon, very soon will the people learn the extent of my madness, when the truth shall come forth openly into their midst.[22]

When matters then took their course and Pisistratus did in fact set up his rule, Solon again showed the people that not the gods but they themselves were to blame for the mischief (8):

If you have met with reverses because of your weakness and folly, do not seek to divert blame for it onto the gods. You yourselves made these men great; you gave them protectors,[23] and you have thereby won serfdom and shame for yourselves. Each one among you can follow the tracks of a fox to his burrow; yet, when taken all together, you are no better than fools. You pay heed to the tongue and the shifty words of a speaker; but you do not heed facts happening under your eyes.

What Solon asserts in the final four verses is the basic phenomenon of what is now called mass psychology; the surprising contrast between the intelligence of each individual and the stupidity of the collected multitude which allows itself to be misled by a clever speaker.

Of the fragments with non-political content several reproduce thoughts that were generally current. So Solon says (17):

Wholly concealed from men is the will (mind, spirit: νοῦς) of the blessed Immortals.

Or he declares (15):

Man who is born of woman can never be happy, but evil, evil, I say, are all under the light of the sun.

The contrast between 'happy' and 'evil' itself shows that Solon is not

κ.τ.λ.—τὸν αὐτὸν τρόπον καὶ τὸ πλῆθος κ.τ.λ. Livy 28, 27, 11: sed multitudo omnis sicut natura maris per se immobilis est, etc., and 38, 10, 5f. where the comparison is called a vulgata similitudo. In Herodotus 7, 16 b 1 it is applied to the king of the Persians instead of to the people. Perhaps the passage of Solon supplied the impulse for all of these. Similar in thought and formulation is Theognis 313f. (see p. 412, below): 'While the rest are mad (i.e., at a wild drinking party: cf. the storms at sea) I am frenzied too (μάλα μαίνομαι, cf. e.g., θάλασσα μαίνεται, Semon. fr. 7, 39); but among the righteous (i.e., in normal circumstances) I am the most righteous of all men.'

[22] The last clause cannot be properly translated because to the Greeks 'reality' and 'truth' fused into a single conception. Hence from one point of view the sentence is saying two kinds of things at the same time, namely that the actuality of the prophesied tyranny would come to the citizens of Athens, and that the truth of Solon's prophecy would soon become obvious to everyone. The irony of Solon's acceptance of the word 'madness' is striking.

[23] Or 'pledges': the meaning of the line is uncertain.

thinking of the values we call 'moral.' Rather he means that no human
life is free of disappointment; if a man is sad and wretched only
transitorily, he is transferred to 'badness' once and for all and can
therefore not be called 'happy.' Only the gods are 'happy'; but even
a man can be 'fortunate' (13):

Fortunate count I the man with loving children, with horses, dogs that
are keen for the chase, and a good guest-friend abroad.

Solon occupies himself repeatedly with the question of men's
fortune—the same question asked of the wise Solon by the fabulously
rich King Croesus when Solon visited him on his travels, in Herodotus'
story. We receive an original answer in the following verses (14):

Equally rich is the man who has gold and silver aplenty, acres of golden
wheat ripening in the rich plain, horses and oxen; and he who counts as
his only possessions something to eat; clothing for his back, and shoes for
his feet, joy when the season comes, in beauty of youth or of maiden,
pleasures in which our youth fitly may take its delight. This is true wealth
for a man: whoever has more to his portion leaves all the surplus behind
when he goes down to the shades. No man buys himself off from death or
painful diseases, and a bribe will not turn back age in its silent approach.

The tone of this piece is light and the style graceful. Balancing three
kinds of property, in silver, gold and land, is the threefold comfort of
being fed, clothed and shod; and opposed to the public splendor of
horses and mules is the private enjoyment of the love of boys and
women. In the contrast of five things on each side we can easily
recognize Archilochus' contrast of imaginary and real values, or, for
that matter, the same turning aside from ostentatious possessions
in favor of personal and private pleasure which is the essential
feature of Sappho's Anactoria poem (fr. 16 LP, p. 185f., above). But
whereas Sappho rates the rapture of a lover higher than admiration
for the pomp of power, Solon shows a much more bourgeois preference for physical well-being over wealth and its display. In his view
the pleasures of a festive hour[24] deserve the preference because they
can be enjoyed directly, whereas nothing more can be done with
excessive wealth than to leave it to one's heirs. What we have before
us is presumably a piece of banqueting poetry (cf. fr. 20, p. 218,
above), to which the references to old age, sickness, and death are
appropriate. Solon assures the diners and drinkers reclining on soft
cushions that at the present moment (cf. πάρεστι, line 3) they possess
the highest fortune available to mortals. They are comfortably fed,

---

[24] The use of the aorist παθεῖν shows that no permanent state, but only an
occasion is intended.

clothed and shod, and the enjoyment of a youthful body is in prospect.[25] No one has reason to envy the richer or to strive for ever greater possessions. In a political elegy (fr. 3, p. 220, above) Solon advised the nobles to spend their time harmlessly at dinner-parties rather than bring the state to ruin by greed for possessions. Something similar is recommended here, without the political implication. And here, furthermore, there is mention of the natural limits beyond which fortune could not rise.

In many respects the fragment shows the influence of Mimnermus.[26] But Solon does not see the pleasure of love as the only thing that makes life worth living, as Mimnermus does, and he does not strike tones of lament. Instead he directs people to a happy fulfillment of all natural, vital urges and to the firm ordinance of nature which, among other things, allows us to enjoy the pleasures of love at the proper season, in the years of youth (line 6). Solon believes in order generally, but particularly in the order of nature (fr. 10; 11; 1, 18–25). While Mimnermus saw aging as a catastrophic transformation from youth to senility, Solon regarded the natural course of life as a succession of many stages differing by degrees. To this theme Solon devoted an entire elegy which is preserved complete (fr. 19).[27] Here the life of a man is divided into ten periods of seven years each. The first seven years bring to the child, still immature and without understanding, the growth and loss of his first teeth. If god allows the boy to complete the second seven years, signs of developing puberty appear. In the third period the young man's cheeks are covered with down, while his limbs are still growing. In the fourth period every man is at the height of his strength, which is the mark of his quality (*areté*) (?). In the fifth period a man should think of marriage and offspring. The sixth gives him clarity of mind and freedom from awkwardness of behavior. The fourteen years of the seventh and eighth periods (age 42 to 56) bring the ripest maturity of understanding and speaking. In the ninth tongue and wit are still competent, but too feeble for high quality ('great *areté*'). After the close of the tenth heptad, so we are told at the end, a man is 'not untimely struck by the lot of death.'[28] The elegy devotes one distich to each

[25] Solon speaks of pederasty in fr. 12 also.
[26] Solon's vv. 5 and 6 sound very like vv. 5 and 4 in Mimnermus' fr. 1.
[27] On this cf. W. Schadewaldt, *Antike* 9 (1933), 297ff. (=*Hellas und Hesperien* [Zurich and Stuttgart, 1960] 41–59). Many parallels from other literature are adduced by Franz Boll, *Die Lebensalter* (1913: not accessible to me).
[28] The apparent discrepancy with fr. 22, 4 (p. 217, above) can be cleared up: there a personal wish is expressed, while here the normal case is stated; there a polemical purpose led Solon to make the divergence between the two ways of life seem as wide as possible.

epoch, except that the seventh and eighth are combined into a single couplet. Artistically the rather dry poem is of no interest; what is notable is the calm and objective way in which Solon accepts natural development in its rise and decline.

There remains a final small moralizing fragment to discuss.[29] It too deals with wealth (4, 9):

Many good men are poor, and many villains are wealthy, yet I would never exchange places with such men as these, and give up goodness for riches: Virtue is something enduring; riches go about from one man's purse to another's.

Solon counted himself not among the rich, then, but among the good. What qualities he had in mind for 'goodness' (*areté*) is not shown; but it implies considerable enlightenment that in his opinion goodness has nothing to do with wealth and that it attaches to its bearer permanently. For, according to the prevailing view, one of the properties inherent in goodness was success and hence wealth, and many believed that failure put the stamp of 'badness' on a man hitherto 'good.'[30]

But here Solon places wealth and goodness on opposite sides of the scale, as he weighed wealth against sensual pleasures in the preceding fragment (14), and a third time (fr. 23, p. 224, above) arrayed wealth and power (lines 5–8) as against reputation (line 10). As yet, indeed, there is no differentiation between 'inward' and 'outward' goods (the time for this was still far off); but the person—its natural pleasures, its virtue, and the reflection of its virtue in reputation—is rated higher than possessions.[31]

A lengthy elegy in which Solon expresses himself on basic questions of human existence is preserved in its entirety. Here is the text (1):

Born to Olympian Zeus and to Memory, fairest of children, you of Pieria's spring, Muses, attend to my prayer. Grant me, I pray, from the gods prosperity, and from my fellow mortals always to have honor and goodly report. (5) Let me always be kind to my friends, to my enemies bitter, held in respect by the one and in fear by the other. Wealth I would gladly possess, but I have no wish to acquire it wickedly. Sooner or later comes the requital for sin. (9) Riches bestowed by the gods make the man

[29] The couplet of fr. 16 admits of widely divergent interpretations between which we cannot decide without the original context.

[30] This view underlies Solon's fr. 15 (p. 229, above); with him, then, the old views went side by side with the emerging new. It is only in Simonides that we find a decisive change in this respect (p. 307–12, below).

[31] This is approximately the Archilochean attitude to self; Solon (fr. 14, 9–10) and Archilochus (fr. 6, p. 137f., above) both use the argument that a man cannot ransom himself from death with money. But the more radical Archilochus disdains honor and reputation (fr. 6; fr. 9 and 65, p. 139, above).

who receives them happy. Strongly founded and fast, they are a good that
endures. Riches that men pursue with violence come not in due order but
pressed and compelled, (13) yielding to actions of sin, follow unwilling. Soon
blindness comes on them that do evil.[32] In the beginning it is slight, like
the first smoke of a fire, scarce to be seen at first, but fearful indeed in its
outcome. Actions of arrogant pride never endure among men. (17) Zeus
looks through to the end of all things, and then on a sudden, just as a wind
in spring rises and scatters the clouds, starts the barren billowy ocean from
its very depths, levels the ripening wheat in the rich well-tilled fields, (21)
reaches up to the pinnacled seat of the blessed immortals, and cleanses
the sky, which shines pure in its brightness again: now the sun shines
brilliantly down on the earth and its richness, not a single cloud is to be
seen anywhere: (25) such is the punishment sent by Zeus. He does not, as
men do, feed his resentment at each several action of guilt. Yet no mortal of
sinful mind can escape him for ever; sooner or late, his guilt comes at the
end into sight. (29) One is punished today; another reprieved to the morrow.
Even if one shall escape, so that the justice of God falls not on him, still,
still it will come: his innocent children or their children in turn pay at the
last for his sin. (33) But we mortals, the good and the evil among us imagine
that it will go with each as he supposes himself (?) till disaster befalls:
then we weep. But up to that moment we are amusing ourselves with the
vain pleasures of hope. (37) So the man who lies sick and plagued by painful
diseases hopes that in no long time vigor and health will be his. So the
worthless wretch supposes that he has talent and virtue; one is handsome to
himself, though to all others he is abhorred.[33] (41) Or if a man is poor and
penury's anguish afflicts him, still he is sure some day that riches and
wealth will be his. Hence they all strive onward in sundry fashions, and
this one hopes to be rich by trade, venturing far in his ship over the fishy
deep, (45) shaken and storm-tossed by gales, and in the hope of gain stakes
on the issue his life. That one, pinning his faith to his well-curved plough and
his oxen works year in, year out, tilling the tree-bearing soil; (49) this one,
versed in Athene's arts and the trade of Hephaestus, lives by the hard won
knowledge and skill of his hands. While yet another, with gifts bestowed by
the heavenly Muses, understands all rules governing music and art. (53)
Another receives prophetic vision from Apollo the archer, and from afar
he foresees evils that come upon men, for the immortals dwell with him;
yet that which is fated omen or auspice never averts from mortal man. (57)
Some discharge the tasks of Paean the healer as physicians; even they have
no power over the end of their work. Often unbearable anguish comes from
trivial pain and their soothing drugs cannot help to diminish the pangs.
(61) Then again, they may make healthy again one tormented by evil and
painful diseases by the mere touch of a hand. Destiny brings her curses
to men, and brings also her blessings. What the immortals send, no-one
can ever escape. (65) All that we do is fraught with danger: no-one can ever

---

[32] Cf. (on ἔρχεται and ἕπεται and the subject-matter) Pindar, *Py.* 3, 105: ὄλβος
οὐκ ἐς μακρὸν ἀνδρῶν ἔρχεται σῶς, πολὺς εὖτ' ἂν ἐπιβρίσαις ἕπηται.

[33] The ideal of καλοκαγαθία is implicit.

know where a thing may end, when it has once been begun. One man seeks
to do well, and never suspecting his danger, runs blindly headlong into
perdition and death. (69) But for another who works but poorly, all under-
takings prosper, and kindly Zeus saves him from folly's reward. For us men
no visible limit of wealth is appointed; we always find that those blessed
beyond others with wealth (73) hunger for double the sum. How then can
one satisfy mortals? To the great gods we owe all that we ever acquire; yet
by success comes Blindness and when Zeus sends her upon us, her who is
punishing guilt, then wealth goes on its travels again.

For long stretches the language of the elegy is flowing and lucid; but
occasionally there are difficult and obscure passages, and sometimes
the connection between the parts is not plain.

The elegy begins with a prayer to the divine powers of the art
which Solon is practising, the Muses.[34] At the opening of their recitation, epic singers prayed for 'goodness' (*areté*) and for the 'prosperity'
(ὄλβος) of rich gain; similarly Solon asks of the Muses 'prosperity'
on the part of the gods and 'good reputation,' that is the reputation
of goodness, on the part of men.[35] With the idea of reputation is
connected the related idea of effectiveness among contemporaries,
which is formulated in a polarized manner: Solon wishes not to be a
cipher but to be loved and respected by friends, hated and feared by
enemies (cf. *Od.* 6, 184f.). Now Solon reaches back to the passage on
heaven-sent prosperity and declares that wealth can be attained in
two ways, and only wealth gained righteously is a gift of the gods;
only such does he wish for himself. This is the last time the first
person singular is used in the elegy, and the character of prayer is
now given up also. The next theme (vv. 8–32) declares that unrighteous gain will 'surely' be punished. According to Solon the
punishment takes place automatically by a built-in mechanism.
Since the wealth was acquired 'not in accordance with order' and

---

[34] The genealogy of the Muses was obviously created by the epic singers. The
Muses are daughters of Memory because the poet tells of old times; and their
father is Zeus because the poet communicates truth, and Zeus holds reality and
truth in his hands. On the other hand the Muses are conceived of as plural because
they were to constitute a chorus; this idea derives not from epic narrators but from
poets of choral lyric.

[35] Heaven-sent prosperity and good reputation are accorded to those who are
pleasing to gods and righteous men; this is attained by a man who represents good
principles in word and deed; Solon hopes to represent good principles in his
poetry. This inference explains the role of the Muses as intermediaries in vv. 3–4.
A similar train of thought underlies the opening of the Theognis-corpus (vv. 15–26
on the morality of the Muses and the reputation of the poet among all men; only
among his countrymen does he meet with no good will). For Solon his musical
art was not a mere diversion but the means of his political effectiveness and his
rise to power.

possession did not come to the man who aquired it in a natural and unforced manner, a flaw attaches to the event which will eventually destroy everything.[36]

In the beginning the fault may seem irrelevant, but even a spark which is trivial at first grows to a great fire. Again, therefore, Solon argues from an analogy with nature: and he does the same thing again when he compares the penalty which finally cleanses, with the spring storm which finally sweeps heaven clean after a long, dark winter and brings the clear summer weather.[37] At bottom is the thought that purifying atonement can be relied upon as surely as the coming of spring and fair summer weather. Here the argument diverges into two parallel paths: *Atê*, that is, a fault which can lead to no good (p. 62, above), avenges the transgression automatically (vv. 13–15); as an injustice it is punished by god (vv. 17–25). To the unexpressed doubt whether Zeus really always exacts satisfaction for violated right, Solon responds in what follows with the assurance that the penalty often strikes only the innocent children and grand-children, but in any case does at some time surely strike.

With the clear and far-reaching vision of the punishing god the next section (vv. 33–70) contrasts the short-sighted illusions of hopeful man. Hesiod (p. 117, above) and Semonides (p. 201, above) had given moving expression to the theme of human illusions. Solon, being specific as archaic poets were, enumerates various hopes and strivings, listing in order all the callings which men follow for gain. In the last two, the seer and the physician, he emphasizes that real success depends not on man but on destiny. In the end the general conclusion is drawn in this same sense (v. 63ff.): actuality with all the good and evil that it brings in the hands of destiny and the gods (again no distinction is drawn between the two); in all men's dealings there is danger,[38] for they set into motion forces of which we cannot know how they will work out in the end. An industrious man falls into grave error and draws unexpected mischief upon himself through his blindness; a fool who fares ill acquires fortune by god's gift and rises high.[39]

The two distichs here paraphrased lead into the elegy's final section (vv. 71–76), which gives expression to a profound thought in

[36] Cf. the commentary of Linforth (p. 218 n. 2, above) on v. 11.

[37] In the archaic fashion, the simile proceeds in ring-composition; it opens and closes with the main point: the storm removes the clouds.

[38] The word κίνδυνος, 'danger,' first appears in Solon and the Lesbians. It does not look like Greek, and may be a term in trade ('risk') taken over from a foreign language. The heteroclite forms in Lesbian also suggest a foreign origin.

[39] The words of v. 70 occur almost identically in Pindar, *Ol.*, 2, 51ff.: τὸ δὲ τυχεῖν πειρώμενον (cf. Solon v. 67) ἀφροσύνας παραλύει.

a formulation all too terse. It answers the unspoken question whether god's rule as just described, with its apparently capricious interplay of violent and irrational transformations in the lives of men, should not be called disorder or even unrighteousness. For this difficult problem Solon finds an original solution. As he explains the matter, man's own lack of moderation is at fault and makes any other procedure impossible. For we do not seek a specific fortune but would increase our wealth without limit (vv. 71–73). We cannot expect god to satisfy all the insatiable (v. 73);[40] to only a few and in succession can he bestow his full blessing, that is why fortune and wealth migrate from one owner to another (v. 76).[41] The impelling force for this interchange and the chain of catastrophes is again *Atê*, human blindness and its consequences, bad attempts and bad fortune. In our blindness we are not satisfied with the gains which the gods of their grace vouchsafe us (v. 74), but only covet more; instead of being content with repose we exert ourselves doubly (v. 73) and challenge dangerous (v. 65) destiny so far that it really goes into action and through the errors which we commit (*Atê*, vv. 68 and 73) causes a reversal of fortune for our punishment (v. 76). Thus god is justified and human guilt for human disorder is demonstrated.[42] Only through restraint and moderation can we break the vicious circle, and this is what Solon recommends in his other elegies.[43]

While Solon's argumentation in this large elegy is very impressive, it is convincing only to the righteous and the devout who always knew that unrighteousness would somehow meet with retribution, and that all the misfortune which the gods allow to take place is the fault of us men. Solon's ideas are consistent to a degree, but only to a degree. Anyone who looks for discrepancies, imperfect logic, and new questions provoked by his answers to the old, will find them in abundance. Solon does not construct a consistent general theory, for he is not a true philosopher. Neither is he a true poet: he does not create a new world of thought and form, but through his writings as through his deeds he plays a distinguished part in the improvement

[40] The subject that Solon means by τίς, 'god' or the 'gods,' is seen from the continuation in the verse following.

[41] On v. 76, 'wealth goes from hand to hand,' cf. fr. 4, 9 (p. 232, above); the same is said of misfortune in Archilochus 7, 7–9 (p. 144, above).

[42] Later Anaximander was to take up the thought that unrighteous advantages always change masters, and that justice is thereby re-established (p. 266f., below).

[43] In 3, 9–10 and 4, 5–7 (p. 220f. and 223, above) Solon admonishes the wealthy to 'moderation' and 'tranquility', namely to comfortable enjoyment of what they can provide, especially at meals. Fr. 14 argues that comfort in food and love is the height of human fortune, and excessive wealth is worthless (p. 230f., above).

of the world as it is. Beginning with Archilochus, poetry had aimed at nearness to life; now it is subordinate to life.

Solon does not transform reality into autonomous poetry, and therefore his poems have neither the pure and lucid transparency nor the fierce passion or delicate inwardness of Greek lyric. Instead Solon possesses a gift which was to characterize the Attic spirit for many centuries—the rich endowment of a balanced versatility, excluding nothing that forms part of a healthy nature. If the poetry of Eastern Greece emits a perpetual radiance, the writings of Attica breathe a fresh, delicate and spicy fragrance that arises from a thousand human qualities, great and small.

V

Period of Crisis, Religious Literature and Philosophy

(a) *The Crisis of Belles-Lettres: the Seven Sages; Aristeas and Pherecydes*

In the early decades of the sixth century there were many poets active in the Greek world—Sappho and Alcaeus in Lesbos, Semonides and Mimnermus in Ionia, and Solon in Attica. They must all have been dead by mid-century, but they died without successors: it was not till about 530 that lyric poetry began afresh with new strength, and even then with considerable changes in thought and feeling. In between, a generation disappeared.[1] There must have been some particular reason for this sudden lack of poets in Greece:[2] clearly the verbal arts must have passed through a crisis: but what its causes were we can only guess. Perhaps a thorough-going realism gained the ascendancy—a realism which despised the arts of language as being of no account when compared with the palpable realities of life: perhaps religious fervour lost itself in unplumbed depths where organized and consecutive language could not follow it.

This temporary cessation of poetry allows us to take note of various phenomena which are hard to date accurately and whose subject matter does not claim a fixed place in any given context. Among these are the Sayings of the Seven Sages (although it is doubtful whether they can be called literature), some obscurantist religious writings, and finally the so-called Homeric Hymns, which shew the long survival of epic language. Afterwards we may trace the

[1] It is possible that Stesichorus, who cannot be precisely dated, belonged to this missing generation.

[2] The tradition was not wholly broken off, of course, but apparently the productions of c. 560–530 were too unimportant or made too little impression to be widely disseminated and passed on to posterity.

history of philosophy in the sixth century—a task which will lead us steadily from the first third of the century to the last.

The stories of the Seven Sages (ἑπτὰ σοφοί) are mostly legendary, and their reputed sayings apocryphal; but the individuals numbered among them are all historical persons, and most of them lived in the first half of the sixth century. Since biographical legends tend to arise shortly after the death of their heroes, we may suppose that the idea of drawing up such a group occurred about 550. The ancient lists of the wise men vary a great deal: if all variants are put together, we have seventeen sages, not seven. Four names are common to all the lists: the reforming statesmen Solon of Athens and Pittacus of Mitylene, the wise judge Bias of Priene in Asia Minor, and the philosopher Thales of Miletus, to whom Herodotus also ascribes practical and political wisdom. Very often Periander, tyrant of Corinth, features in the lists—an important figure, but ruthless and with a streak of cruelty. To belong to this circle demanded not learning in arts or sciences, but practical sagacity and practical success, particularly in politics, and Solon found his way in as a statesman rather than as a poet. But there is no contradiction in calling such people σοφοί. Certainly when Pindar in the fifth century speaks of σοφοί, he usually means poets, and still later the word was used of philosophers; but the usage had not always been such. In earlier times the word referred to a practical mastery of a given subject: thus it was not the thinker who was styled σοφός, but (for example) the carpenter whose knowledge, experience and skill enabled him to build a roof that would not be destroyed by storms. The Seven, therefore, were clever men rather than sages: their distinction was that in the storms of an unsettled period they knew how to build high the fabric of their own success.

It is understandable that men should have awarded the garland of σοφία at that time to the politician rather than the poet; and at the same time we see why poetry fell dumb in those decades. Poetry had contributed to its own downfall. For a long time it had concentrated on the individual life of the speaker and his immediate milieu; many poets had made it their business to take their subject matter from everyday life and to bow to the demands of mere existence. In its logical extension this movement could lead to a devaluing of literature and to taking lessons from life itself—that is, from the lives of great and successful men. The pressure of hard times may have contributed to a distrust of mere words and thus to a hostile attitude towards literature.

But some species of literature, at all events, was ascribed by legend to these seven clever men, although it was reduced to a minimum and

did not need writing to preserve it. They were the reputed inventors
of certain shrewd proverbial sayings circulated by word of mouth;
and anecdotes were current which provided a suitable context for
these sayings. The proverbs might just as well have remained
anonymous, but apparently the age demanded that pure thought
should be given credentials from the worldly success of its exponents.
The sayings are of Laconic brevity: presumably those who despised
words used as few of them as possible.[3] They are nearly all maxims for
private life: very often they show a sober realism, warning against
naive confidence and naive illusions, and enjoining foresight,
reserve and moderation. In Alcaeus (fr. 360 LP, above p. 196) we
found a saying attributed to Aristodamus, who was later included
among the Seven: 'Money is man'; and Pindar (*Isthm.* 2, 11) provides the background: 'as he said when he became poor and all his
friends left him.' A number of apophthegms are assigned to Periander
by Herodotus (3.53, 4), e.g. 'Ambition is a dangerous possession';
'Do not mend bad with worse.' Under other names we find such
proverbs as, 'Nothing in excess'; 'Confidence has folly (*Atê*) at her
heels';[4] 'Measure is best'; 'Most men are bad'; 'It is hard to be good.'
Proverbs of this kind had also been freely attributed to the Delphic
Apollo, or to 'the divine old man of the sea,' the wise sea-god
Proteus. Now, however, they were clothed in the authority of successful men, who had been alive and active a few years earlier. The
realist generation built itself a modern and worldly mythology.

　Only one side of human nature could be satisfied with sober and
sceptical reserve. The other side too claimed its rights: from time to
time men wished to enjoy the heady delights of spiritual bliss. At this
period, when Greek poetry was sinking more and more into the
conventional and practical, ultimately to resign itself to a temporary
death, the emotional life of the Greek people was violently stimulated
by a new and ecstatic type of religious feeling. In the seventh
century the foreign god Dionysus came down from his native haunts
in the North-East to make a triumphal progress through all the
Greek world. Dionysus was not so much the bringer of wine as the
god of ecstatic delight, of unbridled desire, of a kind of madness,
animal-like in its power, that was both in the senses and beyond them.
He had been known to the Greeks for a long time, but at one particular moment his qualities and powers began to gain an unheard-of
ascendancy over the human spirit: first women, then men, finally
the cities themselves were drawn into his service. All opposition was

---

[3] In Herodotus 5, 92 δ2–η1 Periander is given a piece of practical advice from
another intelligent tyrant without the use of words at all.
　[4] Cf. Br. Snell, *Leben und Meinungen der Sieben Weisen* (3rd ed., Munich 1952).

shattered: any defence which could be offered by commonsense or by the love of form and clarity, was in that unprepared age too weak to combat the religious frenzy. The Dionysiac movement burst upon Greece in successive waves: many decades must have passed before it was established everywhere, and centuries before it reached its final development, before the structure of the Greek mind was so re-organized as to harmonize new and old. This movement too must have been non-literary: orgiastic worship must needs reject explanation in words and limitation through artistic forms.[5]

The literary remains of the sixth century also attest a lower and dampened spirituality. The poem of Aristeas embodies a penchant towards the improbable and extravagant which loves to indulge fantasies set in remote and inaccessible regions, while the prose treatise of Pherecydes seeks to reflect the nature of our own world enigmatically in wilfully bizarre images. With such works as these literature relapses into infantilism. In language imperfectly mastered they show a union of absurd caricature and amorphous obscurity.

The poem of Aristeas is in epic form and describes a journey to distant lands with a mixture of realism and fantasy. In this, Aristeas was continuing an old tradition. There had long been a considerable epic on the voyage of the Argonauts to the Eastern end of the Black Sea, and on the remarkable détours by which they returned to Greece. The *Odyssey* was full of voyages and wonders, and there is a close parallel between it and the poem of Aristeas in that he tells the story in his own person, just as Odysseus and Menelaus relate their own adventures in the *Odyssey*. But for all that, the poem of Aristeas was a typical product of its own age. First, it makes a great difference whether an impersonal singer puts narratives into the mouths of great legendary figures or whether a contemporary poet speaks of his own adventures. Secondly, in the *Odyssey* the original religious element in the story (so far as it had a foundation in myth) has shrunken to insignificance, while Aristeas announces himself as possessed by Apollo and led by him into distant countries. Even the worship of Apollo was tinged at that time with enthusiasm, and a similar spirit was later to attach the most remarkable legends to the name of Aristeas—as, for example, that when he lay dead in one place, he had been seen alive in another.

Aristeas came from Proconnesus, a marble island in the Sea of Marmara, and his journey took him from the Northern shores of the

---

[5] Although the dithyramb had existed from of old (cf. Archilochus fr. 77), the dithyrambs of Bacchylides for instance show that poetry when composed as an art form, although dedicated to the wild god Dionysus, no longer expressed any of his own specific character.

Black Sea northwards into what is now the Ukraine and Russia. Two short fragments of the epic have come down to us. The one (in 'Longinus' *On the Sublime* 10, 4) runs as follows:

This also my spirit perceived and mightily wondered: men dwell on the water, far from land, in the ocean, and they are folk to be pitied; exhausting toil is their portion, having their soul in the sea, their eyes on the stars of the heavens. Many a time they raise their hands to the blessed immortals praying from deep in their bowels, and are cast painfully upwards by storms.

Apparently the reference is to a sea-faring people[6] who never come ashore; Aristeas must have heard of ships with living quarters, which caused him great astonishment, and he pitied the wretched life led under such conditions. He has many clever points to make about their life between wind and water: their eyes are devoted to the stars (which show them their way through the waste of waters), and their soul (i.e. their life) is based upon the sea;[7] in a storm, which tosses their stomach upwards, their thoughts and their imploring hands are turned skywards. The other fragment (in Tzetzes, *Chil.* 7, 686ff.) deals with the ethnography of this region:

—the Issedes take pride in long flowing hair as an adornment. And they affirm[8] that there dwells in the hidden heart of the northland, neighboring them, a numerous people, hardy in warfare, rich in horses, with thriving stock of sheep and of cattle. Yet each of them has only one eye to gaze on the heavens. Their hair grows thick: of all men they are the strongest.

These one-eyed people are called Arimaspians, and they must have played an important part in the poem, since it was entitled *Arimaspeia*. Aristeas does not claim to have seen these wonders for himself: he only penetrated as far as the Issedes, and learned from them what sort of beings dwelt in the far north. Beyond the Arimaspians dwelt the Gryphons, guardians of the gold which grew there in the soil, and at truceless war with the Arimaspians. Beyond the Gryphons again, on the shores of the farther ocean, were the holy people of Apollo, the Hyperboreans. While Aristeas' results are fantastical, his methods of work and presentation are respectably scientific. In the manner of that later Ionian *historiê*, 'seeking out,' on which

[6] Not to lake-dwellings on piles: the passage itself and the context in which it is quoted show that Aristeas was thinking of ships in a storm.

[7] It is impossible to decide whether the threefold repetition of the verb ἔχω and the recurrence of ἀνά at the same place in the line are accidental or a deliberate figure of thought. The idea of the 'soul on the water' comes from Archilochus fr. 21: 'When our soul lies in the arms of the waves.'

[8] Read καί φασ', cf. Herod. 4, 13, 1 and 16, 1, and see also *De Simia Rhodio* (Göttingen, 1915) p. 34 n. 1.

Herodotus prided himself, Aristeas went in person as far as he could; on areas beyond his reach he consulted those whose opinion might reasonably be expected to be authoritative. There is nothing absurd in his account of a migration of peoples from North to South, beginning with the Arimaspians; in each instance a stronger people drove its weaker neighbours from their previous abode.[9] But this genuine desire for knowledge is coupled with a prurient love of wonders, and Aristeas underlines the sensational nature of his news-stories by various smart points of phrasing. His attitude towards the fabulous is quite different from that of the *Odyssey*: he does not simply swallow fairy-tales or simply present them in sensible images, but he reflects with obvious astonishment on the phenomena which he has to report. Apart from the point already mentioned, his style is dry and lifeless: one can see nothing of the divine possession[10] which he claims.

There is a certain affinity between the geographical legends of an Aristeas and the religious cosmology of Pherecydes. It seems to have been written in or before the middle of the sixth century, and is thus the oldest Greek book in prose. The author was an Ionian from the little island of Syros near Delos. The work began as follows (*Vorsokr.* 7B1, detailed reference p. 252 n.1):

Zas (=Zeus) and Kronos[11] were always, and Chthoniê. Now Chthoniê was called 'Earth' after Zas gave her the earth as a gift.

In the next fragment (B2) we hear more detail of the bestowal of the earth on Chthoniê:

—and made for him his houses, many and great. When they had finished this all, and furnishings and menservants and maidservants, and all else that is needful, now that all was ready, they held the wedding. And when the third day came for the wedding, Zas made a robe, great and beautiful, and wove upon it in many colours the earth and Ogenos (=Ocean) and the houses of Ogenos—

After a break in the text, Zas is speaking to Chthoniê:

—that your wedding may be (?), I honour you with this. Rejoice then (χαῖρε: a formula of greeting) and be mine. This, they say, was the first

---

[9] Cf. Herod. 4, 13, 2 and Aristeas' statement that the Arimaspians are the strongest of all men.

[10] There was another wonder-worker associated with Apollo in Greek legend—the Hyperborean Abaris, who (says Herodotus 4, 36, 1) 'carried an arrow all round the world without ever taking food or drink.' A seemingly earlier form of the legend has him flying through the air on an arrow (see K. Meuli, *Hermes* 70, 159).

[11] The right reading, cf. *Frühgriech. Denken*, p. 19f.

festival of unveiling. From this the custom arose for gods and men. And she—took the robe . . .

Thus according to Pherecydes a trinity, made up of Zas, Kronos and Chthoniê, and existing from all eternity, stood at the beginning of things. Zas represents the sky, Chthoniê is the power of lower earth and the underworld. These two marry and perform for the first time the unveiling ceremony which afterwards became usual at weddings; the thanks-offering made by the bride also is part of the ritual (cf. Pollux 3, 36). In this case the unveiling-gift took the form of a robe on which Earth was depicted surrounded by Ocean. As the first fragment tells us, Chthoniê was transformed and raised to the status of the complete earth by being clothed in this robe: the foundations in the deep now received the addition of the covering surface. According to Pherecydes the surface of the earth is Zas' creation, and the act of creation is compared with weaving—or rather equated with it, since in the author's primitive way of thinking the thing and its representation become fused. Apparently then this earliest Greek prose treatise, composed in the period of crisis, is more primitive in thought than the much earlier Hesiod.

This impression is strengthened when we read the other remarkable things contained in Pherecydes' religious cosmogony. The earth-garment was attached to a 'winged tree'—was the earth itself thought of as a tree, flying through space like a bird? The cosmos consists of five inner regions (μυχοί);[12] each of them has its gods. The following sentences (B5) come from his description of the structure of the universe:

Within (or beneath) this part is the part called Tartaros; it is watched over by the daughters of the northwind, the Harpies (predatory demons) and Thyella (whirlwind): thither Zeus banishes any of the gods who is rebellious.

The picture of Tartarus as a prison for hostile gods, with storm-winds as its guardians is familiar from Hesiod (*Theog.* 717–44, above, p. 104–107); probably Pherecydes took this detail from him, or perhaps both draw on the same tradition. Just like Hesiod, Pherecydes too speaks of a great war among the gods (fr. B4); but in his version the leader of the one army is Kronos, not Zeus, and of the other a certain Ophioneus (serpent-natured). It was agreed that whichever should be driven into the ocean should be reckoned as the defeated party: the reward of the victors was the possession of heaven.

The little that we know of Pherecydes' book suggests that, com-

---

[12] Or perhaps seven regions. Our reports of Pherecydes' system are confused. μυχός never means 'corner', but rather 'inward parts,' 'lower parts.'

pared with Hesiod, it was a step backwards. Pherecydes was on the intellectual level of that mass of apocryphal material upon which Hesiod drew; but Hesiod raised himself far above it (see above, p. 97 with n. 2).

Since the book is the oldest in Greek prose, we should pay some attention to its style, which is so striking that it is worth while to go into details. The periods are made up of a great number of extremely short separate members, for example: 'and made him his houses/ many and great/// When they had finished this/all//and furniture and menservants and maidservants// and what else was needed/all//when now all was ready//they held the wedding///.' The first characteristic feature is the slow but steady shift of perspective from one sentence-member to another; the second is the very short range of the thought at any given moment, making it necessary to repeat (as the threefold 'all') and recapitulate ('when all was now ready'): the third is the principle of putting something firm at the beginning, then amplifying it by any number of short additions ('and . . . and . . . and . . . and'). This principle appears again in what follows: '—Zeus made a robe/ great and beautiful//and on it wove in many colours the earth and—.' First we are told that a robe was made, then we learn how it was made and what it looked like.[13] At the outset the hearer is given something intelligible and informative in the fewest words possible, so as to put him in the picture; then detail after detail is added, but in such a way that the hearer can readily and completely digest them. It is a style that arouses no tension, because nothing is ever left in mid-air.[14]

This prose style of statement followed by amplification was not the invention of Pherecydes: it appears in very much the same form in inscriptions of the period. It was particularly well adapted to laws and treaties. A rule is first set down, then it is fitted out with provisoes and definitions, limitations and extensions. In this way a text is produced which can be followed section by section, unlike the Chinese-box style often favoured by jurists, which have to be read six times forwards and backwards before one can find one's way in. A treaty from the sixth century will serve to illustrate the slow and methodical accuracy which this style makes possible. The contemporary text on bronze which has been preserved divides the various sentence-sections

[13] One is tempted to see a parallel between this style and the myth of Chthoniê: first, the earth is present without its characteristic features; then these are added to it as a garment.

[14] On this stylistic principle, see W. Krause, *Kuhns Zeitschrift* 52 (1924) 245ff.; W. A. A. van Otterlo, *Griech. Ringkomposition* (*Mededel. Nederl. Akad.*, Letterk. 7, 3, Amsterdam 1944) p. 43.

by marks of punctuation, and we are consequently enabled to read the text in the original rhythm (*Sylloge Inscr. Graec.*, ed. W. Dittenberger, 3rd ed. [Leipz. 1915–1924] no. 9):

'The treaty for the Eleans/and the Herwaioi/there shall be alliance for a hundred years/starting this year/and if anything is necessary/be it word or deed/they shall stand by each other/in peace as in war/and if they do not stand by each other/one talent of silver/shall they pay/to the Olympian Zeus/the breakers of the treaty/the talent falling to the god/but if anyone destroys this writing/be he a private person or an official/or an association of persons/he shall incur the sacred debt/therein written (i.e. shall pay one silver talent to Zeus).'

A style like this is more than a way of speaking; it is a clear and constructive way of thinking, and very probably the men who used it acted as they wrote.[15]

(b) *The Homeric Hymns*

In contrast to the amorphous myths and speculations of Pherecydes, the so-called Homeric hymns are as luminous, serene and clear to comprehend—that is to say, as Greek—as they could well be. We may deal with the hymns at this point since some of them (such as the Hymn to the Pythian Apollo) seem to have been written in the early years of the sixth century. At least one (to the Delian Apollo) is probably older; most of them are more recent. They are not easy to date, they are as anonymous as the old epics themselves.

Their connection with the epics is very close. They use the language and form of epic, and they are familiar with the recitation of epic. On each occasion the singer began his recitations with the praises of one god or another; not until he had 'taken his beginning from a god,' as the *Odyssey* expresses it (8, 499), did he enter upon the proposed theme. Hence the Hymns were called 'prooemia' ('fore-songs'). We possess a collection of such epic prooemia, embracing about thirty pieces. They display their original purpose by their all (or nearly all) ending with a transition to a song that was to follow, e.g. 3, 545:

So I bid you farewell, you son of Zeus and of Leto! I shall be mindful of you and of a new song for my singing.

---

[15] On the bronze tablet letters like A, Y, M, Λ and E have the first stroke vertical like a post, and the other strokes slope downwards away from it. Here also we see the principle of putting something solid first and then adding the distinguishing marks.

Sometimes in the valedictory formula the poet adds a prayer, as in the *Hymn to Aphrodite*, goddess of sexual attraction: 'Grant me beautiful song' (10, 5), or to Demeter, who bestows the harvest: 'Demeter and Persephoneia, grant me graciously heart-warming food and drink as the reward for my song' (2, 493f.); once we read: 'Grant me the victory in this contest' (6, 19f.), and twice: 'Grant me goodness and blessing' (15 and 20, see above, p. 234f.).

As one expects of genuine 'preludes,' most of the hymns in our collection are of very slight compass: five to ten verses, or at the most twenty-two, serve the purpose of paying one's respects to one of the immortals. Two of the pieces are more substantial, with 50 to 60 hexameters. A few have the full extent of an independent poem, running to some hundreds of verses. The reciter who used one of these was in effect making a poem of religious content serve as the first in a series of epic recitations. The long hymns are dedicated to Demeter, Apollo, Hermes and Aphrodite.

Epic hymns to the gods were liable to two opposite tendencies. As religious poems they were of necessity inclined towards broad and systematic exposition, while the stylistic tradition of epic tended to keep them on the narrow path of a single narrative. From the example of the *Hymn to Aphrodite* we can see how well Greek taste and dexterity resolved the conflict.

The introduction to the hymn (vv. 1–52), roughly a sixth of the whole, shows the systematic side, while the rest takes the form of a story. It deals with the amour of Aphrodite with the Trojan prince Anchises. The goddess is overcome with passion and seeks Anchises out by day in the solitary mountains where he tends the cattle at their summer pasture.[1]

So as not to alarm him, she takes on the shape of a young girl, and after some feigned reluctance, is soon lying in his arms. When their union is over, she resumes her form as a goddess. Anchises is terrified and begs to be forgiven; Aphrodite restores his spirits by hailing him as worthiest of mortals, beloved by the gods, and tells him all that he needs to know. She will bear him a son, she says, who will be called Aeneas and will be raised by the Dryads. Aphrodite's speech (and the hymn itself) ends as follows

Yet if someone of mortals should seek to know, and should ask you,

---

[1] While lawful wedlock was a thing of house and hall, the transient liaisons of passion had a different setting. In later pastoral poetry this was a mild and lovely countryside, but in the hymn it is still the heroic wilderness of mountains. Anchises does not guard a flock of harmless sheep: he keeps watch over a herd of cattle. He does not play upon the flute, but on the lyre, like Achilles (80); and he fights against lions and bears, like the herdsmen in the similes of the *Iliad*.

'Who was the mother that carried your beloved son in her body?'
Answer him—do not forget—in this same way as I tell you.
'One of the flower-faced nymphs, they say, is the mother who bore him.
Those that dwell nearby in the mountains shaggy with forest.'
But if you speak out the truth and loudly boast in your folly
How you, a mortal, enjoyed the favours of flower-crowned Cypris,
Then will great Zeus grow angry and smite you down with his thunder.
Now have I spoken all: do you but mark and remember,
Hold your peace, speak not, beware the anger of heaven.'
So she spoke, and arose once more towards airy Olympus.
Now farewell, great goddess, you who rule in beautiful Cyprus:
With you I began, but another story now calls me.

The narrative part of the hymn has a winning charm, in which the
human and the divine, the morally elevated and spontaneously
natural, the serious and the playful side of love, all claim and find
their due place. This one love-passage perfectly illustrates the eternal
nature and workings of Aphrodite. But even the narrative part contains some touches of systematic doctrine. Aphrodite's parting speech,
which with its hundred or so verses makes up a third of the whole
poem, serves not only to instruct Anchises, but to set everything
before the hearer in a context which makes it more easily intelligible.
She refers explicitly to previous love affairs between divinities and
members of the Trojan royal house, the family which had a special
closeness to the gods. Ganymede had been carried off to heaven
because of Zeus' love for him, and Tithonus had been the immortal
bridegroom of Eos. Yet he was not made exempt from the human
burden of growing old (192–238). Aphrodite now draws a parallel
between Anchises and Tithonus, and applies it to the present
situation. She would not wish her lover to be an old man for ever:
if Anchises could remain always young, she would gladly be his wife,
but that is denied to him, and the gods hate old age (239–246). The
conclusion—that man and goddess must now part for ever—remains
unspoken. Aphrodite speaks instead of the shame she must feel
before the other gods: she, who had formerly been dreaded for her
power of making gods fall in love with mortal women, has now fallen
victim to her own enchantment. When her child is born, it is to be
entrusted at once to the nymphs of Ida. Here comes the second digression: Aphrodite describes the nature of nymphs—they are women
halfway between gods and mortals. They join in dances with the
gods, and in the darkness of secret caves they surrender themselves
to Hermes and to the Sileni. Their life is very long, but not eternal:
it is tied to the tree which is sacred to each individual nymph, and
when the tree dies, so does she. Thus the themes of gradation between

gods and men, of mortal old age, and of love-affairs with gods are spun out further in this depiction of the Nymphs; and at the same time the poet completes his spirited drawing of wild nature, passionate and germinal (68–74, 97–99), in the midst of which the child of man and goddess is conceived, and under whose tutelage he will grow to manhood (257)[2].

We may now consider the expository section at the beginning of the hymn. It runs as follows:

> Sing to me, Muse, of the works of fair Aphrodite, the golden
> Cypris, who kindles in gods the flame of joyful desiring,
> Ruling also the races of men who are doomed to be mortal,
> And the air-winging birds and every beast of creation
> All that the earth brings forth and all that dwell in the ocean,
> Eagerly all take their part in the works of garlanded Cypris.

Yet Aphrodite's power does not extend everywhere, and after this opening the poet hastens to add the names of three goddesses who harden their hearts against love: Athene, Artemis, and the goddess of the domestic hearth, Hestia. He stresses that these divinities have other important interests, that they bestow other gifts on men, and that they attach importance to other things than wedlock. Clearly the poet has made it his business to honour all the goddesses[3] and to do justice to all sides. This preoccupation is evident again and again in what follows. To celebrate the powers of Aphrodite, the poet reminds us how even the greatest of the gods fell so far under her sway as to deceive his sister and consort Hera; but scarcely have the words left his lips before he embarks on a panegyric on the respectable Hera. Even so, he must still remove the impression that Zeus himself is ultimately subject to Aphrodite: he therefore tells his readers the story (apparently his own invention) that Zeus deliberately sent upon her the fate that she had inflicted upon others: he filled her with passion for Anchises, so that she could no longer laughingly boast of having ensnared the gods in her toils and made them beget mortal children. This explanation brings out the principle of compensation, which the poet clearly takes very seriously.[4] At the

---

[2] In Sappho (above p. 172) also and in Ibycus (below p. 284f.) we find the specially favoured young thought of as having been brought up under the care of the Nymphs.

[3] The list of goddesses is extended in vv. 93.

[4] The theme of Aphrodite's humiliation is taken up twice more in the narrative (vv. 198f., 247–255). The notion of compensation is worked out also in the story of the rape of Ganymede: the anxiety which Zeus caused to the boy's father is balanced against the honour with which he is recompensed (vv. 207–217, i.e. 11 verses out of the 16 devoted to the story). The legend of the rape of Ganymede was very important to the archaic Greeks, who were much given to pederasty, as

same time it provides a justification for the narrative, which is to show the goddess, conqueror and conquered at once, trapped in the heady infatuation of which she is the primal force, and to relate how the universality of her power was proved in her own person. This also is a kind of compensation.

In our analysis the doctrinal elements come out more coarsely and nakedly than they do in the poem itself. The four other long hymns are even less theological in content than the Hymn to Aphrodite.[5] The Homeric hymns are entirely different from the religious poetry that we find among other nations. The praises of the god never take the form of an endless catalogue of his powers and attributes.[6] Never is any attempt made to draw a definite picture of the god in hard and clear outlines; nor do the writers follow the example of many oriental hymns in heaping attributes and expressions at random on whichever god is being celebrated, in such profusion that his image dissolves in a formless aura of might and majesty. The hymns never claim to enshrine true belief in the only correct form of words and thus establish it for all time. The authors were believers indeed, but poets, not priests. None of the hymns is tied to a ceremonial or harnessed to a cult: none takes on the stiff garment of uniformly devotional feeling. They could be recited as well in a festive gathering as at a public solemnity, since they create of themselves the atmosphere which they demand. They are some of the most original and the liveliest creations of Greek poetry. The unconstrained as well as the majestic side of divine behaviour was turned to just as good account here as formerly by the epic singers (above p. 54f.). Each of the long hymns has its own special quality: they vary one from another more than corresponding parts of the epics do.

Although the style in many features corresponds closely with the language of epic, the poems bear the stamp of post-epic origin. We

we may see from the archaic statue found at Olympia: the god, as he hastens away, carries the boy on his arm: Ganymede has taken his plaything with him, a live chicken: in heaven he is to serve the gods as their cupbearer (see above p. 170 and 180; below p. 292f).

[5] It is in fact an exaggeration if we speak of 'theology' in connection with this hymn, since the word suggests a carefully worked-out system of precise doctrines to be binding on all believers. It was to be many centuries before the Greeks understood or cared about such constructions (see below p. 332 and p. 443 n. 5), and this hymn shows comparatively slight, but interesting, leanings in such a direction. The 'theological' parts of the *Hymn to Aphrodite* have been recently interpreted by F. Solmsen (*Hermes* 88, [1960], 1–13) as a critical counter to Hesiod's *Theogony* and a passage of the *Iliad* (4, 48–61).

[6] Except the *Hymn to Ares*, which is shown by its content to be more recent(e.g. Ares is identified with the planet Mars), and is also different in form (the god is addressed throughout).

find this, for example, in the narrative manner of the *Hymn to Demeter*, which was composed in Attica probably about the time when Solon began to write (above, p. 217f.) and is thus, together with his fragments, our oldest surviving Attic poetry. After losing her daughter, Demeter, plunged in mourning, sits beside the city springs of Eleusis in the guise of an old woman. Three sisters find her there and tell their mother, who says that the old woman must be urged to come into their house to look after the youngest child, who is not yet weaned. The three sisters go back to the spring to fetch the goddess (v. 174):

> They, just as young does or playful heifers in summer
> Bound over the meadows, their spirits lively with pasture,
> Hastened along the sunken lane; the folds of their dainty
> Garments they gathered away from the ground: their beautiful tresses
> Floated about their shoulders, in hue most like to the crocus.
> There by the road they found the divine one, where they had left her
> Sitting before, and back to the well-loved house of their father
> Gently they led her; and she, with deep-felt grief in her heart,
> Followed behind with close-veiled head, her mantle of sable
> Floating about the slender feet of the hastening goddess.
> So, before long, they arrived at noble Celeus' dwelling,
> Entered and crossed the hall in front, where the lady mother
> Sat by the pillar on which the roof's fair frame was supported,
> Holding the child, the flower in bud to her bosom. The maidens
> Ran to her side, and the goddess' head, when she entered the threshold,
> Rose to the beams, and she filled the abode with the lustre of godhead.

This passage betrays the quicker tempo of a more recent, un-epic age of poetry. A series of pictures is presented, pleasing, serious and vividly drawn, fading swiftly one into another. In the concluding verses we have a stage tableau elaborated beyond anything thinkable in the old epics. In a single grouping one sees the mother with the child in her arms, her young daughters at either side, with the pillar supporting the ornate roof as the background: opposite stands the goddess, sufficient in herself to fill the door opening with her majestic form and the light that streams from it.[7]

This style of poetry reminds us of sixth-century painting, with its

[7] The text goes on to say that the mother is frightened at the overpowering appearance of the goddess, as Anchises was similarly affected when Aphrodite revealed her true nature. In both cases the situation in which a god reveals himself arises naturally from the context. The *Hymn to Apollo*, on the other hand, begins with a quite unmotivated scene in which all the gods (not men!) shrink in fear from Apollo as he enters the hall of Zeus with his fatal bow bent. The reason for this dramatic entry is nowhere stated. The poet has simply put into words the standard representation of Apollo in statuary.

lively narrative manner, its elegant grace and dignity and its ceremonious refinement. The further one follows the sixth century, the more one sees its painting and sculpture moving towards the sharing of ideals with its poetry.[8] Before that time—for what reason we do not know—the arts had gone their very different ways.

(c) Pure Philosophy: Thales, Anaximander, Anaximenes and Pythagoras[1]

Shortly after the beginning of the sixth century, probably even before Pherecydes had lit the wretched lantern of his theological cosmogony, there arose in Ionian Asia Minor the daystar of pure philosophy, to bring a light which was to illuminate the world for centuries, or for millennia.

Not until this new stage can we speak of 'pure' philosophy. If we look at what went before, we see that Hesiod's *Theogony* (written about a hundred years before the point which we have now reached) was still entangled in the toils of the traditional mythology; and even when he found out something new for himself, he conceived it and expressed it in mythological terms. It is part of the same attitude that Hesiod only aimed at a complete system where the myths were concerned (although even here he left many gaps), while his philosophy was restricted to a few energetic thrusts this way or that. Thus we find in him theories on force and political power which justify them as being in the service of a god (p. 99–101); on the suffering of humanity, whose means of livelihood Zeus has 'hidden away' (p. 116) and who are constantly beset by evils which can realize themselves by their own will, while 'hope' is denied a free transition into reality (p. 117f.). We may particularly notice the theory of what we call 'being and not-being,' and of the 'threshold' or the frontier between them, from which being takes its origin (p. 102–107). In the period after Hesiod, as we have recently learned, there was

[8] Cf. T. B. L. Webster, *Greek Art and Literature 530–400 B.C.* (Oxford 1939).

[1] Fragments of philosophers are cited according to *Die Fragmente der Vorsokratiker, Griechisch u. Deutsch* by H. Diels, 6th ed. by W. Kranz (Berlin 1951). The philosophers are numbered continuously (e.g., '28 Parmenides'): in the older editions the numbers are ten lower ('18 Parmenides'): The fragments marked 'A' (e.g., 28 Parmenides A47) are statements by other writers on the doctrines of well-known philosophers; the 'B' fragments (often quoted here simply as numbers) are fragments of their original texts. A complete English translation of these is given by K. Freeman, *Ancilla to the Pre-Socratic Philosophers* (Oxford, 1947). A large number of both A and B fragments are translated and discussed in G. S. Kirk and J. E. Raven, *The Pre-Socratic Philosophers* (Cambridge, 1960).

further speculation on the principles to which the universe owes its origin and structure—speculation which inclined more and more towards abstractions. In the latter half of the seventh century we found—surprisingly enough in the choral lyrist Alcman—a complementary pair of basic principles spoken of, *Poros* and *Aisa,* or in another variant *Poros* and *Tekmor,* that is to say, in terms of our notions, 'open possibility' (or 'accessibility') and 'binding definition' (above, p. 163–165).[2] On the one hand, these are the foundations of human existence, since there are certain attractive possibilities open to us (*Poros*), while others are closed to us by Fate (*Aisa*)—a remote modern analogy would be the opposing notions 'freedom and order.'

On the other hand, these same forces, as Alcman seems to have thought, were at work in the separation of 'day' from 'darkness,' in the origin of the sun and moon, in the regular motions and phases of the two in both space and time (cf. τέκμαρ in Apollonius, below, p. 254 n. 5); from these in turn depended of course the seasons and climate and with them the growth and death of plants, beasts and men (cf. e.g. Aristotle, *De gener. anim.* IVa E., 777 b 26ff.).[3] This is

[2] Although the commentators' arguments are confused and although they anachronistically read into the text a later type of thought, the following facts are plain: (1) Alcman did in fact speculate on the natural world; (2) he was well enough at home in speculative thought that he could freely vary the name and nature of one member of the pair; (3) such speculations seemed to him reconcileable with the traditional religion and mythology which was his normal field. The rôle of Thetis, however, whom the commentator speaks of as the ordering power of the world as it came into being, remains puzzling. We may perhaps suppose that Alcman himself did not speak of Θέτις, gen. Θέτιδος, but of Laconian θέτις (or σέτις), with the genitive case (probably not occurring in (the original text) θέτιος, equivalent to Attic θέσις, in the sense of 'placing,' 'ordering' (cf. the common ἔθηκε=*fecit,* 'made'). The word occurs first in Pindar *Ol.* 3, 8: Pindar proposes to create his song in a cunning blend of lyre, flute-music and ἐπέων θέσις ('ordering,' 'forming,' 'arranging'). On the other hand, Doric -τις for Attic -σις is very poorly attested (E. Schwyzer, *Griech. Gramm.* I, p. 270, no. 4), and in Alcman fr. 125 the transmitted text is μαθήσιος, not μασήτιος. We should very much like to know whether Alcman in fact (as the commentator says he did) posited something like an original ὕλη τεταραγμένη καὶ ἀπόητος (the Ovidian *rudis indigestaque moles, Metam.* 1, 7). On the two philosophical passages from Alcman cf. below p. 314 n. 25.

[3] If we were to allow ourselves to look for a distant analogy to Alcman's two principles in modern science, we might think of the interplay of unpredictable chance and rigid obedience to laws, as in modern cosmogony (the 'turbulence' of cosmic material) or in the origin of species. By suggesting such analogies I am not trying to project modern notions back into Alcman's time: such an attempt would be nonsensical. Nevertheless, in trying to grasp this pair of opposed notions from the seventh century, it may help if we regard it for a moment as a potential germcell, from which over many ages the modern pair might have developed—although in reality of course there was no such continuity.

already a different way of thought from Hesiod's, with his doctrine that 'Light-of-heaven' and 'Day' arose from 'Darkness' and 'Night' by an act of begetting (above, p. 102f.), while at a later period the brother and sisters 'Sun, Moon and Dawn' came into existence (*Theog.* 371–74). But in Alcman also the speculations, for all their boldness, are still attached to the framework of the traditional religion and mythology; he calls the pair 'the oldest and most honourable of gods,' and claims to derive his information about them from the Muses, whom he has back-dated for the purpose.[4] However that may be, no one, so far as we know, either before or after Alcman's time has heard of this 'oldest' pair of gods and the thin garment of mythology allows the philosophical content to be seen.[5]

Now however, at the beginning of the sixth century, ideas come forward which are independent and self-supporting and are destined continuously to beget new departures in thought. Greek philosophy is now to influence more and more the heads and hearts of the ancient world. A philosopher steeped in its spirit is to rule the West from the throne of the Caesars. Becoming part of thought and life from Babylon to Cadiz, from Africa to the Rhine, it is fated to survive the conversion of the ancient world to Christianity and deeply to penetrate

[4] In his cosmogonical poem Alcman goes further back into the past than poetry normally does. This is presumably why in the opening he invokes the Muses as children of Heaven and Earth (cf. also Pindar *Nem.* 3, 16b), so that they can give a more authentic account of the first stages in the genesis of the universe than if they were, according to the common notion, younger by two generations— children, that is, of Zeus and 'Memory,' of the lord of reality and of the calling back to existence of what men have experienced in the past (cf. *Iliad*, 2, 485). Even by this device the Muses cannot be made to have been present at the very beginning: Muses living before the world began would be unthinkable. Hesiod felt no difficulty in the notion that the daughters of Zeus should tell him about the very beginning of all things (cf. *Theog.* 53–62 and 114f.). Alcman himself in *Pap. Ox.* 2389 fr. 4, col. 2, 9 (page 8) mentions the Muses and *Mnamosyna* side by side in the nominative.

[5] We still cannot say whence Alcman derived these ideas. In any case, we have here for the first time an authentic testimony to an early cosmological system, comparable with those later ascribed to 'Orpheus' or 'Musaeus' or the like (the expression τὰ εἰς Μουσαῖον ἀναφερόμενα occurs in 2 *Vorsokr.* B2, 14 and 15, detailed reference p. 252 n. 1), in which probably the most diverse theories were thrown together into an amorphous mass. There are three tenuous threads connecting Alcman's material with one or another of these legendary figures: the use of the word τέκμαρ for the rules of stellar motion in Apollonius, *Argon.* 1 496–500, Orpheus being the speaker (ἥδ' ὡς ἔμπεδον αἰὲν ἐν αἰθέρι τέκμαρ ἔχουσιν ἄστρα, σεληναίης τε καὶ ἠελίοιο κέλευθοι); the same word (but in the sense of 'token,' 'distinguishing mark'?) occurs also in 'Musaeus' B7 (from the Εὐμόλπῳ τῷ υἱῷ ἔπη cf. A1)=Hesiod fr. 164 Rzach; an earlier dating of the Muses recurs in 'Musaeus' B15. On Pherecydes' regression to primitive mythical cosmogony see above, pp. 243–245.

the new religion. At its very outset Christianity is to be influenced by Greek philosophy; later it will absorb Platonism and the system of Aristotle. In the Catholicism of our day Greek philosophy is a living force; in our sciences, in our ways of thought, even in our spiritual life,[6] its effects are of decisive importance.

So far as we know, pure philosophy, divorced from all extraneous associations, came into existence suddenly and without visible cause. From a Greek frontier land where the blood of nations was mingled, where the cultures of West, East and South met and interpenetrated in conflict, at a time when exhaustion from within and despotism from without threatened to cripple the adventurous Greek spirit— there and then arose, as if by a miracle, the new and wholly Greek world of thought. Those same Ionian colonies had formerly moulded Homeric religion (which also was in its way a peculiarly Greek construction); from Ionia the epic climate of religious feeling had spread over the whole Greek nation: now it was the Ionians again who first pushed aside this religious outlook to give free passage to their own thinking. In the generations that followed it was still for a long time the colonial Greeks of East and West who carried on the philosophical movement. Mainland Greece hung behind, since, unlike the colonizing peoples, it had not made a clean break with the past, and could not therefore so easily make up its mind to radical innovations.

Radical in all respects that new philosophy certainly was, which now set itself up as a discipline in its own right. In the cosmos and in life it sought intelligible laws, not random chance or personal caprice: hence it could hardly take personal gods as its starting point, and could have no common ground with the national religion. It did not deal in particulars, but in universals; did not communicate by symbols, but by direct statement. Hence it disdained myth, which had provided Hesiod's philosophical notions with part of their substance and more than part of their form. As true and avowed philosophy, it cared nothing for the purely ephemeral in past or present. At the same time, it never simply accepted anything important, but strove

[6] Our inner life is to a great extent determined by our self-interpretation, that is to say, by theories. We may see this most clearly in studying earlier epochs; for example, the various personages of Shakespearian drama, which seem to us not very true to life, are very largely constructed on the typological doctrine (established in antiquity and revived in the Renaissance) of the 'four temperaments'. In principle our own case is the same: there is an interaction between current theories of human nature and our actual inner life of feelings and emotions. We indulge more largely in those emotions on which more stress is laid by the currently accepted theories, either through direct acquaintance with those theories, or through the medium of books or films based upon them.

to see the reality behind the appearance which things present to us. In this respect it diametrically opposes that tendency which we can trace in poetry from Archilochus onwards. The poets encouraged men to accept transitory experience as being of ultimate validity; they represented existence as having only one layer; in our mortal life we should experience, enjoy and suffer all reality to the very dregs. The philosophers saw life and the world as many-layered, and during the temporary silence of poetry they pursued a vigorous and spontaneous metaphysic.

The philosophy of this period was characterized by Aristotle as 'philosophy of nature'; but the term cannot be serviceable to us unless we define the idea of nature so as to make it fit these speculations. At first 'nature' was a term which included man. It was not until the age of the sophists and of Socrates that man was considered as a creature *sui generis*, moving in a world that belongs only to him. This world (as many of the sophists were to emphasize) he had very largely constructed himself by his 'ordinance' (θέσις) and his 'law' (νόμος)— a world of morals and society, which in many respects conflicted with 'nature' and should be corrected accordingly: 'law' must yield to its opponent 'nature.'[7] At this period Socrates was to recall philosophy from the vast tracts of the cosmos, in which it had formerly gone a-wandering, was to bring it down from the skies and make it at home in the houses of men, so that it should, as ethics, give instruction and support to our straying footsteps (Cicero, *Tusc.* 5.4, 10). To a strictly moral philosopher like Socrates, all man's knowledge or conjectures about 'nature' as a whole would seem relatively unimportant. It is with reference to this later reaction, in which all previous achievements were rejected as valueless, that modern scholars have lumped together all the earlier philosophers under the title of 'pre-Socratics'—a title which the latter, fortunately for themselves, could never have imagined. For the so-called pre-Socratics man is still a part of nature: he does not stand in contradistinction to the non-human world, but is a component member of it. He lives in and by the same ordinances which rule all things, even to the stars in the heavens. Thus Heraclitus (fr. 114, below, p. 391f.) taught that all human laws are 'nourished' from the one universal divine law, and that our thoughts and actions should win strength and certainty from union with the all-embracing, rational law. Here 'law' does not mean something set up quite artificially and often in opposition to 'nature': on the contrary, it is 'nourished' by the general sense of 'nature' as a whole, and therefore sets a standard for men also; any deviation from it is mistaken, irrational and in the

[7] Cf. F. Heinimann, *Nomos und Physis*, Basel 1945.

last resort ineffective. Secondly, while man was understood as a part of nature, nature was understood anthropomorphically. The notion of a pure mechanism in nature, radically different from all the classes of things in which there is a will at work and goals being striven for, had not yet occurred to anyone, and consequently the work of the early thinkers was far removed from our modern conception of the physical sciences. They were not content with limited sets of data and limited objectives: what they sought was ideas capable of comprehending at once the mechanical world and the world of will and mind. But at the same time the enquiring spirit of these speculators led them onto many subjects which we should assign to the physical sciences; and, thanks to the extraordinary energy and adaptability of their minds, they had ideas and drew inferences of which many are anything but primitive and ephemeral: many indeed have enjoyed new life to great effect in modern branches of science—even in the most recent of them.

The early thinkers each began and ended with a metaphysical doctrine intended to explain, at one blow, as it were, the universe and its course, including human life.[8] Each of them produced a single comprehensive dictum on the nature of things in general. If he took up the pen, he produced one short treatise,[9] which in a later age, when titles were given to books, would receive the monumental title 'On the nature of things.' In each case the teachings were concerned with the questions, 'What is the real basis of the whole, and consequently of each individual entity?' and 'How is the individual entity derived from the basis?' In each case we find a hypothesis which provides its own justification. The question has a meaning only when the answer is supplied, not before: only when the breakthrough has been accomplished through the manifold variety of phenomena to the uniformity which (according to the theory) lies behind—only then is it shown that the breakthrough was possible and necessary. The doctrine is not arrived at by logical inference,

[8] Cf. G. Misch, *The Dawn of Philosophy* (ed. and transl. R. F. C. Hull, London, 1950).

[9] It seems likely that these books were not intended to be read in private, but aloud before an audience, after which they would be explained and discussed section by section: the content of these very compressed books could not have been properly understood and appreciated in any other way than by examining and discussing with one's hearers the ideas which must at first seem strange. Thus at the beginning of Heraclitus' work (below, p. 371), he refers to discussions with others on his *logos* (with a characteristic remark that his instruction made the hearers no wiser). Even if this were so, this confrontation with his public could hardly fail to help the author himself to clarify his thought and improve his presentation.

but all kinds of facts which tend to support it are very willingly brought forward. Intuitive genius found the goal before finding the road that could lead to it: pure reasoning, without a thorough basis of observation, arrived at a number of the principles employed by science in our own day. When compared with ours, Greek science seems very rich in ideas, but irresponsibly hasty in adopting and proclaiming them. It was not interested in a long and patient construction in which the individual can play only a part, without a hope of living to see the completion of the whole—probably without even any inkling of the meaning and importance of what he is trying to find out. The Greek philosopher of these early days lived in the bold conviction that the full understanding of the nature of the universe was accessible to him personally, and he dared to tread the open and direct road to his objective, not disguising his purpose under utilitarian pretexts. The will to know and to understand needed no external justification among the Greeks.

Concerning the outward forms taken by the study of philosophy we know little or nothing. At first, no doubt, the number of those who felt called to its pursuit was very small, but the supply never wholly gave out: the great thinkers always found someone to echo their teaching. Their words were listened to, their writings were read and disseminated wherever Greek was spoken.

We, however, possess the works of the early philosophers only in fragments—in verbal quotations of individual passages, which we find in a number of later writers. Apart from these we have extensive 'doxographical' material, i.e. statements by later authors on the doctrines of the old philosophers. Plato refers several times to earlier philosophers, and Aristotle gives systematic synopses of his predecessors' theories. His pupil Theophrastus composed a monograph on the 'Teachings of the Physicists' (φυσικοί, natural scientists, philosophers of nature), and to this book may be traced (directly or indirectly) most of our surviving doxographical material. The work itself has not survived, but the numerous treatises deriving from it make a rough reconstruction possible[10] and give us some idea of its character.

The method adopted by Theophrastus was apparently to go through the works of earlier philosophers, from Thales to Plato, making them answer a catechism based on the problems which Aristotle considered the most important.[11] From a mass of excerpts

[10] For this reconstruction see the monumental work of A. Diels, *Doxographi Graeci* (Berlin 1879).

[11] The questions were concerned with: principles underlying the universe; nature of god or gods; origin and constitution of the universe; stars and climatic phenomena; the soul and nature of perception and intellection; the body and its constitution.

thus obtained he assembled, for each Aristotelian problem, the solutions proposed by previous philosophers: those solutions he evaluated critically from an Aristotelian standpoint.[12] It is obvious enough that, for our purposes, the doxographical statements of Aristotle and Theophrastus can be used only with the greatest caution.[13] Any idea is liable to be distorted when it is reported and reformulated by someone else; and this is particularly true of philosophical thought when it is reproduced by another philosopher with different views. In addition, Aristotle and Theophrastus were under the necessity, for their own purposes, of dragging the old ideas, one by one, from their original context, and squeezing them into a new framework, into which all too often they would not fit.[14] Again and again they had to wring from a book answers to questions which had never entered the author's head;[15] and they had to ignore in the books anything that had no bearing on their own problems, no matter how important it might be in the original system. We must also remember that Aristotle and Theophrastus were not concerned with writing the history of philosophy for its own sake:[16] they did not aim at reproducing the views of the early thinkers accurately and in their original sense, but in turning them to account as material for working out the details of their own doctrine. Theophrastus was well aware that he was obliged to misrepresent the old systems in projecting them onto the Aristotelian plane, and sometimes he himself provides a helpful hint.[17] Hence we can never accept a doxographical notice at its face value, but must compare it (if that is at all possible) with passages of the authentic texts. As a second resort, the inner consistency which we must attribute to any given system can help us to

[12] On the structure of Theophrastus' work see O. Regenbogen, *R.-E.* Suppl. 7, 1535ff.

[13] The question of Aristotle's trustworthiness is systematically examined by H. Cherniss, *Aristotle's Criticism of Presocratic Philosophy* (Baltimore 1935).

[14] Aristotle uses in one place (*Metaph.* 1075b 12: cf. Cherniss p. 363) the term ῥυθμίζειν to denote his re-arrangement of the original material.

[15] A particularly crass and very instructive example of distorted presentation, without reference to the context, occurs in Aristotle *De Anima* 427a 25, where he cites *Odyssey* 18, 136f. (discussed above, p. 134): 'For the feelings of every man whom earth produces are ever such as the day he receives from the father of gods and mortals.' He finds in it the theory that perception and thought are the same (see below; p. 363 n. 37 and Cherniss p. 313 n. 86).

[16] This would have been quite superfluous, since the original works were available to anyone who wished to consult them.

[17] 21 Xenophanes A31, 2–3 may be paraphrased thus: 'Theophrastus says that Xenophanes, the teacher of Parmenides, put forward the (Parmenidean) thesis of the unity and completeness of that-which-is (i.e. the cosmos); but he adds that the thesis of Xenophanes does not belong in this context, since Xenophanes was speaking not of the cosmos, but of the unity and completeness of God.'

resolve difficulties and to fill gaps in the tradition. Finally, the logic of historical development can be taken into account. The last two criteria, however, are not easy to apply successfully, since hardly any philosopher follows out his ideas into all their consequences, and the history of philosophy contains as many crooked and broken-off tracks as straight and uninterrupted ones. The general result is that the certainty and completeness with which we can recover the doctrines of these early thinkers fluctuates from point to point, the most important among the variables being the supply of significant original texts.[18]

Of the first of the so-called Ionian natural philosophers we possess not one word of original text. We are not alone in this: the ancient writers also had to rely on oral tradition and on its reflection in other men's works. Thales never wrote a book.

Thales lived at the beginning of the sixth century in Miletus, the greatest and most important of the Ionian cities.[19] We are told that he supposed water to be the basis of the universe (11 Thales A12); but he himself did not use the term ἀρχή ('beginning, basis, principle': 12 Anaximander A9). His doctrine is said to have meant that the earth floated on water, and that earthquakes arose from agitation of the surface of this water (A12; 15). These notices of his teachings sound plausible, but, since we have access to none of Thales' doctrines in their original words, we can say nothing certain about their real meaning. We shall have to be content then with some generalities and with some suggestions which do not claim to be any more than possibilities.

Whereas Hesiod spoke of the earth as the great mother of the whole, not one of the so-called natural philosophers took the earth as the 'basis' or principle of the universe. Their metaphysical speculations sought the root of all being not in something solid, tangible and familiar, but in something subtle, fugitive and hard to grasp. For Thales (if our information is trustworthy) this was water: but by

[18] If we wish to avoid self-deception, we should constantly bear the following facts in mind. (1) Of the first four philosophers after Hesiod (Thales, Anaximander, Anaximenes, Pythagoras) we possess one original sentence. (2) This sentence contains a fundamental notion of which the doxographical tradition takes not the slightest notice beyond merely quoting the passage (see below p. 266). Nevertheless, as soon as we have even a little piece of original material, a critical combination of the direct and indirect tradition can lead, under favourable circumstances, to satisfactory conclusions: for an example which to me seems particularly clear, see *Frühgriech. Denken* p. 183–185 on Parmenides A 37 and B 10–15.

[19] His father had a Carian name: his family could be traced back to Phoenician colonists, but it was one of the most respected in the city.

'water' he did not mean material water in our sense. We should misunderstand the expressions of the early Greek philosophers, if we took them as meaning that the basic stuff of the universe was the substance water, or the substance air, or the supposed substance fire. The notion of substance or matter did not arise until much later, as an antithesis to form or force.[20] The principal philosophical category of those days was quality, and by 'water,' 'air' or 'fire' was meant a possessor of certain characteristic properties. When Semonides (see above p. 203f.) spoke of a type of woman coming 'from the fox' or 'from the bee,' he was indicating certain qualities, not speaking of material substance. Each animal that he names represents a particular natural constitution, distinguished from all other constitutions by a complex of properties composing it. In fact this very doctrine of Thales, with its moving and spontaneously active water and its moved and passive earth, is illuminated by his contemporary Semonides, who provides the earliest authentic text embodying such attitudes of mind. He speaks in fact of women sprung from 'earth,' others from 'sea': 'earth' is the quality of inertness, dullness, passivity, 'sea' of activity, mobility, spontaneity, of that which changes and moves without external stimulus (above p. 205f.). For Thales possibly 'earth' meant the whole complex of lower qualities, including passivity, weight, bulkiness and solidity, while 'sea' meant the complex of higher qualities, including what we should call mobility, force, life and 'soul' (cf. 21 Xenophanes B 29f.). He may have drawn attention to the movement of water—smoothly flowing in rivers, leaping in mountain torrents, dashing violently as waves on a coast; he may have pointed out that its presence animates the soil and produces plant life, while its absence destroys all life, and that when the fluid quality of water is driven off by evaporation, only brittle and lifeless matter remains. We may further suppose that Thales interpreted the whole universe on the basis of an interaction between the opposites 'water' and 'earth,' in which water, so to speak, was the soul and earth the body. We read that from the attractive power of the lodestone and of amber[21] he drew the inference that

[20] In our own day we have seen again the abandonment of the notion that there are a number of substances (possessing certain qualities) and a number of forces (with certain regularities) forming two separate groups of quite independent phenomena; both are recognized now as different manifestations of one and the same thing and as being incapable of definition purely as matter or purely as force. The early Greek thinkers from the very outset, naively but not stupidly, thought in terms of constituting qualities, without distinguishing between matter, properties and immanent forces.

[21] Magnetic ores were found near the city of Magnesia and named after it; the electrical attraction that can be exercised by amber was known at an early date.

there was a 'soul' or 'life' (ψυχή) in the stone (A1, 24; A3). If it is true that he taught that all things were 'full of gods' (A22), he may perhaps have equated the life-force with godhead. But this is no more than a guess.

The next in the series, Anaximander (born c. 610) is much better known to us. He left a written treatise, of which we possess at least one sentence in something like the original wording. Like Thales, he was a Milesian, and the fourth century (projecting its own manners into the past) described him as the 'pupil' of Thales. There is indeed a certain connection between the teachings of the two, since Anaximander adopted Thales' doctrine about water into his own system, although in a subordinate rôle (below p. 264f.). On the basis of the universe, however, he made a pronouncement very different from that of Thales: he declared that the *apeiron* was the 'beginning' or 'principle' (ἀρχή) of each and every thing that exists. The Greek ἄπειρον can be translated as 'unbounded' or 'undefined,' and Anaximander seems to have used it in both senses at once. The word πείρατα also seems to have been used to mean not merely 'boundaries' but also any kind of defining or determining. Transferred into our terms, the theory states that everything which realizes itself in actuality is derived from that which is potential (unlike Hesiod's notion in which the world suddenly and out of nothing comes into the 'void'); or, more precisely, that any defined actuality is evolved from a background of undefined possibilities, which mingle with each other, having no fixed boundaries, so that the sum of them also is indefinable and unbounded.[22] Now being a good archaic

[22] There are some previous approximations to this new conception of an ἄπειρον, an 'unbounded undefined,' e.g. Hesiod's striking reference to the 'boundaries' (πείρατα) which separate all defined existence from empty non-existence (above p. 105–107); and the notion of *tekmor*, 'determining, definition' (above p. 253) is related to Hesiod's idea. As for the notion of an antithesis between reality and possibility, or actuality and potentiality, as we should call it, it is decidedly older than Anaximander (see above p. 118 with n. 11). But Anaximander in the first place elevates the realm of possibilities into a self-sufficing basis of the universe; in the second (if our previous interpretation is correct, which we based on Theophrastus' explanation [A 9a φύσις ἀόριστος καὶ κατ' εἶδος καὶ κατὰ μέγεθος]), he took the undefinedness of pure possibilities one stage further. In his realm of the 'undefined' are not merely those component elements of the whole whose transference to actuality is in any given instance undetermined, but those elements themselves are undistinguished from each other. Thus we do not find there, *inter alia*, something that is capable of being warm but is not actually warm; we find rather an unseparated store of that which is potentially warm and potentially cold —an idea which recurs later in Anaxagoras, although with important modifications (in the beginning, says Anaxagoras, before the separating 'spirit' set to work, everything was mixed and confused together, indefinitely small and indefinitely numerous).

thinker, Anaximander could only conceive a defined group of qualities as accompanied by its polar opposite; that which has to be bounded and limited, must be delimited with respect to its opposite. Therefore, according to his teaching, the evolution of realities took place in the following way: from time to time out of the unbounded-undefined a pair of antithetical qualities or complexes of qualities would arise, and afterwards each individual entity that had thus come into being would sink back into the *apeiron* through the mixing together of the opposites which had engendered it, and which by thus mixing lost their proper nature (12 Anaximander A9; 10; 16). The wide and varied range of perceptible qualities was reduced by Anaximander, as it seems, to one single pair of opposites, 'hot and cold' (A10). Apparently he considered the qualities of lightness, brightness, mobility, life etc. as mere varieties of 'heat,' and darkness, heaviness, passivity, lifelessness etc. as varieties of 'cold.' Being full of the dynamic interplay of opposites, the world of reality is in perpetual change and movement (A11), while the *apeiron*, in which there is no differentiation, is free of coming-to-be, passing-away and change; it 'never dies nor grows old' (A15; B3), just like the Homeric gods. But the 'undefined' cannot take over the positive properties of the gods; where there is no distinction, there can be no positive characteristics.

Anaximander was not content with erecting the thesis of the two worlds—the world of finite reality which we experience with our senses and of which we are ourselves part, and the world beyond, the realm of infinity beyond perception or intellection. Unlike the metaphysicians of the Upanishads, whose prime object was to sink themselves into the cause of all things, who bent all their efforts towards freeing themselves from all thoughts concerning this world, the Greek metaphysicians aimed at a complete interpretation of the phenomenal world also. The truths which they had discovered had to be defensible as true and as explanatory of the actual constitution of the sensible universe. Hence Anaximander boldly and rather violently undertook to outline the general structure of our world, and concerning his sketch we have the following information.

Our earth is shaped like a drum of a column, and we inhabit the upper circular surface. The earth remains suspended: it does not fall, because it is at an equal distance from the other things and has no reason to move from the midpoint. It is surrounded with a layer of air. When the world came into existence, a shell of fire built itself up around the earth and its envelope of air, just as bark grows around a tree. (Thus, by an antithetical differentiation, there evolved from the *apeiron* a pair, 'cold-hot,' with the cold inside.) Later the shell of fire burst (?) and split up into several rings of fire, namely the courses or spheres of the stars. Every ring of fire consists of a kernel and a shell; but a layer of air conceals the fire except at one point where the light sparkles out, through an opening like the nozzle of a pair of bellows: this is what we see as a star. (The stellar sphere, that is to say, is a pair, 'light-dark', with the light inward.) The moon's phases and eclipses are caused by the opening and closing of the orifice. The stellar circles are in rotary motion like wheels.[23] Anaximander went so far as to give measurements: the earth is three times as broad as it is high; the sun is of the same size as the earth; the moon's orbit is 19 $[= 1 + (2 \times 3 \times 3)]$ times as great as the earth; that of the sun 28 $[= 1 + (3 \times 3 \times 3)]$ times as great as the earth (A10.11.21.22).

Anaximander was also the first to draw a map representing the surface of the earth (A6). It has been reasonably surmised[24] that this map, like the later one of Hecataeus, but to a still greater degree, assigned simple geometrical shapes to the seas and continents and squeezed them into symmetry. Just as the individual star-spheres of light were separated from each other by surrounding darkness, so the dry land-masses were surrounded by water. The origin of the earth was also attributed by Anaximander to an opposition and antithesis with water. Originally it was wholly covered by water; then gradually it dried out, except for the lowest parts, which are still covered by the sea; but the seas too will disappear in time. For Anaximander, then, water was in existence before land: this obviously reflects the teaching of Thales. Anaximander attributed the drying-out of the earth to the effect of the sun in drawing out moisture. Winds and weather are also caused by the sun, while in return the winds influence the course of the sun and moon, whose recurring movements are caused by winds that spring up regularly

[23] Here for the first time we find the notion of spheres as the agency through which the several planets are carried in circles around the earth—spheres analogous to the outer sphere which carries the fixed stars around with it. In Parmenides the spheres are called 'rings' (στεφάναι, below p. 361). The idea that the paths of the planets are to be identified with so many invisible rings, in which each planet is fastened, steadily gained in precision during the succeeding centuries, and the mechanism of the rotation of these spheres, coupled one to another, was ever more accurately defined. In order to explain the complicated orbits, with their apparent retrograde movements, further spheres were inserted between the actual planetary spheres. Even the heliocentric theory of Copernicus did not reject the notion of spheres, but reduced their number from 80 to 43. Only in the seventeenth century was it recognized that the stars move freely and independently in space. In early Greece there was a rival view which looked on the stars and planets as freely moving hollow spherical bodies (above p. 213 n. 9, below p. 386).

[24] Cf. W. Jaeger, *Paideia* vol. 1 English transl., 2nd ed. (Oxford, 1945), 157f.

at certain seasons (Anaximander A27; Herodotus 2, 24, 1 and 26, 2).

All life is likewise supposed to have begun in the water,[25] since at first there was no dry land. The original form was the crustacean with a spiny integument; later the shell was cast off. (In the organic world also we see the principle of shell and kernel determining each other antithetically: the opposing pair is of course 'hard-soft.') The origin of animals also takes its course under the animating influence of the sun's heat. Man himself originally arose from an aquatic creature; for a sucking child is unable to live by itself, and therefore the human race could not have begun with a new-born human being, but must have developed from a creature of a different kind. Earlier, human beings passed the first of their life in the sea and then underwent a metamorphosis. Therefore men should not eat fish (seacreatures) because the fish is the father and mother of man (A11; 30).

A further inference drawn by Anaximander from the idea of something unbounded-undefined as the basis of all things was that the *apeiron* could not be limited to producing this one world in which we live: there must be innumerable worlds. His further assumption that such worlds are all mutually equidistant arose no doubt from a notion that the equilibrium[26] of the whole would thus be preserved: certainly his centrally-poised earth was explained on those lines (A9–11; 17).

This then, according to such testimony as we have, was Anaximander's outline of the universe. If several features of it sound strange, the fault arises not from an exuberant fancy, but from the boldness and freedom of thought with which he made the same basic principles apply throughout the whole scheme. We may also suspect that all these notions would make much better sense if we had them in their original form and context, together with his other teachings of which we have not even any indirect information, since they happened not to lie within the field of research of our informants.

The few original words which we possess have great depth and power and a content of which the doxographical excerpts give us no inkling. Thanks to the conscientious accuracy of Theophrastus, we have at all events one short sentence in something like its original

[25] It was not until Darwin's time that this thesis of Anaximander's was received into some esteem again, just as his doctrine of the plurality of worlds has been re-established through the work of modern astronomers. A notion which now is based on cogent reasoning from a wide range of precise observations, was then a bold surmise of a mind pushing forward into the unknown, with only a minimum of known facts at its disposal.

[26] The principle of equilibrium and counterpoise must have been in Anaximander's mind when he made his opposites always appear in pairs. Cf. G. Vlastos, *Class. Philol.* 42 (1947) 168f.

form. While Theophrastus was collecting his material, he came upon a passage where Anaximander's language assumed a poetical tone, where the thought seemed to soar above any prosaic analysis. He therefore abandoned temporarily his transcription into Aristotelian terms, and preferred to quote a few words very much as he found them. His statement on Anaximander's theory of the basis of the universe runs (leaving some aside): 'Anaximander . . . assumed as the principle and basis of the things that exist . . . an undefined complex of qualities, out of which the heavens and the world enclosed within them are composed.

"And from whence coming-into-existence is to those things which are, thither also is passing-away for them according to their debt; for they give right and penance each to the other for their unrighteousness according to the behest of time."

Thus he expresses himself rather poetically.' (A9; B1).[27] In these few lines of the original text Theophrastus has preserved for us a priceless, but not readily intelligible document.

Let us start with the second half: 'for they give . . .' 'They,' of course, are all things and beings in existence at any given time. The expression 'they give right' means in ordinary Greek usage: 'they are punished.' The turn of phrase shows us that the punishment is not regarded as passive suffering, but as something active: the infringer of right 'gives' something to the victim of his misdeed; and he gives 'right' because punishment changes an existing wrong into a restored right. In this instance the 'wrong' consists in coming into existence, and punishment and 'penance' in passing away. The executioner, as it were, who determines the due date of the punishment, is 'time.'[28] 'Time' for Anaximander's contemporaries was not a mere co-ordinate on which the observer's eye could travel forwards or backwards at will. Rather, it was identical with that driving force which never allows the course of events to stand still.[29] The continuing world-process, according to Anaximander, always exacted the appropriate penalty of extinction from that which had come into existence. In a similar vein Solon had often declared his conviction that all guilt found its punishment in the course of time.

[27] Theophrastus gives the quotation in indirect form: Ἐξ ὧν δὲ ἡ γένεσίς ἐστι τοῖς οὖσι, καὶ τὴν φθορὰν εἰς ταῦτα γίνεσθαι κατὰ τὸ χρεών. διδόναι γὰρ αὐτὰ δίκην καὶ τίσιν ἀλλήλοις τῆς ἀδικίας κατὰ τὴν τοῦ χρόνου τάξιν. On the extract and its verbal accuracy see Vlastos, *op. cit.*, n. 119.

[28] On χρεών 'indebtedness' 'rightness', see e.g. Solon fr. 23, 21; on χρόνος as the agent of δίκη Solon fr. 24, 3 ἐν δίκη χρόνου and fr. 3, 16; for κατὰ τὴν τάξιν cf. Plato. *Laws* 10, 904c 8.

[29] Cf. *Frühgriech. Denken* p. 1ff.

But how are we to understand this mutual suffering of penance among all things that exist, whereby in perishing each returns to that from which it drew its being? The guilt seems to consist in this: a thing which comes-to-be, in emerging from the *apeiron* and passing into actuality, selfishly snatches potentialities for itself and denies them to other things which might have come to be instead. The guilt is expiated when the thing that exists passes away by sinking again into the *apeiron* and returns its existence to the common stock of potentialities for some new application.[30] The possibilities which are set free by the extinction of an entity are sooner or later, through the mediacy of the *apeiron*, turned to the account of a successor, which thanks to them can come into and remain in being. Everything that exists is the beneficiary of the annihilation of a previous entity, and each by its death will play its part in filling that shoreless ocean out of which all being is derived. If one views the whole, everything has its justice. Existence, the possession of which is an unfair advantage, is taken away again from its greedy possessor, and thus it is made available for the use of others, whereby the new possessor will incur the same guilt: and in the sum total no one has any ground for complaint. Formulated thus, Anaximander's theory is identical with that stated by Solon at the end of his great elegy (above p. 235f.): it is only that Anaximander speaks of the *apeiron* and the privilege of existence, while Solon speaks of Zeus and the privilege of prosperity. The purpose of the theory in either case is to justify the workings of fate. Anaximander extends the notion of justice to the cosmic process: a problem which was originally social and religious has been transferred to a wider and more majestic context.

The metaphysical doctrines of Anaximander certainly aimed at the highest and the most universal. An infinite number of worlds was not enough for him: he aimed beyond these worlds, at that which is at all times the unformed basis of all form. It was only beyond this so broadly conceived empire of Being (which must always be a defined and therefore limited Being), in the Undefined and Unlimited that an intellect seeking the absolute could at last halt and take its stand. Hesiod previously had caught a glimpse of the basis of being, beyond all being. In his boldest speculations he touched with fear and trembling upon the fearful 'sources and boundaries' of the universe, and looked for a moment into the void beyond the 'boundaries' (above p. 105–107). Where Hesiod saw an 'empty chasm,' Anaxi-

---

[30] The *apeiron* in this context is made plural in form (ἐξ ὧν—εἰς ταῦτα), since it consists of innumerable potential things, which are disadvantaged by the actualizing of individual things from their number, and are later relieved of their disadvantage when those things return to the general 'undefinedness'.

mander beheld an immeasurable plenitude of the undefined, lying in readiness for existence.

This one invaluable sentence from Anaximander's book has been preserved in its original form because of its 'poetical' manner of expression; Anaximenes, the third and last in the series of Milesian philosophers (he died after 530), wrote in a 'simple and unpretentious Ionic,' as we are told (13 Anaximenes A1), and none of his book has survived in the original form.[31] In his case the task of classifying his ideas and modernizing his style seems to have presented no difficulty to later students. The doxographers saw Anaximenes as Anaximander's pupil, and like Anaximander, he posited a basic cosmic stuff out of which all things arose and into which they were finally resolved (B2). For this stuff, however, he did not look outside the world of our experience: air, according to him, was the basic substance of all things. Here he parted company with the metaphysical approach of Anaximander. He seems rather to have agreed more closely with the first of the Milesians; but for his basic stuff he chose something finer, more volatile and, so to speak, more spiritual. Air and wind seemed to him better qualified than water and sea to be equated with the active, creative power that rules all things: after all, our breath of life is air (B2). To correct a predecessor's philosophical system in this way is a proceeding which we find paralleled in Solon. For Semonides and many others before and after his time the sea had been the type of wilfulness and spontaneity: Solon in a political simile pointed out that the sea (the mass of the people) is not in movement and unrest by itself, but is stirred up by storm-blasts, i.e. by demagogues (fr. 11, above p. 228 with n. 21).

On the details of Anaximenes' teaching we know, first of all, the following: 'Undefined (ἄπειρος) air is the principle out of which everything arises, has arisen and will arise—the gods and the divine as well; and everything else will form itself out of the progeny of air. When air is at its most uniform, it is not perceptible to the eyes: it is perceptible only by cold, heat or movement' (A7). Anaximander had distinguished between two levels of existence; but now Anaximenes discovered in air a union of the qualities of both. Being formless and bodiless it was not an object but something unbounded-undefined like Anaximander's suprasensual *apeiron*; but at the same time it is hot or cold like the sensible objects that arise from the *apeiron*. Thus it is at once part of the universe and the source of the universe, at all events when it appears as itself, as air, as the breath of the wind, the

[31] W. Kranz in *Hermes* 73 (1938) 111 and *Göttinger Nachr.* 1938, 145 has not convinced me that the sentence in fr. B2 is genuine. One of the anachronisms in it is the notion that the soul 'rules' us (or 'rules' the body).

breath of life. On the other hand, by cooling, which goes hand in hand with concentration, it can lose its proper form; it becomes 'storm' first of all, then with increasing cold becomes successively cloud, water, earth and ultimately stone. With heat and expansion it turns first into aether (the blue radiance of the sky), finally into fire (A7). In this thesis we can also detect two ideas started by Anaximander. The undefined state is the ideal, and degeneracy sets in with the emergence of heat and cold, which to Anaximander were the basic qualities of the sensible world.

Yet in this conception a wholly new spirit is at work. Determinedly natural in his approach, Anaximenes refuses to look for the essence of things beyond the world of experience: he brings back the 'basis of things' into the realm of things themselves; he transforms metaphysics into physics. He speaks as a physicist from the beginning with the hypothesis that all matter is of one kind, but takes on various properties according to its temperature. Physical phenomena like condensation and evaporation, freezing and melting, compression and rarefaction are brought into a firm mutual relationship by a single comprehensive formula. To support his view that cold goes with compression and warmth with expansion, he points out that our breath is warm when it comes from a wide-opened mouth, and cold when it has to squeeze through a small opening of the lips (B1). The physical statements and references are hasty and disputable; but the manner of thought is startlingly scientific.

In the world-picture which he draws, Anaximenes made his basic notions stick out at every point: by hook or by crook the particular must be forced into line with the universal. Since air is the basis of all things, Anaximenes makes the earth (which he thought of as shaped like a flat dish—a common enough notion) float on a cushion of air. The stars also were to him flat and floating discs; they consisted of fire, but had a central invisible solid body (as a kernel perhaps), which revolved with the star (A7 and 14).[32] Here is the influence of Anaximander again, in whose scheme opposites always had to occur together. The stellar fires are made of moisture heated, vaporized and rarefied to a very high degree. The annual movement of the sun and the varying movements of the stars in general are explained by the pressure of closely-packed air (A15, cf. Herod. 2, 26). Anaximander's thesis of stellar spheres which passed continuously under the earth as well as over it had to be abandoned by Anaximenes, since his earth was no longer freely floating in space. Hence he inclined to the common superstition that at night the sun

[32] Diogenes of Apollonia (64 A12) identified the central solid bodies with meteoric stones.

sails round on the stream of Ocean from West to East (above
p. 102, n. 13), and taught that the stars, after reaching the Western
horizon, travel backwards round the earth just as if (ὥσπερ εἰ) the
cap on a man's head were to rotate (A7, 6; 14). The sun, he says, is
not seen at night because it is so far away and because the raised
edge of the earth hides it (above p. 213, n. 9). We see here that
Anaximenes was willing to use antiquated notions when the details
of his theory required it: the advance of natural science on one front
does not preclude a withdrawal on another. There is one interesting
point in Anaximenes' explanation of lightning. Anaximander (12 A
23) had explained thunder as the noise of a cloud bursting when
wind forced its way through it and lightning as the bright edge of the
tear, which appears particularly bright against the dark background.
Anaximenes was very ready to accept an explanation which made
wind responsible for so striking a phenomenon, and he supported it
by pointing out that the furrow cut by a ship's rudder in the dark
water at night appears to glow brightly (the phenomenon of
phosphorescence). The analogical method here employed with
doubtful validity, was destined to play an important role in later
science.[33]

After a fifty-year sojourn in Miletus, philosophy threw off its local
restrictions and began to expand with that sudden vigour which new
ideas acquire at the moment when the world is ripe for them. The
next two to lead the field, Pythagoras and Xenophanes, were Eastern
Ionians, but not Milesians, and each independently took the new
intellectual movement into the far West. Pythagoras was born in
Samos, one of the islands lying off the deeply indented West coast of
Asia Minor. Having notions of his own on the best political constitution, he escaped from the burdens of life in Samos—particularly the
tyranny of Polycrates from about 540 onwards—and settled in
Southern Italy; at first in Croton, on the East coast of what is now
Calabria, later apparently in Metapontum, near Tarentum. Very
probably he did not leave Samos alone, but took a following of
friends and supporters with him into the wild. His activities fall
roughly within the period 530–500.

At that time the far West of the Greek world offered to enterprising spirits opportunities that the Eastern frontier could no longer
give. In 547 Lydia had become a province of Persia; Sardis, the
home of Alcman, became the residence of a Persian satrap; the great
empire of Persia was now the overlord or the neighbour of the
Eastern Greek cities, and the tensions of political and cultural conflict
in that narrow space along the seaboard of Asia Minor were rising

[33] Cf. H. Diller in *Hermes* 67 (1932) 35.

to danger-point. Southern Italy on the other hand was comparatively speaking a vacuum. Apart from the threat (not yet serious) of the Etruscans in the North and of Carthage in the South, the states of 'Great Greece,' as the Hellenized parts of Southern Italy and Sicily were called from the eighth century onwards, had no confrontation except with each other or with barbarian tribes at a lower level of culture. Rome was still an insignificant capital of a tribe, merely one among many such. Here in the West everything could assume greater dimensions than were possible in the old world. There was no visible limit to the pasture and ploughland. Here states could be planned as the founders chose, not too much encumbered with history. Greek philosophy also found in the West a suitable setting for its bold speculations. After Xenophanes had emigrated to the West, Elea (on the West coast, South of the Gulf of Salerno) became the home of a most important philosophical school (see below p. 326); Croton produced the first physician who aimed at a philosophical basis for his art (below p. 340). The West also became the home of various religious sects.

In the movement which stemmed from Pythagoras many different ends were pursued at once: meditative philosophy, natural science, both practical and theoretical, reform in religious belief and practice, sectarian solidarity among the followers, and lastly social and political reform. In more than one city of Southern Italy the Pythagorean brotherhood was a powerful and often decisive political force.[34]

The teaching of the Pythagoreans was only passed on personally to the adherents of the sect. None of the believers entrusted it to writing, and Pythagoras himself left no written work behind him. It was an exception if a man closely connected with the school made his knowledge public (14 Pythagoras A 17). Hence in the time when the sect was still flourishing, only an incomplete and unreliable picture of its teaching got abroad, and our own knowledge of the subject is scanty. We have in the main to rely on accounts drawn up about 300 B.C., shortly after the demise of the movement, and copied out by writers of late antiquity whose works still survive; there was a Neo-Pythagorean movement from the first century B.C. onwards, and all the available accounts of the doctrine were collected. In these circumstances it is impossible for us to distinguish early, later and much later elements, or to pick out Pythagoras' personal con-

[34] This does not mean that the Pythagoreans as such formed a government, but rather that they put the most important political offices into the hands of their own members. Cf. K. von Fritz, *Pythagorean Politics in Southern Italy* (New York 1940) 94ff.

tribution from the general doctrines of the school. The Pythagoreans themselves would have it no other way: credit must be given to the master for everything achieved by them. It seemed right to them, we are told, that everything should be credited to 'Him,' 'The Man'— for they never pronounced his name—and that 'no-one should take personal credit for any discovery, or only very seldom; hence there are very few of them who are known to have written a book of their own' (18 A 4; 58 D 6, 198).

The founder of the sect received a more than human veneration from his followers, probably even while he was still alive; and even those outside the movement must have been impressed by his striking doctrine and personality. Even today we possess four statements about him made within sixty to eighty years after his death. Only one of them is an enthusiastic acceptance, but even the dissenting and scoffing voices attest the impact of his character and teaching on men's minds.

The earliest of these references comes from Pythagoras' younger contemporary Xenophanes (see below chap. VIIa), who told the following sarcastic anecdote in an elegy (21 Xenophanes B 7):

Once, we are told, in passing he heard a puppy-dog squealing under its master's whip. Full of compassion, he said, 'Leave him; beat him no more! The soul of one of my comrades lives in this dog: I know simply by hearing his voice.'[35]

To pay serious attention to a puppy and treat it as an incarnation of a human soul seemed to the sober Xenophanes the height of absurdity. As to Pythagoras, the four lines show that tradition is right in ascribing to him the belief in transmigration of souls.[36] In all probability the belief is a good deal older than Pythagoras, although certainly younger than the time of Homer and Hesiod. Homer indeed did not even have the notion of 'soul' in our sense (see above p. 76f.). The word *psyche*, which was afterwards used to mean the 'soul,' originally meant 'breath,' 'breath of life.' At first in epic poetry it was used for 'life'—never with reference to any particular vital function (e.g. breathing, perception, motion, thought, feeling or consciousness), but always in connection with the loss of life (e.g. 'they lost their *psyche*'; 'he took his *psyche* from him'; 'I set my *psyche* at hazard').

[35] In its form this is a type of anecdote told of philosophers which afterwards became very popular: 'On such-and-such an occasion (or in answer to such-and-such a question) the great man made the following significant remark.' See also above p. 240 on the saying of one of the Seven Sages (Aristodamus) and the occasion on which he said it.

[36] There is no reason to doubt that the verses do in fact refer to Pythagoras, as Diogenes says.

Accordingly *psyche* was used to mean the undefined something that went away in death or unconsciousness and left an inanimate body behind. Secondly, since the human mind is unwilling to accept in full the idea of total annihilation, the epic writers believed that this something, the *psyche* of the dead man, went off to the dark kingdom of the underworld, where it led a wretched and shadowy existence. Thus a development occurred which was to have important consequences: that which at first meant simply 'life' came to mean an ego which survived bodily death. It was not now a long step to two further assumptions. First came that of Pythagoras, according to which one and the same soul or ego was successively reborn in various bodily shapes; second the notion of a 'soul' in the living man which is to be distinguished from the body. The passage of Xenophanes contains no testimony to the second of these assumptions; for, according to the verbal expression, the dog *is* the soul (not, possesses the soul) of the friend, and the 'soul', not the dog, cries out with the well-known voice. Hence the soul is reborn *as* a dog, not *in* a dog.[37]

Of Pythagoras himself later legend averred that he was previously the valiant Trojan Euphorbus, who in the *Iliad* (16, 806–17, 60) was the first to wound Patroclus and was then slain by Menelaus (see above p. 75); and he was able to remember every life that he had had as animal, beast or plant, since, when he was Aethalides (reckoned the son of Hermes) he was granted a wish by Hermes, and he sought and received a power of memory such as would extend to all his existences and the intervals between (14 Pythagoras A 8, Diog. Laert. 8, 4–5).

We can see the point of the legend about Hermes. The believer in reincarnation must face the fact that we do not remember our previous existences. Hence the thesis was invented that our memory is normally destroyed between one life and the next. Thus Virgil in describing the underworld (*Aeneid* 6, 713) says: 'The soul for which fate has appointed new bodies draw long oblivion from the spring of Lethe.' But the souls of the elect are spared this breaking of continuity. An Orphic inscription[38] from southern Italy, of the fourth or third century, speaks of two springs, one on the left, from which the soul must be careful not to drink (clearly the spring Lethe, i.e. oblivion), and one on the right, 'whose cooling waters flow from the lake of

---

[37] A distinction between body and soul was as alien to this period as one between matter and force.

[38] We have good reason for thinking of this group of inscriptions as Orphic, since they refer to the soul as a son of Heaven and Earth who was slain by thunder. On the Orphic legends of the Titans see I. M. Linforth, *The Arts of Orpheus* (Berkeley 1941) 326 and 254f.

remembrance' (*Vorsokr.* 1 Orpheus B 17, detailed reference p. 252 n. 1). To Pythagoras then, if to anyone, his followers would be likely to ascribe a power of memory which could span all previous existences.

At this point another of our early references to Pythagoras is relevant. Empedocles, who was born about seventy years after him, devotes the following enthusiastic verses to the praises of someone unnamed, whom our ancient source identifies, probably correctly, with Pythagoras (31 Empedocles B 129):

Then was living a man distinguished beyond all for his wisdom, master of untold wealth in the spacious realms of the spirit, skilled to the highest degree in every region of science. When he applied his mind with the force of his whole understanding, he surveyed easily each several thing that had happened during the space of ten or of twenty life-times of mortals.

The knowledge and abilities of Pythagoras are here expressed quantitatively in the archaic fashion, and the range and extent of his powers are connected with his having the total experience of many lives available to him. The remaining two early testimonies also speak of the large, even the unique, extent of Pythagoras' knowledge. Heraclitus, who belonged to the generation after Pythagoras, expressed himself thus: 'Pythagoras, the son of Mnesarchus, practised research (ἱστορίη, 'finding things out') more than any other man, and having excerpted these books (?) he constructed his own kind of wisdom—polymathy and deceit.' In another passage he wrote: 'Knowing many things does not teach understanding: else it would have taught Hesiod and Pythagoras, Xenophanes and Hecataeus' (22 Heraclitus B 129 and 40). We need not concern ourselves here with the reasons for Heraclitus' hostility to Pythagoras (see below, p. 384). What is interesting here is that both Heraclitus and Empedocles ascribe to him an extraordinary range of knowledge, skills of every kind, and a specific method (cf. κακοτεχνίη). In later tradition Pythagoras was reckoned *inter alia* one of the founders of geometry and arithmetic, as being skilled in astronomy and even in medicine (Diog. VIII, 12). There is another respect in which this tradition fits in, in general terms, with the earliest evidence. Empedocles referred Pythagoras' unique abilities to his powers of memory, and, according to later accounts, a good memory was reckoned by the Pythagoreans as the basis of learning, skill (ἐμπειρία) and intelligence; hence they cultivated the memory by systematic exercise. Every morning the Pythagorean was required, before rising from his bed, to call to mind the whole course of the previous day, or the previous two days if possible—every action, every event, every word spoken or heard had to be remembered in the correct sequence (58 D1, 164–166). The adepts, then, tried to follow in their master's footsteps, although a long way behind, by thus aiming at powers of memory which would make their experiences a life-long possession.

The four passages that we have examined are the sum total of our trustworthy early evidence. They tell us something indeed of Pythagoras' person and teaching, but not very much. For the rest, we have to fall back on evidence which is valid only for the doctrines of the school, not for those of Pythagoras himself. Even within these limits the evidence is full of uncertainties, so that we can hardly assert with confidence any single thing about early Pythagorean doctrines.[39] The following paragraphs will try only to give a general picture of some Pythagorean ideas: how much of them is genuinely old, and how they might have appeared in their original guise, are questions beyond our knowledge.

The Pythagoreans, like Anaximander, had their own theory on the 'basis of the universe'; and to them also it seemed inescapable that this basis must be infinite and free from the burden of matter. But, whereas Anaximander had made the undefined, unlimited and potential the basis of all that was defined, limited and actual, they sought their cosmic principle in that which caused things to be defined and qualified. Thus far they were treading a path which Hesiod had trodden in his day, when he made the 'sources' of things the same as their 'boundaries' (above p. 105–107): but they went far beyond Hesiod. Behind our world of things and happenings they saw a ruling world of mathematical order, which, without ever becoming a 'thing' itself, gave to all things their appointed quantity, form and proportion. Now these three, quantity, form and proportion were reckoned as functions of number, and so the principle was formulated: 'Number is the principle of the world.'

Mathematical thought was then still intuitive, and the means of expressing numerical values by symbols were far from satisfactory. Numbers were envisaged as figures made up of points, like those we see on dice or dominoes. Thus the various numbers were associated not merely with particular magnitudes, but with particular areas, forms, structures and proportions. There was no distinction between geometry and algebra, and mathematical thought operated with a mixed terminology in which, for example, 'square' and 'square number' meant the same.[40] For the Pythagoreans, numbers

---

[39] W. A. Heidel, *American Journ. Philol.* 61 (1940) 1–33, gives a very sensible warning against attempts to reconstruct early Pythagorism by arguing backwards from the later stages.

[40] Cf. J. Stenzel, *Zahl und Gestalt* (Leipzig 1924) 25.

constituted not one set, but two opposing sets: the 'even'—or, more literally, 'joined' (ἄρτιοι)—numbers, which composed symmetrical figures, seemed to them different in kind from the asymmetrical odd numbers, which they called 'excessive' (περιττοί). Such a term as 'even' (one of Solon's favourite words) suggests at once order and clearness. The four or square, being a doubly symmetrical figure, seemed to them to represent the most perfect order: hence it was identified by the Pythagoreans with the principle of justice and law—a notion still embodied in the phrase 'a square deal.' The later Pythagoreans justified their identifying the square with justice by the following argument: justice repays like with like, and in square numbers each factor undergoes the same multiplication as it bestows on the other (58 B 4). Another number to which the Pythagoreans gave great importance is the number ten, the basis of our decimal system. Four and ten are connected in that ten is the sum of the first four numbers. This equation, $1 + 2 + 3 + 4 = 10$, can be expressed by a triangle, each of whose sides is four units:

This triangle the Pythagoreans called *tetractys* ('fourness') and they are said always to have sworn by the *tetractys* (44 A 11). Not a god of heaven or hell, but a figurate number, was their highest object of reverence. Of the first three integers, one is reckoned as the creative number, since it brings a defined something out of the indefinite mass (58 B 26). Two brings in difference and opposition, since with two plurality begins to diverge; but at the same time the number binds plurality together; pairs of opposites are the basis of all multiplicity (58 B 1a; B 5 etc.). Three produces a middle enclosed between a beginning and an end (58 B 17). In Pythagorean thought the universe must be dominated, like the numerical system, by the number ten. Hence, in addition to the earth, sun, moon, five planets and the sphere of the fixed stars, they postulated a 'counter-earth' to bring the number up to ten (58 B 4 etc.).

In the cloudy brightness of early Greek philosophy, brilliant discoveries and wilful inventions often appear confusingly alike. In one field the Pythagoreans certainly succeeded in finding a real relation between number and experience: they discovered that musical harmony is based on numerical proportions. If a string be halved in length, its tension remaining the same, the note is raised by one octave; the proportion 4:3 produces a fourth, and 3:2 a fifth. Thus, under the rule of simple proportions, order is brought out of the infinite range of sounds, and harmony is created. In music number takes on directly sensible form, and its powerful effects on the emotions and the will are obvious to our perception. To a nation as artistic, creative and sensitive as the Greeks, music meant a great deal: however simple their monophonic songs may have been, they could exert a powerful force on the soul. 'The Pythagoreans also considered that music could contribute powerfully to health, if it was applied in the manner appropriate to the case' (58 D1, 164). They also believed that music, with its numerical proportion, accompanied and determined the equally well-proportioned course of the celestial bodies; they were convinced that sun, moon and stars went round on their courses amid the 'music of the spheres.' It was from the Pythagoreans that Plato took over the idea of 'mathematics' (roughly = 'things learnable'), consisting of the four disciplines arithmetic, geometry, music and astronomy; and under Plato's influence the middle ages made the similarly defined *quadrivium* the basis of all higher learning.[41]

Thus in the Pythagorean philosophy the various provinces of the real world were brought together into an impressive unity: the very rules of ethics and propriety of manners were brought into the same system. *Aretê*, human goodness, was reckoned by the Pythagoreans as a form of harmony (using a musical metaphor) or as 'quadratic' when they used the language of geometry (Diog. 8, 33; cf. below p. 308, Simonides fr. 542). Since the truths of mathematics were inviolable, the Pythagorean had to consider his own word of honour as sacred—an area in which we cannot say that the greatest strength of the Greek nation lay.[42] Just as in mathematics there is no room for individual whims and fancies, so the life of the Pythagorean was subject to a very strict discipline. 'Silent are they and obedient: he who can listen is praised' (Iamblichus 163). Reverence for the gods, for one's parents and for the law were the three highest duties (Iamblichus 174–176). The relations of men one with another were founded on justice (Iambl. 180), but by no means on equality; in a hierarchy of dignities each individual had his appropriate place and

[41] Cf. E. Frank, *Plato und die sog. Pythagoreer* (Halle 1923) p. III. There could also be a reverse influence of Pythagorean number theory on practical music. According to their notions the first four numbers were the best (together with their sum, the *tetractys*); hence the interval of the third, based on the proportion 4:5 or 5:6, could not be given full recognition. Consequently the third was frowned on for a thousand years: it was only during the middle ages that the objection to its use finally faded away. This theory is, however, rejected by many students of the history of music.

[42] Schiller's *Bürgschaft*, a story of a loyalty to one's word that was no empty form, is adapted from a legend of the Pythagoreans.

had to behave accordingly. Every word uttered had to be correctly adjusted to the equal or different rank of one's collocutor; relations between men must not be carried on according to the feelings of the moment: everything must be thought out and duly ordered (Iambl. 263; Diog. 8, 17; 33–35). Those of lower rank must be gladly co-operative, not sulkily obedient, and those of higher rank must be kind to their inferiors, not harshly dictatorial (Iambl. 180–183). Even the clothing[43] and diet of the Pythagoreans were subject to rigid prescriptions (Iamble. 205); thus they were forbidden to eat beans, and probably had to abstain from all meat. There was a mass of rules governing behaviour, going into the minutest details: 'Take not up what has fallen from the table'; 'Do not break bread,' and many more, intelligible or otherwise.

This selection from the later evidence can only give the most general impression of the Pythagorean movement, without any guarantee of the antiquity of individual features. We may end by trying to understand the place which reincarnation held in the Pythagorean system. Plato in the *Meno* uses the 'theorem of Pythagoras' (or, more accurately, a special case of it) to demonstrate that the truths of mathematics are visible even to one who comes into contact with mathematics for the first time. The content of the theorem is mastered by the young boy in a way which suggests remembering rather than learning something new. In this con-nection Plato says that there is a doctrine (the Pythagorean) which refers all learning to the recalling of experiences that befell the immortal soul in its wanderings through many lives, partly on earth, partly in Hades (81 a–c). From what Plato says we may reconstruct the Pythagorean notions somewhat as follows. The truths of mathe-matics are not subject to accident; they are raised as far above birth and death as they are above doubt and mistake. Man himself, in applying himself to mathematics, frees himself from this impure world of deceit and danger; the conditional nature of his being falls from him, and his separate identity disappears. The human soul comes near to the very basis of things when it takes its stand upon mathematical truth. In showing itself fit to enter the realm of pure incorporeal being, it shows itself as not subject to the flesh and the body; its home is not in this world, but above it. The soul which thus is in peculiar communion with what is timeless can neither have been born nor die. Each of its new births, with an appropriate place in the hierarchy of living things, serves as penance for previous sin and as purification for a higher status to come. When born as a man, it is

[43] On the rule against woollen clothing see J. Quasten in *Amer. Journ. Phil.* 63 (1942) 207ff.

the soul's duty to aim at the truth by remembering, to preserve its purity in a chaste and temperate life, and by every effort to promote the victory of that great world-order which enlightens the confused, beautifies the ugly, and ennobles the humble.

But perhaps we have already carried our speculations too far, and have already said too much about the Pythagoreans, because on Pythagoras himself we can say so very little.

VI

The New School of Lyrists

(a) *Ibycus (and Stesichorus in retrospect)*

The story of Greek philosophy has carried us past the middle of the sixth century, when Greek poetry seems to reach a dead point (see above, p. 238). In the last third of this century lyric poetry re-emerges, and during the eighty years or so until the archaic period ends (c. 530–450) one or more great artist is always active in the genre.

The direction that lyric poetry took in its second period was quite different from that of its first. There is now no trace of an unswerving devotion to real life. We may remember the passionate drive towards actuality which possessed the creator of Greek lyric as we know it. In emancipating poetry from epic forms and ways of thought, Archilochus broke with outworn convention in order to deploy his ruthless directness and unadorned naturalness in one field only—the depicting of the changing phases of his own active life. Not long after Archilochus, however, realism which had begun life with this tone of rude defiance, lost its heroic strength and sank at the last into bourgeois insipidity and feeble caricature. In giving up its artistic purity and individuality, poetry ushered in its own dissolution: if it became a simple copying of life, it must needs soon make its exit and leave life itself in possession of the stage. Now that poetry came forward once again, she had changed and purified her image. She still made herself the servant of living reality, but disdained the banal and the everyday. She was now careful and selective in her attitude; elevated, or at least refined and elegant in her tone. And of the various lyric forms it was choral lyric which took the lead as most dignified and even pretentious. But we must first take a glance backward at the history of this artistic form.

Choral lyric, which so far we have met only in Alcman's hands, had soon found a successor to Alcman in the Western part of the

Greek world. The Sicilian Stesichorus[1] had been widely active in this sphere around 600. His compositions seem, surprisingly enough, to have been of a purely narrative nature, telling stories of the heroes at considerable length. Thus in the subject matter of his poems he carried on the epic tradition unbroken. The only one of the few fragments which we are able to compare with its original shows us how little alteration—at least in one instance—he made in the content of the traditional story while clothing it in lyric dress.

The model here was the fifteenth book of the *Odyssey*. Telemachus there is taking leave of Menelaus and Helen, whom he has questioned concerning the fate of his missing father; according to custom, he received from his host and hostess gifts to make him long remember his visit—one of them is a silver mixing-bowl with a golden rim (115). On parting he expresses the wish, more in sorrow than in hope, that on his return he may find his father already in Ithaca (156); and thereupon comes a most encouraging omen; an eagle flies across from the right with a goose in its talons (v. 160). Helen interprets the omen as indicating a speedy return of Odysseus—he may even be in Ithaca at that hour (which the hearers of the *Odyssey* know to be the case). Now in a papyrus fragment of Stesichorus recently published (1956) we find the following text (fr. 209 Page):

(with joy) she suddenly beheld this wonder
and Helen spoke thus to the son of Odysseus:
'Telemachus, this messenger who from heaven above
winged his way through the desert air
. . . with a loud cry . . .
. . . betokens that to your house . . .
. . . the man
. . . through the decree of Athene
. . . chattering crows
nor will I hold you back[2]
(so that soon) Penelope shall see you, son of your beloved
    father.'

After a gap come some beginnings of lines:

a silver (vessel?) . . . with gold over . . . which from (the treasures of) the Dardanids (i.e. the kings of Troy) . . . Menelaus (carried off) . . .

One sees immediately that the changes from the original in subject matter are quite inconsiderable. For his lyrical presentation Stesichorus has chosen not an epic narrative of heroic deeds or happenings, but a tender scene of almost ceremonious friendship, with a prophetic

[1] For a detailed treatment see Bowra, *Greek Lyric Poetry*[2], 74ff.

[2] The words are: οὐδ' ἐγώ σ'ἐρύξω; in the *Odyssey* (15.68) it is Menelaus who says to Telemachus: οὔ τί σ'ἐγώ γε πολὺν χρόνον ἐνθάδ' ἐρύξω.

foreshadowing[3] of the subject to which the thoughts of the speakers are directed. The second verse has the form of an epic hexameter, and the language is very similar to that of epic, although not identical. It goes beyond anything possible in epic when Helen speaks of Penelope's seeing again the 'son of his beloved father': in this circumlocution, suggested to Helen by her sympathetic understanding, we feel both Penelope's sorrow for her missing husband and her happiness in seeing again, in the person of Telemachus, their only son safely returned.[4]

The fragments, miserable as they are, show that in one respect Stesichorus was possessed by the spirit of the new age. He has a penchant towards factual accuracy, completeness and objectivity in narrative; he does not shrink in one place (fr. 181) from bringing a prosaic measurement into his verses; he loves lists (frs. 178 and 187)— thus he gives a complete list of winners in competitions (fr. 179), of participants in the Calydonian boarhunt (222), of prisoners taken at Troy (197), even of various kinds of food offered to a girl[5] (fr. 179). All this, taken with his geographical interests (fr. 184 and 183), recalls Alcman's manner (above, p. 161f., 167f.); and, as with Alcman, the liveliness and vigour of his descriptions are not devoid of charm.[6]

A pleasing fragment (185) describes the parting between the Sungod, who has arrived at his setting, and Heracles, who has been bidden to journey to the farthest west:

Helios, Hyperion's son, mounted his golden bowl to journey across the ocean to the depths of holy, gloomy night, to his mother, his fair wife and his beloved children; but the son of Zeus went on foot into a grove of shadowy laurel trees.

The poet is as much a participant here as in the former fragment: his sentimental fancy is aroused by the nightly return of the Sungod to the bosom of his beloved family, including his mother. Stesichorus must have supposed that Helios does not spend the whole night on his solitary journey, as had been reasonably surmised (above, p. 212), but that he enjoyed a respite of domestic comfort in the northern deep.

In Stesichorus' 'Palinode' (apology or retraction) a personal element comes forward which contrasts with the reticence of the epic singers. The poet had spoken of Helen as an adulteress; but then he declares (192):

[3] On scenes of prophecy in Pindar see below p. 447 and *Pyth.* 4, 12–57.
[4] See above p. 174 on Sappho's unepic use of the expression 'dear father.'
[5] Is this girl Atalanta? Cf. Apollodorus 3, 9, 2 and 3, 13, 2.
[6] Quintilian (10, 1, 62) praises the power and dignity of his narrative, but finds the detail wearying.

This tale is untrue: you did not ever board the well-built ship and were not taken to Troy's citadel.

'It was not you that ran away with Paris—only a phantom.' This 'palinode' became the basis of a later legend that Stesichorus had been smitten with blindness after his attack on Helen, but that she, having the nature of a goddess, restored his sight after the retraction.[7]

Ancient literary historians associated Stesichorus very closely with his fellow lyrist Ibycus; they could not settle whether certain poems were to be ascribed to the one or the other. This seems surprising, since the poems of Stesichorus sound so much more old-fashioned than those of Ibycus that we can accept those statements which place his *floruit* about 600. Probably the ancient critics relied only on an external criterion, that is, the dialect, which was identical in both. Ibycus also was a Western Greek. He came from Rhegium (Reggio di Calabria) on the strait between Southern Italy and Sicily. He went from there to Samos and wrote at the court of the tyrant Polycrates (c. 537–23)—the same Polycrates whose arbitrary government was the cause of Pythagoras' removing himself, in the opposite direction, to Southern Italy. The courts of the tyrants and of other princes provided natural gathering-points for the socially aspiring lyric poetry of the age, and for choral lyric above all. It could only flourish where it found a well-established circle of art-loving *dilettanti* which was capable of appreciating and producing these difficult choral dances (see above p. 159f.). It presupposed a society which could afford money, leisure and cultivation of the mind, and which took pleasure in elaborate and splendid performances.[8]

We do not have much by Ibycus, but two of the fragments show that he was an artist of the highest order, whether we consider the originality of their tone, the strength and sweetness of their diction, or the concentration of meaning in their stateliness and power. Both seem to be the opening words of poems concerned with homosexual love—the only form in which romantic love was known to the Greeks of that day. The kind of bitter torment that Sappho expressed

[7] Stesichorus may possibly have written in his Palinode: 'following the blind Homer, I failed to recognize you and was myself blind; but now I see again,' and posterity perhaps took the words too literally. Plato's choice of words (*Phaedrus* 243b) ποιήσας δὴ πᾶσαν (!) τὴν καλουμένην Παλινῳδίαν, παραχρῆμα ἀνέβλεψεν probably refers to a particular passage with which the poem ended. The notion of a phantom as a bone of contention between combatants occurs in *Iliad* 5, 449–53: there also it is probably an alteration of an older version (Aeneas slain by Diomede?).

[8] Choral odes were, however, sometimes performed as solos to the accompaniment of a stringed instrument (Pindar, *Nem.* 4, 14–16), but only as an inexpensive second-best to a regular performance by a group of dancers.

is found again in Ibycus' passionate admiration of a young man.

The first of these fragments begins with the image of a hunt in which Love (Aphrodite) is the huntress and Eros entangles the victim in her net (287):

> Once more Eros is at work with his love-kindling glance under blue-dusky lashes, with his every magical wile to compel me into Aphrodite's endless net. Truly, I tremble before him who comes, just as a horse accustomed to the yoke, who has grown old after many victories, is reluctant to enter on the track with the speedy chariot.

Before Plato interpreted Eros as the longing in the heart of the lover, he was more often seen as a force radiating from the object of affection and drawing us towards him (e.g. Sophocles *Antig.* 783f.). Thus Ibycus sees Eros in the form of the youth who has thrown over him the spell of a longing that can never be at rest (cf. above p. 180). 'Once more' the fresh charm of nobility and youth looks with new eyes on the poet, just as for Sappho also passion is ever repeating and renewing itself (above p. 179). The 'blue-dusky' eyelashes of Eros symbolize the dark power with which passion seizes upon Ibycus: in early Greek poetry great and commanding personages are represented with dark hair (above p. 34, n. 24). The net of love is very significantly described as 'endless,' since it encloses its helpless victims like a ring that returns upon itself,[9] and thus makes escape impossible.[10] Ibycus is acquainted with love and with the tremendous demands that it makes on him, just like a horse that has grown old in racing, and he trembles before what lies ahead. It is a task beyond his strength; he is no longer young. For the common run of men love is the crowning glory of their vigorous youth: but the poet has been singled out to remain all his life open to the sacred power of a grand passion, at once favoured and overborne by the gift of the goddess Aphrodite.

The other fragment alludes in even more striking tones to this singular destiny.[11] Here Ibycus begins by depicting an enclosed garden belonging to the Nymphs, the good spirits of living nature, in

[9] Cf. Pindar, *Pyth.* 4, 213: πότνια (Aphrodite) δ'ὀξυτάταν βελέων ποικίλαν ἴυγγα... ἐν ἀλύτῳ ζεύξαισα κύκλῳ.

[10] Cf. Ed. Fraenkel on Aeschylus, *Agam.* 1382.

[11] It is remarkable that the poet makes a distinction between himself and the social group in which and for which he works. Normally the singer is reckoned as the appointed spokesman and leader of the circle, since he knows more of what is good and beautiful than the others do. Here, however, he is marked off by the depth and fullness of his emotions from the many whom he is supposed to represent. In the same way, paradoxically enough, choral lyric was spoken as a monologue. Pindar had the same tragic experience of passionate attachment in old age (see below p. 504, fr. 123), and much the same thing befell Goethe.

which under their careful nurture the buds come forth in springtime and the flowers unlock. As in Sappho, so here we may take the picture as typifying tender youth growing up to know happy love under friendly protection (above p. 172). Then comes the contrast with the poet's own lot (286):

Quince trees watered by the cool[12] ripples of the brook, where the un-ravished garden of the maidens is, and vinebuds growing under shadowing branches, bloom in the spring; but for me Eros slumbers not at any season,

but flashing with lightning, a Thracian stormwind sent by Cypris, with parching madness, dark, unsparing, he holds fast my soul without respite in the bonds of his harsh mastery.

Ibycus is forbidden to enjoy the blessing of the ordered cycle of the seasons; love comes to him not in the balmy springtime of an easy protected youth, but in the rude winter storm (cf. Sappho fr. 47, above p. 183) of dried-up old age, that comes blustering over open wastes.

We find the same three-part structure in both fragments. They begin with a beautiful and highly-wrought word-picture in an elaborate style. The middle section is a short sentence in which the poet's plight is movingly expressed without any veil of imagery; with its simple and unadorned language it gives the effect of a cry of pain, albeit a muffled one. Finally comes a second image which sustains and adorns and completes the thought, and is as careful in its language as the first. What is original here is the way in which the trinity is made into a unity. We have often seen that the typical archaic composition glides from one sentence to another in a juxtaposition of the circumstances which are conjured up and then left behind. Each draws the next in its train, but there is no connexion running through all; the relation between them varies from place to place. The words, to some degree improvised, present a complex of events act by act, connecting the individual happenings by some new device each time. Here, however, in Ibycus the theme was fixed and settled on beforehand, and the language presents a static condition,[13] element by element, on a pre-arranged plan. In this new structure, behind each several element is the one and same idea of the whole, just as in the theories of the philosophers a unitary

---

[12] I read ῥοᾶν ἔκ, and in v. 12 πεδόθεν (cf. *Frühgriech. Denken* 47 n. 2).

[13] Even the individual sentences are built on a pre-arranged plan. In all the four images the necessary finite verb is in the last, or almost the last, place. Thus the sentence is curved like an arch, only finding at the end the abutment on which it can rest. This contrasts with the archaic style in which the first few words give something solid and tangible, and the rest of the sentence adds further elements of definition (above p. 245f.).

metaphysical basis was found behind the multiplicity of phenomena. In one important respect this poetry is no longer archaic: it lacks the fresh directness of earlier art and that dancing suppleness which seems always to be purely concerned with the moment until at the very end, as if by accident, the sequence of figures rounds itself off to a closed circle. Thus these two fragments with their firm and static structure show a composed and conscious self-possession which has a classic ring.

Ibycus needs space to develop the architectural perspective of his poetry;[14] a short extract is no more able here than elsewhere to give a notion of the whole. The shorter fragments—and even of these we have few enough—can tell us nothing of the man's real quality, even if they teach us something about his themes and a little more about his language. A sustained elegance is the keynote throughout, with a wealth of adjectives that are ornate and even magnificent on occasion.

Sappho's symbol of the garden recurs yet again in another fragment (288) celebrating a youth named Euryalus:[15]

Euryalus, flower of the bright-eyed Graces, nursling of the fair-tressed ones, Cypris and warm-glancing Peitho have reared you among roses.

Here instead of the nymphs other fostermothers are named: the Charites or Graces, spirits of charm and attractiveness, with bright eyes and silky hair (alluding simultaneously to the boy's own eyes and hair), Love (Cypris) and seductive charm (Peitho).

We are reminded of Sappho again when Ibycus elsewhere speaks of flowers and trees or of the birds of the air.[16] His tones, however, are rather more solemn than hers (frs. 315 and 317a). We hear (303b) of the morning chorus of the birds:

When sleepless festal morning awakes the songstresses . . .

And he compares the passionate soaring of the soul (?) with the flight of a bird (317b):

[14] One detail still deserves mention. The pictures of the garden of the nymphs and of the winter storm are not marked off from the direct and unsymbolic expression by the formula 'as . . ., so . . .': instead they are integrated with the general exposition and become metaphors or symbols. This procedure simplifies the structure by avoiding parallel tracks, as it were: in this way the presentation gains depth. This integration of similes is regular in Pindar also; but they are never worked out by him in such meaningful detail as by Ibycus.

[15] The whole complex recurs in a different arrangement in Longus 2, 4–5; the identification of Eros with a beautiful boy and the reference to the poet's advanced age reminds us of Ibycus fr. 286 and 287.

[16] The legend of the 'cranes of Ibycus' thus seems to fit in with his manner.

theme, but no mortal man can tell it in all its detail/ship by ship, how Menelaus sailed from Greece from the harbour of Aulis and came over the Aegean sea to horse-breeding Troy, the bronze-shielded heroes with him,/sons of the Achaeans, of whom the foremost in battle was the swift Achilles, and the mighty warrior Ajax (was the second best).

[5] (But who was the fairest of all who came) from Greece to Troy? (It was the same Achilles, and next to him was he) whom/Hyllis bore— Hyllis bedecked with golden ribbons. But in comparison with him in the eyes of Trojans and Achaeans—the winning countenance of Troilus shone like triply refined gold compared with brass. In common with these you also, Polycrates, will enjoy for ever the imperishable glory of beauty, just as in song also my fame (is imperishable).[24]

Thus supplemented, the poem acquires some connexion and unity. What is said about the Trojan war becomes relevant now that it can serve to back up the thesis of the first triad. Nevertheless, the poet will not 'now' sing of the seducer Paris and of the slender Cassandra,[25] or of the unhappy consequences for Troy of this lover's folly, nor yet of the heroic valour (*aretê*) displayed in battle for the fairest of women: for these things he has now no inclination. We may interpret this as meaning that the presence of the beautiful Polycrates has too powerful a claim on his heart and senses. He is also unwilling to apply himself to a task that goes beyond mortal strength; he does not propose, in order to prove the power of beauty, to record the number-less hosts of those who were summoned to war for Helen's sake: in fact he only mentions a few of the greatest among them. He is much more concerned with the question of the most handsome among Greeks and Trojans, and above all with celebrating the youth Troilus, whose appearance captivated both camps alike. 'Them do

[24] Here the poem ends. In the reconstruction of the first triad I have not suc-ceeded in capturing the remarkably flat and unmodulated style of the surviving parts, which differs so markedly from Ibycus' manner. In v. 3 I supplement τηλ]όθεν since we already have ἀπ' Ἄργεος in 28 and 36; and in v. 22 I propose experimentally ἐκπ[ρεπή]ς. What διερός means in v. 26 remains uncertain. In vv. 39–41 we should expect to find Nireus (*Il.* 2, 671–75) instead of the son of the unknown nymph Hyllis, if nymph she be. I cannot follow the grammatical con-struction of these last two lines. The reading of the scholium clearly needs emenda-tion: as things stand, we cannot see what it refers to. Probably it is concerned with the horses of Laomedon and ties up with Τροίαν ἱπποτρόφον in v. 30, or with the horses which Troilus was taking to water when Achilles fell upon him, and with his descent (γένεσιν?) from Teucer and Laomedon.

[25] Cassandra is named as an example of female beauty, as Paris of male. Thus Ibycus praises her beauty in fr. 303a. Probably the poet is also thinking that her beauty was as fatal for Agamemnon (whose name occurs next) as Helen's infatua-tion with Paris. The poet is not going to mention here 'the other children of Priam'; but Troilus he keeps in reserve for his final point.

you resemble, young Polycrates; just as they were glorified in the old epics, so will you be made immortal in this my lyric song.'

The reconstruction which has been attempted here arranges the poem so that the five typical elements of choral lyric (below p. 488) are all represented in it. The poem sets forth a universal statement and supports it out of the heroic sagas; it celebrates the power of the goddess Aphrodite; the singer speaks of his own feelings; finally he takes a man of his own day and places him on a level with those celebrated in old tradition. We found ideas similar to these earlier in a poem of Sappho's, which closely resembled choral lyric in the notions which it expressed (fr. 16, above. p. 185–187). There also the power of Aphrodite over the human heart evoked a reference to Helen and the fall of Troy, and there also the singer valued the charm of youth and beauty above martial prowess. But now the poet goes one step further: he says that lyric poetry is better suited to the glorifying of the present day than to the narrating of events in the past. But even so the rejection of historical narrative is less decided, in this comparatively late period, than it was in Archilochus. The repeated gesture of renunciation[26] cannot conceal the fact that in theme and language the poem is strongly influenced by epic.[27]

Before we leave Ibycus, let us look again at those two great openings of poems, 'Once more has Eros . . .' and 'Quince trees . . .' (frs. 286 and 287). The thoughts expressed reminded us of Sappho; yet the nature of the experience and the style of the expression is so strikingly different in Ibycus that we can infer a revolution in the whole spiritual attitude. While Sappho willingly surrenders to the bitter-sweet urging of passion and lets all her being flow into it, Ibycus feels the passion that seizes him as something alien and abnormal, against which his own self strives in vain. The psychological situation has become more complex, and to understand and express the conflict demands a higher level of awareness.[28] There is a corresponding difference in Ibycus' form of expression. In reading him we no longer have the feeling, as with Sappho, that the facts

[26] For this dwelling on themes which the poet claims to reject one may compare Horace's *Laudabunt alii* (Carm. 1, 7) and Timocreon fr. 1, both probably based on Lesbian originals, cf. *Frühgriech. Denken* 90f.

[27] The poet has in his mind particularly the second book of the *Iliad* with the catalogue of Trojans. The two bravest Achaeans are mentioned in 768f. and the two most handsome in 671–674. The thought of vv. 23–27 of this poem comes from vv. 484–93 in *Il.* 2.

[28] What we have here is not a conflict between different organs of the soul (e.g. between feeling and understanding) or between different motive forces (e.g. duty and desire), but a conflict between two characters: a man growing old and desiring tranquility is compelled to have the feelings of a giddy and vigorous youngster.

are simply put into words one after another in an unaffected style
that arises and falls of its own volition. Rather the individual
sentences are ordered in a framework within which each element has
its allotted place and its defined function. The informing energy of
his art traces complex general pictures in which we do not find only
sharp outlines, as we did before, but a three dimensional inner
structure as well. By this means a richer and more powerful animation is rendered possible.

The lesson which we learn here from the history of Greek literature is borne out by the history of Greek vase-painting. The period
at which Ibycus wrote coincided with the change from black-figure
to red-figure. The figures were no longer placed as coloured
silhouettes with few internal details on a blank background, but the
whole background was coloured in and the figures left uncoloured.
The sharpness and precision of the outlines was thus unimpaired;
but the real difference is that the artist was now able completely to
form his figures with the expressive language of line within the
boundaries that defined them. Thus the way was opened towards a
more organic and animated style of depiction. In the first part of this
new development, roughly from the time of Polycrates to the
Persian wars, 'this artistic handicraft (vase-painting) celebrated its
greatest triumphs and achieved the most perfect synthesis between
conventional ornament and elaborate naturalism.'[29] The finest and
most perfect workmanship, a unique synthesis between naturalism
and convention—such was also the companionable poetry of
Anacreon.

(b) *Anacreon*

Anacreon was an Ionian of Asia Minor from Teos. After Teos had
been absorbed into the Persian empire in 545, a number of the
inhabitants migrated to Abdera in Thrace to escape the burdensome
alien rule. Among their number Anacreon lived for some time in
Abdera; later, like Ibycus, he was active at the court of Polycrates,
tyrant of Samos. When Polycrates was murdered by the Persians
and Samos itself fell under Persian control, Anacreon accepted an
invitation to the Athenian court. Hipparchus (527–510), the son and
heir of Pisistratus, is said to have sent a powerful warship to Samos
expressly to convey the famous poet safely to Athens.

Anacreon was not a master of formal choral lyric: his compositions
were for individual performance, in convivial company especially.
His poems were lively, fresh and attractive. Here is a poem of his for

[29] E. Buschor, *Griech. Vasenmalerei* (2nd ed., Munich 1921), p. 146.

a drinking party, a prayer to Dionysus, god of the vine and sender of vital force and pleasures (357):

Lord, to whom the youthful Eros, the black-eyed nymphs and radiant Aphrodite
are companions in play, you who roam on the mountains, on the high ridges: before you I kneel, graciously come to us, let my prayer be acceptable to you;
and give good counsel to Cleobulus, make him, O Dionysus, receive my love![1]

The prayer, 'Come to us,' refers not to Dionysus alone, but also to other divinities who are addressed in the charming picture with which the poem opens.[2] The cheerful sport which took place on the mountains was to find a counterpart in the room in which Anacreon sang: beautiful boys, as captivating as Eros himself, as lively as young animals, wait upon the drinkers. Young maidens are there also, from whose dark eyes the magic of Aphrodite rains influence on men's hearts. The gift of Dionysus, which the youths pour out, will banish all care and favour the joys of love. The poet himself has designs on Cleobulus, and hopes that in an atmosphere impregnated by such forces the youth will favour him.

A less serious tone is perceptible in this opening (358):

Again Eros with his golden hair throws his purple ball towards me; urges me to play with the maiden of the gay-coloured sandals.
But she (for proud Lesbos is her home) is not pleased with my hair (for it is white); she watches and waits, dreaming of another.[3]

Here again we have the theme of love in old age, but without the passion that it had in Ibycus. The attraction, furthermore (here graphically seen as a ball which Eros throws at the poet), is exercised not by a male member of the party, but by a hired female musician;[4] and the poet thinks not of any grand passion, but of mere play.[5]

[1] The expression of the closing line is difficult. I take Cleobulus as subject of δέχεσθαι (with H. W. Smyth, *Greek Melic Poetry*, [London and New York, 1900] *ad. loc.*).

[2] Dionysus and Aphrodite were reckoned as closely related, both as gods and as natural forces. (E. R. Dodds on *Bacchae* 402–16.)

[3] ἄλλην, that is, another girl (hence the reference to Lesbos). Χάσκειν, 'to gape,' is used by Solon (1, 36) for a foolish indulgence in fruitless hopes.

[4] Lesbos was also celebrated for the quality of its musicians (Sappho fr. 115; Cratinus fr. 243 Kock).

[5] Compare the playful Eros in 357, 4. Correspondingly, the symbol of the ball connects itself with children's games; only a later epoch replaced the ball with a dart, thus uniting the notion of wounds and pain with that of striking from a distance. In fr. 398 (below p. 295) another children's toy, knucklebones, are a symbol of the game that Eros plays with his victims. In Apollonius Rhodius (3, 117ff.; 132ff.) Eros plays with knucklebones and with a coloured ball.

Moreover, the game is still going on: it is not yet clear in whom the girl will take an interest, although the poet pretends to know that his wooing (referred to in the first stanza) has failed; the girl does not like him. Graceful and restrained, the poem hovers in a region of possibilities and hopes which are all equally open. A most social and companionable touch is the charming gesture with which Anacreon, while seeming to retreat half a step from his young competitors for the girl's affections, cannot forbear a friendly tilt against the woman of Lesbos who expects more pleasure from a clumsy youngster than from the seasoned craftsman.[6] In general Anacreon's poetry is pervaded by a lightly jesting tone which in its freedom and self-confidence could only come from a relaxed and cheerful soul with perfect mastery of its chosen forms. This light, bantering manner is here turned against himself: and this is the first example of poetry's successfully treading the attractive but perilous path of irony directed at oneself. Alcman indeed made a move in this direction, but its effect was largely ruined by bombast and self-satisfaction. Hipponax fell into the opposite extreme, into a grotesque clowning devoid of all dignity. Both are often heavy-handed; and heavy-handed irony is a contradiction in terms. Only in Anacreon were the qualifications for true, that is, subtle irony combined: the calm maturity of a master artist, who can unbend without loss to himself, and detachment from the subject matter and from oneself—qualities which Archilochus, the founder of lyric, would have despised and rejected.[7]

The same Cleobulus who appeared in the prayer to Dionysus is the subject also of the following strophe (359):

Cleobulus is my desire, I am half mad for Cleobulus, I hunger after Cleobulus.

This stylistic pleasantry, of bringing in the same name three times in different constructions, we have met already in Archilochus (fr. 70, above p. 149, n. 43). There, however, the tone was of biting scorn against all those who treated Leophilus as the hub of the universe: here Anacreon ironically turns the figure against himself: 'Cleobulus, always Cleobulus.'

A triadic structure recurs fairly frequently in the fragments of Anacreon, though not always so strikingly as in the verses last quoted:[8]

[6] On Anacreon's consciousness of his own abilities cf. fr. 417 and 402c (below p. 295f.).

[7] In Archilochus the manner in which his actual life is portrayed is neither ironical nor frivolous, but deadly, almost fanatically, earnest.

[8] E.g. fr. 388: 'Hat, earrings and cow-hide' at the beginning, 'coach, golden ornaments and parasol' at the end, and in between three sentences each beginning

they convey the notion of well-ordered richness. A like effect is produced by the numerous, but judiciously chosen, adjectives, as for example the three colour-epithets in the strophe cited above; the purple ball, golden-haired Eros, the gaily-shod girl. The language is perfectly fluent and easy, but no longer plain and everyday. There are no gaps or jumps in the composition, but the archaic style of continuous flow is past for Anacreon,[9] as it was for Ibycus. Instead, within the general sequence the members are clearly punctuated, and each element appears once only, in the one place which classical rules would assign to it. Anacreon's achievement was no more and no less than admirable occasional poetry, like pieces of fine goldsmith's work. His pleasant and agreeable strains, with the clarity of their language and the easy brevity of their stanzas, are easy to hear and easy to remember. Their tone is personal without being individual, so that anyone who recites them can think of them as referring to himself.

Other boys besides Cleobulus were honoured in song by Anacreon: in that age love was directed less towards an individual than towards a type. Ever and again, we are told (fr. 402a *test.*), he celebrated the eyes of Cleobulus, the youthful charm of Bathyllus and the hair of Smerdiës. The last-named had cut his hair short, like a man's, when he reached the appropriate age,[10] and the poet reproaches him for so doing (414):

And you cut short the flawless bloom of your hair.

The name Smerdiës suggests western Asiatic influences on the Samian aristocracy, and Anacreon's one line contains two word-plays precious enough to recall the elaborate artifices of oriental poetry. The trite image of the flower is at once taken literally, since the bloom is cut off; and the adjective qualifying 'bloom' is ambivalent in the original:[11] *amômon* means 'perfect, blameless,' but at the same time it is the name of a precious perfume.

Recently (1954) some further verses on the same theme have come to light (*Oxyrh. Pap.* 2322, fr. 1, 1–10 = fr. 347 Page):

. . . and of the hair which hung down shadowing your tender neck.

You are now like a tree shorn of its leaves, and your locks, grasped by a boorish hand are fallen all together into the dust;

patiently did they abide the cutting steel, and I grieve bitterly. What can one do, if one does not [unintelligible].

with 'often'; fr. 395: 'temples, head, teeth'; fr. 396 'water, wine, garlands.' Other poets also were fond of groups of three: e.g. Alcaeus fr. 338 LP, 5–8; Mimnermus fr. 1, 3; Solon fr. 14, 4 and 9f.

[9] cf. *Frühgriech. Denken* 60.   [10] cf. eg Apollonius *Argon II*, 707.

[11] I have not been able to render the *double entendre* in English.

Here the poem ends. Verses like these would be very silly if Anacreon's complaints and reproaches were over nothing but a haircut. What is implied, of course, is that, together with the long hair, the boyish charm of Smerdiës has also gone beyond recall; the pretty boy has now transformed himself, and by his own wish, into a soldierly young man, and thus, in the course of nature, Anacreon's passionate adoration of his adolescent charms is a thing of the past. These poems, after their own fashion, constitute a lover's farewell, like some of the poems of parting that we find in Sappho.

In both these fragments the poet is speaking directly to his beloved Smerdiës; but the poem does not become a private dialogue between the two, with no third party present. Anacreon is instead giving an object lesson in relations with young boys. He feels himself a master and virtuoso in this field (402c):

For my poetry's sake the boys will all love me: I can give pleasure in singing, and pleasure in speaking too.

And he urges his companions, when making advances to a young girl (?), to be tender and tactful. 'You must not be rough with the child,' says he (408), 'but as soft and gentle as to a little fawn, not yet weaned, left in the forest by her antlered mother and wholly undone.'[12] The advice is in keeping with that Ionian humanity which was always alive to the feelings of others.

Just as he looked on his boys as children, so Anacreon envisaged Eros, the embodiment of childlike attractiveness, as a young child, long before he was represented by artists in that guise and finally degraded to a sort of cherub. Eros amuses himself with a ball, as we have seen (p. 292), or, like other boys, with knucklebones, which were used as dice. But in his hands the games become symbolic: anyone who is struck by his purple ball feels the kindling of desire for love-play, and (398):

Eros' knucklebones are called passion and hot-blooded conflict.

The verse points the contrast between the childlike nature of Eros and the violent passions which he arouses in the hearts of men and youths.

A contrast to this attitude and to the simile of the timid fawn is provided by a little poem to a Thracian girl, of whom many must

[12] The antlers of the doe gave trouble to ancient critics; but Greek poets often used their poetic licence in describing nature, as also did Greek artists (schol. Pind. *Ol.* 3, 52a). A late-geometric bronze group in Boston (in Roland Hampe, *Die Gleichnisse Homers und die Bildkunst seiner Zeit*, Tübingen 1952, figure 17a, text p. 34) shows a doe with very large antlers suckling a fawn.

have brought pleasure to the male drinking-parties of Abdera. The poet offers himself as an instructor for her graduation from children's games into more adult pastimes (417):

Thracian filly, why do you eye me askance, why do you coldly shun me and take me for an ignoramus?

Mark my words, I can very neatly slip a bridle on you and draw the reins and get you to the finishing-post.

But now you graze about the meadows childishly, playing and frisking about, because you have no practised horseman to mount you.[13]

The passage shows that the graphic vigour of early Greek poetry still lives in Anacreon, despite the late-archaic prettiness which often appears in his style. Here he avoids indelicacy by elegant periphrasis; but when he feels inclined, he will call a spade a spade without embarrassment or making a mystery of it (fr. 407). Yet again he talks in metaphors to a young girl when he is in a fever of longing (389).

'You are hospitable: I am thirsty—let me drink.'[14]

When the poet, who thinks that he should win every heart by his personal qualities, wants to complain of the filthy competition for lucre, he draws a picture of a good old time (384):

When Peitho did not dart her rays from flash of silver.

Peitho (Persuasion) is the power of bending another's will to one's own.[15]

In the poetic style of all the fragments which we have quoted, one is struck by the grace and variety of Anacreon's similes and metaphors. They do not adopt the circumstantial form of Homeric similes, with an explicit 'Like as . . .' followed by an explicit 'Even

---

[13] In v. 2 it is better to take μ' as με than as μοι. The comparison of a young girl with a race-horse, already known to us from Alcman's sensually attractive Spartan girls (above p. 165), is here applied to a naive and inexperienced Thracian. The poem served as a model for Lucilius 1041f.

[14] Expressions such as 'hospitable' as a polite indication of the general accessibility of such girls are also found in Archilochus (fr. 15, above p. 145) and Pindar (fr. 122, 1 below p. 469).

[15] πείθειν basically has a wider meaning than 'persuade.' It is one of those active verbs which have been back-formed, with a causative sense, from middles: from πείθεσθαι 'fall in with someone's will' came πείθειν 'make someone willing.' To win someone over there were more ways than talking: e.g. bribery (Herod, 9, 33, 3 μισθῷ πείσαντες); and Peitho as the traditional attendant upon Aphrodite wins over her victims by physical charm, without saying a word. Anacreon amusingly transforms this well-known Peitho into another one, who operates simply with 'silver,' i.e. hard cash.

so ...': the *as* and *so* are fused together, and the actual thing described is replaced by a sensible image. Ibycus does the same (above p. 286 n. 14), but in Ibycus the images open up a further perspective: in Anacreon they serve only to create an atmosphere. He sometimes uses images from myth and religion, but he does so in a light tone, somewhat with tongue in cheek. When the boy to whom he is inclined will not heed his entreaties, the poet imagines himself appealing to the gods in heaven (378).

I mount now to Olympus on easy pinions to be heard on love's behalf. My boy will not be young with me.[16]

Anacreon's images usually contain something moving, floating or poised in mid-air (379):

Eros, who sees that my beard is now grey, flies
before me in the drift of his gold-flashing pinions.

It was an old superstition among the Greeks, that to leap from a certain mythical cliff was a cure for unhappy love; and Anacreon sings (376):

Again I climb up, to hurl myself from the cliff of Leucas down into the grey waves, drunken with love.

Anacreon, so far as we know, is the first poet who treats love as a kind of mild intoxication. Yet he is no stranger to the impact and violence of passion (413):

With his great hammer Eros struck me once again, like a blacksmith, and quenched me in the ice-brook.

The image is of iron which is heated in the forge, shaped with hammer and anvil, and quenched in cold water,[17] and Anacreon makes it a parallel to the game that love plays with the human heart,[18] as it

[16] I.e., will not share the joys of youth with me. In *Iliad* 9, 511 likewise, prayers which are not given a hearing appeal to Zeus. Pseudo-Julian, *epist.* 193 Bidez-Cumont (263) seems to allude to this poem; cf. also Pindar fr. 122, 4f.

[17] Cf. τύπος ἀντίτυπος, πῆμ' ἐπὶ πήματι in the oracle quoted by Herodotus 1, 67, 4, where the doubled 'storm' of the bellows is spoken of; also Hippol. *Ref.* 8, 29. Other parallels to particular points are εὕει ἄτερ δαλοῖο (wife to husband): Hesiod, *WD* 705; an uncomfortable dip in a stream (metaphorical): Aristoph. *Ach.* 381; the expression χαράδρη χειμερίη in a simile, implying 'impassible': Apollon. Rhod. 4, 460; hardening (of bony substance) produced by alternate heating in the fire and cooling in water: Plato *Tim.* 73e. It is doubtful whether Anacreon had in mind the hardening effect (on iron and on the lover) produced by the blows of passion.

[18] A late Greek romance (Longus 2, 7, 5) has a lover speaking of his feelings as follows: 'My soul hurt me, my heart smote me, my body froze me; I cried out like one struck, I was silent like one enchanted, I plunged into rivers like one burned.'

had been felt and expressed from Sappho onwards. But in Anacreon the play of opposites—hammer and anvil, heating and cooling—which was properly the essence of the image of iron being laboriously forged, receives very little emphasis. The new world of ideas had no room for the archaic polarizing manner. Sappho, again, had spoken of love as something bitter-sweet, a power before which we are helpless (fr. 130); but Anacreon declares the opposite in another passage (428):

I love again, and yet love not, and I am mad, and still am sane.

This is no longer a struggle between rapture and anguish as in Sappho, but a coexistence of feeling and unfeeling. Beside the self that is entangled and defeated stands another self that is quite free, rational, and capable of describing the dissociation. Such an attitude is very close to irony.

In this more modern world of ideas we cannot be surprised to find Anacreon using the word 'soul' with the same associations which it has today (360):[19]

Boy, dear boy with your maiden's eyes, I love you, but you hear me not, knowing not that you hold the reins which my soul obeys.

The theme of the poems hitherto examined was a favourite one with Anacreon, and most of his fragments come from drinking-songs. By the normal usage of his times, masculine society found its choicest pleasures in the relations that were entered into on such occasion. with women and with boys. Anacreon makes it a matter of principle that wine, women and song go together (96 Diehl):

I have no love for the man who, when the wine bowl is flowing, talks about battle and war, subjects for sorrow and tears:
Rather for him who attends to the Muses, and bountiful Aphrodite, whose beautiful gifts waken but pleasure and joy.[20]

In his poetry Anacreon recommends to his companions the refined behaviour which he would like to see practised in love and elsewhere. As an *arbiter elegantiarum* he often strikes a didactic note (356):

Come, my boy, and bring the wine bowl: set it here, that I may drink long and deep. Ten parts of water, added to five parts of wine—mix it so: then[21] I will serve Dionysus with no coarseness.

And later in the same poem we read:

[19] On the development of the notion 'soul' see above p. 272f.
[20] On this distaste for war as a theme cf. Stesichorus fr. 210, Xenophanes fr. 1, 19–24; Theognis 763–766.
[21] The reading and interpretation of δεῦτε or δηῦτε in Anacreon are uncertain (cf. L. Weber, *Anacreontea*, Göttingen 1895, p. 41ff.).

No, we will not shout and quarrel as we sit and drink our wine like a crowd of vulgar Scythians, but with tuneful strains of song let us drink in ease and comfort.

To one of the company he says (416):

I detest such people, with their barbarous, quite unpolished manners. But I can clearly see, Megistes, you are none of their kind.

He is still more outspoken in rebuking the women present for their talking among themselves, for their chatter which 'like the surf of the ocean' never comes to a standstill (427). Presumably in order to compose a quarrel, he proposes that one of the men should favour them with a dance (375):

Who would like to fit his heart to youthful pleasure and dance to the melting strains of the flute?

It is also important, if the party is to go off properly, that one should know when to stop (412):

I've drunk too much, so let me now go home.

These party-poems of Anacreon's, with their preaching of moderation and propriety, are very different from the simple and basic drinking-songs of Alcaeus. Anacreon's party is no longer hasty improvization; and the drinking parties for which his poems were intended were not haphazard meetings, but social occasions arranged long beforehand[22] and demanding much art and expense. In the late-archaic period pompous display and elaborate elegance were in fashion:[23] it was not until the beginning of the classical period that a simpler taste reasserted itself. Thus the drinking-parties were by no means unpretentious affairs, and Anacreon heightened the enjoyment of all the good things by dwelling on them in his poetry. Thus we learn that tables are set before the guests, 'loaded to overhanging' with various dishes and sweetmeats (435). The revellers bedecked their heads with myrtle wreaths (fr. 410), and hung 'perfumed garlands' on neck and breast (fr. 397), made out of roses and other flowers (fr. 434).[24] One also anointed one's breast with

[22] The long list of quotations from Alcaeus in which he advances various personal justifications for drinking (above p. 194f.) finds only one counterpart in Anacreon (fr. 362).

[23] The sons of Pisistratus, for example, who had Anacreon conveyed to Athens in a state galley, 'invented festivals and processions,' and the luxury of Athenian high society, with 'horses and all sorts of other things,' was a sore burden on their subjects (Athen. 12, 532f.).

[24] The detail and accuracy of description in fr. 434 and elsewhere (fr. 356, 3–4; 383, 2 etc.) reminds one of Alcman (cf. Alcman fr. 19 etc.); Anacreon fr. 373 and 144 Gentili invite comparison with Alcman fr. 17, for example (see above p. 167f.).

perfumed unguents, to comfort the stormy beating of one's heart (363). It is from Anacreon that we first hear of the game of *Kottabos*, a Sicilian invention.[25]

To heighten their pleasure in life and youth, the early Greeks used to keep the image of old age and death before their eyes. Anacreon in his old age offered himself to point the contrast to his comrades in the following verses (395):

Now are both my temples gray, my head of hair is whitened, my teeth are old, and youth with all its happiness has left me. Therefore I often lament and fear the darkling hall of Hades. There dwells horror, and the road is hateful that conducts men hither. For it leads in one direction, downward, going only downward.

These mournful and commonplace verses produce an unpleasant effect,[26] even if we suppose (so as to leave no possibility excluded) that the passage is ironical, that Anacreon is making fun of his own self-pity. What a contrast with Mimnermus, who wished to die the moment that old age took from him the power of making love!

In later antiquity Anacreon was thought of as the poet exclusively of wine and love;[27] but in fact his themes were not so narrowly limited. We have evidence of his writing on much more various topics: among the fragments, for example, we find a number of satirical pieces in which some of his contemporaries (from the petite bourgeoisie, apparently) are mentioned and ridiculed by name (frs. 424; 394b; 387; 431; etc.). A rather longer piece than these has been preserved (388):

He who used to wear a pinched-in pointed hat upon his head, wooden dice in his ears, a hairless cowhide round his sides,

the new-washed covering of a rotted shield; who used to go about with bakers' girls and pretty boys, who made his money in backstairs ways, the young crook Artemon;

often he had to put his neck in the pillory, often in the wheel, often was

[25] A disc of bronze was balanced on a stand. When a guest had drained his glass, he held it between two fingers and, without leaving his place, tried to throw the last drops of the wine onto the disc. If he struck it successfully, it fell down and struck against a metal figure with an audible clang. As he threw the wine, the guest would call out the name of a boy or girl in whose honour he was trying his skill, with a tender expression or two. The game certainly lent itself to love-prophecies and badinage of all kinds.

[26] In *Gött. Nachr.* 1924, p. 86n. I questioned the genuineness of the fragment. Paul Maas has since convinced me in correspondence that it must be Anacreon's.

[27] Later times brought forth a crop of 'Anacreontic' poems which were softer and sweeter than the genuine product, and their metre likewise was more of a jog-trot even than the examples last cited. These effusions became a model for the German Anacreontic fashion of the eighteenth century.

his back marked with stripes, his hair and beard dishevelled and plucked out:

now he rides in a coach, bedecked with ornaments of gold, the son of Cyce, and sits under an ivory parasol, such as only he and women use.

Here is a *levée en masse* of descriptive detail, fitted into the framework of a single sentence and rhythmically ordered in neat and tidy clauses. There is none of that calculated economy of movement with which the invectives of Archilochus[28] stalk and seize his prey: and this poem is equally far removed from the genial rough-and-tumble of Aristophanic comedy. It is only the smooth continuity of the form that binds the disparate elements together.

We are all the more pleased, therefore, with a delightful new find. A short poem began with these two stanzas (Pap. Oxy. 2322, fr. 1, 11-19 = fr. 347 Page):

Pitiable are her feelings—her we know of—so men tell me; often she speaks of her misfortune with indignation:
'Well were it with me, dear mother, if you cast me into the sea, overwhelmed me in its cruel waters, where the purple billows rage!'

The original text has a fineness of detail (e.g. in the correspondence between the openings of the two stanzas) and an elegance of presentation that we find only in Anacreon. In the last three lines the style rises to high poetry: the young woman's grief is expressed in pathetic strains which Anacreon lends her with a half-serious sympathy. What her misfortune had been was possibly revealed in the course of the poem, possibly not. The original audience must have known the facts well enough to detect on whom she was modelled, since where her name might be expected, Anacreon uses instead a form of words which I have rendered very feebly with 'her we know of.' Literally ἀρίγνωτος means 'very recognizable,' i.e. 'identifiable without any further explanation or the like.' It is a purely poetical word—the only such word that the poet uses in the first stanza, speaking in his own person; and in so doing he puts an aura of epic memories around his heroine, with a keener ironical effect than in the second stanza.

We also find dramatized conversation in verse among the fragments of Anacreon, as in fr. 354:

Through you I shall become the talk of all the neighbours,

and 432:

A woman tainted am I now and quite undone by your desires.

---

[28] We can, however, detect in Anacreon something of Archilochus' power, on occasions when he gives free outlet to his basic emotions (frs. 407; 389; with fr. 439 compare Archilochus fr. 72). The theme of Archilochus fr. 22 seems to recur in Anacreon fr. 361.

One would hardly expect elevated religious tones in Anacreon, and very probably he never wrote any regular hymns[29]—hymns, that is, whose proper purpose was to honour the higher powers. We have the beginning of a prayer to the primordial 'mistress of beasts' who had a famous shrine by the river Lethaeus in Magnesia (Asia Minor): how it went on we do not know (348):

Huntress of stags, o Artemis fair-haired daughter of Zeus, I pray kneeling, Mistress of Beasts, to you.

You gaze with a kindly eye from Lethaeus' rolling stream on the city of daring men: you care not for dominion over tame and submissive folk.[30]

This opening seems characteristic (418):

Hear an old man's prayer, o maid with curling locks and robe of gold!

This sounds more like a piece of gallantry addressed to some pretty girl than a prayer to a goddess; yet such it must be, since epithets involving 'gold' are used in Greek poetry only with reference to gods.

A remarkable contrast to the softness and delicacy of Anacreon as we knew him is afforded by a number of fragments (all regrettably short) which strike a martial note. The songs from which they come were no doubt occasioned by the conflicts between the Greek settlers in Abdera and the Thracian natives.[31] A song of lamentation over the fallen warriors (or, more precisely, a song expressing sympathy with their misfortune) began as follows (419):

Out of all my gallant friends, for you I grieve first: you Aristoclides, gave your youth to keep servitude from your country.

Here we are in a very different atmosphere: youth (*hêbê*) is not enjoyed, but is sacrificed to higher ends. The language is strong and concise: ornamental epithets, such as 'chaste' youth, 'bitter' servitude, 'beloved' country, are not used: the things speak for themselves without any help. Another poem (fr. 401) called on the citizens to arm for battle. Political topics also appear: Anacreon complains (fr. 353) that 'the insurgents have the upper hand in the holy city' (Samos), or that 'the crown (the circuit of walls) of the city has perished' (fr. 391); he fears disaster: 'I shall see my country suffer sorely' (fr. 505c).

---

[29] C. M. Bowra, *Greek Lyric Poetry* (2nd ed., Oxford 1961) p. 273, with reference to Schol. Pindar *Isthm.* 2, 1.

[30] I read οὐ γὰρ ἂν ἡμέρους ποιμαίνοις πολιήτας.

[31] Pindar's second paean refers to a severe setback in the war of the Abderites against the native Thracians.

Finally[32] we quote a few peculiar fragments from unknown contexts.

I slide over blind cliffs. (403)

My spirit is blunted. (421)

I am (?) not so inclined, yet I wait for you without wavering. (97 Diehl)

And finally a distich (411a) with rhyming repetition and with a striking melancholy charm:

I wish that death would come: my release from these my sorrows cannot come otherwise, cannot come by any other way.

(c) Simonides

The late sixth century was the time when Greek archaic civilization reached its maturity. In politics it saw the brilliant courts of the later tyrants; in the plastic arts it produced marble groups of compelling beauty and the charming black-figure and early red-figure vases. In literature the polished poems of Ibycus and Anacreon, with their firm, clear structure and their luminous profundity, bear witness that a goal had been fully achieved. In these self-sufficient masterpieces there is nothing that looks outside themselves.

If the development of the Greek spirit was to be carried further, men were needed who would break with tradition and lay on new foundations roads that led to other ends. Such a figure was Archilochus at the beginning of the archaic period: at the start of the classical epoch the choral lyrist Simonides and the philosophical rhapsode Xenophanes held a similar place; both, like Archilochus, were apostles of a new simplicity. But while Archilochus was a heroic revolutionary, the torchbearers of the classical period were enlightened critics and reformers.

Simonides came of good Ionian stock. He was born about 557 on the island of Ceos, which can just be descried from the Attic promontory of Sunium as the nearest of those Cyclades which glimmer on the horizon. Simonides seems to have been the first to write choral lyrics by appointment and for pay to honour human beings, not

[32] Of the pieces in *Pap. Oxyrh.* 2321 (first published in 1954=346 Page), Nos. 1 and 4 have not, to my mind, been interpeted in any way which fits the surviving remains. In fr. 6 we may be right in suspecting a similarity of theme with Bacchylides fr. 20B and Pindar fr. 124: the speaker wishes to enjoy during 'the whole night' at a symposion the waking dreams of drunken euphoria—dreams of sea voyages, with a glimpse of the acropolis of Athens (?) visible from afar off, blooming gardens (?), lofty palaces, or the like.

hymns in praise of gods. He composed songs to celebrate the achievements of men or boys who had won contests in the national games.[1]
But his principal bent was not in this direction: he was particularly
famed for his choral lyrics on the occasion of funerals, the *threnoi*.
It was part of the career of a choral lyrist that he was often invited
abroad to rehearse and produce his songs at the appropriate place
and time; often he would stay for a long period in one place which
offered him better opportunities for practising his art than his own
little island. Hipparchus prevailed on him by rich gifts and high fees
to come to Athens, just as he had previously gained Anacreon for
his court. During the last twenty years of the sixth century Simonides
spent some time in Thessaly; at the time of the Persian wars he was
working for the Athenian democracy, and he ended his long life in
Sicily, where he had gone to the court of the tyrant Hiero.

In the wide Thessalian lowlands the descendants of the defeated
natives were under the sway of an aristocratic ruling class, in which
two great families had distinguished themselves by rank and power—
the Aleuads and the Scopads. Simonides wrote poems for both these
families. At a banquet celebrated by the Scopads, their palace
collapsed, and the head of the family, Scopas, and many of his kin
met their death beneath the ruins. The *threnos* which Simonides
wrote on this occasion began thus (fr. 521):

You who are a man, think not to know what the morrow will bring, nor,
when you see a man happy, to know how long it will last: our change of
state is faster than the flight on outspread wings of a fly from one place to
another.

In these few verses we hear tones which remind us of Christian
preaching; the opening, indeed, is almost like those of many of the
psalms. We feel personally addressed as never before in Greek
literature. The warm *you* of Simonides is not directed to an individual
friend or to the assembly of mourners, but to his fellow-man: 'You
who are a man . . .'; and the poet clearly includes himself. Deeply
moved, he reacts to the deaths as if he himself had been touched by
the hand of fate: that which touches one of us, cannot be matter of
indifference to any. The conception of humanity developed in
classical Greece is here foreshadowed. The concluding image is
highly individual:[2] a change in human life is no more significant or
important than the sudden darting flight of a fly, when it goes from

---

[1] The brief fragments that we have of such epinicia by Simonides will be discussed later in connection with the epinicia of Pindar (p. 434–36).

[2] According to the examples in Liddell and Scott *metastasis* as a euphemism for
death does not occur before Polybius. They wrongly give Euripides fr. 554 under
that head: clearly it belongs under II 2 ('change').

one place to another. Pindar later was to declare with gloomy pathos that man, subject as he is to violent change, is the 'dream of a shadow' (*Pyth.* 8, 96). Simonides says something rather similar here, but the particular turn of phrase is characteristically different. He has no notion of denying the reality of our existence: instead he sets man on a level with the most insignificant of creatures that inhabit the earth.[3] This again is an attitude which finds a parallel in Christianity, as for example in the humble and brotherly spirit of Russian Christians, which finds expression in similar images.

It may appear that we have laid too great a burden of meaning on this short fragment; but when we look further afield, we find confirmation for the impression that we have received here.

The limitations of humanity are a favourite theme in the *threnoi*. When Simonides speaks of these limitations, again and again we could fancy ourselves listening to the Psalmist:

Slight is the strength of men, unsuccessful their struggle, in their short lives sorrow comes upon sorrow, and inevitable death hangs over them all alike. For the good have their share of death, even as the wicked man has. (520)

There is no misfortune that may not be expected in human life: in a brief space God turns all things about. (527)

Everything is sucked down into the same cruel whirlpool, the virtues (*aretai*) of men and their riches alike. (522)

It was even beyond their power, theirs who lived of old, demigods begotten of great gods, to lead a life free from grief, calamity and danger, up to the goal of old age. (523)

The last fragment clearly shows that Simonides is intending to comfort, not to dispirit. The clear recognition of what is denied to us makes human pride bow before the omnipotence and majesty of God, but it encourages us vis-à-vis our fellow men, who are all under the same limitations: even the sons of gods are not exempt.

It was in fame that the Greeks sought their consolation for the transitoriness of personal existence: through fame the gateway was opened to a kind of immortality. Here also Simonides sets a limit. The fame and memory of a dead man will not last for ever (594):

(The only thing that does not perish at once with our death is the fame which we gain in our lifetime. It remains for a time,) like a splendid funeral monument;[4] at the last it sinks beneath the earth.

[3] Formally, the basis of comparison is the swiftness and suddenness of the flight, but the comparison goes further, since the idea of the fly cannot be mentally dissociated from the flight and put out of the picture. Similarly in Homeric similes of lions, regardless what particular element is the basis of comparison, we cannot forget that it is a lion which acts as the hero does.

[4] καλὸν ἐντάφιον must be part of the quotation, cf. 531, 4.

The comparison of fame with a sepulchral monument echoes momentarily the thought that our memory of a man, if it is to endure, must be put into an artistic form, be it a statue or a poem,[5] such as that from which these words are taken. In another poem Simonides directs a heavy fire against the presumptuous claim made by an inscription ascribing immortality to the grave-monument of which it formed part. Somewhere in Asia Minor stood a tomb crowned by the figure of a woman in bronze, with an inscription making her speak thus (Diog. Laert. 1, 89):

> I am a maiden of bronze, and I lie on the gravestone of Midas.
> Long as water shall moisten, as long as trees shall be leafy;
> While the sun and the moon shall shed their rays upon mortals,
> While the rivers shall flow with rushing streams to the ocean;
> So long shall I remain on the grave, at the place of lamenting,
> Saying to him that shall pass, 'In this grave Midas is sleeping.'

The lines were ascribed to Cleobulus, tyrant of Lindus, who was reckoned among the Seven Sages. It probably dated from the time when the casting of large figures in bronze was a recent invention, and in the pride of discovery an artist boasted of the permanence of this new technique. The poem was well known, and was current in several versions: it had thus come to Simonides' knowledge.

Simonides pays no heed to the circumstance that a new technical advance was announcing itself in triumph;[6] the boast of immortality is abhorrent to him, and it receives all his attention. To rebut it, he enters into a verbal wrangle with the old poet. Solon earlier had taken issue with Mimnermus (above p. 217f.), but in a light-hearted and urbane manner. Here, however, the tone is severe and didactic, almost schoolmasterly (581):

No-one who bases himself on reason can agree with Cleobulus of Lindus when he compares the ever-rolling streams, the flowers of spring, the rays of the sun and of the golden moon and the salty deep itself with the strength to endure (*menos*) of a pillar. All things are weaker than the gods; but a stone—even human hands can destroy a stone. This is a notion held by a fool.

So one of the Seven Sages is branded as a fool because his ideas are not based on reason. We can see at once how intellectual this polemic is. The mistake lay in assigning to mere human handiwork the same vital energy (*menos*) as that which dwells in the infinite

---

[5] Pindar proudly boasts that his odes are not, like statues, tied to one place (*Nem.* 5, 1ff.) and are not exposed to destruction by the elements (*Pyth.* 6, 7–13); Horace's 'exegi monumentum aere perennius' (*Carm.* 3, 30) is well known.

[6] This appears from his talking of stone instead of bronze.

power of the gods. Here again the poet is reminding us of the limits prescribed for all that pertains to man.

The texts studied so far have all been concerned with death and decay, and they necessarily therefore laid stress on what is forbidden to man.[7] But this is only half of the message which Simonides felt called to convey to the Greek people. In renouncing the unattainable, and thus freeing ourselves from extravagant ambitions, he sees reason for demanding a greater charity in judging ourselves and others. To gain acceptance for this greater toleration, it was necessary sharply to correct the system of norms and values then in force. This task of revision is essayed in the longest and most important fragment of his that we possess.

This very interesting piece deserves detailed consideration. But before we examine it, we must clearly picture to ourselves the ideas which Simonides opposed.[8] Values, it is well known, are not always determined by the reason, but rather, in many cases, by the will. The lords of archaic Greece devoted themselves with vigour and passion to all the pleasures of life, and especially to that most aristocratic pleasure, the possession and display of power. Manly worth (*aretê*) comprised for them achievement, rank, dominion, wealth, brilliant and conspicuous success—in a word, greatness. Every proud heart joined in the titanic struggle for the kind of distinction which raised its fortunate possessor to a felicity little below that of the gods; while failure and ill-luck, it was felt, branded the loser with the stigma of inferiority. In this scheme of values, no distinction was made between fortune and merit. If the gods heaped blessings on a man, it was like a mint-mark saying: 'This is pure gold.' Misfortune brought disgrace, made a man small and exposed him to pity. The middle way between triumph and disaster, a modest prudence which sought its standing on firm rather than high ground, was to holders of such views contemptible. He who was not 'good,' i.e. great and powerful, was automatically 'bad.'

Simonides' poem is directed against such views. In order to set out his thought methodically, he takes an old proverb as his starting-point. Again it is a saying ascribed to one of the Seven Sages. Pittacus of Mytilene, the target of Alcaeus' bitterest attacks, had said, 'It is hard to be good'; and Simonides begins (542):

[7] To judge from two other fragments (522 and 594) the passage may have continued: 'No, the monument is mortal too, like human worth and human fortune. Longest-lasting is the fame bestowed by poetry; but that too finally perishes as if it had never been.'

[8] We are accurately enough acquainted with these ideas, since they find their fullest expression in Pindar (cf. below p. 475, 500), at a time when forward-looking men, who shared Simonides' views, had already abandoned them.

It is hard to become a truly good man in arms and legs and understanding, foursquare, built without flaw.

Almost every word in this version needs to be interpreted more precisely. What is meant by 'a good man' we have already seen. Good will and hard work are not enough to make a man 'good'; visible achievement and success were also needed.[9] This proving of oneself in action was called, in the language of that time, 'becoming good.' By 'arms and legs' Simonides implies bodily action, by 'understanding' (*nous*) the working of will and intellect.[10] To express perfection and agreement with the norm he uses the Pythagorean term 'four-cornered, square.'[11]

In the original poem this introductory passage was followed by a personal address to the person for whom it was written;[12] but this has not been preserved. After this interruption Simonides comes back to Pittacus. But this time his acceptance is more qualified: it is not that the saying is untrue in its general direction, but that it does not go far enough. In the explanatory clauses of the first extract Simonides defined the requirements of 'being good' in their most stringent sense. Now, as he considers them again, he finds himself compelled to regard the fulfilment of them not as 'difficult' but as quite impossible.[13] The second strophe runs as follows:

To me the saying of Pittacus is not quite true, even though a clever man said it. He said, 'It is hard to be good ("noble").' Only to god can such a description apply.[14] For a man it is impossible that he should be other than bad, if he is cast down by a calamity against which he is without

---

[9] A definition of *aretê* in which Theognis (683–86; 695f.) and Pindar (*passim*) concur, is 'a passion for greatness and the achievement of greatness.'

[10] Cf. *Iliad* 15, 642f.: παντοίας ἀρετᾶς, ἠμὲν πόδας ἠδὲ μάχεσθαι καὶ νόον, and above p. 77 n. 5.

[11] Above p. 277. Similarly Polyclitus, wishing not to portray individuals but the 'canon,' is said to have sculpted 'square' (*quadratas*) figures (Plin. n.h. 34, 56). Polyclitus also wrote a book in which he based the 'canon' on numerical proportions, after the Pythagorean fashion: the term 'quadratic' may in fact have come from his original book.

[12] It was addressed to Scopas. It seems odd that a feudal lord should be the one to whom ideas ultimately destructive of his scheme of moral values were directed. We may well suspect that Scopas had met with a setback to which Simonides alluded: in that case the arguments that he put forward would be quite appropriate.

[13] There is thus no logical contradiction in Simonides' procedure. At first he agrees with the saying, then he goes a stage beyond it, i.e. he disagrees with it, but he still recognizes it as the 'saying of a clever man': he does not reject it like the poem of Cleobulus. Seneca corrects a dictum of Epicurus' in exactly the same way (*ep. mor.* 22, 13–15). At first he says of it *nescio utrum verior an eloquentior*, then he says *falsum est* and goes one better himself.

[14] Cf. Matth. 19, 14: 'Why callest thou me good? None is good, save God alone.'

resource. Every man is good who has succeeded,[15] and every man bad who has failed. But most often (are they successful) and do best, whom the gods love.

Almost everything that Simonides says in this strophe was an old and bitter truth to his audience. Since the gods never grant uninterrupted success to any mortal, we are each and all, strictly speaking, 'bad' (cf. Solon fr. 15, above p. 229). One single word, however, in the strophe looks beyond the common view. Simonides does not speak simply of a calamity (or misfortune or mischance), but of one against which human wit is resourceless (*amêchanos*). Only then are we all equally 'bad,' when we are overthrown by forces to which even the best must yield. This significant proviso becomes the basis of Simonides' further conclusions, which are entirely new and revolutionary, and were to be basic assumptions for all time to come. So modern are they, in fact, that they sound quite banal. The poet continues thus (third strophe):

Therefore will I not seek that which cannot possibly be, and pin my share of existence on an unrealizable hope: the wholly blameless man as one of us who live by the fruits of the broad and fertile earth—I will not say that I have ever found one such. But I love and praise him who does nothing shameful of his own free will. Not even the gods fight against necessity.

'I will not seek' is much the same as, 'In my firm conviction one should not seek'; and 'seek' is used in the same sense as when Diogenes went about with his lantern 'seeking' an honest man: the word implies the establishment of standards by which one can judge others and live oneself. The human race is characterized as, 'we who eat the fruits of the earth': by deriving nourishment from the earth we owe our debt to earth (above p. 54 n. 4) and are thus faulty and unlike the gods. Hence we must not base our limited life-span upon the illusion of a perfection that is denied to us. One withdraws from the field where compulsion and necessity hold sway; for not even the gods take up arms against the inevitable. The question is no longer whether we are 'bad' through our failure or 'good' through our success, but whether we willingly do what is shameful. Unlike the ambiguous term 'bad,' 'shameful' (or 'hateful') means only that which is morally objectionable; and by adding 'of his own will' Simonides makes it clear that only those actions come under consideration in which the agent can use his free will.[16] The man who,

---

[15] Read πράξας μὲν εὖ. The γάρ is inserted by Plato (who cites, and thus preserves, the poem for us in *Protagoras*) for the sake of his context.

[16] It is worth noting that Hesiod brings in the criterion of will in deciding whether the breaking of an oath deserves punishment (*Theog.* 232, *WD* 282; cf. R. Maschke, *Die Willenslehre im griechischen Recht*, Berlin 1926).

so far as in him lies, keeps himself clean from morally wrong behaviour, 'him do I praise and love'—which again means, 'he ought to be praised and loved.' For the outside world, not the individual conscience, is still the court which gives the final judgment on a man's worth.

But now the new position has to be more accurately defined. So far we have heard what the poet rejects as unacceptable, and the norm of morality has been only negatively defined as abstention from willingly doing wrong. Is such an abstention, even if it is devoid of positive achievement, to be reckoned enough? The last strophe answers this question. Unfortunately it is not preserved completely and word for word:

I am not zealous to censure . . .; for me it is enough if a man is not weak ⟨in understanding⟩[17] and not incompetent; one who understands the laws of society, a sound man . . . in such a one would I not find fault, for the generation of fools is beyond number. All that which has nothing hateful (shameful) mixed with it is good.

By saying, 'I am not zealous to censure,' Simonides declares himself against those critics who condemn their fellow-men for failing to measure up to unreasonable standards. He then states his own requirements. Again the formulation is partly negative, and deliberately so, in order not to aim at completeness in his thought. First, to deserve praise a man must not be weak in understanding (or sentiments: the word is in any case a conjectural supplement) or quite incompetent. These words supplement what he said before about 'misfortune against which one is without any resource.' The only thing which makes no diminution of a man's worth is that which he does or suffers under the compulsion of an irrestible force. If the victim goes under through his own incompetence, through not being clever or able enough, that is another story. For an intelligent Ionian like Simonides it went without saying that a man who wanted to be respected must have a certain amount of ability and savoir-faire.[18] Thirdly Simonides prescribes that one must understand the laws of society. By 'laws' he does not mean simply written enactments, but

[17] The gap may be plugged fairly confidently with νόον. The supplement is necessary first to qualify κακός more closely and thus to distinguish it from the κακός in v. 8; secondly we have to supply a reasonable antithesis to ἠλίθιος; thirdly the expression must be parallel to οὐκ ἀπάλαμνος. In Solon 19, 11 f. νόος and οὐκ ἀπάλαμνα ἔργα are put together.

[18] A contemporary proverb (Theognis 1027f.) declares: 'The accomplishment of badness is easy: but the encompassing (παλάμη) of good is hard.' This παλάμη in doing good and shunning evil is the thing which the οὐκ ἄγαν ἀπάλαμνος of Simonides must possess to some degree. (The note on ἀπάλαμνος in Wilamowitz, *Sappho und Simonides* [Berlin 1913] p. 175 n. 3, followed by Liddell and Scott s.v., is mistaken.)

in general terms all the obligations of justice and fair dealing towards one's fellow-citizens; and 'understanding' includes, as always, its practical applications. The fourth requirement, 'a sound man' is expressed too vaguely for us to render it precisely.[19] At all events Simonides was not thinking of the average man, whom (rather too optimistically) we now call normal: his reference to the vast predominance of fools shows that he had in mind men of more than ordinary qualities. He ends with a further extension of his previous statement ('Him do I praise and love, who does nothing shameful of his own will'), declaring that every thing is 'beautiful' (i.e. morally good, superior) which contains no mixture of what is 'hateful' (i.e. shameful).

The last conclusion rests on the logic of polarized thought, of the type which Simonides' contemporary Parmenides carried to its extreme limits. In this system the basic qualities, e.g. light and dark, are absolute, and where we think we see a lower or higher degree of brightness, there is in reality a mixture, varying from case to case, of absolute light and absolute dark. Hence there is no neutral ground lying between the opposites: if one quality is entirely lacking, then its opposite is wholly present. Consequently for Simonides that which contains no admixture of the ugly is for that very reason beautiful. By using this conclusion he is able to extend the idea of the good and beautiful so that it begins immediately where the ugly and blameworthy leaves off. In human affairs one will look no longer for the absolute beautiful as the opposite extreme from the ugly. In this subtle manner Simonides employs the formal logic of polarized thought to overturn polarized thought itself and to substitute a relative mode of thinking.

Thus in his ideas and attitudes Simonides left far behind him the archaic way of thinking in antitheses. Only one great antithesis was retained, or even increased its importance with him—that of god and man. This became for him the antithesis of absolute and relative. God alone is in the absolute sense 'good': men are never *sensu stricto* good—in the most favourable circumstances they can be 'best of their kind,'[20] that is to say, when the gods love them. We cannot hope for more than that one or two individuals should rise above the vast mass of the stupid.

---

[19] The word ὑγιής is very rare in early Greek poetry (Radermacher on Sophocles *Phil.* 1006).

[20] Simonides did not have the terms 'absolute' and 'relative' at his disposal. In the one place he solves the problem by opposing the absolute form 'good' to the relative superlative 'best of the kind'; in the other he puts the absolute term 'beautiful' with its new definition, 'better than ugly.'

The awareness of our human limitations, which provides others with a theme for complaint and lamentation, sets off in Simonides a train of thought which leads to a calmer, warmer and more confident humanity. It is a mistake, he tells us, to aim at things beyond the confines of our limited existence and to dash ourselves in hopeless longing against the bars of our cage. Human objectives must be within the circle of fate that encloses us. One cannot lay to a man's account anything forced upon him by the general laws of the human condition: we should honour and love anyone who acquits himself well in the rest of his actions.

This sensible and tolerant (but not soft) attitude takes away from men an unbearable responsibility. The deep feeling of guilt possible in one to whom such doctrines were yet unknown is to be seen in an anonymous elegy of Simonides' time. In the Theognis collection we find this moving outcry and complaint (Theogn. 373ff.):[21]

Great Zeus, I am bewildered: you are the ruler of rulers; you have the glory alone, you have the lordship and might; you know the thoughts and desires of each man: Lord, over each and all boundless your kingdom extends. Why then is it your will, Cronides, that the unrighteous and they that do your commands should be rewarded alike? Whether a man is modest in heart or violent and haughty, practising deeds which set law and religion at naught, still such a man wins glory and keeps it. But him who is righteous, keeping aloof from guilt, loving the honest and good, him poverty grips, the mother of impotent weakness, binding him hand and foot, cheating his will to do good, laying his reason low by her overpowering compulsion. So that against his will he must bear shame and reproach, under compulsion of need which brings him much that is hateful, lies, dishonest deceit, shameful contention and strife, even against his will. There is no other misfortune like unto this, which brings helplessness in its train.

The writer of these lines sees no way out. He is burdened with 'helplessness' born of poverty, 'helplessness' which destroys his natural character and compels him by 'necessity' to do evil deeds against his will and to suffer the shame that attaches to them. He thinks in the same terms as Simonides. But Simonides, because of his creative vision, is able to untie the apparently inextricable knot. The gods themselves do not fight against necessity, and things against which even the valiant are helpless are not to be laid to a man's charge. It is not divine misgovernment, but false human value-judgments that strip the blameless but unsuccessful man of his

---

[21] The verses have previously been cited in this connection by Karl Reinhardt, *Parmenides* (Bonn 1916) 130.

honour. Human beings should always be judged by human measure and no other.[22]

The result of the polemical tone adopted by Simonides is that the negative side of the new doctrine—abstention from unrealizable ambitions—comes out more strongly than the positive injunctions, which were to remain later in undisputed possession of the field. It is all the more pleasing, therefore, that a fragment has survived to show that Simonides had no intention of letting human ideals slide downwards into the abyss of what came easiest. In this piece he adopts the often-quoted dictum of Hesiod (*Works and Days* 289ff., above p. 122) which says that the road to Virtue (*aretê*, 'manly worth') is long and steep, made so by the gods, and not surmounted without sweat and toil (579):

There is a saying that *Aretê* dwells on a cliff hard to climb, and on a steep crag (?) alone (?) she rules her pure domain.[23] She is not visible to the eyes

---

[22] A fragment of choral lyric of similar content has recently come to light in *Oxyrh. Pap.* vol. 25, 1959, no. 2432 = fr. 541 Page (on which see Max Treu, *Rhein. Mus.* 103, 1960, p. 319–336; Bruno Gentili, *Gnomon* 33, 1961, p. 338–341; H. Lloyd-Jones, *Class. Rev.* 11, 1961, p. 19). This interesting piece, which comes either from Simonides or from his nephew Bacchylides, deals with the theme that many human failures are pardonable as arising from circumstances beyond a man's control. It probably began with the thought that the progress of time, by bringing the true facts of a case to light sooner or later, finally passes a true judgment on the moral rightness or wrongness of any action. The new text may provisionally be rendered as follows: '(Time?) distinguishes the beautiful from the ugly: if anyone with loose tongue casts calumnies upon another, the smoke (i.e. smouldering ill-will) achieves nothing, the gold (i.e. true worth) remains untarnished, and truth is ever victorious. Only to a few does (god?) grant flourishing continuance in *aretê* to the very end. For it is not easy to be good, since the irresistible lure of profit or the poisoned darts of deceitful Aphrodite or the swelling love of power coerce us against our will. Since it is scarcely (possible) for a man to tread the path of rectitude all his life, (it is enough) if he (keep away) from the crooked (path) . . . rightly . . .' On individual points: For the supplement 'time' as the vehicle of victorious truth cf. Solon's appeal against unjustified reproaches to 'the judgment-seat of Time' (fr. 24, 3: above p. 226); Pindar, *Ol.* 1, 33: 'The coming days are the wisest witness (against envious detraction, v. 47f.)'; *Ol.* 10, 53. In line 2 κακ]αγορεῖ Treu and Gentili. In line 3 we should probably write ποτι]φέρων. On the 'smoke' of envy and ill-will see below p. 460, n. 39. The connection supplied between lines 4 and 5 (Gentili) is supported by the similarity of structure, the general sense, and the parallel in Bacch. fr. 14, where also there is a reference to pure gold; and in all the passages cited the same ideas and expressions occur repeatedly. Lines 7–11: the three impulses that militate against a blameless life (cupidity, erotic passion, ambition) are illustrated by Treu p. 327–9 with parallels from later Greek poetry; to his passages we may add the three dangerous urges in Theognis 29f. (below p. 403) and what Pindar says in fr. 123, 7–9 (in a different connection) about the love of money (βιαίως 'unnaturally,' like βιᾶται in our fragment) and the love of women (below p. 504).

[23] Wilamowitz, followed by others, has introduced nymphs into this landscape:

of all mortals; only to him who has come at the cost of much sweat to the summit of manhood.

What is new here since Hesiod is the reverent tone in which Simonides speaks of *aretê*, as of a goddess.[24]

Aretê, however, cannot be won through the efforts of those who strive for her: the blessing of the higher powers who rule all reality is needed if she is to be realized (526):

No man has won *aretê*, no city, no mortal, without the gods. God is the all-wise (*or* all-clever), but among men nothing is invulnerable.

The second sentence is peculiarly Simonidean: 'No human endeavour is exempt from destructive forces which can cheat it of success; god, on the contrary, is—.' We expect to be told 'all-powerful,' his strength is always successful and brings what he plans to fruition: that is approximately what Pindar says (*Pyth.* 2, 49ff.). But Simonides does not speak of power and might: he talks of the 'cleverness' or 'resourcefulness' of god. He takes the Homeric epithet of Odysseus, *polymêtis*, 'very clever, inventive, wily,' and intensifies it to a superlative, *pammêtis* 'infinitely clever and resourceful.' No one else ventured to follow him. God, as seen by the clever Ionian Simonides, is a super-Odysseus, and his all-power is based on his all-cleverness. While even the keenest-witted man is often at a loss, god is the only being ('only' is implicit in the definite article) who always finds a way.

In this supreme practical cleverness which Simonides ascribes to God, we see the projection of that practical cleverness which he demands from men of distinction.[25] It is the Odysseus-ideal again, but at another level. We are not now concerned with wild adventures

they are charming but out of place. There is no reason to attack Μιν (sc. Ἀρετάν) χῶρον ἁγνὸν ἀμφέπειν when there is such an exact parallel as Pindar *Pyth.* 5, 68 (Apollo μυχὸν ἀμφέπει μαντεῖον). Could Simonides ascribe to Hesiod in *oratio obliqua* a statement that he never made? And what meaning could the nymphs have in a picture otherwise so clear and simple? Instead of νῦν one could write, for example, τραχύν, and μόναν for θοᾶν; both would fit the passage of Hesiod.

[24] Hesiod spoke of the acquisition (cf. ἐλέσθαι v. 287) and possession of *aretê*, and Simonides expressed himself similarly elsewhere (fr. 526, 2). Here, however, he does not speak of gaining and holding, but with a modest reserve makes the very sight of the highest moral value the supreme end of human endeavour. It is like a foreshadowing of Plato to hear Simonides saying that the good in all its beauty reveals itself only to him who devotes all his strength to realizing the good.

[25] Intelligence and flow of ideas in practical problems (μῆτις, μηχανή, παλάμη, cf. 542, 29), is clearly in Simonides' eyes the most potent weapon in the struggle for success and greatness; and the limits of humanity appear to him in the fact that no intelligence can cope with an ἀμήχανος (542, 9) ἀνάγκη (542, 20): necessity imposes a limit even on the gods. The interplay of compulsive necessity and inventiveness trying to slip through is basically identical with Alcman's remarkable pair of divinities Αἶσα (or Τέκμωρ) and Πόρος (above pp. 163f. and 253f.)

and fairy-tale triumphs over every kind of obstacle, but with the mastery of common life by uncommon faculties, with distinction won by hard, painful struggle, with position in the community maintained by decency, honesty and humanity.

The humanity of Simonides is felt in the *threnoi* as an audible undertone; in his theoretical discussion of the idea of a good man it is the unspoken assumption underlying all the conclusions at which his acute criticism arrives. A narrative fragment from one of his choral odes shows this basic trait of his nature in a new light. The fragment gives a brilliant illustration of the poet's ability to feel sympathy, in a concrete instance, for human suffering and human confidence, to set forth a given human situation in poetry with vitalizing power, and to convey human emotion springing from strange circumstances in all the lustre of elevated language without detracting from its natural spontaneity. The subject comes from the story of Danaë. Danaë was shut up in a tower by her father after an oracle had foretold that her son would slay his grandfather. Zeus himself fell in love with her beauty, and came into her prison in the form of a shower of gold. When she bore the infant Perseus and her father learnt of it, he shut up mother and child in a chest and had them thrown into the sea. The chest floated, and was cast up on the island of Seriphos. Simonides depicts their voyage in the tossing chest over a stormy sea: it is the first Madonna-painting in Greek literature (543):

As in the skilfully-made chest the rushing wind and heaving waves filled her with fear and her cheeks were wetted, she put her loving arm around Perseus, and said: 'Child, what an ordeal for me: but you are sleeping. Baby-like, noticing nothing, you sleep in this joyless, bronze-riveted wood, shining in the night, in blue-black darkness where you lie. The salt flood over your curling locks, when the wave breaks over us, does not disturb you, nor the roaring of the gale, while your pretty face lies there, bright against the purple cover. If you were frightened by what is indeed frightening, your little ear would also hear my words. I say to you, 'Sleep, my child, the sea shall sleep, our measureless suffering shall sleep. May a way of escape appear, father Zeus, sent by you. If I am too bold and demanding in my prayer, forgive me.[26]

In this striking picture the first novelty is Simonides' choice of just this moment in the story as his theme. Usually, when poetry has to tell of fairy-tale happenings, it passes lightly over the least believable turns of events. The miracles themselves are only touched upon in covert allusion; the astonishment of the onlookers may be more graphically depicted; but the main emphasis is on the contrast

[26] The text is uncertain in several places.

between the situations before and after the improbable happening. Simonides, on the contrary, does not first relate how Danaë and her child were thrown into the sea and condemned, as it seemed, to certain death, in order then to describe the opening of the cast-up chest by fishermen and their astonishment at finding persons alive inside: his imagination dwells with the mother and child in the midst of their frightening voyage. The miracle is seen by him not as a momentary event, not from an external standpoint, but as a continuing state, and from the viewpoint of those immediately affected. He places himself quite unreservedly in the heart of the incredible situation, and tells us how, inside the chest, love, hope, and prayer look for a successful deliverance from the perils outside.

The picture itself is built up from a very few elements with typical Ionian clarity. Even the colours are few in number, but strong and simple: the ornaments of the choral-lyric style are used with strict relevance to fact. The chest is 'skilfully made' and 'bronze-riveted'; the sea foams, the gale roars, the darkness is blue-black; the child has a pretty face and curly hair and lies on a purple blanket; the mother has only her tears, her loving arm, and the words that she speaks. While she is overwhelmed with anxiety, the child sleeps on in ignorance. A single word tells us that things in themselves frightening do not frighten him—an echo of the principle of subjectivity. The transition to unselfish tenderness is full of warmth and mother-love: 'Sleep on then, even if you leave me alone with my fears.' The thought suddenly soars upwards with the sublime transition: 'May the peace that rests on this little sleeping creature descend on the elements outside and silence their raging fury!' Out of this comes her prayer to 'father Zeus'—the bodily father of her child. After this upsurge of feeling the note changes to one of meek piety: 'Forgive me, if I ask for too much.' This precious scrap of poetry shows a rare combination of dignity, truth to life, and humanity; at one point the formulation almost touches on the sublime.

During Simonides' lifetime the epoch that revelled in the bizarrerie of an Aristeas or an Abaris was drawing to a close; the meteors of miracle faded before the dawn of the classical age, and mythology began to lay aside many of its absurdities and to become more man-like, in art as well as in poetry. When old standards break up, frontiers tend to become confused: things mutually incompatible are left side by side to sort out their differences as they may. Simonides often has to handle traditional tales of wonder; he brings out in clarity and detail the strangeness of the happenings, but at the same time he breathes into their barren thaumaturgy the living warmth of his own new feeling for man and nature.

Two of his fragments describe the miraculous power of music. Orpheus sings and plays on his lyre, and (567):

birds beyond number flew over his head; straight up from the dark blue water jumped fishes to hear his beautiful song.

Here human action radiates into its physical environment and produces effects upon it. In another fragment the world of nature holds its breath as if under a spell, to let the sounds pass freely (595):

No leaf-rustling breath of wind stirred itself to interrupt the honey-sweet voice or prevent it spreading out[27] and insinuating itself into the ears of mortals.

Simonides admits the miraculous not merely when it has a fairy-tale attractiveness and advances his poetical purposes; he also employs it to make our blood run cold. The apparition of Achilles' ghost over his grave before the assembled Achaean army receives a vivid and graphic life from him as from no other Greek writer (557). He tells the story of the brazen giant Talus, who was forged by Hephaestus for the king of Crete as a fleet-footed watchman to patrol his shores, a robot of superhuman strength. He relates how this monster seized the Sardonians who refused to obey his master's will and leapt with them into a fire, and how the tortured wretches, with mouths open and distorted, died with a 'sardonic grin' (568).

The painter of so many vivid and animated scenes could not but have something of the dramatist in him; and the infancy of Greek tragedy in fact fell within his lifetime. In a choral ode dealing with the homecoming of Theseus from Crete he included a messenger's speech like those familiar to us from tragedy. The ship has sailed into harbour, but by the negligence of the steersman (550b) not the white sail, as prearranged, had been hoisted in token of success, but (as Simonides puts it with all the pomp of choral lyric, 550a):

a purple sail, steeped in the liquid flower of the strong-growing scarlet-oak.

A man comes from the ship with the good tidings, but too late: the young hero's father, supposing that his son is dead, has thrown himself into the sea. Beside his body the messenger tells the story which he would have told if he had been alive, and in an apostrophe to the dead man, he expresses his own sorrow (551):

If I had come before, I could have helped you to a happy life instead of this.[28]

[27] Read κιδναμέναν.

[28] The genitive βιότω is explained by the genitive after the middle ὀνίνασθαι, whose active form is here used with causative sense ('make one enjoy'): on this causative see J. Wackernagel, *Sprachl. Untersuch. zu Homer* (Göttingen, 1916) 130ff.

We know of a number of poems composed by Simonides on the occasion of the Persian Wars, and it is very interesting to find out how a spirit like his reacted to circumstances greater than any individual, particularly to self-sacrifice for one's country. Poems were written on the Athenians fallen at Marathon (490) by Aeschylus and by Simonides, then nearly sixty years old: both poems were elegies, just as Archilochus had composed an elegy in honour of the drowned soldiers (above p. 143). In the latter poem the note of lamentation over the dead was soon silenced and overborne by the advice to enjoy life while one might. But times had changed. Athenians of the early fifth century would not welcome an abrupt transition from the death of one's fellows to one's own pursuit of pleasure; they would prefer to remember their dead in quiet sorrow. The story goes that Aeschylus came second in the contest: the lofty emotions of his verses were found lacking in that 'tenderness of compassion' which the occasion demanded (*Vita Aesch.* 8). From Simonides' elegy one single verse has survived (63 D):

Only god never fails but prospers wholly and surely.

'Man, on the other hand,' for thus we may complete it, 'has no perfect achievement, no unalloyed pleasure, no gain without loss.'[29] The loss of brave men to achieve victory is regarded by Simonides as a tribute to which humanity is subject: here also we find his general philosophy of the limitations placed on human existence.

Ten years after Marathon the Persians again sent their fleets and armies against Greece; and this time it was to be a war fought out to its final decision, with each side now aware of the other's real strength. While the Greek warships at Artemisium lay ready to bar the further advance of the Persian fleet, at the coastal pass of Thermopylae, not far away, a hand-picked Greek army under the Spartan king Leonidas barred the way to central Greece. Even before the fleets met in battle, a northerly gale blew up and severely damaged the Persian ships. The story was later told that the Athenians had previously made a sacrifice to the North wind (Boreas) and had asked for his help. He was in fact their son-in-law, having taken (as the legend had it) an Athenian woman as his bride—he had swept down upon Athens and had carried off Orithyia, a daughter of the king, to be the wind's bride in his Thracian home. After the war the

---

[29] Thus in Apollonius Rhodius we read (4, 1165):

For, as we wander abroad, we troops of suffering mortals, we nowhere lay our hands on unmixed pleasure, but always hard at the heels of joy come grief and bitter repining.

Athenians raised a temple to Boreas, and Simonides composed a choral ode describing the sea-fight and the god's intervention. Unhappily, almost nothing of it has survived.

The Persian army, after long and bloody battles, was able to outflank the Greek position of Thermopylae and thus make it untenable. But the Spartans did not budge: dismissing the other contingents, they with the Thespians chose a soldier's death at their post. On the stone that marked their grave the following epitaph was carved (92 D):

> Tell them at Sparta, you that pass by
>   That here obedient to their laws we lie.

The 'laws' were the Spartan traditions of a warrior's honour and duty, and the wonderful simplicity with which the discharge of that duty to the very end is indicated, gives weight and dignity to the pentameter. Of the first verse we may think differently. Greek epitaphs were commonly addressed to the passer-by, since graves were in open country, beside the roads. Here, however, the traveller is not bidden to stop and think quietly for a moment about the dead; he is asked to take a message, to bring news of their self-sacrifice to their far-off home, since not one of that devoted band had escaped the fate of them all. The notion of a message makes us think again of drama; and in fact the 'messenger's speech' was a device much used in tragedies on the Persian Wars: but on a gravestone immovably fixed and intended to stay for ever in its place, such a dramatic element seems inappropriate and rather far-fetched. Even more artificial is the fiction that, without the chance-led passer-by, who also happens to be going to Sparta, the Spartans must remain ignorant that their brave men are all slain. This touch of ingenuity is in the manner of Simonides, to whom the epigram was ascribed in later antiquity: but the ascription has no solid authority.

On the other hand the epitaph written by Simonides for a friend who had also fallen at Thermopylae is undoubtedly genuine (83 D):

This stone honours Megistias: him the Persians slew, when they carried war into the Melian land. He was a seer, and knew that his death drew nigh; but he would not flinch from his duty: he stayed here with the Spartans, and died.

This epigram, as beautiful as it is untranslatable, needs no commentary: it speaks directly to our hearts.

What is new in Simonides' thoughts comes out more clearly in a fragment of a choral ode for a memorial service to all those fallen at Thermopylae (531):

Of those who died at Thermopylae famous is the fortune, beautiful the destiny: an altar their grave, instead of tears, remembrance; for compassion, praise. Decay, and all-consuming time cannot deface such a monument of brave men, and in the consecrated place has the glory of Hellas chosen its dwelling. Witness thereto is Leonidas, king of Sparta, who left behind him the great glory of manly valour (*aretê*) and imperishable renown.

The manner in which Simonides examines and interprets the great achievement once again reminds us of a sermon. The death of the heroes is represented as something quite unlike any ordinary death, and there is no allusion to these limitations of humanity which were touched on in the other *threnoi* (see above p. 304–306). The five short clauses at the outset make up together a five-fold inversion of commonplace value-judgments: bitter sorrow is turned to glory, and extinction to eternal life. The form is strong and sure, the rhythm rapid and uniform; but the content is brilliant and ingenious in a most complex manner. The five-fold inversion is not brought about between unmistakable opposites in the archaic fashion: very often the things contrasted with each other differ rather in magnitude and degree.[30]

The clauses that follow continue the pattern of inversion in word and sense. The grave which has just been consecrated as an 'altar' now receives a 'monument' of glory, longer-lasting than a monument of stone or bronze could be (above p. 306f.); those who sleep in the grave are not dead men but 'the glory of Hellas': they are elevated thereby to the rank of protective heroes, like the mighty dead of mythical times, whose graves were at the same time shrines.[31] But it is not merely for the brave men of Thermopylae that Simonides proposes such honour, but for all those who died like 'good men'— the simple words *anêr agathos* were enough in that age to denote and to reward sacrifice of life for one's country. The general statement is then proved (not perfectly logically) by a reversion to the previous topic as an illustration.[32] No Greek could doubt that the memory of

[30] Τύχα, referring to death, ought to equal ἀτυχία, but the description of it as εὐκλεής elevates it to εὐτυχία. Πότμος, being unavoidable compulsion, cannot properly be the object of moral judgment (καλός); but the heroes of Thermopylae willingly drew their fate upon themselves. Τύχα as arbitrary chance and πότμος as necessity are not easily reconciled, but here they are parallel. 'Lamentation' over the loss and 'remembrance' of the departed are no more mutually exclusive than 'compassion' and 'praise'; but they figure here as opposites since they represent opposite states of mind.

[31] C. M. Bowra (*Greek Lyric Poetry*[2], 346) refers to the yearly sacrifice offered to those fallen at Plataeae, who were treated as heroes.

[32] This way of developing one's thought is archaic: cf. *Frühgr. Denken* 72–74; Leonhard Illig, *Zur Form der pindarischen Erzählung* (Berlin, 1932) 61; an early example is *Odyssey* 11, 425–9.

Leonidas the Heraclid would be imperishable: from this the poet concludes that anyone who died in the same way would have a like reward.

All the individual reinterpretations and inversions in this remarkable poem serve one single end. The naive way of regarding the facts—'The hard fate of the fallen and the sight of their grave give occasion for pity and lamentation'—is step by step corrected and replaced by another based on ethical and religious values: 'The heroism of the fallen and their altar enjoy everlasting glory and honour.' Physical death is transfigured into moral life, just as in the poem to Scopas on the nature of human greatness, physical defeat, if not associated with anything dishonourable, is elevated to moral victory (above p. 309–312). This is deeply and powerfully felt, and is startlingly new. The language and style of the two poems also show a victory, hitherto unheard-of, of the intellectual over the material. The thought is no longer tied to the picture and to the physical situation, as it had been before.[33] Emancipated from the clay, it soars upwards to a height from which it sees things stripped of their heavy earthliness, leaving only the bright colours of their true meaning. This eagle's view makes it possible to bring together into the picture things widely separated from each other; and in so free a flight through space the perspective can be chosen as the need or the wish arises. The sophistic movement is here foreshadowed—the sophistic movement which we may define as the emancipation of the intellect from any and every shackle laid upon it. The movement was to begin immediately after mid-century, when it would apply the methods of abstract thought, as they had been developed by speculative philosophers in explaining the physical universe, to questions of the practical conduct of life.

This inquiry into moral values and into the truly good life is associated with another question: 'What is happiness, and where should one look for it?' Two fragments (584, 604) give at least an inkling of the answer:

Without joy no kind of human life is desirable, no *tyrannis*; without it even the life of the gods is not enviable.

In an earlier time the haughty domination exercised by a tyrant had been reckoned the crown of human existence: it was all things in one, all that was great and lovely and enviable.[34] But Simonides is shrewd enough to realize that not everyone is made happy by his

---

[33] We may compare, for example, the expression of a somewhat similar thought in pseudo-Tyrtaeus fr. 9 (below p. 337–339). The elegy is certainly more abstract than the genuine poems of Tyrtaeus, but much less so than Simonides' Thermopylae ode.

[34] Cf. *Frühgriech. Denken* p. 67 n. 3.

good fortune: one must have happy and pleasurable sensations, otherwise the highest rewards of life are a hollow sham. He tells us further:

There is no *charis* (charm, pleasure) in beautiful *sophia* (wisdom, skill), if
one has not good health, that is worthy of honour.

The great respect accorded to good health here is very singular. For
Simonides 'health' is not a value purely of our lower, animal being;[35]
and it is characteristic in both pieces that he lays stress on the mutual
connexion of those elements which together make up the vital sum of
natural human good fortune. Certainly Simonides played his part,
if ever anyone did, in producing the Greek of classical times—
harmonious, healthy, with the tranquillity of deep and clear waters,
and with an earnest awareness of the boundaries of his being.

On Simonides' religious notions we have only an unsatisfactory
argumentum ex silentio. In the extant fragments no particular deity is
apprehended purely as a person. The gods whom he mentions by
name are all forces of life or nature, as Poseidon (576) and Boreas;
as the Muses, who 'with spotless cup draw the longed-for, love-
kindling water from the ambrosial deep' (577b); as Eros, whom he
calls the son of Ares and Aphrodite, because love and strife go together (575); as Zeus himself, whose name occurs once as a synonym
for the weather: 'When Zeus is reasonable in a winter month,' i.e.
when the weather is calm and mild in the middle of the winter (508).
For the rest, Simonides talks simply of 'god' and 'gods' in antithesis
to men. For absolute godhead he had a passionate reverence which
rejected all application of purely human standards: but he prudently
directed his creative activity towards man and his works. In politics
as well he could show what his experience was worth even at an
advanced age.

In 476, when over eighty, Simonides in a dedicatory epigram
(77D) referred to the victory gained in a choral competition by an
Athenian men's chorus with a song composed by him and under his
direction; and at about that time he could boast of fifty-six victories
in all with male choruses (79D). Shortly afterwards he left Athens
and went into the West to the powerful king Hiero of Syracuse. Here
he succeeded in acting as mediator between Hiero and the tyrant of
Acragas, who had taken the field against Syracuse, and in re-
establishing peace between them. He lived for about eight years in
Sicily, mostly at the court of Hiero, where Pindar and Simonides'
nephew, Bacchylides, also wrote. He died at Acragas in 468, almost
ninety years old.

[35] At the end of the poem to Scopas (542, 26) he summed up all attributes of
the normally good man in the one word 'a sound (healthy) man.'

The impact of Simonides on his own and succeeding generations must have been extraordinary, and was not produced by his poetry alone. His personality made a lasting impression, and in consequence a mass of anecdotes came to be spun about him, some friendly, some hostile. We hear of his almost miraculous powers of memory, of the dignity of his personal appearance, and of his great love of money. We can well believe that the clear-headed and realistic poet was equally realistic in turning his abilities to account. On the other hand, the adherents of older-fashioned ideals might have interpreted the sober moderation with which he deprecated overweening ambition as base materialism.[36] How true or false the anecdotes are, we cannot tell. Likewise we have no means of checking on the stories current about Simonides' relations with his younger competitor Pindar; and in the texts of the two poets men found reflexions of a supposed feud between them.[37] At all events it was not easy for two characters so widely different to have harmonious relations.

Viewed in terms of its function, the poetry of Simonides was occasional poetry: in terms of economics, it was a commodity bespoken and bought at a high price. His choral songs attended on the important stations of an individual's journey through life; they enhanced the brilliance of festivals and social gatherings; and their texts were disseminated in writing, like broadsides. But this description of externals does little more than touch the inner nature of the thing. The poetry of Simonides aimed at more than the adornment of life for a temporary pleasure: is set out to teach and to educate. 'Not from fragrant painted flowers, plucked in the dew-fresh meadow, do I twine fast-fading, fruitless garlands, but from the bitter thyme, like the subtle bee, I suck the sweet honey of my poetry.'[38] These are roughly Simonides' own words about himself.[39] Drop by drop from

[36] Such an interpretation was possible, cf. Pindar fr. 123, 5. A materialist element in Simonides' spiritual brother Xenophanes is indisputable, cf. fr. 2, 22.

[37] The interpretation put forward by the testimonium to Simonides fr. 602 does not square very well with the thought expressed in the two passages.

[38] Fr. 593. The negative expressions in Plutarch Moralia 41e: μιμεῖσθαι μή τούς στεφηπλόκους—συνείρουσι ἐφήμερον καὶ ἄκαρπον ἔργον—ἴων καὶ ῥόδων καὶ ὑακίνθων λειμῶνας, and 79c: ἄνθεσιν—χρόαν καὶ ὀσμήν, probably come from Simonides: witness their recurrence in a parallel passage in Pindar (Nem. 7, 77f.: εἴρειν στεφάνους ἐλαφρόν—λείριον ἄνθεμον—ἔερσας); the wording of Plutarch 494a suggests that σοφήν also is a quotation. Thus here again a curiously sketchy passage in Pindar can be understood as an allusion to a well-known passage of Simonides.

[39] The bee-simile by which he characterizes his own poetry was taken over by Horace in the ode in which he declines to celebrate Augustus in Pindaric strains (4, 2, 29-32, cf. E. Fraenkel, Horace, Oxford, 1957, p. 435, n. 1). Thus Horace felt himself not to be a Roman Pindar, but perhaps something like a Roman Simonides.

[Footnote continued on page 324.]

experience and reflection he distilled the full load of thought which gives such a close concentrated texture to his poems. In one place, speaking in the maturity of his manhood, he uses a different image to reject the loud claims of youth to know better (602): 'The new wine does not quarrel with the gift of last year's vines: this is but the chatter of children.'[40]

Simonides in his poetry is more decidedly and directly a reformer than any other Greek lyrist. A new orientation was necessary if men were to escape from inert oscillation between polar opposites. Lines of thought which led nowhere had to be broken off and replaced by others more practical. The older methods of public education by poetry were inadequate to accomplish such a revolution. Unlike the earlier poets, who put their doctrines before the public in a confident and magisterial manner, as if they were laying down laws, Simonides is lively, critical, contentious, always ready to argue. Dicta of the old sages, brash assertions of the young, all are grist to the mill of his ready dialectic. He examines, approves or rejects, gives the question a new turn, seeks and finds. Just as (in his metaphor) the very sight of the highest human excellence can only be gained by a hard climb demanding toil and sweat, so our powers of mind and understanding must be exerted prudently and skilfully, honestly and accurately if we are to come in sight of our goal and learn how we ought to live. In this way he broke free of the archaic feeling of helplessness and abandonment. He also put an end to a sublime sleep-walking confidence in intuitive thoughts and actions: no longer did men accept what offered itself; they exercised discretion and choice, and justified their choice.

The parallel between Horace and Simonides is in many ways instructive, and deserves the more consideration if Horace himself felt it.

[40] For a similar turn of phrase in rejecting someone else's view cf. fr. 581, 6 (above p. 306).

VII

Philosophy and Empirical Science at the end of the Archaic Period

---

(a) *Xenophanes*

The same tendencies which appear in Simonides are found also in a kindred spirit in a different field—the rhapsode, philosopher and theologian Xenophanes.[1] The lives of the two very nearly coincide: Simonides lived approximately from 557 to 468, Xenophanes roughly from 570 to 475. Like Simonides, Xenophanes was an apostle of enlightenment, directing an incisive criticism against rooted prejudices; they both fought for a rational ordering of values and for a practical code of ethics; both emphasized the relativity of all things human, and contrasted it with the absoluteness of god.

Xenophanes also was an Ionian. He was born in Colophon in Asia Minor, the birthplace of Mimnermus, and he was an exile from the age of twenty-five, after the satrap Harpagus had conquered the Greek settlements in Asia for his master Cyrus, king of the Medes and Persians. Thenceforward he led an unsettled and wandering life as a singer, earning his bread by his talents. He says of himself (8):

Seven and sixty years are gone with their summers and winters, driving my thinking head this way and that in Greece. Twenty years had I lived and five years more when it started, if it is in my power rightly to reckon it up.

Clearly Xenophanes was very proud of his ninety or more years. In another fragment we read (22):

---

[1] We know nothing of personal relations between them; but in one of his poems Xenophanes is said to have referred to Simonides as a skinflint (*Vorsokr.* 21 Xenophanes B 21).

These things one should say by the fire, in the season of winter, resting at ease upon one's couch when dinner is over, sipping the honied wine and munching chick-peas: 'Pray, who are you, and where do you come from? How old are you, comrade? Tell me how old were you then, when the Medes came into our country?'

In the established manner of the rhapsodes, the narrative was to be set going by questions (p. 12–14); and Xenophanes prescribes some questions which will give him another opportunity to speak of his great age and of his wanderings in the far-off days of his youth.[2] The weary exile at last found a new home in the Western colonies, perhaps at Elea, a recent Ionian settlement in Southern Italy (see above p. 271).

The evening drinking-circle had always been among the Greeks the setting of cultivated intellectual companionship, of cheerful or reflective conversation or poetry. Odysseus, when he prepares (*Od.* 9, 5–10) to entertain the company 'like a well-skilled singer' (11, 368), begins with an elaborate encomium upon the festal occasion; and Xenophanes does the same thing in the longest of his fragments (1):

Now is the floor swept clean, and clean are the hands of the diners; spotless the cups: chaplets of flowers are laid on our heads, myrrh with its subtle scent is handed to each by a servant. There stands the bowl of wine, full to the brim with delight; yet more wine in reserve (the store can never be exhausted), flower-perfumed and sweet, waits in its pitcher of clay. Heavenly savours arise from the incense smoking before us; cool is the water to drink, sweet, translucent and pure. White loaves lie there before us: the generous welcoming tables groan with their burden of cheese: thyme-scented honey is nigh; there in the midst is the altar, covered everywhere with flowers; all about the hall is filled with friendship and music and joy.

These introductory verses, in the archaic objective manner, do not depict the pleasurable feeling of the guests, but list instead all the physical objects which give rise to those feelings. The rule is violated in only one effective instance, where 'delight' is put instead of 'wine.' A great stress is laid on cleanliness: after dinner the floor was swept clean and hands washed; the cups and drinking water are spotlessly pure, and the air is cleansed and sanctified by incense. This aware-

---

[2] The parallelism of the two fragments leads us to conclude that Xenophanes left his home upon the Persian invasion. That was an important historical event, and thus gives a firm point of reference for the reckoning in fr. 8. But the poet knew the date of his birth only approximately (8, 4), which is not uncommon for Greeks now as then.

ness of physical cleanliness paves the way for the notion of spiritual purity which appears in the following verses:

Men of good will should first of all praise god in their singing, praise him with reverent tales and with pure speech, pouring the due libation and praying that they may be granted power to do right, for that we should desire above all. Then it is no presumption to drink as much as lets each man, saving the greybeards, go safe to his dwelling alone. Him should we praise among men, who, speaking of things that are noble, shows his concern for worth (*aretê*), and proves his memory's strength: not by talking of battles, by fables of Giants and Titans or of Centaurs—tales bred by men's folly of old—stories of bloody strife, which do no good in the hearing. All a man does should have the good for its goal.[3]

The externals in this piece follow the usual pattern;[4] libations, hymns and prayers open the proceedings, and then each man makes his own contribution to entertaining and amusing the others. But some of the details are unusual. According to Xenophanes one should not ask the gods for protection and help, for success and prosperity, but should pray that one's own efforts may meet with success if—and only if—they aim at a virtuous purpose.[5] The prayer has some resemblance to an oath—'So help me God as I am

[3] In v. 19 ἐσθλὰ πιών is impossible on several grounds: the word-order is wrong; Hermann's law is violated; ἀναφαίνει has two objects, ἐσθλά and the substantival clause. Transposition of the ι (=ει) gives ἔσθλ(α) εἰπών. In v. 24 θεῶν προμηθείην ἔχειν could only mean 'have consideration for the well-being of the gods' (in Herod. 1, 88 προμηθίη is 'thoughtful consideration'); and this is nonsense. I propose: χρεὼν δὲ προμηθείην αἰὲν ἔχειν ἀγαθήν (ἀγαθήν is the ms. reading) = 'one should always have a good purpose before one's eyes' (poetry should not only *delectare*, but also *prodesse*).

[4] See the references given by C. M. Bowra, *Class. Philol.* 33 (1938) 353ff., = *Problems in Greek Poetry* (Oxford, 1953) 1ff. A close parallel is Theognis 760–767 (where the injunction not to talk of war is meant for the particular occasion). Cf. also Theognis 765: ὧδ' εἴη κεν ἄμεινον, which helps us to understand v. 16 ταῦτα γὰρ ὧν ἐστι προχειρότερον, cf. the translation given above. Προχειρότερον (a polar comparative?) reminds us of the Homeric ἐπ' ὀνείαθ' ἑτοῖμα προκείμενα χεῖρας ἴαλλον; what 'lay to hand' is described in vv. 1–12. The idea underlying vv. 13–24 is a more general one: ὅσια δρῶν εὔφραινε θυμόν (Bacchylides 3, 83), or δίκαιος ἐὼν τὴν σαυτοῦ φρένα τέρπε (Theognis 794f.); that is to say, 'If one behaves piously (here=sings a hymn) and righteously (here=prays for righteousness), there is nothing wrong in enjoying harmless pleasures (οὐχ ὕβρις πίνειν ὁπόσον etc.)'. Compare the converse in Solon fr. 3, 7–10 (above p. 220f.): ἄδικος νόος—ὕβριος ἐκ—οὐκ ἐπίστανται παρούσας (cf. προχειρότ ερον) εὐφροσύνας (cf. μεστὸς εὐφροσύνης in verse 4) κοσμεῖν δαιτὸς ἐν ἡσυχίῃ. Cf. also Ion of Chios (ap. Athen. 10, 447f.).

[5] On πρήσσειν, 'accomplish, realise' see B. Snell, *Aischylos und das Handeln im Drama* (Leipzig, 1928), 10ff., 17f. Parallels to τὰ δίκαια δύνασθαι πρήσσειν:—Theognis 1027f. (above p. 310 n. 18)—'the πρῆξις (or παλάμη) τοῦ ἀγαθοῦ is hard'; and the definition of *aretê* as ἔρως καλῶν καὶ δύνασθαι (above p. 308 n. 9 and below p. 418). But while the others use the ambiguous notion of the ἀγαθόν or καλόν, Xenophanes speaks of the δίκαιον.

righteous.' What Xenophanes has to say next on the choice of themes for recitation reminds us of Plato's strictures on poetry.[6] He would like to see a great many of the old myths excluded, as being mere inventions of our fore-fathers. Thus at one stroke he consigns to the rubbish-heap the whole tradition on which the art of his fellow-rhapsodes had been based from the very beginning. The antiquity of a belief, for him, did not confer authority on it, but rather the reverse: what had been worked out long before would no longer satisfy a progressive mind. A further objection to conventional recitations is that such poems as the *Iliad* and *Theogony* deal with war and conflict, and these themes are not 'useful.' It is a pity that the fragment breaks off here: the positive recommendations which followed have not been preserved.

In the verses of the practical and down-to-earth Xenophanes we find again and again criticism of 'useless' things. He attacks the extravagant ostentation with which the ruling citizens of Colophon (the Thousand, as they were called), used to dress themselves up for meetings of the general assembly (3):

While they as yet stood free from the hated yoke of the tyrant, off to the council they went, proud in their purple attire. They were tricked out in useless finery picked up from their Lydian neighbours, numbering, all in all, just one thousand men, pleased with themselves, and peacock-proud of elaborate hair-styles, every inch of their skin wet with the costliest scent.

Here we see before our eyes the 'head-adorning' Ionians, with the long hair that marked the citizen with full voting rights. Since Homeric times it had been customary to give a baroque weight and fullness to one's person by elaborate finery, especially where the head was concerned. This artificial pomp was only heightened by the refinement of the late archaic age and of the Lydian kingdom. But now the classical period was approaching, when the taut and well-knit forms of nature were to find favour again and short hair was to become normal for men. Xenophanes is already rejecting the old fashion, but not so much through a purer taste[7] as on a principle of rational economy.

His criticism of conventional schemes of value cuts deeper when he questions the importance which men then attached to the national

---

[6] Cf. *Republic* bk. 3; *Theaetetus* 175e 7 etc. Xenophanes' reference to memory in v. 20 indicates that guests who were unable to make up their own, recited passages of other men's poetry.

[7] This fragment is our oldest example of a notion afterwards commonplace— purple and perfume are condemned as perversions of pure wool and oil respectively: cf. *Frühgr. Denken* p. 242, n. 1.

athletic contests. A particular target was the granting of official distinctions to the successful competitors (2):

> If any man is the winner by fleetness of foot in the races,
>> Or gains the pentathlon, where the enclosure of Zeus
> Lies beside Pisa's bank in Olympia; if he in wrestling
>> Or in that painful skill, boxing, defeats his rival,
> Or wins the pancration, most dreadful species of conflict;
>> Fame and renown are his—worth in the citizens' eyes;
> His is the foremost place in times of public rejoicing
>> His are the meat and drink lavished at public expense,
> Yes, and good cash besides, paid out from the purse of the city.
>> Or if his horses come first, still his reward is the same,
> Though he is not my equal in worth: for the wisdom (*sophia*) that I have
>> Far excels all strength either of man or of horse.
> Wilful folly is this and great injustice, to value
>> Fleetness of foot and strength higher than wisdom and sense.
> Grant there be one in the city of wondrous skill as a boxer,
>> One who excels in wrestling, or in a mixture of both,
> Or comes first in the footrace (for this is reckoned the highest
>> In men's trials of strength, and the most honoured of all):
> Yet are the city's affairs run none the better for all that,
>> Nor does it have much joy out of a man of this sort;
> Though he may win great fame in many Olympian contests,
>> Never a penny he brings into the coffers of state.

The circumstantial but effective manner of writing is typically archaic. Xenophanes does not deal in general notions like 'athletic performances' or 'the honouring of athletes': he takes his reader through a great part of the programme of the Olympic games in their actual sequence, and lists all the various rewards of the victors, before plunging into general concepts and developing his criticism; and the justifying arguments deal another blow at the enthusiasts for games. But the long-drawn-out sentences are far from the archaic style, and another modern feature is the expression εἰκῆ νομίζεται, 'wilful folly,' with which Xenophanes brands the opposite view to his. The sophists who fought for reason in human affairs in the later fifth century thought of themselves as the champions of natural order against the artificial, accidental or wilful 'statutes' (νόμοι) issued by human societies. To the sober and practical Xenophanes the honour acquired by a community from the sporting victory of one of its members appeared a mere fiction;[8] to him good order (*eunomia*, 'well-lawedness') and prosperity are the only real goods. For his own

---

[8] Xenophanes was not alone among his contemporaries in condemning the overestimation of athletics: an equally critical attitude is expressed in a remarkable elegy which we shall shortly study (p. 337–39).

skill or wisdom (*sophia*) he clearly claims the ability to improve laws and manners and to increase the prosperity of the community.

What we have seen of Xenophanes stamps him as a utilitarian. He values only those activities which contribute to good order and prosperity in the community. Personal displays he condemns as useless luxury; the national games, so highly valued in his day he reckons as a wilfully stupid pastime; the national mythology he rejects as fabulous and injurious to morals. His prayer, to be able to perform what is righteous, fits in with this utilitarian philosophy, since righteousness, according to Simonides (above p. 310f.), benefits the community. But there is nothing homespun about his theological views. His search for moral purity and intellectual precision drove him to purge religion also of preconception and prejudice, and he was led by way of unsparing criticism to become an apostle of monotheism.

We saw earlier that the divine personages of Homer, lawless to the point of outrage, and the sombre apocalyptic myths of Hesiod will not satisfy even the least demanding of moralists (p. 53f. and 97). This difficulty provides Xenophanes with a starting point for the rejection of traditional religion (fr. 11):

All those acts which among us men are wicked and shameful Homer and Hesiod lay to the charge of the blessed immortals—stealing and lying and wenching and each one cheating the other.

This is as forthright as it can be, but it is only a beginning. Xenophanes is not content simply to reject: he exposes thoroughly and methodically the anthropomorphic fallacy that makes such errors possible (14):

We men suppose that gods were born, like us, dress themselves just like men, and look and talk as a man does.

To Xenophanes this seems primitive and barbaric, and he therefore neglects the distinction between Greek and barbarian, and points out that all men imagine the gods after their own likeness: the negro sees his gods as black and snub-nosed; the Thracian has blue-eyed gods with red hair (16). Finally, to render the anthropomorphic view wholly ridiculous, he crosses even the boundary between man and beast (15):

Now suppose oxen had hands like ours, suppose that a lion knew how to work with his hands and carve out statues as we do: horses would make their gods like horses, oxen like oxen, giving the self-same shape in which they themselves had been moulded.

The imaginary example shows, with Greek wit and by the

peculiarly Greek device of an experiment in thought, exactly where the mistake lies. Human qualities are assigned to god, and god is thereby dragged down to an earthly level and made subject to change and multiplicity. In some instances gods are depressed even below the human level: the worshippers of Bacchus plant little cuttings of spruce in a circle round a building and honour them as embodiments of the god under the name of *bacchoi* (17).[9]

In opposition to such views Xenophanes puts in a single word his contention that god is one, and that he is not in the least like us:

One god—greatest of all in the world of gods and of mortals, resembling man neither in mind nor in outward appearing.

The one true god is far above the many anthropomorphic gods of traditional belief, just as he is far above human beings: compared with him, men and the so-called gods shrink into equal insignificance.[10] The dividing line between him and all else cannot be too sharply drawn. He has to be one, because the existence of others at his level would make him restricted and specialised; in the same way he has no limitation or specialisation within himself (24):

He sees as a whole and hears as a whole, and thinks with his whole self.

For 'thinks' one could as well put 'perceives' or 'wills': the Greek νοεῖ embraces all three meanings. The expressions 'sees' and 'hears' are not to be taken literally: it is the usual story of words being inadequate to describe the absolute nature of divinity. But it is hardly accidental that Xenophanes should speak of sight and hearing, but not of feeling, smell and taste, the senses involving bodily contact. God, even in his actions, is independent of bodily contact: he operates through his spirit only (to put it in modern terms) from somewhere outside space upon this spatial world (26/25):

Dwelling in one place ever, he is exempt from all movement; for it would not be fitting for him to go from one place to another. No: unmoved he accomplishes all by the will of his spirit.[11]

[9] This cult-practice is attested also by Hesychius 127 and probably Eurip. *Bacch.* 109.

[10] It is a little difficult that the one god should be 'greatest among the gods'. I have suggested a solution in the paraphrase. The words ἐν ... ἀνθρώποισι, coupled together with τε-καί, can only refer to the false notions of deity by which the gods are thought of as superior human beings: thus 'gods' means 'the gods of popular superstition.'

[11] The double expression νόου φρενί seems to have been chosen in order to exclude any taint of materiality: 'with the mind of his mind.' Κραδαίνω is a poetical word of rather vague meaning, since the nature and manner of God's operation upon the world cannot be closely defined.

The force of this expression becomes apparent if we remember that in Greek philosophy the word 'movement' included all forms of change. Hence in god's sphere no physical event takes place: it is only when his effortless will impinges on our world that it is translated into movement and event. In exerting his will he is the spirtual source of all that happens; in 'hearing and seeing' he is aware of all that happens; but he himself never moves.

This line of thought, beginning with an attack on anthropomorphism, led Xenophanes naturally enough to monotheism, and thence to an idea of god transcending all human conception. The final result was hardly calculated to be popular.[12] Scarcely anyone seems to have accompanied the bold speculator even halfway on his long road: his one god found no worshippers.

There was some foreshadowing of monotheism among the Greeks at least from Homer's time. The higher intellectual levels represented in the literary monuments could always see beyond the diversity of gods and form a notion of the divine in its generality: to such a notion they attached the name of 'the gods', 'god', or 'Zeus';[13] at a later period τὸ θεῖον, 'the divine' was also current. On the other hand, it seemed obvious enough that many different divine powers were at work in nature and in the individual human life, and that very often such powers might be in conflict one with another. In general men were content to leave this state of affairs unexplained.[14] From Homer until the end of paganism monotheism and polytheism were not mutually exclusive opposites, and the problem of the one or the many aroused little interest. Xenophanes was an exception, and one consequence of this was that his militant monotheism produced virtually no effect.

The idea of the absoluteness of god brought in its train the clear recognition that our world was conditioned and limited. Simonides laid equal stress on both sides, and Xenophanes also drew the sharpest of distinctions. But in exposing the folly of anthropomorphism and in demonstrating the relativity of earthly values he uses the same highly original approach. In a modernized form his argument may be represented thus. Suppose that we were negroes or horses: then we should consider not the white man, but the negro or the horse as a

[12] But a philosopher of Aristotle's eminence adopted the notion of the unmoved mover; and the doctrine of Anaxagoras, νοῦς (πάντα?) κινεῖ, parallels Xenophanes' statement, θεὸς νόου φρενὶ πάντα κραδαίνει. The sophist Antisthenes taught κατὰ νόμον εἶναι πολλοὺς θεούς, κατὰ δὲ φύσιν ἕνα (Diels, *Doxographi Graeci* 538, 9).

[13] References in G. F. Else, *God and Gods in Early Greek Thought*, Trans. Amer. Philol. Assn. 80 (1949) p. 24–36.

[14] We saw above (p. 250 n. 5) that it was not for a long time yet that the Greeks had any feeling for theology.

creature if not perfect, then approximating to perfection.[15] Our ideal would then be a lower one, and we should honour as divine that which we now despise, since the untutored intelligence establishes norms according to its accidental experience: on a smaller scale the same dimension assumes a greater significance. Now for the Greeks, who knew of nothing sweeter than honey, honey seemed the very essence of sweetness. Xenophanes accordingly proposes another of his acute mental experiments (38):

Let us suppose that god had never created honey: then we should think that figs were very much sweeter . . .

sweeter, that is, than we do now. It follows that men do not have knowledge of sweetness in itself, but only of more sweet or less sweet.[16] Thus those pure qualities with which Greek thought constantly operated, are removed from the realm of experience.

It was the strength of the Greeks that they always tried to penetrate into the nature of things, and their corresponding weakness that they neglected the quantitative aspect of measure and degree. They speculated on 'the' hot and 'the' cold, but they never troubled themselves to determine how hot or how cold a given body was at a given moment. The achievements of civilization were seen by them in equally absolute terms. They looked upon any discovery as a unitary whole, as basically complete in itself. So, for example, agriculture was regarded simply as a thing given, a unit, which was expressed mythologically in the story that the goddess Demeter taught men how to till the fields. But Xenophanes has a penetrating correction to make (18):

Man is not taught by the gods to know things whole from the outset; little by little advances are made with time and with trouble.

We did not receive 'civilization' as a gift from the gods (cf. Eurip. *Suppl.* 201–15): rather, we are always engaged in seeking a higher civilization. Xenophanes was one of the few men in antiquity who believed in steady progress. It must have been this belief that fed his reforming zeal and gave him that bold confidence with which he championed his unconventional ideas.

In one respect Xenophanes entangled himself in the web of his own principles. Just as he freed his god from the fetters of worldliness

[15] A similar notion occurs in the comic poet Epicharmus (fr. 3 Diels): just as men find pleasure in creatures of their own similitude, so do dogs and asses, oxen and swine, each reckoning its like as the most beautiful object in creation.

[16] In the same vein Simonides said that only god was good, men being more or less good.

and raised him to a sublimity beyond perception, so he purged the physical world of all traces of godhead and rationalized it into a wretched simplicity. Those two elements that are nearest to us, the earth that we tread and the air that we breathe, for him compose the whole: there is nothing above the air, nothing below the earth (28):

Here, at our feet, we can see the broad earth's uppermost surface, meeting the air up here, but below it touches the boundless.

He probably took air to be a rarefied form of water, since he says (29):

Earth and water are all that ever arose and developed.

Apparently Xenophanes is adopting again the primitive notion expressed by Semonides of Amorgos concerning the interplay of the passive element earth and the active element water. Earth and sea, according to Xenophanes, are in perpetual interchange. From fossils found in various places he drew the inference that what was now dry land had once been water and mud. Hence he came to the conclusion that the sea periodically inundated the earth and all things on it, and that living forms periodically built themselves up from earth and water. He invoked water also to explain the phenomena commonly assigned to the heavens: in fact he denied the existence of the heavens. Wind and rain, he thought, come from the sea; clouds, rainbows, lightning, St. Elmo's fire, all come from vapours arising from the sea; even the sun and stars are formed anew each day from rising vapours. The paths of the sun and moon he considered as being so close to the earth that he postulated different suns and moons for the different zones.

This is an extraordinary cosmology, daring and poverty-stricken at once. Apart from a strong empirical tendency, which is shewn in the logical, if too general, conclusions drawn from fossils, it is forced and unconvincing. Our world had to be made as near, as present, as commonplace and unmysterious as it could, in contrast to god. Everything is explained on the basis of everyday experience, and every effort is made to prevent any considerable widening of our ideas concerning the world about us. Thus Xenophanes came to the dull conclusion that the sun was useful in the origin and sustenance of the world and its living creatures, but the moon was superfluous (A42). Clearly the sight of the celestial bodies awakened in him no edifying sense of wonder; just as he criticized the 'useless' festal attire of the burghers of Colophon, so he saw in the sublime nocturnal luminary only a piece of self-indulgence on Nature's part. For Xenophanes it behoved the universe to be strictly practical.

The postulate that god was of a different order of being from the things of our world drew with it the consequence that the nexus between god and the world was incapable of definition. All that Xenophanes knew was that god moved all things with consciousness and volition, while he himself was exempt from all happenings. On further details he committed nothing to writing, as we are credibly informed: when he spoke of unity and completeness, it was in reference to god, not to the world.[18] He was more a theologian than a metaphysician; and even as a theologian he was very little inclined to sit and brood over the inconceivable nature and workings of god.

He was, after all, a staunch empiricist at the same time, as we can see from those verses with which his didactic poem began. He there answers the question how far his contentions can be proved in the following way (34):

Certainly no man has clearly seen it, nor will there ever be one who has eye-witness knowledge concerning the gods and (concerning) what I say on each and every matter; since even if one should be so fortunate as to make a true (statement about things beyond the senses), this would be without a knowledge based on observation;[19] all (that I shall put forward in what follows) is based upon acceptable inference. (God, on the contrary, has immediate observational knowledge of all things.)[20]

[18] Cf. A 31 (and above p. 259, n. 17). The valuable remark of Theophrastus, which has received too little attention, shows quite clearly, first that the doctrine of the unity of all things was not put forward by Xenophanes; secondly, that it was attributed to him by a deliberate manipulation of his teachings. This knowledge eliminates at once many of the statements made by the doxographers on Xenophanes' supposed cosmological views. Cf. also A 30, where the looking upward to heaven is probably an Aristotelian interpolation; see W. Jaeger, *Journ. of Rel.* 18 (1938) 133. Thus when Plato (A 29) and others attribute this monistic doctrine to the entire Eleatic school from Xenophanes onwards, 'and even before him,' it is an anachronistic back-projection.

[19] On (αὐτὸς or ἐγὼ) οἶδα in the sense 'I know by observation (either my own or credibly reported)' cf. *Frühgriech. Denken*, ed. 2, p. 345; also above, p. 19, n. 26, and Heinrich Stein on Herodotus 1, 20, 1.

[20] The last sentence is not preserved in the original. For the overall interpretation of the fragment cf. *Frühgriech. Denken*, ed. 2, 342–349. Further parallels are (for τὸ σαφές = accuracy and trustworthiness resting on eyewitness knowledge) Aeschylus, *Seven* 40 ἥκω σαφῆ τὰκεῖθεν . . . φέρων, αὐτὸς κατόπτης δ' εἴμ' ἐγὼ τῶν πραγμάτων; (for εἰ τύχοι . . . οὐκ οἶδε, and the negated τὸ σαφὲς εἰδώς) the end of the first chapter of the introduction to περὶ ἀρχαίης ἰητρικῆς: ἃ (scil. τὰ ἀφανέα καὶ ἀπορεόμενα) εἴ τις λέγοι καὶ γινώσκοι ὡς ἔχει, οὔτ' ἂν αὐτῷ τῷ λέγοντι οὔτε τοῖς ἀκούουσι δῆλα ἂν εἴη εἴτε ἀληθέσ ἐστιν εἴτε μή, οὐ γάρ ἐστι πρὸς ὅ τι χρὴ ἀνενέγκαντα εἰδέναι τὸ σαφές; (for 'where the gods are concerned, we can only go on δόκος, not on τὸ σαφές') Thuc. 5, 105, 2 ἡγούμεθα γὰρ τό τε θεῖον δόξῃ, τὸ ἀνθρώπειον δὲ σαφῶς; (for εἰ τύχοι τετελεσμένον εἰπών . . . δόκος δ' ἐπὶ πᾶσι τέτυκται) Plato *Symp.* 202a (condensed) τὸ τοῦ ὄντος τυγχάνειν (ἄνευ τοῦ ἔχειν λόγον δοῦναι) οὐκ ἐπιστήμη ἐστιν ἀλλ' ὀρθὴ δόξα.

Xenophanes, of course, was convinced that he had been fortunate enough to hit upon the truth with the theories that he advanced (34, 3). But he was well aware that only a part of his doctrine rested upon observed facts, since for mere mortals the limits of what they can observe are tightly drawn. For everything beyond those limits 'plausibility' (δόκος) had to suffice. He therefore distinguished between the percepts of the senses (cf. fr. 36: 'All the things which show themselves visibly to mortal eyes'), which he takes unquestioningly as certain, and that which is merely inferred or surmised. The last can at best be merely probable; and thus we find in Xenophanes for the first time a clear explanation of 'probable' or 'plausible' (35).

Let these things be assumed, which look like those that are certain.[21]

Hitherto thought had operated intuitively, seeing the phenomena in the light of an interpretation decided on beforehand: now, however, a methodical distinction was made between observation and speculative assumption. At the same time different degrees of knowledge were recognized: there were some unqualified statements, and others with a limited claim to validity. The word used for knowing by experience is (w)eidenai (cognate with English witness, German wissen), which literally signifies the position in which a man is placed through having seen—'witnesshood,' as it were. This word, with its derivatives historein, 'to hear witness,' historiê, 'hearing of witness,' 'establishment of facts' at once took a leading place in a new empiricism in the fields of medicine, geography and history.

The pious desire of Xenophanes to free god from earthliness led him to banish god from the world. In return he emptied our world of all transcendent qualities, and thus opened the door to the empirical approach.[22] His new critique of intellection was important not only for what it excluded and rejected, but even more for what it included and adopted. With this deliberate and conscious limitation,

---

[21] δεδοξάσθω in 35 is parallel to δόκος in 34, 4, and δόκος, δοκεῖν, δόκιμος etc. are derived from δέκεσθαι 'to accept'; cf. Hecataeus fr. 1: τάδε γράφω ὡς μοι δοκεῖ ἀληθέα εἶναι (A. Rivier, Revue de philol. 30, 1956, p. 48f.). Hence δόκος implies here a positive probability. The negative notion of something that seems true but is not, appears as early as Hesiod Theog. 27.

[22] A chain of accidents brought it about that Xenophanes was regarded in late antiquity, paradoxically enough, as the founder of scepticism. Not long after his time the verb eidenai lost its restriction to knowledge by observation (cf. Parm. 1, 3; 6, 4). It now seemed as if Xenophanes in fr. 34 was casting doubt on all knowledge, and the last two lines must have been misunderstood as follows: 'Even if someone should chance to say the truth, he does not know (that he speaks truth); all (so-called knowledge) is pure supposition' (thus Sextus Empricus Adv. math. 7, 49–52; but in 7, 110 the fragment is rightly understood, 'in the way it is interpreted from another viewpoint').

within which a new kind of mastery could be developed, we are leaving the archaic world and taking the path to classical Hellenism.

INTERLUDE: AN ELEGY ('TYRTAEUS' FR. 9) ON THE NATURE OF VIRTUE

In fr. 2 (above p. 329f.) Xenophanes ridiculed the exaggerated importance attached to athletics. The high esteem in which success at games was then held was based on an attitude which we know from Pindar. On that theory *aretê*, 'goodness,' i.e. excellence or manly worth, was considered not as the sum total of various desirable attributes, but as an ideal indivisible unity; from time to time it showed one or other of its sides and thereby showed itself (cf. Solon 19, 8?). Thus a victory in the games was regarded not as an achievement of technique in one particular branch, but as a valid proof of general *aretê*, sealed by the blessing of the gods, without which no achievement could be successful. Similarly power and riches or the grace of a youthful body were considered as unquestionable proofs of *aretê*, since one and the same radiance was shed by them all upon the admiring beholder.[1]

The author of an interesting elegy which has come down to us under the name of Tyrtaeus, but which probably belongs to the time of Xenophanes,[1a] saw the danger of exaggerating the evidential value of such achievements and of taking this or that individual virtue as if it were all in all:

I would not talk of a man or value him for the virtue (*aretê*) of his feet or his skill in wrestling, even if he had the strength and size of a Cyclops, and ran more swiftly than the Thracian north wind; (5) if he were more handsome in form than Tithonus, richer than Midas or Cinyras; if he were more regal than Pelops the Tantalid and had the persuasive eloquence of Adrastus:[2] (9) or if he had all fame except that of warlike prowess. For a

[1] In Plato's dialogues the question is often raised whether *aretê* (the word is commonly but very unsatisfactorily translated as 'virtue') is a unity or a multiplicity of individual qualities: if the latter were true, then a man could possess one of the qualities without the others. Nowadays we pose the question whether the 'greatness' of a distinguished individual is confined to the field of his greatest achievement, or whether we can take him as a model in other departments of life also.

[1a] However, for a defence of this poem as a genuine work of Tyrtaeus cf. W. Jaeger, *Sitzungsber. Preuss. Akad.* 23 (1932) 537ff.=*Scripta Minora* II. 75ff.=*Five Essays* 103ff.

[2] The writer concerns himself with conspicuous talents and striking abilities; the humbler virtue of moral rectitude, which was later seen as the essence of *aretê*, is not mentioned. Correspondingly, the reward of *aretê* (27–42) consists predominantly in honours and distinctions.

man does not become (i.e. does not show himself) good in war unless he
is able to gaze upon bloody death and longs to stand face to face with his
foe. (13) This is manly worth (*aretê*); this is the prize[3] that is best among
men; this is finest for a young man to win. This is a credit to the city and the
whole people, when a man stands astride in the front line unflinchingly, (17)
with no thought of shameful flight, when he sets his soul and his enduring
will as the gage, and has a heartening word for the comrade standing
beside him. Such a man becomes (shows himself) good in war. (21) Quickly
he puts to flight the savage phalanxes of the enemy and breaks the wave
of battle by his valour. He who falls in the front line and loses his life,
bringing credit to his city, his people and his father, (25) who is pierced with
many a wound in his breast through his cuirass and heavy studded shield
—such a man is lamented alike by young and old, and the city mourns for
him in lasting grief. (29) As his grave is distinguished, so are his children and
his children's children and his whole line; never is his name and fame
brought to nothingness; though he is under the ground, yet is he immortal
(33) who, distinguishing himself in standing and fighting for country and
children, is killed in cruel war. But if he escapes the fate of cruel death and
encompasses the glorious victory of his spear, then all honour him alike,
both young and old, and he has many joys before he descends to Hades.[4]
When he grows old, he is distinguished among his people; no one thinks of
impairing his dignity or his rights: (41) all alike, the young and those of his
own age, make room for him upon the benches—even his elders. To such
a height of worth (*aretê*) should a man aspire by never faltering in his
valour for war.

The elegist, like Xenophanes, vigorously controverts the devotion to
athletics, but he follows a very different line. He has no notion of
claiming a leading role for the intellect, and he cares little for
skill in words: *aretê* for him is most fully realized in courage shown in
battle. He does not start by proving the axiom that prowess in war is
the highest virtue, but he takes it as a self-evident basis for his arguments in v. 9 and following. What he is concerned to prove is that
no other quality can guarantee that a man will acquit himself well
in battle.[5] Not in play, not on the arena, but only in deadly earnest on
the battle-field does true worth prove itself. The poet's sole concern is
moral achievement. Unlike Tyrtaeus, he does not draw an animated
battle-picture complete with technical details: it is warlike spirit that
forms his constant theme, together with the situation in which
determined courage can evince itself (11–19).[6] Such achievement as

---

[3] The word *athlon* makes one think of the competitive games.

[4] Only here and in v. 40 ('rights') are practical benefits referred to. The content
of v. 38 comes from the seventh century, see above p. 139 with n. 18.

[5] ἀλκή (v. 9) denotes not physical strength, but martial spirit and achievement.

[6] Apart from the concentration on the spiritual side (διαβάς in v. 16 is the only
exception) the recent date of the elegy shows itself in some other features. The poet

this is of great value for the whole citizen body, since it leads to success in attack or defence (15; 21–22).[7] The second half of the poem sets out the advantages which accrue to the brave man himself from his actions, whether he falls or survives. The closing distich contains an admonition to strive for the highest form of *aretê* with fierce determination (*thymos*, cf. *Iliad* 5, 135 and its context).[8]

(b) *The Beginnings of the Empirical Sciences: Medicine, Geography and History*

As a practical philosopher, Xenophanes showed a happy knack of illustrating abstract ideas with cleverly devised examples from the real world. Like Socrates later, he made great play with the various races of men and animals, with the taste of honey and of figs. His speculations were supported by instructive imaginary examples from the sensible world; and he gives us clearly to understand that our theoretical knowledge can never be more than an airy superstructure over a basis of trustworthy perception. The empiricism thus displayed is undoubtedly connected with the rise of the empirical sciences which began in the early years of the fifth century. The national penchant for constructing general theories did not, of course, cease to operate; but it was now united with a readiness to take into

is not combating cowardice and indifference, as Tyrtaeus was, but rather a false theory of *aretê*—a theory which could hardly have been current during the Messenian War, but which is obvious in almost everything that Pindar ever wrote. Also, there is no direct address, no 'you' or 'we,' nor do we find the Spartan division of the army into young men and old; the poem applies just as much to young men (14) as to fathers of families (29). The way in which λόγος is used in v. 1. and v. 9 is scarcely possible for Tyrtaeus. See also note 8.

[7] Xenophanes also spoke of benefit to the community, but he meant economic advantage.

[8] The style of the elegy is mature archaic. A steady forward movement is maintained in the archaic fashion, but the long drawn out introduction (1–14, like Xenophanes 2, 1–11), the clear articulation and the pleasing balance of the whole indicate the end of the period. The first ten couplets are devoted half to saying, 'Not this . . .,' and half to saying, 'But that instead.' Both halves, the negative and the positive, end with the same declaration (10 and 20). After a couplet on the advantage to the community, there come ten more (6 +4) distichs on the personal rewards of valour. The section on the rewards of the fallen is framed by two distichs saying much the same thing (23–24; 33–34); and all the positive section (achievement and reward) is similarly framed by distichs of like content (13–14; 33–34). The sentence-construction is decidedly modern, with much subordination of clauses. With a remarkable consistency only judgments and conclusions are put into main clauses, all the factual basis being in subordinate clauses. This is in itself a kind of spiritualizing process.

account masses of details and to evaluate them methodically. In the scientific study of medicine the two became fused.

Some relation to Xenophanes is quite obvious in Alcmaeon (*Vorsokr.* 24, detailed reference p. 252 n. 1), a medical writer born at Croton, the Pythagorean centre in southern Italy, while Pythagoras was still living. He seems to have been the first Greek to write a book on medicine: he began it with an account of his basic method which agrees closely with the epistemological fragment (fr. 34) at the beginning of Xenophanes' poem (1):

Alcmaeon of Croton, son of Pirithous, said these things to Brotinus and Leon and Bathyllus.[1] Of things unperceivable (just as) of things human the gods have knowledge; but those who are merely men have to interpret signs.

Here is a deliberate statement of the scientific method: from facts that can be perceived inferences are drawn about things not subject to direct observation.

As regards Alcmaeon's medical theories, we are told that he reduced the multiplicity of possible conditions to a system of contrasted pairs, such as white and black, sweet and bitter, great and small. It was typical of the time to regard qualities, not objects, as primary and determinative, and to group them into polar dualities. In early Greek speculation it was usual for one pole then to acquire overtones of value; that is to say, white, sweet, light, etc. commonly formed the more positive and active group, while the others expressed the more negative qualities of passivity and materiality. It is not surprising, then, if Alcmaeon makes the light, bright and warm elements responsible for the development of sense-perception. Air bears sounds to the ear-opening; indrawn breath carries smell to the brain; the tongue, warm and moist, melts the things tasted and conveys the taste through its porous substance; the eye sees by means of the aqueous humour and the fire enclosed in the eye. Perceptions find their way to the brain through openings and 'ways' (pores).[2] From the impairing of the senses caused by damage to the brain Alcmaeon concludes that the brain is the receptacle of all sense-impressions. Semen also, which clearly must at the outset contain the whole man within it, he considers as a secretion of the central organ, the brain. This is the account that Theophrastus gives (in a modernized form, presumably) of Alcmaeon's teachings on sense-perception. Morbid conditions he considered as being brought about by

---

[1] The book is a committal to writing of teaching given orally by its author to three pupils. Two of them are known to have been Pythagoreans.

[2] On this point see now F. Solmsen, *Mus. Helvet.* 18 (1961) p. 151-153.

the one-sided, 'monarchical' predominance of a particular quality, health by 'isonomy,' i.e. possession of equal rights, between wet and dry, cold and hot, sour and sweet, etc. (B 4).[3]

The conceptions of Alcmaeon had considerable influence in subsequent medical theory. He taught that a disequilibrium in the natural qualities, i.e. an illness, was caused either by inner disordering or by influences from outside, e.g. through physical force, or by drinking water with some particular quality. A treatise now passing under the name of Hippocrates, which deals with the influence of soil, air and water on health, has the following to say about water: (*Airs, Waters, Places*, ch. 8):

So much for spring-water: now I shall discuss rainwater and water from snow. Rainwater is the lightest, sweetest, finest and clearest, since the sun has sucked it up previously and extracted from the water the finest and lightest parts. This is shown by salt, since the salty part of water remains behind because of its thickness and heaviness, while the finest part is lifted up by the sun because of its lightness . . . There is another point. When it has been taken up and set into motion, moving this way and that and mixing with air, the thick and dark part of it is separated out and becomes cloud and mist, while the clearest and lightest part of it is left and becomes sweet through being heated and cooked by the sun; for everything that is cooked becomes sweet. . . . This is naturally the best, but it should be decocted and filtered: otherwise it has an unpleasant taste and makes the voice of those who drink it hoarse and husky.

But all water from snow and ice is bad. Once it has been frozen, it never returns to its old characteristics; the clearness, lightness and sweetness separate out and are lost, and the thickest and heaviest parts remain. This may be seen from the following. Put a measured quantity of water into a vessel in wintertime and place it in the open, where it will freeze as quickly as possible. Next day bring it into a warm place so as to melt quickly: when it has melted, measure it again, and you will find appreciably less. This is an indication that in course of freezing the lightest and finest parts disappear and dry up—not the heaviest and thickest, for that is impossible.[4] For this reason water from snow and ice and the like is the worst for all purposes.

---

[3] Cf. G. Vlastos, *Class. Philol.* 42 (1947) 156ff.

[4] It is interesting that we have here a question put to nature herself in the form of an experiment, and that the conclusion is arrived at by measurement, when neither experiment nor measurement were commonly found in Greek science at that time. The conclusion, however, which is drawn from the experiment is false. It is true insofar as only pure water evaporates off, while the impurities remain; but the writer had no notion that only pure water turns into ice, and that the salts previously dissolved in the water are separated out. Instead he postulates the opposite, that only the earthy parts can coagulate into ice. In consequence he attributes the loss of volume occasioned by evaporation during the experiment to the expulsion and evaporation of the lightest parts occasioned by freezing. This

It is reminiscent of Alcmaeon, to find the assumption here that the qualities light–sweet–clear and heavy–bitter–dark are united in water. A little earlier we were told that the sick should drink water of an opposite quality to their disorder (p. 61, 30 Heiberg, ch. 7). The reference to 'indications' (p. 63, 16, ch. 10) also reminds one of Alcmaeon's method. Thus the little treatise, although more recent than Alcmaeon's book, may give us at least some notion of his ways of thinking.

We find Greek medicine here at a level where it has wholly out-grown magic. The emerging science of history found it less easy to free itself from the tradition of myth and legend. The Greeks could not go on long believing in the gloomy and incomprehensible forces of diseases caused by demons and cured by spells; but they could not so soon cut themselves off from their mythology, with all its clarity of form and significance of content. The physician also had nature on his side, since she gave every day opportunity to verify the assumptions of yesterday, whereas the historian could assault tradition only with a scepticism based on general principles. Thus it came about that the radicalism of Xenophanes in rejecting the 'inventions of antiquity' was long in finding disciples; only haltingly and step by step was a critical attitude developed towards the traditional legends.

The study of geography was rather more fortunate. Knowledge of the earth, of countries and of peoples is naturally a field of empirical study, since it deals with primary facts which can be immediately verified. These studies first ripened in the fifth century. From ethnography the Greeks passed to history with a geographical groundwork (Herodotus), and finally arrived at the scientific writing of their own history (Thucydides).

The founder of Greek geography was Hecataeus.[5] He was a citizen of the great Ionian port of Miletus, the centre of the Greek world of Asia Minor, carrying on trade with all the world, with colonies covering all the shores of the Black Sea. His family tree, which was traced back to the Greek mainland, had a god as its originator. As a member of one of the leading families, he took part in the political direction of the city. In 499, when the notables of the Ionian cities were planning a rebellion against their overlord, the Persian king Darius, Hecataeus disagreed, and sought to prove the hopelessness of the undertaking 'by enumerating all the peoples over

he thinks has been proved by his experiment, and he goes on to the further conclusion that water from ice and snow is unhealthy.

[5] On Hecataeus, Xanthus and Charon see L. Pearson, *Early Ionian Historians* (Oxford 1939).

whom Darius rules, and his power.' When his warning was disregarded, he maintained that Miletus must ensure her naval supremacy and assemble the materials for a great fleet, for which purpose they should lay hands on the costly votive offerings to Apollo which the Lydian king Croesus had formerly made at Miletus: it was better to use them themselves than to let them fall into the hands of the enemy. This proposal was also rejected; and a third suggestion, as unconventional and as acute as the others, equally failed to gain acceptance (Herodotus 5, 36 and 125–6). In the event Hecataeus was justified on every point. All these opinions attest a sober realism in politics, and they show also the connexion between Hecataeus' geographical interests and the practical problems with which his city found itself faced.

Hecataeus composed a book describing the whole earth as far as it was known, and added a map to it. The main feature of his picture of the earth were taken over from Anaximander (above p. 264); and he also thought that land and sea were distributed over the world with great regularity. The earth was round, and the river Oceanus flowed round its margin. A waterway made up of the Mediterranean and Black Seas divided it crossways and separated Europe from Asia; these two seas were connected with the outer ocean by the straits of Gibraltar in the West and by the river Phasis (in the Caucasus) in the East. The Nile, which also originated in the ocean, divided Asia into two halves;[6] exactly corresponding to the Nile, and flowing from the north into the Black Sea, came the Ister (Danube), dividing Europe also into East and West quadrants. The outer edges of the world were waste and desert and inhabited by fabulous beings. As early as Herodotus this neat packaging attracted derision, but it was hardly avoidable as a first approximation to the truth.

Hecataeus' description of the world is built on the notion of a sea voyage beginning from the Straits of Gibraltar, along the north shores of the Mediterranean and Black Seas as far as the Phasis in the East, then back along the southern shores to the West again. The description always starts from the coast; then it tells what lies 'above' (i.e. inland), and so further and further until the margin of the world is reached. This manner of description was called for essentially because the coasts were the parts best known.

The style is normally of the driest, e.g. (1 F 113a Jacoby):

And after that the Locrians, and there (i.e. in the land of the Locrians) Chalaeon, a city; and there Oeanthe, a city.

[6] Not long after Hecataeus' time (cf. Pindar, *Pyth.* 9, 8 from the year 474) Libya (Africa) was recognized as a third division of the earth (below p. 441f. n. 2).

One is surprised to see how consistently Hecataeus refuses to avail himself of the opportunities which language offers to shorten the repetition of similar material. Thus he does not say here, 'And the cities of Chalaeon and Oeanthe,' but his list registers each detail in its own right, just as one would repeat the same symbol close together on a map. Instead of using pronouns to connect with what has gone before, he repeats in the following passages (291, 305) the words 'mountain' and 'island':

Around the so-called Hyrcanian (i.e. Caspian) Sea (are) mountains high and covered with timber, and on the mountains artichokes.

In Butoe (in Egypt) near the temple of Leto is an island called Chambis, sacred to Apollo, and the island (is) moving and floats about and moves over the water.

In his geographical statements Hecataeus writes almost wholly in main clauses, and each clause has the narrowest imaginable horizon. While the general picture of the world was forced into quadrants with a splendid disregard for facts, the filling in of this frame is characterized by a minute pedantry. No attempt is made to give any living form to the presentation, and objectivity is carried to an extreme.

Hecataeus was not content with pure topography: some ethnographic details were included, e.g. (154):

The Paeones (a Thracian tribe) drink beer made from barley . . . And they anoint themselves with oil from milk.[7]

Hecataeus was particularly detailed in his description of Egypt, whose ancient civilization made a profound impression upon him. He travelled in Egypt himself, but he could see little of the architecture, since the Egyptians concealed their temples behind massive enceinte walls and allowed no strangers inside.[8] Only in Thebes did he gain admission at least into the forecourt of the great temple. There he conversed with the attendants of the temple and received an explanation of the statues of the priests, to the number of 345, which were alleged to represent that number of generations of Egyptian history. This confounded Hecataeus, whose own pedigree went back to a god at the sixteenth generation. Compared with the long history of Egypt, the origin of the Greek nation seemed as a thing of yesterday.

[7] The Greeks were not acquainted with butter and consequently had no word for it. Our word *butter* is ultimately derived from Thracian (?) *butyros.*

[8] Cf. Sourdille, *La durée etc.* (Paris, 1910). Herodotus fared no better; hence his delight when he was once enabled from a point of vantage to look into a temple enclosure and see the architectural features (2, 137, 5ff.).

From Hecataeus' description of Egypt we possess two rather longer extracts which Herodotus adopted almost unchanged from his predecessor's book. They are concerned with two remarkable creatures, the crocodile (324) and the fabulous bird, the phoenix:

(The crocodile is hunted a great deal and in many different ways; I will relate the way which seemed to me most remarkable.) When he (the hunter) has fastened the back of a pig on a hook, he drops it into the middle of the river; he himself, standing on the river bank and holding a live pig, beats the latter. When the crocodile hears the cries, he hastens towards the cries and, finding the back, swallows it; and they (the hunter and his mates) pull; and when it is dragged up on land, first of all he plasters its eyes with loam; if he has done this, the rest follows easily; if not, it is very difficult. (Herod. 2, 70).

As for the sacred phoenix, Hecataeus was told that it dwelt in Arabia and came once every five hundred years to the 'city of the Sun,' Heliopolis, in Egypt; i.e. it came on the death of its father, to give him the last honours in the temple of the sun. The transportation of the body is described by Hecataeus as follows (324):

First he makes out of myrrh an egg as big as he can carry; then he tries it to see if he can carry it; when he has done this successfully, he hollows out the egg, lays his father inside, and plugs up with fresh myrrh the place in the egg where he made the hole and put his father in; the father being inside, the weight of the egg is the same as before. Having plugged it up, he carries it to Egypt to the temple of the Sun.

In these passages we see at once the same atomizing tendency in style; each element is short and practically independent, and the nearness of the horizon at any given point makes frequent repetition necessary. But all the same, in both passages the individual elements form a neat enough sequence and one which fits the subject matter. The compelling logic behind the complex operations of the phoenix or the crocodile-hunter emerges with perfect clearness. The same pleasure in accurate detail and in a precise ensemble can be seen in the early red-figure vase-painting of the same period.

The language of this work has no form of its own, but is dictated by the subject matter at any given moment. Sometimes the grammatical level sinks so low that the sentences do not make correct syntax (324):

The riverhorse is four-legged and cloven-hoofed; having the mane of a horse; showing large incisors; the tail and voice of a horse; size that of the largest ox.

Hecataeus' love of listing and classifying occupied him also in the field of legendary history. Apart from his work on geography he wrote another four books, entitled *Genealogies*. In this the family-tree of noble houses, peoples and cities were traced back to various heroic progenitors who in turn were reckoned as the sons or grandsons of gods. Some primitive etymologies were thrown in:

(15) Orestheus, the son of Deucalion, came to Aetolia and became king; and a bitch belonging to him gave birth to a log, and he had it buried, and there grew from it a vine with many clusters of grapes, and he therefore named his son Phytius (from *phyton* 'plant'). Phytius' son was Oeneus, so named from the vine, which the Greeks formerly called *oenae*. Oeneus' son was Aetolus (the progenitor of the Aetolians). (22) . . . and when Perseus took hold of the hilt of his sword, he found that the cap (*mykes*) had fallen off. (Hence the place came to be called Mycenae.)

He found the authority for his statements in old epic poems in the manner of Homer or Hesiod, but he subjected this extensive and often self-contradictory mass of data to a critical examination, as he states in his introduction (1):

Hecataeus of Miletus relates as follows. I write the following believing it to be true; for the things said among the Greeks[9] seem to me numerous and absurd.

His criticism cannot have been very consistent, since it was so lacking in the story of the bitch and the vine. In other places he adopted a rationalizing approach. Heracles is said to have defeated the hound of hell Cerberus (representing death, see above p. 105) at the command of Eurystheus, and to have dragged the beast up from Hades to the upper world. Hecataeus explains thus: there was an unpleasant snake living on the promontory of Taenarum, and it was called 'the hound of hell' since anyone who was bitten by it immediately expired because of its poison; it was this snake which Heracles brought to Eurystheus (fr. 27). Another of Heracles' labours was to defeat the fabled water-snake Hydra. On this topic, it would seem, Hecataeus had this to say:

I think, however, that the snake was not so big and . . ., although more formidable than other serpents, and this is why Eurystheus gave the order, thinking that it was impossible to carry out.[10]

In the following fragment (19) a heroic tall story is made to toe the line:

Aegyptus did not come to Argos himself, but most likely his sons: Hesiod says there were fifty of them, but I doubt if there were as many as twenty.

---

9 That is, among the Greek general public; cf. Ion of Chios in Athen. 13, 604b.
10 Pap. Cair. in B. Wyss, *Antimachi Colophon. Reliquiae* (Berlin, 1936), p. 83, 38ff.

It is quite obvious that Hecataeus' scepticism did not extend to the substance of the legends; he only rejected the fairy-tale elements. If his scepticism had gone deeper, of course, he would never have written the *Genealogies* at all.

The fragments of Hecataeus show what a struggle the nascent science of history had with myth and legend even after the establishment of empiricism as a theory. They also show how far prose lagged behind poetry in fluency and elegance. For all that, the Ionian Hecataeus seems almost modern if we compare him with a rather later prose writer from the mainland. Not long after the *Genealogies* had been written, Acusilaus of Argos composed a similar work, in which he followed closely the *Theogony* and *Ehoiae* of Hesiod, by now some centuries old, but occasionally 'corrected' him in details (2 T 6 Jacoby; F 4; 6 etc.). Just like Hesiod, he began his story of the universe with the 'void' (F 5), and continued it through the world powers and divinities to the heroes of mythology. The spirit of Hesiod (above p. 102) appears also in his deriving all rivers from the great original river Oceanus (1):

and Oceanus wedded Tethys, his sister; from them were born three thousand rivers; and Achelous is the oldest of them and the most honoured.

In the same way he derives all poisonous snakes from the blood of the monster Typhon (F 14). The rationalizing explanation of Cerberus as a snake, which Hecataeus found necessary, is not adopted by Acusilaus (F13). The primitive level of his thought and language can be judged from the following example (22):

Poseidon married Caene, the daughter of Elatos ('pine-man'). Then, since it was not . . . for her to bear children either to him or to any other man, Poseidon handed her over to another man who was invulnerable and had the greatest strength of anyone then living, and if anyone tried to injure him with iron or bronze, he had no success (?). And this man was king of the Lapithae and waged war all the time with the Centaurs. Then he set up his spear (in the middle of the market place and commanded sacrifice to be made to it: to pray to the gods was not permitted. And) Zeus, when he saw him do this, was angry and urged on the Centaurs against him. And they drove him upright into the earth and put a block of stone over him as a monument, and he died.[11]

Acusilaus is here recounting an extremely ancient legend. The Lapithae, of whom Caeneus was one, appear even in Homer as representatives of a yet more primitive antiquity, of a cruder and

[11] The supplements proposed by Jacoby do not fit Acusilaus' style: I suggest something like: ἀκόν[τιον ἐν μέσῃ ἀγορῇ, τούτῳ κελεύει θύειν· θεοῖ]σι δ' οὐκ ἦεν [εὔχεσθαι. καὶ] Ζεύς . . .

rougher humanity: even the proud heroes of the *Iliad* cannot compare themselves with Caeneus and his like for self-will and self-confidence (*Il.* 1, 260ff., above p. 35f.). To an age in which the individual was not yet severed into soul and body it was not hard to imagine that the physical constitution of a man partook of the unyielding hardness of his character. In this way one arrived at the notion of a hero like Caeneus: overwhelmed by the numbers of his savage assailants, pounded with beams and great stones, he remains unbent and unbroken, and at last is driven into the earth like a tent-peg.

The work of Acusilaus represents a step backwards, not forwards, in Greek historiography. The progressive development which led from the Eastern Greek Hecataeus to the Eastern Greek Herodotus, was accomplished in the East. The history of Lydia was written before Herodotus by the half Lydian, half Greek Xanthus, who even used original documentary material (cf. Nicolaus Damasc. 90 F 44, 7 Jacoby). We know little more about the Greek Charon of Lampsacus (on the Asiatic shore of the Dardanelles), who wrote about 460 (?)[12] a work on Persian history and a chronicle of his native city. We possess an entertaining passage (262 F 1 Jacoby) from this latter work:

(Year . . .) The Bisalti (a native tribe) marched against Cardia (a Greek city northwest of the Dardanelles) and were victorious. The leader of the Bisalti was Naris. He had been sold in Cardia as a child, and was the slave of a Cardian and became a barber. The Cardians had an oracle that the Bisalti would attack them, and they often spoke of this oracle when they sat in the barber's shop. He ran away from Cardia to his own country, and urged the Bisalti to make war on the Cardians, after being himself chosen as leader by the Bisalti. Now the Cardians had trained all their horses to dance to the flute at banquets; and they stood up on their hind legs and made dancing movements with their forelegs to the tunes that they had learned. Naris was aware of this, and he bought a flute-girl from Cardia, and the flute-girl came to the Bisalti and trained many other flute players. When battle was joined, he ordered them to play all those airs to which the Cardian horses were accustomed. And when the horses heard the music, they got up on their hindlegs and began to dance. Now the main strength of the Cardians was in their cavalry; and so they were defeated.

In style this narrative is far above the muddy flow of Acusilaus, while considerably below the easy charm and freshness of Herodotus. Several times the storyteller has to break off or deflect the course of his narrative. The content and character of this amusing story show that the anecdotal element in Herodotus' work was already present in that of his predecessors. Anecdote and romance began to take the

---

[12] Jacoby puts him considerably later.

place of legend and fairy-tale. Formerly Aristeas, as a poet possessed and driven on by Apollo, had found his inspiration in the wonders of far-off places; the same attitude recurs in Hecataeus (F 327f.) and in Herodotus, who both (the latter with reference to Aristeas) describe the fabled dwellers on the margins of the earth; the myths, as retold by Hacataeus and Acusilaus, were packed with wonders. But now a more modern kind of narrative took the field, still aiming at surprising the reader, but at surprising him over something that he could understand. Men were now to be told with what address and ingenuity difficult tasks had been accomplished—how crocodiles were caught; how a bird conveyed a spiced and embalmed body through the air; how horses learned to dance to the flute, and how this feat of dressage was turned to account by an ingenious enemy. The love of wonders was now combined with the practical spirit of the new age, and the result was a keen interest in things striking and instructive.

This was the path which development was to take, leading beyond the merely marvellous or remarkable. The anecdote acquired an historical and general significance: as a sophisticated substitute for myth, it developed into a short story full of meaning and point. It was not until the highest development of historiography under Thucydides that narrative ceases to be pointed and that interest in the marvellous disappears. This is of course the death-sentence of the short-story in historical writing: there are episodes in Thucydides, but no anecdote, no romance. It is only then that history acquires its full seriousness and strength, with emotion not less deep for being implicit, with power that is elevated but controlled. Medicine began to arise as a science and a technique when it began to be sober and mechanical: history for a long time was to derive much of its motive power from the love of novelty and a passion for the strange and unusual.

(c) *Parmenides*

For sixty years Xenophanes carried his 'thinking head' around the countries of Hellas and his earnest message could be heard everywhere. Born in the archaic period, he lived on into the beginning of the classical age, and worked indefatigably in bringing about that great transformation. He helped to create a new type of humanity, capable of drawing a clear distinction between our world here and the transcendental world beyond. The gain for the empirical sciences from this new attitude has already been considered; and in the process we have gone beyond the frontiers of the archaic age. We have now to consider its effects in philosophy, and in so doing we return chronologically to the point from which we started.

As Theophrastus expressly states, the metaphysic of Xenophanes was directed not at the world, but at god (above p. 335 with n. 18). The transformation of these theological speculations into philosophy was accomplished by Parmenides, who is reckoned as Xenophanes' 'successor' in 'the Eleatic school.' But it means very little to talk of schools and successors in this context. Certainly one can clearly see connexions between the theology of Xenophanes and Parmenides' ontological doctrines of Being and Seeming; but in all essentials what Parmenides created was so new, so important, and so self-contained, that Xenophanes' contribution to it sinks into insignificance.

Parmenides was born in that same Southern Italian city of Elea in which Xenophanes became a citizen after his long wanderings. His lifetime falls in the latter half of the sixth and the first half of the fifth century. We are told that he was 'of a noble family and possessed of a noble fortune'; that he was a pupil of Xenophanes and a Pythagorean (the Pythagorean sect was very well established in Southern Italy); and that, in accordance with Pythagorean doctrines, he lead a retired life. How much of this is true we cannot say. What is more important is that, owing to two lucky accidents, we possess Parmenides' work to a large extent in its original words,[1] and thus we have an incomparably fuller and more trustworthy picture of his doctrines than we have of any other early Greek thinker. We can read them in the form in which he himself presented them—a poetical form, since he enshrined his majestic teachings in an epic poem.

The core of Parmenides' philosophy is metaphysical in its nature. To come face to face with that reality beyond the senses which had disclosed itself to him, the poet had to mount in spirit beyond this world in which we live. Whenever he reflected upon his lofty ideas, he felt himself carried away into a realm of light beyond all earthly things. In the introduction to his poem he describes this experience,

---

[1] The whole introduction was cited by Sextus Empiricus (2nd century A.D.), who imagined that he could use it to support his own ideas. In the sixth century a number of citations were made by Simplicius, who also transcribed the central passage on ontology complete, wishing to preserve it for posterity: copies of the work, he says, were becoming very scarce. The Christian emperor Justinian, who built the church of Hagia Sophia with the utmost magnificence, forbade in 529 all teaching of (heathen) philosophy, and shut down the Platonic Academy in Athens, to put an end to the 'madness of the Greeks.' Simplicius and some others subsequently migrated to Persia, in the hope of finding a patron of Greek culture in Chosroes I. After some years he returned disillusioned to Greece and devoted himself to writing on philosophy.

and since ordinary words are incapable of conveying anything so far beyond the ordinary, he conveys it in images and symbols.[2]

Some of his metaphors he was able to borrow from the conventional language of poetry.[3] The poetical form and language are conveyed symbolically by the image of a glorious and exciting chariot-ride,[4] in opposition to plain prose, which was described as 'pedestrian language.' The poem begins as follows (28 B 1):

The steeds which convey me as far as my will goes forth,[5] carried me, when they had borne me on the sounding (?) way, the way of the Goddess who brings the man who knows through all cities (?).[6] On that road I was conveyed, for my very clever horses bore me along it, drawing the car, and maidens led me on my journey. The axle in the hub blew a clear note from the pipe, glowing hot, since it was impelled by the pair of whirling wheels on either side, whenever the daughters of the Sun hastened it onward, leaving the abode of Night, towards the light, throwing back with their hands the veils from their heads.[7] There is the gate of the paths of Night and Day; the doorframe and stone threshold surround it: heavenly-bright itself, it is filled with the great halfdoors. Avenging

---

[2] Probably this was why Parmenides chose verse: fr. 1 could not have been expressed in the Greek prose of his time.

[3] Parmenides 1, 1–2; 5; 17–18 have an exact parallel in Pindar *Ol.* 6, 22–27 (cf. *Frühgriech. Denken* p. 158).

[4] This image was probably in Hesiod's mind when he wrote *Works and Days* 659.

[5] Probably Parmenides is boasting that his thought will go as far as he likes to send it (cf. Solon 3, 30 and the opening lines of Ovid's *Metamorphoses*). The first verse is quite general; the second passes to the intellectual journey which is to be the theme of the poem.

[6] The third verse is very difficult. Reading ἄστη, it could mean that the message of which the man-who-knows (Parmenides) is the bearer has reached all lands (cf. Theognis 23f.) through his writing (see the following note); and the epiphany of the goddess may have ended with some such instruction as 'Go now and open the eyes of the blind.' But these are only possibilities.

[7] The imagery is as impressive as it is readily intelligible to anyone acquainted with this kind of language. It is concerned with thought; and in the archaic manner no distinction is drawn between (a) the process of thinking; (b) the content of the thought; and (c) the formulation and expression of the thought in the poem. Thus we hear of the 'way' or 'journey' of the thought (the cogitative process, the method of thought, and probably also the attraction of the poem on its hearers and readers); of its kinetic energy (the swift horses), and of the radiant and keensighted maidens ('daughters of the Sun') who point out the route for the journey from darkness into light, who hasten the traveller onwards, and who also unveil themselves in the course of the ascent (see below p. 480f., n. 22). The tempestuous power of his thought (we shall soon see how remote and alien from this world are the conclusions to which it leads) is symbolized in the speed of revolution of the wheels, which makes the shrieking axles glow redhot (cf. n. 9, and Aeschylus *Suppl.* 181 and *Septem* 153; the central hole drilled through the hub was denoted in Greek by the same word (*syrinx*) which also means the shepherd's pipe; this fact influenced the wording of the line).

Dike bears the requiting keys. To her now spoke the maidens with gentle words and addressed her with knowledge, so that she drew back swiftly for them the firm-pegged bar from the gate.[8] The doors made the opening gape wide as they swung back, turning in their sockets the bronze-plated posts in turn (?), both strengthened with rivets and nails.[9] And through them straight forward the maidens propelled the car and horses.

Dikê (v. 14) is the power of law and rightness. She bears the 'requiting keys' to the door of knowledge because the righteousness of a man's thought determines whether he opens up the truth or shuts it off from himself.

Without any transition, the reception of the traveller at his destination is now depicted. 'The Goddess' greets him as a young man for whom access to truth has been granted by a fortunate accident (his abilities) and by *Dikê* (the rightness and justice of his thinking):

In friendly wise the Goddess received me, and took my right hand in hers, and addressed me and spoke in these words: 'Young man, who have come with immortal guides to my dwelling with the horses that carried you, greeting, for no unfavourable fate sent you to travel this path, which lies far from the tread of men,[10] but right and justice. It is fated that you learn all—both the convincing and infallible heart of Truth[11] and the opinions of men which have no trustworthiness in them.

[8] By convincing arguments (cf. Πειθώ 2, 4, and see n. 11) the daughters of light (=thoughts) authenticate themselves to Dike. Their words are 'gentle' (just as light is 'mild,' 8, 57) in contrast to the βίαιον of falsehood (cf. Parmen. 7, 3; Simonides fr. 598; Pindar *Nem.* 8, 34; *Il.* 23, 576 etc.), because on this occasion they are addressing a power that thinks as they do, while on other occasions Parmenides' dialectic is 'hard' (see below p. 368 with n. 42).

[9] The gate of decisive understanding opens to the thinker and lets him into the realm of light. Here again the importance of the thing is brought out in the archaic style by the writer's going into minute detail. He describes every feature of the door as it stands closed and as it opens. The essential elements in the construction of a gate were the posts and sockets of the hinges, just as in vv. 6–8 the essential features of a chariot are the axles and hubs. The imagery is richer than need be, since the passage through the gate, the emergence from the realm of night, the journey into light and the unveiling all represent approximately the same thing.

[10] πάτος is not used here in its normal sense of a path or track from place to place, but of the walking or treading of bustling men; see W. Kullmann, *Hermes* 86 (1958) 159f.

[11] On the text see K. Deichgräber, '*Das Prooimion des Parmenides*,' *Abh. Mainz. Akad.* 1959 p. 22. I read now ἀληθείης εὐπειθέος (cf. in the next verse πίστις ἀληθής and 8, 50 πιστὸς λόγος ἀμφὶς ἀληθείης, in the same contrast as here; 8, 28 πίστις ἀληθής; 2, 4 Πειθώ as an attendant upon Ἀληθείη) ἀτρεκὲς (cf. Pindar *Nem.* 5, 17 φαινοῖσα πρόσωπον ἀλάθει' ἀτρεκές) ἦτορ. It is interesting to see the variants—(εὐπειθέος:) εὐκυκλέος: εὐφεγγέος and (ἀτρεκὲς:) ἀτρεμὲς, all prompted by a good understanding of Parmenides' doctrines. But εὐκυκλέος (instead of εὐκύκλου as in 8, 43) is a *vox nihili* (Deichgräber), concocted under the influence of εὐπειθέος, which was replaced by two conjectures probably because it was misinterpreted as meaning 'obedient.'

This serves to introduce the lecture which Parmenides puts into the mouth of 'the Goddess.' We may see in her the Muse of this poem, or the power of truth or of understanding or insight—it makes little difference, since 'the Muse' in poetry represents all these things at once: art, wisdom, knowledge, truth.

The 'truth' which was vouchsafed to Parmenides was the outcome of an extraordinarily bold speculation. It will be helpful if we make its main lines intelligible beforehand in a partly modernized form.

What the philosopher ultimately strove to grasp was truth or reality, or in other words, Being. Hence an understanding of the nature of Being became the cardinal point of philosophy. Now Parmenides' view on Being was that it had sense only in the positive form, as affirmed Being: if one tried to deny a state of affairs and thus to negate a state of Being, one destroyed in so doing the subject of the statement, and in fact did not make a statement at all. Thus there could be no such things as a negative statement. Even statements which contained an implicit negative destroyed themselves.[12] The statement, for example, that something has begun to be, contains the implicit assumption that previously it was not; and the assumption that an object not previously existing began to be an object at a given time is nonsensical and false. The same argument applies to motion and to all forms of change, since here again is an implicit statement that a state of affairs existed at one time and at another time did not. There cannot even be a plurality of objects, since this would imply that one object is not, or is not like, another object. Among qualities we can only have those which are wholly positive, such as 'whole,' 'full,' 'all'; the others, e.g. 'green' are automatically excluded by their negative corollary—'not red,' 'not blue', etc. Among things and happenings there is only Being, which can be expressed in the one-word sentence 'Is';[13] among numbers, only the monad; in time, only the eternal; in space, only the universal. From all this it

[12] In the exposition of his ontology Parmenides uses only statements which contain no negative, or which contain a doubled negative, e.g. 'Being exists, and Nothing does not exist' (6, 1–2). Where a single negative appears, a second is implicit, e.g. 'It is not deficient' (8, 33): 'deficiency' is a negative idea.

[13] The sentence 'Is,' as the kernel of Parmenides' teaching, has no subject; it is an impersonal verb, like ὕει '(it) rains.' If one puts in a general subject, such as 'Being is,' or 'Everything that is, is,' the statement is degraded to a tautology: on the other hand, a defined (and therefore limited) subject would inadmissibly specialize Being. In the language of his day Parmenides found the verb 'to be' used in three distinct functions. (1) Unaccented, as a copula (but the use of a copula was not obligatory, cf. Parm. 2, 7; 8, 16; 9, 4; 12, 3). (2) Accented, meaning 'to exist': this also might be left out (8, 42). (3) Accented, with infinitive or ὅπως, meaning 'it is possible (or permissible) that . . .' (2, 2 εἰσι νοῆσαι; 6, 1 ἔστι γὰρ εἶναι; 2, 3 οὐκ ἔστι μὴ εἶναι, 8, 47 and 8, 9 οὐ φατὸν οὐδὲ νοητόν ἐστιν ὅπως . . .).

follows that the world in which we think we are living cannot be real. Hesiod had postulated that our world of things had a counterpart in a world of void and negativeness (above p. 102–107); but Parmenides, while denying the existence of anything void or negative, concluded with similar logic that our world also does not exist.

As soon as the question of Being is posed, Parmenides can see only two 'ways' to be considered for seeking an answer: we have to choose between unqualified assent and radical denial (2):

Now I will tell you—and remember what you will hear—what are the only thinkable ways of enquiry. The one, that says, 'Is, and Not-being is not,' is the path of Conviction, who is a handmaiden to Truth; the other, that says, 'Is not, and Not-being is necessary,' is a path, I tell you, utterly inscrutable; for you cannot know that which is not (that is beyond accomplishment) nor can you express it.[14]

A further fragment[15] appears to begin with the demonstration that any thought or statement must have a positive entity as its subject; but the verbal expression is strange (6):

It is necessary that a thought and a statement of that which Is, Is; for Being exists, but Not-being Is not. I bid you take this to heart, for this is a path of seeking against which I warn you at its outset. I warn you also against that on which men who know nothing wander, double-heads; for helplessness within their breasts drives their unsettled spirit: they are borne abroad deaf and blind, bewildered, an undiscriminating herd, to whom Being and Not-being count the same and not the same, whose path is ever backwards as much as forwards.

The first path of which Parmenides disapproves is probably the one named second in the previous fragment, namely the negation of Being. It leads to nothing, and nothing does not exist. A third path is that of compromise. For those who choose it Parmenides has nothing but contempt. A man who will not face the clear decision between yes and no shows himself as being helpless and lacking all direction. Parmenides cannot sufficiently express his contempt for these vacillating characters whose ambiguous thoughts drift first in one direction, then in the other. Probably he had often found that men to whom he expounded his strange doctrines (above p. 257, n. 9) fought against admitting the unreality of the world in which we live, trying to escape from his merciless logic; and when he put to them the question, 'IS, or IS not?', they committed the mistake (appalling in his eyes) of considering not Being itself, but the things of this world

---

[14] Cf. in a later passage (7, 1–2): 'So that which is Not-being cannot be proved (??); therefore keep your thoughts firmly away from this path.' (7, 1–2 is a fragment on its own: cf. *Class. Phil.* 41 (1946) 170, n. 9).

[15] On fr. 3 see below p. 357. I cannot satisfactorily interpret fr. 4.

while attempting to answer. In the debates that followed they were compelled to ascribe positive reality even to negatives (e.g. death), and thereby they half distinguished between, and half identified, Being and Not-being.

We cannot trust our daily experience and the evidence of our senses, which present us with a world of multiplicity and change (7, 3):

Let not custom with its many experiences drive you onto this path so that you are ruled by the unseeing eye, the sounding ear and the tongue. Judge rather by thought the much-contested argument put forward by me.

Once the logic of pure thought has taken over, it leads us along the one correct path. The text continues (7, 6 = 8, 1):

It now remains to speak of one way only, that says 'IS.' On this are many tokens that it cannot either come to be or pass away, since it is all-in-one, immovable and endless (?), it never 'was' nor 'will be,' but IS now all together, one and continuous. What sort of a beginning will you seek for it? How and from whence did it grow? I will not permit you to say or think, 'It came from nothing,' for it is unthinkable and unsayable that Is-not IS. What necessity gave it cause to arise later or sooner, beginning out of the original nothing? Hence it is necessary either that IS (i.e. Being exists) or it does not, and the power of certainty will never allow that from Not-being anything other than itself can arise. For this reason Dike has not relaxed the fetters and left Being free to come to be or to pass away: she holds it firmly.

Many details in this section are doubtful, and both here and in the continuation the sequence of the thought cannot always be seen. The general sense, however, can hardly be doubted. At the end of the passage *Dikê* (above p. 352) comes forward again as the norm of logical correctness. She rules not only our thoughts, but the relation of things themselves: things are as they must be. All that follows turns on our answer to the basic question (8, 15):

The decision turns on this question, 'IS, or IS not?' The conclusion is necessarily that the one (sc. Is not) must be given up as unthinkable and unsayable, for that is a false road; but that the other IS and is right. How could that which IS later pass away? How could it come to be? If it had a beginning, it IS not, nor if it will not arise till later. Thus coming-to-be is destroyed and passing-away disappears; nor can distinctions be made, since it is of the same kind throughout. It is never in a higher degree— for that would destroy homogeneity—nor in a lesser degree, but everything is full of Being. Thus everything is continuous, and Being jostles against Being.[16]

[16] πελάζειν never means 'to approach,' but 'to bring close' or 'to arrive at,' sometimes even conveying direct contact (e.g. *Od.* 14, 350): and the present tense

The unbroken continuity of Being applies as well to time as to space (8, 5 and 22–25). Since each and every Being exists now, and since it is as impossible that Being should come into existence or pass away as that it should be fragmented (fr. 4?) or cut short, the passage of time can have no power over Being; and it is equally impossible that Being should be in a higher or a lower degree in one region than in another.

This leads to the exclusion of all events or happenings. The Greek term for happening or change in any form was 'movement' (8, 26):

> But it is unmoving, without beginning, without end, in the bonds of great fetters, since coming-to-be and passing-away were driven far away: true certainty expelled them. It remains the same in the same and dwells in itself and will remain immovable.[17] For powerful necessity holds it in the bonds of the limits that surround it, for it is not permissible that that which IS should be without bounds. For it IS, and lacks nothing: but that which Is not would lack all (?)

By 'boundaries' (*peiras*, v. 31) Parmenides obviously cannot mean temporal or spatial boundaries, since beyond such boundaries Not-being would begin. Rather, he seems here, as he does later (8, 42–49) to attack those theories which assumed various strata of being, and transformations from lower to higher being, or conversely from a higher grade of existence to a lower (in v. 23f. he expressly denied variations in intensity of Being). Anaximander in particular had assumed that our world of defined and complete actuality had its basis in an 'unbounded' or 'undefined' (*apeiron*), in which all possibilities existed side by side and unseparated. But for Parmenides Being cannot be potential, undefined and incomplete: it must be actual, defined and whole. In this sense it has its fixed 'boundaries,' i.e. finality.

Next some very obscure remarks on the nature of intellection,

---

may regularly denote not movements towards, but rest at something. This notion I have sought to render in my translation. The same holds good of the cognates, viz. ὁ πέλας which in the N.T. means not 'the man who is near,' but 'the man who is nearest'; ἔμπλην (*Il.* 2, 526)='close by'; πλήν='up to (but not including),' 'except.'

[17] Read ταὐτὸν δ' ἐν ταὐτῷ μίμνει, καθ' ἑαυτό τε κεῖται, χοὔτως ἔμπεδον αὖθι μένει (see *Frühgr. Denken* p. 191 with n. 1). Parmenides' ideas recur in Plotinus *Enn.* 5, 1, 4: ὁ δὲ νοῦς πάντα · ἔχει οὖν ἐν αὐτῷ πάντα ἑστῶτα ἐν τῷ αὐτῷ (= Parm. 8, 29), καὶ ἔστι μόνον· καὶ τὸ ἔστιν ἀεί · καὶ οὐδαμοῦ τὸ μέλλον, ἔστι γὰρ καὶ τοτε · οὐδὲ τὸ παρεληλυθός, οὐ γάρ τι ἐκεῖ παρελήλυθεν, ἀλλ' ἐνέστηκεν ἀεί (= Parm. 8, 5) and in Augustine *Conf.* 9, 10, 24: (The wisdom of God) *ipsa non fit, sed sic est ut fuit, et sic erit semper* (= Parmen. 8, 29–30); *quin potius fuisse et futurum esse non est in ea, sed esse solum, quoniam aeterna est* (= Parmen. 8, 5). This connection between Plotinus and Augustine was pointed out in a lecture by J. H. Taylor.

which can only be translated and interpreted with the greatest diffidence (8, 34):

Knowledge is identical with knowing the fact of Being; for you cannot find knowledge apart from that which IS, within which is the thing affirmed. Nothing IS or will be apart from that which IS, since even this is bound by Fate to be whole and unmoved.

For Parmenides all knowledge is a knowledge of Being; for the affirmation or negation of any fact indicates a recognition that the fact belongs to the realm of Being (i.e. of actuality): clearly there is nothing beyond and apart from Being. The quality of being immovable, which reigns in the realm of Being (vv. 26, 38) brings as its consequence that there can only be 'knowledge' or 'being-aware' (νοεῖν vv. 34, 36), not 'learning' or 'becoming-aware' (which would be νοῆσαι).

From the unity and completeness (36–38) of Being the conclusion is drawn that Being and the knowledge of Being are not two things, but one. This is expressed in a different fragment, which I insert here (3):

For knowledge (more accurately: recognition as a state) and Being are the same.[18]

The Being of Parmenides' philosophy is thus conceived from the outset as known Being, and there is no true knowledge other than that in which Being understands itself as Being.[19]

If this quiet awareness of Being is the only true knowledge, then the notion with which we face the restless ferment of this world of perception, with which we accept unquestioningly its self-destroying contradictions, can be no better than figments (8, 38):

Mistaken are the appellations[20] which men have set up thinking them true—coming-to-be, passing-away, being and not (being), moving from place to place and changing of bright colours.[21]

[18] Unfortunately this important sentence contains a grammatical difficulty. Can τε, despite its position, be taken with νοεῖν? To have τε standing after the verb that is common to both subjects is considerably more troublesome than (e.g.) the postponed τε in Il. 3, 80 (ἰοῖσίν τε instead of ἐπετοξάзοντό τε) or Il. 21, 559 (Ἴδης τε instead of ἵκωμαί τε), or the examples in Denniston, The Greek Particles, 1934, 517f.

[19] In the world of appearance each of the two elements has a knowledge of its own nature, see below p. 363.

[20] The simplest emendation of the corrupt reading seems to be τῷ μάψ ὀνόμασται (if the unaugmented form is acceptable here and in 9, 1); other proposals are too far from the ductus (e.g. πάντ' ἀπέωσται after 8, 18, or πάντα πέπλασται after Xenophanes 1, 22). A new interpretation of the transmitted text is put forward by L. Woodbury in Harvard Studies in Classical Philology 63 (1958) 145–160.

[21] A colour-change from white to black (e.g. in the melting of snow) here serves to represent the general notion of change of quality or situation (Frühgr. Denken p. 206, n. 2).

This is the number of words that sufficed the ruthless logician to demolish our whole universe. The starting-point of his destructive reasoning is not sought in any objects, materials or forms of life; he does not tell us that earth, water, sun and stars or men and beasts are mere illusions: he knocks away instead the very pivots on which the world had seemed to turn to the theoretical thinkers of his day; he kicks out the duality of Being and Not-Being; he tramples on motion and change, and denies the reality of opposing qualities. The constituent elements of the archaic view of the world had been not objects, materials and creatures, but forms of being, active forces and qualities.[22]

Now Parmenides comes back to his 'boundaries' (cf. v. 31 and my interpretation of it), i.e. to the universal completeness of Being, in contrast to the 'unbounded' and 'undefined' of Anaximander which was purely potential and a preliminary stage to full reality (8, 42):

But since (there is) a final boundary, it (Being) is complete (realized) on all sides, like the mass of a well-rounded ball, from the middle outwards of equal strength in all directions; for it would not be right for it to have any part greater or less. For there is no Not-being which could hinder it from achieving evenness, nor is it possible that Being can here be stronger and here lighter than other Being, since it is exempt from all harm. Equal to itself in all directions, it meets its boundaries uniformly.

In other words, Being rests like a perfectly made ball in equilibrium about its centre, without any internal play of forces or pressures of stronger against weaker parts, uniform and balanced in itself. It makes contact with its 'boundary' all round: i.e. it never falls short of the end-form assigned to it by its own nature.[23]

This transcendental image of a homogeneous actuality, securely poised within the limits of its full realization, brings to an end Parmenides' teaching on 'truth.' But he has not yet come to the end of what he has to tell us (8, 50):

Here I relinquish reliable statement and knowledge concerning truth (actuality); from now on hear assumptions after the fashion of mortals, listening to the deceptive ordering of my words (verses).

Parmenides' intuition and his labour of understanding does not make a halt at that point where he denied the world of the senses and declared it to be an illusion: he wishes fully to understand this world

[22] Cf. above p. 260f.

[23] Parmenides is very far from saying that Being has the outward shape of a ball: he compares it with a ball explicitly in respect of the equality of mass in all directions, in which no energy tending to produce motion can arise. For the linguistic expression cf. Plato, *Phaedo* 109a.

as well, so far as it is conveyed to us by 'custom with its many experiences' (7, 3). In his analysis of that world in which we fancy that we are living, through the testimony of our irrational senses, Parmenides has a three-fold aim. He explains the structure and the regularity of the world of appearance; he discloses the fundamental error on which its system goes astray; and he shows how this mistake, once made, cannot but perpetuate itself.[24] The text continues (8, 53):

> They (sc. men) according to their notions[25] have decided to name two forms—that is one too many, and it is here that they have gone astray—and have divided their appearance as (if they were) opposites and have set marks on each of the two separately: on the one side the sky-bright ('aetherial') fire of flames, which is gentle, very agile, the same as itself in all directions, but not the same as the other; but rather that other stands by itself, in opposition to fire: gloomy night, a dense and heavy thing. I will give you an accurate account of this view of the world,[26] so that no opinion of mortals may escape you.

In the last two verses the goddess makes the claim that the theory which she advances is perfect except for its describing only the human view of the world, i.e. a mistaken view. There is no real contradiction in the presenting of this world-view at once as a new revelation and as a well-established production of the common human imagination. The exposition sets forth for the first time the categories with which our clumsy human nature has hitherto been forced to operate in ignorance of what it was really about. It also proposes to show how from those false assumptions the world in which we fancy we live must necessarily arise.

The basic mistake is in positing[27] a basic duality. Two principles ('forms' or 'ideas') have been introduced which are distinguished by their specific qualities ('marks'). 'Night' is the negative counterpart of 'fire.' But instead of seeing that there should be only one principle underlying the cosmos and that the negative character of the second takes away its actuality, men ascribed to Night a nature 'by itself' and made it an independent partner of fire in the structure and

---

[24] See below p. 364. This is also hinted at in the verses with which our first fragment ends (1, 31f., following on from the text translated on p. 352): 'You must also acquaint yourself with the assumptions of men, in which is no real trustworthiness; but nonetheless you must learn also this—how that which is accepted as true must have Being in an acceptable way, insofar as it penetrated all things completely' (1, 30–32 according to K. Reinhardt's interpretation). Very probably B11 and 10 came after 1, 32.

[25] Read γνώμαις, and cf. Pind. *Nem.* 10, 89: οὐ γνωμᾷ διπλόαν θέτο βουλάν.

[26] ἐοικότα πάντα probably as in *Od.* 4, 654: 'similar in all respects.'

[27] By 'posit' I am roughly rendering the combination καταθέσθαι and ὀνομάζειν which Parmenides uses three times (8, 38–39 and 53; 19, 3).

function of the universe. Each of the two principles is identical with itself throughout; and the various qualities which it possesses are superficial variations of its one specific nature. Parmenides names three such qualities on each side, but one could extend the list indefinitely. 'Fire' is bright, warm, light, mild,[28] and active both physically and mentally: 'Night' contrariwise is dark cold, heavy, stiff, passive and in the grip of dull ignorance (ἀδαῆ). The reduction of all multiplicity to a pair of polar opposites (reminding us to some extent of such pairs as 'force and mass,' 'mind and matter') was a persistent feature of early Greek philosophy,[29] and with his choice of 'fire' and 'night' as basic constituents Parmenides put himself in line with tradition.[30] What is original in his theory of the world of appearance is not the first assumption, but the strictness with which it is worked out and systematized.

The lengthy original fragment breaks off here, but there is no doubt about the next step. The two principles mingle in varying proportions and thus give rise to things of every sort. Even if several things are juxtaposed homogeneously, they do not become one and the same, but there may be something of another kind between them and separating them. Space and time become significant factors; by regrouping of the elements the new is created and the old modified or destroyed. At the same time a postulate is satisfied which is as valid in the world of appearance as in that of reality: the unprovable assumption of a void can be excluded here also (9):

But now that all things have been called light and night, and whatever corresponds to their forces (the qualities of light and night) has been distributed to these or those things, light and unperceivable night fill all things, each of them equal (in power), for there is nothing that belongs to neither of them.

All things (or parts of things) are understood as composed of light and darkness, according to the 'powers' of light and darkness displayed in them. Now light and darkness are complementary: an excess or deficiency of brightness, lightness etc. necessarily implies a deficiency or excess of darkness, heaviness, etc. Since in the world of illusion the

[28] It is 'mild' just as light and life are in opposition to night and death as objects of fear, or as clearness and truth are opposed to stupidity and ignorance which do violence to reality (above p. 352 n. 8).

[29] The opposites are 'sea' (or 'water') and 'earth' in Semonides (above p. 205) probably also in Thales (above p. 261) and certainly in Xenophanes (above p. 334).

[30] Hesiod had made 'night' a principle of negativity (above p. 102–105); and 'fire' is only another way of expressing one side of the duality 'hot and cold' which was fundamental in Anaximander's system (above p. 262–65), or one of the two basic qualities of Anaximenes, 'hot and tenuous' against 'cold and dense' (above p. 268). On Heraclitus and Empedocles see below p. 385f., n. 36.

negative element, night, is reckoned as of equal standing, one can immediately conclude that any vacancies left by light are at once filled up by darkness. Thus a kind of continuum is retained in this realm also.

These principles being laid down, the goddess can explain (11) how earth and sun and moon and the aether common to all and the Milky Way and uttermost Olympus and the hot power of the stars began to come into existence.

You will know the nature of the aether and all the constellations in the sky, the radiant (?) works of the pure shining sun and from whence they had their origin, and the works of the round-eyed Selene, the wanderer, and her nature; and you will learn of all-surrounding heaven, whence it came to be, and how Necessity constrained it to contain the boundaries of the stars. (10)

In the earliest days the vault of heaven enclosing the world had been thought of as made of stone, and Homer speaks of the 'brazen' or 'iron' heaven; Parmenides shares the notion of a material sky, and he is able to understand also the 'necessity' which erected this bounding 'wall' (A 37). His conclusions on this score have not been preserved, but we can guess what his thoughts were. Behind the stars the All comes to an end and strikes against Nothing in every direction; for in the world of appearance the negative has an apparent existence, and is even thought of as material. Hence it follows that the boundary of the world, the absolute negative on which the waves of positive Being and living movement break, must be an absolutely hard, absolutely passive, and absolutely dense mass.

Within the spherical universe and below the sky Parmenides thought that all things had ordered themselves in layers according to their density. The light and fiery parts had been driven upwards and outwards by their 'hot power' (11, 3), while the dark and heavy sank downwards, i.e. towards the middle (schol. on 8, 56ff.). Highest of all, immediately under the sky, was a region of pure aether, through which the fiery spheres ('rings') of the stars pursued their courses. Further inwards concentric rings of mixed nature followed each other in sequence; the fire-content became steadily less; in the centre was the cold and unmoving earth (A 1; 37; 44).[31]

Only a few verses from his description of the universe have been preserved. His account began with the outermost layer, the bounding

[31] Theophrastus (fr. A37) misunderstood one of the verses preserved for us by Simplicius (fr. B12, 2). Once this has been understood (cf. *Frühgriech. Denken* 183f.), we can set aside those statements made by Theophrastus in A37 which are derived from his interpretation of the verse. He also misunderstood the words ἐν μέσῳ τούτων in the following verse (op. cit. 185). Both his mistakes arise from a real ambiguity in the original text. On the spheres see above p. 264 n. 23.

heaven, and then passed on to the 'narrower' (i.e. inner) spheres—first the pure and then the mixed (12):

For the narrower (rings) are filled with unmixed fire; those that follow them, with night to which a portion of fire is added; and between these (between Fire and Night) is the goddess who rules all things: in all things she rules over hateful birth and comingling, leading the female to the male for union, and again conversely the male to the female.

That is to say, below the aether of pure fire and the fiery rings of the stars are various dirty and contaminated layers. In these every power is at work which engenders all sorts of things and creatures from the abominable and mistaken duality of the universe. Parmenides sees it as a kind of aphrodisiac compulsion. The close juxtaposition of the two elements, the female soft-and-warm and the male hard-and-cold (A 53), unleashes forces of communion and commingling which by their uncontrolled (A 34) interplay call into existence all that is transitory.[32] In a similar vein Hesiod had made practically everything arise from matings and births, and had set up Eros as the great creative force. Next to the goddess of sexual union Parmenides places the god of sexual desire (13):

First of all gods she created Eros.

This pair of divinities has its opposites in War and Contention, the powers of division and destruction, dissolution and death. (A 37).

The outermost of the 'mixed' spheres, according to Parmenides, was that marked by the circle of the Milky Way. A slender stream of fire trickled through the night and caused the 'heavenly milk' to shine with a dull radiance, unlike the sharp and brightly sparkling stars of the higher spheres (A 37; 43; 43a). The pure sun revolved above it, and the impure moon in strict correspondence below it. The moon, he says, shines only with borrowed light, being itself more of the nature of night. With a heavy pathos he describes the ambiguous double nature of the moon:

Night-shining, wandering about the earth, alien light, (14) always looking towards the rays of the sun. (15)[33]

[32] Parmenides, considering only unmoving Being to be real, stigmatizes the unceasing reproduction found in the world of the senses as 'abominable' or 'hateful.' In this connection we should remember that in the archaic epoch the union of man and woman had no high ideals attached to it: it was only the sterile passion between members of the same sex that was regarded highly. The indirect testimonies give us no notion of this strong revulsion, since they only pass on the dry groundwork of his teachings. On the emotional content see below p. 367f.

[33] W. Jaeger (*Rhein. Mus.* 100, 1957, 42ff.) thinks that a description of the sun as περὶ γῆν ἰὸν νυκτικρυφὲς φῶς went before this passage. On the double nature of the moon cf. (e.g.) Plato, *Symp.* 190b.

It is as if Parmenides saw here an image of sublunary humanity,[34] tied to its dark and cloudy sphere, but still turning with longing to the purer light of heaven, to which the nobler qualities in man's peculiar nature are akin. The bright part of us strives towards illumination through the whole truth, while the other side of our mixed nature, the night side, as it were, darkens and corrupts our understanding of the world.

This brings us to a consideration of Parmenides' theory of cognition, which naturally occupied a key position in his double system of Being and Appearance.

It has long been observed that we can only understand or indeed perceive certain things if we have them in our own nature: the idea of benevolence can only be grasped by the benevolent, and one who does not hate cannot understand hatred. In the most general terms, such observations lead us to a theory of perception by correspondence between likes. Parmenides refines the notion to this point, that light reveals itself to light, and darkness to darkness. 'He who is dead seeks not light, warmth and sound, but cold and silence and opposite qualities'; this was Parmenides' teaching according to Theophrastus (A 46). The two 'forms' light and darkness have a kind of awareness with which they feel and perceive themselves and their like. Since man is made up of light and darkness, he knows and sees around him an equally dual universe.

With this in mind we can turn to a difficult fragment on the theory of perception (16):

For as from time to time the mixture of our inconstantly wandering[35] members chances to be, so is a man's thinking set up.[36] Identical with what a man thinks is the nature of his members, in all men and in each.[37] That

[34] The notion of the 'sublunary world' is common in later philosophy. An echo of it comes in Kotzebue's *Gesellschaftslied* of 1802: 'Es kann schon nicht alles so bleiben/hier unter dem wechselnden Mond.'

[35] On πολυπλάγκτων cf. *Frühgriech. Denken* 31 and 34.

[36] On παρέστηκεν (for the reading see B. Snell in *Glotta* 37, 1958, 316) compare B1, 24: Parmenides comes escorted by the maidens personifying light and thought. The medical writers use προσίστασθαι of disorders 'set up' by a particular mixing of the humours (Hippocr. I p. 50, 20 and 63, 8 Heiberg).

[37] The language and thought of the fragment are along the same lines as *Od.* 18, 136f. and Archilochus fr. 68 (on both see above p. 134f.). There we are told that the feelings and thoughts of men are conditioned by the circumstances in which we find ourselves from time to time. What the writers had in mind was our varying attitudes in practical life—sometimes confident and daring, sometimes diffident and spiritless. Parmenides now replaces the variations of external circumstances by the varying constitution of our own members; furthermore, he is talking of changes in our view of the world, sometimes containing more of light and truth, sometimes of darkness and falsehood. It is not surprising that Parmenides' thesis

which is greater is the thought (?)[38]

Thus our manner of thinking varies according to the proportion of light or darkness in our human constitution; for what we perceive and think is of the same kind as the constitution of that which perceives and thinks, since the individual receives impressions and constructs ideas from those constituents which are akin to himself. All men consequently have a dual world-picture (cf. fr. 8, 52–59 and fr. 9), and each individual's world-picture is clear or clouded by illusion in a greater or less degree according to his individual constitution and its variations from time to time.[39]

Parmenides' system of the illusory world is rounded and complete. Since we men are a product of the false world, our nature is prone to error; and again that defective nature projects upon the outside world the faults of its own constitution, and thinks that it finds its own nature confirmed in the world of illusion. In the system of the real world the subject and object of cognition, namely Being and awareness of Being are even more wholly one (see above p. 356f.). In this way every statement in the double system of doctrine coheres logically with every other, and Parmenides can make the proud claim (5):

It matters naught to me whence I begin, for thither shall I return again.

The explanation of the sensible world ends with these verses (19):

Thus these things arose according to appearance (or: assumption) and are now, and in time to come, since they grow, they will come to an end; and for each of them men have introduced a name as a token.

He seems to be saying that the world of deception and of mere names is heading towards its dissolution, for the very reason that movement and growth necessarily entails death and dissolution. It is explicitly stated (A 23) that Parmenides gave no further details about the coming end of the world.

should crop up again among medical writers: 'In Galen's opinion, Chrysippus owed his right understanding of the world to the right mixture of the elements in his body,' says L. Edelstein (*Bull. Hist. of Medicine* 1952 p. 306), with reference to Galen *De sequela* c. 11 and 4 (4 p. 814ff. and p. 784 Kühn). On individual points in the text and on the interpretation of fr. 16 see *Frühgriech. Denken* p. 173–179.

[38] This last sentence is hard to understand: for a provisional interpretation see the following note.

[39] The fragments do not tell us directly how Parmenides was able to emancipate himself from all human fallibility. Probably he assumed that in a state of enlightenment like that in which he depicts himself in the opening verses our power of judgment (λόγος and κρίσις, 7, 5; 8, 15f.; 8, 50) sees through and renders harmless all errors imposed upon us by the night side of our nature, thanks to the victory of the 'more' (16, 4?) or preponderance of light in it. Cf. G. Vlastos, *Trans. Am. Phil. Assoc.* 77 (1946) 66ff. and *Gnomon* 31 (1959) 193–195.

We have now in all essential points come to the end of our information about the philosophy of Parmenides. It unites grandeur of intuition with strictness of logic. He had gazed upon Being in all its plenitude and glory, but also in all its austerity and exclusiveness. Just as Xenophanes had chosen to believe in god as god and as nothing else, so Parmenides worked out his notion of Being as pure Being and nothing else; and he used his razor-edged dialectic to defend it against all common-sense doubts as the unique and perfect actuality. The metaphysical spirit here rules supreme.

This metaphysical spirit (cf. 1, 1 θυμός) is most completely expressed in the opening, in which the philosopher describes his own ascent into pure and inerrant reason in dramatic and vigorous images. There is a sequence of three scenes: the furious journey from night into day; the passing of a gate that opens to one man only; the gracious reception on the other side. The autobiographical 'I' at first appears quite openly; then it is latent and implied in the horses, chariot, maidens, etc.; then directly again in the address (1, 22ff.), where it is ennobled by the goddess' hand-clasp, to be replaced by 'you' on the lips of the divine speaker. This 'you' has a personal character as long as it is denoting (as in 24–32) the recipient of an exclusive favour, one who has raised himself above the fluctuations of humanity. But when the 'you' recurs later, as it sometimes does, it denotes only the audience of the lecture—in one instance Parmenides particularly (8, 61), elsewhere anyone who through his intermediacy will hear or read the poem.

The description of the journey and the expounding of the revelation complement each other precisely. The personal and the objective never interfere or overlap. The introduction is practically devoid of any didactic quality: it merely describes how the philosopher freed himself from all the ties of his darkling existence in this world and came through the gate of understanding to his shining goal beyond the world. All this is expressed as pure event and experience, without a word about the content of the reasoning processes which carried the narrator out of this world to the world beyond. Conversely, in the doctrinal part the element of personal experience disappears under the intellectual argumentation; although here and there among the proofs and disproofs something of that great effort shows through which Parmenides put into his spiritual battle (see below p. 367f.). Nevertheless we can venture to fill the gaps and reconstruct the culmination of the experience, since the logical strictness of Parmenides' system leaves little room for doubts and hesitations.

Being was, according to Parmenides, conscious Being, and the single but sufficient content of its consciousness was the fact of existing. We can only render this consciousness as, 'I am, and I am the All-One; apart from me is nothing.' Thus there is no room for anything else, no room for a someone to stand beside this Being and be cognizant of it. On the contrary, Parmenides in his time of ecstatic inspiration must have felt himself identical with Being. This implies that in his ecstacy he lost consciousness not only of his being part of the world and of humanity, but also of his existence as an individual and in time.

That Parmenides in fact attained this condition can neither be proved by documentary evidence nor decisively disproved.[40] But there are powerful arguments to support our assumption that Parmenides personally experienced the *unio mystica* with true Being.[41]

---

[40] Apart from general considerations which could be urged this way or that, I see two possible objections: (1) Parmenides makes no mention of such an experience; (2) by his own account he received this doctrine as a young man (1, 24 κοῦρε—this is the word used by Penelope in addressing the suitors, e.g. *Od.* 19, 141) and a disciple (1, 31 μαθήσεαι), and is treated as one who still needs enlightenment and conversion.

(1) But we could not expect the archaic thinker to speak openly of his experience, when Plato himself, at a much later period, recognized that the highest and most individual elements of his doctrine could not be expressed in his published works (cf. J. Stenzel, *Kl. Schriften* 151–170).

(2a) To the best of my knowledge no one has yet taken literally the matter of Parmenides' being instructed by a goddess (cf. W. Kranz, *Neue Jahrb.* 1924, p. 65ff.). Instead it has been considered that the doctrine which he puts into the mouth of the goddess is his own original thought; that the goddess who confronts him represents objective truth as he recognized it; and that this truth had never entered his mind until he had worked it out for himself. (This is not contradicted by his having felt this understanding as a gift from above, cf. B. 1, 26f. We should not nowadays deny a man credit for his accomplishments because we considered him 'gifted,' nor would the early Greeks: Agamemnon's remark in *Il.* 1, 178 is prompted by spite.)

(2b) Insofar as the Parmenides of the introduction is a favoured mortal who has achieved the great end of his hopes, he is Parmenides in person; but while Parmenides is putting the doctrine into a poem for recitation and study, he is communicating the 'goddess's' revelation to the public, and it is thus the hearer or reader, not Parmenides in person, to whom the statements, arguments, pieces of advice (2, 1; 6, 2; 7, 5) and warnings (6, 3ff.; 7, 2; 7, 3–5; 8, 7f.) are addressed while the author in presenting the poem becomes merely the voice of the 'goddess,' i.e. the voice of truth.

Hence neither point 2a ('The goddess apparently an external and alien power') nor point 2b ('Parmenides appears as one who learns, not one who knows') is relevant to our enquiry whether Parmenides' knowledge represents his own experience.

[41] Of the arguments favouring the thesis I select the following three (very briefly) as the most important.

(1) The representation of the journey upwards has all the marks of experience:

If that had not been so, he could only have postulated and argued for the unity and uniqueness of pure Being, not have actually conceived it, and the Parmenidean Being could never have attained that self-sufficing maturity which, according to him, it had possessed from all time (8, 42–49). We may further suspect that he aimed at this *henosis*—for how else would he have come to achieve it? It is only such an intention which renders truly intelligible his thesis of the identity of thinking and being, and of a Being which is aware of itself alone. It is a matter therefore of some importance philosophically, not a mere detail of biography, that we should answer affirmatively the question whether Parmenides intended and achieved in personal experience the culmination of his system of thought.

Only for a very short time, probably only for moments, would Parmenides, as a Westerner, have experienced the mystic union: speedily he would sink back into the lower level of the world of appearance, which then laid hold upon him and mastered him like any other. But he would still retain his theoretical knowledge of the truth and the ability to advance arguments for it such as those contained in the main part of the poem. Moreover, he would retain the memory of the reality of his former ascent and the hope that the experience described in the introduction would be repeated (cf. the present tense in the first verse). For the critical and constructive analysis of the world of appearance, on the other hand, he had no need of ecstatic experience: for that purpose the 'ice-cold logic' (Nietzsche) which he had at his command was quite sufficient.

Thanks to the accident which has preserved so much of the original text, we can form in this case some idea of the emotional background

is Parmenides' experience likely to have ended abruptly before its consummation? Would this inward perception have died away at the very moment of crossing the threshold to his goal?

(2) Could Parmenides actually have believed in his theory, which compelled him to deny what he and everyone else saw and heard around them at every moment (cf. 7, 4f.), if the ultimate point to which his conception could soar was this, that in addition to Being, outside that which suffers nothing outside itself, there was nevertheless a Parmenides to whom this state of things had been revealed? This, be it remembered, is the Parmenides who boasts in the first verse that his thought can carry him as far as he will.

(3) Parmenides' thought displays a radical, even brutal, consistency. His most powerful argument against the existence of the world was that a recognition of the world of appearance necessarily involved the recognition of Not-being, and that Not-being cannot be because the conception of a Not-being is 'utterly inscrutable' (2, 6 παναπευθέα, cf. also 8, 21 ἄπυστος) and 'beyond accomplishment' (2, 7 οὐ γὰρ ἀνυστόν, cf. also 8, 8; 8, 17). Would not so consistent a thinker have been compelled to abandon the central core of his ontology if he had not actually experienced and realized this conception? Such a realization could only occur in personal experience of Being.

to the processes of thought from which his doctrines emerged. The realm of Parmenidean truth is pervaded not by the pious tranquillity of a *nirvana* attained by the 'awakened' Indian sage (*buddha*), or, in Greek terms, it is not the windless calm (γαλήνη) of a beatific peace after the flight from the storms of coming-to-be and passing away. We feel rather the triumph of a great binding and controlling power over something that struggles wilfully against its supremacy. This something that is defeated we may identify with that natural Being which reveals itself to us in all our experience and all our own energies as something made up of a thousand basically different components, something that can only be grasped fragment by fragment, restlessly moving and changing, moving and moved at random, embracing at once coming-to-be and passing away, life and death. Of the masterful violence of Parmenides' thinking the texts speak in unmistakable language, which we shall now render word for word as accurately as possible. The compelling decision has been taken; an overpowering (κρατερή) Necessity (ἀνάγκη, which could also be rendered 'compulsion') has laid upon Being the bonds (these 'bonds' or 'fetters' are mentioned several times) of a boundary which surrounds it on all sides; Right (δίκη) does not unloose the bonds so as to give Being the power to come into existence and to pass away, but instead holds it tight; Fate has constrained Being to be complete (= all-embracing) and unmoved. This Necessity (or 'Compulsion') is 'subject to much contention' or 'much given to contention' (πολύδηρις); true conviction has banished afar off all coming-to-be and passing away; the goddess will not permit (a false statement of thought); the strength of conviction will not allow that there should be anything else apart from Being. If in addition we consider the headlong career described in the opening, so furious that the axles scream and become red-hot, we see that it was no dreamy and airy wafting away that carried Parmenides to his goal, but the impulsion of hard and vigorous powers. These powers are the illuminating force of his thoughts, presented symbolically as the horses which draw his chariot and as the daughters of the Sun who hasten his team onward, who do not merely draw back, but hurl aside, the veils from their heads.[42]

This bold thrust into the open space beyond the world of men did not merely win for Parmenides his knowledge of ultimate reality; it

[42] The door, on the contrary, does not open with a thunderous crash (as in *Od.* 21, 48–50); it is not even burst open, but Right (or Righteousness) obediently opens the gate to allow passage to the man whom the sun-maidens escort: i.e. to correct thinking the door of truth is opened without fuss or resistance (see above p. 352, n. 8).

also enabled him to survey our world of appearance and to explain its structure, its laws and it origins with equally rigorous consistency. But the further problem of the relation between reality and appearance has to remain unsolved. Just as in Xenophanes' system the relation of the unmoved god to the moved world is never explained, so the crack that yawns in the Parmenidean system cannot be plastered over by any stretch of ingenuity. For Xenophanes god and the world had differed greatly in their degree of accessibility to human thought, but both were equally real: for Parmenides, however, only the one Being was firmly established in true reality, while the world and every object or event in it hung in the void suspended by a rope of misconception fastened only to itself.[43]

Xenophanes was as spiritual as could be in his theology and as earthly as could be in his narrow cosmology; Parmenides' metaphysic is richer and broader beyond comparison, and it is all cast in one mould. Yet in many ways he is the pupil of Xenophanes. There is one characteristic feature common to both their critical methods: for the one the gods of common belief, for the other the world of common experience appeared as an anthropomorphic illusion. If a modern illustration may be used, human nature is looking through a window into the twilight, and is not aware that the appearance of what it thinks it sees is overlaid with its own reflected image. Only by standing outside can we dispel this naive illusion.

That unique escape upwards from the earthly world which Parmenides accomplished removed him also in some sense from the continuity of history. His thought is conditioned and sustained by an objective, abstract consistency which has nothing to do with accidents of time or place. Hence it is impossible to draw a line between the direct influence of his doctrines and the effect which the problems that he raised produced spontaneously on later generations. The latter has lasted until our own time.

Of his immediate pupils there are two of whom we can form some notion, Melissus and Zeno of Elea. Zeno sought to prove the homogeneous continuum postulated by Parmenides by presenting with much wit and ingenuity the difficulties that arise if one assumes, on the one hand, infinite divisibility, or on the other, elementary quanta

---

[43] Another, but less serious, difficulty is that in the analysis of the sense-world he equates not-being with opposite-being, non-perception with perception of the non-existent, and (this being the boldest assumption) 'night' with material. Parmenides did not need to fear attack on these peculiarities, since they result from an assumption which he declares to be basically false and which therefore must lead to inconsistencies—namely the recognition of negatives as quasi-positive and having a real existence.

which are incapable of further division.[44] On the former assumption Zeno's contemporary Anaxagoras built his original system, while the latter led to the atomic theory. But these things are beyond our scope: we will examine them no further, but turn instead to Parmenides' great contemporary Heraclitus.

(d) *Heraclitus*

From Parmenides' poem we possess at all events two continuous sections of a page or two in length: the prose treatise of Heraclitus 'the dark' has left no single fragment longer than a few lines. Yet these detached sentences exercise a compelling power. They lay hold on the reader before he yet understands their matter; but for all that, Heraclitus' teaching is one sustained call to sober and vigilant awareness.

The fragments are monumental even in their isolation. Each bears its own full load of meaning and moves to a rhythm of its own creation. One might naturally call them sayings or proverbs rather than fragments. But in the best archaic tradition these component parts have a family kinship with one another. The hundred or more sentences could be arranged in almost any order that one chose: in any arrangement one would see many significant connexions, anticipations, reminiscences, and the thoughts set in motion by one are continued and developed in the others. The experiment speaks volumes for the consistency and unity of the doctrine and for the compelling eloquence of its author; but it also shows that the structure of the work cannot be recovered by conjecture. The book is lost, yet some basic outlines of Heraclitus' philosophy can still be traced.

Heraclitus was contemporary with Parmenides (c. 500?). He was a citizen of Ephesus, the Ionian city of Asia Minor, and no ordinary citizen. It accords with the regal haughtiness of his language that as the scion of the ancient ruling house he possessed the rank and title of king, and rejected it. He resigned the honour—which since the establishment of the democracy had become a kind of archpriest-hood—in favour of his brother. The treatise in which he formulated his doctrine was not intended for a disciple, or for the Greeks, or for humanity at large. Instead he dedicated it to his native deity Artemis (the 'Diana of the Ephesians' mentioned in the *Acts of the Apostles*) and deposited it in her temple.

---

[44] Cf. *Frühgriech. Denken* p. 198–236. While for millennia it seemed that the alternatives of infinite divisibility or indivisible elementary quanta were of purely speculative interest, they are now more real than ever as one of the most urgent concerns of descriptive physics.

The human public had shown itself inaccessible to the *logos* that Heraclitus preached; his words had always fallen on deaf ears. His book began thus (1):

This logos, which is true for ever, men are alike unable to understand before hearing it and after they have once heard it.[1] For although everything happens according to this logos, yet they are like those who have never known it, though they experience words and actions of such kind as I set forth here, treating severally each thing according to its nature and describing its relation; but to other men all that they do in their waking hours escapes them like the things which they forget when asleep.

Human beings—so we are told in this, the longest of all the extant fragments[2]—do not understand the sense of life by themselves, nor do they receive the explanation when it is offered to them, as the philosopher offers it in this book.[3] He is going to analyse all things and describe them according to their nature, and thereby establish the *logos*. *Logos* is a word belonging to everyday speech: the early philosophers did not concern themselves to develop terms of art. It meant *inter alia* the content of an expression and the motive or end of an action; if one said that there was no *logos* in something, it meant that the thing had no sense or no relevance. *Logos* is also the reckoning-up that one gives, i.e. the explanation and justification of one's actions or statements. Since the *logos* provides explanations, it is first and foremost of a rational nature ('logical'); secondly, it is not always on the surface of things, but has to be looked for in and behind the phenomena; if one has the luck to find it, it will reduce seeming confusion to order and bring within one purview what seemed to be widely different. Heraclitus' *logos* is the sense and basis of the world; the norm and rule which determines everything, by understanding which we make everything comprehensible. In speaking of this *logos* at the outset of his book he signifies at once the content of the book and the subject which it treats—the cosmic law.

Heraclitus often attacks in a similar vein the incomprehension of the stupid, who even in their own lives are virtually 'not there' (34):

---

[1] I take τὸ πρῶτον in the same sense as in *Il.* 4, 267; 6, 489; 19, 9 and 136: it denotes the deciding first event from which later things follow—or ought to follow, in this case, since surprisingly enough, no effect is produced.

[2] The style is typically archaic—a sustained concatenation by antitheses, e.g.: they do not *perceive* the world in which they *live*; the world in which *they* live, *I* explain to them; *I* explain it, to the *others* it is unperceived; unperceived in *waking* as if they were *sleeping*. The style corresponds to Heraclitus' view of the world, since for him all life is an oscillation between opposites, following each other in a continuous flux.

[3] In this connection cf. p. 257, n. 9.

Those without understanding hear and are as the deaf: the saying fits them, 'Here and not here.'

For perception does not at once imply awareness (107):

Poor witnesses for men are the eyes and ears of those whose souls understand not their language.[4]

From his own standpoint Heraclitus contradicts the saying of Archilochus: 'What men think is of like kind with what befalls them'[5] (17):

What they think is not of like kind with what befalls them, nor does instruction help them to understanding: they imagine things for themselves.[6]

Archilochus had meant: 'We have no genuine self, since our thoughts and feelings radically alter corresponding to the real circumstances to which we are from time to time exposed.' Heraclitus, enmeshed in his own ideas, read something quite different into the text of the old poet, and replied: 'The thoughts and feelings of men wholly fail to correspond to the realities in which they move; they set something up of themselves and consider it as true.'

Heraclitus alludes to the same notion in recounting a traditional joke. According to an amusing story, Homer in his old age passed by a group of fisher-boys who on that occasion were pursuing smaller prey than fish. The lads proposed a riddle to him, and in his chagrin at being unable to solve it, he died upon the spot. Men in general, Heraclitus thought, were in the same position (56)

as Homer, who was the wisest of all the Greeks. Boys who were hunting lice made a fool of him by saying, 'What we saw and caught, we leave behind: what we neither saw nor caught, we take with us.'

The wisest of men, outwitted by verminous children—that was a situation after Heraclitus' heart (cf. fr. 83; 117; 121). But he felt that the paradoxical riddle had a special relevance for him: it was couched in a style like his own, and could be made the vehicle of his own ideas. 'What men see with their eyes and grasp with their hands, they throw away without understanding it and making it their own; but the true realities in which and from which they derived their existence they carry like lice in their clothing, which escape both their

---

[4] For the interpretation of βαρβάρους cf. Bruno Snell's translation in *Heraklit, Fragmente*, Munich, 1926.

[5] Archilochus fr. 68, see above p. 134f.; on Parmenides' inversion of Archilochus' idea see above p. 363, n. 37.

[6] Probably we should read (with Bergk) τοιαῦτα ὁκοίοις; πολλοί was added by Clement in citing it.

eyes and their hands. They do not grasp what they are concerned with: what they have they do not possess; for they do not understand the *logos* in accordance with which all things happen.'

Now what is this *logos*, this norm of all existence? What is it that is the reality of all realities and the very life of our life? It is the *coincidentia oppositorum*, the coming together of opposites to make a two-sided unity.

In the philosophy of Heraclitus that polarized way of thought and perception which had dominated the whole archaic period attained its sharpest definition and its most complete theoretical expression. What Hesiod had begun, Heraclitus brought to fulfilment. The opposites 'night and day', excluding, yet supporting and complementing each other, were finely pictured by Hesiod as a compelled union of contraries in his image of the gate.[7] They are never in the house together, but they come face to face on the threshold, when one goes out into the world, into existence and activity, while the other passes into the region beyond the world, into cessation and rest. In this image Hesiod almost, but not quite, reached the Heraclitean Truth. He had come to a stop immediately before the decisive realization (57):

Hesiod is most men's instructor; he is acknowledged as having known most—he who did not know day and night: for they are one.

Day and night are not each a thing in itself: they are the two sides of the same thing. Both have their end and their beginning in the tension that unites them. The transformation from night to day and from day to night, their recurrent arising from and passing away into each other is the basis of their existence and the content of their being.

Living and dead, waking and sleeping, young and old are the same. For this being transformed is that, and that being transformed is this. (88)

The cold is heated, the hot cooled, the moist dried and the dry moistened. (126)[8]

Heraclitus and Parmenides adopted the most widely divergent positions imaginable in facing the same problem. Parmenides considered opposition and antithesis as meaningless; if however, such an assumption was made, as in the world of appearance, each of the opposites existed 'in itself' (above p. 359f.). But for Heraclitus

---

[7] *Theog.* 748ff., above p. 104. Parmenides also in his own way adopted the image of the gate of the universe, the gate of night and day (above p. 351).

[8] That these two fragments belong together may be inferred from the polemic of Melissus (30 B8, 2–3) against them; cf. also Plato, *Phaedo* 71 bc.

opposition is the very stuff of reality, and the opposites continually pass one into another. For Parmenides there can be nothing but a unitary unmoving Being; for Heraclitus nothing exists but difference and change in events.

The teachings of Heraclitus are not concerned with substances, but with qualities and conditions, such as warm/cold, wet/dry in the sphere of what we should call the inorganic, or living/dead, waking/ sleeping, young/old in the biological field. What was important to him was that one should be aware of the dynamic in the interplay of opposites, and should recognize and welcome it as the law of all existence.

On the same principle values only exist by virtue of the negative values that are their opposites (111):

Sickness made health a good and pleasant thing, hunger fullness and exertion rest.

A similar feeling had made Mimnermus and Anacreon regard old age and death as a spice to the confident strength of youth and as the price paid for the enjoyment of life. For Heraclitus, all pleasurable feeling was derived from pain,[9] and he who valued the one was not entitled to protest against the other.

With equal logic the relation could be turned the other way round, so that pain was dominant and pleasure appeared only as its reverse side. But the philosophy of Heraclitus is not the expression of a morbid languor, but of a powerful and earnest vitality. He lays the stress on the positive side. He regards transformation not as an oppressive necessity, but as a restoring of strength:

It is exhaustion to serve and be subject to the same things. (84b)

In changing it takes repose. (84a)

A uniform existence, like that postulated in its extreme form by Parmenides, an existence which necessity has cast one for all in a rigid mould, seemed to Heraclitus a harsh servitude. He also scornfully rejected a third possibility—that good and evil added up to an indeterminate nullity in between, like the *apeiron* of Anaximander, to which opposites ultimately returned as a kind of mutual penance. Heraclitus was not interested in a compromise in which positive and negative values disappeared.

The rule that the negative value gives rise to the positive, as the night to the day, is equally valid for him where moral values are being considered (23):

[9] Cf. also e.g. Plato's *Phaedo* 60b and 70e.

They would not know even the name of justice, if this (injustice) did not exist.

Here again the positive side is uppermost (102):

For god all is fair, good and just; but men (call) some things just and some unjust.

What he means is apparently that man and god have different things in view. Man considers individual events, and thus he thinks them good or bad from instance to instance. God sees all evil at once, and at the same time sees all good; and the wider the horizon that a thought takes in, the truer and clearer, according to Heraclitus, is the picture that it gains (below p. 390f.). For god, who takes all things together, wrong becomes the basis for the existence of a moral code, and thus right triumphs: not as a victor over wrong and in despite of it, but together with and thanks to wrong. That there exist both good and bad, is good.

Here we enter on a new area within the Heraclitean theory of opposites. Day and night, waking and sleeping, health and sickness change one into another and put an end one to another in temporal sequence; good and wicked actions, on the contrary, have no such alternation, but each can exist as either single or multiple acts without the other. Yet even so, for Heraclitus right and wrong, good and evil, are only the two sides of the same thing, since in their very nature they are related one to another by the tension of their opposition.[10]

We can now unriddle a very striking and obscure-sounding fragment (62):

Immortal mortal, mortal immortal, living the death of the others, and dying the life of the others.

Gods and men, by virtue of the gulf of oppositeness that separates and unites them, are one; and the human/divine lives in the gods the death of men, just as in men it dies the indestructible life of the gods.[11]

Heraclitus speaks again and again of opposites, but the word 'opposite' does not occur in the extant fragments. The relation is denoted by other, less intelligible names (fr. 10). It can be called 'war' (53):

[10] In the realm of values Heraclitus' theory is substantially true. If, for example, all men were 'good' and were unable to be otherwise, there would be no merit in being 'good.' The value thus disappears, and 'men would not even know its name.'

[11] The dictum of Heraclitus is historically quite true, since the gods were created by the Greeks (and others) as counterparts to men (see above p. 53–56). Pindar's formulation of the position was that gods and men were dissimilar brothers, born of one mother, but set apart by their very different characters (*Nem.* 6 1ff., see below p. 472f.).

War is father of all things, king of all things; he has made some to be gods, others to be men, has made some slaves, some free.

Gods are sovereign rulers over men, and men equally sovereign over slaves. The power which creates the relation (as father) and regulates it (as king) is 'war' or struggle. The struggle and mutual contention of opposites have caused gods to be called gods and men men; and all slavery in antiquity went back directly or indirectly to captivity in war. In addition, discord governed the relations of masters and slaves at all three levels, fed by the caprice and jealous maintenance of privilege of the former and the envy and spirit of revolt of the latter.[12]

The thesis of the identity of opposites, in itself paradoxical, brought further paradoxes in its train (80):

One must know that war is common to all and that justice is strife—

For the first part of this dictum Heraclitus adopted the old Greek saying that war is common to all.[13] War is a common undertaking of the opposing parties, who agree that killing shall be permitted and submit themselves to the decision of battle. For the expression 'Justice is conflict' Heraclitus found a starting-point in the fact that the same word *dike* in Greek means justice and a lawsuit. The administration of justice would lose its meaning and function if it were not counteracting a chaos of conflicting interests.

'War is a thing in common.' If we understand 'war' here in the wider sense, the sentence means that opposition is composition. The following then is also true (10):

Combinations (?) are whole and not-whole, agreeing disagreeing, consonant dissonant, and one out of all and all out of one.

Parmenides would only allow wholeness and unity to be real; but in Heraclitus' eyes wholeness and parts belonged inseparably together, and the unity of the all rested upon its embracing multiplicity. Musical harmony (Greek *harmotto* 'to fit together') was based on the difference of high and low notes (A 22; B 8). The instrument of musical harmony, the lyre, has tension in the essence of its construction (51):

[12] The words 'father of all' and 'king of all' applied to war contradict the most cherished convictions and stand them on their heads. Ares the slayer and destroyer becomes the begetter and father of all: war, the most violent opponent of law (e.g. *Vorsokr.* 89, 7, 6 p. 403, 32ff.) steals from law the honourable title of 'king of all' (Pindar fr. 169 Snell).

[13] Cf. *Iliad* 18, 309 and Archilochus 38 (above p. 148). The same idea is implicit in Pindar *Nem.* 4, 30ff., where the formulation is obviously influenced by Heraclitus (cf. ἄπειρο- and λόγον ὁ μὴ ξυνιείς as in Heraclitus fr. 1.)

They do not understand how that which differs is of one sense (*logos*) with itself; backstretched (reading παλίντονος) harmony as of bow or lyre.

'back-stretched' is a Homeric adjective for the bow, and stretching or tension (Gr. *tonos*) gives the bow its speed and the lyre its sound. The double illustration involves at once a new opposition. The bow is the weapon of battle and death, while the lyre stands for peace and harmony, and the two together were the emblems of Apollo, the god of death and of music.[14] But this duality in unity can be seen in the bow itself (48):

The bow's name is life, but its work is death.

This untranslatable dictum is based on the accident that the same four letters (*bios*) spell the words for 'bow' and 'life' in Greek, and that *ergon* 'work' can also mean fact or actuality as opposed to mere words or names.

Despite this gloomy saying, the positive side is predominant in the interplay of conflict and harmony (54):

Unseen harmony is mightier than seen.

By 'unseen' he certainly meant here that deeper harmony in which the principles of accord and discord find themselves at one. Here the doctrine of opposites reaches its third and highest level. Not only does that which can change into its opposite (e.g. night and day) form a unity with its opposite; not only does that which derives its very nature from its opposite (as right from wrong) likewise form a unity with it; but the principle of harmony itself is inseparable from that of opposition. The notion of 'harmony' becomes void if it is applied to things which were already of like kind and in agreement (cf. A 22).

Parmenides' philosophy looked on life with disfavour: that of Heraclitus, on the contrary, was the first, as it were, to put life into life. His philosophy certainly derived much also from the characteristic way of living of his age, which was accustomed to think in terms of black and white, and in its emotional experience embraced the principle of polar opposition with passionate abandon (as we have seen many times and shall see again). Thus most of the sayings of Heraclitus, although they deal in universals, are in immediate contact with life; they are not dealing with extraordinary things, but with the customary things of our existence, which they seize upon

---

[14] Cf. Pindar *Pyth.* 8, 1–20, see below p. 497–99 with note 10. For juxtaposition of bow and lyre cf. *Od.* 21, 405–11 and Theognis Trag. p. 769 Nauck: φόρμιγγα ἄχορδον = τόξον.

with a new and dramatic intensity, revealed in the necessary inter-play of opposites. The reader is at once carried along with the dynamic movement of Heraclitus' assertions;[15] and, although he is never addressed in person—the book was dedicated to Artemis, not to human beings—the content and style of the work impress the author's individuality upon the reader so forcibly that we need not illustrate the point by specific examples.

We are told that Heraclitus expounded the theory of opposites with especial exhaustiveness because he reckoned it as his greatest discovery (*Vorsokr.* II, p. 422, 37ff.); and it is true that, as soon as we adopt his theory, we see life and the world in a new perspective. With startling simplicity the *logos* reveals the hidden order behind seeming disorder. Evil and suffering are not explained away, but rather logically justified as the necessary ground for what is good and beautiful. Heraclitus could bring this realization to meet a crying need of his generation. The feeling of being stretched between opposite extremes constituted the greatness and the tragedy of archaic man, and the burden that one bears becomes more tolerable if one can recognize it as inevitable, as arising from the basic nature of the things to which it applies.

Many other of Heraclitus' doctrines can be derived without difficulty from his theory of opposites. If, for example, we turn round his statement that opposites come together in a kind of identity, it then tells us that identity only exists through opposition. All being for Heraclitus consisted in a perpetual alternation of change or in a tension never to be relaxed. Even a seemingly uniform existence is in reality a continuous process of self-destruction and self-renewal:

[15] The effortless power which Heraclitus exerts over the reader becomes some-times quite tyrannical. If ever another writer adopts part of Heraclitus' doctrine or refers to his sayings, he is liable to start writing like Heraclitus himself. This can be seen in the contexts of our fragments of Heraclitus and in the 'imitations' (*Vorsokr.* under 'C', detailed reference p. 252 n. 1). This makes it all the more difficult to distinguish the genuine quotations from the half-genuine paraphrases and wholly false imitations. Among the B-fragments in Diels we can recognize some as belonging to the last two groups. This applies for example to some of the pieces coming from the *Meditations* of Marcus Aurelius. Thus B 73, coming from the fourth book of the *Meditations*, was derived by the emperor from the ending of the genuine fr. 1 (G. S. Kirk, Heraclitus, *The Cosmic Fragments*, Cambridge, 1954, p. 44f.); and B 75, from the sixth book, is a further development of the emperor's from B 73, as Gerhard Breithaupt has shown (*De Marci Aur. Anton. Commentariis . . .*, Göttinger, Diss., 1913, p. 21–23). In B 71, from the same group, I propose to reduce the citation somewhat. The emperor tells himself 'to remember' not 'the man who, according to Heraclitus, forgot . . .,' but 'that which I am accustomed to forget': τοῦ ἐπιλανθανομένου is passive (like ἐπιλελησμένον in *Luke* 12, 6) and middle: the passive use does not occur elsewhere in Marcus Aurelius, but it is typical of him to reproach himself for forgetting good teaching, as in 12, 26.

New waters are always flowing into the same rivers;[16] so also souls steam upwards from moisture. (12)

Our life (or our 'soul'—*psychê* serves for either) maintains itself and its identity only by the continuous afflux of new coming-to-be, while it is simultaneously in continuous decay:[17] 'Souls steam upwards from moisture' (see below p. 385). Fed from below and vanishing away above, our soul is a phenomenon that in continuous passing-away presents the false appearance of continuous existence.

The physical preconceptions connected with the life-process in Heraclitus' philosophy will concern us later. At present let us find in this dictum only the idea of a continuous exchange, giving and receiving, between our self and the external world. The soul is not a separate entity; rather, the cosmic process in one of its many passages from a lower to a higher state ('steaming' or 'evaporation') causes something to arise which we feel as our personal life. Consequently the nature of things is accessible to us by way of self-knowledge (101):

I have sought out myself.

In the 'I' which is aware of itself in clarity and certainty the subject and object of recognition coincide. Here, in the individual existence, the general existence may be immediately experienced in seeing and feeling, in doing and suffering, in the tension of opposites and in the creative power of transformation.

If by looking into our own soul we can gain access to the very core of reality, this implies that everything that cannot be attained by such introspection is comparatively speaking unreal. The whole world of mechanical nature, which is only given to us from outside, is thus unreal. Even the greatest of the heavenly bodies, which rules over the regular cycle of the seasons (fr. 100) is a wretchedly small object when compared with the soul (3 and 45):

The sun is as broad as a man's foot; you can find no boundaries to the soul in whatever direction you may wander, so profound a sense (*logos*) has it.[18]

[16] I follow André Rivier (*Un emploi archaique de l'analogie chez Héraclite et Thucydide*, Lausanne, 1952, p. 13ff. and *Mus. Helv.* 13, 1956, p. 158–60) in striking out ἐμβαίνουσιν.

[17] Basing themselves on this image of a river, later interpreters embraced this side of Heraclitus' doctrine under the catch-phrase 'All things flow,' but the formula is ill-adapted to express his philosophy in general.

[18] Diogenes Laertius (9, 7) quotes fr. 3 and 45 together; cf. also (in a different application) Seneca *ep.* 88, 13: *intervalla siderum dicis; nihil est quod in mensuram tuam non cadat. Si artifex es, metire hominis animum.* For the wording cf. Lucret. 1, 958: *nulla regione viarum finitum.*

If a man lies on his back and holds his leg aloft, the breadth of his foot will cover the sun from side to side. But that same foot could never reach the boundaries of the soul, for in the soul lives and is conscious the meaning of the All. Like all things that are not known experimentally from outside but experienced themselves from within, the 'meaning' or 'sense' that is thus known is without measure or boundary; so indeed all the feelings that we have in any lively way are incapable of measurement: they fill us to the brim, overflow, and flood our entire world. But for Heraclitus the grounds for saying that the soul is immeasurable are objective rather than psychological. The individual soul, the only part of us that is not merely subject to, but an active bearer of the *logos*, becomes the 'seeker of itself' (above p. 379) and finds the one infinitely profound shaft through which it communicates with the cosmic *logos* and unites with this *logos* in a common understanding of existence—although on the part of the human soul this must remain an imperfect understanding. This is a very different communion from that of Parmenides with pure Being.

The notion of the 'depths' was associated in the thought of Heraclitus' time[19] with the idea of something inexhaustible and elemental that had its stable foundation in itself and completed itself from its own stores (115):

The soul has sense (*logos*) which increases itself.

Understanding leads by itself to greater understanding, and insight to deeper insight.

The world of physical nature, on the other hand, has had firm boundaries appointed by the decree of justice.[20] The sun again serves as an example. While the soul can plumb fathomless depths, the magnitude and course of the sun are narrowly defined, and the cosmic police, as it were (cf. *Il.* 19, 418) are on patrol to see that he keeps within them (94):

Helios will not overstep his measure. If he did, the Erinyes, the ministers of Dike (Justice), know where to find him.

The sun, the light of the physical world, must therefore be content with a subordinate role, when compared with the *logos* and its spiritual world. Homer glorified Helios as the god who 'sees all things and hears all things.' But the sun is a mere diurnal phenomenon (below p. 386). When Heraclitus says (16):

How can a man conceal himself from that which never sets?

[19] Cf. *Philologus* 87, 1932, 475; B. Snell, *Gnomon* 7, 1931, 81ff.
[20] Cf. G. Vlastos, *Class. Philol.* 42, 1947, 164ff.; K. Latte, *Antike und Abendland* II (Hamburg, 1946) 70.

he is thinking of the inextinguishable *logos*, the sense and the norm of all happenings below or on high.

Xenophanes also had assigned the least possible importance to the heavenly bodies in order to make as sharp a cleavage as possible between the worldly, to which they belong, and the divine (above p. 333f.). Heraclitus replaces this crude dichotomy by a division into three levels. First we ascend within the sensible world to the highest that we can find in it, only to learn that a further and similar ascent is necessary to reach the sphere of the transcendent. The first step is referred to in the following fragment (99):

If there were no sun, then despite the other stars we should live in darkness.[21]

The next step was probably seen in some such terms as, 'He for whom the light of the *logos* does not shine lives, despite the sun, in darkness like an animal.'[22]

The example which we have just given is to some degree a reconstruction, but the form of thought exemplified in it is known to be typical of Heraclitus.[23] Another example occurred in the very first fragment. Starting from the commonplace contrast of sleeping and waking, Heraclitus declared that the clear and wakeful state in which we imagine we live and do our business is like a heavy and troubled sleep when compared with the clearness possessed by one who has been awakened to the *logos*. Like the algebraic formula of the mean proportional (a:b = b:c), this image involves three terms representing each a different level upon the scale of a particular value.[24] The first term is one generally admitted to be of little or no value; the second is one recognized as valuable and high in the scale of everyday values; the third is a transcendent, to which the multitude is a stranger and towards which the philosopher wishes to direct our attention. The middle term units opposite qualities, according as it is compared with the first or the third; in fr. 53 (above p. 376) the free

[21] εὐφρόνην ἂν ἡγομεν as cited by Plutarch, *Mor.* 98c; in 957a also εὐφρόνην ἂν ἡγομεν would fit better than the transmitted εὐφρόνη ἂν ἦν, which probably is a mere manuscript corruption.

[22] I take the second step (cf. fr. 29 and others) from Plutarch, *Mor.* 98c; in 957 also the association of the quotation from Heraclitus with the notion of an animal existence is perceptible (πάντων ἂν ἀγριώτατον ζῷον κἀνδεέστατον ὁ ἄνθρωπος ἦν). We may add Clement, *Protr.* 113, 3 (vol. 1, p. 80 St.), adduced by Kirk, *Cosmic Frag.* (above n. 15) p. 162. No reliance can be placed upon Heraclitus fr. 134.

[23] Cf. *Frühgriech. Denken* p. 251–283.

[24] What is implied is a contrast rather than a ratio of magnitudes, and to this extent the comparison with the algebraic formula breaks down. Also the second contrast is incomparably more important than the first, and to this extent the 'equal' sign is inapplicable.

citizen, for all his pride, is master of his slave, but himself a slave to god. When a man takes his stand on the transcendent, the two lower terms recede into almost equal worthlessness, since the second contrast is much sharper and more decisive than the first. The awakened mind sees no difference between the sleep and the waking of other men; whether they have heard or not heard, seen or not seen, is all one (all this is in fr. 1); when they hear, they might as well be deaf, when present they might as well be absent (fr. 34, cf. fr. 107); the wise poet was outwitted by louse-ridden children (fr. 56); Hesiod, the teacher of the nation, did not know what was really important (fr. 57); the average man is no better than a cow (fr. 29 etc.).

The outline of the thought is completely visible in the following two sayings:

Men appear childish to god, as children to a man. (79)

The handsomest and wisest man is ugly and stupid compared with god, as the handsomest ape is when compared with a man. (82 and 83, paraphrased).[25]

In Heraclitus' day children were not considered as creatures of a different kind from adults, with different and positive characteristics, but only as a useless contemptible preliminary stage to maturity. As for the ape, that was rendered absurd and despicable to the human observer by the very fact of its looking and behaving almost like a man.[26] In a similar sense man is a caricature of god: in god's eyes the fairest human countenance is like an ape's grimace, and man's highest wisdom is infantile folly.

This trick of thought using the mean proportional was probably taken over by Heraclitus from the Pythagoreans.[27] He found it useful for a species of extrapolation. The ultimate objective of his thought lay beyond all values; in such expressions as 'god' or 'logos' it is not properly grasped, and human speech cannot do more than help the hearer to make the discovery for himself. For this purpose the form of the mean proportional is ideally adapted. The first, everyday contrast, e.g. child: man, points out the direction in which the thought has to travel and imparts to it an upward motion which is to

[25] Plato also (*Theaet.* 161c) alludes to this saying (baboon—man—God, in respect of wisdom). On the image of the ape cf. W. C. McDermott, *Trans. Amer. Philol. Assoc.* 66, 1935, 166ff.

[26] For the ape as ugly and ridiculous cf. Semonides fr. 7, 73ff.

[27] The Pythagoreans probably discovered the mathematics of musical harmony (above p. 276f.). In a sequence of similar intervals, e.g. octaves, the lengths of the strings would be in geometric ratio, and the application to geometry and algebra would quickly follow. We should remember that *logos* was the Greek for 'ratio,' 'proportion.'

carry it in the same sense, but with increasing velocity, along the second stage out of this everyday world to the distant goal.[28]

To break through the shackles of the world of the senses is in fact beyond human power, since (78)

The human kind has no understanding, the divine has.

A tremendous demand is made of him who would see into the true nature of things (18):

He who hopes not for what is not to be hoped will not find that which is untraceable and inaccessible.[29]

It is Heraclitus' way not to speak so often of the enlightenment itself as of commonplace men who are incapable of it. In several sayings he compares them with practically every domestic animal one after the other, excepting only the noble horse. For those who deride the teacher of a new doctrine he has the following contemptuous words (97):

Dogs bark at anyone whom they do not know.[30]

Elsewhere he says: 'The pleasures of such men are like those of oxen who have found some particularly juicy grass' (fr. 4, not preserved in the original form). Likewise in fr. 9:

Donkeys would value chaff more than gold.[31]

The standard scheme occurs twice in this saying: 'The donkey is to the ordinary man as the ordinary man is to him who has been awakened,' and 'Chaff is to gold as gold is to real values' (cf. fr. 29). Remaining fast in the world of experience is pilloried by Heraclitus in an allusion to swine wallowing in the mire and enjoying it (fr. 13); or he speaks of farmyard fowls and swine that bathe in the dust (fr. 37, cf. also fr. 5, see below p. 396). Just as they do, so does the unenlightened man root deeper and deeper in worldliness and stupidity;[32] he 'digs himself into the dung.'[33] This simile, with its

[28] Plato later continued the proportion (a:b=b:c=c:d) and applied it to the connections of the four elements (see below n. 36): in this mathematical form it appears in the *Timaeus* (31b ff.), and in the image of the cave and the divided line (see *Frühgriech. Denken* p. 280–282).

[29] Plato uses similar terms (ἀπορώτατά πη, δυσαλώτατον) to describe metaphysical intuition in *Tim.* 51 ab.

[30] The translation loses the sharpness of the original, where γινώσκω means both to recognize and to understand.

[31] The donkey was a stock illustration of stupidity (ἀμαθία, cf. Plutarch *Mor.* 363c) and gluttony (cf. Semon. fr. 7, 46f.; Plato *Phaedo* 81e).

[32] Cf. Plato, *Phaedo* 82e, ἐν πάσῃ ἀμαθίᾳ κυλινδομένην (ψυχήν).

[33] See *Frühgriech. Denken* p. 251–256 and p. 267 with n. 1. The filth of worldliness into which the unenlightened man sinks makes it harder for him to raise himself

archaic earthiness, inspired Plato later to his famous parable of the cave.

For Heraclitus, as for the other early Greek metaphysicians, the breakthrough to knowledge was a sudden one. The assembling of data alone could not force the pass into the higher world (40):

> Much learning does not teach understanding: otherwise it would have taught Hesiod and Pythagoras, or Xenophanes and Hecataeus.

For the new method of study, based on extensive observation, passing under the name of *historiê* (p. 336, 339ff.) Heraclitus has only a savage contempt. As often happens, he takes great figures of the past as typifying what he objects to in his own time. He ignores the fact that Hesiod and Pythagoras too were in their way metaphysicians, and he puts the contemporary theologian Xenophanes cheek by jowl with the empirical Hecataeus. Of Pythagoras as a representative of *historiê* he had this to say (129):

> Pythagoras, son of Mnesarchus, practised investigation (*historiê*) more than any other man: he selected these writings (?) and made for himself a wisdom of his own, an accumulation of learning, a harmful craft.[34]

From his own standpoint, Heraclitus (like most of the so-called natural philosophers) takes only a very specialized interest in the problems of the physical constitution of the universe.[35] Our principal informant, who went through Heraclitus' work for answers to Aristotle's questions, said resignedly: 'He doesn't say anything definite' (A 1, 8). The one thing to which Heraclitus attached any importance was clearly the demonstration that physical nature was subject to the same rule of law that obtained elsewhere. Here also a fixed reason and *logos* lay under all things; all seemingly static existence is to be interpreted as a continuous event, as regular change and movement, and particularly as a transformation of opposites into one another.

Heraclitus found the same ordering of three levels, as in the formula of the mean proportional, in the three forms or conditions of the one element of which he supposed the cosmos to be made up. What we should call matter in its solid, liquid and gaseous forms, he called earth, water and fire. When the dead and rigid earth was exposed to vivifying fire (warmth), it lost its rigidity and became

---

up to higher things, and the more the latter escape his vision, the deeper in the mud he sinks. The opposite to this vicious circle is the virtuous circle, as it were, of the *logos* which makes its own increase (fr. 115; cf. also Empedocles B 110).

[34] The saying is probably only authentic in part; in the phrasing cf. 86 Hippias B 6 and Plato's seventh letter 341b (συνθέντα ὡς αὐτοῦ τέχνην).

[35] See above p. 256–58.

mobile. It changed from dry to moist and took the form of a flowing stream or billowing sea. But it was only with the second transition, when in boiling it was transformed from cold to hot and became raging fire, that fluid substance attained the complete fulfilment of free movement and energy.[36]

The highest and truest form of all being is in Heraclitus' scheme 'fire,' which is at once warm and vivifying, and hot and destroying. 'Fire' is the informing principle of the world, but it is not an *archê* (beginning, principle) in the sense of a temporal beginning (30):

This world-order (*kosmos*) was no more created by a god than by a man; it always was and is and will be ever-living fire, flaming up in due measure and being quenched in due measure.

By the flaming-up and quenching of fire he means not the coming-to-be and passing-away of the element, but its transformation into a higher or lower form (31):

Fire's transformations: first sea, but of sea half is earth, half whirlwind.[37] Earth dissolves into sea (?) and fits itself to the same *logos* (relation, correspondence, proportion) as it was before there was earth.

In its highest form, as air and warmth, as the breath that enters our lungs, and in its transition to the highest form, namely as nourishment whose assimilation is accompanied by the evolution of heat,[38] the element is life and soul for man and beast. Thus Heraclitus could say that the soul also was not a thing, but a process, a transformation of water into fire: 'Souls also steam upwards from moisture' (fr. 12, above p. 379).

[36] In contrast to the systems that worked with two opposite principles—e.g. water/earth (Semonides) or hot/cold (Anaximander), or fire/night (Parmenides, see above p. 359–63), Heraclitus has three forms making two sets of opposites— fire—water—earth. The three members of this series are considered by him as transformations of a single element, rather as Anaximenes (above p. 266f.) supposed that a single element, 'air,' formed the different kinds of matter according to its condensation or rarefaction. The medieval orthodoxy of four elements came originally from Empedocles (c. 440 B.C.). According to him 'fire, air, water and earth' ('hot and cold, moist and dry') were four distinct substances, which could not change one into another; in addition to the substances there were forces of union and separation, which he called 'love' and 'strife.'

[37] Half of the sea evaporates and returns to its original form, fire. The reason why Heraclitus chooses the *prêstêr* (a waterspout in which water is drawn upwards, accompanied by electrical discharge) is probably that in this not uncommon phenomenon the ascent of water and its regression to fire seemed to be manifested in its most striking form.

[38] According to ancient belief breathing and assimilation of nourishment were closely connected. The liquids that we drink pass into the lungs, according to Alcaeus fr. 347 (above p. 195) and Plato *Tim.* 70c, 91a (on which see Gellius 17, 11 and Macrobius 7, 15).

In sinking down to the two lower levels the element dies two deaths, and on the way upward it is twice born (36):

To become water is death for souls, to become earth for water; but from earth comes water, from water soul.

The sea, as a mean proportional, unites in itself the opposed qualities of the extremes (61):

Sea is the purest and the foulest water, drinkable and sustaining to fish, undrinkable and deadly to man.

In the sea the rivers discharge all their dirt, yet its waters are not soiled (Bacch. 3, 86) and the sea is called the 'unstained' (Aesch. *Pers.* 578); in Greek belief and cult-practice it was capable of purifying what had been stained. Seawater is nourishment and life for the lower, earthly[39] creatures which dwell in the sea, just as it is poison and death for those with a fiery soul.

If one is at the middle stage, two directions of transformation are open. By its medial position the sea becomes again, as it was with Thales and others, the origin and source of things. The upper world of the stars and of pure fire also, according to Heraclitus, fed upon the vapours that arose from the sea. Thus the stars also are not things but events: fire continuously gathers at the top and is radiated back from thence. The sun is extinguished every evening and lights itself up again every morning (fr. 6). Heat evaporating upwards forms itself into hollow hemispheres which give the sun and moon their form and magnitude: when the hemispheres turn the lighted side away from us, eclipses occur. Where the moon is concerned, the hemisphere is constantly turning, thus producing the phases (A 12).[40] Heraclitus expressed no view on the heavenly sphere bounding the universe, nor did he leave any description of the earth (A 1, 9 and 1, 11).

For him it is the cosmic process that is interesting, not the outward form of the cosmos.

The cosmic process for Heraclitus is without direction (60): the way up and the way down are one and the same.

Everything maintains itself in equilibrium going and coming (30). The Stoics were the first to read into Heraclitus' text the thesis that the cosmic process periodically reached its consummation in a universal conflagration, with the heavenly fire on each such occasion

[39] Cf. Empedocles B 76; Plato, *Republic* 10, 612a; *Tim.* 92b.

[40] Parmenides had given the true explanation of the moon's phases (above p. 362). On the bowls or hollow hemispheres of the stars see above p. 213, n. 9, and cf. p. 264, n. 23.

returning from its various lower forms to its original nature. According to Heraclitus' own view, the everlasting life of fire consisted in its eternal changing out of one form into another (90):

Everything is exchange for fire, and fire for everything, as gold is for merchandise and merchandise for gold.

Just as in the purchase of goods a certain quantity of the goods corresponds to a certain quantity of gold, so the changing of things into fire and vice versa is regulated quantitatively by the *logos* (fr. 31, above p. 385). And just as in this world gold, even if not exchanged for things, is still reckoned valuable, so for Heraclitus fire is in itself valuable and divine. In words of apocalyptic obscurity he speaks of the paramount power of fire (66):

Fire will come upon all things to judge them and fasten upon them.[41]

Taking a hint from the popular superstition which reverenced in the lightning the weapon of the supreme god and the symbol of world rule, Heraclitus wrote (64):

Lightning steers all things.

Here is a remarkable paradox, bringing two opposites together: the annihilating thunderbolt is said to be the 'steersman,' i.e. the guider and sustainer of the universe;[42] rather as the far-striking bow of Apollo signifies at once death and life (fr. 48, above p. 377). Thus

[41] The last word can mean 'seize upon,' 'consume,' 'convict' or 'condemn.' The genuineness of the fragment has been questioned on substantial grounds, probably correctly. It does not seem to have been noticed, however, that in the transmission of the series of fragments derived from Hippolytus between nos. 63 and 66 two quotations from Heraclitus have been put into the wrong place in the text, namely B 64 (together with the preceding words λέγων οὕτως and the explanations of οἰακίζει and κεραυνός that follow) and B 66. Probably the extracts from the original were at one time written in the margin, and were then inserted at the wrong points. The text can be restored to order by the following transpositions.

(a) After Hippolytus' sentence λέγει δὲ καὶ τοῦ κόσμου κρίσιν καὶ πάντων τῶν ἐν αὐτῷ διὰ πυρὸς γίνεσθαι we should read not fr. 64 but fr. 66: πάντα γάρ φησι τὸ πῦρ ἐπελθὸν κρινεῖ καὶ καταλήψεται.

(b) Next should come λέγει δὲ καὶ φρόνιμον τοῦτο εἶναι τὸ πῦρ καὶ τῆς διοικήσεως τῶν ὅλων αἴτιον and not until then comes λέγων οὕτως (B 64) τὰ δὲ πάντα οἰακίζει κεραυνός, τουτέστι κατευθύνει, κεραυνὸν τὸ πῦρ λέγων τὸ αἰώνιον. (κατευθύνει was an old gloss on οἰακίζει since the word occurs in a similar context in v. 8 of Cleanthes' Hymn to Zeus.)

(c) After this, as the last member of the series, should come fr. 65 with the explanation belonging to it as transmitted in the text, from καλεῖ δὲ αὐτὸ (scil. πῦρ τὸ αἰώνιον) to ἡ δὲ ἐκπύρωσις κόρος.

[42] Here (and probably in fr. 94, above p. 380) we may be reminded of the myth of Phaethon, in which the lightning that struck the incompetent driver of the sun saved the earth from being consumed by fire.

also in the hands of the divine shepherd the cudgel serves as an instrument of his careful supervision (11):

Everything that crawls is tended by (god's) activity.[43]

Heraclitus' views on god are not at all clear, since he says very little on the theme, and most of that is very obscure.[44] The following fragment, however, clearly and forcibly describes the relation of god to the world (67):

God is day and night, winter and summer, war and peace, fullness and hunger. He changes his properties (?) just as (oil), when mixed with perfumes, is named after the odour which it then possesses.

The four pairs of opposites which Heraclitus names represent all the others also. Not only do the two sides of any given pair of opposites coincide, but in god all opposites come together. The comparison with oil may be understood as follows.[45] Perfumes were put up in the form of unguents composed of the scent itself and an olive-oil base. Hence perfumes were, so to speak, mere variants of olive oil, which was in general use for cleansing and massaging the body. Perfumed unguents, says Heraclitus, are named after their specific scent, while the oil which serves as a neutral base and which gives them their effect and utility is forgotten. In the same way one experiences and gives names to the obvious individual phenomena, and forgets the god behind them, who continuously takes on and lays aside the contradictions of existence, and in so doing remains always neutral and unspecific. In the opposite individuations[46] into which god enters, he is the real substance and power; everything else turned out by the restless mechanism of the cosmos and of life can only by considered as a transitory accident; but even these accidents are god,[47] and only

[43] This notion is alluded to by Plato, *Critias* 109b (condensed): θεοὶ οἷον νομῆς ποίμνια ἡμᾶς ἔτρεφον, πλὴν οὐ καθάπερ ποιμένες πληγῇ νέμοντες, ἀλλὰ πειθοῖ οἷον οἴακι (cf. οἰακίζει Heraclitus fr. 64) τὸ θνητὸν πᾶν (cf. πᾶν ἑρπετόν Heracl. fr. 11) ἐκυβέρνων. Shortly before the quotation of fr. 11 in the treatise *De mundo* we find something that is clearly derived from Heraclitus fr. 114 (400b 27–31).

[44] How Heraclitus envisaged the relation between 'god,' *logos* and 'fire,' and indeed how far he concerned himself with the problem is not known.

[45] Cf. *Frühgriech. Denken* 237–250. The palaeographical consideration that πῦρ might very easily have fallen out after περ, but that there is no reason why ἔλαιον should have done, is trivial when weighed against the arguments from the subject matter in favour of the supplement 'oil.' Anyone who is well acquainted with the ways of Greek manuscripts (or with his own slips of the pen) could amass a score of instances where words have been omitted without any obvious reason.

[46] Specific quality ('odour') and appellation or notion ('is named') are the *principia individuationis*.

[47] Cf. the last verse of the *Trachiniae*.

from him do they have the power to be something different and specific and to discharge their different and specific functions.

The last fragment that we read gives us no indication whether god is wholly merged in the phenomena of the universe and is nothing more than the principle of reality in whatever happens, or whether he transcends the world and, despite his 'mixing' with events, has a separate life of his own. We find the answer to this question in the two following fragments:

Of all the men whose words I have heard, none succeeds in understanding that there is one thing that is wise, separated from all. (108)

That which is alone wise is willing and unwilling to be called Zeus (Life?) (32)

In other words, there is, according to Heraclitus, a pure spirit ('that which alone is wise'), which can be in some sense identified with Zeus, and this intelligence has an existence of its own over and above nature and the world. This is exactly the answer which Heraclitus' notion of different levels might have led us to expect.[48]

So far we have heard of pairs of opposed forces as the form in which all phenomena present themselves, of the *logos* as the norm of all events, of god as the essence of them, and finally of intelligence existing by itself. We have also been able to trace how these acute and powerful doctrines can give a man a new and positive grasp on this fragmented and unquiet world. Even if we derive no specific precepts of action from it, it is important that we learn to understand god and the ruling 'meaning' which produces those sharp contradictions without which there is no life, and which yet gives to all things unity and harmony, not in spite of the contradictions, but because of them. Now we must examine some sayings which deal more directly with individual existence, some of which are concerned with the practical conduct of life. These aphorisms are very far from forming a regular system of ethics; man is considered in them not as a special creature with unique properties, but rather as a part of the cosmic whole. Anthropology and cosmology are not yet distinguished, and the attempt to explain the cosmos is animated at least as much by an interest in man as by a wish to advance in the knowledge of physics.

[48] Anaxagoras, who lived after Heraclitus, also posited a spirit that did not mingle with phenomena (59 B 12). But even before Heraclitus' time Xenophanes proclaimed a purely spiritual god who kept the world in motion yet was himself outside the world (above p. 331): Heraclitus had no doubt 'heard' these 'words' (cf. fr. 40), but he ignored them here. Apparently he thought that Xenophanes' theology was very unsatisfactory compared with his.

As we saw earlier (p. 379 and 389f.), life or the soul is for Heraclitus a phenomenon of transition from depth to height and of transformation from 'water' to 'fire.' Life is fed by the light and subtle vapours which we draw in with our breath and breathe out again when we have derived sustenance from it. In a similar way the stars catch their share of rising vapours in their hollow hemispheres and from that source sustain their fires (A 12). Thus every thinking man is in some sense a tiny star; but since he is condemned to this troubled level of life on earth, far below the bright sun, far below even the imperfectly shining moon, there is much that is dull and watery in his composition. The purer and brighter the fire of the soul, the more valuable and effective it is (118):

The dry soul is the wisest and best.

From this principle we derive a valuable sidelight on the phenomenon of drunkenness (117):

When a man is drunken, he is led by a halfgrown boy; he goes unsteadily he knows not where, for his soul is wet.

In the original text probably the grown man served as the mean proportional between the child and the fully enlightened sage, and sobriety as the mean between drunkenness and godlike comprehension: compared with the insight of the pure fiery soul, our ordinary sober sense is like the fuddled wits of a drunkard who does not know where he is going.[49]

Thus in our soul there burns a portion of the celestial fire, which it is our duty to keep pure; in it there lives a part of the life of the universe, and we must keep ourselves in accordance with it. As long as our senses are awake and alert and the breath of fire passes into us, we are like coals set glowing by the fire around them (A 16, 129f.). Heraclitus emphasizes communication with the universal (cf. above p. 379f.). At the very outset of his work he wrote as follows (2):

One must follow the universal; reason (*logos*) is universal, yet many men live as if they had a special understanding of their own.

Later we find:

Being rational is common to all. (113)

Those who are awake have one common world. (89)

---

[49] Plato (*Phaedo* 79c and 82d) says that those who are sunk in worldliness are like drunkards, not knowing where they are going.

In sleep, on the other hand, one cuts oneself off and goes into a private world; the memory, which is responsible for continuity, is extinguished (B 1, A 16, 129) and irrational delusions of dreams have a free hand.

Heraclitus demands of men that they should be wide awake, rational and truthful (fr. 112), which for him implies strict adherence to the universal. What we say can only be rational, and thus valid and effective, if it is consonant with the truth and reality that encompasses all things (114):

One must speak with reason and thus strengthen oneself by that which is common to all, as a state by its constitution, and even more so, for all human laws are nourished by the one divine law; for this has power as far as it wills, it extends to them all and extends beyond them all.[50]

The notion of 'law' is narrower in Greek than in English: *nomos* signifies a basic norm (as it might be, a constitution), in opposition to a regulation or enactment deciding a particular issue. The notion of a 'divine law' appears here for the first time in the scanty remains of early Greek literature which the accidents of destruction and preservation over the ages have left to us. The multiplicity of constitutions and the variety of notions of law in the thousand and one sovereign states naturally suggested the idea of a higher ordinance from which the various separate human laws were derived (or 'fed,' as Heraclitus puts it); and the amoral use of power given by the laws led to the postulating of overriding divine laws (cf. Sophocles, *Antigone*, 450ff., 77).[51] By his 'divine law' Heraclitus must have meant that universal ordering of the world and of justice which he had discovered (cf. fr. 94; 102; 80); this both has and is 'meaning.' Only the man who 'speaks with reason' speaks and thinks validly and in the sense of the cosmic order; and any deviation from reason leads what

[50] The original Greek uses two verbal similarities to underline the important relationships with which it is concerned. The two expressions 'with reason' and 'common' sound almost the same (ξὺν νόῳ and ξυνῷ), and the words 'reason' and 'law' have only a difference of one letter (νόῳ and νόμῳ, cf. Plato, *Laws* 12, 957c, 5–7). The sense of the passage and the omission of the definite article both show that χρή governs λέγοντας as well as ἰσχυρίζεσθαι. 'That which is common to all' is of course 'being rational' (fr. 113); and those who already spoke with reason would not need to be specially admonished to strengthen themselves (i.e. their words and ideas) with reason. Rather, the construction is like that in Aesch. *Prom.* 659f. (τί χρὴ δρῶντ' ἢ λέγοντα δαίμοσιν πράσσειν φίλα): *through* speaking rationally one makes oneself more strong and sure.

[51] Behind and above individual enactments of course stood law as a thing in itself, arising from and guaranteed by Zeus, according to Hesiod (*Works and Days* 1ff., cf. above p. 114). Hesiod developed a theory according to which all legitimate power consisted in the service of Zeus (above p. 100f.).

we say into the void of unreality and robs it of all force.[52] Heraclitus
helps us towards a notion of the divine law by his method of a mean
proportional: just as the law or constitution of a city overcomes the
destructive conflict of self-interest and brings individuals together
into an organized community, so does the divine law operate in
respect of the various human enactments (as individual citizen is to
law, so is individual law to divine law). The law of the state is the
only thing that gives strength and support to community life, and a
breach of the law leads to the dissolution of the state just as much as
an enemy's bursting through a breach in the walls (44):

The people should fight for the law as for the walls.

Transgression of law should not be tolerated: otherwise it will spread
like wildfire (43):

It is more needful to quell arrogance than to quench a fire.[53]

Only he who leads his life according to the universal law is strong,
sure and free. Individual pecularities, on the other hand, condemn
him who has them to a corresponding peculiar destiny for good or for
evil (119):

Character (*êthos*) is fate (*daimôn*) for men.

Further dangers threaten a man from his *thymos*, the organ of desire,
mood and feeling (85):

To fight against desire (*thymos*) is hard, for it stakes the soul (=life) on
what it wants.[54]

[52] Here and elsewhere we notice that there is no mention of a consistent *will*
towards justice and the law, although consistent thought and language are often
prescribed. 'Will,' however, is a concept that is missing in the intellectual horizons
of early and classical Greek thought. What we call will was taken as immediately
implied in all intellectual acts and emotional states from which action originated.
Hence there was no special word for will—only other words which included it
with some other concept, e.g. βουλή, 'plan, proposal' (also 'advice,' 'counsel'
etc.), μένος 'impulse' (beside εὐμενής, 'well-wishing,' 'kindly'), θυμός and many
others. We may add also verbs such as epic μήδεσθαι 'intend as a gift,' 'make ready.'
Of the two verbs which come nearest to the notion of willing, βούλεσθαι is rather
'to wish' (used also of utopian wishes), while ἐθέλειν can also mean 'to engage in
something of one's own free will' and even 'to be prepared,' 'to be able' (e.g. *Il.*
21, 366, Heraclitus fr. 32).

[53] This metaphor of quenching can also be used by Heraclitus in a good sense,
since fire also must not overstep its bounds (fr. 94). Thus K. Freeman, *The
Pre-Socratic Philosophers* (Oxford, 1946), p. 127.

[54] For ὠνοῦμαι 'I am willing to buy' (like δίδωμι 'I offer') cf. Herodotus 1, 69; for
ὠνοῦμαι and θυμός together cf. Herod. 1, 1, 4. Ψυχή in this context can only mean
'life,' cf. *Il.* 9, 322; Hesiod, *Works and Days* 686, Herod. 1, 24, 2 (so understood
by Aristotle, *Pol.* 1315 a 30 taken together with a 26): otherwise there is no justi-

Many of our wishes, moreover, are in conflict with themselves. In contrast to the standard complaint of human weakness and inability (ἀμηχανίη), the success or failure of our enterprises resting with the gods alone, as in Theognis 139f.: 'There is no one among men who achieves all that he desires'—in contrast to this hackneyed lamentation Heraclitus declares (110):

It would not be good for men if all that they desire took place.

Many are infected with the 'holy sickness' (epilepsy) of prejudice (fr. 46), and most men take their mistaken views as seriously as children take their playthings (fr. 70, cf. A 1, 3). Thus it is no wonder if our life plays games with us according to equally arbitrary rules (52):

Life is a child playing, playing at draughts; a child holds the sceptre.[55]

For the opinions of the generality Heraclitus had only contempt; the universal of which he spoke (fr. 2 and 114) was something of universal objective validity, not the subjective judgment of the majority (49):

One is ten thousand for me, if he be the best.

In Heraclitus' day Ephesus was ruled by the community of those born as full citizens, i.e. the men of established and landed families. Such a constitution was based upon the assumption that an unofficial leadership would establish itself through the majority's sensibly taking second place to some able individual. Heraclitus says (33):

It is law also to submit to the counsel of one.[56]

But it could easily happen that the mass of mediocrity would not allow any leading personality to emerge. On some event otherwise unknown to us Heraclitus makes the following mordant comment (121):

fication for the γάρ. Any contrast between 'body' (the word does not occur in the B-fragments) and 'soul' is alien to Heraclitus; Ψυχή embraces both physical (fr. 12) and spiritual (fr. 45) life. Cf. W. J. Verdenius, *Mnemosyne* series 3, vol. 11, 1943, p. 115ff.

[55] So far as I know, αἰών in the earlier literature refers only to the existence, life or fate of the individual; thus in a passage of Pindar (*Isthm.* 3, 18) which resembles this fragment we find: αἰὼν κυλινδομέναις ἁμέραις ἄλλ' ἄλλοτ' ἐξάλλαξεν. For the rest this fragment, whose context is unknown, is capable of several different interpretations.

[56] There is an allusion to fr. 49 and 53 in Aristotle *Pol.* 3, 1284a 3–15 and b 27ff. (εἰς τοσοῦτον διαφέρων—κατὰ τῶν τοιούτων οὐκ ἐστι νόμος αὐτοὶ γάρ εἰσι νόμος—πείθεσθαι τῷ τοιούτῳ πάντας); immediately afterwards (a 17–22) he speaks of ostracism, cf. Heraclitus fr. 121 and Plato, *Gorgias* 490a.

The Ephesians would do well to hang themselves every man, and leave the city to boys, since they drove out Hermodorus, the ablest man that they had, saying, 'No one shall be the ablest of us; or, if there be such, let him be able somewhere else and with different people.'

A historical legend makes this Hermodorus indeed play an important part 'somewhere else and with different people.' The fact that Roman law arose and developed under powerful Greek influence was given concrete expression in the story that Hermodorus helped the decemvirs in drawing up the Twelve Tables.

Heraclitus did not hope for anything good from the majority, whose limited outlook enabled them only to accept the most commonplace instruction (104):

What kind of intelligence or understanding do they have? they believe in the singers of the common people and they take the masses as their instructors, not knowing that most men are bad and a very few good.

By the 'singers of the common people' Heraclitus probably meant the epic rhapsodes; for in his time the old epics had long become public property. On the open competitions in which Homer, Archilochus and other poets were recited, he had this to say (42):

Homer deserves to be beaten out of the contest with a stick, and Archilochus likewise.[57]

These are his words on the valueless existence of the multitude in the cyclic sequence of generations[58] (20):

When born they wish to live and to have their deaths, and they leave behind children, so that there shall be deaths.

This is a grim inversion of the common view by which a man lives on in his descendants. By the law of the unity of opposites the awakening of new life serves rather to ensure that death shall not die.

The eye of the philosopher beholds different perspectives from those of the stupid rabble (fr. 87): death is not an end (27):

There waits for men when they die that which they neither expect nor believe.

---

[57] The first syllable of 'rhapsode' sounded like *rhabdos* 'a cudgel,' and hence came the erroneous notion that the rhapsodes thumped out the rhythm of their verses with a stick (cf. Pindar, *Isthm.* 4, 38). Fr. 17 was aimed at Archilochus (see above p. 372).

[58] The 'circle of being' is closed, in Heraclitus' view, when the contrast of the generations moves on one stage in the standard scheme, i.e. when the son, about thirty years after his father begot him, becomes in his turn the father of a son (A 19 and cf. *Frühgriech. Denken* p. 251f.).

The more noble the death, the more noble its sequel (25):

Greater deaths receive greater portions.

He who is struck down by the 'father and king of all,' war, (fr. 53), goes to a higher dignity (24):

Gods and men honour those fallen in war.

Honours are far more valuable than physical objects as rewards. They are living spirit, not transitory things; they renew themselves like an ever-flowing stream (29):

The best men value one thing above all—the never-dying fame of mortal things; but the masses fill their bellies like cattle.[59]

The main theme of Heraclitus' philosophy of life seems to be the advance from the individual to the universal, from disorder to order, from animal enjoyments to intellectual values, from the superficial ways of thought of the multitude to the penetrating insight of the few; an advance to a fuller and stronger reality, towards which our words and actions ought to be directed.

His views on religion are not dissimilar. He takes exception to the common rituals of worship, since they remain wholly on the surface. The reality of the divine nature is not so easy to grasp as people think, since

by its strangeness it[60] escapes being known. (86)

It was one of the duties of the 'king' of Ephesus to preside over the festival of the Eleusinian mysteries (A 2). We can understand that Heraclitus resigned the dignity, since he could not approve of such rites (14):

The mysteries that are commonly celebrated among men are celebrated in no holy manner.

It must have seemed a sort of blasphemy to Heraclitus that one should attempt to come closer to god by being present when holy objects were displayed. External behaviour cannot bring a man to the holy of holies of the spirit.

Nor did irrational enthusiasm lead man to god. Heraclitus had hard things to say to 'night-wanderers, magicians, maenads, bacchantes, enthusiasts' (fr. 14). Ecstasies and extravagances were to him no substitute for clear understanding: the powerful dynamism of his teaching and the heightened vitality which he preached had nothing in common with ignorant fanaticism. The wild Dionysiac

[59] For the simile cf. fr. 4 and 9. and see above p. 383.
[60] The context in Plutarch compels us to interpret it thus (cf. fr. 18).

rituals in which the mere agitation of the passions was credited with religious value earned nothing but contempt from Heraclitus (15):

If it were not for Dionysus that they make their procession and sing a song to the phallus, their actions would be reckoned quite shameless. But Dionysus, for whom they hold their mad revels, is the same as Hades.

When human beings err so crudely, it may well be that the concealed double nature of things, the unity of opposites, corrects them without their knowing. With triumphant scorn Heraclitus points out that the swelling powers of procreation are identical with death and decay;[61] so the fools may continue in wild intoxication to hail their own deaths.

For Heraclitus Greek religion and Greek worship were mistaken, since they sought god where he was not to be found. God is not in any individual thing; he is in the creating and reconciling union of all transformations and oppositions with which our life makes contact day by day and hour by hour; god is what we live and what we die.[62] Yet men in general never catch sight of the true, pure side of things that gives them their meaning; they wallow deeper and deeper in the mire of this world (above p. 383). Even those actions which they perform for religious motives lead them into the contagion of worldliness, not away from it. To cleanse himself of bloodguilt, a murderer would sacrifice a pig and wash himself in the creature's blood (5):

They cleanse themselves by staining themselves with fresh blood, as if a man who had fallen in a dung-heap were to cleanse himself with ordure; he must seem a madman to one who understands what he is doing.[63] And they pray to such images of the gods as these, as if one were to talk to a building: they have no idea what gods and heroes are.

Anyone who submits himself to such a purification is like a swine rolling in filth (above p. 383), and anyone who prays to images is confusing lifeless objects with gods and heroes. Men even honour lifeless corpses with prayers and offerings over their graves, and call them 'heroes.' But (96)

corpses should be thrown aside like dirt.

Men cling to what is immediately presented to them, without knowing or learning what it really means (above p. 371–73). They are satisfied with mere words, thinking that all reality can be con-

[61] Cf. fr. 20, above p. 394.

[62] Cf. fr. 67 (above p. 388f.) and 62 (above p. 375).

[63] That is: a man performing such a ritual must appear insane to anyone who understands that he is washing off filth with filth. On the verbal structure of the fragment cf. *Frühgriech. Denken* p. 77f.

veyed in them. But the god who imparts the truth speaks otherwise (93):

The lord of the Delphic oracle neither speaks nor conceals; he points (σημαίνει).

Apollo points or gives tokens, which the hearer must translate into terms of that which is shown or indicated. Like reality itself, the god's oracle is sometimes so ambiguous as to unite opposites.

The teachings of Heraclitus 'the obscure' had the same difficulty as the Delphic oracle. As a metaphysician he could not truly impart what he had understood; he could only give tokens. To complete the message demanded an act of understanding from the hearer, if he was capable of it.

Heraclitus' doctrine of the *logos* demanded one decisive intellectual transformation—no more, no less. One of its many paradoxes is that the immeasurable depths which it opened up begin immediately behind the flat surface of our common sense-experience (cf. A 9). The surface that we have to break through is paper-thin, and at whatever point we penetrate it, we come at once to the reality of the universe. True understanding does not do violence to the testimony of the senses, and it does not wheel away on world-forsaking pinions to distant voids. It affirms all things as they are by grasping the meaning they incorporate. The nature of things is understood anew as a process and a transformation. Even our own self is not a thing, but a process, through which it is in continuous communication with the life of the whole. Thus we experience in ourselves the unity and regularity of the universe. But the law of unity is called contradiction. All opposites stand fast with unrelaxed rigour: higher and lower, justice and injustice, life and death both attract and repel each other with perpetual tension; yet that tension is revealed as a secret harmony which brings them and binds them together. When we possess this knowledge, our actions and experiences are more earnest and living, more powerful, more elevated. In conflict and transformation we see no longer the brutal violation of truces, but the logical ordinances of the one unifying force of creation. Bitter conflict, even if we physically perish in it, becomes a play, a tragedy, which pleases even while it frightens.

Sophocles was the lawful heir and successor to Heraclitus. He did not, of course, take over the structure of his dogma, but rather his spirit and direction. The stark conflicts of Sophoclean tragedy, admitting no resolution of the conflict except that by the catastrophe the hero shall be compelled to see that conflict and catastrophe have always been inevitable; the stubborn anger of Sophoclean personages, the unyielding hardness of fate and of the gods; the declaration after the play of annihilating forces that, 'Nothing has happened that was not Zeus'—all this shows kinship with Heraclitus.[64]

In the history of philosophy the teaching of Heraclitus, after influencing every thinker in one way or another, found a later avatar in the Stoa. In its new Stoic guise it conquered the conquerors of mankind, the citizens, senators and emperors of Rome, and found its way into the nascent doctrines of Christianity. In the opening words of the fourth gospel—'In the beginning was the Word . . .'—the philosophy of Heraclitus speaks even now from the pulpit.

[64] The Heraclitean elements in Sophoclean tragedy deserve a careful investigation.

VIII

The Last of Archaic Lyric

(a) *Poetry of the Transitional Period*

At about the same time that the Asiatic Eastern fringe of the Hellenic world heard the solitary thinker Heraclitus put forth his majestic doctrines in words that have reverberated through the ages, the sacred dancing-floor of Dionysus in Athens saw Aeschylus present his first tragedies to the assembled people. Attic drama was raising its proud head.

In the rise of tragedy two very dissimilar factors played their part: the highly literary genre of the choral lyric, and the mumming dance which was not literary at all. The ground on which they met as partners was the cult of Dionysus. Colourful and uninhibited plays with masked actors were presented as part of his worship, both to amuse the people and to honour the god who was the engendering and animating force in plant, beast and man. In his service, as much as in that of any other, we find the choral lyric, which from the very beginning had been religious and almost liturgical in nature. It did not present the poet's words in a simple recitative, but underlined their content while singing by dance and symbolic mime. Thus this form of poetry contained at least the kernel of a dramatic element,[1] and this achieved a rapid development as soon as choral lyric in the service of Dionysus entered into competition with the rustic farce. First, taking a hint from the mumming dances, one individual stood apart from the chorus to take on a particular role; the chorus in return gave up its neutrality and began to represent a particular

---

[1] One of Bacchylides' choral odes (18), composed at a time when tragedy was already well established, gives the impression of representing posthumously, as it were, a halfway stage between choral lyric and tragedy: the chorus in alternate strophes represents the citizens of Athens and their king Aegeus, the father of Theseus. This is a step towards a possible lyrical drama; but we cannot therefore assume that the actual evolution of tragedy took place along these lines.

group of people. Next passages of recitative dialogue[2] were inserted between the sung and danced sections, and the number of actors was increased. This union between a high art-form with immemorial traditions and a naive popular entertainment was singularly blessed by fortune.

Both by their date and their content the tragedies of Aeschylus should find a place in this book; but an adequate treatment would demand more space and prominence than can be reconciled with the plan of the work. Accordingly I propose to leave tragedy out, and to consider here only Theognis, Pindar and Bacchylides as representatives of lyric poetry at the end of the archaic and threshold of the classical period. All three poets lie open before us, for we have extensive and continuous texts of them; but one of them, Bacchylides, has no special importance for the history of Greek thought and sentiment. To form our first notions of where the other two stand in that time of change we must look back for a moment at Simonides as we came to know him earlier (p. 303–25).

Simonides was some forty years older than Pindar, yet he was far the more modern in spirit; he worked consciously to prepare the way for what was to come. He was the clever and lucid advocate of a rational revision of prevalent modes of thought and behaviour. Proud ambition was to yield place to calm conformance with nature; the arrogance of self-conscious nobility must be replaced by bourgeois propriety; from the dream of a success that would put man among the gods, from the nightmare of a defeat that would annihilate him, one should awake to a clear understanding of the human limitations of every man, an understanding which in all modesty still recognized man's true worth. In Pindar, however, the old habits of thought which Simonides had assailed survived; indeed, they found in him their most complete expression. Yet Pindar treats them as obvious and timeless truths, and scorns even to take notice of the rival notions which were meanwhile gaining the ascendant. Theognis, finally, seems chronologically to belong between Simonides and Pindar. His writings show an embittered advocacy of the old against the new, for which he had no sympathy or understanding. He could see only the destruction which the intellectual and social revolution brought in its train, and fought against it without any real hope of victory. Savage indignation, scornful derision, and some sniping from behind cover are the feeble weapons which he deploys; but in

[2] What we call the spoken verses in tragedy were not delivered like ordinary speech, but intoned in a special modulated recitative. This can be established from the caesurae (four to each line) which careful research can detect in the tragic trimeter.

his wide-ranging discussion of the social and moral questions of his day he has many things to say which deserve our attention.

(b) *Theognis*

The work which we possess under the name of Theognis is a loosely connected sequence of poems or sayings in elegaic metre. Most are of only a few couplets, many of one only. Their content may be briefly described as threefold: comment on contemporary events, philosophy of life, and personal affairs. The political poems mostly give vent to a bitter and brooding resentment over the course of events; the poet's philosophy of life is partly ethical, partly utilitarian. What he says is meant not so much to be philosophical and speculative as practical and realistic; yet his views are mostly expressed in quite general terms and are consequently somewhat vague. One topic does achieve concrete reality in his poems—the companionship of the table, to which many of his sayings refer; for the drinking party was the normal setting for the recitation of poetical apophthegms of the kind that we find in this collection. In many of them a boy called Cyrnus is addressed. The basic theme is that the mature man Theognis places the wisdom of his forefathers and the fruits of his own experience at the disposal of the handsome young Cyrnus, the son of Polypaus, and that he communicates this wisdom also to the public. Love between man and boy was an important factor in upbringing in those aristocratic circles. Many of the pieces are of an erotic nature.

Theognis did not write his book all at once; it took shape under his hands over many years of work, which can explain the inconsistencies even in the genuine parts. He wrote at the end of the sixth and beginning of the fifth century,[1] in Megara, a small but not insignificant neighbour of Athens. In composing his work he must have taken over much that he heard from others, and he may well have incorporated actual quotations from books that were known to him. At all events a good deal of alien matter found its way into his book after his time, partly from lateral transmission, partly from new production. The purpose of the book and the looseness of its structure laid it open to amplification. A tidy division into genuine Theognis and forgery is not possible. Neither as thinker nor as literary artist was Theognis of the first rank, but for this very reason his writings are instructive, since his conservatism led him to follow a highly developed tradition. The historical value of the collection

[1] Cf. the note in David Campbell, *Greek Lyric Poetry* (London, 1967) 345f.

is considerable, for the spirit of the transitional period speaks in it through many voices; and indeed its human value is not negligible. We find among the sayings striking phrases, interesting observations and shrewd remarks that deserve our considerations. Among the voices that we hear some speak to us directly.[2]

After the fashion of the Homeric rhapsodes, Theognis begins his work with a prayer and short hymn of praise to Apollo; then he invokes Artemis, and finally the Muses and Graces. To the latter he attributes the following dictum, apparently as a sort of motto (17):

That which has beauty is loved, and that which has none shall be unloved.

The verse is not so banal as it appears. In early linguistic usage the notion of loving was bound up with the idea that a man would behave in a way corresponding to his feelings; and 'the beautiful' implied at once physical and moral beauty. Thus the motto, which sets the tone for the whole work, means roughly, 'I love what is beautiful, and my heart is set on noble deeds; I detest all that is ignoble.'[3]

The poet goes on to introduce himself to the reader (19):

Cyrnus, I set my seal on these my verses enshrining lessons of life,[4] whereby no one may take them for his. And men cannot put bad verses to stand in place of my good ones. Each will say to himself, 'Theognis composed this, he whom Megara bore, whose name is known in all countries.' Only at home my works do not find favour with all. Be not surprised, Polypaus' son, since even immortal Zeus, sending rain or sun, does not give pleasure to all. Yet to you will I strive to convey the things that were taught me, Cyrnus, by men who were good when I myself was a boy.

The 'seal' is the author's name, which Theognis deliberately puts in the mouth of his public so that he can praise himself indirectly.[5] This seal, as a component part of the text itself and hence not easy to remove, was to protect the author from plagiarists who might borrow parts or even the whole. Also, the original text was supposed by its literary quality to maintain its integrity against alterations, which in Theognis' eyes could only be changes for the worse.[6] Thus Theognis

---

[2] Cf. the passage discussed above p. 312f. (vs. 373–392).

[3] On the 'love of beauty' see below p. 418.

[4] σοφιζομένῳ is impossible to translate.

[5] Precisely the same thing was done by the author of the Homeric hymn to Apollo (v. 172f.; the similarity extends further, cf. F. Jacoby, *Berl. Sitzungsber.* 1931, 115, n. 1) and by Alcman (above p. 161f.).

[6] This seems to be what he means. To the modern scholar the notion involved is not a strange one: our textual criticism is based upon the postulate that the best attainable variant must be what the author wrote.

foresaw the dangers to which a book of this kind was exposed; but his hope that it would withstand them was only partly fulfilled.

Cyrnus' lessons begin with a fundamental admonition (29):

Reason well: do not encompass achievements (*aretai*), honour or riches, Through an unworthy act, or by infringement of right.

One must act by the light of reason and not be carried away by the desire for greatness to reach one's goal by foul means or by depriving others of their rights. The wishes of an ambitious man can be divided into three principal classes, aiming at three things: at honour, i.e. office, dignity, distinction; at *aretai*, i.e. unusual abilities which declare themselves in achievements and are recognized by society according to their merits; finally at riches.[7] Much later Aristotle could still pose the question whether honour, *aretê*, or wealth should be the goal of life (*Nic. Eth.* 1, 5).

Theognis has just said (28) that he received the teaching which he now imparts from 'good' men, i.e. from distinguished members of the upper classes. Cyrnus must now apply himself to getting a similar education (31):

This then comes first; but next: never mingle with bad men; banish them far from your side, staying with good men alone. Always eat and drink in their company: sit with them always; make it your task to please those who have might in the land. You will learn good from the good; but once you mingle with bad men, even the wits that you had speedily vanish away. Bear this in mind; consort with good men: so you will sometime say that I counsel well those whom I love and esteem.

This is the clear expression of a way of life based on social stratification, of a philosophy which took it for granted that the 'good' were those who had power, and that their attitudes were the only valid ones.

The two passages which follow give warning of threatening revolution and collapse. The first foresees a despotism deriving support from the discontented masses (39):

Cyrnus, the state is in labour: I fear she may bear the avenger—him who shall make us pay dear for our folly and sin. The citizens are still sound of heart, but those who have power drive headlong to the cliff where our destruction awaits us.

The second (43ff.) laments the progress of dissolution: the arrogance, self-seeking and avarice of the 'bad' is constantly increasing, and the

---

[7] In the new fragment of choral lyric (above p. 313, n. 22) we find the same list of three types of desire that can seduce us from a virtuous life.

processes of law have lost their integrity: party strife, political assassination and a tyranny are bound to come.

The next poem, however, reveals a totally changed situation: the rule of the 'good' has been overthrown (53):

Still is our city a city, but far changed, Cyrnus, the people. Those who formerly knew nothing of justice and law, they who used to clothe their naked bodies in goatskins, scattered outside the walls, living like beasts of the field—they are the 'good men' now, and those who were formerly reckoned good are become the mob. Who can endure such a sight? Now they cheat one another, and smile as they do so,[8] and are not mindful of paying kindness or injury back. Do not take as your friend, dear Cyrnus, one of these people, no matter what you desire, no matter what you intend. Practise instead with them all the feigning language of friendship, yet breathe never a word on any matter that sits close to your heart: you will quickly learn how false are their feelings if one wants deeds, not words, none can rely on their faith. Cheating and lies and deceit are all that they love, arts that men always ply when they have nothing to lose.

What was formerly the lower class has now gained full citizen-rights and with them a majority and a dominating position in the community. In reality these people must have been peasants and small farmers, fishermen and artisans; but Theognis depicts them as skin-clad shepherds, subhumans with no notion of law and justice.[9] They were equally ignorant of the game of *quid pro quo* as played by the aristocratic cliques which had formerly dominated political life, and instead each sought without scruple to take advantage of his fellow.

Now what is Theognis' attitude towards the new state of affairs? Does he call on the truly 'good' to rally their ranks and fight tooth and nail against the hated regime? Does he most earnestly adjure Cyrnus to avoid any contact with the rabble, for fear that the contagion would corrupt his own true nature? Not a bit of it. In the sharpest contrast to his former precepts he inculcates a show of

[8] γελᾶν in both ancient and modern Greek can mean 'cheat,' 'delude.' In Sparta someone said to me, νὰ μήν σε γελάσῃ, 'See he doesn't pull the wool over your eyes.' Instead of γνώμας I have adopted μνήμην from the repetition in 1114, since it gives better sense (cf. 112; Herod. 5, 74, 2 and such expressions as μνησικακεῖν and ἀμνήστεια). Since μνήμην ἀγαθῶν is much the same as χάρις (cf. Euripides, *Alcestis* 299), the phrase μνήμην εἰδέναι may be interpreted as χάριν εἰδέναι. On the difficult reading γνώμας cf. B. Snell, *Ausdrücke für den Begriff des Wissens* (Berlin, 1924), p. 34, n. 4.

[9] The notion that shepherds were lawless savages occurs in the *Odyssey* (9, 112, referring to the Cyclops). A scorn like that of Theognis is expressed in Menander, *Epitr.* 52–54 (in Körte's third edition). In pastoral poetry, of course, this very simplicity was reckoned a virtue in shepherds.

friendship towards all; the only proviso is that Cyrnus should not enter into any binding alliance with the now dominating class, on the practical ground that in the long run it is impossible to work with them. Without any attempt at palliation he says that a man must go and howl with the wolves until normal times return. The author of this advice was not an aristocrat by conviction, but an undisguised opportunist: and that the author was other than Theognis himself is highly unlikely.

Next comes appropriately enough a series of fifteen sayings with the same leading idea: 'Be cautious in dealing with men, for very few are trustworthy: mere word-friendship has no value.' 'Good' men in this context are those who return friendly services with corresponding services; to do a kindness to a 'bad' man is just like sowing the sea.[10] It is pleasantly naive that it is only the other partner's trustworthiness that is being considered throughout: a later saying (439f.), on the other hand, advises us, 'Before all things, test your own self.'

Now comes a long string of sayings (129–136) whose principal theme (there are others) can be characterized as 'man and destiny.' By good luck and bad luck here the author means particularly riches and poverty. Complaints over the loss of wealth are frequent in the collection; apparently the former privileged classes had been to a great extent impoverished under the new order, and they were smarting under the double loss of power and prosperity. Under the economic re-arrangement the former class-distinctions could not be maintained (183):

Horses and asses and sheep we value according to breeding, Cyrnus, and wish them to be bred from the finest of sires. Yet our nobles gladly accept bad women, of low birth, to be their wives, if only the dowry is great. And a woman does not refuse a base companion in wedlock if he is rich: she admires wealthy men rather than good. Gold is what men adore: the base now mates with the noble; nobles mate with the base: money confuses the breed. So do not wonder, Cyrnus, to see the breed of our townsmen daily grow worse: for excellence is mingling with worthlessness.

Another hand has put in an answer to this saying, to the following effect: 'The man who marries a rich woman from a low family knows very well what he is about, but necessity knows no law' (193–196). One receives the impression that the man who inserted this rejoinder was inclined to deprecate the lordly didactic tone.[11]

---

[10] Alcaeus (fr. 117(b), 27 LP) uses this image similarly.—In v. 111 ἐπαυρίσκουσι seems to be used as a causative (see above p. 317 n. 28) to the middle ἐπαυρίσκεσθαι: 'They cause you to enjoy the fruit of what they received from you.'

[11] Vv. 193–196 were written to be read at this point; the ταύτην is meaningless unless it is referred to v. 185f.

After the series on man and destiny, riches and poverty, we find in immediate sequence the following elegy, which undoubtedly formed part of the original work of Theognis (237):

My gift to you was wings, wherewith you might soar at your pleasure over the boundless sea, over the regions of earth. Where men drink and rejoice, there will you for ever be present; there shall your name be heard still on the lips of all men; there, while the shrill pipe sounds, fair youths will sing of your praises, praising the well-tuned voice high in harmonious song. Even when you descend to the dark earth's gloomy foundations, down into Hades' halls, full of lamenting and tears, even in death men will not forget you; your name will forever dwell in the mouths of men, always immortal and new, Cyrnus; through Hellas' land you will journey; forth to the islands over the barren and grey depths of the fathomless sea, needing no ship or horse: the noble gifts of the Muses decked with violet crowns—these will convey you abroad. All who delight their hearts with song, both now and hereafter, all will hear Cyrnus' name while earth and sun shall endure. Yet I get from you in return not the smallest kindness or regard; just as you might deceive a little child, so you put me off, with words.

The last distich, demanding a *quid pro quo*, may seem to us an abrupt descent. But Theognis thought otherwise. At the very outset, the words 'My gift to *you* . . .' lead the way to the point which is to come at the end; and for Theognis the connection was simple and direct.

The elegy 'I gave you wings' gives the impression that it was intended to close the collection; but in fact there are still a thousand verses before the end of the first book. In the very middle of the first book we find a collection of sayings of the same type as those with which the Theognis collection begins.[12] This second beginning represents the start of a drinking-party even more clearly than the first one did. The author does not give his name, but he is probably not Theognis. The verses are better and fuller, the articulation clearer and richer, the progress of the thought is quicker and firmer than we are accustomed to find in Theognis: it seems as if a second and similar collection had been tacked on to that by Theognis. The city to which it is addressed is still Megara, and the period is around 480, the year in which the Persians attacked Greece and penetrated deeply into the country. The series begins as follows (757):

Over the city, our home, from danger for ever to guard it,
Zeus, great lord of the sky, stretches his favouring hand—
He and the other blessed immortals: may great Apollo
Lead our hearts and our tongues still in the way that is right.

[12] And of the same type as those verses which inaugurate a drinking-party in the first fragment of Xenophanes (above p. 326–28).

Now shall the flute and the lyre in sacred harmony mingle;
We too, when we have poured red-glowing wine to the gods,
Making our holy libation, will drink and talk and be merry,
Fearing not for the war which we now wage with the Medes.
These are the things that are meet for the hour: with untroubled spirit
Enjoy comradely pleasure; drink to the last drop
Pleasure's cup, and keep far distant evil powers,
Baleful old age and death that ends all.

Now the speaker declares himself ready to entertain the assembled company with his poetry (769):

If one, as servant and friend of the Muses, has gifts of the spirit more than others have, one must not hoard them alone. One must always be busy inventing, composing, imparting; knowledge is worth little if it is kept to oneself.

Then follows another prayer (773):

You, lord Apollo, yourself did build our high citadel,
To gratify Alkathoös, the son of Pelops:
Now do you guard against the Mede and his arrogant army
The city, so that the people in festive spirit
May, when the springtime comes, bring a hundred oxen before you,
Delighting in the lyre and the lovely joyful dance
About your altar and in the cry of the paean.
I am fearful when I see such folly around me
And strife destroying our people:[13] but you, great Apollo,
In your mercy and grace shelter our city from harm.

After this concern for 'our city' we find some lines expressing love of country (783):

I have been once as far as the land of Sicily
And I have been to Euboea of the vine-covered plain;
And famous Sparta by the sedge-grown banks of Eurotas:
Always was I met with kindness and warmth wherever I came,
But my heart found in all these no joy:
Nothing, I find, is more dear to a man than his own land.[14]

We now find a *confessio fidei* in accordance with the motto (v. 17) and the first admonition (v. 29f.) given by Theognis (above p. 402f.). The ideals of this speaker are *sophia* (wisdom, cleverness, skill) and *aretê* (789):

May no goal ever be nearer to my heart than these two—wisdom and

---

[13] Some of the Greek cities had made common cause with the Persian invaders.
[14] Here again we find impersonal grandeur, represented by three examples, depreciated in favour of personal nearness and affection (see above p. 138–40, 185f.).

manly worth. In service to them always, I delight in the tones of the lyre, in singing and dancing; may then my spirit for ever nobly abide with the good.

Theognis at the outset made it clear that he had enemies in his city, and consoled himself with the reflection that even Zeus cannot please everyone (above p. 402); this theme is variously conveyed in the four following sayings (793):

Never inflicting harm by injurious act on a stranger or on a man of your land, but giving justice her due, do what delights your heart.[15] When the citizens chatter about you, some will indeed find fault, others will name you with praise.

Good men will be reviled by many, and praised by others; if one is bad, his name is never spoken at all. (797)

Here 'good' means virtually great and important, while 'bad' means the commonplace man in the street, whose existence nobody notices; Pindar expresses a similar attitude in fr. 104c, 8–10 Snell. Bourgeois sentiment, on the other hand, must above all have the peace and ease that it loves: this spirit informs the following distich (799):

No one who dwells upon earth is exempt and free from all censure; all the better for him who shall offend but a few.

The solemn first verse repeats an old and melancholy truth; the second, in a slightly mocking tone, derives a comforting inference from it. Finally, the last saying of this group tells us again that it is impossible for a mortal to win nothing but approval in the whole course of his life, since even Zeus, the ruler of the universe, does not achieve such success.

The examples already provided are enough to give some impression of the form and character of the collection.[16] Old ideas and new,[17]

[15] Cf. above p. 327 n. 4. With 795f. cf. Archilochus fr. 9 (above p. 139).

[16] The book as we have it so carelessly put together that several pieces occur twice over, with variants of the kind that tend to arise in an oral transmission (in this case it is by no means certain that the version which occurs earlier in the collection is in fact the more original, see above n. 8 and below n. 20). The arrangement is often stupid: e.g. the distich 381f. is thrust in the middle of a poem; 219f. has crept in between a saying and the rejoinder to it; 979–982 has no business between 973ff. and 983ff. The arranger was obviously more concerned with increasing the volume of the collection than in preserving its unity. This is understandable if we suppose that the written text was not intended for continuous reading, but as a poetical thesaurus from which the user could select what he would like to recite at a party.

[17] The transposing of old ideas into distichs has not always been successfully accomplished. v. 169 repeats the traditional saying, 'When a man has received gifts from the gods, envy itself cannot grudge him his fortune' (see above p. 138

original verses and borrowed,[18] follow each other without any principle; and the sequence is made more kaleidoscopic and bewildering because the points of view vary and the themes are constantly changing.[19] The book often assumes the character of an open discussion such as would take place at the table, where each participant had some contribution to make to the entertainment. There are some direct contradictions.[20] The tone is lively, but the stylistic level of serious literature is maintained, and jokes or indecencies are therefore excluded. The argumentation is not too strictly logical nor yet too negligent; elaborately pointed phrasing (453ff.; 1207f.; 351ff.[21]) is relatively rare. A specimen unique in its kind is a quatrain that plays upon words and ideas as significantly as a Shakespearean fool (267):

> Poverty is well known, and yet at the same time a stranger;
> Seldom is she beheld either in market or court.
> Always she comes off worse, wherever she goes she is spit on;
> Wheresoever she dwells, there is she hated by all.

n. 14); but the pentameter carries on as if the sense of the hexameter had been, 'The gods often throw good fortune into men's laps without their doing anything to earn it.' The Theognidean distich was later turned into two (Byzantine?) trimeters (Apostol. 8, 89 i = 2, 456 Leutsch): Θεοῦ διδόντος, οὐδὲν ἰσχύει φθόνος, καὶ μὴ διδόντος, οὐδὲν ἰσχύει κόπος.

[18] The culling of citations did not always result in complete distichs, and the gaps had to be filled by hook or by crook. In v. 626 τοῦτο γὰρ οὐ δυνατόν is not only flat but quite wrong, since ἀργαλέον of 625 did not mean 'difficult' but 'awkward,' 'painful' ('It is ill-mannered to claim to know better all the time, but on the other hand one puts oneself in a false light if one lets every foolish statement pass uncorrected'). In v. 424 ἢ τὸ κακόν is unnecessary and unsuitable (ἠὲ λαθόν would have been more tolerable); but πολλάκι also is objectionable, and one expects rather the idea of Heraclitus B 109.

[19] Frequently two adjoining sayings have a striking word in common, the recurrence of which makes some kind of link in sense between the two. In one case (305) a verbal expression is brought in which repeats something said a little earlier (300), but the words are now used in a different sense and the two sayings have in fact nothing else in common. The second quatrain must have recurred to the arranger's memory through a purely mechanical word-association with the former.

[20] v. 193 (above p. 405 with n. 11); 221ff. (below p. 415); 931f. and 1155f. (p. 419f.); probably also 799f., 313f. (above p. 408, below p. 412) and 393ff. (below p. 421 n. 46). It is remarkable that in these instances the arranger allowed the sayings which he disapproved of to stand unaltered, contenting himself with a rejoinder, instead of suppressing, altering or rewriting the objectionable material. In other places the text appears to have been corrected: thus in v. 1074 we probably have the genuine form, which in v. 218 (see below p. 414f.) has been replaced on moral grounds by one which is meaningless. For interpolated rejoinders in a collection of sayings cf. also Hesiod WD 379f.

[21] With this now cf. Menander Dyscolus 208–211 with Handley's note.

Irony also is uncommon (e.g. 523f.). Genuine humour is either absent or so dry that we do not detect it; the analysis of his own condition made by a drunkard in 503ff. sounds almost pedantic. There is, however, perhaps an undertone of kindly humour in this consolatory distich (293):

Even the lion has not always meat, but on some occasions even he, strong as he is, finds himself quite at a loss.

The content of a work like this can only be described in the most general terms; I have selected some striking examples, grouped according to subject matter.

The passages which are directly concerned with the pleasures of the table are intended to diffuse a happy and genial temper. At the same time they have a didactic element, giving instructions on the behaviour best calculated to enhance one's own and others' enjoyment of a happy occasion. Thus we find the following elegy (467):

Do not force a guest to remain if he has no wish to stay longer; and send no-one away if he would like to remain. Do not wake one of us up, Simonides, if in his drinking, heavily burdened with wine, gently he sinks into sleep; make no-one sleep who is wide awake and unwilling: painful is all constraint which puts our freedom in bonds. If a man wishes to drink, let his cup be filled: not every night have we such pleasure as this. But for myself, I have drunk my measure of honey-sweet Bacchus; I will go home and seek slumber that frees from all ills. Now I have reached that point where wine is best in its working: not too drunken as yet, still I am sober no more. If anyone neglects due measure in drinking, no longer he is able to rule his tongue or to keep charge of his wits; he says many tactless things, offending those who are sober; and loses all sense of shame, once he is fuddled with wine. He who had sense before is now turned childish. Recalling this to your mind, do not drink more than a due measure of wine. Rise from the table before you are drunk, and let not your belly rule as it rules a slave living from this day to that. Or, if you stay, drink nothing. Instead I constantly hear you cry, 'Fill it up!' You fool, that's how you come to be drunk. Now you declare, 'I must drink my friend's health,' now, 'Everyone's drinking,' now, 'A libation to Zeus!', now, 'For a special event': have you not heard of 'No?' You need to be one of the heroes if you would keep your wits when you have honoured each pledge. So let the talk be good among you who remain by the winebowl; shun like the plague all words leading to quarrel or strife. Let what one says to another be fit for everyone's hearing; if they are managed like this, parties give pleasure to all.

The instructions are given, according to archaic principles, in the form of vivid, concrete illustrations,[22] and again in the archaic

---

[22] In the same way the two personages, the speaker and the imaginary drunkard, dramatically represent the right and the wrong attitude.

manner, the development of the thought is largely determined by the interplay of opposites.[23]

In the middle of the festivities we find a man who has been asked, as his contribution, to sing to the flute (211):

I cannot sing clear and sweet as the nightingale; last night I attended a great drinking of toasts. I will not find fault with the flute-player as an excuse; I do know how to sing, but my voice is gone.

All sorts of theories are put forward concerning wine. It unites opposite qualities (211):

Very much wine is bad for a man; but if he has studied how he should drink, then wine changes from evil to good.

—but it also removes distinctions (497):

Foolish heads and wise men's heads, if once they have taken more than their measure of wine, both are made empty alike.

Wine demands that everyone shall be in a like frame of mind (627):

He is wanting in manners who is drunk when his fellows are sober; nor is it fair to remain sober when others are drunk.

—but it also distinguishes men's character (499):

Craftsmen who know their trade test silver and gold in the furnace: so in wine we find proof of the mind of a man, clever though he may be; for if any baseness was hidden, wine brings it out and shames him who was formerly wise.[24]

Under the melting influence of wine and the spirit of social gaiety each man shows himself as he really is; and a cool head can turn this to his advantage (309):

Use your wits above all when the festive table receives you: act as if you observed nothing of all that occurs. Bring with you laughter and jokes; take away what adds to your power; learn to know how each man's passions are kindled or quenched.

This is a shrewed piece of advice: instead of joining in the relaxed gaiety, a man should only pretend to do so. One can hardly imagine that such a piece of advice was openly given at the table: it would destroy the atmosphere and put the victims on their guard. Here, then, the collection contains more than merely pieces for party recitation; when it was crystallized in writing it afforded entry to

[23] The formulation of the opposite pairs is overstrained at 471, where to 'tell a man to sleep' means no more than 'tell him to go home to bed' (cf. 468, 476, and Panyassis fr. 13, 11).

[24] The distich 501f. as rendered in the Theognis MSS only repeats the thought, and partly the words of 497f., while, in the rendering of Stobaeus the two halves of the saying fit together perfectly. κακότητα δὲ πᾶσαν ἐλέγχει means, 'The depravity of all who are depraved comes to light'.

pieces of advice which could only be given in quiet and confidential moments. Immediately after this quatrain comes a reply from a man who for his part rejects this underhanded reserve; his maxim is *desipere in loco* (313):

When men are mad about me, I will be the maddest among them; if they choose to be just, no one is juster than I.[25]

There are quite other reasons why the following fine passage cannot be reckoned as table-poetry (825):

What? Would you venture to sing, with the strains of the flute-player to guide you, when from the market place we see the bounds of our land, land which keeps you and feeds you? And you in your festival garments twine in your golden locks garlands of purple and red? No, my Scythes, shear your tresses and still your rejoicing; mourn for the fertile and fair lands which the city has lost.

After the early Greek fashion, concern for the misfortunes of one's country[26] is not expressed in tones of melting sorrow, but in sharp expostulation (cf. above p. 152f. and n. 2), as the poet presents an imaginary scene of gay revelry in direct contrast to the sorrow that he feels in his heart.

Earnest anxiety for the welfare of the state is the basis of this elegy also (667):

If I were possessed of wealth, Simonides, such as I once had, then I should fear much less speaking with those who are good. Now I can only look on. Though I see what passes about me, poverty closes my lips. I can tell better than most why we are driving on, with our white sails struck from the masthead (?) out of the Melian sea into the darkening night. No-one will work at the pumps, but the waves dash over the gunwales, starboard and larboard at once. Scarcely can anyone in the ship hope to escape while they act as they do: the capable helmsman, he who kept skilful guard, now is relieved of his post. Each one is seeking to profit, the common good is forgotten, now there is no notion of true justice or of sharing alike. Orders come from the crew, the base rule over the worthy; shortly, I fear, the wild billows will swallow the ship. This I have veiled in riddles in order that good men may use it; bad men may learn from it too, if they are clever enough.

[25] Cf. above p. 228 n. 21, p. 327 n. 4.

[26] The enemy has annexed so much of the speaker's homeland that one can see from the city as far as the border. For v. 826f., cf. the borders and fruits of the land called to witness in the Attic oath of the ephebes (M. N. Tod, *Greek Hist. Inscr.* II [Oxford 1948] no. 204, 19f.). The import of the saying ('When one's homeland is in danger, one should not wreathe one's hair, but cut the hair and mourn') became a commonplace to the extent that Aeschines could apply it to the wreath of Demosthenes (3, 211: οὐ γάρ δεῖ, ἐφ᾽ οἷς ἡ πόλις ἐπένθησε καὶ ἐκείρατο, ἐπὶ τούτοις ἐμὲ στεφανοῦσθαι).

The ship of state serves as a symbol for the community of fate which binds all citizens for weal or woe—including those who in their blind self-seeking would rather know nothing of this bond. The simile was no new invention of this poet's (above p. 190, n. 4); but he assumed that the 'bad' and uneducated men who now held the upper hand were not familiar with it. He speaks vaguely and obscurely, because in his economically dependent position he cannot venture on open criticism. But on the other hand, the danger to the city and its people is so manifest that he cannot refrain from uttering his covert warning.

The two poems last cited, the second opening (757–788) which we read earlier (p. 406f.), and a few detached short poems,[27] are nearly all the indications there are of patriotic feeling in the *Theognidea*, if we disregard those poems in which, behind the furious party-political feeling, there are possibly traces of a purer emotion.[28] In general there is little indication of a feeling of responsibility for others or of service to a cause. Family relationships are very seldom mentioned,[29] and there is no mention of the duties of office.

Friendship and its complement enmity play a correspondingly greater part. Individuals grouped together for mutual advantage, and there were also larger alliances whose members took each other's part in conflict with other cliques for advantages of all kinds, and probably also in the common battle of all 'good' men against the whole class of the 'bad.' A poem of Solon's (above p. 232–34) comes to mind when we find the following prayer, based equally on the assumption that the measure of a man's greatness is his ability to benefit friends and injure enemies (337):

Zeus be my help to reward the friendship of all those who love me: may I, in fighting my foes, always be stronger than they. Then, when I die, all men will call me a god among mortals, if I have paid back all, Cyrnus, both evil and good.

Similar assumptions underlie these two passages (561, 361):

This is my wish: to maintain my own, and in generous bounty to enrich my friends greatly out of the spoils of my foes.—
A man's heart sinks when a hurtful wrong is inflicted: but greatly it leaps in joy when he has taken revenge.

[27] 865ff. (below p. 417); 945ff. (below p. 416); 1044; anxiety for one's native city is expressed in 151ff.; 541f.; 603f.; 855f.; 1003f.

[28] Cf. 233f. (below p. 415). Hatred of a tyrant, or of tyrants in general, is expressed in 823f., 1179ff. and 1203. Euboea and the Cypselids are spoken of in 891ff. A war is going on in 549ff., 887ff.; 1043ff. (This is to complete the list of passages dealing with significant political events.)

[29] 'Be patient with a friend as if he were your brother' (99); an unbrotherly brother: 300; a father advises his son: 1049; choice of a wife: 183–196; 457ff.; 1225f. On 409f. see below p. 419.

The trustworthiness or lack of it in friends is naturally of decisive importance, and the theme is fully developed in the collection. One speaker complains that he cannot find an honourable companion; he himself is as true as gold, but the other has shown himself as false as lead (415ff.). This kind of self-advertisement (cf. 447ff.) should not surprise us in a group whose members were always canvassing for partners in fresh alliances. Thus someone declares (529):

I have never betrayed any friend or true-hearted comrade; I do not in my breast carry the heart of a slave.[30]

Another invokes the Dioscuri, the prototype of brotherly affection (1087):

> Castor and great Polydeuces, who dwell in fair Lacedaemon
> In the valley of Eurotas, by its murmuring stream:
> If I should ever wish harm to a friend, may my own head receive it;
> If he should wish it to me, may it fall doubled on him.

The invocation of the Dioscuri makes the third line a prayer and the fourth a curse. In his naive selfishness the speaker makes the oath that is to bind himself only half so strong as the curse by which he is to be protected against his partner. A man who has been left in the lurch by his own group informs them (or threatens them) that he will find satisfaction by going over to the enemy (811):

Death may indeed be worse than the fate by which I am stricken, but it is crueller far, Cyrnus, than all other wounds. I am betrayed by my friends; to my enemies let me go then: I shall find whether their hearts are friendlier.[31]

A prudent reserve (cf. 118) is often inculcated. There is nothing more dangerous than the false friend (89):

Either love me with unfeigned heart or refuse me and hate me and make our battle open. He who is single in tongue but double in thought—such a companion can be grim, Cyrnus; he is better an enemy than friend.

The attitude forcibly expressed here seems to us no more than an elementary requirement of decent behaviour. But then we find such a piece of advice as this (213 = 1071):

Cyrnus, to all your friends show a shifting, changeable nature; when you converse with a man, model your feelings on his. Practise the wiles of the boneless polypus:[32] when he is clinging fast to a rock, he always adopts its colour. Alter your colour according to changes of times and of places; if you desire to have power, better be clever than good.

[30] To be like a slave would imply unscrupulous pursuit of one's own advantage.
[31] The same meaning is probably conveyed by the quatrain 1013ff.; but τ'ἐχθρούς and τε φίλους must be transposed ('before having to humble himself before his friends and be compelled to abandon his loyalty').
[32] On the text and meaning of 213–218 cf. *Frühgriech. Denken* p. 32f.

Literally translated, the last verse says, 'Cleverness is superior to great *aretê*.' This is a questionable maxim: and in one branch of the transmission (218) the verse has been recast into a more innocuous form: 'Cleverness shows itself superior to inflexibility'; but this only removes the most obvious objection which a moralist might make to the maxim. Here again we find that the next piece in the collection is an animated rejoinder (221):

If you suppose that the man next door is an ignorant fellow; if you think only you know what it is to be wise; then you are greatly mistaken and wrong in your thinking; all of us, I dare say, know a few tricks of our own. Many refuse to pursue their advantage by shady dishonesty, but there are others who find crookedness more to their taste.

There are several such instances, where conflicting views were put forward which have left their mark in the book. We read (963ff.) that the policy of changing like a weathercock (of being ἐφημέριος) cannot be successful for very long; sooner or later a man's true nature will come to light, and until then one must keep one's judgment of others in abeyance: 'I made a stupid blunder when I called you good before being fully acquainted with your character; but now I avoid you as a ship (avoids a dangerous bay).' Then again we hear this piece of advice (365):

Be not excessively shrewd; let your tongue speak nothing but kindness: only the meanest of men nourish a choleric heart.

Or the hearer is advised to make himself unpredictable—presumably to make people keep their distance and protect oneself from being exploited (301):

You must be bitter and sweet, be kindly and harsh in your manners dealing with servants and slaves or with the neighbours around.

The last distich is inspired by the wish to cultivate a lordly superiority: by being deliberately difficult and wilful one is to gain a reputation as an independent personality. This is an aristocratic notion, in direct opposition to the doctrine that one must be in all respects agreeable to one's company at any given time. There are, however, a few detached poems in the collection which breathe a spirit of aristocratic pride, independence and conscious superiority: witness the following:

Never will I submit to the yoke of those who oppress me; no, not if Tmolus itself were to bear down on my head. (1023)

Trample upon them, this dull-witted people; prick them with ox-goads; lash them and round their necks fasten the burdening yoke. Never could anyone find a people so fond of its masters,[33] not if one searched through all those upon whom the sun shines. (847)

He is a bulwark and tower who has brains to the fools about him, Cyrnus, and yet small is the honour he gains from them. (233)

I cannot understand what feelings are held by this people; I am unable to please, whether I treat them badly or well. I am derided by many, by good men as well as by evil; still, among fools there is none who could do what I have done. (367)[34]

Finally, a solemn vow which defies translation (945):

For me the road to my goal is straight; I will not swerve to this side or that side: I am bound only to do what is right. I will put into order this our rich land, and never surrender power to the mob or do what unjust men desire.

'Order' (κόσμος) was a party slogan of the aristocracy, and the passages just cited presuppose an aristocratic regime in force.

We hear quite different tones when bitter disappointment makes itself heard in the confused conflict of the leading parties (341):

Zeus of Olympus, listen and grant my timely (?) entreaty:
Let me, for all I have borne, now be repaid with success.
Rather would I be dead than find no respite from anguish
Nor to have power to inflict woes in requital for mine.
This is but fair and just; yet I have no prospect of vengeance,
No hope of punishing those who by compulsion and guile
Robbed me of all that I own . . .[35]
Might I but drink their blood! Ah, may some favouring daemon
Swiftly arise who will bring to pass all that I pray for.

Chivalry towards their foes was not to be expected from men of this stamp. Cunning and cruelty unite in this dictum (363; cf. Solon fr. 23, 15, above p. 224):

Have fair words for your foes; but if they should be in your power, use no fair-sounding phrases; drink your revenge to the dregs.[36]

An equally coarse spirit is shown in the exclamation (1041):

Come, bring the fluter along; let us laugh and drink and be merry, sitting with him who mourns: let us rejoice at his woes!

Yet there is something of greatness in the harsh forcefulness of such

[33] 'Fond of its masters' probably refers not to a single individual master or tyrant, but to a ruling class.

[34] The word-play between μωμεῖσθαι ('deride') and μιμεῖσθαι ('imitate') cannot be rendered in English. For the thought cf. 24ff. and 793–804 (above p. 402 and 408).

[35] The next verse and a half are unintelligible.

[36] The behaviour of the god towards his opponent in Euripides' *Bacchae* is strictly consonant with this advice.

sayings. A mild and tolerant attitude is very seldom recommended, as in 323:[37]

Do not condemn your friend, being vexed for some little occasion, Cyrnus; do not indulge petty resentment or spite.[38] If we take to our hearts each trivial fault of our comrades, friendship and mutual ties could not exist among men. While there are men, each one will be marked by various mortal weaknesses: only the gods, Cyrnus, are unwilling to pardon.

A further reflection is the following (305):

Not all those who are bad were bad from birth and conception; rather, when they have once chosen the bad for their friends, they learn evil works and evil words and injustice, thinking that what their friends say cannot ever be false.

From a strictly logical standpoint, the content of this poem is no more than a necessary consequence of the view previously put forward by Theognis (35f., above p. 403) that evil conversation corrupts good manners. But it is remarkable that anyone should actually have drawn the conclusion, since it presupposes a concern with the right theoretical attitude towards men whose conduct has to be opposed by practical measures. An equally elevated standpoint is taken in this distich (1079):

I would revile none of my enemies if he should be honest; nor would I praise any friend if he should show himself base.

This thought is most fully developed in a saying reminiscent of Socrates, which seems to forbid the returning of evil for evil (547):

Do no harm in malice to any: for him that is righteous nothing is better than this—kindness and goodness to all.

We have seen many maxims dealing with the relations of men one with another. We turn now to the question of the goals and ideals of life of the individual,[39] and in particular of the nature of manly worth, of *aretê*. As we might have expected, we find a wide range of different answers.

In one passage, and one only, we find *aretê* understood as courage in the field, just as it was in Pseudo-Tyrtaeus (above p. 337–39); and here only we find the same stress laid on the eternal fame conferred by *aretê* (865):

Often the gods send blessings to men who are totally worthless, making

[37] An opposite injunction (1217) says that we should never sit rejoicing with anyone who is grieving, feeling happy at out own good luck.

[38] The primary meaning of διαβάλλειν is 'drive asunder,' 'alienate': the notion of 'slander' is secondary (cf. Liddell & Scott s.v.) and does not fit this context.

[39] We exclude from this question the purely physical pleasures of wine and love, as well as the enjoyment of power and the delight in revenge.

them useless to their friends and to themselves. But manhood's glory is never forgotten; city and land are often saved by the warrior's arm.

For all the idealism of the sentiment, there is a sober and manly clarity in the argument. The accidental blessings of riches, which often turn out the reverse of a blessing to those who receive them, are contrasted with the achievement of the warrior which wins security for the city and at the same time assures itself of lasting remembrance.

Another definition of *aretê* comes very close to the Simonidean doctrine (above pp. 308–11):

If you should never do or suffer anything that is shameful, Cyrnus, there is no proof greater than this of your worth. (1177)

Then again we find 'goodness' equated with righteousness in the sense of later moral teachings, and *aretê* thus becomes 'virtue' (145):

Hold to your honesty, choosing to live with scanty possessions rather than revel in wealth acquired by infamous means. All virtue (*aretê*) is gathered together in righteousness, Cyrnus; if we can call a man good, righteousness earns him the name.

Two further sayings presuppose a very narrow definition of *aretê*, one which was then in vogue among aristocratic circles. The formula was, 'Passion for beauty and power'—the power, that is, of 'the beautiful'; in other words to realize in one's own life what was noble, great and refined.[40] *Aretê* accordingly demanded first a soul receptive of all things noble and elevated and striving vigorously to pursue them; secondly the ability to translate one's will into action. We find a quatrain lamenting that these two requirements are seldom simultaneously satisfied (683):

Many have wealth who have no sense of beauty; some who are seeking beauty are lacking in means, oppressed by poverty. Thus in this way or that the gates of achievement are bolted: some have a shortage of gold, others a shortage of wits.

In the following distich the speaker reckons himself as a member of one of these two classes (695):

I cannot muster, my heart, the resources for which you have asked me; do not despair: there are more lovers of beauty than you.[41]

In several places the various desirable things of life are weighed against one another, with varying results. Wealth, we are told (149f.), is often bestowed by fortune on men of no account, but only a few

---

[40] ἐρᾶν καλῶν καὶ δύνασθαι, cf. Plato *Men.* 77b ff. This definition of *aretê* underlies many passages in Pindar (cf. *Frühgriech. Denken*, 2nd ed., 361f. and below p. 474); cf. also p. 327f. with n. 5.

[41] Cf. Pindar *Pyth.* 4, 288f.

possess *aretê*.[42] In one place (933ff.) high praise is given to the few who combine *aretê* with beauty (*kalokagathia*). On the other hand, we were told earlier that *aretê* and cleverness are the highest goals, but then again that cleverness is better than great *aretê* (p. 407, 414, vs. 789ff. and 1074). A rather lengthy poem (699ff.) lists the possible blessings both of body and of mind, in order to tell us that in most people's judgment wealth is the one *aretê*.[43] The next step is taken by a poem (903ff.) which sees the highest *aretê* in a just balance between getting and spending: if one makes too much money, one's rejoicing heirs will have the profit, but if one spends too much and lives longer than expected, he will die in poverty. A rather waspish rejoinder takes another view (931):

Saving and sparing is best; for if you should die without leaving wealth to your heirs, who then drops a salt tear on your tomb?

In sharp contrast another distich values the respect earned by a good life more highly than wealth and possessions, even for the children who inherit (409):

Finest of all things, Cyrnus, to lay up as wealth for one's children is the respect which men always bestow on the good.

This view is several times expressed elsewhere: Pindar makes use of it in the eighth *Nemean* (35–39, see below p. 489), and in Sophocles' *Antigone* (701–704) Haemon uses it as an argument against his father. In the Theognis collection itself we find a witty parody, which defies effective translation (1161):

Finest of all things, Cyrnus, is laying up naught for one's children; what they demand should be rather bestowed on the good.

In an alternative transmission (Stobaeus, 3, 31, 16 = III p. 672 Hense) the parody runs as follows:

Finest of all things, Cyrnus, for laying up wealth in your chamber, is the respect which a man always bestows on the good.

Both these revised versions amount to roughly the same thing: one of the 'good' is using the argument to ask for a friendly service. The 'respect' mentioned in the second version shows itself in financial and other favours; good men will in due course richly repay what has been bestowed on them; consequently the man who is ready with favours, although his bank balance may be reduced, can place

[42] Cf. also 315ff. from Solon.
[43] The style is strikingly like that of Pseudo-Tyrtaeus fr. 9. The excursus on the inevitability of death is perhaps preparing the way for a continuation which may have said, 'Life must be enjoyed as long as it lasts, and this is where money counts.'

what he has done on the credit side of the ledger; it is wrong to think of them as losses or sacrifices.

Success and prosperity—that is the interpretation of *aretê* in the following poem (335):

Desire nothing too much; hold firm to the mean, and in this way, Cyrnus, you reach the goal (hard to encompass) of worth.

The poet seems to mean that a man will only do well for himself if he trims his sails carefully and steers clear of great risks.[44] This is a piece of true bourgeois sentiment; but at all events *aretê* is still thought of as a good which a man can win for himself. Another distich (653f.) makes it no more than a gift of the ruling powers, giving this advice: 'Do not allow yourself to long for any other *aretê* than the favour of Destiny and the goodwill of the gods.' Next *aretê* itself is given up (129):

Pray not for virtue (*aretê*), Cyrnus, or that the gods may endow you richly with noble estates: pray for good fortune alone.

A step further, and *aretê* ceases even to be mentioned (1153):

Grant me enjoyment of wealth, and freedom from sorrow and evil; may I do no man harm, safe from all burden of woe.

Even this seems too ambitious to the next speaker, and he rejoins (1155):

I neither desire nor pray for wealth. No, may I rather live with a few things content, safe from all burden of woe.

The speaker presumably wants to avoid the dangers which attend the pursuit of great wealth. The question of risk is treated in another and rather singular distich, which gives pointed expression to a thought expressed by, among others, Solon (1, 65ff., above p. 254). It runs approximately thus (637):

Danger and hope in human affairs resemble each other: dreadful divinities they are, one and the other alike.

We are often led by a tempting opportunity to do something which turns out badly; and in this way the two opposite aspects of a new enterprise, the enticing and the threatening, are reduced to the same thing. Religion no longer offers any support in such chaotic relations as many of the poems reveal.[45] We are told that no sacrifice can alter

[44] This kind of trimming is recommended in 401ff. and 557ff., and as a political maxim in 219f.

[45] There is seldom any expression of the idea that the gods are the supporters of the moral order (399f.; 1170; 1179ff.; 1195f.). The Delphic oracle is mentioned 805ff.; *theoroi* are spoken of in 545.

the determination of the gods once they have decided to send suffering (1189f.) Zeus does not reward and punish according to desert; he inflicts hardship on the just, and 'leads the poor man into guilt.'[46] Another speaker feels justified, in face of a threatening political catastrophe, in throwing overboard all the usual rules of decent behaviour (235):

We are not bound to behave like men who are going on living: what suits us may befit men whose whole city must die.[47]

Finally one has ceased even to believe that any moral orientation is possible (381):

Nothing has been decided for man by the powers above us (daimôn), not even how we can best earn the good will of the gods.

What is there left then? Only what a man can give himself; a specific form of courage and resistence which the Greeks called τολμᾶν (441ff.; 555f.; 591ff.): we have no corresponding idea, and thus a rather lengthy periphrasis is needed. What is meant is a strong and composed attitude of mind; a spirit of resistance which sets the oppressed on his feet again; a kind of active patience which strengthens those who have been weakened, and gives freedom again to those who are in bonds. All this is based upon a peculiar elasticity which is produced by simultaneously recognizing and disregarding the ugly truth. This quality when achieved does not display itself outwardly in its own shape, for in the behaviour of the self-controlled man the dark depths of sorrow are concealed behind calmness. A practical consideration is urged in support of such an attitude (355):

Cyrnus, be strong in sorrow, as once you rejoiced amid pleasures, when fate willed that of these also a share should be yours. Just as misfortune succeeded to happiness, so now from sorrow seek in turn for relief, praying for help from the gods. Do not show your pain too much: if you make a display of your sorrow, there will be few who will feel sympathy with your distress.

With this edifying advice we end our selection of sayings on particular themes.[48] Lastly we must see what impression the collection gives as a whole.

[46] 373ff., above p. 312. A rejoinder to this saying comes in the next (393ff.). It declares that the upright man keeps himself free from guilt even in the direst need, and that the ultimate test of character is in such trials as this.

[47] For the expression cf. v. 68.

[48] Among those poems which we have omitted are many good ones, as the verses renouncing a previous friendship, 595ff. and 599ff.; sharp rebuke in 453ff.; 1247.; 295ff.; and many others. The paederastic poems are in general slight and uninteresting; the few concerned with love of women are rather better: I have omitted those of both classes.

Many hands over many generations contributed to the formation of the work, and for that very reason the general picture is in many respects bewildering. In order to simplify and clarify it somewhat, I shall pick out a few characteristic features and sharpen the outlines here and there.

The Theognis-collection contains little that is great poetry, but much that is valuable out of the stock of ideas of the periods from which it comes. In its verses we find 'many of human concerns, tricked out in the brightest of plumage,' so as to flit like birds from place to place and to sing as they do, 'pleading for daily bread, something to keep us alive.'[49] Poverty and other hardships are among the most frequent themes, but there are many others; all the sayings are concerned with practical problems of life. The private interests of the individual are predominant, although party politics also come onto the stage; major political issues remain in the wings. On the other hand, the experiences and situations of which we hear are not individual but typical, and the persons, the 'I' and the 'you,' represent either man in general or a human type. Even when individuals are addressed by name, the words are aimed at a wider circle which was also listening to them: in one place (495) this is expressly stated. The versified address is not allowed either to degenerate into familiar conversation, nor yet to take on the tones of a public oration, as we saw it do (for example) in the elegies of Tyrtaeus.[50]

The manner of thought is abstract and conceptual, and the speakers are extremely sparing of illustrative detail. The most graphic of them are those which deal with the drinking party, although even these pass over many of the appurtenances that we hear of elsewhere—the table with bread, cheese, honey and nuts: the wine-jug and the drinking-bowl; the altar with its incense, the garlands and perfumes.[51] There is no trace of the specific detail found in archaic poetry. We hear constantly of 'riches,' 'wealth,' 'poverty,' 'distress'; never of wheatfields, herds of oxen, flocks and

[49] 729f. The text of the distich is partly corrupt (ἔχουσαι), and its meaning is disputable. For the thoughts taking wings we may compare v. 237; 939 Pindar, *Pyth.* 8, 34 etc.

[50] We find no collective audience addressed, as 'Megarians,' 'fellow citizens,' 'young men' (the opening of 1160a is corrupt). Nor are there any allusions to particular places (exceptions: 879ff., 1002) or the like, which would limit the applicability of the poem. Such references were either avoided from the first or weeded out later. This does not apply, however, to those pieces intended to set the scene, which are defined in place, as 11ff. and 773ff. (Megara) or in time, as 764 (the Persian wars).

[51] The two alien hexastichs 879ff. and 997ff., which recall the style of Xenophanes fr. 1, form an exception.

sheep, ships bearing produce from country to country; not a word of tillage, industry and trade, in fact not a mention of working for one's living, or of crop failures, losses, or the burden of debts.[52] We are indeed told that a man should not associate with unreliable persons in any 'serious business' (62, see above p. 404), but we are given no hint whether a political or a commercial transaction is meant, or indeed what business the poet had in mind at all. This lack of graphic and concrete detail cannot be laid at the door of the elegiac form, which knows no such limitations. We must rather suppose that a gnomic universality was the dominating purpose of the collection. Although the maxims were intended for practical application, this leaves us very ill informed about the actual circumstances with which the recipients of all this instruction were supposed to cope.

In proportion as the external circumstances were left undefined, more stress was laid on attitude of mind (νόος); and the attitude of mind which informed the book as a whole can be easily detected. It may be termed 'aristocratic' in so far as the speakers reckon themselves as belonging to the social upper stratum, and many of them display a contempt for the lower classes and the 'empty-headed' masses (κενεόφρων δῆμος, 233). Now and then they speak of a leader and leadership (above p. 415f.). But if by an aristocratic attitude we mean that spirit which speaks so clearly in the poems of Pindar, the tone of this collection can more fitly be called bourgeois. This can be seen if we take some particular examples of what is in it and what is missing.

There is an abundance of angry resentment and grumbling complaints; but of lofty ideals there is very little. The specifically aristocratic ideal of discipline and tight order is never mentioned, with one solitary exception (947, see above p. 416). No one reminds himself or his fellows of the duty of obeying the law, or of maintaining the traditions of one's fathers. There is no appeal for peace and harmony in the community.[53] Scarcely anything is so frequently and sharply denounced in the collection as violent encroachment on the rights and property of others (ὕβρις), but no one has the notion of recommending benevolence and collaboration instead.[54] On the contrary, the warfare of 'enemies' one against another seems to be taken as normal, and there seems to have been violent competition for

[52] There are a few exceptions or partial exceptions, as travelling and sea-borne trade in 511ff.; 1166; agriculture 1197ff.; 'working' or 'striving' (in a general sense) in 135; 914; 1116; 'one must not deny one's debts' 1195f.; but ships, for example, only appear in similes (114; 457ff.; 576; 970; 671ff.).

[53] Verses such as 43–52 are exceptional. The pacificism of 885f. has a narrowly personal motive.

[54] As Pindar does in the hymn to *Hêsychia* (*Pyth.* 8, 13f.).

riches, which one strove to snatch from ones' enemies in order to line one's own pockets or to give largesse to one's own friends.[55] In the sharpest contrast with the poetry of Pindar, we find no expression of a desire for a reputation which will outlast the span of bodily life.[56] Again in contrast to Pindar, we find no celebration of the aristocratic virtue of liberality (except in 1162, above p. 419), none of the pomp and circumstance of princely life, nothing of culture and the arts. The wealth that supplies a man with more than the mere necessities of life serves in Theognis merely to purchase personal pleasure (903ff.). Sport and the national games are never mentioned; the writers were not concerned with exerting and proving themselves in contest, but only with pleasure. They are apparently not princes or great lords, nor do they have any ambition to be. Thus we hear nothing of that shadow cast by greatness and domination—the envy felt by others.[57]

Strength and greatness of feeling is shown only in two things, but in those repeatedly—in endurance and conflict. To pay back good with good and harm with harm is the greatest satisfaction known to the members of this circle. This is the end forwarded by their friendships, which are not ties of the spirit but partnerships for the pursuit of advantages on both sides. Consequently no human quality is so strongly stressed as trustworthiness in friendship, meaning a readiness to stand by in difficulties and to repay in full the services done to oneself.

If we read through the Theognis collection continuously, we feel ourselves in the company of men who are involved in a severe struggle for existence and are determined to carry it on ruthlessly. Overthrown and ruined by revolutionary changes, embittered by poverty, sharpened and hardened by unhappy experiences, they had ceased to be squeamish about their methods or pretentious about their objectives. For the greatest part, the contributors to the collection are not concerned with contributing to the victory of moral values or political ideals. Such ambitions are far beyond their storm-narrowed horizon. Their efforts are bent rather on achieving personal success and personal influence for the individual, and yet more vigorously

[55] See above p. 413 (for 561f.). Exceptionally 331f. enjoins righteousness irrespective of party.

[56] Exceptions: the warrior's renown, 865ff.; Cyrnus' posthumous survival in poetry, 237ff.; children inherit the respect which their father enjoyed, 409f. (above p. 417; 406f.; 419).·

[57] 797f. is rather like a passage of Pindar (see above p. 408), but where Pindar speaks of φθόνος, the distich uses the word μέμφεσθαι. Μωμεῖσθαι etc. occur often enough in the collection, but φθονεῖν is never used. Cf. however μωμεύμενος in 169 (above p. 408 n. 17) and ζηλωτός in 455.

on saving him from ruin. In social life the maxims do not so much tell us how to create confidence and warmth as encourage cool distrust and prudent reserve. The dominant spirit is of practical realism that does not expect much pleasure from life. In such periods there is more truth than ever in what a fine couplet declares (1027):

Dear Cyrnus, the working of evil is easy and simple for men, but to encompass good—that is the difficult task.

(c) *Pindar and Bacchylides*

I. THE POETS AND THEIR VOCATION AS CHORAL LYRISTS; THE EPINICIANS OF SIMONIDES

The linguistic form in which the maxims of the *Theognidea* are cast is simple and unpretentious and in consequence it was able to withstand the vicissitudes of time. Through the rest of antiquity poets and laymen continued to clothe their thoughts in the convenient form of the elegiac couplet, which provided the author with a wide range of standard figures ready to hand. With choral lyrics (above p. 159f.) it was a different story. Its forms were complex and, unlike elegy, it tended towards the unusual and the distinctive. Rhythm and melody varied from one ode to another, and consequently it was impossible to repeat word for word turns of phrase which had once been hammered out. The numerous possibilities of free modification encouraged a special development of the genre, and a specific choral-lyric style was developed. The language is that of high poetry, and thus free from the tyranny of schematism. It prefers variation where everyday language would require exact correspondence, and it glides over in silence a great deal that the cultivated listener can easily supply from the context. But this makes the odes difficult to read; one must work hard to understand them, but the labour is richly repaid. Choral lyric had a high sense of its own dignity, and its production accordingly had certain closely-defined prerequisites. It required a poet-choirmaster who should be at home in all the traditions of the art, in word, music, gesture and dance; wherever it was performed, it needed well-trained amateur choruses to present it, and it relied upon a public who by long experience had qualified themselves to understand the difficulties of the text and to be judges of the elaborate performance. All these reasons conspired to make choral lyric also more representative of its age than any other literary form; and as the most characteristic and highly-bred product of the epoch it did not attain its finest development until the epoch itself was near to its climax and its decline. Thus the archaic age of Greek literature found its ultimate crown of poetry in the choral odes of Pindar; and in their thought and expression the archaic ideal was expressed in impeccable purity. Throughout his creative period (c. 498–446) Pindar remained untouched by the revolution in ideas that was going on around him. As one born out of due time, he lived on into an age that became more and more alien to him. Attic tragedy, with an entirely different basis, had already entered upon the heritage of choral lyric when Pindar was bringing his older art to perfection; and not only Aeschylus, but Sophocles and Euripides had made their voices heard before silence fell on his. It is true that tragedy took over choral lyric and developed it further (above p. 399), but only to tie it to tragic dialogue and make it serve other ends to which it had originally been a stranger. In its new setting choral lyric flourished for a while, but died away quickly with the passing of that generation which had been brought up to know the independent choral lyric. From then on this type of poetry served only to provide feeble entr'actes in drama or as an insignificant exercise for the literary virtuoso.

Of Pindar's literary production we have four complete books and a considerable collection of fragments, which is being constantly increased from papyrus discoveries. Egyptian papyri have also restored to us considerable remains of the work of his contemporary Bacchylides. Bacchylides, like Pindar, was a choral lyrist, and he wrote for some of the same employers and even competed with him several times upon the same occasions; furthermore, Bacchylides was clearly much influenced by Pindar. Consequently it is permissible to treat Pindar and Bacchylides together, although not to put them on the same level. The contrast is very great. Bacchylides possesses an easy and lucid art, while Pindar matches depth of content with his mature and masterly skill as a poet.[1]

By origin Bacchylides was an Ionian from the island of Ceos, and we cannot fail to detect in him the light elegance of Ionian artists, the sensible clarity and graphic qualities of Ionian writers. He presumably learned his craft from the aged Simonides, whose close kinsman he was; but of that reforming zeal which marked the precursor of the sophists there is no trace in Bacchylides. Indeed in all his writings we can find no trace of any purpose directed elsewhere than to the writing of elegant poetry and achieving recognition thereby. Pindar was a Boeotian from the neighbourhood of Thebes: thus

---

[1] For this reason we shall not concern ourselves very much here with Bacchylides, and not devote a separate section to him, but deal with him from time to time where he serves as a foil to Pindar.

he came from that same region of Greece in which the respectable thinker and poet of the countryside Hesiod had lived. Boeotia was still a backward and provincial district; Pindar had to study his art abroad, probably in Athens. But his heavy earnestness, his inward strength and stability and his high aspirations can well be reckoned as part of his inheritance from his landlocked peasant ancestry.

Despite his coming from such a remote province, Pindar quickly gained a pan-Hellenic reputation. Several times in his poetry he was able to allude to his having made nonsense of the contemptuous nickname 'Boeotian pig.' By his art and personality[2] he won a reputation and respect which enabled him to talk to kings as an equal and to give them advice and instruction almost *ex cathedra*. The Greeks of that time gave to the poet the place that he deserved, and Pindar was well aware of his own worth. He also knew that what he had to give was more than the great ones of the earth could either

---

[2] Not through his supposed descent from the legendary Theban noble family of the Aegeidae (or from the Theban phratry of the Aegeidae, cf. schol. *Pyth.* 5, 101b fin.). This modern supposition is based upon one solitary passage, which the ancient seekers out of biographical allusions never interpreted in that sense—indeed the ancient biographers do not agree on the name of Pindar's father, and give us three names from which to choose. The four words 'descendants of Aegeus, my fathers' in *Pyth.* 5, 75 could by themselves be taken as referring to Pindar's fathers just as much as to the fathers of the Cyrenean chorus: there are parallels for both— on the one side *Isthm.* 1, 1 and *Olymp.* 6, 84; on the other *Pyth.* 8, 98, *Nem.* 7, 85 and probably *Paean* 2, 28. But both the immediate and the wider context of the passages are decisively in favour of the fathers being those of the Cyrenean chorus. The sentence runs: 'Thence (i.e. from Sparta) sprung, came my fathers, the Aegeids, to Thera.' Now the Cyreneans derived their origin from Sparta and Thera, whereas a Theban Aegeid, descended from someone who had left Thebes and gone first to Sparta, then to Thera, is quite unthinkable. The wider context (vss. 80–90) is in praise of Apollo Carneus (80) as the god closely associated with the Cyreneans from the beginning, and Pindar's ancestors have no business here at all. Callimachus' *Hymn to Apollo* (71–73) has a close parallel: '(Apollo has many cult-names, but I as a Cyrenean name him) Καρνεῖον· ἐμοὶ πατρώιον οὕτω. Σπάρτη τοι Καρνεῖε τὸ δὴ πρώτιστον ἔδεθλον, δεύτερον αὖ Θήρη, τρίτατόν γε μὲν ἄστυ Κυρήνης, etc. There is nothing surprising in the Cyrenean chorus' styling itself, on behalf of the whole people, a descendant of the Aegeidae; such a thing was common, as when Tyrtaeus, for example, describes the Spartan youth collectively (8, 1) as 'descendants of the never-defeated Heracles', although strictly speaking only the two royal families were so descended. (This could be applied to Pindar also: even if the kinship to the Aegeidae referred to him, he could style himself thus *qua* Theban, not as claiming descent from a noble family.) Perhaps we can follow the scholiast in taking this mention of the Spartan–Cyrenean Aegeids as a hint that Pindar, as a countryman of the Theban Aegeids, felt himself akin to the Cyreneans and thus associated with the victor. Thus we have no notion from what sort of a family Pindar came; but it is perfectly clear that the ideas which he expresses are solely those of the leading families (K. Latte, *Gött. Gel. Anz.* 207, 1953, 40); see below p. 474–76.

give or deny him. He often reminds us that man and his deeds are transitory unless a poet's words bestow on them immortality in whatever sense the poet is willing to impart.[3]

Since all Pindar's poems were occasional pieces, many of them can be dated to a particular year. There are no less than fifty-two years between the first date and the last, and we cannot fail to see a certain development of the poetical style. But in general the changes are trivial compared with the very great uniformity of his work as a whole. Pindar's art, like Pindar's world, is wholly pure and wholly self-contained.[4] To enter the realm of his poetry is like going into an enchanted circle. It is not easy to gain entrance; but he who has once succeeded never leaves it again. One cannot escape from the strength and power of Pindar's language, the abrupt soaring of his thought, the sharp rigour of his laws and the earnest humanity of his feeling. And the very uniformity of his work makes it possible for us to learn to understand the frequent obscurities of his language better and better as our acquaintance with the work grows. The meaning of his words, the significance of his images, the connections underlying his violent transitions—all these become steadily clearer as we compare kindred passages from different poems and draw inferences one from another.

Pindar always has the whole in mind, even when he is speaking of the part; every ode, almost every strophe, is directed at the whole that lies behind them all. Pindar's 'darkness' is not, as the German romantics thought, the swirling mist of a thundercloud that drives onward it knows not whither, and discharges its fury into the void. Pindar is no Ossian, no 'original genius' unconstrained by tradition. The difficulties of his language arise rather from his speaking as a supreme master, at the very end of his epoch, knowing and believing, to others who understood and believed, in a comprehensive and abbreviating art-form which did not deal in description and explanations, but in allusions and reminiscences. Two hundred years of the richest Greek experience culminated in his genius. His work is the expression of a power comparable with that of a Parmenides or Heraclitus.[5] While the theories of the philosophers strove to throw

[3] In *Nem.* 4, 83 we read (paraphrased): 'The praise of great deeds in song, such as my song in honour of Timasarchus, bestows on the man thus celebrated a rank comparable with that of a king.' If the poet by his art is able to bestow kingly rank, then he himself by his art is the equal of kings, and we need not inquire by what personal patent of nobility he was able to take such a high tone towards Hiero and the young ruler of Aetna as he does in the first Pythian.

[4] But very far from being rigid; see below p. 470 n. 8.

[5] 'Pindar's true spirit and profound insight are greatly misunderstood by those who, in imitating or interpreting him, see him as an unreflecting enthusiast, as a

light on the basis of existence and to make visible the active principles in nature as a whole, Pindar set forth an image of the nature of men, heroes and gods, modelled in lights and shadows, heights and depths, lit by the rays of beauty and sublimity.

Of the choral songs which Pindar wrote and composed, only the words have survived; the music has perished. His entire output was arranged by ancient critics into seventeen books according to their several types. Of these only the four books of ἐπινίκια ('victory-songs') have been preserved in manuscript: odes in honour of victors in the games at Olympia, Delphi, Nemea and the Isthmus—the so-called Olympian, Pythian, Nemean and Isthmian odes respectively. The reason for the survival of these books particularly was their popularity in late antiquity, 'since they are more human, less mythological and less unconscionably obscure than the rest' (Eust. *Vita* p. CVII 20 Christ).

A suitable occasion for the public performance of epinician odes was the return of the winner to his city. The successful athlete entered in a joyous procession, and the chorus of friends and compatriots that escorted him sang the epinician to welcome him and sing his praises during the procession.[6] There were, however, many other occasions suitable for a performance: a social art like choral lyric did not wait passively on external circumstances for an opportunity to exert itself, but made its own openings as it thought fit.[7] And the festal public performance was not the end of the matter; the purpose of the poem was to immortalize the achievement and the performer. The text became an heirloom in the family, which found glory for itself in the glory of individual members; the poets will hardly have

man intoxicated with his own sound and fury. His step is so steady and bold, the plan of his poems so profoundly and architecturally laid out, his images are so skilfully chosen, the arrows of his poetry have such a sure aim, that to emulate such a Daedalus is, as Horace found from his own experience, a most dangerous exploit. He is sustained and borne onwards by the winds of heaven and by his own spirit, not stormy, but strong and sublime.' Thus the acute and judicious Herder in 1803 (*Adrastea* 11).

[6] The second *Nemean*, for example was written for a procession of this kind (cf. v. 24). This short ode was written so as to be repeated *da capo* as often as necessary, so that all the spectators lining the streets along the route might hear it in its entirety. This is shown by the way in which the end of the song forcibly directs us back to the beginning again: (v. 25) 'Begin (!) the pure-sounding strain (v. 1) with that with which the Homeric singers most often begin—.' On a song of Sappho's for the ceremonial conducting of a bride, which probably was also designed for repetition, see above p. 174 n. 13.

[7] Performance of an epinicium before the victor's door: *Isthm.* 8, 1–4, cf. *Nem.* 1, 19f.; at the temple of a god: *Pyth.* 11, 1ff., etc. From *Pyth.* 1, 97f. we can gather that young people when gathered together socially sung choral odes for their own entertainment and edification.

thrown away their own copies after one performance; and anyone who took pleasure in the ode could make his own transcript of it. The victor's native city, on whom, according to Greek notions, a great deal of the glory was reflected, might place a copy of the ode in its archives.[8] From such manuscripts the poem could be re-awakened into life at any time; for there was nothing to prevent an individual from singing it to his own accompaniment. The melodies were purely monophonic, and every member of good society had been trained in singing and the lyre. Thus Pindar could say to a victor whose father was no longer living (*Nem.* 4, 13):

If your father Timocritus were yet warmed by the flaming rays of the sun, often would he strike rich melody from his lyre and celebrate in the words of this song his son blessed by victory.

Just as the victory ode was intended to carry the fame of the achievement to the remotest posterity, so also it carried it, while the event was yet fresh, far abroad into the Greek lands and islands. Of an Aeginetan ship-owning family which had distinguished itself in many contests, Pindar says that 'they took songs of their own glory as their cargo' (*Nem.* 6, 32); apparently they had sung the new songs in the evenings at the houses of their friends overseas, celebrating the more ancient glories of their line together with the latest achievement, and distributed texts where they found people interested in them. Another of Pindar's odes, again for a victor from the great trading island of Aegina, begins as follows (*Nem.* 5, 1):

I am no bronze-caster, I make no unmoving statues to abide for ever rooted to their base. Nay rather on every boat and vessel, sweet song, fare forth from Aegina with the news that Lampon's son, the mighty Pytheas, has won the crown in the pancration at the Nemean games.[9]

The chorus that rehearsed and publicly performed the ode was discharging thereby a debt of gratitude to their compatriot who had contributed so much to the fame of their common homeland. In more than one place all the citizen body, even the personal or political enemies of the victor, are called upon to join in his praises. The situation is less clear for the composer of the ode, if like Pindar he plied his art as a trade and placed it at the service of people with

---

[8] Pindar's ode in honour of a Rhodian athlete was deposited in a temple in Rhodes, written in letters of gold (schol. *Olymp.* 7, p. 195, 13 Drachmann).

[9] These verses again reflect the rivalry between the two arts which serve to immortalize a man: the art of the statuary and that of the poet (cf. above p. 306f. with n. 5 and 7). In *Pyth.* 6, 5–14 Pindar maintains that the 'treasury of songs' provides a more secure protection for the fame of those whom it celebrates than the treasury of Delphi does for the statues of victors.

whom he had otherwise no common bonds. What was it then, apart from the expected fee, that impelled him to contribute his poem to the celebration?

It was Pindar's conviction that great achievements have a 'thirst for song' (*Pyth.* 9, 103f.; *Nem.* 3, 6ff.) and a claim to be praised in poetry. This claim was naturally made to those men who possessed the gracious gift of musical art. In this sense Pindar describes his contribution as the discharge of a debt (*Pyth.* 9, 104; *Olymp.* 3, 7; *Pyth.* 8, 33). He also considered that noble qualities can only flourish if they are recognized and praised (*Nem.* 8, 39ff., see below p. 489f.). But the poem is more than the actual offering of a service; it is a gift of friendship (χάρις). Pindar participated personally in the happiness of the victor: 'I rejoice in the new good fortune' (*Pyth.* 7, 18).[10] Thus the gift of the poem established a tie, even if there is no other, between the giver and the receiver. One victory ode begins thus (*Olymp.* 7):

As when a man, drinking to his young son-in-law,[11] holds in his lavish hand a bowl pearled with the dew of the grape, and gives from his own possession to the other's the heavy golden treasure of his possessions to adorn the feast, to honour the new kinship, and in the presence of friends to wish good fortune to the harmonious wedlock; so do I send the Muses' gift of a draught of nectar (=immortality), the lovely fruit of my soul, to men who have won for themselves the prize, and I beg the favour of the gods for victors at Olympia and Pytho. Happy is he whom good repute guards.[12]

If the victor is a boy, then we may discern something of a lover's homage in the poet's attitude towards him.

Pindar must have travelled a great deal in maintaining contact with the circles for whom he wrote his poetry. He will often have been a spectator at the games, so that he could himself bear witness to the achievement and he must often have been the guest of those who commissioned him, in order to train the chorus in person and then, dressed in the long ceremonial garments of the chorus-master, to direct the presentation and accompany it on the lyre. If he could not go there himself, Pindar sent 'the Muse' (i.e. the MS. of his

[10] This is probably what is meant by *Pyth.* 9, 89, 'I have received something lovely for my share.'

[11] It was a Greek custom at the table that one 'drank to' presents, i.e. symbolized one's acceptance by drinking to the giver. The giving of a golden bowl filled with wine serves as a symbol of the choice of a husband in an exotic romance in Athenaeus 13, 575c (from Chares) and similarly 576a (from Aristotle).

[12] θῆκε ӡαλωτόν (6) = ἐμακάρισεν, 'expresses pleasure in the good fortune of the other.' Correspondingly ὁ δ' ὄλβιος (10) is a μακαρισμός. Ἰλάσκομαι (9) is correctly explained by Julius Stenzel (diss. Breslau 1908), p. 11; for the dative compare *Iliad* 1, 147, for the subject cf. *Pyth.* 12, 4ff. (ἵλαος), *Olymp.* 2, 12ff. etc.

poem, to journey there by itself). One of his poems begins thus (*Nem.* 3):

> O Muse, powerful one, my mother, I beseech you, travel to the Dorian isle Aegina in the holy month of the Nemean games; for on the banks of the Asopus young men await you, craftsmen of sweet-sounding songs of triumph, yearning to hear your voice.

In strict logic such things as the address on the poetical parcel and its delay in being delivered have no place in the song to be performed, but Pindar is not in the least concerned with this sort of logic. The epic singers permitted themselves at most an invocation of the muse, but Pindar's choral poetry takes the liberty of expressing every attitude of the poet's that was in any way connected with his art, and the hearer can, as it were, be present at the composition of the poem. One opening (*Olymp.* 10) admits that Pindar had forgotten his task:

> Behold me, where the Olympian victor, the son of Archestratus, is written in my heart! I owed him a sweet song, and forgot it. Do you, O Muse, and you, Truth, daughter of Zeus, hold me with just hand pure from the reproach of lying and sinning against my friend. Future time that has come upon me from a distance (=the passing of the stipulated time) has brought upon me the deep shame of a debt unpaid. Yet still has payment with interest the power to still sharp reproach.

Personal expressions of this kind give the charm of intimacy to Pindar's poems, and they are at once winning and dignified. On another occasion the poet was working on a choral ode to be performed in honour of Apollo of Delos, when he received a commission for a victory-ode for a fellow-Theban. He set aside his work on the ode for Apollo, and began his poem for the Theban as follows (*Isthm.* 1):

> Thebe of the golden shield, my mother, your desire will I set nearer to my heart than any other. Be not angry with me, rocky Delos, to whom I am now under obligation: what shall be nearer to a just man than his revered parents? Yield place, o island of Apollo; with the gods' help will I bring both tasks to full accomplishment, and dance both for Phoebus of the unshorn locks in sea-girt Ceos with its sailor sons and for the wave-washed strip of the Isthmus (where Herodotus of Thebes won the prize).

Pindar makes no bones about referring to the payment that he expects for his poems by praising the liberality of the person addressed and reminding him that no expenditure is better directed than that which brings him recognition and fame. The exchange of poem against fee did not belong to the world of commerce, but to the whole philosophy of the 'guest-friend.' Generosity and hospitality ranked among the highest virtues in the circles in which Pindar worked, and the poet, like any other honoured visitor, received the appropriate guest-gift (*Pyth.* 10, 64):

I trust in the kindly hospitality of Thorax, who concerns himself to win my favour and has yoked this four-horsed car of the Muses (=commissioned the poem); his service and his invitation do I willingly repay with the like . . .

Thus speaks Pindar, somewhat circumstantially, in the earliest of the dateable poems that we possess.[13] And just as great nobles, even without visiting each other, could set up a guest-friendship simply by interchange of gifts (cf. *Iliad* 11, 23 and *Odyssey* 21, 34–38), so the poet sent his poem when he could not come in person, and the recipient sent a gift in return to his 'guest-friend.'[14]

In general the poet worked on direct commission, whether for individuals as in the victory odes, or for communities, which must have been normal with hymns for religious occasions. But it sometimes happened that he addressed a poem uninvited to some great noble. Wherever he went, however, or wherever he sent his poem, he could be sure of a good reception, since the reputation that he and his art enjoyed seems to have been extraordinarily high. In Syracuse he was a guest of the most powerful Greek ruler of his time, the tyrant Hiero, who in Pindar's words (*Olymp.* 1, 12):

wields the sceptre of judgment in Sicily rich in sheep, picking the flower of all manly excellence and delighting in the bloom of the Muses' gifts, such as we often enjoy in sport around his hospitable table.

What we know about the externals of the choral lyrists' profession is easy enough to understand. What is harder is to achieve any clearness on the inner content of the poems. The victory odes contain a great deal which seems to have little or nothing to do with the occasion of the poem, a victory in an athletic contest. How are we to explain this fact? And what in general terms is the dominating idea in the odes of Pindar? Where is there a unity in all this multiplicity? We will not attempt an *a priori* solution of this question, but we will try to obtain it gradually, piece by piece, from the texts and from the other facts which we shall meet in the course of our investigation. In connection with this problem there is another that

[13] The conception of the guest-friend relationship was helpful in getting round the deep rooted Greek prejudice against performing services for foreigners for pay. It was generally felt that a man should place his gifts exclusively at the service of his countrymen (cf. Plato's objection to the travelling sophists).

[14] It follows that a reference to guest-friendship cannot be at once taken as showing that Pindar had visited the person concerned. Cf. also Theocritus 7, 129: ἐκ Μοισᾶν ξεινήιον=payment for the poem.

must be solved at the same time: Why did great poetry apply itself to such ephemeral topics as victories in the field of sport?[15]

The religious element in the poems is the easiest to understand. In the Greek world all high art had a religious element, and the ceremonial performance of an ode was from the first an action connected with worship. Seen from this viewpoint, the topical element, the reference to particular contemporary men and circumstances, appears as an alien element, and one is surprised that victory odes came about. Historically speaking, the genre was relatively late in appearing. Simonides is said to have been the first who applied the art of the choral lyrist not merely to the praises of gods and heroes of legend, but also to celebrating human contemporaries, by lauding victors in the games or by praising the dead in funeral dirges. It was Simonides also who gave to humanity a new dignity within the limitations of its nature. The victory ode has a special justification in that the athletic contests were under the particular protection of gods and heroes, and in themselves ranked as expressions of religious sentiment.

Of the victory odes of Simonides we possess only a few sparse fragments; but a legend attaching to them gives us some welcome information. We are told that Simonides once wrote a choral ode for a victorious boxer, but the latter refused to pay more than a part of the fee, and scornfully bade him ask for the rest of it from the Dioscuri, since Simonides had permitted himself 'digressions such as are common among the poets,' in which he sang the praises of Castor and Pollux, who were the prototypes and divine protectors of all boxers. 'Just is the race of the gods,' wrote Pindar once with reference to Castor and Pollux (*Nem.* 10, 54), and on this occasion they proved it in Simonides' favour. Shortly after the feast in celebration had begun, two young men appeared at the door and asked to speak to Simonides. When the poet came out, they were nowhere to be seen; but at that very moment the house collapsed and buried all those within under its ruins.[16] Thus the blasphemer received his punishment and the pious poet his reward.

[15] For the answers to both questions see below p. 488–90.

[16] This element in the legend (which occurs in Quintilian 11, 2, 11ff., Callimachus fr. 64 Pfeiffer, and other places) took its origin from a *threnos* of Simonides' which we have discussed above (p. 304), lamenting the death of one of the Scopads who perished with others in the fall of a house. The story goes on to say that by his wonderful powers of memory Simonides was able to identify the unrecognizable corpses by remembering the exact order of seating at the table. Simonides was famed as the inventor of a system of mnemonics: a choral lyrist needed of course to have a wide knowledge of mythology, and the nine Muses were reckoned to be the daughters of Mnemosyne, i.e. power of memory or recollection (=tradition).

From this delightful anecdote we can infer that in many of Simonides' victory odes there was remarkably little about the actual victor, but a great deal about the Dioscuri by whose grace the victory had been won.[17] The oldest victory odes were primarily hymns in honour of the Dioscuri or other gods and heroes, and the human victor was only mentioned and praised in passing. In Pindar we can still find clear vestiges of this attitude.[18]

Viewed historically, the victory ode is a particular variety of hymn to god or hero, and Pindar was following a well-established tradition in incorporating a generous measure of religious or legendary material in his victory-odes.[19] Nevertheless, the historical explanation is not in itself enough. Pindar did not burden himself with the mere lumber of tradition: everything in his poem had to be justified by his own principles. For him victory in the games must have possessed some importance to entitle it to this religious and heroic celebration. Simonides was able to take athletic successes less seriously, since for him the ideals of humanity were to be sought elsewhere. This is obvious enough even in the meagre fragments that we possess of his victory odes.

Four of the surviving fragments strike a note of wit and badinage. On one occasion he had to celebrate a victory gained by a mule-team in the chariot race. Now mules are useful, but not very romantic, creatures; only twice (in 500 and 496) were teams of mules admitted to the Olympic games. Simonides devised a way to avoid calling a mule a mule and reminding the victorious coursers of their asinine ancestry, by thus apostrophizing them (515):

All hail to you, daughters of wind-swift steeds!

[17] From Quintilian's account we learn that four different poems had been identified as the one in this legend. Thus the apparent disproportion that underlies the story must have been not an accidental and unique, but a typical feature.

[18] In *Isthm.* 1, 18 Pindar describes his victory ode as a 'hymn to Castor or to Iolaus,' into which he will 'insert' the present victor in the chariot-race (Iolaus of course was a charioteer of the heroic age); next, vv. 17–32, come the praises of Iolaus and the Dioscuri. This throws light on the expression Καστόρειον in *Pyth.* 2, 69; the word is simply synonymous with ἐπινίκιον. At the beginning of another ode (*Olymp.* 3) the poet expresses the wish that his poem may find favour with the Dioscuri and their sister. The dedication to the Dioscuri is readily understood from what we have already seen, and it is moreover justified by Pindar himself in vv. 36–41. (But the inscription which *Olymp.* 3 bears in the manuscript arises from a misunderstanding of v. 34 on the part of the ancient commentators; cf. *Hermes* 89, 1961, p. 394ff.)

[19] The first *Olympian* (for Hiero) represents itself as a hymn in praise of Zeus (vv. 9–10) and of Pelops (vv. 25–95: he is apostrophized vv. 36–51), whereas only thirteen verses in between (11–23) and a score at the end are concerned with Hiero.

In a poem to a wrestler called Krios Simonides played upon the meaning of the name as a common noun (= 'ram'); referring to the severity of the contest which the winner had had to endure, he wrote (507):

Our Ram was well and truly shorn.[20]

A charioteer had been victorious in the games at Pellene which were held in the winter; the prize was one of the specialities of Pellene—a woollen cloak. The driver who braved the winter's cold in order to win a garment to keep him warm is compared by Simonides to the man 'in the Carian fable' who in midwinter plunged into the icy sea to catch an octopus to feed himself and his family in their winter distress.[21] We have become accustomed, from Pindar's time onward, to the elevation of athletic successes to the heroic level in literature: Simonides contrariwise jokingly brings the achievement down to the level of the simplest humanity and estimates the reward purely at its practical value;[22] this is in tune with the attractive realism that we recognized in him earlier.

The fourth and last example of Simonides' playful treatment of his subject is the following fragment (509), which praises a victorious boxer:

Even the strength of Polydeuces would not raise a fist against him, nor the iron son of Alcmene.

The sons of Zeus, who in current belief kept watch over the games as prototypes of athletic fortitude, and as higher powers bestowed victory on their favourites, are here ranked by Simonides not merely beside, but actually below a contemporary mortal. This cannot have been meant seriously; it was written tongue-in-cheek to contain its own refutation.[23]

[20] 'Shear' in the sense of 'thrash' is common in Latin comedy (Terence, *Heaut.* 951; Plautus, *Capt.* 896 etc.).

[21] Simonides 514 (fr. 11 Bergk), cf. *Gött. Gel. Anzeigen* 1928, 264f. (where unfortunately Pellana in Achaea is confused with Pellene in Chalcidice; corrected by Kurt Latte in Gött. Gel. Anz. 1953, 39). For the fable cf. also Macarius 5, 9; that the games were held in winter is also attested by schol. Pind. *Olymp.* 9, 146g and Nonnus 37, 149–151.

[22] Pindar follows him, at a discreet distance, in a passage which also alludes to the cloak as the prize; but Pindar's way out is through heavy stylization (*Olymp.* 9, 96ff.): 'Epharmostus proved his wondrous might . . . when in Pellene he bore off the prize, the gale-stilling remedy against cold winds.' For the expression we may compare Hipponax 25, 1–2 and *Il.* 16, 224; *Od.* 14, 529.

[23] But even so the statement comes near to being sacrilegious. To explain it we must remember that for Simonides 'god' was the absolute, in comparison to which the heroes of legend, subject to all that humans suffer, seemed much closer to men, as we can clearly see in fr. 523 and 543 (above p. 305 and 315f.). Thus in

2. TWO SHORT VICTORY ODES BY PINDAR

Wit and irony of the kind that we have seen in Simonides are wholly lacking in Pindar.[1] Instead, many of his poems are distinguished by a quiet and delicate grace. As the first of his poems that we shall read in full, we take one of the shortest and simplest.

When the Olympic games were celebrated again for the first time after the great Persian war in 476, the winner of the boys' boxing contest was the young Hagesidamus from 'Epizephyrian' (= Western) Locris in Southern Italy. The prize was a chaplet of olive leaves. The ode in his honour runs thus (*Olymp.* 11):

[*Strophe*] There are some times when winds are most needed by men; at other times heaven-born water, the rain-children of the cloud; but when a success is gained by hard striving, then hymns with honeyed voices founding future praise are presented, a trustworthy pledge for great virtues (*aretai*).

[*Antistrophe*] Unstintingly to the victors at Olympia such praise is offered. My tongue is eager to furnish yours; but it is through God's grace that a man attains clever understanding as anything else. Hear now, Archestratus' son Hagesidamus: for the sake of your boxing contest.

[*Epode*] I will pour the sweet adornment of melody on the garland of golden olive, respective to the race of the Zephyrian Locrians. Go there in festal procession, O Muses. I will be your surety; no inhospitable company are they, nor unacquainted with the beautiful; but high in wisdom and also spearsmen are they whom you will visit. For never has a tawny fox changed his inborn nature, nor a loud-roaring lion.

[*Strophe*[2]] The song satisfies Hagesidamus' desire like a favourable breeze (filling the sails of the boat of his popularity); it descends like gentle rain (quickening and nourishing the noble growth of his lofty aspirations).[3] By the authority of his words the poet attests before all

Simonides men of his own day and heroes of legend stand cheek by jowl in the same hymn because the same circle of humanity includes them all; in Pindar the reasons are very different.

[1] When for example in *Isthm.* 4, 52f. Pindar allowed himself to allude to the mean stature and appearance of the victor, he blunted the point of the statement by adding, 'But Heracles was not very tall either,' without abandoning the seriousness of his panegyrical style.

[2] The strophe and antistrophe have exactly the same rhythm, while the epode is different. The pattern is thus a–a–b. The group, composed of strophe, antistrophe and epode, is called a triad. The longer odes consist of several triads (pattern a–a–b. a–a–b, . . .); there are commonly five of them.

[3] For those familiar with this stylized language the images of wind and rain have a special meaning. 'Wind' signifies will and state of mind (cf. *Die Homerischen*

the world, as if on a sworn statement, the achievement and the qualities (*aretai*) by virtue of which it was achieved.

[*Antistrophe*] Pindar will make his contribution to the praises of the victor; but in the last resort his art, like every good thing, comes not from himself, but is to be credited to the gods. Now does Pindar for the first time give any details of the Olympic victor who is his theme —his name, the nature of the contest, and later [*epode*] his native country. The poet sends 'the Muses' (that is to say, his poem) to the Locrians, so that it may be sung at the *joyeuse entreé* of Hagesidamus. The Muses are not to be apprehensive about their voyage to Italy, for the Locrians are hospitable and acquainted with 'the beautiful.' The notion of the beautiful in Pindar embraces all that is pleasing, elegant, honourable and cultivated. In reference to the reception of the Muses, 'acquaintance with the beautiful' implies a refined appreciation of art; Pindar's ode will be skilfully performed and fully appreciated by its audience. Furthermore, the Locrians are as clever as they are bold in battle. How is it that Pindar can pledge himself in this way for the far distant Locrians? It is because Hagesidamus at Olympia gave proof of the four virtues in question, both for himself and for his people, since virtue breeds true to type.[4] He is skilful and brave; in the boxing contest he showed the intelligence of a fox and the courage of a lion (cf. *Isthm.* 4, 46f.). Moreover, he is acquainted with the beautiful: in his case this means he has devoted himself to athletic pursuits, which possess no practical, but only ideal, value. Finally, he is not inhospitable, since he has promised the poet a suitable 'guest-gift' (i.e. a fee).

The poem is of small compass, and its one basic thought is simple *Gleichnisse* [Göttingen, 1921] 19f.), and especially popular favour (see above p. 43 n. 39) and fame (cf. the 'wind' of praise in poetry, *Pyth.* 4, 3; 1, 90ff.; *Nem.* 5, 51 and 6, 28f.; 7, 11–18; see also *Frühgr. Denken* 360f.). The laudatory poem resembles 'rain' because every great deed 'thirsts' for recognition (*Nem.* 3, 6f.; *Pyth.* 9, 103f.), and because *areté* only grows up like a tree towards heaven when it is watered with praise and poetry (*Nem.* 8, 40; cf. also *Nem.* 7, 12ff.; *Isthm.* 7, 19); see below p. 489f. Cf. now also the study of *Olymp.* 11 by Bundy, *Univer. of California Studies in Class. Phil.* 1962, I.

    4 Pindar can only go bail to the Muses for things falling within his direct knowledge, as here his personal acquaintance with the boy (cf. *Olymp.* 10, 100 to the same Hagesidamus). If he were thinking of earlier poets and musicians in Locris, then his personal guarantee could not apply, and v. 17f. would have to mean: 'Muses, you will not for the first time become guests of the Locrians, and you have long known for yourselves how skilled they are in things of beauty.' For the sake of his chosen stylization Pindar ignores the familiarity which the Muses already had with the people to whom he was sending them. But how dull, and how much less true, would the poem be without such simplification! (In fr. 140b on the other hand Pindar expressly mentions the cultural traditions of the Locrians: circumstances were seen under different lights according to the dominating poetical idea.)

and joyous: 'A poem for Hagesidamus of Locris is due; I am writing it; thither it is bound; there it will be artistically performed and favourably received.' Yet it is not poor in the ideas that are represented in it: the play of the elements and the fidelity to type in man and beast; longing and the desired fulfilment, obligation and achievement, performance and praise-giving; martial spirit and poetic feeling; the divine giver of all good things, and many others. In the lively flow of the poem this pious expression forms a static midpoint; the first and the last of the three strophes give assurance of the virtues of the victor and his nation; the opening and the conclusion are each adorned with a double simile. But the symmetry is not obtrusive; the poem flows gracefully and lightly. When he wrote this poem, Pindar's abilities had already reached their full development.

Not very much later (probably about 470) Pindar wrote another short victory ode for Ergoteles of Himera in Sicily, who had won the footrace at the Olympic and other games. Here we find a fuller and more serious tone; Ergoteles was a mature man with many vicissitudes of fortune behind him. The city of Himera also had gone through a stormy period and had been under foreign rule, but was now again free. Many of her citizens perished in the troubles; to make up the lists, immigrants were invited and accepted into the citizen body with equal rights. Among these was Ergoteles of Cnossus in Crete, who had suffered exile in the civil conflicts and now had the chance of having a home again. He acquired some land in Himera—a privilege only accorded to full citizens—and as a Himeran citizen he won for himself and for his adopted country the glory of athletic distinction. Near the city there are hot springs, called the 'bath of the Nymphs,' in which Ergoteles could wash off the dust of his old country and his wanderings; to bathe oneself in a new country was a symbol of successful settlement.[5] The essential quality of vicissitudes such as he had undergone, from prosperity to disaster and back again, was called in Greek *tychê*: the word can also denote the destiny of whole communities. After these preliminary remarks the text will be intelligible without comment (*Olymp.* 12):

[*Strophe*] I pray you, saviour-goddess Tyche, daughter of Zeus the Liberator, watch over Himera and increase her strength. By you is the swift ship ruled on the sea, and on land violent wars and assemblies of men in counsel. The hopes of petty men roll up and down in turn, cutting through the waves of the lying sea of vanities;[6]

[5] Cf. *Frühgriech. Denken* 97f.
[6] On the image of the 'sea of lies' (of illusions) see below p. 468 n. 2.

[*Antistrophe*] no dweller upon earth ever found by divine grace a trustworthy token for future events; plans for the future are struck with blindness. Often things fall out for men contrary to their expectations; happiness is often reversed, yet often again, having been entangled in bitter troubles, it swiftly changes into high good fortune.

[*Epode*] Son of Philanor, in truth the glory of your swift feet would have shed its leaves,[7] as unknown as a cock that fights at home, if strife among citizens, setting man against man, had not robbed you of your Cretan homeland. But now, crowned at Olympia, and again at the Pythian and Isthmian games, Ergoteles, you take pleasure[8] in bathing in the warm spring of the Nymphs, which you visit near your own domain.

The opening consists of a brief prayer to Tyche for Himera; then follows a long series of maxims on the power of the incalculable. It is not until the epode that Pindar speaks to Ergoteles, when he takes the man of the hour as a living example of the timeless truth that is formulated in the strophe and antistrophe.[9] The praises of the victor are only one theme among many.

In the two poems that we have read, we have met elements of many different kinds. These are typical of the genre, and they constantly recur, varying in their number and distribution. Victory odes are concerned with the victor, his family and his country; the poet also speaks of his own skill and of the particular poem; he makes general reflexions on life and the powers that determine the course of events; finally, he turns his eyes on the divine in prayer and meditation. Of these four components three are intrinsically of a general nature: everything earthly is subject to the higher powers; the maxims are of general validity; and the poet's artistry provides the medium for every word and every note of the ode. The only specific element is the victor and the circle to which he belongs; this is the first point at which individual persons and facts are mentioned. There is another specific element in a fifth class of material which we have not yet encountered, namely myths of gods and legends of

[7] The origin of the metaphor 'to shed its leaves' lies in the fact that the victor was crowned with leaves and that leafy boughs were held over him by the spectators.

[8] βαστάζεις does not mean ἐπαίρεις καὶ αὔξεις (thus the scholiast 27a), or 'extol, ennoble' as the dictionaries have it, quite inappropriately to the context, but literally 'deal with' (as *Od.* 21, 405, cf. 393–395), 'make oneself familiar with'; and Pindar uses verbs expressing contact in the most varied connexions (cf. F. Dornseiff, *Pindars Stil* [1921] 94–96, and below p. 495f., also T. Holy, *Harvard Studies in Class. Phil.* 70 (1965) 235ff.), e.g. *Nem.* 8, 3 and *Isthm.* 3, 8. Here it only expresses the contact between the bather and the hot water.

[9] Ergoteles, we might say, is merely 'fitted in' to a hymn to Tyche (see above p. 435 with n. 18).

heroes. Every choral lyrist made use of myth and legend, and Pindar is no exception; but only the longer odes gave him room to develop this element fully.

3. MYTH IN THE CHORAL LYRIC

The aspect which myth[1] assumes in Pindar's victory odes, together with the general construction of his longer poems, may be understood by studying the ninth Pythian. It was composed in 474 and thus falls in the middle period of Pindar's creative activity, when he was in his forties.

The victor here celebrated came from the Greek city of Cyrene in what is now Libya, which was then a land of fertile plains with rich ploughland, lush meadows and extensive hunting country. The beliefs of the inhabitants invested Cyrene, the goddess of the city and country, with the honours due to a huntress and conqueror of lions. By her side stood another tutelary god, Aristaeus, a god of shepherds, bee-keepers and huntsmen, and in some respects akin to Apollo. Consequently Aristaeus ranked as an aspect of Apollo, or alternatively as the son of Apollo and Cyrene. An old legend represented Cyrene as a mountain-nymph in Thessaly; from there Apollo had brought her as his mistress to Libya, where she received under her protection Greek settlers from the island of Thera, who had migrated to North Africa at Apollo's behest. So the story ran in the *Ehoiai* attributed to Hesiod. Pindar has put the epic narrative of the *Ehoiai* through a lyrical transformation. His poem begins by hailing the victory of Telesicrates of Cyrene, who had won the prize at the Pythian games in the foot-race for men in full armour; in Pindar's language the armour is represented by its heaviest single component, the shield of bronze (*Pythian* 9):

[*First strophe*] In company with the deep-girdled Graces will I proclaim aloud as Pythian victor with the brazen shield Telesicrates, blessed by the gods, crowning glory of Cyrene, of her who was once carried off from the storm-echoing vales of Pelion by Leto's son of the flowing hair. In a car of gold he bore the wild maiden (? or: the virgin huntress) hither, where he set her up to be mistress of the land rich in pasture, most rich in crops, and gave her the third branch of the firm-set earth[2] for her lovely and blessed abode.

[1] The term 'myth' in the present context includes legends of gods and of heroes.
[2] This is the oldest witness that we have to the notion of a three-part world, made up of 'Asia,' 'Europe' and 'Libya' (usually meaning Africa West of the Nile). This threefold division was truer to the three cardinal points East West and South (North was omitted because the Mediterranean world had no intercourse with the

[*First Antistrophe*] Silver-footed Aphrodite welcomed the guest from Delos (Apollo), touching with gentle hand the chariot built by god's skill, and decked with winning modesty their delightful bridal bed, twining the uniting band of wedlock for the god and the daughter of mighty Hypseus, who was then king of the haughty Lapiths, an heroic grandson of Oceanus; him (Hypseus) once in the far-known valleys of Pindus Creusa bore, a naiad who had enjoyed the love of Peneus,

[*First epode*] a daughter of the earth. He (Hypseus) reared a child, Cyrene of the white arms. She loved not the coming and going of the shuttle, or the pleasures of receiving guests in the house with her companions; no, rather with spear of bronze and with sword she raged among the creatures of the wild, bringing much peace and tranquillity to her father's herds, but that sweet companion of the bed, sleep, she cut short and banished from her lids as soon as the red of dawn began to approach.[3]

[*Second strophe*] He saw her once as with a monstrous lion she wrestled alone and unarmed, he with the broad quiver, the far-shooting Apollo. At once he called Chiron from his rocky hall: 'Come, son of Philyra, from your holy cave and wonder at a woman's courage and at her great achievement: what a battle she endures with heart unafraid, a maiden defying toil and danger! No storm of fear troubles her heart. Who is the man that begot her? From what lineage was she severed

[*Second antistrophe*] that, hidden away in these shadowy mountains, she makes trial of her unconquerable warrior-spirit?[4] Is it impious if I lay upon her my far-famed hand and break the sweet wildflower of the bed of love?' Speedily the mighty Centaur answered him, laughing merrily with mild glance, and declared to him his thoughts: 'To sacred love

Northern peoples) than the old dual division into 'Asia' and 'Europe,' in which Africa, so far as it was known, was lumped in with Asia. The conception of the regions of the world seems to have begun with 'Asia,' whose separate territories, so far as they fell within the purview of the Greeks, were politically united from the sixth century onwards in the Persian empire, including Egypt and what lay to the West of it; as its counterpart, according to the archaic two-fold division, the non-Persian territories were given the general name of 'Europe.'

[3] ἀναλίσκω (25) means 'give up, sacrifice in order to gain something else instead'; a hunter goes to his business before the dawn and the dew (cf. Apollonius Rhodius 4, 109–113; for the expression cf. Bacchylides fr. 4, 36–38 and Hesiod *WD* 574). Παῦρον (24) is predicative ('proleptic'): Cyrene allows herself little rest in order to bring much rest to the herds (22). On σύγκοιτον see below n. 10. The sleep which shortly precedes the dawn was reckoned as the most beneficial (*Rhesus* 554–556; Moschus *Europa* 2–4 with Bühler's commentary).

[4] For the meaning of ἀλκή (not physical strength) cf. Passow-Crönert s.v. Ἀπείραντος denies the achievement of the end and purpose pursued (cf. ἀτελής in a similar application *Nem.* 3, 42), and can be used of exertions without end or without realization of their purpose (*Nem.* 8, 38; a formal parallel also *Isthm.* 4, 11: ἀπλέτου δόξας—τέλος). Cyrene then is testing herself on ἔργ' ἀτέλεστα, as Theognis 1290 says of Atalanta in a passage (1287–1294) very similar to this passage of Pindar in thought and expression (e.g. νοσφισθεῖσα Theognis, ἀποσπασθεῖσα Pindar);

subtle Persuasion brings the stolen key, O Phoebus, and among gods as among men one blushes to enjoy openly the sweet bed for the first time.

[*Second epode*] So you yourself, for whom to deal in falsehood is forbidden, were led by agitation of feeling to use that word amiss, when you enquired whence the maiden came, you know, great lord, the appointed end of all things and of all paths, how many leaves of spring the earth puts forth, and how many grains of sand in the sea and rivers are tossed about by waves and the buffeting of the winds, and what is to come and whence it will come—all you know unerringly. But if I must measure myself against the wise,

[*Third strophe*] this I will say: As her husband you have come to this valley, and it will come about that you will bring her over the sea to the chosen garden of Zeus. There you will make her mistress of a city and gather nearby an island-people on the hill beside the plain. Now will broad-meadowed Libya the commanding one, graciously receive the glorious maiden in her golden palace; there she will grant her straightway the right to her native place and shared possession of the land, where the earth repays with every crop and is rich in beasts of the wild.

[*Third antistrophe*] There shall she bring forth a son, whom splendid Hermes will take to himself from the child's dear mother to bring him to the high-enthroned Seasons and to (the goddess) Earth. These will lay the little one on their knees, drop nectar and ambrosia on his lips and make him an immortal, another Zeus or holy Apollo, bringing blessing to those whom he favours, a fatherly protector of their flocks, to be called Agreus and Nomios (=god of the chase, god of meadows), and by others Aristaeus.'⁵ With these words he prevailed on him to bring about the joyful consummation of the union.

[*Third epode*] When gods are in haste, speedy is the accomplishment and the ways are short. The same day saw the fulfilment; they mingled in love in the gold-adorned chamber of (the goddess) Libya, where she

the elegist seems to be basing himself also on the type of the virgin huntress as described in the *Ehoiai*, which was no doubt identical for Cyrene and Atalanta (cf. also Hesiod fr. 21 Rzach). The lover in Theognis says that the huntress' life pursued by the girl is ἀτέλεστον because it denies wedlock as the natural destiny (τέλος) of a woman (1289f., 1294). The enamoured god in Pindar probably thinks the same; v. 36 ('Is it impious . . .') follows without a break.

⁵ There is nothing particularly surprising in a comparatively obscure god's having three different names (Agreus, Nomios, Aristaeus); but it does rather take us aback that the god should be at once a son of Apollo, (an) Apollo and (a) Zeus. The passage strikingly illustrates how little weight was attached in Pindar's time to the distribution of the divine into distinct persons, if even the great Olympians shared names with third parties or with each other. The poet and his public were clearly conscious that the name of a god did not denote a person so much as a living and acting power.

(Cyrene) now rules that city of beauty which also enjoys the fame of athletic contests; just as now in the holy place of Pytho the son of Carneades (i.e. Telesicrates) has adorned it (the city) with flowering success. There he won the victory, and the name of Cyrene was proclaimed—Cyrene which will joyously welcome him when to his homeland, the land of fair women, he brings brilliant fame from Delphi.

[*Fourth strophe*] Great manly virtues (*aretai*) ever give rich matter for song, but from that richness to take a little and illuminate it is a whetstone (?) for the skilled; in every action alike the right choice bears the crown. Seven-gated Thebes learned how to him (Telesicrates)[6] Iolaus' honour granted (a victory). He (Iolaus), after he had cut off Eurystheus' head with the sharp edge of his sword, was buried under the earth in the grave of his grandfather, the charioteer Amphitryon, there where he (Amphitryon) as a guest-friend of the Sown Men lay, having moved his abode to the streets of the horse-breeding Cadmeans.

[*Fourth antistrophe*] Having lain with him (Amphitryon) and with Zeus, the wise Alcmene brought forth at one birth the victorious strength of the twin brothers (Heracles and Iphicles). Ignorant indeed is the man whose tongue knows not the name of Heracles and thinks not constantly of the waters of Dirce, which nurtured him and Iphicles. To them will I discharge my vow with festal notes when some joy falls to my lot; may the pure light of the sounding Graces never abandon me! In Aegina, I declare, and at the rock of Nisa (i.e. in Megara) you (Telesicrates) have three times caused glory to shine upon your city,

[*Fourth epode*] having by your achievement saved yourself from the silence of your fellowmen, who have nothing to say of those who do nothing. Therefore friend and foe alike among your fellow-citizens must not conceal the success which is a glory to all, contrary to the advice of the old man of the sea (Nereus); for he declared: 'With unfeigning heart shall a man with justice praise even a foeman for a great achievement.' Often the maidens saw you at the recurring festival of Pallas (in Athens) and silently each one wished that you might be her husband or her son, Telesicrates;

[*Fifth strophe*] so it happened also at the Olympian games and at those of Earth the deep-bosomed and in all the contests at home. But from me, while I was busy in slaking the thirst for song, a glory of your ancestors demanded its due re-awakening:[7] how for the sake of a Libyan woman they came to the city Irasa as suitors for the famous fair-tressed daughter of Ancaeus. For her many noble men of her own nation, and likewise many from afar, contended; for wondrous

[*Fifth antistrophe*] was her appearance, and all wished to pluck the ripening fruit of her gold-crowned youthful prime. But her father devised for his

[6] Thus Wilamowitz, *Berl. Sitz.-Ber.* 1901 1291 (but he advanced a different interpretation in *Pindaros*, Berlin 1922, 264.)

[7] Read καὶ παλαίων δόξα τέων προγόνων, cf. *Frühgriech. Denken* p. 79 with n. 2.

daughter a wedding more worthy of renown. He had heard how once Danaus in Argos accomplished a speedy wedding for his eight and forty daughters before the noontide came upon him.[8] He ranged the entire company (of his daughters) at the end of the track and bade all those who had come to be his sons-in-law to decide in a footrace which hero should marry each daughter.

[*Fifth epode*] Even so the Libyan contrived to give to his daughter a bridegroom. He set her, richly adorned, at the mark to be their final goal, and proclaimed that he should take her who first in leaping should touch her garment. There Alexidamus, after running swiftly over the course, took the high-born maiden's hand in his and led her through the press of the Nomad princes. The people bedecked him with many a green leaf and garland; many winged trophies had he won before.

Instead of a single triad, like the poems previously considered, this one has five. It is incomparably richer, and in parts difficult. We shall try to come to grips with it by explanations and free paraphrasing, and at the same time to form some judgment on the style.

[*First strophe*] The poem declares itself as a victory ode at the very outset by beginning as an artistic announcement (the Graces favoured artistry of all kinds) of a victory. As soon as the name of Cyrene is mentioned, there is an easy transition to the first myth; for 'Cyrene' is at once the city community, the city-goddess, and a nymph with a personal life-story. Apollo carried her off from Thessaly to the third part of the world. [*First antistrophe*] When the couple arrived in their new land, Love herself (Aphrodite) 'laid her light hand on the divinely driven car' and blessed the consummation of the union. An epic poem, instead of representing the one action with its static pictorial quality, would have described the reception in a flow of narrative.[9] Pindar's lyrical manner in dealing with myth is selective, allusive, and subtle in the means it employs, but very powerful in its effect. When the high point is reached, the narrative breaks off, and again there is an easy transition to Cyrene's genealogy. Her father, a savage Lapith, was a son of Peneus, the principal river of Thessaly, and a Naiad, and thus a grandson of the primal river Ocean and the primal mother Earth. [*First epode*] Now Cyrene's history begins again, this time from the beginning. The daughter of

[8] Pindar was no doubt thinking of the programme at Olympia where the footrace had to end before midday, cf. Pausanias 6, 24, 1. The fixing of a definite term justifies the expression ἑλεῖν as νὺξ αἱρεῖ etc.

[9] Something to this effect: 'Aphrodite came down from Olympus to Libya, went to meet them as they arrived, and spoke the following words: . . . And Apollo answered thus: . . . Then he unharnessed his steeds and set ambrosia before them; and meanwhile Aphrodite decked the couch, and then led the twain to the bridal chamber.' On Pindar's stylization and its parallels in contemporary painting see T. B. L. Webster, *Class. Quart.* 33, 1939, 176. See also below n. 11.

Hypseus was no ordinary girl; she despised the normal female occupations, and instead of leading a sheltered life while waiting to be married, she lived as a huntress in the wild. The Greeks associated hunting with a rejection of love. [10]

[*Second strophe*] An accident, which afterwards reveals itself as a disposition of providence, leads Apollo to the place where Cyrene is wrestling with a lion. Pindar does not describe the course or event of the struggle, and thus he leaves it to the imagination of his readers to picture a group in statuesque immobility. He is less interested in the physical outcome of the adventure than in erecting, as it were, a monument to the heroic spirit of Cyrene. [11] The god is aroused to passion by the vigorous masculinity of the young girl; for Pindar's ideal world is a world of men and boys, and the truly feminine remains unsung in his works. The plastic art of his time represented girls and women with an almost boyish appearance. [*Second antistrophe*] Apollo suggests that a limit ought to be set and an end imposed on the girl's insatiable devotion to fighting by providing her with a husband; but he is not sure whether he is the one who should enjoy her love, and he consults the wise Chiron. [12] Chiron is known to mythology as a wise old Centaur, skilled in the lore of forests, herbs and men, who brought up the great heroes Achilles and Jason and trained them for a life of adventure. He had already appeared as giving good counsel to Apollo in the story of Cyrene in the *Ehoiai*, from which Pindar took this legend. From Chiron Apollo receives the answer that he wanted: 'As the all-knowing prophet you know very well that you may and will taste the love of Cyrene; and your timid enquiry only shows the retiring modesty in which first love conceals itself.' [13] In Chiron's words the conflict between the human and

[10] The 'sweet companion of the bed, sleep' in v. 24 thus has a special point. The expression occurs at the same point where in the third, fourth and fifth triads marriage is mentioned (see below n. 20).

[11] A relief has in fact been found depicting Cyrene wrestling with a lion. Pindar's narratives are often as stylized as if a relief or vase-painting had been transmuted into verse (see above n. 9). But it is not that Pindar had any notion of competing with the visual arts in his technique. What the painter and sculptor did from necessity, Pindar did by his free choice: for his own purposes he concentrated the entire weight of a story on one telling moment.

[12] The management of the scene is strikingly similar to that familiar to us in the drama. Just as in a tragedy, Apollo calls the old Centaur out from his cave to speak to him of Cyrene's extraordinary character and to put his question to him; and it is not until Apollo speaks that we find out that Chiron's dwelling is also the background of the stage. An epic poet would first describe the locale and then bring on the personages.

[13] Myths of this kind very seldom waste words on the feelings of the girl; it was reckoned a distinction for a woman to bear a child to a god.

divine natures in Apollo is at once brought to light and clarified. The *second epode* celebrates the all-embracing spirit of the god, just as the first depicted the powerful character of Cyrene.

[*Third strophe and antistrophe*] The Centaur's speech completes the story of Cyrene. He prophesies her establishment in Africa ('Libya'), the arrival of Greek colonists, and the birth and apotheosis of Aristaeus. Pindar could have brought all these things into a direct narrative, in their appropriate places according to the sequence of events; instead he halts the action in mid-course immediately after Apollo and Cyrene have seen each other for the first time, in order to cast a significant glance forward and to bring into the present stage of the treatment the lasting blessing that is to be founded upon the previous union of the two. In this way one and the same scene is loaded with other material of real importance for the story as a whole, whether it went before or came after in time. In general Pindar deals very cavalierly with time-sequence, even when he does not motivate it specially by inserting a prophecy: for him it is the value and significance of events that is really important. Thus he looks upon even that remote past in which the myths are set as something actively influencing his own time. Thus in the part of this ode which we have so far studied, the treatment which begins with the recent victory of the Cyrenean at the Pythian games goes first forwards and then backwards in time in the first strophe, and then, in the antistrophe and epode up to the connexion with the second strophe, backwards and forwards once again. [*End of the third antistrophe; epode*] As soon as Chiron has finished speaking, Pindar makes us aware of the immediate situation again. Apollo is in a hurry, and the poet, falling in with the divine sense of urgency, brings him as fast as narrative will permit to the goal of his wishes. This brings us back to the same point where we were in the middle of the first antistrophe; in typically archaic fashion the ring of composition has bent back on itself, as a token that the tale of Cyrene is at an end. Another ring is closed immediately afterwards, when the Pythian victory of Telesicrates is mentioned again as it was at the beginning. [*Fourth strophe and antistrophe*] A list of Telesicrates' previous victories is now in order; but Pindar states in advance that he will only mention the most important of them: 'Where there are great deeds to praise, one is tempted to speak of them at great length, but true art demands that a little be selected from the store. *Kairos* (i.e. the rules of accurate choice and prudent restraint, the sense of what suits the circumstances, tact, discretion etc.¹⁴) alone produces maturity and

---

¹⁴ The meaning 'opportune moment' is more recent, but this has often been ignored. Pindar's expression (v. 78) ὁ δὲ καιρὸς ὁμοίως παντὸς ἔχει κορυφάν has a pre-

perfection in any field.[15] Telesicrates gained a victory in the games in memory of Iolaus, who was buried in Thebes.' Taking Iolaus as his starting-point, Pindar gives an honourable mention to other heroic figures associated with Heracles;[16] then he justifies this intrusion of mythology into the list of Telesicrates' victories. The sequence of thought is something like this: 'Iolaus and Amphitryon are buried in Thebes; Thebes was where Heracles and Iphicles were born and brought up. A poet would have to be stupid not to take every opportunity of mentioning the great Heracles and his kinsfolk, together with their (and my) native city. I promise to express my reverence for them in the future (just as I do now) if I have the good luck (as I have now) to be able to celebrate a noble victor' (see above p. 431 n. 10). Jubilation at good fortune and at the thought of future poems might arouse the sleeping 'envy' of fate and invite calamity; hence Pindar lowers his tone to that of a prayer that his activity as a poet may continue a long time.[17] Then he continues the list, and explains: 'Through three victories at Aegina and Megara you have won fame, Telesicrates, for your city and yourself, (*fourth epode*) and have given men good reason to praise you.[18] All citizens

cursor in Hesiod, *WD* 694) καιρὸς δ' ἐπὶ πᾶσιν ἄριστος (above p. 127) μέτρα φυλάσσεσθαι occurred a little before, the general purport of 689–693 being: 'A man should not load all his stock in trade on a ship, but only half of it or less; otherwise the loss in case of shipwreck becomes too great.' Clearly there is nothing about opportune moments here. On καιρός in Pindar see also the following note and p. 474 n. 11, p. 498 with nn. 8 and 9, and p. 504.

[15] The sense of the sequence: ἀρεταὶ πολύμυθοι—βαιὰ ἐν μακροῖσι—ὁ καιρὸς παντὸς ἔχει κορυφάν (76–79) cannot be mistaken if we look at the parallels from other passages immediately before or after a list of victories: πλήθει καλῶν—ἐν ἑκάστῳ μέτρον—καιρὸς ἄριστος (*Olymp.* 13, 45–48); καιρὸν εἰ φθέγξαιο, πολλῶν πείρατα συντανύσας ἐν βραχεῖ (*Pyth.* 1,81f.); παύρῳ ἔπει θήσω φανέρ' ἀθρόα (*Olymp.* 13, 98); μακρὸν πάσας ἀναγήσασθ' ἀρετάς—εἰρήσεται πόλλ' ἐν βραχίστοις (*Isthm.* 6, 56–59). The preposition ἐν is thus used in two different senses, either as in βαιὰ ἐν μακροῖσι ('a little chosen out of a large mass', cf. ἐν πολλοῖσι παῦρα in a similar context in tragedy, Soph. *El.* 688), or as in πόλλ' ἐν βραχίστοις ('abundant material [expressed] in fewest words').

[16] Alcmene had intercourse during the same night with Zeus and with her husband Amphitryon, whence resulted the twins Heracles and Iphicles. Iphicles' son Iolaus was the friend and shieldbearer of Heracles; after the latter's death he slew Eurystheus, the hero's former taskmaster and enemy.

[17] He does much the same in *Isthm.* 7, 39. On the notion 'quod di bene vortant,' cf. W. Schadewaldt, *Der Aufbau des pindarischen Epinikion* (Halle, 1928) 288.

[18] The evidence of parallel passages compels us thus to interpret Pindar's terse expression in v. 92: σιγαλὸς ἀμαχανία is λόγου (cf. *Isthm.* 5, 27) ἀμαχανία, and silence enwraps the fainéant (fr. 104c, 9 Snell 83, 5 Bowra etc.). In a positive application, σιγαλὸν ἀμαχανίαν φυγών would be equivalent to κελαδεννὰν (cf. 89) ὕμνων καὶ αἴνου εὐμαχανίαν (cf. *Isthm.* 4, 1–3) φάνας. The negative manner of expression here, as often elsewhere, can be explained by the fact that the polar habit of thought always has

of Cyrene must unite in your praise, even your personal enemies, according to a saying of the old man of the sea.' (The divinities of the sea had been always reckoned as possessing profound wisdom and knowledge of the future). 'In Athens also you have won victories, and the admiration which women feel for the victor drew many a tender glance in your direction.'

[*Fifth triad*] While Pindar is thus proclaiming the achievements of a Cyrenean of his own day, an old tale of Telesicrates' ancestors (probably meaning an early settler in Cyrene) presents its claim to be re-awakened in song—a claim which the poet must meet *ex officio*. In the delightful story from Cyrenean local tradition a reference to a similar Greek legend[19] has been inserted, relating how Danaus, who came from Cyrene's neighbour Egypt, married off eight-and-forty daughters in a forenoon.

We shall now survey in retrospect the ninth Pythian as a whole— not in order to analyse the artistry of the presentation, for its solemn yet warm beauty speaks for itself, but to give some account of its content. What is the real subject of the poem, and what is the uniting element in it all?

In each triad the theme of love and marriage recurs,[20] and three times it takes the form of a rapid choice and wedlock (Apollo, the Danaids, Alexidamus). But the rhythm of these repetitions has not binding strength enough to secure the cohesion of the whole; the predominating impression is of a material excessively copious, indeed bewildering.

All five stock themes are represented: the here and now (Telesicrates); religion (Apollo, Cyrene, Aristaeus); poetry (Pindar as herald and artist); the so-called gnomic element (Chiron's dictum on young love, Pindar's views on *kairos*, Proteus' words on praising one's enemies); and finally the mythological element. The myths, which are sometimes briefly alluded to (Heracles and his kin, the

the opposite in mind; thus we find in v. 94 (μή) βλάπτων for 'obeying,' and μή κρυπτέτω for 'let him declare.'

[19] The bride-race was a regular ritual among many primitive peoples; among the Greeks of the historical period it survived in various slightly differing forms as a theme of legend (the Danaids, Atalanta, Hippodamia).

[20] It is also placed with great symmetry within the triads—five times in the five antistrophes: ant. 1, fourth and fifth verses (bed); ant. 2 vss. 3–4 (sexual desire); ant. 3, vss. 1–5 (childbirth); ant. 4, vss. 1–3 (sexual intercourse and birth of twins); ant. 5, vss. 1–3 (sexual desire). It comes four times in the five epodes: ep. 1, 7 (the bed-companion sleep, cf. above p. 446 n. 10); ep. 3, 8 (the victorious runner comes home to the 'land of fair women,' cf. *Pyth.* 10, 59); ep. 4, 8 (Athenian maidens would like the victorious runner for their husband); ep. 5, 6–7 (the victorious runner takes his bride home). (We may notice here the parallel drawn between an athletic victory and a wedding in *Olymp.* 7, 1ff., above p. 431.)

Danaids), sometimes related in detail (Cyrene, Alexidamus), take up here not less than three quarters of the entire poem. Their themes are very various, and the connecting links are diversely attached. Cyrene is the native city and city-goddess of the victor; Apollo is her husband, a principal divinity of the Cyreneans and the god of the Pythian games; Aristaeus is their child; Alexidamus was a mythical ancestor of the victor's and, like him, a great runner; Danaus served as a model for Alexidamus' father-in-law; Iolaus granted a victory to Telesicrates; Heracles, Amphitryon and Iphicles are kinsmen of Iolaus, and all four are Pindar's countrymen. Apparently the motley material and disparate connexions are deliberate (cf. *Pyth.* 10, 53f.). If we compare other victory odes of considerable length, it becomes apparent that the themes diverge even more strikingly than they do here; and the more poems we read, the more we are troubled by the absence of any unity—as long as we look for it in the different subjects of the individual poems. Is there perhaps a unity of a different kind? Is there an idea which by its nature remains the same in different fields? Before grappling with this question, we must examine further tests and become better acquainted with the lyrist's world of thought in all its breadth and depth.

There were also choral odes which included only a myth and virtually nothing else; such odes were sung and danced in honour of a god on a festal day. Some of this kind have been furnished by the Bacchylides papyrus. For an example we may take a charming poem (*Dithyr.* 17 Snell) concerned with the Athenian national hero Theseus, who according to the legend was a son of Poseidon. The opening plunges *in medias res*, the previous incidents being taken as known. Minos, a son of Zeus and king of Crete, had imposed a cruel tribute on the Athenians: at regular intervals they had to send seven youths and seven maidens as victims of the Minotaur, a creature half man and half bull. Once again Minos has set sail for Crete with fourteen young Athenians. Among these is Theseus, who has volunteered to be of their number; he is to slay the Minotaur and put an end to the tribute.

[*First strophe*] With dark blue prow the vessel was cleaving the Cretan sea, bearing Theseus and twice seven fair children of the Ionians (Athenians), and the North wind blew into the far-shining sails, thanks to glorious aegis-shaking Pallas: then the wild (?) gifts of Cypris, the goddess who bears desire in her diadem,[21] began to play upon the heart of Minos.

[21] ἱμεράμπυκος θεᾶς Κύπριδος δῶρα means the sexual attraction (ἵμερος) diffused from Eriboea thanks to the grace of Aphrodite (cf. Plato *Phaedrus* 255c). Aphrodite's diadem is the sensible symbol of this power, much as the goddess in the *Iliad* (14,

With unrestrained hand he seized upon a maiden and touched her pale cheek. Eriboea cried out to Pandion's bronze-armoured grandson (Theseus). Theseus saw what was happening, and his eye rolled dark beneath his brow, indignant grief entered into his heart, and he spoke: 'Son of Zeus on high, you direct the wishes of your inmost heart no longer in the permitted path: use no despotic violence, hero.

[*First antistrophe*] What the all-powerful destiny of the gods has approved for us, what side the beam of justice inclines to, the portion meted out to us, that we must fulfil, as soon as it comes; bid yourself check what you have violently begun. Just as the daughter of Phoenix, she of the charming name (Europa), sharing the bed of Zeus under the brow of mount Ida, conceived and bore you as the greatest of mortals, so did the daughter of wealthy Pittheus bear me to the sea-god Poseidon, and the Nereids with violet-dark hair brought her (as a wedding gift) a golden head-dress. Therefore I require of you, ruler of the Cnossians, that you abstain from presumption that brings sorrow in its wake. I am no longer willing to gaze on the immortal lovely light of the dawn if to any of these youths or maidens you do violence. Sooner we will make trial of our strength in arms, and what shall be the issue, the gods will decide.'

[*First epode*] So spoke the hero skilled in arms, and they who were in the ship looked in amazement at his proud valour. But anger seized the son-in-law of Helios (Minos), and spinning a web of guile he answered: 'O mighty father Zeus, hear me! If truly the Phoenician maiden with white arms bore me your son, send down to me from heaven the swift thunderbolt with mane of fire as a clear sign. And you, Theseus, if indeed Aethra of Troezen bore you to the earth-shaker Poseidon, bring that fair golden adornment of her hand back from the depth of the sea, boldly casting yourself into your father's realm.'

[*Second strophe*] Mighty Zeus heard and despised not his prayer: willingly he granted before all eyes crowning honour to his son Minos, and thundered. He, as he saw the wonder that he had desired, spread wide his arms to the godlike azure of the sky, he the hero swift in battle, and said: 'Theseus, here you see clearly the gift which Zeus has given me. Now make your leap into the raging sea, and your father, the king and son of Cronos, will bestow on you the greatest fame wherever the earth is adorned with standing trees.' So he spoke, and Theseus' soul had no

216) bears sexual attraction (ἵμερος) in her girdle, and lends this girdle and its power to Hera; in Hesiod's *Works and Days* Pandora receives from Aphrodite attraction (πόθος) and *charis* (65f.) by being adorned with a necklace and crowned with flowers by the Charites (73–75). When a woman puts on attractive adornment, she does so in order to heighten her own attractions and render them more effective. This detailed explanation of a simple Greek expression was necessary because we moderns have forgotten how to see the play of forces simply and directly as forces; instead our crude ways of thought operate with discrete objects and the qualities attaching to them.

thought of retreat; he stood on the firm-rigged bowsprit and sprang, and the meadows of the sea received him gently. The son of Zeus was amazed in his inmost heart, and he bade them let the well-made ship run before the wind. But destiny had prepared another way.

[*Second antistrophe*] The vessel fared swiftly; the North wind blowing from aft drove it along; fear fell upon the Athenian youth as the hero leapt into the sea, and the tears fell on tender cheeks, for they feared a cruelty that they could not escape. But dolphins, dwellers in the salt deep, swiftly bore great Theseus to the abode of his mighty father, and he came to the palace of the gods. When he beheld there the daughters of divine Nereus, he felt fear, for from their bright bodies came a radiance like fire, and their locks were bound with fillets of gold; with supple foot they took delight in the dance. He saw his father's beloved consort, the divine Amphitrite with her large eyes, in her beautiful chamber; and she hung about him a mantle of purple,

[*Second epode*] she pressed into his thick locks a perfect band which at her wedding cunning Aphrodite had given her, adorned with roses. To mortals of right mind nothing that the gods undertake seems unworthy of belief: beside the slender ship he now appeared! Ah, with what troubled thoughts he filled the mind of the leader of the Cnossian host, when dry he came from the salt flood, a wonder to all, and on his body gleamed the gifts of the gods. The maidens in fair garments cried out with new-won joy, so that the sea echoed, and the young men, forming a circle about him, sang with lovely voices a paean. O lord of Delos, in heartfelt rejoicing at the chorus of Ceans, give us god-sent good fortune to be our guide!

The end brings a surprising twist: the narrative ends with a paean, that is, a choral song to Apollo as helper and deliverer; and the poet adds a prayer to Apollo. It is as if the chorus of Athenians on the ship, calling upon Apollo, had unconsciously changed into the chorus of young men (and girls?) of Ceos who were performing this ode of Bacchylides.22

The art of Bacchylides in relating this legend is truly Ionic—generous of detail, full of clear and graphic images, and readily intelligible from the first. More than a third of it is in direct speech, elaborate and occasionally dragging. The action, however, is very lively, and the feelings of the actors are brought out by the poet with great care. Desire, anger, courage, astonishment, disappointment and joyous delight succeed one another in rapid sequence, especially

22 The legend recounted and the actual choral performance are yet more closely connected by the fact that the fourteen young Athenians on their homeward journey landed in Delos and there danced a 'crane-dance' in honour of Apollo. This ritual dance to the Delian Apollo was, so to speak, dramatically represented in the choral dance of Bacchylides. See above p. 174 for the 'song within a song' at the end of one of Sappho's poems.

towards the end of the ode. As a final touch, the chorus from the story becomes a chorus in real life and utters its prayer. The language of the poem is too much bedecked with the elegant adornment of adjectives, which we recognize as a feature characteristic of the late archaic period. Both the form and the content[23] lack the strength and power and the measured pace of epic, just as they are lacking in the dignity and profundity of thought found in Pindar. In general, Bacchylides' poem is rather insignificant in comparison with either epic or Pindar. The narrative leaves no lasting impression, unless it be of the clear radiance that shines upon the children of the gods.

From Bacchylides and his pleasant occasional poetry let us return to the fuller tones of Pindar. One of the greatest poems of those we have is the first Pythian, written in 470 in honour of the most powerful Greek ruler of his time. Hiero, the ruler of the prosperous city of Syracuse and of much of Sicily besides, had won a victory at Delphi with a four-horse chariot. Pindar's poem, however, is relevant not merely to the success of Hiero's steeds, but it celebrates a promising innovation in the political sphere. In order to give his dynasty stronger support, Hiero had founded a new city-state at the foot of Etna, and had established his son Dinomenes as its king. He called the city Aetna, and in order to let it profit from the new success, he had himself styled 'Hiero of Aetna' when the victory was announced in Delphi, not as 'Hiero of Syracuse.' When Pindar composed his poem, Hiero was himself on campaign; despite a respiratory disorder that troubled him severely, he was pursuing in person a feud with some other Sicilian dynasts. The poem begins with a panegyric on music:

[*First strophe*] Golden lyre, truest possession of Apollo and the violet-tressed Muses, whom the dancer's step obeys in beginning the glorious festival, and whose guidance the singers obey, when you are struck and give the opening to the prelude that leads on the chorus; you quench even in the thunderbolt its flash of everlasting fire, and on Zeus' sceptre sleeps the eagle; he lets his swift wings droop on either side,

[*First antistrophe*] he the prince of birds, for you pour a dark cloud over his bent head, gently closing his eyes; in slumber he rocks his supple back, entranced by your rhythms. So also the wreaker of violence Ares: the sharp point of his spear he allows to rest, and refreshes his heart with sleep. You ensnare the weapons and the souls of the gods through the masterly skill of Leto's son and of the deep-girdled Muses.

23 The ring that Theseus is supposed to fetch from the bottom of the sea is entirely forgotten; this is a most awkward business, and not comparable with Pindars' omission in the ninth *Pythian* in failing to tell us who won the fight with the lion. In describing the fear felt by Theseus at the sight of the shining daughters of Nereus, Bacchylides is trying to combine the miraculous with the naturally human, after the manner of Simonides.

[*First epode*] But all that is hateful to Zeus is destroyed by the voice of the Pierian maidens, all on earth and in the cruel sea, and he that lies in grim Tartarus, the foe of the gods, Typhus with the hundred heads; he who once was nurtured in the far-famed Cilician cave, but now on his shaggy breast the wave-dashed cliffs of Cyme press and the isle of Sicily. A pillar of heaven presses him down, Aetna white-bedecked, the yearlong nurturer of biting snow;

[*Second triad*] from whose depths burst forth pure fountains of unapproachable fire, and flowing streams pour forth by day a dark torrent of smoke, but by night the red rolling flame hurls rocks into the deep plain of the sea with a great roar. That monster sends up these fearful streams of flame, marvellous and wonderful to behold, strange even to hear of from them who have seen it,

that he lies there, crushed beneath the dark-leaved ridges of Etna, and the earth, and the place where he lies rips the back that is cramped against it. Permit us, Zeus, permit us to be pleasing to you, to whom this mountain, the forehead of the fruitful land, belongs, from which mountain is named the city below, on which its famous founder conferred dignity when at the Pythian games the herald cried out its name together with that of Hiero the victor

in the chariot-race. For seafarers it is a first joy if at the beginning of their voyage a favourable wind attends them, for then they can hope that at the end also a good homecoming will be granted to them. In the same way this happy event brings with it the hope that she (the city Aetna) will in future be distinguished by victory-crowns and by her coursers, and will make her name heard in the joyous singing of the festival. Lycian, ruler of Delos, Phoebus, you who love also the Castalian spring on Parnassus, may your will grant this prayer and bless the land with great men!

[*Third triad*] For from the gods came the possibilities of human excellences (*aretai*) whether it be that a man is gifted with wisdom, with strength of arm or with skill of tongue. If for my part I purpose to sing the praises of that man (Hiero), I have confidence that my brazen-cheeked spear, when my art directs it, shall not fly outside the course, but that in length of cast I shall overshoot my rival. May all time to come preserve him in such good fortune, in enjoyment of his abundance and forgetfulness of pain!

May he remember great battles in war, in which he stood fast with unflinching heart, when they (Hiero and his men) found through the god's devising honour such as no other Greek enjoys, the proud crown of rich possessions. And now, like Philoctetes, he has taken the field, and compelled by necessity many a proud heart seeks his favour. It is told that godlike heroes came to bring back from Lemnos

the wound-stricken son of Poeas, the bowman, who sacked Priam's city and brought the toils of the Danaans to their consummation, treading weakly with enfeebled body: thus had it been ordained. May God preserve Hiero in the time to come, as then Philoctetes, and bring within his grasp what he desires. Muse, let me pray to you also that before Dinomenes I may raise my voice in requital for the victory of the four steeds; the crown that his father bears is his truest joy. Let us therefore for the king of Aetna devise a song of friendship,

[*Fourth triad*] for him, for whom Hiero has founded the city and set it up in god-appointed freedom with ordinances framed according to Hyllus' rule. The Doric sons of Pamphylus and of the Heraclidae are determined in their dwelling-place at the foot of Taygetus ever to remain faithful to the laws of Aegimius. Coming from Pindus they laid hold successfully upon Amyclae, where they became the glorious neighbours of the Tyndarids who ride on swift steeds, and the glory of their spears has won fame.

Granter of prayers, Zeus, vouchsafe that in all future time by the waters of Amenas the true judgment of men may accord this destiny to the people and king. May he who commands (Hiero) with your help and by the hand of his son hold the community in honour and lead them to peace and harmony. To you I pray, son of Cronus, grant that the battle cry of the Phoenicians and the Tyrrhenians (Etruscans) keep their overmighty battlefleet tamely at home, considering what befell at Cyme,

where they suffered grievously, smitten by the leader of the Syracusans who hurled their youth from their swift ships into the sea, freeing Hellas from heavy servitude. Salamis would be my theme, if I wished to give due gratitude to the Athenians; in Sparta would I speak of the battle at Cithaeron (Plataeae), where the Medes fell, those warriors of the curved bow: but from the banks of murmuring Himera I take my song of praise for the sons of Dinonemes (Hieron and his brother), which they earned by manly courage (*aretê*) when their enemies were laid low.

[*Fifth triad*] If in speaking a man make the right choice, embracing in small compass a multitude of things, less disfavour of men is thus earned. For dangerous satiety oppresses lively expectations, and what citizens hear of another's good fortune weighs heavily on their secret thoughts. Nevertheless, since to be envied is better than to be pitied, do not give up noble ideals. Shape your language on the anvil of truth.

If even something slight goes amiss it will grow much greater as coming from you; you rule over many, and there are many trustworthy witnesses of both things (i.e. of good and of evil). Abide in the great-souled ardour that animates you, and if it be granted that you enjoy the long endurance of good report, set not too narrow bounds to your expenditure. Like a seaman, let the sail out full to catch the wind. Be not deceived, friend, by the gains of the moment: the glorious fame that remains after us

can alone declare the quality of the departed to men who are masters of word and song. The virtuous magnanimity (*areté*) of Croesus does not perish; but he who burned men in the bull of bronze, the savage Phalaris, is ever held in the grip of hostile report, lyres under the roof do not welcome him, as the sweet theme for the voices of boys singing. To become prosperous is our first goal; that men speak well of us, the second; but he who achieves and retains both, has received the highest crown of life.[24]

[*First triad*] At the opening of the poem Pindar speaks not of that lyre which he is holding in his hand (as in *Olymp.* 1, 18), nor does he call on the Muse to stand by his side, but instead he celebrates in hymn-like tones the 'golden' (i.e. divine, heavenly)[25] lyre in the hands of Apollo, the god of music and of the Pythian games, and at the same time celebrates the chorus of Muses on Olympus. In this way the present choral performance is traced back to its original source, or to 'Music itself,' to speak in Platonic terms; but if we adhere to Pindar's terminology, to those forces to whom the lyre belongs as by right.[26] The power of Apollo's lyre is shown in soothing by its harmonies the wild forces of the divine world, quenching the blaze of the lightning, and causing the war-god to lay aside his spear and sink into a pleasant slumber. The music of Dionysus is very different in its nature and effects, and it uses different instruments. When its animating tones are heard in heaven, lightning and battle with its

---

[24] The text: in v. 12 I read θέλγεις, since I cannot see that κῆλα without a possessive can mean 'your melodies.' Κῆλα then becomes an accusative and refers to the thunder of v. 5, as in *Il.* 12, 280 and Hesiod, *Theog.* 708. In v. 72 there are three arguments against the common interpretation. 1) The intransitive use of ἔχω does not occur in Pindar except in εὖ δ᾽ ἔχοντες in *Olymp.* 5, 16, which is different in construction and meaning, which probably is not by Pindar, and furthermore is shown by the metre to be corrupt (Boeckh proposed εὖ δὲ τυχόντες). 2) ἰδών with two objects, ὕβριν and οἷα πάθον, is implausible; and if instead we attach οἷα δαμασθέντες πάθον to the στόνος in ναυσίστονον ὕβριν, the construction becomes still more peculiar. 3) ναυσίστονος ὕβρις as a hypostasis of νεῶν ὕβρις στένει (= 'is defeated') is more than bold. Now στόνος with its derivatives is a typical attribute for murderous combat (e.g. *Il.* 4, 445; 11, 73; Pindar, *Isthm.* 8, 25) and for weapons (e.g. *Il.* 8, 159), and since ἀλαλατός precedes (cf. στονόεσσαν αὐτήν = 'war,' *Od.* 11, 383), ναυσίστονος ὕβρις can easily be understood as 'aggressive war-fleet.' The sentence κατ᾽ οἶκον ἔχῃ ναυσίστονον ὕβριν has a close parallel in πολύστονον ἐρύκεν ὕβριν in Bacchyl. 17, 40. It is only necessary to write τὰ (instead of τὰν) πρὸ Κύμας, and οἷα πάθον fits exactly into place.

[25] Cf. Paul Jacobsthal quoted by E. R. Dodds on Eurip. *Bacch.* 553–555.

[26] σύνδικον κτέανον is what they possess σὺν δίκᾳ (*Pyth.* 9, 96; *Nem.* 9, 44). It is nonsense to talk of Apollo and the Muses having a 'common right' to the lyre.

spear will join in the ecstacy of dancing. This scene also was depicted by Pindar in a dithyramb which has been recovered in papyrus. The contrast with the Pythian ode is so instructive that the verses deserve to be quoted (fr. 70b, 5):

... we know how the children of heaven under the sceptre of Zeus (in Olympus) celebrate the feast of Bromius (Dionysus). It begins with the rolling of drums for the Great Mother; then come rattling of castanets and flaring torches of gold-flaming pine-slivers;[27] the echoing shrieks and groans of the Naiads tossing their heads in frenzy; the all-compelling thunderbolt breathing fire, and the spear of Ares; and the warlike aegis of Pallas sounds with the hiss of a thousand serpents. Swiftly comes Artemis who dwells alone, having yoked the race of lions in Bacchic ecstacy ... Bromius takes delight in the dancing women and the hordes of beasts ...

The papyrus text, published in 1919, when compared with the Pythian ode, strikingly confirms Friedrich Nietzsche's theory (published in 1872) of the double nature of Greek music. According to Nietzsche the one type of music (the Dionysiac) helped towards the discharge of destructive (although divine) forces in life—thus in this dithyramb the lightning of Zeus and the spear of the war god take part in the wild dancing at the feast of Dionysus—and the other, that connected with Apollo, 'quenches by the sound of the lyre' (to use Pindar's words) 'the eternal fire of the thunderbolt and laps Ares in tranquil slumber, so that he lays aside his grim spear'; for Apollo's instrument 'enchants the weapons and the souls of the gods by the art of Leto's son and of the Muses.' At the end of the antistrophe we find Apollo and the Muses mentioned again, as they were at the beginning. This, in Pindar's style, is an intimation that the scene is now finished and complete.

Next, in the true archaic manner, comes an antithetical picture. That power which brings joy and tranquillity to the Olympians, irritates and enrages their foes. According to the legend a monstrous being named Typhus had once contended with Zeus for the mastery of the world. Zeus had overthrown him with the lightning and had buried his defeated enemy under Etna and the Pithecusae (the modern Ischia and Procida, islands off Cyme).

[Second triad] The origin of the legend is obvious in Pindar: volcanic phenomena and earthquakes were interpreted as the fiery breathing and convulsions of an infernal monster lying under the mountain and the islands. There had been an eruption of Etna shortly before this poem was written, and the Pithecusae also (the

---

[27] Sappho (fr. 98, 6) describes a girl's hair as ξανθοτερα δαιδος, and Bacchylides (3, 56) writes ξανθὰν [φλόγα].

'sea-washed cliffs of Cyme'[28]) had given clear tokens of their volcanic nature.[29] Thus in this case Pindar's myth has a topical bearing; but at the same time the myth of Etna serves to introduce the new city of Aetna. The god of the mountain is enthroned over his defeated and tormented adversary; the warning picture of what happens to those who 'are not loved by Zeus' evokes in response the impassioned prayer to Zeus: 'Permit us to be pleasing to thee.'[30] By 'us' Pindar means men in general, but particularly the inhabitants of the new city. Hiero's Pythian victory has been a promising start; Apollo, who granted that victory, is now entreated to bestow on the city further great achievements and great men.[31]

[*Third triad*] The name of Hiero has already been spoken, but first we hear a pious reflection on the divine origin of all human gifts, before the favoured poet addresses himself to praising 'that man' as he deserves. When Pindar makes this cast, the 'bronze-cheeked'[32] spear of his poetry will fly further, without departing from the truth, than when other poets praise other men; for in fact no other Greek can be compared with Hiero for greatness and power.[33] In praising

---

[28] Ἁλιερκής (v. 17) can only denote an island as in *Olymp.* 8, 25 (or a narrow isthmus, as in *Isthm.* 1, 9).

[29] After the naval victory over the Etruscans off Cyme (474 B.C.) Hiero planned to bring these strategically important islands permanently under his control. For this purpose he sent Sicilian settlers; but earthquakes, eruptions of hot springs and other alarming occurrences so terrified the settlers that they went home again (Strabo 5, 248).

[30] Compare the transition in *Pyth.* 8, 17–18 from Apollo's defeated enemy to Apollo's favourite blessed with good fortune. On the interweaving of themes that runs throughout this poem cf. G. Norwood, *Pindar* (Berkeley, 1945) 102–105; R. A. Brower, *Class. Philol.* 43 (1948) 25–27.

[31] In v. 40 νόῳ is instrumental (like γνώμῃ in *Nem.* 10, 89): 'Be thou in thy commanding spirit disposed to do this and to make the land εὔανδρος.'

[32] A Homeric adjective for the spear is 'bronze-helmeted' (κεκορυθμένα χαλκῷ), since the spear is imagined as a warrior; and the helmet in Homer is often called 'bronze-cheeked' because it had cheek-pieces of bronze. Pindar combines the two, and is probably thinking of the tongues by which the point was secured to the end of the shaft.

[33] The other poets with their other themes are called 'opponents' only in the framework of the simile of competitors in a spear-throwing contest. There is certainly no allusion to conflict with Simonides and Bacchylides as competitors with Pindar for Hiero's favour, who are to be beaten off the field by his superior art; the context forbids such a small-minded interpretation. On the other hand, our interpretation, according to which Hiero's unique greatness will bestow a uniquely compelling power on the praises of him in Pindar's poem, is supported by many parallels. In *Isthm.* 2, 35 we read: 'Hurling the discus mightily I will throw it even so far as Xenocrates overshoots all men in amiability of temperament'; Bacchylides 5, 14–37 says approximately this: 'My song of praise for Hiero wings like the eagle over all distances, since Hiero's greatness is so lofty and boundless.'

Footnote continued on page 459

the king an expression of the type 'quod di bene vortant' is brought
in as usual,[34] 'May it so remain for all future time,' before we come
to present hopes and anxieties: 'and may Hiero be able to forget his
sorrows! He can look back upon glorious victories won by stubborn
endurance. He must still show great steadfastness, for he is yet once
again in the field,[35] although smitten with sickness. Just as once the
most powerful Greek leaders before Troy paid court to the suffering
Philoctetes, since they could not achieve their purpose without him,
so proud men (other Sicilian dynasts?) have found themselves
compelled to ask for Hiero's personal support. May recovery and
success, which were part of Philoctetes' destiny, also be part of the
king's'!

The poet now turns to the young Dinomenes to congratulate him
also as son of the Pythian victor and as king of Aetna.

[*Fourth triad*] Pindar praises the Dorian constitution which Hiero
had appointed for the new city, and recalls the establishment of the
Spartan state in Laconia, which served as a model for all Dorian
constitutions. He looks forward to internal harmony among the
well-ordered young citizens, and prays for freedom from external
attacks. This prayer brings him back to Hiero, who had inflicted
decisive defeats on the two most dangerous enemies of his kingdom.
In 480 the Carthaginians ('Phoenicians'), in trying to expand East-
wards from their colonies in Western Sicily, had been defeated at the
river Himera by Hiero and his brother Gelo (their father had also
borne the name Dinomenes); and six years later, four years before
this ode was written, Hiero's fleet had crushed the naval power of the
Etruscans ('Tyrrhenians') in a naval battle off Cyme, near Naples.
Pindar alludes to the latter first, and then delays for a while before
touching on that of Himera, speaking first of two other battles of the
previous decade, in which also Greek warriors had hurled back by
sea and land the onset of barbarians seeking to enslave Greece:
Salamis in 480 and Plataea in 479. In this way the poet makes a chain
of three links, tying together the glorious feats of arms of the
Athenians, Spartans and Syracusans. Chains of this kind are common
in Pindar, where they indicate that certain great values correspond
to each other, each in its own particular sphere.[36] This stylistic

Pindar's remark here then refers to the subject of his poetry, not to its formal art:
the notion of form as separate from subject matter was alien to early aesthetic
theory.

[34] See above p. 448 with n. 17.

[35] νῦν γε μὰν ἐστρατεύθη (50f.) can scarcely be taken to mean that Hiero is now
home again.

[36] Cf. the opening of the eleventh Olympian (above p. 437): 'Often is it favouring winds that are most needed, often rain, and at this moment a poem.'

device has been christened 'priamel,' after a similar figure much favoured in the middle ages.[37]

[*Fifth triad*] Pindar now breaks off from the praises of Hiero's achievements, since an excess of praise can easily turn the admiration which the hearers feel for the man thus eulogized into envy and ill-will. If the exceeding greatness of a prince makes too powerful an impression on the consciousness of his subjects, then the animation of personal hopes is checked, and in the emotions thus brought to a halt envy takes firm possession of the soul. The train of thought, in the archaic manner, has now drifted away from the particular subject which set it going; we do not hear anything more about moderation in praising people, but instead the delicate relation between an ambitious ruler and his people is treated in general terms. Pindar now turns to the young king of Aetna, and addressing him in person, says, 'Do not give up high ideals'! thus answering the implicit question whether it is worth while to expose oneself on a solitary eminence to the cold winds of envy and malevolence. In other odes Pindar declares earnestly that glory and envy are inseparable: 'Good fortune brings equal envy' (*Pyth.* 11, 29); 'On every man rests the envy of his greatness (*aretê*); but the head of him who has nothing is hidden in dark silence' (fr. 104c, 8). Either a man is great and exposed to malice, or he is void of value and forgotten even in his lifetime. It was this attitude among aristocratic circles at that time which gave rise to the proverb, 'Better be envied than pitied.'[38] At the same time the inescapable question poses itself: 'How is a king to behave in facing the envy and malice which aims at his overthrow?' As his answer Pindar gives four pieces of advice: 'Be righteous' (*iustitia fundamentum regnorum*); 'Speak truth'; 'Be conscious of your exposed position even in small matters'; and finally, 'Practise liberality.' It is the last maxim that detains Pindar longest. The notion recurs elsewhere in his poetry: a great man, if he wishes to lessen the malice felt against him, should share his good fortune in princely fashion with others: unstinting hospitality is 'water on the smoke of those who are ill-disposed towards whatever is noble'; by 'smoke' Pindar means smouldering ill-will that does not venture to burst forth in the bright flame of rebellion.[39] In this passage Pindar

---

[37] The term was first introduced by F. Dornseiff (*Pindars Stil*, Berlin, 1921, 97).

[38] That this was in fact a current maxim we can learn from its appearance in Herodotus' splendidly acid story of Lycophron (3, 50–53; cf. *Frühgriech. Denken* p. 67 n. 3). The tyrant's young son had by his stiff-necked opposition gotten himself into a position which left him only the alternatives of becoming a beggar or a ruler; and his father told him: 'You will soon learn how much better it is to be envied than to be pitied.'

[39] *Nem.* 1, 24; cf. *Gött. Gel. Anz.* 1928, 273f. and W. A. Stone, *Class. Rev.* 48

makes use of another current image. The king is to set all sail so as to catch the favouring wind of friendly feeling.⁴⁰ What is saved by the man of narrow soul who shrinks from expense (meaning the cost of lavish hospitality, including 'guest-gifts,' or in other words, the poet's fees); is only a momentary gain: in the long view it shows itself to be a loss, since it gives away the chance of posthumous fame.⁴¹ The words of speakers, the songs of poets give to men a duration that transcends physical death. Croesus of Lydia is named as an example of benevolence and generosity, and the cruel tyrant Phalaris serves to set him off by contrast. Pindar now takes the notion of entering upon immortality bestowed by poetry and raises it to a sharp and concrete picture. At the opening of the poem we had Apollo striking his golden lyre; at the end we are told that noble and handsome boys (here was an erotic undertone for Pindar and his public) entertain the guests at banquets with their playing upon the lyre, taking into their musical companionship the great and good men of earlier times and honouring them by dwelling on their memory. The closing words glorify the fame which accompanies greatness as the highest fulfilment of earthly good fortune. To the laurels that crown the victor, poetry adds its own unfading diadem.

If we compare the structure, matter and thought of this ode with other victory odes, we cannot fail to recognize the generic likeness.

(1934) 165f. The Nemean passage, previously rather puzzling, can be understood from the standard comparison of envy or malice with smoke (Plutarch *Mor.* 787c: 'Many compare envy with smoke'). The closest parallel to our passage is Alcaeus fr. 74, 6 LP: 'Now, while the wood is first beginning to smoke, you Mytileneans must quench it so that it does not burst out in a bright blaze,' alluding to the flame of a revolution of the commons against the aristocracy, in which they would set up a tyranny. Of other passages which develop the theme in various ways the earliest (setting aside the linguistic equation θυμός ('anger') =Lat. *fumus*) is a striking remark in the *Iliad* (18, 109f.) on the two phases of the same feeling—first anger, then ill-will. Violent anger, says Achilles, is a real pleasure, one of the most pleasurable feelings that a man can have, and it comes in 'sweet as honey'; but as a consequence a feeling of ill-will establishes itself which is constantly renewed and 'waxes inwardly' (cf. Sappho fr. 158 LP), troubling him who feels it like a burning, suffocating 'smoke.' The occasion of this speech is Achilles' anger and ill-will towards the overbearing Agamemnon. Cf. also Lucretius 3, 303f.: *irai fax ... subdita percit fumida, suffundens caecae caliginis umbram;* Ovid *Metam.* 2, 809: *felicisque bonis non lenius uritur Herses* (scil. Aglauros), *quam cum spinosis ignis supponitur herbis, quae neque dant flammas lenique tepore cremantur.* We have now a further example of 'smoke' used to mean hatred and reproach, see above p. 357 n. 22.

⁴⁰ On this image see above p. 437 n. 3.

⁴¹ Just as Pindar speaks here of gains which 'change with the weather,' i.e. are deceptive, so in *Nem.* 7, 17f. he says: 'The wise know also the future wind (of fame) that will blow tomorrow, and they will not let themselves be led from gain to loss' (cf. *Frühgriech. Denken,* 2nd ed., 360).

Again we find the five standard themes treated: the art of lyre-playing and of choral song are impressively treated in the powerful opening and the intimate picture of the third triad; the religious element is fully and powerfully represented; maxims for the conduct of life are laid down; the person and family of the victor are clothed in a bright radiance; myth and legend are not lacking, since mention is made of Typhus, of the early history of the Dorians, and of the half-legendary Croesus of Lydia. In this poem, however, the gnomic element takes the form of a 'mirror for princes', addressed to the young king of Aetna; the Dorian constitution of antiquity has been reborn, full of promise, in the new city; and instead of bringing out old legends of heroes from the mists of tradition, Pindar is able as a contemporary to bear his poetical witness to the great deeds of a king yet living. Compared with the secular importance of the victories gained over the Carthaginians and Etruscans, the victory of Hiero's horses at the Pythian games recedes into the background. Pindar has fully exploited the unusual material which here lay to hand, and out of it he has created a poem of uncommon greatness and unity. We can clearly see here how flexible the form of the choral ode was, and with what supreme mastery Pindar handled all its rich possibilities.

This same victory of Hiero's in 470 was also celebrated by Bacchylides in a short poem (3), just as both poets had been active in honouring an earlier success in 476 (Pindar *Olymp.* 1, Bacchylides 5). In 468, when Hiero's life was nearing its end, his team of coursers brought him home from Olympia the third and most coveted victory of all. On this occasion Pindar remained silent, and Bacchylides alone celebrated the king's last triumph in the pan-Hellenic games. Probably the king, whose taste for poetry developed rather late in life,[42] found the readily intelligible poems of Bacchylides more to his liking than the less accessible art of Pindar.

The victory ode which Bacchylides wrote for Hiero's Olympic victory begins by paying homage to the principal goddesses of Sicily, Demeter and Kore (Persephone):

[*First strophe*] O Clio, you who bestow lovely gifts, praise Demeter, the ruler

---

[42] Aelian (4, 15) tells us that Hiero was by nature a rough and unmusical soul, but that in the enforced leisure of sickness he had works of poetry read to him and acquired a complete 'musical' education. It is at all events clear that about 476 he invited Simonides to his court, and made use of him occasionally with excellent results in diplomatic service; that from the same period both Pindar and Bacchylides wrote for him and for a time resided at his court; and that in 470 Aeschylus was invited by him to compose and present a drama there in honour of the newly founded city of Aetna.

over wondrously fertile Sicily, and the violet-garlanded Muses, and Hiero's swift Olympic coursers,

[*First antistrophe*] thundering with the glory of their success and fame beside the swift-eddying Alpheus, where to Dinomenes' son they brought the fortunate possession of the crown,

[*First epode*] and they who watched happily shared in his rejoicing. Thrice fortunate is he who, blessed by Zeus with the greatest kingdom in Hellas, is too wise to let his towered prosperity be covered in concealing darkness.

[*Second triad*] The holy places are bright with festival where the sacrifices fall, the streets are bright with hospitable plenty. There shines forth in lustre the gold of cunningly fashioned tripods, set up in the temple where over the sublime dwellings of Phoebus beside Castalia's brook the men of Delphi rule. God himself shall we deck in glory, for his blessing is the best; just as once the prince of horse-yoking Lydia, when Zeus fulfilled the decision that was destined, and Sardis fell before the Persian might —just as then the god of the golden sword, Apollo, kept Croesus safe.

[*Third triad*] The king, overtaken by the never-expected day, was not minded to endure the miseries of servitude. A pyre he ordered to be raised before the brazen-gated palace, and with his beloved wife and his fair-tressed daughters who shrieked aloud in woe, took his place thereon. Raising his hands to the vault of heaven, he cried aloud: 'O too powerful deity, where is the gratitude of the heavenly ones? Where is the mighty son of Leto? The house of Alyattes is humbled in the dust . . .
[*Gap here in the papyrus*]

[*Fourth triad*] . . . the city; reddened with blood is the gold-eddying stream of Pactolus. Women are dragged with violent hand from their bowers. What was formerly hated is now desired: to die is the greatest joy.' So he spoke, and bade an attendant kindle the fire. The maidens shrieked and flung their arms about their beloved mother, for the cruellest death is that which one sees approaching with open eyes. But as soon as the flaming might of the terrible fire took hold of the pile, Zeus brought a black rescuing cloud and quenched the yellow flame.

[*Fifth triad*] Nothing is beyond belief that the will of the gods accomplishes. In that hour the Delos-born Apollo bore away the old man with his slender-footed daughters to the Hyperboreans and gave them a new home, as reward for his piety, since of all mortal men he sent the richest gifts to holiest Pytho. Of all that dwell in Hellas, no one, most famous Hiero, will boast that he has sent more gold than you to Loxias. Each man that does not feed on malice has good to say of you, the lover of horses, the great warrior, to whom all-ruling Zeus granted a sceptre,

[*Sixth triad*] and to whom the violet-wreathed Muses give their share. . . . what the day brings . . . thou devisest; short (is delight); but winged hopes . . .⁴³ us creatures of a day. The lord Apollo . . . spoke to the son of Pheres (Admetus): 'If one is mortal, one must have two ways of thinking: that you will see no more than tomorrow's sun, and that you will live for fifty years a rich and full life. Acting with piety enjoy what gives you pleasure: this is the greatest gain.'

[*Seventh triad*] What I declare to you, the thinking man will understand; the deep aether is without stain; the waters of the sea suffer no blot or contamination; gold is joy: but to man it is not granted to lay aside grey old age and put on vigorous youth again. Yet the glory of greatness (*arete*) passes not away with the body, but is cherished by the Muse. Hiero, you have shown forth before men the fairest blooms of good fortune. It is not silence that brings adornment to those blessed with success. Praising you with words of truth (?), men will also perform the friendship-gift of the sweet-singing nightingale of Ceos.⁴⁴

Bacchylides' ode has seven triads against Pindar's customary five, but the strophes are considerably shorter. The language correspondingly moves with a lighter and more rapid step.

[*First and second triads*] Sicily and her goddess are praised very briefly,⁴⁵ and in the same breath the poet sings also of Hiero's horses and of the race-track at Olympia. Bacchylides, like Pindar, praises Hiero as the greatest of Greek rulers; and he compliments him on not hiding his light under a bushel. It is not only that he practises the expensive sport of chariot-racing: splendid entertainments and

⁴³ Probably βραχὺ γὰρ τὸ τερπνόν. πτερόεσσα (this supplement, proposed in the first edition, has been confirmed by a further discovery) δ' ἐλπίς . . . (cf. *Pyth.* 8, 90f.).

⁴⁴ The last two lines are difficult. Κόσμος is (as in Pindar, *Olymp.* 11, 13 and fr. 194) the adornment which the ode confers on the man whom it celebrates (φέρει in the same sense as in *Nem.* 8, 14; *Isthm.* 5, 62; *Pyth.* 2, 3). 'Not silence' means 'resounding praise,' as in *Nem.* 9, 7ff.; *Isthm.* 2, 44; *Pyth.* 9, 92–94. It cannot possibly be meant that anyone should sing 'songs of praise to the delectable artistry of Bacchylides'; χάρις is much more likely to signify the ode itself as a pleasure and a gift of friendship, as so often in Pindar (*Olymp.* 10, 78; *Pyth.* 11, 12; *Nem.* 7, 75 etc.; with possessive *Pyth.* 10, 64; with genitive *Pyth.* 2, 70); and just as the transitive κελαδέω can mean both 'sing about' (*Nem.* 9, 54: ἀρετὰν κελαδῆσαι) and 'perform' (*Olymp.* 11, 14: κόσμον ἀδυμελῆ κελαδήσω; *Nem.* 4, 16: ὕμνον κελάδησε καλλίνικον), so ὑμνήσει here must mean 'perform the ode' (cf. Ovid's *canar* in *Am.* 1, 15, 8). For the thought: 'Someone will also sing this song of mine,' cf. *Nem.* 4, 13–16; *Isthm.* 2, 45 (also in conjunction with 'no silence'). The expression σὺν ἀλαθείᾳ gives no trouble, since Bacchylides often affirms the veracity of his statements (e.g. 8, 19–25; 9, 82–87), but καλῶν cannot be right: perhaps one might read or conjecture κλέων.

⁴⁵ In Pindar's slower and heavier manner the same theme is handled like this (*Nem.* 1, 13): 'Shed now flowers of brightness on the island which Zeus, the ruler of Olympus, bestowed on Persephone: he nodded his waving locks, promising her that he would cause Sicily, most fair of all lands blessed in crops, to raise high its head crested with noble cities (etc.)'

hospitality on a grand scale witness to his generosity, and he has dedicated golden tripods to the Delphic Apollo.[46] It was about eighty years since the fabulously wealthy Croesus had set up votive offerings in Delphi of solid gold, and the value of these gifts was the wonder of every visitor. Consequently the legend of Croesus was an obvious choice for the mythical element in this poem: Pindar in the first *Pythian*, two years before, had alluded to the kindness and generosity of Croesus (above p. 456). The transition is provided by the dictum that pious gifts bring their reward; the narrative then proves Apollo's gratitude towards Croesus.

[*Third, fourth and fifth triads*] As far as the crisis of the action, the story is told with animation and feeling, and presented with graphic clarity; but then the miraculous deliverance is sketched in with a few hasty strokes. It is a general rule of art that doubt and difficulty need to be presented at length and in detail, while the listener's sigh of relief at the happy ending calls for only a very little help from the artist. Here however the principle seems to have been carried a little too far; the poet disposes all too summarily of the sudden rescue and the blessed existence which those who had so nearly suffered a horrible death were now to lead in the land of faery 'beyond the north wind.' Hence, unlike its counterpart in the poem about Theseus, the startling *dénouement*[47] fails of achieving its full effect.

[46] 'Hiero of Syracuse wanted to dedicate to the god a tripod and a statue of Nike ('Victory' in gratitude for his Pythian success, see above p. 453) made of refined gold; but for a long time he could not procure the gold. Finally he sent men to Greece to look for it, who came after many vexations to Corinth and tracked down a quantity of gold in the possession of a Corinthian Architeles, who had bought it up in small quantities over many years and had collected a considerable amount. This man sold them as much gold as they wanted, and then gave them as much gold as he could grasp in one hand as a gift to the purchasers. Hiero in return sent him a ship with wheat and many other gifts from Sicily' (Theopompus, quoted by Athenaeus 6, 232 a–b).

[47] Bacchylides' narrative clearly shows the emotional motivation of the legend. In 547 the Persian Cyrus conquered the armies of Lydia, took the Lydian capital Sardis, and (as our oldest authority tells us) put Croesus to death. The devotees of the Delphian god could not come to terms with this event. 'Where was the gratitude of the gods? Could Apollo permit such a thing?' they too may have asked, and their religious belief supplied an answer—the pious monarch was saved by a miracle. In Bacchylides' poem (written in 468) two gods take a hand: Zeus sends the rain, and Apollo frees Croesus from the alternatives of death or slavery by spiriting him away. The second by itself would have been enough. A generation later Herodotus (1, 87) told the story again, and in his narrative also there are two themes twisted together. Cyrus is going to burn Croesus to death, but (1) when the pyre has already been kindled, he changes his mind; (2) the attendants cannot put out the flames; Croesus prays to Apollo and appeals to the gratitude that the god owes him (as in Bacchylides); then clouds appear from a clear sky and extinguish the fire.

Bacchylides was probably in a hurry to pass on to the parallel between Croesus and Hiero: as the Lydian had given more to the god than any other mortal, so the Sicilian had given him more than any other Greek. Some other flattering expressions are added.

[*Sixth and seventh triads*] When the ode was written, Hiero was a dying man, and he did not survive the next year. This critical situation is taken into account in the moralizing reflections of the final section. At the opening, where the papyrus is badly damaged, the line of thought can only be conjecturally restored: 'A man must accept what the passing day brings him (Croesus also saw a 'day that he had never expected'); pleasures do not endure for long, but our plans and projects boldly take wing towards the future; a man therefore must take simultaneously the long view and the short.' The one bids us happily accept everything of beauty that the moment offers; the other bids us piously eschew anything that could later bring ill in its train.[48]

To unite these two outlooks is 'the highest art of life.'[49] This theory is put into the mouth of the god whom the narrative glorifies, Apollo.[50] At the start of the seventh triad a more obscure style of language sets in, modelled presumably upon that of Pindar. The poet points out that the elements never change their nature; they regenerate themselves from their inexhaustible depths. The blue of heaven is often obscured by clouds, but it always renews its radiant purity; the waters of the sea receive all the impurities of the earth, yet they are never soiled, but purify man from sin.[51] In the same way gold is not subject to rust and decay (cf. Pindar, fr. 222, Theognis 451f.), but remains what it is—simple 'delight.' (Hiero had just been advised to pursue pleasure, and he was not short of gold for the purpose.) But man cannot preserve or renew himself; he must tread the path from carefree youth to burdensome old age. Nevertheless, where there is true greatness, reputation does not grow old or decay, since the Muse nourishes it. The king whose liberal maintaining of his dignity has 'shown to the world the fairest blooms of good fortune' will not forget poets in his generosity. 'Not silence,' but celebration

[48] For Ὅιασ δρῶν εὔφραινε θυμόν (83) cf. Theognis 793–795; 1121f., and above p. 327 n. 4.

[49] The Homeric ἅμα πρόσσω καὶ ὀπίσσω λεύσσει is probably meant in the same sense (*Il.* 1, 343; 3, 109; 18, 250; *Od.* 24, 452): πρόσσω is that which lies immediately before our eyes, and ὀπίσσω that which comes later. This becomes clear when we compare *Il.* 18, 250 with the detailed account given in 259–265.

[50] It is remarkable that Zeus, the granter of any Olympic victory, is only mentioned here and there, without any regular context.

[51] On the last see above p. 386 on Heraclitus fr. 61; for the theme in general see *Philologus* 87 (1932) p. 475f.

in poetry bestows on a man's successes the form in which they will best endure. Among the songs that will be sung of Hiero in future years will be that of the Cean nightingale.

The themes of the closing section are like those in the corresponding part of Pindar's ode, but Bacchylides remains always on the surface. The narrative of Croesus' escape is melodramatic beyond anything of the sort in Pindar: the king has decided to make his entire family a sacrifice to his pride; his lovely daughters scream at the visible approach of death, as we might well expect, and by the miraculous deliverance they also are translated to an earthly paradise, thanks to their father's piety and his costly gifts to the Pythian god. The figure of Hiero makes only a weak impression, since nothing is clearly stated about his achievements or his cares and sufferings: all we hear of is his god-given greatness, his splendour and liberality. In general terms, if one sets long poems of Bacchylides beside comparable poems of Pindar, one cannot fail to see the great difference in depth. The talent of the one cannot be compared with the genius of the other. The agreeable art of illusion which Bacchylides handles with skill cannot stand up against the earnestness with which Pindar embraces and interprets, orders and assesses the most diverse elements of reality.

4. POEMS OF A LESS SERIOUS CAST

It is only where the subject demands a light touch that Bacchylides has any prospect of competing successfully with Pindar. We have fragments of drinking-songs from both. Bacchylides wrote one for Alexander the son of Amyntas, king of Macedonia, intending it to be sung by the circle of the king's intimates at their revels. It began as follows (Bacchyl. fr. 20B):

Lyre, you have hung from your hook long enough and allowed your clear seven-stringed voice to be mute: Come to my hand! I am resolved to send to Alexander a golden winged gift of the Muses,

a fair adornment for the assembly of revellers, for hours when the welcome despotism of the flowing bowl warms the young and susceptible heart, when feelings that herald Cypris are kindled in our sense,

as companions to the gifts of Dionysus. The thoughts of men then swiftly travel upwards: in a moment one levels to the dust the bulwarks of cities and feels that one is destined to be the ruler of the human race;

one's dwelling shimmers all gold and silver; deep laden with wheat, ships from Egypt bring over the sparkling sea great store of riches; such are the pictures that crowd into the drinker's soul.

O son of high-souled Amyntas . . . what is there better for mortals than to grant themselves delight? . . . darkness (of death); no man remains in good fortune for the whole span of his life; but he who receives his right (share) . . .

When Bacchylides assigned these kingly daydreams to Alexander— that cities would fall before his conquering armies and that world domination would appear to him as a goal within reach—he could never have suspected that another Alexander, the grandson of this one's great-grandson, was destined to turn this vision of world monarchy into reality and to distribute great kingdoms to those who shared his table.

Now let us turn to Pindar. His verses also are addressed to a young prince, the son of the tyrant of Acragas (Agrigentum) in Sicily (Pindar, fr. 124ab):

O Thrasybulus, I send you here an after-dinner vehicle of lovely song. It may delight the whole circle of boon-companions and be a spur

for the draughts of Dionysus and the Attic bowls in hours when the anxious cares of men vanish from their breasts, and on the ocean of gold-spangled wealth

we all alike set sail for the shores of deception. He who has no wealth at once acquires it; they who are well to do . . .

. . . The soul becomes great indeed, when the shaft of the vine overmasters it.

Comparing the two, we see at once a generic resemblance, which extends even to the sentence-structure and the choice of words;[1] apparently there was a firm tradition of this kind of poetry. Yet the feeling of the language is characteristically different. In Bacchylides the drinker's fancies become crystallized into sharp and concrete detail: a fleet of vessels loaded with wheat ploughs the bright sea bringing unheard-of wealth. In Pindar on the other hand the sea is not a real sea, but a symbol of the deceptive medium of wine-warmed daydreams, which bears the dreamer, cradled in it waves, towards the shores of deception.[2] A further difference is that Bacchy-

[1] The following more or less close correspondences: 'I send,' 'bowl,' 'for hours when,' the daydreams, 'despotism of the bowl'='the vine overmasters.'

[2] Wind and waves had been from time immemorial symbols of everything inconstant, changeful and deceptive. In *Olymp.* 12, 5 (above p. 439) Pindar says that human hopes, bobbing up and down, float across the 'sea of lies' of vanities. The comparison of the drinker with a seafarer recurs about the end of the fifth century in Choerilus (fr. 9 in Athenaeus 11, 464 a–b):

lides is happily content to give free play to the self-deception; he yields to the moment without spoiling it: the more serious mind of Pindar is from the very outset looking soberly on the hilarity of the revellers, and stresses the unreality of their dreams. But in the very act of shattering the illusion, he can produce a sentence of such powerful irony as, 'On the ocean of gold-spangled wealth we all set sail for the shores of deception.'

There is a second occasion on which we see Pindar handling a topic which seems strangely at variance with the elevated character of his art. In 468 a Corinthian named Xenophon was victorious at Olympia, and he commissioned Pindar to write him an epinician (*Olymp.* 13); but this was not the only task which he set the poet. Before setting off to the games, he vowed to Aphrodite of Corinth that, if victorious, he would endow her temple with a hundred hetaerae.[3] After the victory Pindar had to compose a poem to celebrate the handing over of the girls to the goddess. Of this poem two portions have survived. Pindar began with an address to the slaves themselves (fr. 122):

Most hospitable young maidens, ministrants of Persuasion in wealthy Corinth, who often kindle on the altars the yellow tears of fresh frankincense, while your thoughts soar upwards to the mother of the Loves, the heavenly Aphrodite,

to you it is granted (?), my daughters, on the lovely couch to pluck blamelessly the flower of youthful delight. Where necessity compels, all things are fair. [*lacuna*]

Yet I ask myself in surprise, what will the lords of the Isthmus (the Corinthians) say of me, that for my song I have devised such a beginning, which consorts with women who consort with all. . . .

Χερσὶν ὄλβον [ἄνολβον] ἔχω κύλικος τρύφος ἀμφὶς ἐαγός,
ἀνδρῶν δαιτυμόνων ναυάγιον οἷά τε πολλά
πνεῦμα Διωνύσοιο πρὸς ὕβριος ἔκβαλεν ἀκτάς.

From the agreement with Pindar we can infer that this comparison was a current one. This gives a surprisingly simple explanation of the subject of the well-known black-figure drinking-vessel of Exekias with Dionysus as a seafarer from the late sixth century (P. E. Arias and M. Hirmer, *A History of Greek Vase Painting* [London, and New York, 1962] plate XVI), which cannot be satisfactorily explained from mythology: the happy tippler is sailing over the sea of daydreams. In cult processions Dionysus was carried in a boat on wheels (M. P. Nilsson, *Gesch. d. griech. Religion* I 539 and 550; K. Latte *Gött. Gel. Anz.* 207 (1953) 41, with a different interpretation).

[3] If we take the number of a hundred (on γυῖα='body,' 'person' cf. *Olymp.* 8, 68 with numeral, and *Gött. Gel. Anz.* 1922, 194) quite literally, the establishment of this corps must have been desperately expensive. Prostitutes in antiquity were generally slaves, and they were hired out by their owners. In this case the goddess became the owner, and the girls' earnings went into the temple coffers.

. . . gold on the pure touchstone . . .

Mistress of Cyprus, a hundred-head herd of roving girls has Xenophon brought into thy sanctuary, blessed by fulfilment of his prayer.

The extraordinary task here assigned to Pindar has been most delightfully discharged. In the very first sentence he defines, unmistakeably but charitably, the profession to which the girls are dedicated.⁴ The allusion to their activities is then developed into a little scene pleasantly portrayed: the girls who have been assigned to a party to entertain and gratify the guests, stand around the altar which flares and sends up the smoke of incense in the midst of the revellers.⁵ As they drop beads of frankincense into the flame, they pray in silence to the 'Mother of the Loves' to make them attractive.⁶ After this picture, which includes an expression of homage to the goddess, Pindar poses the question of morality, and gives an indulgent answer on the lines of the new rules represented by Simonides: reproach can only attach to our actions if we are acting by our own free will; compulsion exonerates us (see above p. 308–10). The poet then frankly admits that his poem may cause raised eyebrows. The few words that survive of his justification can probably be supplemented (from *Pyth.* 10, 64–68) to the following effect: 'My friendship pure as gold with Xenophon bids me take on the embarrassment to which I expose myself by this poem; that is the touchstone on which my friendship must be tried.' Thus the poet also was acting under compulsion. The closing lines of our fragment complete the dedication of the 'herd.'⁷ In the complete poem there must have been an expression of gratitude to the goddess for the Olympian victory and a prayer for further divine grace. We should very much like to know whether the poet addressed any prayer to Aphrodite for her favour towards himself and his art (cf. *Paean* 6, 4; *Pyth.* 6, 1).

This delightful fragment of the scolion to Aphrodite shows once again the highly personal character of Pindar's poetry. Bacchylides knew his trade, but Pindar was the complete master.⁸ He had the

⁴ For 'hospitality' as a euphemism for promiscuity see above p. 296 n. 14.
⁵ For the altar compare Xenophanes 21 B 1, 7 and 11 (above p. 326).
⁶ Chamaeleon refers this burning of frankincense to the act of handing over the girls to the temple. But this interpretation founders on the word πολλάκι, which must go together with θυμιᾶτε (cf. πολλάκις in *Pyth.* 4, 295); to depict their thoughts as soaring up to Aphrodite is not very suitable if they are standing in front of her temple; and it is illogical that they should make an offering precisely at the moment when they are themselves being offered up.
⁷ For the expression φορβάδων [κορᾶν] ἀγέλαν cf. Plato, *Laws* 2, 666e.
⁸ Apart from this short section, I have not tried to go into the question of how far Pindar was able and willing to vary his art according to occasions, persons and audiences, or according to the different genres of poetry. The 'perceptibly lighter

power of making its conventions serve highly unconventional ends. With a manly boldness and self-confidence he keeps his natural dignity even when he merely aims to amuse.

5. SOME PINDARIC WAYS OF THOUGHT

Pindar's poetry has character and substance because it is animated by a definite will and gives voice to definite ways of thought. In order to understand the spirit of his poetry better, we will look at some striking excerpts from the texts.[1]

'Best of all things is water,' is the opening of the poem that stands first in our collection; but what this means is not apparent until one reads the whole context of the strophe (*Olymp.* 1, 1):

Best of all things is water; gold gleams like blazing fire in the night as the shimmering crown of nobility and wealth; and if you desire, my soul, to sing of contests, look not over or beyond the sun for another hotter star of light in the solitary aether, nor let us celebrate any games higher than the Olympian.

The 'priamel' figure (above p. 460) is obvious: to lead up to the Olympian games, in which Hiero had won the victory here cele-brated,[2] a sequence of things is named, each being the best in its kind: water, gold, fire at night (stars), the sun in the solitary heavens, the Olympic games. What this implies in more precise terms can be understood from the ideas of that time;[3] and in fact, as often in

stylization' of the songs for girls has been noticed by K. Latte (*Gött. Gel. Anz.* 207, 1953, 40).

[1] Many of these will be the opening words of poems, since these parts are often characterized by particular force and originality: the vigorous impetus of the opening phrases makes itself felt, and the poet has complete liberty in form, since the metre and melody are not yet hard and fast. In addition it is desirable that the first verses should be impressive, as Pindar himself says at the opening of the sixth *Olympian:* 'We will set up as it were golden pillars to sustain the forecourt of the well-walled building, since we would fain erect a building that can be seen, and the countenance of a work that is beginning must shine afar.' We have already seen some striking examples of this: 'I am no bronze-caster . . .,' 'As when a man holds a bowl pearled with the dew of the grape . . .,' 'Often need we favouring winds . . .,' 'Lyre of gold . . .' (above p. 430f., 437, 453f.).

[2] The emphasis here laid on the place of the contest, and the choice, as a mythical subject, of the origin of the games, can be explained from the circum-stances. Hiero's victory of 476, his first up to that time, was in a comparatively unpopular event, the race for saddle-horses; hence the especial significance of the victory was in its being an Olympic one.

[3] The series 'aether, (sea) water, gold, fame' appears in Bacchylides 3, 85ff. (above p. 464); gold, sun, and aether are associated with victory and fame in Simonides fr. 64 Diehl, where the sun is called 'the valued (τιμήεις) gold in the

Pindar, Heraclitean notions are just below the surface. According to Heraclitus water is the element of vegetative life in opposition to the lifeless and passive earth, while fire is the element of higher life in opposition to earth and water. Heraclitus also, as Pindar does here, compares gold as the ideal of material value with fire as a metaphysical yardstick of value (fr. 90, above p. 387). Thirdly, another characteristic saying of Heraclitus' (fr. 99, above p. 381) provided the model for another pair of contrasts occurring in Pindar. A 'fire in the night' represents light set in opposition to darkness; but the sun by day 'in the solitary aether' is the one light, set over against all the lesser lights of heaven; no star can even be seen when the sun shines. In the same way an Olympic victory outshines all victories in other games. The opening of the poem then is intended to inculcate the notion of a supreme value by examples from different fields, in order to elevate the victory now being celebrated into the class of supreme values.[4] Pindar's thought is consistently directed towards values, and this attitude dictates his choice of subject matter, both in what he admits and what he excludes.

The values of Pindar's world are personified in the figure of the gods in heaven, while in men value and non-value, heavenly and earthly, are curiously mingled. The theme of 'god and man' is touched on by Pindar in the opening of a victory ode for Alcimidas of Aegina (*Nem.* 6, 1):

One and the same is the origin of men and of gods; from one selfsame mother we breathe, of both kinds, but divided by great difference of power; for what is here is nothing, but the brazen heaven has eternal duration as an unshaken place of abiding. And yet in many things we come near to the great mind or nature of the immortals, although we know not where, according to what the day or the nights bring to us, fate has appointed the end towards which we hasten.

Witness of this truth is now again Alcimidas, in whom it is shown that the inborn nature is like to crop-bearing fields, which in alternation bring now the nourishment of life in abundance for men from the ground and now, suspending their strength, repose in tranquility.

Here is the archaic swing of the pendulum from opposite to opposite[5] as men and gods are understood according to their affinities and

aether' and is made to bear witness to a man's fame; in Simonides fr. 51 Diehl, 'The best guest-witness is the gold that shines in the aether,' and in fr. 605, 'The sun is alone in heaven.' On the opening of *Isthm.* 5 ('sun, gold, contest, fame') see below p. 485–88. Cf. also *Olymp.* 3, 42ff.

    [4] See below p. 488.
    [5] The scheme is this: 'Man and god are akin—but yet wholly different—often man is like the gods—but yet he is helplessly exposed to every change.'

differences.[6] The purposes of high-principled men are like those of
the gods; but for the gods life and fulfilment of purposes are certain,
secure and free, while among men they are uncertain and dependent
on chance happenings that can be brought about by a single day or
night.[7] The antistrophe names the Nemean victor to whom the ode is
dedicated. Alcimidas' family had a remarkable number of athletic
victories to its credit; but from the list that Pindar gives it is obvious
that not every generation had had its share. The family talent
skipped some members, passing from grandfather to grandson, or
from uncle to nephew. Pindar often speaks of heredity[8] as the
decisive factor in producing men of noble qualities; here, however,
he sees a further indication of human frailty in that noble qualities
often remain latent even in members of a gifted family. Just as
previously the unshakable security of the gods was symbolized by
the 'brazen' heavens (see above p. 361), so here a comparison with the
irregular productiveness of the earth serves to characterize the
changing and unreliable nature of man. That which is always completely and abundantly present among the gods is to us earthly
creatures often granted, but often withheld.[9] In another passage
Pindar says: 'Our life changes and alters all things in the whirlwind
of the day; yet the children of the gods are free from all hurt

[6] In the opening words many commentators have taken the repeated ἕν in the
sense of ἕτερον μὲν—ἕτερον δέ. But is it conceivable that the sequence 'one—one—
one' should mean 'one—a different one—the same one'? Can we suppose that in
the anaphora ἓν γένος—μία μάτηρ the exactly corresponding initial words are to be
taken in opposite senses? Cf. also Hesiod, WD 108.

[7] For the expression ἐφαμερίαν—μετὰ νύκτας cf. Hesiod, WD 102 and Theognis
160. On the theme in general see Frühgriech. Denken 30 n. 2.

[8] Τὸ συγγενές in v. 8 acquires its true sense from the comparison with ἀρχαῖαι ἀρεταί
in the parallel passage Nem. 11, 38. Cf. also ἀρετὰ σύμφυτος—δόξα παλαιά—ματρόθε
σύννομοι in Isthm. 3, 14–17.

[9] According to ancient views man is mortal because he receives into himself
the products of the earth (above p. 54 n. 4). Here the notion is refined: 'Like
the earth which nourishes him, so the nature of man himself sometimes fails.' In
v. 11 it is usual to follow the explanation of the scholiast (σχολάσασαι τὴν ἑαυτῶν
δύναμιν ἀνέλαβον), which unnecessarily complicates the thought and does violence
to the words, Μάρπτω means 'grasp,' 'hold firm' (as an action in the aorist, as a
continuing state in the present); cf. Iliad 21, 489: 'held her hands fast (so that she
could not move)'; 23, 62 'sleep held him in bonds'; Soph. O.C. 1681: 'the earth
has taken him to itself and made him unseen (ἄσκοπον)'; Il. 8, 405 'holds fast
(and does not permit recovery)' (cf. Il. 13, 439). The parallel passage Nem. 11,
37–42 mentions fruit trees along with fields; fruit-trees bear a heavy crop only
every other year (cf. Varro R.R. 1, 55, 3 if the fact has to be attested). Plato
similarly speaks of cyclical φορά and ἀφορία in a passage where the Pindaric simile
recurs (Rep. 8, 546a). Aristotle (Rhet. 2, 1390b 25ff.) paraphrases the Nemean
passage in the same way as the scholia do (ἀναδίδωσι is 'produces,' cf. Plutarch,
Camillus 15, 3 etc.).

(*Isthm.* 3, 17, cf. above p. 393 n. 55). The gods have at their command that certainty of achievement which is denied to us: 'God achieves every purpose according to his wish' (*Pyth.* 2, 49).

In comparison with the gods, man is a mere nothing, according to the opening of Pindar's ode to Alcimidas; but Pindar is very far from the Christian notion of self-denial and contrition. For him the gods are our cousins, as it were, from the reigning family, since we all come ultimately from the same mother.[10] Noble men are impelled by the divine inheritance in their blood to try to be like the Olympians. Their earnest will towards greatness and noble achievement is often disappointed, but Pindar does not on this account condemn lofty ambitions as improper; he takes them as a token of noble qualities of mind. But one should not set one's heart on too remote a goal: thus the poet prays (*Pyth.* 11, 50f.): 'God grant that I strive towards what is noble, aiming at that which is accessible according to my age.' This is in accord with the teaching which defines manly worth (*aretê*) as a union of two things: of striving towards lofty ends and of the ability to encompass them.[11]

Thus Pindar is no advocate of pusillanimous prudence or of the golden mean of bourgeois contentment, nor does he applaud happiness in obscurity. This is certainly not the implication of the passage where he says: 'I will look for those pleasures which the day affords, and fare on tranquilly to old age.' This sentence has to be read in its context. We will cast back some distance, and begin where the poet is speaking of a kinsman of the victor's who had been slain in battle (*Isthm.* 7, 25):

. . . he for whom a fate was appointed by Ares of the brazen shield, but for brave men honour is compensation. For each man should know, who has undertaken in such darkness to keep off the bloody hail from his beloved homeland.

[10] The gods are descended from the Earth and Sky, and the earth is also the mother of the human race; it is not possible to make out more precisely how Pindar viewed the origin of man.

[11] See above p. 308 n. 9 and p. 417. According to *Olymp.* 1 Hiero possessed both: a feeling for what was noble (on the expression ἴδριν cf. Theognis 683, *Pyth.* 4, 288), and power to do it. Pindar speaks of a man's time of life in *Pyth.* 11, 50f., since he is speaking for both young and old (see the next note). Passionate desires are only justified and capable of fulfilment if they are appropriate to the age of him who feels them (the norm of ἁλικία, cf. fr. 123, see below p. 504, and fr. 127, as also Solon fr. 14, 6); if they are moderate (the norm of μέτρον, cf. *Nem.* 11, 47, see below p. 502; *Pyth.* 2, 34; *Isthm.* 6, 71); and if they are in accordance with the circumstances (the norm of καιρός, cf. above p. 447f., below p. 497–99, and again frs. 123 and 127). Fr. 127 corresponds closely in its prayer-form to *Pyth.* 11, 50f.

... [corrupt passage] ... that he wins for himself the greatest fame among his people whether he now lives or dies. Son of Diodotus [Pindar is now addressing the dead kinsman], following the example of the warrior Meleager, of Hector and of Amphiaraus, you have given up the blood of your young life,

fighting amongst the foremost, where the bravest went into the fiercest fighting with the least hope. Beyond words was the sorrow that struck me at your death. But now [now that an Isthmian victory has been won] Poseidon [the god of the Isthmian games] has granted me peace after the storm. I will sing and adorn my hair with garlands. May no ill-will of the immortals do me harm!

Such joy as the day brings I will pursue, and journey on in tranquillity to old age and the life appointed for me. We are all mortal, the one as much as the other; yet the daemon (the destiny of our life) is unequal. But he who directs his eyes to the far distance, he does not attain to treading the brazen floor of the dwelling of the gods. The winged horse threw off

his rider Bellerophon, when he would fain have flown to the company of Zeus, to the heavenly mark of his journeying. A most grievous end awaits forbidden enjoyments. But to me, Loxias, proud in your locks of gold, in your contest at Pytho, grant the flower-rich coronet.[12]

Here, at the end of the archaic age, we hear the same notes that were struck in an ode of Alcman's at the very beginning: 'Never shall a man fly to heaven,' 'There is a resentment of the gods: fortunate is he who lives one day in happiness without tears.'[13] If Pindar here does what Alcman did in his day, in pointing out the limitations of our human condition, at the same time he sets the limits wide enough at least to come near to full divinity. He does not bid our wishes come to a halt until they dream of treading the 'brazen floor' of heaven and forcing an entry into 'the company of Zeus,' as Bellerophon in the legend sought to do. On another occasion he advises the victor: 'Seek not to become Zeus' (*Isthm.* 5, 14). In great and noble men he

12 Here the poem ends. The 'me' in the final prayer refers to the Isthmian victor, who proposes to essay his powers next in the Pythian games. The first person can have several references in Pindar. Most commonly it refers to the poet himself; but it can often refer to the chorus performing the ode and to the community that the chorus represents (above p. 427 n.2); sometimes, as here, it denotes the person celebrated in the ode, in whose name Pindar and the chorus address the gods; lastly, expressions such as 'I shall,' 'I will' and the like can mean 'one ought to,' where the poet's words express a widely-held conviction and reflect a moralizing philosophy of life. Thus in this poem, 'I will pursue the joys ...' means in effect, 'One ought to pursue ...'; and in *Pyth.* 11, 50 (above p. 474) the prayer, 'God grant that I strive towards the highest ...,' is intended not as a private prayer of the poet's own, but as a wish that should be adopted by every hearer and reader of the ode.

13 Alcman 1, 16 and 37 (above p. 163 and 164).

expects to find a titanic drive to storm the heights of heaven, since it is part of our half-divine nature to strive ever upwards. Even if there is a warning of the bitter end that awaits measureless ambition, the tragic tension between ideal and accomplishment remains, and there is no attempt at a reconciliation. Thus we must not see a Stoic detachment from the individual's life or an Epicurean resignation of worldly ambition in Pindars declaration that he intends, knowing what our human lot is, to meet with tranquillity whatever may be attached to his destiny; nor must we do so in the advice that he gives elsewhere (*Pyth.* 3, 107), that one should adapt oneself to the moment, 'be great in great fortunes, and lowly in lowly.' He does not enjoin indifference, but understanding of the uncertainty of our existence, together with a noble courage in adversity (fr. 42):

Let not strangers see what misfortunes are approaching us. This counsel will I give you: all that befalls us of happiness and success we should openly show to all men; but when there falls upon a man, by the gods' devising, insufferable calamity, this it is right for us to hide in darkness.

To the suffering Hiero he has this to say (*Pyth.* 3, 80):

You know the saying from ancient times: 'For one joy the gods send upon man two sorrows.' The fool cannot endure this becomingly, but the noble soul can, turning that which is good outwards.

The continuation of the poem (103–106) lays further stress on the basic instability of human fortune. The 'resentment' of the gods, i.e. the jealousy with which they guard their superiority over men, is ready at any moment to fall on him whose rash self-confidence provokes it; and then by the sternness of their chastisement they remind us of our limitations and of their power. Hence every cry of rejoicing must be accompanied by some such pious prayer as we heard before (*Isthm.* 7, 39, p. 475): 'May no ill-will of the immortals do me harm!' Perhaps the finest expression of this pious humility is in the ode to Theia which will occupy us later (p. 485ff.). Pindar is singing the praises of Aegina, with its great naval power; he has just referred to the great feats of arms formerly accomplished by the sons of Aegina. Now he turns to the most recent deed of valour, the naval victory of the Greeks at Salamis, in which the Aeginetan vessels played a distinguished part (*Isthm.* 5, 46):

Many a shaft is ready for my singing tongue to glorify the men of Aegina. Thus might even now the home of Ajax, Salamis, bear witness on their behalf as a monument raised up to the sea-people in battle, in the deadly storm of Zeus, that hailed death upon countless men. But let your boasting be drowned[14] in silence. Zeus granted this as all else, Zeus the lord of all.

[14] On βρέχω 'choke,' 'drown' (cf. βρόχος 'noose') see *Glotta* 14 (1925) 1.

We men should not pride ourselves too much upon our advantages, since our existence is governed by the day ('ephemeral,' fr. 157), and the lord of all, Zeus, sends us days of very different kinds. All reality comes from above: 'To all things should thou assign Zeus as the cause' (*Pyth.* 5, 25), and reality is basically of changeable nature (*Pyth.* 2, 88):

A man shall not strive against god, who often advances now this one, and then to another grants great honour. But not even this soothes the feelings of the envious.

The resentment of the gods takes care that our tree shall not grow up to heaven, and in this way it takes away any ground for envy on the part of our fellow men.

But how and why particular pieces of good and bad fortune come to us, is a question that Pindar does not answer, and does not even ask. He has no thought of attributing precise and detailed justice to the divine rule; what falls to the human lot is not reward and punishment, but change and reversal, and the law of reversal seems to the poet a kind of substitute for the principle of divine justice, as it formerly did to Solon (above p. 235). But this doctrine permits only an overall justification of the rather wilful divine government; in particular cases any lively moral feeling must be tempted to 'strive against the gods.' In one passage Pindar is telling the story of Heracles and Geryon. Heracles, the son of Zeus himself, had been commanded by his taskmaster to bring him the cattle of Geryon; he simply took them, without paying or asking leave; Geryon took up arms against this theft, and was slain by Heracles. At this point in his narrative Pindar makes it clear that he sympathizes with Geryon— with the man whose death was decided by Zeus; but in the same breath he beats a retreat, saying: 'Yet will I never say anything that is unpleasing to Zeus.' But again he says that a just man will not sit idly by while his property is stolen. Obviously the legend of Geryon had troubled Pindar; he was grappling with the same contradiction that Hesiod also had tried to resolve (above p. 98–101): divine rule and amoral force can neither be separated nor united. In another passage where he refers to Geryon again (fr. 169), he tries to sidestep the difficulty by speaking of the supreme power of *nomos*, which controls even the gods, and which can legalize even the worst act of violence (cf. also *Nem.* 9, 14f.). *Nomos* in Greek is anything that is current and accepted: usage, custom, norm, rule, constitution, law. Exactly what it means here is not clear, but in any case *nomos* is an ordering power. Pindar believes in order and rules, and he shrinks from radical questioning of any rule that he finds current.

Pindar is no critic and no theologian. Towards the Olympian gods he carefully keeps a measured distance.[15] He does not try to work out how the gods exist in themselves or in relation to one another. His world of gods has no system, no articulation, no spatial depth. Everything is on one surface that is directed towards man and his world.

With reference to the doctrines held and the myths related of the gods, as also in reference to the legends of heroes, Pindar's belief is receptive, adaptable and free from speculation. He takes these things as they come, accepting any of them that he can turn to his uses.[16] If he comes up against some story of dubious morality such as the despoiling and slaying of Geryon, he first protests against it, and then prudently declares that he has nothing to say. This pointed silence is one of his characteristic features. In an ode for the Aeginetans he speaks of the great heroes of Aegina; the narrative leads up to a point where he would have to tell of a fratricide whose perpetrators had to seek refuge in exile. Here Pindar, with a very obvious omission, tells us that he is ashamed to relate the abominable action which drove the Aeacidae from their native island, and he breaks off with a declaration that he prefers to ignore what is ugly and devote himself wholly to what is beautiful. These are his words (*Nem.* 5, 16):

Here I stop; not every truth may with advantage show its face, and silence is often the best path that a man can tread. Yet when the purpose is to praise the blessings of the gods or the might of arms or iron war, a long leap may be marked out for me; spring and strength are then in my knees; eagles wing their way over the sea to the other shore.

Pindar was not able entirely to escape the tendency towards criticism of the old legends, as we see it practised by his contemporary Hecataeus. In one instance we see him correcting before our eyes a legend which did not satisfy him in its current shape (*Olymp.* 1, 24ff.). According to legend Tantalus had once bidden the gods to dinner

---

[15] There is only one of the gods of whom Pindar speaks with personal warmth, as of a respected friend—namely Apollo, 'who grants men recovery from the burden of disease, who gives us the lyre and grants the power of music to whom he will, bringing order without strife into our hearts, and who is lord of the oracle among the mountains' (*Pyth.* 5, 63). His particular feeling for Apollo becomes obvious if we observe his treatment of this god in the Pythian odes, where he presided over the games, and compare it with that of Poseidon in the Isthmians.

[16] In the poems written for different places Pindar readily adapts himself to local traditions and interests, without being greatly concerned about what he has said in other odes for other places. It sometimes happened that the readers in one city might feel themselves offended by what he had said for other audiences in other cities (cf. e.g. *Nem.* 7). This was another respect in which his pan-Hellenic activity involved him in difficulties (cf. above p. 433 n. 13).

and served up to them the body of his son Pelops (it was probably meant as a pious offering); all the other gods perceived the abomination and withdrew from the accursed banquet, but Demeter, whose anxiety for her lost daughter made her oblivious of everything else, helped herself to a little of the shoulder. The gods brought the boy back to life, and gave him a shoulder of ivory instead; in consequence a white birthmark was hereditary in the family. It is instructive to see how Pindar sets about his improvement. First he tells us that Clotho (the power of fate) took the resuscitated child, with his bright shining shoulder, out of the cooking-pot. Then he comes to a stop, full of doubt at the gross and crude miracle of bringing a cut-up body back to life; his final decision comes from the thought that it is not good to say that the gods sat down at a table where human flesh was served. Accordingly Pindar gives the story a new form, and tells it, 'contrary to tradition,' in a shape that leaves out the human sacrifice;[17] he found it quite impossible to credit the gods with a cannibal gluttony.[18] The reason that he gives is not that the story is impossible, but that 'it is fitting for men to speak good things of the gods, for thus one avoids offence' (35), and that 'speaking evil has often brought misfortune upon its authors' (53).

If Pindar is not given to theorizing about the gods, he is at least equally far removed from speculation concerning the mechanical ordering of the universe. He speaks of the natural philosophers as 'breaking off the withered fruits of wisdom' (fr. 209). So far as he concerns himself at all with physical phenomena in his poems, he interprets them in a moral or religous sense. A striking natural occurrence which exercised the scientists of his time was the yearly inundation of the Nile. They asked how it was possible that the river flowed in greater volume during the dry north African summer and autumn than at any other time. Pindar gave the naive answer that a *daimon*, a figure in human shape a hundred fathoms tall, ruled over the river and regulated it according to the seasons (fr. 282).[19] What he must have meant was that a divine power released the water and provided the fertile flood-plains when it was needed in order for the Egyptians to survive. To a solar eclipse of the year 463 Pindar could

[17] This is not all. Pindar also puts up a well-reasoned hypothesis to account for the rise of the traditional false story (46–51) and for its wide acceptance (30–32). The critical method is excellent, although the material is ill-adapted to it.

[18] Γαστρίμαργος referring to cannibalism recurs in Xanthus (Athen. 10, 415c), again in a Lydian story. Pindar's re-telling of the tale was the second time that humane sentiments had modified it: the first was when the gods were represented as not being pleased with a man's sacrifice of his own son.

[19] I am at a loss to imagine from what tradition this theory was ultimately derived. It was possibly Egyptian.

only react with undisguised consternation: he wholly ignores the theories which had already been advanced to account for the phenomenon. The catastrophe set his thought moving along purely religious lines. At the request of his native city he addressed a prayer to Apollo and his son Teneros, who jointly possessed a shrine and oracle in the Ismenion in Thebes; and the purpose of the ode seems to have been to ask the oracle for an explanation of the prodigy—how the eclipse was to be interpreted, and what should be done to avoid the disasters that it seemed to portent.[20] The opening of the poem (*Paean* 9) was as follows:

Lamp of the sun, what purpose do you have as you gaze, mother of the eyes? Noblest of stars, snatched away in the daytime you have made helpless the strength of men and the path of wisdom; treading a road of darkness you wander on new and unwonted ways. As a suppliant I come, swift guider of the car, to implore you: turn to some scatheless blessing for Thebes, commanding one, this terror to all mankind.

[*Two lines missing*]
Do you bear the sign of a coming war, or withering of the harvest? or depth of snow beyond measure, or the abomination of civil war? or . . . of the sea? or frost in our soil, or a summer season of rain, streaming with angry waters? Or will you overwhelm the earth in floods and make the race of men begin anew?[21]

The Greek chorus does not approach its god with fantastic rites of purification or magical formulae; it voices its anxiety and its desires in human and natural terms. It even permits itself the liberty of ignoring, at least at the outset, Apollo and Teneros, the dwellers in the very temple in which the ode was performed. Instead of addressing them, he addresses in his opening words the power actually concerned, the 'lamp of the sun' (ἀκτὶς ἀελίου fem. = 'sunbeam,' 'sunlight'). The 'lamp of the sun' had no temple and no place in the Greek pantheon, since in myth and cult Helius was a male divinity. Pindar, however, is speaking not of a person, but of the power of sunlight working in our lives; and in consequence he directs his prayer not to the god Helius, but to the 'mother of the eyes' who illuminates the universe for us.[22] How differently a prayer like this moves us by

---

[20] This may be inferred from the verses found in the papyrus, which celebrate the oracle, pray to Apollo as its god, and honour Teneros as a prophet.

[21] The construction in v. 6 is uncertain; no convincing restoration of v. 16 has yet been proposed.

[22] From the standpoint of ancient ideas there was a closer relation between sunlight and the human eyes than we might suppose on the basis of our more advanced science. The gaze directed by the eyes was thought to illuminate, casting an active ray, which like a beam from a light-source, went from the human eye, impinged on the object, and then returning brought an image of it

its warmth and intimate tone, compared with Pindar's celebration in an ode for a Rhodian victor, of the principal deity of the island, Helius, as 'the father, the begetter of sharp rays (ἀκτῖνες) of light, the lord of fire-breathing steeds' (*Olymp.* 7, 70)!

6. THE 'POWERS' IN PINDAR

The transformation that Pindar essayed in the ninth *Paean* is a remarkable one. To the poet and his public the image of Helius as a shining male figure driving a car of fire was familiar from a thousand representations in poetry, painting and sculpture; yet in his prayer Pindar diverges from the ruling tradition in a cardinal point. The image of the horses was indeed retained in allusions to the 'path' or 'way' of the sun; but for a male figure he substitutes a female, or rather he substitutes a certain something that has scarcely anything personal about it. He straightforwardly and naturally approaches and addresses the sunlight, conceiving it without any external trappings as that which it really means to men, as 'the mother of the eyes.' Here we come upon a feature that is very important in Pindar's thought.

Previously (p. 61ff.) we had occasion to draw a distinction between the anthropomorphic divinities, conceived as persons, and the powers which were identical with natural phenomena and forces. Such a power, for example, is *Eris*, the love of conflicts and battle: a violent force which brings its victims so under its spell that they are set at variance with their normal nature and take on instead her spirit and perform her work (above p. 64f., 102f., 115f.); another is the compelling power of chance (*Tyche*, above p. 439f.), which suddenly alters the whole course of our life. Others are self-blinding which draws calamitous consequences after it (*Atê*, above p. 62f.); the charm and attraction (*Charis*, above p. 163f.) that can proceed from men or things or actions; the winning power of persuasion and conviction (*Peithô*, above p. 296, 469); the power of art (*Mousa*), and

to the mind that was ready to receive it. Conversely, it was thought that the sun did not merely illuminate the world with its rays and render it visible to us, but saw everything by the medium of those rays, just as men saw things with their 'eye-beams.' Helius was reckoned as the god 'who sees all things.' This notion underlies Parmenides' image of the illuminating thoughts as 'daughters of the sun' (above p. 351 n. 7). Properly the 'daughters of the sun' are the sunbeams (cf. Pindar, *Olymp.* 7, 70); but in Parmenides' image they are the rays of the 'light of the world' and of true perception, acting as vehicles of clear understanding in both directions —to the object towards which they direct the thinker, and back again to the mind of the thinker, which they illuminate as they unveil themselves.

many others as we find them named and described especially in the *Theogony* of Hesiod. Their names in Greek are mostly feminine.[1] We might call them simply 'beings,' since they all have a clearly marked being or nature which is easy enough to grasp, though less easy to describe. 'Powers,' however, has become the technical term.[2] The 'powers' are in truth no fictions or creations of art, but realities of timeless validity; each man may perceive them repeatedly when once his eyes have been opened to them.[3]

Among the Greeks of the archaic period the reverence which they felt towards such powers clothed itself in religious forms. These realities, as super-personal powers in life, belong alike to heaven and to earth. They are so natural that we can grasp them entire, yet they have a depth that goes beyond the mechanical universe. Pindar likes to interpret human life on the basis of 'powers' which work themselves out in it. In regard to these 'powers' his god-fearing ways of thought display an active originality which strikingly contrasts with his adherence to tradition in other respects. He has constantly something new to say of them; not a little of what he says is surprising: all is meaningful and convincing.

A boy whose thoughts are yet at play with the dreams of childhood[4] has been victorious in the pentathlon; scarcely yet at home in the world, he has won great reputation in it, thanks to his inborn qualities (cf. *Nem.* 5, 40). Hence the poet at the opening of his ode addresses in terms of gratitude and honour the power who presides over birth (Elithyia), who at first moment of life imparts to each human child its peculiar qualities and thus helps to determine its destiny in life (*Nem.* 7, 1):

Elithyia, enthroned with the deep-minded Fates, daughter of mighty Hera (the goddess of marriage), hear me, bearer of children! Without you we do not behold the light or the darkness of night, we do not receive your sister Hebe (the prime of life between childhood and old age) with her shining limbs. Yet we do not all strive to the same ends: Different qualities divide us, binding each to his destiny. Thanks to you greatness (*aretê*) is

[1] So-called abstract nouns are generally feminine in European languages. The term 'abstract' is, however, rather misleading, since it presupposes that there is an act of abstraction between perception and the formation of a concept, when in reality such forces as pugnacity, attraction, persuasion are experienced no less directly than hunger or thirst.

[2] And I have no desire 'to add unnecessarily to the confusion of terminology which is rampant enough already in the history of religion' (Kurt Latte, *Gott. Gel. Anz.* 207, 1953, 34).

[3] We moderns have to a considerable extent lost the sense of the elementary phenomena and factors in life, partly because we carry our analysis so far that we can no longer see the wood for the trees.

[4] On v. 91 in this ode (*Nem.* 7) cf. Wilamowitz, *Pindaros* 161 n. 2.

ordained for Thearion's son Sogenes, and he is glorified in song among the pentathletes.

The powers will not be isolated, for they have their meaning only in the framework of the great whole that we call 'life.' Thus Birth is here enthroned together with Fates, is the daughter of Wedlock and the sister of Hebe: the coming into existence of the individual and the fulfilment of the qualities born in him are understood as sister powers (cf. also Hesiod, *Theog.* 922) The end of the poem (99f.) completes the expression of the wish that a prosperous *hêbê* and a blessed old age may be in store for the boy.

In the actions and reactions of life the Pindaric powers sometimes become dynamic to a startling degree. The archaic law of polar ambivalence and the Heraclitean notion of the identity of opposites bring it about that the most mild and friendly of powers have a gloomy and insidious counterpart. The music of Apollo, which softens and tranquillizes all the forces of good, arouses the imprisoned prince of darkness to flaming and earth-shaking rage (*Pyth.* 1, 1–16, above p. 453f.). Peaceful 'Tranquillity' can fight savagely when it is necessary to restrain a violator of peace (*Pyth.* 8, 1–13, below p. 497–99). 'Comeliness, who grants to mortals all that is graceful, lends dignity' even to malicious falsehood, when she dresses it in the garb of pleasing legends (*Olymp.* 1, 30–51). *Hôra*, the season of youthful strength and vigour in men who have just matured, with the gay courage that she imparts and the winning charm that she sheds over them, is thus apostrophized in the opening strophe of an ode (*Nem.* 8, 1):

Sublime Hora, you bring the ambrosial joys of Aphrodite, dwelling in the eyes of youths and maidens, many a man you touch with mild hands of compulsion, yet others you touch otherwise.

The *hôra* which beams from the eyes of beautiful girls and boys brings with it a power and compulsion of two kinds, leading to beatitude or martyrdom.[5]

The Pindaric powers are no bloodless allegories, dragging their weary feet across a puppet's stage; nor are they figures conjured up by the violent postulates of metaphysics from an unapproachable other-world, to stand shapeless and scarcely comprehensible before the eyes of the initiate.[6] They are always in our midst, they work

[5] Cf. Ibycus fr. 286, above p. 285. On κᾶρυξ cf. Aeschylus, *Suppl.* 1001. This idea of the two kinds of 'hands' with which Love touches us helps one to understand Propertius 1, 9, 23f. (*facilis* corresponds to ἀμέροις).

[6] The one exception is Theia in *Isthm.* 5 (below p. 485–87), a conception which arises from a radical abstraction. But even she makes herself directly perceptible to human feeling.

directly upon us and through us. In one of his dithyrambs (fr. 78) Pindar addresses the war-cry 'alala,' shouted by Greek armies before joining battle, in the following terms:

Hear me, Alala, daughter of Ares, prelude of the spears, you to whom men fall as offerings for their homeland in death's holy sacrifice.

As 'prelude' to the holy self-sacrifice of brave men, and as the first beginning of a decisive event whose outcome only god knows, the battle-cry is a power of high rank; but it is from our own throats that it comes, by our own will that it is uttered.[7]

The 'powers' thus become intermediaries between men and the great personal deities; intermediaries to whom no altars smoke, no worship is paid, but which in our souls we honour with pious reverence. Pindar is ready to see the powers as 'daughters' of the Olympians. He calls *Alala* a daughter of Ares; on the occasion of the eclipse he prays not to Helius, the father and begetter of the rays (*Olymp.* 7, 70), but to the radiance itself and to the god's daughter 'lamp of the sun' (*Paean* 9, above p. 480f.), he prays to *Tyche*, the idea of fortuity in life, as a daughter of Zeus (*Olymp.* 12, 1–2, above p. 439) who is lord of all reality; Truth also he addresses as 'daughter of Zeus' (*Olymp.* 10, 13).[8]

A power is by its very nature specific; it has its own laws and is master of a particular domain. The more clearly each of these figures is developed, the more powerful and realistic is the perspective afforded of the field in question. But clarification of details leads to confusion of the whole. The more 'powers' are discovered, and the more intensively one works out their characteristic properties, the more fragmented does our picture of life in general become. Music, a war-cry, tranquillity, fortuity, birth, truth, the charms of *Hôra*—all these have little in common, and a great deal of systematic work would be necessary if one wished to arrange all these disparate entities in their proper places in a general scheme. Pindar is no constructor of systems. He does indeed separate out the individual powers, but in setting them into an ordered arrangement he takes scarcely more than the first step. He is as far from having a systematic world-picture on this level as on the level of the gods or of physical nature.

[7] We may recall the beginning of the eleventh book of the *Iliad* (above p. 64f.). There the dreadful significance of the war-cry that drove the army to mortal combat is represented in a metaphysical and religious image; it was a power sent by God, the power of conflict (*Eris*), that joined with the war-lord and his heralds in uttering the fateful cry.

[8] Cf. further 'Report, daughter of Hermes' (*Olymp.* 8, 81f.); gold, which is mighty and never passes away, as a son of Zeus (fr. 222), and many others.

Yet his work as a whole has a kind of uniformity which the reader perceives at once. However, to say that it lies in the style or the technique would obviously be unsatisfactory. There must be behind it a way of looking at things which makes a uniform style possible.

This attitude is not hard to find. Pindar's poetry is directed towards what is noble, great, beautiful, good and godly—in a word, towards values; and this attitude is so rigidly maintained that he excludes everything which does not have a positive or negative correlation with values. Just as Plato later directed the whole power of his philosophical thought towards the idea of 'the good,' so Pindar's poetry has the one aim of helping to realize all that is of value in life. It is from the uniform golden glow of values, shed equally over all his poems, that his creations derive their unity, both overall and in detail.[9]

From a poet as innocent of abstract theorizing as Pindar, we should not expect a didactit verbal formulation of the notion that all values were essentially one. Yet on one occasion he does give such a formulation, so important did he reckon the conception to be. In the small portion that we possess of his entire output we find the opening of one ode pushing metaphysical speculation as far as a 'mother' of all values (*Isthm.* 5, 1):

Mother of the sun, Theia of the many names, thanks to you men have learned to value gold as great and mighty beyond all other things; hence are the competing ships in the sea and the horses straining at the chariot in the circling contest objects of admiration, because of your worthiness;

hence (because of your worthiness) he on whose head many crowns are laid lays claim to the coveted glory in contest, having conquered by strength of arm or by fleetness of foot. But the contention of men is decided by their daemons (inborn fates).

Two things are there that bestow the fairest flower of life with the bloom of happiness: that a man should prosper and that he should receive praise and reputation. Seek not to become Zeus; you possess all if of these two splendours a part falls to your lot. Mortal fortunes become a mortal.

The idea at the end of this extract is one with which we are familiar from the end of the first Pythian. Everything that a man may wish for himself is comprised in the double achievement of the victor: He has 'prospered' in the success and the favour of the gods which has befallen him in the shape of his victory; and he has 'praise and reputation' now bestowed by Pindar's poem in his honour. The opening of the poem is managed in 'priamel' form to lead up to the notion of the glory justly claimed by a victory in the games. But who is Theia?

9 On this point see below p. 488–96.

Hesiod in his epic of gods and cosmic forces, of their origin and their kinship one with another, includes among the numerous names that make up his genealogies the Titans who were parents of the sun, the moon and the dawn. Old tradition gave him a name for the father, Hyperion: but no firm tradition prescribed the mother's name, and so Hesiod gave her the colourless general appellation of Theia, 'divine one' (*Theog.* 371). Pindar took up Hesiod's 'mother of the sun' and elevated her to a 'power.' While he saw in the other powers the daughters of the great personal gods, and in his prayer for Thebes addressed the daughters of Helius (above p. 484), he now took an opposite direction and raised his eyes towards the 'mother of the sun'.

For what Pindar intended to express by this personage it was convenient that Hesiod had given her a name meaning only 'divine one' without defining her any further. Since there are many individual values based upon her, the 'power' of value is in Pindar's eyes truly 'rich in names,' as there was no all-embracing expression in Greek for value in general.[10] The closest approach is the word *timê*, which can mean 'honour,' 'dignity,' 'reward,' 'value' in a variety of shades of meaning. Pindar accords a key position to the word *timê* in the important opening verses of this Isthmian ode, which we must now examine more closely.

The sun is Theia's child: thus in the last resort all light in this world comes from her; but not only light, as Pindar now declares. This power of imparting and bestowing worth and merit is very clearly brought out by the way in which Pindar has arranged his words. 'Gold,' he says, is indebted to you for the fact that men have adjudged to it (νόμισαν) unique force (that is, the highest material value); (you are the value of values) for it equally (καὶ γάρ) comes about through your *timê* that the splendour of swift-moving ships and chariots provide a spectacle to arouse our admiration;[11] (it is through your *timê*) that a victor in the games gains glorious fame as his becoming tribute (ἔπραξεν).' The examples chosen are representa-

[10] The notion of 'worthy', 'possessing value' is adequately conveyed in Pindar's language by καλός, but there is no corresponding term for 'worthiness,' 'Possession of value' (as it might be τὸ κάλλος). Instead the notion is splintered through a variety of special terms, as ἀρετά for persons, κέρδος, καρπός or μισθός for actions, and such other terms as κλέος and δόξα, χάρις and τὸ τερπνόν, κόσμος and στέφανος, φέγγος, αἴγλα and τὸ λαμπρόν, κορυφά and ἄωτος etc.

[11] Ships and chariots were from earliest times a symbol of pride and splendour; Sappho began a poem thus: 'Many say that an army of war-chariots is the fairest thing upon the dark earth, others an army of foot-soldiers, yet others a fleet of ships' (fr. 16, above p. 185). And Pindar himself elsewhere (fr. 221) says: 'Some take delight in the honours (*timai*) and garlands of wind-swift steeds; others delight to dwell in golden chambers; others delight to cleave the salt flood in a swift ship.'

tive of all other things to which a value attaches; thus Theia, in Platonic terms, is proclaimed as the very idea of value, that is, as the power which in every field creates and establishes value as something valid and binding. In the realm of material values she is the basis of the great purchasing power of imperishable gold and of the pride and power of those who possess it; her power is equally felt in everything through which a claim to praise and reputation (κλέος) can be put forward, or by which our sense of admiration is aroused (θαυμασταί). Now at last we are fully able to appreciate what it means that the verses which begin our collection of Pindar's odes should parade such a rapid and exuberant series of values before our eyes: water, the best of all; fire in darkness; gold as the crown of wealth; the one sun in the empty aether; the Olympian games.[12] Thus the priamel figure can be understood at a deeper level: by enumerating the best things in a variety of fields the poet points towards that which is common to them all, the supreme value (above p. 459).

Nowhere else has Pindar advanced so far towards a Platonic conception of ideas as in this address to Theia. It can hardly be accidental that Plato himself speaks of the idea of the Good, the summit of all ideas, as the mother of the sun (Helius): 'In the world of higher perception the last and scarcely able to be perceived is the idea of the Good; he who has beheld it knows that it is the basis of all virtue and beauty; in the sensible world it gave birth to light and to him who is the ruler of light (Helius)....'[13]

If all values by their very essence are of one and the same nature, in which each individual value participates (to use Plato's expression) in the same way human value (*aretê*, manly worth, virtue) is a unitary whole. Of course, Pindar nowhere says this expressly, but this is probably because to him it was self-evident; many of his trains of thought rest on the presupposition that individual virtues cannot be severed one from another. It is only in this way that we can understand the high value that Pindar and his world set upon victories in the games. They thought not in terms of a specialized technical ability, but in terms of the demonstration, in this particular way, of the worth of an individual.[14] If a man throws all that he has to give into pursuing a wholly ideal end; if he gives up his time and money,

[12] See above p. 471f. In n. 3 on that page a passage is cited in which Simonides ascribes to the sun a *timê* comparable with that of gold.

[13] *Republic* 7, 517 b-c, cf. also 506e and 508b. Probably both Pindar and Plato are adopting Heraclitean ideas, cf. *Frühgriech. Denken* p. 282 n. 2 and p. 361f.

[14] See above p. 438: the boy Hagesidamus in Pindar's eyes demonstrates not only to his own, but his whole people's possession of every virtue, for men breed true to type.

if he takes the risk of defeat and disgrace, if he undergoes the long and severe discipline of training with all its pains and privations and efforts, and puts out every ounce of his strength in the event itself;[15] and if then the grace of the gods, without which no achievement is possible, chooses him as victor from all his competitors, then in Pindar's eyes he has given convincing proof of his *aretê*.[16] And proofs of this kind were necessary, for the values in which Pindar believed were no other-worldly abstractions; they had to be fulfilled and realized in life.

7. THE ART OF PINDAR

From the point which we have reached in gaining this understanding of Pindar, it is but a short step to the end of our long quest for the unity of his various poems.

As we saw earlier, the material content of the longer poems differs enormously from one to another; there is, as it were, no vanishing-point towards which the various lines converge. If there is any general perspective which can confer unity on the poems, it must be one which transcends the individual poems. This applies not only to the victory odes, but to other varieties of choral lyric as well, since the same problem of unity presents itself in all.

It has been shown that the society for which Pindar worked believed in the unity of all values and that they were realized as examples in individual fields. In dealing with any such example it was tacitly assumed that the particular proof of worth, whatever it might be, represented the unity of all, as in the corn-market a single handful may represent the quality of a whole cargo. In each of his great choral odes Pindar sets forth the whole world of values—not in a theoretical outline of its basic features, but in concrete examples from its most important areas; and the proofs of worth may be adduced either at random or according to the accidental context of events. Any myth, represents the legendary past which contained all the models of all that could happen.[1] Every pious reference to the

---

[15] In races for horses and chariots the personal achievement of the owner was missing (in the early period the victory was adjudged not to the owner but to the team); but the enormous expenditure necessary, the prestige which horse-breeding and training had enjoyed from time immemorial, and the splendid spectacle of blood horses at full gallop were some sort of compensation.

[16] This view that *aretê* can prove itself with equal validity in any given field is opposed by pseudo-Tyrtaeus in fr. 9 (above p. 337–39).

[1] From the earliest times Greek fancy had been at work to make the world of myth a treasury of examples of every important happening of human life under gods and powers.

gods contained, in principle, all religious feeling. Timeless truths of a general nature are incorporated in the various maxims. The words of the poet serve to typify all skills and abilities, all thought and language. The particular occasion of the poem is of course alluded to; it provides the nearest illustration of the ability of values to realize themselves in any present set of circumstances. It is in order to achieve this kind of completeness that we find in the typical Pindaric ode those five standard elements of subject matter which feature in it together.[2] The victory ode, then, has also the particular purpose of taking up the recent achievement into the realm of values and of bringing the victorious athlete to his due place among the noble company of famous men, heroes and gods.[3]

Pindar's art is thus an act of homage to values,[4] and to human values in particular. Through this fact function also is more precisely determined.[5] Values live in and upon the estimation that they enjoy; they have to be recognized and understood in theory, and realized and encouraged in practice; without this they would be as dead as a law that scarcely anyone knew or respected. It is the function of the poet, as the voice and conscience of the community, to make sure that the good is honoured, and with correct judgment to allot praise or blame to men and things. In the ode addressed to Hora Pindar declares (*Nem.* 8, 32):

. . . Hateful deception was practised from the earliest times, companion of crafty speech, hypocrisy, injurious slander, she who destroys that which shines brightly and raises to a hollow eminence that which lies in darkness.

Father Zeus, let not such a nature be mine! Let me cleave to the simple path of life, so that in death I may not leave to my children an evil reputation. Others strive for gold or for possession of land insatiably; but

[2] We encountered these five themes on pp. 290, 440 and 449. They were all present (except the theme of poetry) in a short monodic poem of Sappho's (above pp. 185–187). On the logical connection between the various themes see below p. 495f.

[3] Cf. *Olymp.* 2, 1–5 and above p. 435 with n. 18 on the 'insertion' of a victor into a hymn to the gods, in connection with the theory of the victory ode.

[4] This could be said of choral lyric in general. Pindar is the only choral lyrist of whom we have any complete poems, and everything suggests that in him choral lyric achieved its consummation. Thus it is better to interpret the nature of the art from the beginnings to Pindar on the basis of what we find fully developed in him, rather than to explain what at first sight puzzles us in Pindar as arising from the supposed force of tradition to which he had to adhere (above p. 435); in the latter case the significance of the traditional forms is left unexplained, and the real question is evaded rather than solved. Cf. *Frühgriech. Denken* 350–362.

[5] Cf. the observations above (p. 426–435) on the calling of the choral lyrist.

I make my ambition that I may be pleasing to my fellow-citizens[6] until my body is robed in earth, praising what is praiseworthy, and strewing blame on the impious.

Virtue (*aretê*) grows upwards as a tree grows up watered by the lifegiving dew, rising up with the help of the wise (i.e. poets) and righteous among men to the fresh blue of heaven.

On behalf of the community the singer rewards the good that men do with sounding acclaim and undying glory, and thus animates those whom he addressed to ever continuing achievements. It is his hand that bestows the fairest of crowns (above p. 456)—not a quickly fading garland like that which physically adorns the head of the victor, but an imperishable diadem (*Nem.* 7, 77):

It is easy to twine garlands—let it be; the Muse is forging for you gold together with white ivory and with the lily-flower from the dew of the sea (coral).[7]

The special view that Pindar takes of goodness and greatness assigns a central position to his art in another sense also. To maintain a splendid appearance is also for him part of the noble character. Choral lyric, of which he is master, with its words and music and dancing of noble and richly attired performers, was for him and his circle itself something of value and reality, comparable with the proud pomp of the national games. Just as Heraclitus in his awakened consciousness·experienced in his own existence the meaning of the cosmos, in Pindar's choral odes the idea of the good and great achieves self-awareness and triumphantly displays its own significance. Promise and performance here become one. It is for this reason that Pindar's art can so often and so explicitly speak about itself.

Pindar's poetry is a piece of life; it serves life and is nourished by life present and past. But it has no thought of taking reality as it is and representing it in its actual size and shape. Its subject matter is selected by a rigorously critical method and set out by a highly specialized art.

We virtually never hear in Pindar of men working hard for their daily bread[8] or of working for a living at all. Pindar often celebrates

---

[6] That is to say, Pindar submits even his own office to the judgment of the community in whose name he is speaking.

[7] This is a variation on the theme sounded by Simonides (above p. 323): 'Not from gay and perfumed flowers, plucked in the dew-fresh meadow, do I twine my songs as transient and fruitless garlands . . .'

[8] The one exception, I think, is *Isthm.* 1, 47ff., where the tone is contemptuous, as the coarse expression γαστήρ shows. The meaning of the passage seems to be something like this: 'Every activity is directed towards a reward that befits it. The

the great merchant families of Aegina, and speaks of their trading vessels sailing to every port (*Nem.* 5, 1ff.); but he never mentions their cargoes or the bargains that were struck for them. Pindar knew his way about the markets: in one passage he enumerates the most famed products of the various regions of Greece—one produces the best hunting dogs, another the best milch goats, others the finest weapons or chariots, or the most exquisitely made mule-carts[9] (fr. 106); but he is not thinking of the commercial value of these things, only of their unsurpassable quality. His poetry never stoops to the level of everyday life. It remains always on the lofty peaks of life, and even when it has to speak of the jovial atmosphere of a five-day banquet celebrated by the princes and nobles of the Argo's expedition, it speaks in religious accents of their 'culling the hallowed flower of goodly living' (*Pyth.* 4, 131).

Among progressive circles of that day the notion of *historiê*, that is, an empirical stocktaking of all accessible reality (see above p. 336) was finding enthusiastic acceptance. The exclusive art of Pindar had no sympathy for such curiosity, and in contrast with Aeschylus, he was quite uninfluenced by the lively interest in geography then current.[10] Here again it was not ignorance that was the cause: the much-travelled poet was no stranger to geography. His many passages in praise of cities and countries are true to nature, and he attributes to them the features that they actually possessed; but their spatial location receives no attention from him—the points of the compass are never mentioned.[11] He never gives a continuous account of any land or people and its peculiarities; we almost never find in him (here also he differs sharply from Aeschylus[12]) any mention of the strange

great majority of men (πᾶς τις) are contending only for the bare necessities of life; once they have satisfied their hunger, they have gained their reward (shepherds, ploughmen, fishermen and wildfowlers are then mentioned as examples, since their work is directed immediately at gaining food); but the activity of those who aim at glory and success in war or in the games is of a quite different kind; their gains and rewards are the noblest of all.'

[9] Sicily is cited for this last, and the remark still holds good: such can be the longevity of a tradition.

[10] We may compare for example Pindar's account of the expedition of the Argonauts with Aeschylus' description of the wanderings of Io (*Pyth.* 4 and *P.V.* 707ff.).

[11] In these circumstances it is a paradoxical accident that Pindar should be our earliest source for a new geographical theory, the doctrine of the three continents (*Pyth.* 9, 8, above p. 441f., n. 2; Hecataeus had only two, above p. 343). Apparently to Pindar the fact that there were three 'roots of the earth' was not something of merely geographical interest.

[12] On Aeschylus cf. Walther Kranz, *Stasimon* (Berlin 1933) 71–108. For a juxtaposition of the achievements and characteristics of these two poets see John H. Finley, *Pindar and Aeschylus* (Cambridge, Mass., 1955).

and unusual things to be found in the wide world, of exotic costumes, manners or religion.[13]

The one exception is of so peculiar a kind that it proves the rule. In his earliest datable poem (written in 498) Pindar comes to speak of the Hyperboreans, the chosen people of Apollo, and he gives a detailed picture of them (*Pyth.* 10, 27):

(Happy is he who has won in the great games and lives to see his son victorious in the Pythian contests.) The brazen heaven will he never scale, but in the realm of those gains which become our mortal estate he has sailed the longest voyage. Yet wandering by ship or by land you could not find the wondrous way to the folk of the Hyperboreans,

among whom once Perseus dined, the leader of the people, bidden into their dwellings. When he came, he found them offering hecatombs of asses, a lordly sacrifice. In their feasts and songs of praise Apollo constantly takes most delight, and laughs to behold the braying wantonness of the creatures.[14]

The Muse is never absent from the life that the Hyperboreans lead; everywhere sound the choruses of maidens and the call of the lyre and the echo of the flute. They bind their hair with golden laurel for their glad-hearted festival. Neither sickness nor wasting old age is found among that sacred race. Far from pain and warfare do they dwell, freed from the anger that overtakes men on behalf of righteousness.[15]

The people 'beyond the north wind' (for that is what *Hyperborean* means) do not dwell in our world but beyond it; the advantages which their 'sacred race' enjoys embody those joys which mortals long for in vain. Thus Pindars' description of their life and habits has nothing to do with ethnography, any more than the route to their country is a concern of geographers. The poet in fact says that one cannot get there by sea or by land; only Perseus, with his miraculous winged sandals, found the 'wondrous way' thither. This

---

[13] Probably only in fr. 203, where a particular kind of double-dealing is compared with a practice among the Scythians.

[14] The insatiable lasciviousness (ὕβρις) of the donkey was proverbial. In Herod. 4, 129, 2 it brays while copulating; in Xenophon *Anab.* 5, 8, 3 the author says that he would have had to be τῶν ὄνων ὑβριστότερος, οἷς φασιν ὑπὸ τῆς ὕβρεως κόπον οὐκ ἐγγίγνεσθαι in order to cudgel a man without cause when the whole army was suffering from cold, hunger, thirst, exhaustion and enemy attacks; in less precise terms Plutarch *Mor.* 363c. Cf. also Plato *Phaedo* 81e.

[15] Here, and here only, ὑπέρδικος means not ὑπὲρ δίκην but ὑπὲρ δίκης. We should have to postulate the existence of an ὑπέρδικος in this sense from ὑπερδικέω, which is formed analogously to ἀδικέω from ἄδικος. For *Nemesis* as a plague of mankind cf. Hesiod *Theog.* 223; the Hyperboreans are exempt from it because they do no wrong.

flight is for Pindar a parallel to an ascent to the 'brazen sky.'[16] From the empirical point of view this represents a step backwards from the earlier notions of Aristeas, who made personal researches into the far North and on that basis assigned to the Hyperboreans a local habitation and a name (above p. 242). Pindar is not concerned with physical location, only with a symbol and its meaning. In the same way the 'pillars of Hercules,' the mountains which guard the straits of Gibraltar at the Western end of the known world, become for him a symbol of the farthest attainable good fortune (*Olymp.* 3, 44; *Isthm.* 4, 12). As in one instance the imaginary Hyperboreans, so in another the real facts of geography serve merely as a help towards expressing the concept of values. In another passage Pindar makes similar metaphorical use of the names of two rivers. In the cold North-East, where one would gladly take refuge in the heat of summer, the Phasis was the *ne plus ultra* of navigation, as the Nile was in the warm South for which one longed in winter. With a delicate humour Pindar praises a prince in these terms (*Isthm.* 2, 39):

At his hospitable board the blustering wind never compelled him to reef his sail; he continued none the less, sailing in summer as far as to the Phasis and in winter to the Nile.

The image of the 'wind' of popularity which one attracts into one's sails by noble liberality is one with which we are already familiar.[17] Here it is given a new turn. The wind of popularity began to blow too strongly, and the number of guests increased alarmingly, but Xenocrates did not consider reefing the sails of his generosity.

Just as Pindar neglected geography and spatial orientation in general (unless it had some further significance, such as neighbourhood), so he ignored chronology whenever he chose. His manner of presentation springs instantaneously from one point in time to another, and in dealing with a coherent sequence of events he is as likely to go backwards as forwards, and to make constant changes of course.[18] Our sense of time is cruelly abused, but it is the price paid for the emergence of other and more important cross-relations.

The empiricist finds his satisfaction in the particular and the non-

---

[16] The pattern of thought of vv. 22–31 is as follows: 'A victor gains high good fortune; but he cannot get to heaven; but he goes to the limit of what men may gain; but no one can find the way to the Hyperboreans, neither by sea nor land; one would have to be able to fly like Perseus, for whom the impossible journey was rendered possible by a divine miracle.' The transition to a new theme is effected by a series of see-saw movements: statement—antithesis—antithesis—antithesis.

[17] Cf. *Pyth.* 1, 90ff. (above p. 461); also p. 437 n. 3.

[18] Cf. for example the story of Cyrene, above p. 445, 447, and *Gött. Gel. Anz.* 1922, 197f.

recurring: for Pindar on the other hand the individual instance is no more than an example, a test case. He treats the athletic contests with reference only to their significance; very seldom does he give details of a particular event. The victors whom he celebrates remain equally without individuality.[19]

The graphic detail of description which Bacchylides indulges in for its own sake is used only sparingly by Pindar. Shape, colour, movement, light and dark, sounds and smells, scenes and physical objects—all such elements are brought in only occasionally, but for that very reason with the more telling effect. Two examples may be given from one poem. In an ode for a Rhodian victor Pindar happens to speak of the legend of Tlepolemus. Tlepolemus had incurred the misfortune of banishment for a homicide; but in the end his act turned into a blessing for him, since he became the founder of a flourishing settlement beyond the sea, in Rhodes in fact. The idea of bad luck changing to good is conveyed by Pindar in maxims (*Olymp.* 7, 24):

Around the spirit of man drift endless errors; he has no art to find out

what now or at the last will be the best for him. Thus formerly the founder of this land with a staff of hard olivewood struck and slew in Tiryns in his anger Alcmene's bastard brother Licymnius coming from Midea. Bewilderment of the soul has often led the wisest astray. And he went to the god and asked of the oracle.

Pindar here talks partly in generalities and vague symbols, while the remaining part, the narrative, is in a dry chronicler's style: in its barren expanse only one detail stands out with terrible sharpness— the murder-weapon.[20] Now to the continuation of the story. Apollo's management brings about the happy ending.[21] He commands Tlepolemus to go to Rhodes. The oracle does not specify the island by name, but describes it as the place where (according to an old legend) the war-goddess Athene had been born from her father's head; the blacksmith-god Hephaestus contributed to the delivery by splitting Zeus' skull. Here is a second blow, but this time life, not death, results. In Pindar's text (*Olymp.* 7, 33) Tlepolemus is sent off

[19] Just once Pindar tells us that a victor in the pancration was of small and unimpressive appearance, although a powerful fighter (*Isthm.* 4, 49ff.).

[20] We may compare *Nem.* 11, 32 (below p. 502 n. 18).

[21] The complete revolution is underlined by a significant verbal responsion: 'Man is entangled in error; he cannot find his right way' (24f.)—'Man is misled by error; Tlepolemus has himself put on the right road by God' (30f.). Another significant responsion is 'in the beginning' (20) and 'at the last' (26). By the Θάλαμοι Μιδέας Pindar means the city of Midea (*Gött. Gel. Anz.* 1922, 196 n. 5).

to the sea-washed land where once the king of the gods covered over the city with golden snowflakes, at that hour when, thanks to Hephaestus' art and the brazen stroke[22] of his axe, Athene issuing from her father's head raised the battle-cry in ringing tones, and fear of her came upon heaven and mother earth.

Here the scene[23] is depicted as factually and graphically as can be, but only because the greatness of the event justifies this lavishness.

In general Pindar appeals not to sensuous fancy but to spiritual understanding and appraisal. For this very reason the natural dimensions of space and time are neglected, as in general things that have no dignity and importance are ignored. Phenomena are as it were denatured, and empirical data serve only as the raw material from which his operations will extract the value-content. Instead of calling things simply by their names, Pindar likes to speak of their 'flower,' 'peak,' 'bloom' (ἄωτος, ἀκμά, ἄνθος), or however else we choose to render laudatory expressions.

A further peculiarity of Pindar's language deserves attention in this context. In his way of thinking, as in Plato's, which was very similar, an important part was played by the fact that someone should receive or possess or acquire a quality, that he should be distinguished by some value or disfigured by the lack of it. The indefiniteness of the Platonic 'participation' as an intermediary between the quality as an idea and the bearer of it found its primitive counterpart in Pindar in the deliberate vagueness of a great many terms expressing contact or association: a family 'mingles itself' (ἔμειχθεν) with eight victory-garlands (Nem. 2, 22), and a victor is worthy 'to be mingled' with the praise of his fellow-citizens (Isthm. 3, 3); sweet-voiced songs 'are familiar' with Hiero (Olymp. 6, 97), a house is 'not unfamiliar' with festal pageantry and song (Isthm. 2, 30), and Libya is 'not unacquainted' with beasts of the wild (Pyth. 9, 58); sick men are called 'partners of self-generated pains' (Pyth. 3, 47); and there are many other expressions of this sort in Pindar.[24]

The doctrine of values imports a certain systematic element into Pindar's ideas of the world and of life. In this way his ethic makes at least some approach to a system; but his dogma of the gulf between man and god, with all the conclusions that he draws from it, tends

---

[22] χαλκελάτῳ πελέκει is probably to be taken as meaning that the bronze of the axe penetrated the skull, cf. Odyssey 22, 295.

[23] On Pindar's habit of restricting himself to isolated and static momentary scenes see above p. 445f. with n. 11. The scene of the birth of Athene is a common subject in the visual arts.

[24] See above p. 440 n. 8.

to set a counter-system going: the man who strives towards the heights of heaven is again and again hurled down into earthly abasement. In addition there are further and more special truths which are valid in their own spheres. Despite all this, Pindar sees all essential reality as being quite coherent. The general connections, in his view, come about through an immense number of individual connections of all kinds and all directions; and to demonstrate such relationships is a major concern of his art, which helps us to understand many of its peculiarities.

The poet brings out the connections both between values (or their opposites) and their manifestations in life, and between the 'powers' and their working out in particular instances. A web of inter-relations is spun between the lively present and the venerable past, between an event (whether present or past) and a general rule which the event serves to illustrate. Religion, very appropriately, is brought into everything, and poetry, as the universal medium, concerns itself with all other things. Cross-relations connect one value with another and one piece of reality with another; a network of inter-actions connects the powers both with the gods and with values; the list could be greatly extended. To do justice to this multitude of inter-relations, 'the flower of songs of praise flits like a bee to ever new subjects' (*Pyth.* 10, 53). The erratic flights with which Pindar's poetry darts from theme to theme illustrates by its example how, within the world of values, even those things remotest from each other possess a true connection.[25] This fine but strong web of relations weaves the disparate elements of the odes together into that unity over which the one light of 'Theia' sheds its lustre. This then is the complete answer to our question concerning the inner bond of unity of Pindar's poetry, which we posed at the beginning of this section.

We have tried to trace back some characteristic features of Pindar's art to the thoughts and purposes which underlie them. But neither the beauty and charm of his poetry nor its power and greatness can be grasped in the abstract, and we therefore turn back again in conclusion to some specimens of his poetry, which are among the last he wrote.

[25] The connections are often not readily visible, because Pindar only justifies by intimations his apparently abrupt changes of direction. But the connecting links which are missing in one place can be supplied from others. Pindar's trains of thought are constantly repeated, each time in a differently abbreviated form. A fundamental principle of his art is the inexhaustible variation on a few standard features, with which the reader becomes so familiar that he recognizes them under whatever mask.

8. PINDAR'S LAST POEMS

When Pindar wrote the ode to Theia he was about forty years old. His career as a poet lasted another thirty years and more. By the end of his life his powers as an artist, far from declining, had risen to greater heights.

Pindar's last dated epinician was written in 446 for a boy from Aegina who had won the prize for wrestling at the Pythian games. It was to men and boys of this Dorian island that Pindar had dedicated many of his finest poems and his deepest reflections.[1] What did he now in his old age have to say to Aegina and to the world, when for the last time he had to sing the praises of a victor and to set his fame in the universal context of values? (*Pyth.* 8, 1):

Kindly-hearted Peace, daughter of Justice, fairest ornament of cities, you who hold the master-keys both in counsel and in war, receive Aristomenes' honour for his Pythian victory. For you know how to do what is gentle and receive it with unfailing sureness of choice (*kairos*),

just as on the other hand, when a man fills his heart with pitiless rage, sternly you confront those of hostile heart[2] and with overmastering strength crush their arrogance to the dust. Porphyrio learned this lesson[3] when he roused you beyond measure to anger. The most welcome gain is that which one receives from the possession of one who gives it willingly;

but violence brings in time even the haughty to a fall. The hundred-headed Cilician Typhus did not escape you, nor did the king of the Giants; they were laid low by the thunderbolt and by the arrows of Apollo, who with friendly kindness received the son of Xenarces (Aristomenes), who is come crowned from Delphi with leaves from Parnassus and Dorian songs of joy.

This is the first triad of the ode. Its first and last words tell the world and posterity that Aristomenes the son of Xenarces has been favourably received by the Delphic god at the Pythian games (i.e. that he has been blessed with victory), and that he is now holding

---

[1] The following odes discussed above were addressed to Aeginetans: 'I am no bronze-caster' (above p. 430), 'One and the same is the origin of gods and of men' (p. 472), 'Elithyia, enthroned with the deep-minded Fates' (p. 482), 'Sublime Hora' (p. 483) and 'Mother of the sun, Theia having many names' (p. 485ff.). The full list of odes for Aeginetans is *Olymp.* 8; *Pyth.* 8; *Nem.* 4, 5, 6, 7, 8; *Isthm.* 5, 6, 8.

[2] κράτος is almost always, and regularly in Pindar, 'superiority' and 'conquering strength.' Consequently I read (although with some doubt) δυσμενέσιν after the parallel passage *Paean* 2, 21, where ἐχθροῖσι is the dative object of τραχὺς ὑπαντιάζει.

[3] I translate as if we had τὸ καί σε; I can make nothing of τὰν οὐδέ.

his festal procession into his native city of Aegina to the Dorian strains of Pindar's poetry.[4] The opening calls on the community to give a friendly welcome to Aristomenes and the honour that he brings with him.[5]

The city of Aegina is not, however, addressed under its own name and character, but Pindar addresses himself to the spirit that rules the citizens, the spirit of 'kindly-hearted Peace,' and the triad celebrates Peace as a 'power.'[6] By peace he means conciliation and harmony in contrast to hatred and party strife.[7] Harmony is the 'ornament' of cities, i.e. makes them prosper and have a fair appearance; she carries the 'master-keys' because only a régime at unity with itself possesses real authority. Harmony's authority is based not on strength but on justice, for she herself is a 'daughter of Justice.' Furthermore, mild Harmony is able 'with unfailing *kairos*,' i.e. with subtle tact and a sure feeling for what is proper to any given case, to strike her finger upon that which is equally acceptable to all interested parties.[8] But her judgment is equally sure when it becomes necessary to put down a determined rebel by main force.[9] Thus the inner nature of peace develops its own antithesis and complement in a Heraclitean manner. Mild by nature, she can also harden her

[4] For the expression 'gracious reception'='vouchsafing of victory' cf. Bacchyl. 11, 15; a similar phrase in Pindar, *Isthm.* 2, 18. The crowning is a consequence of Apollo's bestowing his grace, just as in *Olymp.* 7, 30 the settlement of Rhodes is a consequence of the murder, yet in both cases the cause and effect appear in the same clause: 'the man (now) celebrated found grace in Pytho'; 'the "subsequent" founder of Rhodes slew his great-uncle.' The construction is not really more abnormal than when we say, '*Pope* Leo XIII was *born* in 1810.'

[5] Cf. *Olymp.* 5, 1ff.; *Pyth.* 9, 73f.; *Nem.* 4, 11ff.

[6] In the Hellenistic period it became quite common to represent a city as a 'power,' in fact as the power of *Tyche*. This symbolized the fact that the prosperity of all members of the community was dependent on the various vicissitudes to which the city was exposed in the wavering course of politics great and small. For the equation of city and *Tychê* a model was provided by Pindar, *Olymp.* 12 (above p. 439).

[7] Cf. fr. 109: 'One must establish the community of citizens in a summer calm, must seek out the bright light of proud peace, uprooting from one's heart the angry spirit of faction, the bringer of poverty, a hateful fosterer of youth.' (In destructive party-strife the younger generation perishes, while peace, according to Hesiod, *WD* 228, is a 'good guardian of youth.')

[8] In *Olymp.* 8, 22 it is made one of the praises of Aegina that *Themis* (the norm in law and custom) is particularly honoured there; 'for in a matter that sways much in different directions, to decide with right judgment without diverging from *kairos* is a difficult undertaking.' Here *kairos* can be rendered as 'due measure.'

[9] Not grammatically, but according to the sense, *kairos* is to be understood in the antistrophe also, as we can infer from the parallel passage *Paean* 2, 30–34: 'If a man, in order to protect his friends, sternly confronts the foe, his exertion brings about peace, entering the fray with *kairos* (i.e. with proper choice).'

heart if she is unable otherwise to prevail; peace brings about peace through war. As examples from mythology Porphyrio and Typhus are brought forward, two monsters who in earliest antiquity rose up against the gods. The thought of Porphyrio's arrogant challenge draws in its train, according to archaic rules, its own antithesis: friendship and harmony. The pendulum then swings back to force, which lays the evildoer low with his own weapon—force. This is illustrated by the fall of Typhus, who was defeated in battle by Zeus with his thunderbolt and Apollo with his arrows. At the end the punishing Apollo changes into the benevolent god who makes the Aeginetan Aristomenes win the prize at the Pythian games.[10]

We pass over the following three triads. The fifth and last comes back to the victory gained by the boy Aristomenes as a wrestler, the event which motivated the poem (v. 81):

On four bodies did you throw yourself from above to do them hurt. For them the decision in the Pythian games fell out not in favour of a happy home-coming; no happy laughter about them awakened joy when they came home to their mothers; through the lanes, avoiding their enemies they stole homeward, wounded by the bite of misfortune.

He to whom recently great good luck has fallen soars up to the greatest bliss in high self-confidence on the wings of his distinctions (aretai); his mind dwells on things better than riches. For a little time our mortal joys blossom. Even so they are cast down and shattered by a turning aside of purpose.

Creatures of the day: what is man? What is he not? Man is a shadow in a dream. But when glory comes, sent by the gods, then a bright radiance and a happy existence is granted to men. Beloved mother Aegina, protect this city in its free course, with the help of Zeus, of mighty Aeacus, of Peleus, stout-hearted Telamon and Achilles.

The last triad also goes in opposites, this time with a dynamic heightened into grandeur. The strophe casts a harsh light on the pride displayed by the procession in honour of the returning victor, by the powerful contrast of the shame and humility with which the defeated contestants go sneaking home.[11] Nowhere else does Pindar so cruelly celebrate a victory;[12] we can detect the hard and bitter feeling of old age.

[10] See above p. 458 with n. 30.
[11] The reference to the boy's 'enemies' can be explained from the mutual hostility of cliques such as we read of in Theognis; the peaceful tranquillity for which Pindar praises Aegina was a rare phenomenon in other communities. In *Pyth.* 9, 93ff. the enemies of the victor are urged to forget their rancour and join in his praises.
[12] *Olymp.* 8, 67ff. is identical in its thought, but less direct in presenting the

The antistrophe brings in some general reflections. With a sharpness reminiscent of Archilochus[13] Pindar gives opposing pictures of joy and sorrow, whose swift interchange is the lot of every passionate and ambitious man—and with other men Pindar is not concerned. A recent victory fills him with joy and self-satisfaction swelling into a chimerical optimism; then his habits of thought swing back to their opposite, and they sink into a faint-hearted despondency.[14] It was a fundamental tenet of the archaic period that a change of outward circumstances brought about a radically new quality in man. At the beginning of the period a late epic writer and Archilochus (fr. 68) put it in the form that our thoughts and feelings make themselves like the day which Zeus sends us.[15]

The epode begins abruptly with the word which contains the essence of that view of human nature: 'creatures of the day'. As the day changes, so do we change; we are not really anything, since there is nothing into which we cannot at some time be changed: 'What is man, and what is he not?' Since we have no firm and enduring substance, we are dreaming shadows in a dreamer's mind.[16] This is expressed by Pindar in a verse which for weight and brevity has no rival even in his poetry. He then comforts his hearers again by swinging back to the brilliant fortune and delightful existence which a favourable day sent by the gods can bring to us—such a day as that which has now dawned for the young Aristomenes and the people of Aegina.[17] To conclude the poem, after the expression of joy comes the regular expression of fear lest evil befall, here a pious prayer for the

picture: 'He who, thanks to the grace of the daemon, but not lacking in his own manliness, thrust off upon the bodies of four boys (the burden of) bitter homecoming, contemptuous speech and a furtive homeward path.' The ode was composed fourteen years before the eighth Pythian, and is also for an Aeginetan.

[13] Cf. Archilochus fr. 67 (above p. 143), where we also find a contrast between the public rejoicing of the victor and the shrinking shame of the defeated.

[14] On the 'turnings' of the human γνώμα cf. fr. 214; that the γνώμα is that of the gods is less likely, considering the verbal expression and the context. For excess in confidence or despondency cf. Nem. 11, 29–32 (below p. 502); for ἐλπίς in the sense of an illusory hope see (e.g.) the material in F. M. Cornford, Thucydides Mythistoricus (1907) 167f.

[15] See above p. 134f.

[16] The conclusion that anything liable to change was unreal was developed to its ultimate consequences by Pindar's contemporary Parmenides. In his philosophy phenomena (and men along with them) are no more than phantoms (see above p. 353ff.).

[17] Pindar will not hear of any other consolation for the basic nothingness of man except that pride and rejoicing are very pleasant while they last. He does not seek to interfere with extremities of joy and sorrow, unlike Archilochus, who in the fragment cited above (n. 13) urges that they should be moderated (fr. 67): 'Do not rejoice nor be cast down too much.'

country's continued prosperity: 'May our mother Aegina, animated by the spirit of quiet and harmony in the community, may Zeus himself, her husband, together with the heroic sons and grandsons of them both, maintain the island in its freedom!' Pindar's prayer was not granted, for fifteen years later the Aeginetan community lost not only the last remains of its freedom, but its very existence, to the neighbouring great power, Athens. Pindar did not live to see it.

In this late poem there is no trace of calm and gentle exposition; the thought and emotion are brought out with elemental force, and the contrast between light and shade is sharper than ever. We find a like bitterness in a shorter ode from the same period, which was written to be performed at an official function in a provincial community. On the little island of Tenedos the new government was entering into office, which it was to hold for one year. At its head as *prytanis* was Aristagoras, a man still young and belonging to one of the patrician families. The solemnity which opened the governmental year was performed with sacrifice, prayer, a choral ode, and a festal libation in the *prytaneion* or town hall, which housed the 'hearth' (Greek *hestia*) of the community. In the home of the community, as in every private house, the hearth-goddess Hestia by immemorial usage received the first offering. It is with an invocation of Hestia that Pindar begins (*Nem.* 11):

> Daughter of Rhea, Hestia, you under whose care are the halls of cities, sister of Zeus most high and of Hera enthroned by his side, welcome with a blessing Aristagoras to your dwelling-place, blessing too his brothers in office about his radiant sceptre, them who, attending to your honour, concern themselves with Tenedos' welfare,

> honouring you with libations before all other deities, with the smoke of incense, while song and the lyre resound, and the commands of hospitable Zeus are discharged at the never-failing table. Let him carry through with acclaim his twelve months labours with uncorrupted heart!

> Among men I praise the good fortune of his father Hagesilas and the wondrous beauty and native fearlessness of Aristagoras. Yet he who enjoys blessings and surpasses others in beauty and has shown his might as the best in contests must remember that he is clothed in perishable members and that at the last he will be wrapped in earth.

> [*Second triad*] It is becoming for the citizens to praise him with good words and to adorn him in the honied tones of skilful songs. Sixteen shining victories in neighbouring games have crowned Aristagoras and his land with a glorious name, in the wrestling contest and the pancration proud of its fame.

Yet the hopes too hesitant of his parents forbade the boy's powers to be proven in the contests at Pytho and Olympia. Surely, by oath, I say, he would have returned from the Castalian spring (i.e. from Pytho) and from the wooded hills of Cronus (from Olympia) with greater honour than his rivals in the fight.

He would have celebrated in festal attire the four-yearly festival founded by Heracles (the Olympics), his hair bound with purple sprays of flowers. But many men are cast down from the possession of fortune by their hollow boasting, and many likewise, too greatly diffident of their powers, are made to stumble past the glory that is properly theirs by a spirit lacking in boldness, that drags them back by the arm.[18]

[*Third triad*] It would have been easy to trace the old Spartan blood in him, derived from Pisander who came with Orestes from Amyclae, bringing with him an Aeolian host with weapons of bronze, and to see his inheritance from his mother's Theban ancestor Melanippus. But excellences (*aretai*) that are handed down

bring powers to light alternately among the generations of men. Even so the dark soil of the firm earth does not bring forth its fruits in every turning year, and the trees do not bear fragrant blossoms in constant abundance, but changing with the occasion. According to a like rule destiny behaves

towards the human race, and Zeus has not placed in the hands of mortals any sure distinguishing mark. Nevertheless we indulge a lofty spirit and plan many deeds; for insolent hope holds our body in its yoke, and the spring of thoughtful foresight is beyond our reach. Moderate should be the gain that we pursue; insatiable desire breeds madness all the more violent.

The form given to the poem is unique. The language is simpler than elsewhere, the sentence-construction is uncommonly direct and regular for Pindar, and each of the three triads ends in the same way, on a dark and grave note.[19] No other poem is so accurately and consistently constructed; it is as if Pindar on this one occasion had let himself be influenced by the new classical spirit. But this is true only of the form, not of the thought.

The first strophe and antistrophe are addressed to a goddess; the

[18] The ironical bitterness of the happening—the self-mutilation, as it were, of a human existence—is made concrete in Pindar's language by a metaphor that turns into a sharp physical image: 'dragging back by the arm.' Here again the one concentrated picture comes in the middle of a passage devoid of imagery (cf. above p. 494 on *Olymp.* 7, 28f.); the nearest concrete expressions, before and after, are at a considerable distance and in different contexts (v. 28 the adornment of the victor's hair, and v. 35 'with weapons of bronze').

[19] In the performance, when the meaning and melody of the language were underlined by the corresponding music of the triads and the meaningful symbolism of dance and gesture, the effect must have been overwhelming.

epode finds the objects of its praise among men. A congratulatory address to Aristagoras' father and the *prytanis* himself[20] leads to an admonition beginning with a subordinate clause to this effect: 'When to anyone are granted such blessings as to him. . . .' As the main clause we expect (judging from parallel passages[21]) something like: 'then he must wish for no more, having reached the heights of human felicity; all beyond that is set apart for the gods.' We are not prepared for such a cruel twist and such a cutting contrast as the close of the triad brings.

The new triad begins afresh with a note of rejoicing. The assembled citizens are called upon to join in the praises of Aristagoras as sung by Pindar. The poet is able to specify a considerable number of victories, but they have all been in insignificant local contests. Aristagoras' parents did not venture to enter him for the pan-Hellenic games, since they had no confidence in his being successful. Pindar avers on his oath that they misjudged the matter; it is as common for human beings to make mistakes of this as of the opposite kind. From this point on the poem is dominated by the ideas of excessive diffidence and overbold self-confidence of wonderful possibilities and the uncertainty of their achievement, of the lure of the unattainable, of longings that cannot be laid to rest.

At the opening of the third triad Pindar hails Aristagoras as being descended from great heroic figures and as the inheritor of noble qualities. But (he then tells us) one can never know for sure in which generation or in which individual the noble ancestry will manifest itself; for it is the law governing all earthly things that the finest qualities often remain dormant. Thus no prediction is possible, as indeed the power to judge and plan correctly in advance has been denied to mortals in general. Yet we still indulge ourselves in grandiose hopes and projects.[22] Our desires and ambitions are like those of the gods, although divine knowledge and understanding are not ours. Such notions as these had been expressed by Pindar before,[23]

[20] The grammatical object of the felicitation is first the father, then the good qualities of the son. This peculiar construction recurs identically (apart from the order), in Herod. 1, 31, 1: Ἀργεῖοι μὲν περιστάντες ἐμακάριζον τῶν νεηνιέων τὴν ῥώμην, αἱ δὲ Ἀργεῖαι τὴν μητέρα αὐτῶν, οἵων τέκνων ἐκύρησε.

[21] *Isthm.* 5, 14ff.; *Nem.* 9, 46f.; *Olymp.* 3, 42ff. etc.

[22] I do not properly understand why Pindar speaks of the 'body' in v. 45. The image of binding is occasionally used by him in the sense of coercion in general, not merely holding still, but also driving along (cf. *Pyth.* 4, 71; 3, 54; cf. also Ixion bound to the wheel in *Pyth.* 2, 40).

[23] In *Nem.* 6, 1–12 we find the same ideas, including the reference to periodical infertility of the soil (above p. 472f.). Another and a strikingly close parallel to the end of *Nem.* 11 occurs in the fragment of an unknown Hermolochus preserved in Stobaeus 4, 36, 66 (4, 2 p. 845 Hense).

and so early a poet as Semonides of Amorgos had expressed them in his pedestrian way (above p. 201). What is novel and surprising is the tragic intensification at the end of Pindar's poem: 'We ought to control ourselves, yet no desire burns so fiercely as the senseless longing for the unattainable.'[24] The aged poet ends his sombre ode with a reference to consuming burning passion.

Although couched in general terms, the concluding words sound like an outburst of personal feeling. In praising the beauty of the young *prytanis*, Pindar may have had in mind Aristoxenus' brother, the boy Theoxenus.[25] Like Ibycus, Pindar remained to the last susceptible to the charms of handsome and noble young men. The closing thought of the eleventh Nemean is picked up again by the opening of a poem (fr. 123) to Theoxenus of Tenedos:

Only in due season and measure (according to *kairos*) should one pluck the bloom of passionate longings, o my soul, in accordance with one's age;[26] but if a man has seen the love-light darting from Theoxenus' eyes and is not consumed with passion, his dark heart has been forged of steel or iron

in a slow fire. Despised by Aphrodite of the ensnaring eyes, he either toils for the sake of gold, or is a slave to female haughtiness.[27] But I, thanks to the goddess, melt like the wax of the holy bee

under the bite of warmth, when I look upon the fresh beauty of boys' bodies. So it seems that Peitho (persuasion) has taken up her abode also in Tenedos together with Charis (attractiveness), blessing the son of Hagesilas (Theoxenus).

We are told that it was at Argos, in the gymnasium, amidst the youths exercising themselves, that Pindar peacefully breathed his last, with his head on the knees of this very Theoxenus of Tenedos. The thought which legend has cast into this mould is thus put into words by Greek tradition: 'He was not only a poet of genius, but a man beloved of the gods.'[28]

---

[24] *Quod non licet acrius urit* is Ovid's formulation (*Amores* 2, 19, 3); the apophthegm no doubt had become proverbial. The last sentence of Pindar's ode is often strangely misunderstood.

[25] For the general context see Wilamowitz, *Pindaros* p. 430.

[26] On the meaning of *kairos* and time of life in this context see above p. 474 n. 11.

[27] The interpretation of the sentence is uncertain: a word is missing in the transmission, driven out by the repetition of ψυχρά(ν) from v. 4. On the contempt felt for heterosexual love see above p. 175f.

[28] Cf. Suidas s.v. Πίνδαρος; Valerius Maximus 9, 12 ext. 7, and the *Vita* p. 21, Drachmann.

IX

Retrospect and Prospect

Pindar died about 445, after producing poetry for at least fifty-two years. In the art that he had practised with incomparable mastery he found no successor of a like stature; the day of choral lyric as the leading poetical form was over.[1] But it was more than a literary genre that died with Pindar: a whole age became dumb when his lips closed. The archaic period of Greek literature found in him its last great exponent and its consummation.

In Pindar's poetry archaic art reached its pinnacle. The subtlety and complexity of the form are late archaic; so is the luxurious ostentation of artistry in works of art. The pomp of language is a mature archaic feature: the thoughts are, as it were, draped in the folds of a costly robe, hung with finely-wrought adornments. Essentially archaic too is the animated course of his poems. The opening is abrupt and striking; then come constant changes of pace; he walks slowly in contemplation; then rushes furiously on; strides out with vigour, each step opening a new perspective; takes a zig-zag course between the attraction and repulsion of opposites; circles slowly round, to find himself at the end where he first began; or in one swift leap attains his distant goal. The basic principle of these choral songs is not the classical one of architectonic strength and visible construction, but the archaic one of fluid movement and development of numerous figures, following after and out of one another. In Pindar this play of form is made the vehicle of an important content; its changeable course reflects the active progress and completion of the ideas, makes them develop out of each other according to the sense, connect with one another or turn back upon themselves. But what is greatest and most personal in Pindar's poetry is of a spiritual nature: its dignity, now serious, now serene; its wilful

[1] On the fading of interest in Pindar's poetry and in choral lyric generally among the Athenian public of the later fifth century see J. Irigoin, *Histoire du texte de Pindare* (Paris, 1952) 12f.

abruptness, and then, on occasion, its heavy sweetness; and lastly, often restrained but always detectable, its titanic power.

Thus at its end the archaic epoch brought forth a literary phenomenon which displayed that period, already marked for extinction, in its most powerful and brilliant development, self-assured, clear and entirely pure. Unlike his Athenian contemporary Aeschylus, Pindar was and remained entirely an archaic Greek. In those tendencies which during his lifetime powerfully contributed to the advance of the human spirit he took no part at all. For the teachings of speculative cosmologists he had no sympathy, as he had no interest in enlightenment, in any empirical rationalizing of the world-picture. His was not a soul that could poke and peer and find fault: he was interested only in what he could admire. A pious and respectful adherent of tradition, he felt himself the chosen voice of the Greek race when he bore witness to the beliefs and purposes of the age that was to die with him.

It is not unique in history that a movement in its final development should in some respects have become the opposite of what it was at the beginning. Archilochus helped to introduce the archaic manner of thought and paved the way for lyric poetry by a revolutionary turn to the solid reality of primary and immediate data. The *I*, the *here* and *now*, were upheld with brutal rigour as the whole content of existence. Pindar replaced the first person by the impersonal 'one' of society; the transitory and the unique were to him no more than illustrations of the universal and eternal. He selects, interprets, re-arranges, praises and glorifies: the hatred and carping of Archilochus is repugnant to him (*Pyth*. 2, 55). While at the beginning reality, starting with physical objects, was on principle accepted in all its earthiness, now, starting from physical appearance, it was equally on principle denatured and spiritualized. Parallel with this movement was the swing from deliberately naive directness and simplicity in expression to a challenging indirectness and complication. By now the epoch had run the gamut in this respect from one extreme to the other. The end had been reached, and from here no road leads farther.

From the regions to which Pindar had soared, from the thin air and burning light which the value of values cast over these dizzy heights, no path led to a further resting-place. The age that followed did not set out from this point, but from a station much nearer to earth. This position was established by a greater sobriety of thought, such as had been long represented by such men as Xenophanes and Simonides. Empirical enquiry widened the intellectual horizon and corrected many errors. Men took their bearings again in a richer and more variegated world; they became more versatile and practical. Instead of thinking in terms of mutually exclusive polar opposites, they preferred to quantify the one or the other, or looked for the golden mean. Thus the notion of the two social classes, the 'good' and the 'bad' became an anachronism; ambition and display of wealth came to be regarded as arrogance, and the democratic ideals of the middle-class virtues and proprieties were put into practice; dress became simple. Criticism and discussion replaced the unquestioning acceptance of the norms represented by the class which set the tone of society; intellectual ability came to be respected. Men learned to distinguish and analyse what they had formerly viewed only as a whole. Probably the most consequential of all the innovations was the definitive division of man into body and soul. Out of these and many other elements came gradually the classical ways of living and thinking.

From its predecessor the classical age took over and developed a great deal; but there were other things which, in accordance with a harsh law of history, it carelessly let fall or deliberately rejected and destroyed in order to fulfil its own being. Much that was valuable perished in this way. In our treatment of the archaic epoch our main purpose was to bring out those elements of value which were realized in that period as in no other. We have sought to understand the epoch on its own merits, as an independent, closed system, distinguished from the epic age which preceded it and the classical which followed. Historical treatment can indeed make a great contribution to the interpretation of a phenomenon by bringing to light the connecting threads which bind it to what went before and what was to come after. We have traced many such threads, but we have not chosen as the principal elements those which appear most conspicuously in the classical age; only pseudo-history can result from fixing our gaze elsewhere than in the centre of the picture. Any view of a subject can only give order and clearness to that towards which it is directed; everything else it distorts or conceals. We miss the true nature of the archaic age if we see it essentially as an earlier stage, not yet fully developed, of the classical period.

Within the archaic epoch each personality and each movement has its own special character and its special relations with others; and during the two centuries that it endured, the archaic mind underwent many changes.[2] Every time that we turned to the productions

[2] We have also met, even within the archaic period, not only precursors of classicism such as Simonides (see e.g. p. 311f., 321f., 323f.) and Xenophanes (e.g. p. 328–30, 333, 336f.), but also classical traits of thought and form coming before their time, e.g. in a fragment of Solon (p. 226f.) and in the poetry of Ibycus (p.

of a new poet or thinker, we found ourselves transported to a new intellectual climate; yet an underlying uniformity is there if one views this period as a whole. As soon as one has recognized some characteristic elements of structure (as the habit of thinking and feeling in polar opposites) and of form (as the continuous smooth movement of thought), one begins to detect them as determining factors throughout the epoch.

The literary monuments of the archaic age have revealed to us a mode of being that is in its own way complete and which is able to give meaning to a man's living and dying. It is one of the noblest primal images and patterns of humanity that are known to us. It has been rendered intelligible and instructive through that extraordinary gift which the Greeks possessed, the gift not merely of giving form and content to their own existence, but of knowing what men are and what they do, and of expressing it with equal clarity and beauty.

285f., 290f.) and Anacreon (p. 294, 298). Historical epochs always in some measure overlap.

X

Indices

Index A: Systematic Index

The index presents some part of the contents of the book in a systematic arrangement: consequently the order does not always correspond to that of the book, which followed a more historical presentation. I have made no attempt to be exhaustive.

The numbers which follow colons refer to the pages. 'Th.' denotes the Theognidean corpus.

509

Opposite forces. [-3.] Things of note from other authors. [-3.1.] Positive. [-3.2.] Negative.

[5.7.] *Areté*, and 'good' or 'bad' men; the 'beautiful' and the 'ugly'. [-1] Typical definitions of *areté* and of 'good' and 'bad'. [-2.] The doctrine of Simonides. [-3.] Further individual points. [-4.] The 'beautiful' and the 'ugly'.

[5.8] Good and bad luck. [-0.] Expressions for 'good luck' in Pindar. [-1.] In what does good luck consist? [-2.] Ill fortune. [-3.] Good and ill fortune as gifts of the gods and powers, of destiny or chance. [-4.] Deserved ill fortune.

[1.] CHRONOLOGY AND PERIODS OF EARLY GREEK LITERATURE

From about 530 B.C. onwards we can date some few authors fairly confidently; but before that time fixed dates are almost wholly lacking, and we must be content with rather doubtful dating of authors.

'Early Greek' literature here means that which preceded in time the 'classical' literature, i.e. up to about 450 B.C. Early Greek literature begins with the 'epic' period, from which the *Iliad* and *Odyssey* have been preserved: 3 f. About 650 B.C. there is a violent change ushering in the 'archaic' epoch (c. 650–c. 450 B.C.), with lyric as the leading branch of literature: 93, 132–136. About 550 B.C. a new trend sets in, in which lyric ('late' and 'latest' archaic lyric) shows substantially different traits: 238, 280.

The literature of the archaic period displays a characteristic manner of thought and a characteristic style: 507, see below under [3.], [4.] and [5.]. But the scheme just outlined of a sequence of different and distinct periods cannot claim to be perfectly valid. The war-elegies of Callinus and Tyraeus (cap. IV.b.) and the so-called Homeric Hymns carry on the epic tradition; original thinkers like Hesiod in the Theogony: 96 f., the later philosophers, and in general those whose writings are concerned more with things than with literary art, like Hesiod in the *Works and Days*, Solon: 220 f., 236 f., or the younger of the nascent sciences (cap. VII.b.), emancipate themselves in particular features from the spirit of their age and from the 'historical development'. Fore-runners of the classical period like Simonides: 323 f., and Xenophanes: 332 f., 336 f., have more of the coming age in them than their dates (c. 557–468 and c. 570–475) would suggest. On the other hand Pindar, who was active down to 446, adhered uncompromisingly to the archaic tradition: 504 f. (perhaps with one exception: 502 f). Solon, whose poetry in other respects bears the typical stamp of the archaic period, expressed himself once (c. 585) in thoroughly classical forms: 226 f.; about 530, in the persons of Ibycus: 285, 290 f., and Anacreon: 294, representatives of classical ways of thought and expression appear on the archaic scene.

Aeschylus and the other dramatists of the first half of the fifth century had to be excluded from this book for compelling practical reasons, although in fact they should come within its scope: 399 *f.*

[2.] LITERARY GENRES

[2.1.] Heroic epic.

[2.1.1.] *Function of epic.* The epics served for entertainment and edification during long hours of leisure: 8–11, 21 f., 557; they aimed at arousing terror and pity by telling of 'sufferings': 14 f., 84.

[2.1–2.] *Development of the epic* in the colonial East: 25 f. Origin of epic subject-matter: 44–53. Epics and cycles: 6, 13, 17 f., 22–25.

[2.1–3.] *The singers of epic:* 6–25. Thanks to the 'Muse' (= tradition and inspiration) the singer is able to sing of the activities of the gods also, and thus has a wider horizon than the heroes of whom he sings: 53 with n. 1. Epic action takes place on two stages, on earth and in heaven: 53–56, 64–68. Epic recitals were preceded by a hymn to a god: 246–250.

[2.1–4.] *Form and language of epic.* Verse: 30–34. Linguistic form: 25 f., 27 f. Formulae: 28–30, 32–33. Speeches: 39 f., 62–64. Similes: 40–44, 305³. Linear representation: 41. Openings of lays: 14 f., 85 f.

[2.1–5.] *Stylization in epic.* Epic does not simply and straightforwardly represent the knowledge and thought of the epoch in which it was composed; rather, its content, form and attitudes are deliberately stylized on literary grounds according to certain definite tendencies, particularly in the *Iliad*, from which some considerable constituents of contemporary life were excluded: 5, 34 f., 36 f., 39. Epic narrative affected a cool objectivity of narrative, under which the feelings and reflexions of the singer were concealed; questions and problems are left untouched by the narrative: 36 f.; the personal element is brought out onesidedly in the world of the gods: 53–56, 58–62, 63 f. The heroic figures are not only made typical and given a monumental simplicity: 34, 84 f., but romantically made independent of common reality: 36 f. Another romantic idea is that the old times of which the poet sings were greater than the present day, and that men were bolder and stronger: 35 f. In consequence the epics archaize in representation of culture and material objects: 21, 35, 44–47.

But this selection and artificial stylization is not carried through completely. In the first place, the archaizing tendency was partly counteracted by the considerable advance in civilization by the time epic received its final form: 36, when it gave more humane traits to its heroes: 51 f., and made them more rational: 81 f.; the heroes of the epic which developed in the colonial east were so advanced compared with those of the ancient sagas of the mainland that Hesiod, in his retrospect of human history postulates not one but two ages of heroes—a brutal 'age of bronze' and a 'god-like age of heroes' of whom the epics speak: 120. Secondly, in the form of seemingly objective reporting epic poetry does find room for hints and interpretations: 37–39; thirdly the speeches of epic characters are relatively free from the usual stylistic constraint: 39 f., 62–64; as also are the similes: 40.

In the more realistic *Odyssey* stylistic fetters are generally loosened: 85–87, 93, although this poem too has a marked romantic element: 128, 135 f.

[2.1–6.] *Developments in epic.* In each epic recitation the singer came to grips anew with the traditional material and made greater or lesser changes in form and content: 8, 12 f., 15–17; even when the epics were already written down, they remained to some extent fluid: 23–25. What we possess is only the final stage, in which all levels from oldest to newest exist side by side or overlapping: 51 f. This applies to language also: 27. It is therefore unlikely that any old section should have been preserved for us line for line in its original form. The content changed by accretion of new material and by the new treatment and modernizing of the old: 47, 50 f. The singers regarded their innovations not as deliberate invention but as an intuitive interpretation of the tradition: 18, 21, 57 f., 66 f., 70 f., 73. The story was enriched by introduction of new minor characters, the main characters were differentiated, motivation was altered or improved: 17 f.; offensive features of the story were mitigated: 50–53; scenes expressing character or situation make the presentation more graphic: 18 f., 37 f., 51. A new animation could be given to elements fixed by immemorial tradition: 18 f., 66 f., and the poet of the *Patroclea* wrestles with his hero's destiny: 74 f. In the *Odyssey* a new ideal of humanity achieves ascendancy: 85 f., 88 f.; this change of outlook is projected backward into the epic narrative, *see under* [4.2–2.]. In its content, style and attitude the *Odyssey* is very different from the *Iliad*: 85–93.

[2.1–7.] *Construction of the epics in general.* The story consists in the main of a series of episodes which the singers put in or left out as they chose and related in such sequence as they chose, often with very loose connexion: 25; a framework which might itself be variable held a number of episodes more or less firmly together: 24, 50 f. Although there were always slight contradictions, the epics remained unitary in the main features of their story: 17 f., 24 f., 89 f., since individual innovations either failed to establish themselves or became the common property of the bards, who in some measure reconciled the new and the traditional material: 21, 24, 133³.

[2.1–8.] *Decline of epic poetry.* Epic as a literary form lost its raison d'être when the romantic admiration for ancient valour and violence (:34 f.) gave way to the newer ideal of a practical, adaptable and more human type of man: 85–90, 93; when men ceased to project themselves unreservedly into the actions and words related by epic and accepted by them as true: 79–81, 84 f., and began to be reserved, many-valued and unsure of themselves: 90–93; and when they no longer believed in an unalterable individual character, but in one that changed with changing circumstances ('ephemeral'): 133–136.
For Hesiod's didactic epics the reader is referred to the text of cap. III.

[2.2.] Lyric (*the term here embraces monodic and choral lyric, elegy and iambus*).

[2.2–1.] *Overlap of lyric genres:* 170³.

[2.2–2.] *Function and significance of lyric poetry* vary considerably, since the medium lends itself to various purposes: for detail see the relevant sections of the text, where we discuss the function and significance of early monodic lyric in general: 151; the poetry of Archilochus (which contributed to the victory of a new idea of human nature and a new scale of values): 134–151; Alcman's choral odes: 168–170; Sappho's songs: (e.g.) 171 f., 176, 187 f.; those of Alcaeus: (e.g.) 199; the poetry of Solon: 218–223, 234³⁵, 236 f.; the monodies of Anacreon: 291–303 passim; the choral lyrics of Simonides: 323 f., 434–436; Pindar's choral lyrics: (e.g.) 428–431, 488–490. No deep significance in Bacchylides: 426. Poetry aiming only at entertainment: 200, 207 (Semonides), 214, 216 f. (Hipponax).

[2.2–3.] *Early lyric.* The rise of lyric goes hand in hand with the recognition of the impermanence of human nature (see under 5.5.): 134 f. (Archilochus), and with a shift of interest from the past, the remote and the strange to the here, the now and the self: 133–140 (Archilochus), 210 f. (Archilochus, Sappho, Mimnermus), cf. also 289 (Ibycus); from public pomp to private intimacy: 138 f. (Archilochus), 185–188 (Sappho), 229 f., 232³¹ (Solon), cf. also 407¹⁴ (Th.). At first its sights are set on immediate actuality: 177 f., 186 f. (Sappho), 199 (Alcaeus), *see under* [3.1–1.] and [4.1–1.]; but it soon begins to go further afield: 187 etc. The requirement of nearness to life leads in time to domestication and triviality: 200, 280; and in the end to a temporary surrender of poetry, which capitulates in the face of reality: 238 f.

[2.2–4.] *Later lyric*. When lyric starts on its second career (c. 530 B.C.), it has become elevated and fastidious: 280. The poetry of Ibycus tends towards majesty: 283 f., and that of Anacreon towards elegance: 291–300.

[2.2–5.] *The self in lyric poetry*. Greek lyric, even the monodic lyric, is not a soliloquy but an address to others, on things that are of importance to others as well as to oneself. Thus the person who experiences is often meant not as an individual but as a type, and the person who judges does not express individual views or feelings, but tells us how we ought to judge or feel, e.g.: 151^{50} (Archilochus), 151 (general), 196 (Alcaeus), 294, 295, 298 (Anacreon), 309 (Simonides), 410^{22}, 422 (Th.), 475^{12} (Pindar).

[2.2–6.] *Choral lyric*.

[2.2–6.1.] *Choral lyric in general*. The poet composes a new melody for each new ode: 160, in which department Alcman took inspiration from birdsong: 162; at the rehearsals and performance he acted as choirmaster; the chorus was composed of trained amateurs in festal attire: 160, 283, 425 f.; they sang the text and interpreted it at the same time by dancing and eloquent gestures: 160^1 (thus the ode does not 'exist', but 'happens', corresponding to the archaic style of a continuous flow in many various figures, *see under* [3.3.]). The chorus-master with his lyre gave them the beginning, the melody, rhythm and time: 453 (opening of Pindar's first Pythian); the *aulos*-accompaniment was provided by professional musicians: 162. During rehearsals the choristers could take an active part in the working out of the ode: 162 f., 166^{20}, and they certainly had the opportunity to make a deeper study of the difficult texts, perhaps to ask the poet himself for elucidation (so also probably the members of tragic choruses): 160. Professional poets mostly wrote to order for a fee (so-called 'guest-gift'): 432 f. (Pindar), 434 f. (Simonides). If he did not train the chorus himself, he sent the manuscript to the place concerned: 431 f., 467 f. (Bacchylides fr. 20, Pindar fr. 124), and reckoned on a competent rehearsal and performance with the help of local talent: 437–439 (Pindar *Olymp.* 11). Occasionally an individual might sing a choral ode for his own pleasure: 429 f. When the archaic period was over, the independent choral lyric rapidly died out: 505^1.

[2.2–6.2] *Varieties of choral lyric*. Opportunities for performance of choral odes arose spontaneously; otherwise they were easily found or invented: 429. The purpose for which the ode was intended dictated its extent, structure and style: 470^8, as also the character and instrumentation (?) of the music: 456 f., the type of dancing and the presentation. Thus there were odes for religious ceremonies, e.g. the dedication of an offering to a god: 166 (Alcman, for a chorus of girls), 469 (Pindar), and there were songs of prayer: 480 (Pindar); dirges (threnoi): 304–307, 317 f., 319 f. (Simonides); songs for drinking-parties: 467–469 (Bacchylides and Pindar), and many others (e.g.: 501, Pindar). The best known to us, because more of them have survived, are the victory odes to celebrate a victory in the pan-Hellenic games: 429–437 (Simonides and Pindar; p. 434 on the origin of this genre); they were sung in procession at the homecoming of the victor: 429, or at other victory celebrations: 453 (Pindar, *Pyth.* 1, which combines the victory celebration with the dedication of a newly established city community). There were also choral odes which comprised a narrative from mythology in lyrical form:

280–282 (Stesichorus), 450–453 (Bacchylides, from whom we have several such 'dithyrambs'); cf. a similar phenomenon in the monodic lyric of Alcaeus: 197 f., which is hard to understand.

[2.2–6.3.] *Choral lyric—miscellaneous*. Particularly impressive treatment given to the openings of poems: 471[1]. A short ode has its beginning fitting on to the end again, so as to repeat *ad lib.*, so that the spectators of a slowly moving procession would be able to hear the whole: 429[6] (Pindar, *Nemean* 2). Unexpected twist at the end of an ode: 452 (Bacchylides *Dith.* 17). The ode violates the dramatic illusion and speaks of its own origin: 162 (Alcman), 431 f., 437 f. etc. (Pindar). Strophic responsion subject matter in Alcman: 165 f., triadic responsion in Pindar: 449[20] (*Pyth.* 9), 494[21] (*Olymp.* 7), 502 (*Nem.* 11). Five classes of themes in victory odes: 440, 449 f., 461 f. The question of unity posed: 433 f., 449 f., and answered: 487 f., 495 f.

[2.3.] Philosophy.

[2.3–1.] *Apocryphal notions*. An amorphous mass of world- and nature-myths, mostly very primitive, was in existence in the epic period: 97[2], 102 notes 13 and 14. These myths were developed or modified in oral tradition, but sometimes also served as the substratum for literary purposes: 254[5]. In written works such apocryphal speculations turn up in Hesiod: 96–99, Alcman: 163–165, 252 f., Pherecydes: 243 f. and Acusilaus: 347 f. *See also under* [4.2–2.1.].

[2.3–2.] *Philosophy as literature*. The history of Greek philosophy as literature begins not with Anaximander but with Hesiod: 108[30], who set out in a mythical form ideas partly inherited and partly original: cap. III.b. and p. 114 f. (*on the mythical form see under* [4.2.]), including a remarkably mature ontology: 102–107. Conceptions utilized by Hesiod had a part to play in later philosophy: 262[22], 360[30]. In the early sixth century philosophy became separated from myth: 252–256, with the exception of the regression seen in Pherecydes and Acusilaus (see above [–1.]).

[2.3–3.] *The primary aim of the 'natural philosophers'* was rather an intuitive metaphysic than a search for physical principles on the basis of which nature could be interpreted; a metaphysic of postulates, applying itself to the nature of the universe and the nature of man without distinction: 255–258, 389 f. It was presumed that one and the same order must be valid for nature and for human life; moral norms were included: 131[32], so that (e.g.) Anaximander postulated a 'cosmic justice' (G. Vlastos): 266 f., *see under* [4.5–2.] and [5.1–2.]. The thinkers began and ended with a metaphysical knowledge by which the world and its course, including human life, could be explained at a single blow: 256 f. There was even a depreciation of mechanical nature in Xenophanes (in contrast to the power of God): 333 f., and in Heraclitus (in contrast to the Logos): 378–381. On the other hand, the system of Anaximenes, if we can believe our sources, was one-sidedly mechanistic: 267–270.

[2.3–4.] *The philosophical book*. Each thinker put his system briefly into a book: 257. The books were widely disseminated and found interested readers: 258, but were primarily intended to serve the author as a basic text for oral presentation with explanations and discussions on the doctrines (thus in Plato's *Parmenides* Zeno reads out his own book and discusses individual sections with Socrates): 257[9], 354 f., 371. The books were generally apodictic in tone: 98; but natural phenomena and observations were also brought to bear in confirmation of the theory: 264 f. (Anaximander), 268 f. (Anaximenes), 334 (Xenophanes), 362 (Parmenides

fr. 14 and 15), 390 (Heraclitus fr. 117). Similarly theories were supported by
mental experiment: 265 (Anaximander), 330 f., 332 f. (Xenophanes). So far as
we know, it was Parmenides who took the greatest pains to support his doctrine by
argument.

[2.3–5.] *Our materials for reconstructing the philosophical systems are very far from being
satisfactory.* The 'doxographical' tradition, i.e. a tradition in which the elements
of doctrine in the pre-Socratics were catalogued at second and third hand, was
never intended as real history of philosophy and cannot be treated as such. It
takes the doctrines of philosophers before Aristotle and applies them to Aristotelian
problems, selecting them and distorting them on this basis: 258 f. Examples of
misleading doxographical reports: 335[18] (on Xenophanes, this time going back
as far as Plato): 361[31], (on Parmenides, going back to Theophrastus). Our
knowledge of philosophical doctrines is only trustworthy insofar as we possess
pieces of the original text and can rightly understand them, thanks to fortunate
but all too infrequent (:260[18]) accidents (:350[1]). An example of an important fact
not mentioned by the doxographical tradition: 265 f. (Anaximander). Furthermore, the doxographers at best only give us the dry bones of the doctrines, while
original texts give us some indication of how the philosopher's mind worked:
362[32], 367 f. (Parmenides). Anecdotes of the philosophers: 272[35].

The philosophical systems themselves are not given in this index; some references under
[4.6–3.] *and* [4.7–4.].

[2.4.] Mutual influence of the various literary genres.

The lyric poet Simonides and the rhapsode, philosopher and theologian
Xenophanes were working at the same time in the same reforming spirit: 325.
The empiricism of Xenophanes keeps company with the empiricism of contem-
porary medicine, geography and historiography: 339–340. Working out of a
philosophical idea in later medical theory: 363[37]. Pindar influenced by the
thought of Heraclitus: 471 f.
   Ideas in poets as precursors of philosophical theories: 187 (Sappho/Protagoras);
266–267 (Solon/Anaximander); 268 (Solon/Anaximenes); 363[37] (*Odyssey* and
Archilochus/Parmenides); 556 f. (Pindar/Plato).
   Philosophical notions occurring in lyric poets: 163–165, 253 f. (Alcman),
205–206, 261 (Semonides).
   For our understanding of the period and its ideas it is advantageous to let the
philosophy throw light on the other literature and vice versa, e.g.: 206, 377–379,
on things conceived in dynamic terms (in philosophy and literature) *see under*
[4.6.]; on the habit of thinking in opposites *see under* [4.7.].

[3.] SOME CHARACTERISTIC FEATURES OF ARCHAIC STYLE

[3.1.] The subject matter.

[3.1–1.] The presentation is mainly concerned with primary data (*see under*
[4.1–1.]), e.g.: 167, 169 (Alcman), 176 f. (Sappho). This applies particularly
to the earlier part of the period; in Hesiod we find a dryer objectivity than in
Homeric epic: 126; in Archilochus' case one can speak figuratively of selfportraiture
in heroic nakedness: 150 (cf.: 138).

[3.1–2.] From Archilochus onwards a large part is played by physical objects,
such as clothing, ornaments, equipments, etc. (but not just to give a more vivid

picture; the objects represent their function and the forces that dwell in them, *see under* [4.6–2.]: 165–168 (Alcman), 171, 174 f. (Sappho), 188 f., 194 (Alcaeus fr. 350), 299²⁴, 294, 300–301 (Anacreon fr. 388); cf. also Solon fr. 26 (not mentioned in text).

[3.1–3.] *Lengthy enumerations.* Alcman has lists of geographical names: 161 f.; of eleven heroes: 163; of ten girls: 165; Alcaeus gives an inventory of his arms and armour: 189; Sappho consoles her friend at parting with an enumeration of the pleasures which they had enjoyed together: 179.

Writers were not content with a general formula, but listed each individual thing. Semonides describes exhaustively nine types of bad wives: 202–204, and lists five areas in which human hopes suffer disappointment: 201; similarly Solon devotes twelve distichs to showing that in all walks of life human effort cannot be sure of success, and that in deprivations and sorrows we tread the path of illusion: 235–236. In order to declare that too much importance is attached to the national sporting contests, Xenophanes twice runs through the entire Olympic program, and separately lists all the various honours paid to victors: 329. In Pindar lists of individual high virtues represent worthiness in general: 459, 459³⁶, 471, 487, 491.

[3.1–4.] A more elegant method than writing a catalogue of indeterminate length is to represent a totality by a triad of concrete entities: 185–186 (Sappho fr. 16, first strophe); 194 (Alcaeus fr. 338, rain, storm, forest; fire, wine, pillow); 209 (Mimnermus fr. 1, 3 and again vv. 6–8) 209 f. (Mimn. fr. 2, 11–15); 229 f. (Solon fr. 14, silver, gold and land, plus draught-animals and horses, contrasted with comfort in belly, sides and legs, plus love-making with girls and boys); six triads in the fragments of Anacreon: 293 f. with n. 8; 437 (Pindar, wind rain and poetry).

[3.1–5.] *Depiction of scenes.* The nature of the matter being described (event, attitude or situation) is represented by a word-picture conveyed with the utmost power of expression: 124–126 (Hesiod), 141 f. (Archilochus), 156–159 (Tyrtaeus), 176–180, 184 (Sappho), 251 (Homeric hymns), 281 f. (Stesichorus), 292–293, 295, 300 f. (Anacreon), 315–318 (Simonides), 326 (Xenophanes), 431, 445, 446, 453 f., 469 f., 494–495 (Pindar).

[3.1–6.] *Later trend away from things and actions.* Late archaic style emancipated itself from a close concern with physical objects and other primary data. Simonides, with his strongly intellectual tendencies, turns what had once been palpable realities into airy notions and juggles brilliantly with them; the purpose is transfiguration: 320 f.; his victory odes play with their theme: 435 f.—Pindar subordinates the given realities to the idea of value, and onesidedly makes them appear in a uniform golden light of moral worth: what does not fit this treatment is left outside his poetry: 485–497.—The didactic sayings of the Theognidea, which could apply equally well to a number of situations, for this reason seldom go into special details: 422 f.

[3.2.] The diction of archaic literature and the style of performance.

In the seventh and early sixth century Archilochus (:149) and Sappho (e.g.: 176–180) speak a language as simple and unassuming as that of prose; it is as if the things themselves turned into words without any help from the poet, although in fact the material is transmuted into the purest poetry. The language of Alcaeus is equally direct, but in him the transformation of the raw material into poetry is sometimes imperfectly accomplished, sometimes not accomplished at all: 199, 193 f. In the last third of the sixth century the style of presentation favoured by Anacreon is charming by reason of its lively but at the same time elegant play with situations and feelings; his sociable and unconstrained poetry has an undertone of subtle and friendly irony directed against others (:300 f.) or against himself (:293, 297 f.). (Irony against oneself occurred as early as Alcman: 161, 214.) In the comic choliambics of Hipponax naturalism of language is forced in the direction of the vulgar and commonplace; side by side with a lively scorn for others we find clowning with himself as butt: 214.—In elegy the traditions of epic form do not permit any great naturalism of diction.—Choral lyric had a poetical language all its own, which it followed as a matter of principle, and which moved further and further away from everyday language. Nevertheless, in Simonides, the fore-runner of classicism, only the narrative sections (:315–317) are set forth in the full typical tones of choral lyric, while the didactic and explanatory parts are more akin to prose.

Adjectives. The extent to which the language of poetry is simple or artistically elaborated can be read off directly from the employment of adjectives—whether they are few or many, necessary to the thought or unnecessary, borrowed from normal language or artificially formed. Archilochus hardly uses adjectives at all: 141, except in his elegiac pieces: 143 f., 145; Sappho uses them more freely, but hers are all relevant to the context in which they appear. Anacreon employs adjectives in considerable quantity, but they always contribute some element of beauty: 294, 301. In choral lyric the addition of adjectives to the more important nouns was obligatory; in Bacchylides the practice becomes automatic: 453. In Simonides adjectives appear in the narrative sections, but in the argumentative parts they are rare or lacking (see above).

[3.3.] Continuous flow of archaic style.

[3.1–1.] *The law of continuity.* The unbroken continuity of subject matter and expression is for us the most remarkable feature of archaic style, since it runs counter to our demand for clear articulation and division in language.[1] This continuity does not arise from incapacity ("Men had not yet learned to articulate the text distinctly and to achieve that end by constructing periods with firm subordination of side-issues"); it is visibly the result of a specific stylistic ideal. Nothing is to be dragged along as a mere side-issue, since the writers wished to devote themselves unreservedly to every single thing that appeared on the scene (*see under* [4.1–1.]); there should not be an unpleasant hiatus in the presentation when it shifts from one subject to another; in real life also everything hangs together one way or another, and the connections between them should be visibly brought out rather than severed. For these reasons the archaic style makes a connection in sense, not merely in grammar, betweeen what has just ended and what is newly beginning; or rather, it passes gradually and by a gentle transition from the one to the other, and there is no definite point at which the former passes from sight and the latter engages our whole attention. Gradual transitions (e.g.): 129–130 (Hesiod), 176 (Sappho, "He . . . you . . . I"), 445 (Pindar).

---

[1] Epic narrative is already more continuous than our modern manner of narrating; and we find this hard to estimate properly, since we have no bump of continuity, as it were. This continuity is more marked in the speeches in epic, which are less subject to the stylistic despotism of the old epic manner, and are already 'archaic' in thought and language.

Whereas classical Greek style produces a series of separate pictures, of which each is tectonically ordered in itself like a static structure (thus e.g. Ibycus, who already deals in classical forms: 285–286), archaic style puts something in motion which can more fitly be compared with a dance (choral odes were in fact danced) with a sequence of figures passing one into another without a break: 505, cf. also: 226.

[3.3–2.] *Figures in continuous sequence.* Since in archaic thought opposites lay side by side and each of them demanded its counterpart (*see under* [4.7.]), the figures often form an oscillation between opposites, e.g.: 227 (Solon), 317 n. 2 (Heraclitus), 457 f. with n. 30, 472 n. 5, 493 n. 16, 498–499, 499 f. (Pindar).

Since archaic poetry liked to pass from the individual instance to the general rule and then again to illustrate the principle by the concrete example, the figures often form an oscillation between the general and the particular, e.g.: 112 f. (Hesiod), 320–321 (Simonides), 460 (Pindar).

Circling around the subject matter, so that different aspects of the same thing successively receive attention, e.g.: 105 (Hesiod) and Solon fr. 1: 232–234 (cf. also B. A. van Groningen, *La composition littéraire archaïque grecque*, 2nd ed., Groningen 1960, 94–97).

Ring composition (cf. W. A. A. van Otterlo, *Untersuch. über griech. Ringkomposition*, Amsterdam 1944). The thought takes a direction which leads it further and further from the previous context, but then comes round in a circle to its starting-point, in such a way that the original context can begin its progress again without a break, e.g.: 234 n. 34 (Solon), 447, 457 (Pindar).

The sentence-figures in Pindar have now been analysed by Asta-Irene Sulzer, *Zur Wortstellung und Satzbildung bei Pindar* (Zürich 1961).

[3.3–3] *Style of earliest Greek prose.* The reader is first given something tangible, and then more and more things are tacked onto it: 245 f. (Pherecydes and an inscription; on the bronze tablet the letters of the alphabet are shaped in accordance with the same principle); in the atomistic style of Hecataeus the chains of appended details consist of more or less independent clauses: 343–346.

[3.3–4.] *Unity of composition, how far achieved* (this we can only judge insofar as the pieces extant are of sufficient extent). The principle of placing all things on the same level as of equal value and of annexing things to each other on grounds of mere proximity could produce no rules for organization of a work as a whole. The degree of artistic unity over any long distance depended on the skill of the author and the strength of his artistic self-discipline, which in Alcaeus, for example, was unequal and in Solon slight (:199, 236). Ideally the course of the developing picture was directed along the right track without visible compulsion, and it rounded itself off into a unity as if by itself: 141 on fr. 79, 149 f. (Archilochus); 176–180, 184–187 (Sappho); 193–194, 197–198 (Alcaeus); 436–440, 501–504 (Pindar; *on the question of unity in Pindar see under* [2.2–6.3.]). The artistic unity of the sayings of Heraclitus rests not only on the masterly art of their construction, but also on the strict logic of the thought: 370.

[4.] EARLY GREEK THOUGHT

[4.1.] Dimensions of thought.

[4.1–1.] *Reality as a single layer.* Epic narrative is concerned in general with the visible side of the world and with the effects of things and happenings: 37 f., and it assumes that the nature of a man is wholly contained in what he does and suffers, speaks and 'knows': 78–82, 84 f.; it was not till later epic that man had anything below the surface: 89–93. In early lyric the thought and feeling of the poet moved essentially on one single level, and what he was occupied with presented itself to him in absolute actuality (*see under* [2.2–3.]): 150 (Archilochus), 176–179, 184 (Sappho), 199 (Alcaeus); for Archilochus even gods were physically present: 147, and so they were for Sappho: 177–180, 184 f.

In the early period there is seldom any mention of a depth of thinking or feeling (:144 'to the very bones', 176 'through my body'), and often the poets do not speak of intensity but of quantity (number, magnitude, repetition), e.g. 'many sorrows' in epic: 14 f., 'much' in Archilochus: 150 n. 49; the Homeric hero picks up a stone which many men could not lift (*Iliad*), a great warrior achieves by himself as much as many others: 153 n. 3 (Callinus); the importance of a thing makes it assume gigantic size to the imagination: 173 (Sappho fr. 111, 110), 194 (Alcaeus' brother killed a giant); repetition of love-experience: 179 (Sappho), 283 f. (Ibycus), 294 (Anacreon), 503 f. (Pindar).

[4.1–2.] *Reality as more than one layer.* Philosophy on the other hand assumes that reality is many-layered (two-layered) and enquires into what lies behind the phenomena, e.g.: 255 f., 397.

[4.1–3.] *Compromise between the two.* The world of epic is one-layered only as far as its stylistic principles are fully realized (*see under* [2.1–5.]); and the radicalism of early lyric was a phase that soon passed. Philosophical myths have in principle two layers—that which is narrated, and that which signifies; but the two layers are fused, e.g.: 98 n. 3. A further fusion is between the concrete foreground layer and the more remote abstract layer in so-called 'hylozoism', e.g. in the identification of 'water' with activity and spontaneity, *see under* [4.6–3.]. The little that we know of Anaximenes, leads us to suppose that in reaction he may have wished to force everything onto one stratum so as to interpret all happenings in mechanical terms: 268–270.

[4.2.] Myth as a medium of thought.

Terminology. '*Myth*' *is used here as necessary to signify one or more of three things:* (1) '*Mythology*', *i.e. the assumption of particular gods or powers, whether individually or in a system:* (2) *The recounting of important (not merely transitory) happenings in the world of gods and powers; and* (3) *Stories from heroic saga, or allusions to them.—On 'powers' see under* [4.6–4.].

[4.2–1.] *In general.* In the earliest period philosophical thoughts could only be defined in the form of myth; and those who used this form could not distinguish between the literal truth of what was said and its function as an image expressing something else: 98 n. 3.

Apocryphal myths of the gods: 74 n. 14, 96 n. 2, 99 n. 4. Mythical narratives and approaches to systematization in the *Hymn to Aphrodite*: 247–250. On apocryphal *myths of nature and the world see under* [2.3–1.].

Hesiod retells old myths, modifies them, and invents new; sometimes he means them literally, sometimes they are a deliberately chosen garment for what they signify: 97–108, 114–121. *On the Hesiodic genealogies see under* [4.5–1.]. The mythology of war in the post-Hesiodic *Shield*: 109–112. The increasing abstractness of myth after Hesiod is attested in Alcman: 252 f. Regression to a primitive level in Pherecydes: 243 f. and in Acusilaus: 347 f.

Stories from heroic saga appear in many lyric poets, either for their own sake:

197 f., or because they are connected with present circumstances (e.g. founding of an athletic contest referred to on occasion of a victory in it), or as an example to support a general statement, or as a parallel to a present happening (*on this head see under* [4.5–4.]), e.g. example: 195 f. (Alcaeus), parallel between Hiero and Philoctetes: 458 f. (Pindar). All the choral lyrists make use of legends of heroes and myths of gods: 440 f.

Sympathetic interpretation of the life of Helios: 212 f. (Mimnermus), 282 (Stesichorus). External nature thought of as in sympathy with man: 168 n. 25 (Alcman?), 316–317 (Simonides).

[4.2–2.] Presentation in myth-form.

[4.2–2.1.] *Examples of new creation of myths concerning nature and the gods.* Mythical interpretation of anomalies of nature: 457 f., 479–481 *bis* (Pindar); a river from their old home supplies the colonists in a new country: 287; the Athenians helped by their son-in-law Boreas: 318; the historical Croesus turned into myth: 465 n. 47.

The speaker's experiences seen in mythical form. The Muses come to Hesiod and call him to be a singer: 95 f.; Athene is present in one of Archilochus' battles: 147; Sappho experiences epiphanies of the gods: 177–179, 179 f., 184 f. (But in Parmenides the mythical elements of the treatment—the Heliad nymphs, the gate, Dike, the goddess etc.—are intended only as symbols: 350–353, 365–367.)

[4.2–2.2.] *Epic.* What took place in the singers' own time or before is incorporated into the epic action by retelling it as myth (just as later tragedy made its traditional material express ideas of its own age). Thus the conflicts of colonists and natives were projected into the Trojan war before there were any colonies: 47. A life like that led by the singer is ascribed to Odysseus as a wayfarer: 11. A change of attitude leads to the addition of an episode of much more modern type at the end of the *Iliad*, and reshapes the latter stages of the action in the *Odyssey*: 51 f. The change in ideals of human excellence between the *Iliad* and *Odyssey* is reflected in the epic narrative, when we are told that the inheritance of Achilles fell to Odysseus, and what conflicts and new possibilities arose from this change of values: 88–90.

[4.2–3.] *Manipulation of myth and saga.* Hesiod makes many innovations, *see under* [4.2–1.] *above*; he decides after all that there are two Erides: 114 f., and he extends the field of operations of the Muses: 107 f. Alcman makes a well-grounded alteration in the genealogy of the Muses: 254 n. 4; an unorthodox genealogy of Eros is found in Alcaeus: 199. Stesichorus, having second thoughts in his 'palinode', radically modifies the legend of Helen: 282 f.; Pindar corrects an objectionable myth: 478 f.; and in other places he expressly declares that he is suppressing something: 477 f.

[4.2–4.] *Movement away from myth.* Xenophanes rejects myths as fantastic and slanderous inventions of early times: 327 f., 330 f., or because they falsify the gradual development of human culture by representing it as a single gift from the gods: 333. Hecataeus zealously enlightens his readers by violent reductions of myth to natural terms: 346 f. Philosophy from Thales onward is free from myth: 255, and uses mythological terms very rarely (e.g.: 380 'Erinnyes', 396 ('Hades is Dionysus')); occasionally employing symbolic language (e.g.: 351 f.). Myth is secularized by the substitution of successful men of one's own time for the gods or figures of saga as guarantors of general truths: 238–240 (the Seven Sages).

[4.3.] Attitudes towards the miraculous.

[4.3–1.] Miracles and quasi-miracles are performed by the gods in epic, within certain limits: 70–75; even Hecataeus, who normally explains away the miraculous (:345 f.), has a miracle to relate in fr. 15 (:346); "Nothing is beyond belief that the will of the gods accomplishes" (Bacchylides in 468 B.C.): 463; "Many wonders are there" (Pindar, *Olymp.* 1, 28, from 476 B.C.).

Marvels of faraway places: 49–50 (*Odyssey*), 241–243 (Aristeas), 491–493 (Pindar).

Un-epic intimacy in entering into the details of traditional miracles, in Simonides: 315–317; in Bacchylides: 453 n. 23.

[4.3–2.] *Substitutes for miracle.* Ibycus celebrates not a true miracle, but a miraculous technical achievement: 287; Hecataeus tells of amazingly clever solutions to difficult problems: 344; so does Charon: 348 f.

[4.4.] Scientific thought.

[4.4–1.] *In general.* Strong tendency towards scientific thought in Hesiod: 117 f. (diseases lie in wait for human beings and fall upon them 'of their own accord'); 124 n. 22 (careful analysis of meteorological processes and their varied effects on plants, animals and man), 127 (the path of the north wind).

Achievements of the new empiricism from the beginning of the fifth century: 339–346. Alcmaeon's discovery that the brain, not the heart, is the central organ: 340; (a scientific experiment, leading, however, to a false conclusion, from the post-archaic period: 341 n. 4). The scientific element in speculative philosophy: 256 f. (*see also under* [2.3–3.]), e.g.: notion of a plurality of worlds: 265 (Anaximander); life-forms originated in the water: 265, 334 (Anaximander and Xenophanes); theories on the paths of the stars: 102 n. 13, 269 f.; on star-spheres or rings: 264 n. 23, 361 f.; conversely on stars as hollow bowls, to explain phases and eclipses: 213 n. 9, 386, but a correct explanation of the phases of the moon in Parmenides: 362.

[4.4–2.] Schematism in the supposition of a symmetrically divided earth: 343 (Hecataeus), *see also under* [4.7–4.]; in the supposed magnitudes and distances of the heavenly bodies: 264 (Anaximander).

[4.4–3.] Spontaneous origin or creation? For Hesiod and later philosophers the world had arisen spontaneously; for Heraclitus it was uncreated and existing from all time: 385. According to Xenophanes civilization was not bestowed readymade on our forefathers by the gods, but man constantly devises better things by his own efforts: 333.

In the primitive notions of Pherecydes, Zeus, Kronos and Chthonie ('the deeps of the earth') had indeed existed from all time, but Zeus first turned Chthonie into 'Earth' by giving her an embroidered garment with Ocean on it, and enveloping her in this: 243. According to Hesiod Zeus created the primal mother of women, Pandora: 117, and Semonides explains the different types of women as created by the gods: 202–206.

[4.4–4.] *Analogies drawn from the regularity of nature and applied to human life.* Assuming that the same logic and regularity hold sway in human life as in nature (:131 n. 32), Solon argues by analogies with the connection of cause and effect in the weather to place the responsibility for political events where it belongs: 228 *bis*, and to lay down the principle that every sin necessarily finds its retribution: 234 f. The same meteorological phenomena were already in epic similes put in parallel with happenings in the world of man, and an inclination to use them as an argument appears in *Iliad* 2, 396 f.: 43 f.

In one passage Pindar infers from the truth to inborn type in animal species that the qualities of a nation are uniform: 437 f.; while in other passages, on the contrary, the observation that the same fields or trees in different years bear sometimes excellent and sometimes scanty crops is placed in parallel with the appearance or non-appearance of noble qualities in succeeding generations within the one family: 472 f., 502.

On the analogy between human types and animal species see under [4.5-3.].

[4.5.] Classification and typology.

[4.5-1.] *Mutual relation under the image of human kinship.* The richest material comes from Hesiod's Theogony, where family pedigrees with many branches provide the backbone for an analysis of the world and of life: 99–103; the parent-and-child relation typifies different things, either subsumption of several notions or objects ('children') under a more general idea ('mother'), or alternatively, 'mother and children' means cause and effects, etc.: 103. Different pedigrees are assigned to the warlike powers that serve Zeus and to the evil ones: 99–103, as also to useful and harmful winds: 103 n. 19. As an afterthought Eris was divided into two sister powers of the same name, one good, one bad: 114 f. (But Hesiod also uses a local grouping as a symbol, as when he names Tartarus as the common dwelling-place of the negative powers, and symbolizes the boundary between Being and Not-being by the boundary between the upper world and Tartarus: 104–107.)

Both before and after Hesiod's time the symbol of blood-relationship was often employed; e.g. all rivers are the children of Oceanus, as in Hesiod: 102 n. 14, so in Acusilaus: 347. From a very early date the Muses were reckoned the daughters of Zeus: 234 n. 34, and in general terms many divine powers were called daughters of deities, e.g. 63 f., 131 n. 32, 182, 482, 484, 501; and in the same way powers having some real connection with each other were denominated sisters, e.g.: 131 n. 32, 482.

[4.5-2.] *Different entities as accidental varieties of one entity.* The bipolar cosmologies (see under [4.7-4.]) distribute all qualities so as to group them under one or the other basic quality; the two basic qualities include in this way many subvarieties, without losing their own identity. All this is explicitly stated by Parmenides in connection with his system of the world of appearance: 359–361; in other systems it is assumed as being obvious: 261 (Thales?), 263 (Anaximander); varieties of the negative in Hesiod: 102 f., in Parmenides: 369 n. 43.

The natural order, the biological order, and the moral order are reckoned not as independent systems but as varieties of one and the same universal order: 127, 131 n. 32, 256 f., 389 f.; in Parmenides consequently the same norms of 'righteousness' (*dike, themis*) operate in different areas: 352 f., 355, 366 (fr. 8, 32). *See also under* [5.1-2.]

[4.5-3.] *Human types in analogy with animal species.* In the complex world of human character and behaviour men steered themselves by the analogy of the animal kingdom, which with its various species had clear distinguishing marks for different types of nature and behaviour. This typology was made use of in the epic animal-similes: 41–43, and in the beast-fables of Hesiod: 121 f., Archilochus: 146–147, and Semonides: 207. The device was employed most systematically of all by Semonides when he distinguished eight types of women derived from eight different animals: 202–204, in which to some extent animal types are imported to the exclusion of real human types: 205.

[4.5–4.] *Reality presented under types drawn from myth and saga (see also under* [4.2–1.]). For everything occurring in the experience of our own day myth and legend provide prototypes: 488 n. 1, and poetry makes extensive use of this recourse to events of the same type in antiquity in order to interpret and glorify the present, since a high esteem attached to persons and events of the legendary past, cf. e.g. 437 n. 1, 489.

[4.6] Persons, things and elements understood as vehicles of forces; specifically forces as 'powers' (*see also under* [4.7] *on the dynamic of opposites*).

[4.6–1.] *The person as a force-field.* In the *Iliad* the person is understood not as something which, with its inner life, is set over against the outside world, but as an open force-field whose lines of force extend without limitation into the outside world, and which is equally open without reservation to forces acting upon the person: 79–82, and to influences coming from the gods: 68 f., 77 f., 80. This conception of the person is variously modified later (as in the *Odyssey*: 90; and Archilochus sees himself, in reference to the revenge which he was able to take, in the image of a hedgehog rolled into a ball, presenting its spines to the outside world: 140), but a considerable part of it holds its ground, cf.: 255 f. *See also under* [5.] *passim.*

Two individual points of interest. The gaze of the eye is thought of as an active ray: 480 n. 22. In the force-field of love the seat of the force is reckoned not as the feelings of the lover, but as the person from whom the attraction emanates: 180, 284, 450 f. n. 21.

A man's good qualities (or lack of them) are consequently shown in his effect on friends and enemies, e.g.: 234 (Solon fr. 1, 5f.), and is attested by the attitude of others to him, e.g.: 310 (Simonides, 'him do I praise and love'), and by his posthumous reputation, e.g.: 456 (Pindar on Croesus and Phalaris). (On the contrary, Archilochus declares that [for him and his like] there is no fame after death: 139.)

[4.6–2.] *Things as vehicles of forces.* To a large extent the objects of which poetry deigns to speak (*see also under* [3.1–2.]) are thought of not simply as objects, but as the vehicles of forces and achievements (referred to often by their epithets in epic: 34); thus in epic: 38 f. (cf. also: 28), 61 with n. 21, 69 f., 110 (the arrows in the *Aspis*); also: 179 f. (Sappho, fr. 2 and 81), 189 f. (Alcaeus, stockpile of weapons = 'war'), 326 (Xenophanes fr. 1, 4, 'jollity' = 'wine'), 351 n. 7 and 352 n. 9 (Parmenides), 453 f. and 456 (Pindar, the 'golden lyre'); particularly pointed: 136 (Archilochus fr. 2, the spear); also: 294 on the significance of Smerdiës' hair.

[4.6–3.] *Elements dynamically conceived in philosophical systems.* Even when the postulated basic elements, instead of having such names as 'void' and 'night' (Hesiod), 'light' and 'night' (Parmenides), 'hot' and 'cold' (Anaximander), are called e.g. 'earth' (Hesiod), 'water' (Thales) or 'sea', 'fire' (Heraclitus), the philosophers do not mean substances, but particular forces, qualities and modes of being: 295, 260 f.; even 'number' was understood dynamically by the Pythagoreans with reference to what it performed: 276. *See also under* [4.7–4.].

[4.6–4.] *Specific world- and life-forces conceived as independent divine 'powers'.* The 'powers': 481 f. The one-sided stylization of epic narrative pushes the powers into the background as compared with the personal deities, but they are not wholly absent: 61–64. Poets particularly concerned with the powers are Hesiod: 96 f., 99–105, 121 (Aidos and Nemesis); and Pindar: 481–487. *See also*: 111 f. (*Aspis*), 163 f. and 252 f. (Alcman), 351 (the Heliads) and 361 f. (Parmenides). Particular powers, e.g. the Muses: 95 f., 107 f. (Hesiod), 187 (Sappho), 254 n. 4 (Alcman), 44 f., 437 f. (Pindar); the Graces: 450 n. 21 (Hesiod), 164 (Alcman), 180, 182 (Sappho), 441 (Pindar); Ate: 61–64; Peitho: 296 (Anacreon), 469 (Pindar); Tyche: 439 f. (Pindar); Dike: 122 (Hesiod), 221 (Solon); Peace: 497 f. (Pindar). Gods as powers, e.g.: 53–61 (Epic), 322 f. (Simonides).

In reflecting on a situation the speaker discovers something new about a power, e.g.: 62 f. with n. 25 (epic speech), or he discovers the power itself, e.g.: 114 f. and 129 (Hesiod, v. 11 ff. and 764).

The commander's cry alerting his troops is transposed into the descent and battle-cry of the power *Eris*: 64 f. (*Iliad*); Pindar prays not to the god Helios, but to the power 'sunbeam': 480 f.

On powers as the 'daughters' of gods and on their mutual relations, see under [4.5–1.].

[4.7.] Thinking and feeling in opposites.

[4.7–0.] *In general terms.* An interplay of polar (absolute or extreme) opposites is a basic constituent of early Greek (especially archaic) thought and feeling; values, and qualities in general, could only be conceived together with their opposite: 54. Where values are concerned, this was in the very nature of things: 375 n. 10, since justice (e.g.) is only a value if there is injustice as the corresponding negative value. For qualities the basis of the view was that (for example) the opposition between hot and cold is more easily perceived than the difference between more hot and less hot, although the latter is more true physically: 333. It was a self-evident truth, for example, in the archaic period, that any living man had enemies just as much as friends.

[4.7–1.] *Contrasting foils.* As a consequence thought constantly operated with contrasting foils. The persons of the gods, eternal, heavenly, happy and free, are *inter alia* conceived as antitheses to those of men, mortal, earthly, unhappy and in thraldom, e.g.: 53–56 (epic), 309 (Simonides), 472 (Pindar); divine knowledge set against human stupidity: 201 f. (Semonides), 381 f. (Heraclitus); divine absoluteness against human limitations: 163 f. (Alcman), 304–310, 313 f., 318 (Simonides), 330–334 (Xenophanes), 340 (Alcmaeon), 472–476 (Pindar), etc. The gods maintain the contrast in all its rigour: 116 f. (Hesiod), their 'grudging spirit' imprisons man in his limitations: 476 f. (Pindar).

A former paradisal existence postulated as a foil to the present misery of mankind: 117 (Hesiod); imprisonment of (illusory) hope and free outlet for (real) evils: 118 (Hesiod); men who live for their belly contrasted with those who aspire to higher things: 96 n. 2 (Hesiod, referring to shepherds and poets), 490 n. 8 (Pindar). Depiction of peace as a foil to a scene of war: 110 f. (Shield of Heracles); chastity contrasted with unchastity in an epithalamium: 172 f. (Sappho); Thetis and Helen antithetical: 197 f. (Alcaeus); similarly Penelope and Clytaemnestra, Telemachus and Orestes in speeches in the Odyssey. *Ate* and the *Litai* antithetical: 61–64 (speech in the Iliad). The joy of the victor contrasted with the humiliation of the vanquished: 499 (Pindar); in choral lyric often one does not state a thing, but denies its opposite: 448 n. 18. *See also under* [3.3–2.].

Real or imaginary contrasts to spur the hearer to action: 171 f. (Callinus), 152 (Tyrtaeus), 208 (Mimnermus), 411 f. (Theognidea). The thought of old age and death as a spice to the enjoyment of life and youth: 195 f. (Alcaeus), 202 (Semonides), 209–211 (Mimnermus), 300 (Anacreon); cf. also 373 f. (Heraclitus).

[4.7–2.] *Opposing forces imminent in the same thing:* 411, wine is both bad and good (Theognidea); 183 'bitter-sweet' love (Sappho), 232 'sweet to friends, bitter to enemies' (Solon), 457 Apollo's lyre delights the Olympians and torments their enemies (Pindar); powers change into their opposite: 498 (Pindar). In Heraclitus the mean proportional unites opposing qualities: 381 f., 386.

[4.7–3.] *Life as a sequence of alterations between opposite extremes.* The labile nature of archaic man swings to and fro between extreme opposite states of feeling: *see under* [5.5.]. Correspondingly human life is seen as subject to the natural law of a sequence of radical transformations: fortune turns to misfortune, and misfortune often back to good fortune (cf. also, from classical tragedy, Sophocles, *Trach.* 129–135): 135 (Archilochus fr. 58), 143 (Archilochus fr. 67 and 7), 223 f. (Solon vv. 63–76), 439 f., 473 f. (*Isthm.* 3, 17 f.), 499 (Pindar). *See also under* [5.8.].

[4.7–4.] *Cosmic structure and cosmic process interpreted as the interplay of opposites.*
Structure of the earth. Since water is the opposite element to earth, an ambient river Oceanus was postulated as the boundary of the whole world: 102 n. 13, 212. Later the earth was divided into two opposed components, Asia and Europe, divided by bodies of water and each one divided into halves by a great river: 343, 441 f. n. 2.
Pairs of polar cosmic principles in philosophy. 'Water' (or 'sea') and earth as opposite principles (*see on this point under* [4.6–2.]) in Semonides (and Thales?): 205 f., 261; 'everything is earth and water' according to Xenophanes: 334. Doubling of the antithesis (earth/water/fire) in the pattern of the mean proportional (:380–383) in Heraclitus: 384–386. 'Hot' and 'cold' as cosmic principles in Anaximander: 262–265. 'Odd and even' in the doctrines of the Pythagoreans: 275 f. 'Light and night' (= being and not-being, knowledge and ignorance) constitute the world of appearance according to Parmenides: 358–364. Opposite powers as constituents of biological life in Alcmaeon of Croton: 340. The positive world (earth, sea and sky) opposed to the world of the negative (void, Tartarus and night), including their inhabitants and descendants on both sides, in Hesiod: 101–107; here not-being is the primary: 102 with n. 12, 105 f. *Aisa* and *poros* in Alcman: 163 f., 252 f.; cf. also: 314 n. 25 (Simonides).
Opposition itself is the basic principle of the universe and of life according to Heraclitus: 372–379 *et saepe; see under* [5.5–2.].

[4.7–5.] *What is between or behind the opposites?* Hesiod speaks of the 'threshold' between night and day: 104, and of a 'threshold' between not-being and being as the source of the positive worlds: 105–107. According to Anaximander the original source of opposites, from which they arise and into which they return, is an 'unbounded—undefined': 262–268, which is neutral: 374. According to Heraclitus opposites are the two sides of the same thing: 372 f., and God is the essence and the perpetual carrier of all opposing realities: 388 f.

[4.7–6.] *Abandonment of the polar principle in particular instances.* Opposites become less sharply antithetical in Anacreon: 297 f. Instead of opposite qualities we find varying degrees of the same quality playing a part in Anaximenes (greater or lesser compaction of a single element, 'air'): 268 f.; Xenophanes (gradations of sweetness, progress from lower to higher civilization): 332 f.; Simonides (gradations of 'goodness' in men): 308–311, 324. Health as an equilibrium between opposites in Alcmaeon: 340. A step on the road towards quantification is taken by Parmenides when he allows a complementary mixture of the opposites light and night, so that an excess of the one is compensated by a deficiency of the other: 359–364, but Parmenides himself considers such a line of thinking as fallacious.

5. EARLY GREEK MAN

[5.1.] The person.

[5.1–1.] *Structure and function of the person.* In the earlier period there is no dichotomy of the person into body and soul; instead, the organs of body, mind and soul issue immediately from the one self: 76–80, 82 f.; spiritual and physical behaviour are undifferentiated in a passage of Tyrtaeus: 158 f. A 'plan' puts itself automatically into action without having any threshold to pass: 78 f., so that the notion of a 'will' is not required: 392 n. 52. To 'know' things as if objectively, serving a wide range of concepts in connection with Homeric man: 81 f. Epic stylizes its characters uniformly, so that external beauty or ugliness correspond to the real nature of the person: 84 f. The new realism of Archilochus behaves differently: 137, while Tyrtaeus enjoins the Spartans to behave in a way corresponding to their appearance: 155 n. 7.

Later a 'soul' constitutes itself as a part of the living human being: 272 f; Anacreon speaks of the 'soul' that directs him: 298, and about the same time Pythagoras expounds the doctrine of metempsychosis: 272 f., 278 f.; for Heraclitus the existence of a 'soul' is self-evident: 379 f., 390, 392 n. 54. (There is no hint of a contrast between 'body' and 'soul' in the contrasts between achievements in battle and in counsel in the epics, or between strength and wisdom in Xenophanes: 329, or between animal and spiritual life in Hesiod: 96.)

[5.1–2.] *Man and the world.* Even after man had acquired a 'soul', there was at first no essential change in his relation to the outside world; he still remained an open force-field (see under [4.6–1.]) among other force-fields (see under [4.6–2] to [4.6–4.]). It was not until Socrates' time that man began to distinguish between himself as a moral being and the mechanical world outside; but to the very end of our period he still felt himself to be part of an overriding order of the whole, in which he participated actively and passively: 131 n. 32; he felt himself subject to the same laws as everything else: 256 f., *see under* [2.3–3.] *and* [4.5–2.].

Xenophanes contrasts mechanical nature not with human nature but with God: 333 f.; for Heraclitus also the contrast is not between man and nature, but between the unenlightened man, who only blindly obeys the Logos that rules all things, and the man who recognizes the Logos and communicates with it: 371–398 (passim).

[5.1–3] *Individuality.* Unitary types in epic: 34, 84 f. One must live according to what the gods have given, either for good or for evil: 39 n. 34, 67 n. 4. A man's inborn nature determines his achievements: 437, 482, 485 (Pindar); the inherited qualities can in any individual either break through or remain latent: 503 with n. 23 (Pindar). A man's nature becomes his destiny: 392 (Heraclitus). Individual temperament and behaviour as 'knowledge': 82 (epic) and capable of being learnt: 403, 417 (Theognidea).

[5.2.] Great men.

[5.2–1.] *In what does 'greatness' consist and how is it spoken of?* (A selection). Epic poetry freely bestows such epithets as 'god-like', but these are more sparingly

applied in the post-epic period. Sappho describes Hector and Andromache as godlike at their marriage-feast: 174; the bridegroom arrives on his wedding-day like
Ares, much taller than a tall man: 173; he gives the appearance of being like the
gods: 176. According to a dictum in the Theognidea, anyone who throughout
his life pays back good and evil in the same coin is as a god among men: 413 (cf.
also 'sweet to friend, bitter to foe' in Solon: 232); Archilochus takes pride in his
'great' art of returning harm for harm in frightful measure: 140. Solon is convinced that by his selfless discharge of the highest office he has kept his fame intact
and will surpass all other men: 224; Sappho is assured by Aphrodite that the
'great' gift of her poetry will keep her memory alive among all people: 188.
Theognis declares that his name is known among all men by his book: 402.
Hesiod tells of his being called by the Muses, who raised him above the animal
existence of a shepherd: 96. Alcman boasts of his coming from lofty Sardes: 160 f.;
Anacreon boasts of his mastery in the arts of love: 295 f., Xenophanes of his skill
or wisdom (sophia) which is useful to the community: (on the other hand, the
greatness of the Seven Sages (sophoi) lay in the personal success of their skilful
management: 239 f.). Parmenides brings in the goddess saying to him that as a
chosen favourite of Fortune he has trodden a path far from the steps of men:
352 f., and that the cosmology imparted to him cannot be replaced with a better
by any mortal: 359; Heraclitus represents himself as a man who sees among the
blind: 371 etc. By addressing his poems to Cyrnus, Theognis has given him wings
which will carry his name through the whole Greek world, and the poet expects
gratitude for it: 406; (contrariwise in the wishful dream of the aged and failing
Alcman the girls of his chorus lend him the lifting power of their wings by singing
and dancing his songs: 162). Bacchylides' ode to Hiero wings its way like an eagle
over all lands, since Hiero's greatness is so infinite and sublime; a similar thought,
sometimes on other images, recurs often in Bacchylides and Pindar: 458 with n. 33.
According to Pindar Hiero has gained by his victories such honour as no other
Greek has enjoyed: 454.

Epic has its own tricks of stylization to make characters great: 34–37, 85; but
the ideal of manly worth in the *Odyssey* is different from that in the *Iliad*: 85–90.
On greatness arising from abundance of vital force see under [5.4–1.], *from* areté *see under*
[5.7.]; *on the highest mortal good fortune see under* [5.8–1.], *on the fragility of human
greatness see under* [5.2–2.], *on achievement, esteem and reputation as criteria of greatness
see under* [4.6–1.].

[5.2–2.] *The leader type.* The unqualified and exclusive pursuit of power is
dramatically expressed by Solon, who puts it into the mouth of an opponent,
since he himself rejects ruling as tyrant as a personal ambition: 224–226. The
leader type is praised in one or two poems of the Theognidea: 414 f.; *cf. also under*
[5.7–1.] *on 'the good'.* Heraclitus heaps scorn on the dull masses of 'cattle' and on
democratic levelling, e.g.: 370, 390 f., 393–395; let the decisions be made by one
man only, if he be the best: 393.

[5.2–3.] *Pindar's conception of greatness.* Although Pindar accepts in all its rigour
the archaic doctrine of the fragility of mortal greatness (*see under* [5.5–1.]), the
men whom he celebrates are animated by a basic urge to scale the heights of
human felicity, and are tempted to aim at godhead; they take into account the
danger of being hurled back into the depths, and a middle way is despised: 460,
474–476.

[5.3] The Middle-class man; the lower strata.

[5.3–1.] *The middle-class man.* Hesiod's *Works and Days* does not go beyond the concerns of men who have a hard struggle for their daily bread: 116 f., 123–125, and among whom no disgrace attaches to physical work; the highest goal of human ability is to achieve a moderate 'wealth', which brings *areté* and prestige (κλέος) to those who are successful (v. 311–313); the qualities required are industry and intelligence (v. 289–298); also righteousness (*see under* [5.6–1.]) and a peasant respectability (v. 342–360, 707–723).

From the late seventh century onward Ionian lyric sinks more and more to a bourgeois level, *see under* [5.4–4.].

The sayings of the Theognidea are intended for the upper stratum, but their spirit is bourgeois rather than aristocratic: 623 f.

[5.3–2.] *The lower strata.* The scazons of Hipponax choose their grotesque heroes among the coarsest of mankind: 214–216. Parvenus are assailed with ridicule by Archilochus (:138 f.). Anacreon: 300 f., and Theognis: 404 f. As an antithesis (*see under* [4.7–1.]) to the higher life we find devotion to the belly censured in Hesiod: 96 n. 2, Theognis: 410 (v. 486), and Pindar: 490 n. 8.

[5.4.] Vital power (*see also under* [4.6–1.])

[5.4–1.] *Vital power shown in warfare.* The self gains strength by conflict with others: 84, 85 f. (epic); the wholly unrestrained vital forces of the epic gods: 53–56 (although in later epic a brutal indulgence of the passions was already considered as repellent: 51–53); vitality and enjoyment of a fight in Archilochus: 140–143, and Alcaeus: 188–194, 199 (but a slight attack of pacificism after a defeat: 193). Hipponax entertained his public with scenes of coarse wrangling and indecency: 214–217.

[5.4–2.] *Sappho.* Sappho's nature is passionate and volatile, but not pugnacious: 183, she yields without a struggle to whatever befalls her, lives through it, and transmutes it into the purest poetry, e.g.: 186–188, 211. The pleasures of the circle in which Sappho moved: 179–183.

[5.4–3.] *Innocent vitality.* Without becoming too much involved with each other, men could indulge themselves socially in eating and drinking and in the love of women or boys. The principle: δικαῖος ἐὼν τὴν σαυτοῦ φρένα τέρπε (Theogn. v. 749 f.: 408) and similar injunctions (:327 n. 4, cf. also: 211, Mimnermus) is strongly represented by Solon: 220 f., 229 f.; Solon does not want conflict, although he has waged it vigorously, but rather the means to eliminate conflict through self-discipline and social adjustment: 222; his healthy vitality contrasted with the weakness of Mimnermus: 217; his elegy on the ten phases in the natural course of a man's life: 232. Mimnermus considers life worth living only as long as the sex instincts can be satisfactorily gratified: 209–211. Without pleasure and health life is not worth living for Simonides: 322.

Instructions for behaviour at a party so that it shall be enjoyable for everyone: 410 f. (Theognis); good conversation and recitation of poetry are also part of a proper symposium: 327 f. (Xenophanes); the Theognis-collection in itself bears witness to this: 400–402. The drinkers revels in daydreams of greatness: 466–468 (drinking songs of Pindar and Bacchylides). A mature archaic elegance in form and content is exemplified by the party solos of Anacreon, many of which are concerned with love-play: 291–300; he also draws ironical portraits of personages of local reputation: 300–301.

Pleasure taken by the performers in the singing and dancing of choral odes: 160 n. 3.

[5.4–4.] Decline of vital power in Ionia from the late seventh century onward: 199 f. (But the mild gravity of Simonides' tone arises not from lack of vitality but from a clear-sighted humanity of a new kind: 323 f.).

[5.4–5.] *Love* (from the viewpoint of the speaker himself). Passionate love, felt by a man for boys or by a woman for girls, for different objects in succession. Sappho: 175–180, 182 f., 185 f.; Ibycus: 283–287, 287–290 (?); Pindar: 504 f., 431 (erotic undertone), 483 (both boys and girls).

A middle position between homosexual and heterosexual affection. Mimnermus: 209–212; Anacreon: 291–298; Theognis: 405 f. and book II (not discussed in the text).

Trifling love affairs with boys or girls. Solon: 218 (fr. 20), 230 (fr. 14).

[5.5.] Archaic man as 'a creature of the day'.

[5.5–1.] *'Ephemeral' man.* Just as archaic man saw the world as the battleground of absolute opposites (*see under* [4.7.]), so his emotional life was dominated by extreme opposites; every change in his fortunes radically transformed his nature, so that his identity became questionable, and he recognized himself as a mere product of the 'day' that God sent him: 133–136, 150–151 (Archilochus). He was tossed to and fro between proud confidence and humble abasement: 143 (Archilochus), 499 (Pindar); his heart swells and shrinks in turn: 413 (Theognidea).

By the fragility of what he is and what he does man reveals himself as a nothing: 472–474, a shadow in a dream: 499 f. (Pindar); his mind is begirt with errors: 494 (Pindar); Zeus has not set any distinguishing mark on the hand of mortals: 502 (Pindar); the higher power has not taught us the way to find favour with the gods: 421 (Theognidea).

Man is helpless against passions (:182) and temptations: 313 n. 22; against misfortune (cf.: 309 ἀμήχανος συμφορά), *see under* [5.8–3.], and quite helpless when in the grip of misfortune, *see under* 5.8–2.

[5.5–2.] *Means of alleviating misfortune.* (a) The divine gift of victorious endurance (τλημοσύνη, 'long-suffering', 'composure'), by which one rejects grief and throws oneself, by a swing of the pendulum, into pleasure and enjoyment: 143 f. (Archilochus); in epic the powers of endurance of Odysseus take the form of a control exercised by the calculating reason over the violent emotions of the heart: 87 f. (b) Self-control is made easier by the recognition that change is the law of life: 143 *bis* (Archilochus), 421 (Theognidea); for Heraclitus the recognition of the nature and necessity of opposites makes possible a clear and definite attitude towards reverses and misfortunes: 377 f.; from the realization that human capabilities are limited Simonides derives the principle that no man should be blamed for something against which even the most able could do nothing: 307–311. (c) Damping down the oscillations of emotions: 143 (Archilochus), or adapting oneself philosophically to changing situations: 134 (Odyssey), 475 f. (Pindar). Enjoyment of such pleasures as the day brings: 475 f. (Pindar), cf. 164 f. (Alcman); living on two levels, taking the long and the short view at once: 466 (Bacchylides). (d) The wise and noble man shows his good fortune to the world and conceals his misfortune in darkness: 476 *bis* (Pindar); similar advice on practical grounds: 421 (Theogn. 355 ff.).

[5.6.] Morality.

[5.6–0.] *The question posed.* What is the basis, in feeling or ideology, of the conviction that moral behaviour is demanded of men and is of the greatest value for them, although there is yet no such thing as a conscience (:84, 221 n. 8, 224) and no Decalogue? By way of illustration we will outline the notions of Hesiod and Solon.

[5.6.1.] Hesiod (the verse references are to the *Works and Days*).

[5.6–1.1.] *Instinctive feeling for justice* is represented by the postive and negative pair of ideas *aidos* (i.e. respect for rules and limits) and *nemesis* (i.e. contempt for or violation of the norms of good behaviour; the meaning 'punishment' is later); if man is abandoned by these two, all protection against evil has gone: 121, 122 f. The peculiar value which Hesiod attaches to productive work (*see under* [5.3–1.]) is connected with his doctrine that the *nemesis* of men and gods is directed against the lazy as well as the wicked, vv. 289–311. The man who is true to his word, righteous and good finds 'favour' (*charis*), cf. v. 190 f.

[5.6–1.2.] According to the general view justice as such possesses an *objective obligation*; it is one of the aspects of the all-pervading world-order: 131 n. 32.

[5.6–1.3.] *The gods, and the power* Dike (*Justice*) *herself, help the rules to become effective.* Zeus as the guardian of justice: 114; it was he who gave justice to man, and who made preying upon each other the rule only for brute beasts: 122 f.; his eye watches over questions of justice, when he chooses to do so: 122. The maiden Dike, the daughter of Zeus, is honoured and respected (*aidoie*, from *aidos, see under* [1.1]) by the gods in Olympus; she tells her father of every transgression, so that he may punish it, v. 256–260; Justice (*Dike*) triumphs at the last over *hybris* (that is, arrogant violation of another's rights), v. 217 f.; *Dike* brings destruction to unjust judges who distort the law, v. 220–224. Zeus makes a community prosper in which justice and integrity are practised, and visits with pestilence and destruction the whole community for the sins of individuals, v. 225–247; the rewards for honesty or the punishment for oath-breaking may be visited on the man's posterity, v. 282–285. There are 30,000 invisible watchers observing the just and unjust actions of men, v. 249–255: 122.

[5.6–1.4.] *Opposing forces.* As forces compelling or tempting man to sin, Hesiod mentions: *hybris* (*see above*, [–1.3.]); the temptation of a gain, which ensnares the mind so that *aidos* is suppressed (?) by her opposite, and a man gains great wealth by violence or 'tongue-robbery' (fraud), v. 321–324; the sexual urge, v. 328 f.; and a 'wickedly contentious, hateful ardour, rejoicing in injury' (clearly distinct from the 'ardour' shown in service to the gods: 99 f.), v. 195 f. Cf. similar later lists: 313 n. 22. In a corrupt society might goes before right, v. 202, 212, the law of the stringest prevails, and the evil-doer is in honour, v. 190–192 (:121 f.).

[5.6–2.] Solon.

[5.6–2.1.] Terms for an instinctive apperception of justice are not found in the extant verses; at most fr. 23, 20 (:224): 'It does not please me (to behave with despotic force, or to place the bad on a level with the good)'. But on the other hand his hymn-like eulogy of good order is filled with strong emotion: 222.

[5.6–2.2.] *The power* Dike *and* Zeus 'surely' (:222) *help the moral rules to become effective.* Dike is silently aware of all that is done, and brings about retribution: 221 with n. 8. Zeus infallibly sends punishment sooner or later upon the evil-doer or his posterity: 234 f.

[5.6–2.3.] *Virtue rewarded and vice punished by their natural consequences.* Unrighteous conduct has a fatal flaw (*ate*) attached to it, which develops in the course of time until the catastrophe is reached (a similar view in Hesiod, *Works and Days* 215 f.) : 234 f.; asocial behaviour brings a political catastrophe that strikes even into the private life of every citizen: 221 f. (*see under* [5.8–4.]); good order masters all evil impulses and establishes justice in all things: 222.

[5.6–2.4.] *Solon's personal morality* will be witnessed before the judgment seat of time by his historic achievements: 226; he has discharged the highest office without selfishness or party spirit: 224–226, in order not to stain his reputation, and to raise himself above all other men: 224. He prays to the Muses for a good reputation among all men: 234 f. with n. 35.

[5.6–2.5.] *Opposing forces.* Hybris: 233 (fr. 1, 16); 'satiety' (self-satisfaction), 220 (fr. 3, 9; also fr. 5, 9); love of gain: 220 (fr. 3, 6), 223 (fr. 4, 4), 233 (fr. 1, 11 ff.): which lays hands on public and consecrated property: 221 (fr. 3, 12); absence of moral feeling: 220 (fr. 3, 7); unrestrained ambition: 224 (fr. 23, 1–7).

[5.6–3.] Things of note from other authors (*see also under* [5.7.]).

[5.6–3.1.] *Positive.* Glorification of the moral achievement of the warrior in actual battle above all other achievements and qualities: 338 (Pseudo-Tyrtaeus). Righteousness as the essence of *areté*: 417 f. (Theogn.). The righteous man does only good to others: 417 (Theogn. v. 547 f.). To injure no one: 420 (Theogn. v. 1153 f.); *see also under* [5.4–3.]. One should not revile enemies or praise friends unless they deserve it: 417. (Theogn. v. 1079 f.).

[5.6–3.2.] *Negative.* Poverty drives a man to lie and cheat and fight, no matter how alien such things may be to his nature: 312 (Theogn.). The same norms do not apply to men in security and to a nation which is facing catastrophe: 421 (Theogn. v. 235 f.).

[5.7.] *Areté* and 'good' or 'bad' men; the beautiful' and the 'ugly'.

[5.7–1.] *Typical definitions.* For the complex notion of human 'goodness' (:417–420, *see also under* [5.2.]) there are four main classes of definition.

(a) *Areté* is first and foremost martial prowess: 157 (Tyrtaeus, fr. 8, 14), 337–339 (Pseudo-Tyrtaeus), 417 (Theogn. v. 867 f.); 'good men' is the title of honour of those fallen in battle: 320 (Simonides), 474 (Pindar).

(b) *Areté* (and the respect that goes with it) is possessed by anyone who achieves successes thanks to his own abilities and the favour of the gods: 123 (Hesiod); 'Every man is good who has succeeded, and every man bad who has failed. But most often (are they successful) and do best, whom the gods love': 309 (Simonides). Since all men are liable to failure, they are all bad: 229 (Solon), and only God is good: 308 (Simonides). On 'bad by bad luck' see also under [5.8–2.].

(c) *Areté* defined as 'a passion for the beautiful' (for all that is noble, great and refined), coupled with the 'power' to realise it in one's own life: 418 f. (Theogn. and Pindar).

(d) *Areté* in a moral sense, as righteousness, the eschewing of all that is ignoble: 418 (Theogn. v. 1177 f. and 145 ff.). Bad men behave in a vulgar way, trespass on other people's rights, and talk of evil things: 417 (Theogn. v. 307).

(e) Where adjectives are concerned, we may add: 'the good' and 'the bad'.

meaning the upper stratum of society (possessing the power: 403, Theogn. v. 34) and the (uneducated, unreliable) lower stratum: 225 (Solon), 403–405, 412, 419 (Theogn.); cf. also: 156 f. (Tyrtaeus fr. 8 on loss of status).

[5.7–2.] *The doctrine of Simonides:* 307–314. It is not possible for any man to be 'good' and remain so; therefore we should love and honour the few who, as 'healthy' men, act intelligently and skilfully and understand justice which benefits the community; ill success (type b) which even the cleverest cannot avoid, and actions contrary to good morals (type d) but taken against one's will, cannot be held against a man (on the last see also: 470, Pindar).

[5.7–3.] *Further individual points. Areté* lasts as long as wealth is the only *areté*: 418 (Theogn.). Only a few possess *areté* as well as beauty: 419 (Theogn. v. 933 f.); on *kalokagathia* see also 233 n. 33 (Solon). *Areté* (probably type b) is attained by avoiding exaggerated ambitions: 419 (Theogn.). Cleverness (or wisdom) and *areté* as the highest goals: 407 (Theogn.). One should wish for no other *areté* than the favour of destiny and the goodwill of the gods: 420 (Theogn.); one should not wish for distinction through *areté* or through riches, but only good luck: 420 f. (Theogn.).

(Moral) badness is not necessarily inborn in a man, but may have been acquired by associating with bad men: 417, cf. 403 (Theogn.).

Simonides speaks of *areté* with timid reverence: 318 n. 24. According to Pindar, *areté*, if she is to find followers, needs recognition by contemporaries and posterity: 490. The question of the unity of *areté*: 337 n. 1; it is a unity, according to Pindar: 487 f. For Simonides the good man must be 'foursquare in arms and legs and understanding, put together without flaw': 308.

[5.7–4.] *The 'beautiful' and the 'ugly'*. In the *Iliad* Thersites is represented as being just as hideous in appearance as he is objectionable in his behaviour: 85. The expressions 'beautiful' and 'ugly' (etymologically = 'disgraceful') are also used for things laudible or objectionable in a moral view: 154–158 (Tyrtaeus). The motto 'that which has beauty is loved' (Theognis v. 17) is probably meant in a moral sense: 402.

Sappho's quest for what is most beautiful is aimed at that which most pleases and elevates those who look upon it: 185 f. By 'the beautiful' in *Pyth.* 1, 86 Pindar means kingly power: 460; likewise in Solon ἐσθλά = power and wealth: 224 with n. 12. In the formula ἐρᾶν καλῶν καὶ δύνασθαι (*above* [–1. type c]) the καλά embrace all that is excellent. Pindar's notions of value and valuable: 485–488.

[5.8.] Good and bad luck.

[5.8–0.] *Expressions for 'good luck' in Pindar*, e.g. εὐζοία, εὐαμερία, μείλιχος αἰών, γλυκὺς βίοτος, ἁβρότας, εὐφροσύνα, εὐθυμία, ὄλβος (ὄλβιος, μάκαρ, μακαρίζω). τέρψις (τὸ τερπνόν), εὐδαιμονία, εὐτοχία (Τύχα).

[5.8–1.] *In what does good luck consist?* It is looked for in different directions and on different levels, e.g.:

In power and wealth, in the ability to achieve what one wants ('revenge expands the heart': 413, Theogn. v. 362; achieving something desired makes us happy: 499 Pindar); in status and prestige (the exiled Alcaeus longs for the folkmoot and the council: 191); Solon prays for a variety of things: the favour of the gods, good reputation, effective influence over friend and enemy, and possessions: 232 f.; 'He possesses all who has these two: shining success, and the praise of men': 485 f. (Pindar). *See under* [4.6–2.], [5.2.].

Or in the possession of *areté*, *see under* [5.7.].

Or in the indulgence of vital force, in friendly social rejoicings (a dinner-party with one's friends amounts to 'culling the hallowed flower of goodly living' according to Pindar: 491), in the 'beautiful' activities of which Sappho reminds her friend in fr. 94: 179. *See under* [5.4.].

Or in the domestic happiness of the landowner who has four things: children, horses, hounds, and a guest from abroad (for conversation and to keep in touch with the outside world?): 230 (Solon fr. 13); or in a happy marriage: 204 (Semonides).

Or the conclusion is reached, in face of the uncertainty of our destiny, that 'happy is he who cheerfully weaves the day to its end without tears', 164 (Alcman); mere freedom from pain: 420 (Theogn. v. 1153–56). See under [5.5–2(d)].

[5.8–2.] *Ill fortune*. List of various misfortunes that afflict humanity: 201 f. (Semonides). Old age as a misfortune: 209–211 (Mimnermus). Poverty, and the helplessness which it brings, a great and incomparable evil: 196 *bis* (Alcaeus), 312, 405 f., 409, 412 (Theogn.). Misfortune destroys our thoughts and character: 134 f. (Archilochus); the necessities of poverty corrupt men against their will, even the virtuous: 312 (Theogn.). Misfortune shames us, because it makes us small, contemptible, powerless, 'bad': 308 f., *see under* [5.7–1(b)]; Simonides is the first to remove the stigma from undeserved misfortune, *see under* [5.7–2].

Posthumous fame in epic poetry earned by misfortunes: 15 (*Iliad*).

[5.8–3.] *Good and ill fortune as gifts of the gods and powers, of destiny or chance* (a brief selection). Zeus distributes pleasures and pains: 118 (*Iliad*), on which: 476 f. (Pindar). Divine interference in human actions and fortunes in the epics: 64–75; fate in the epics: 56–58. Pieces of good luck as 'works of the gods': 138 f. (Archilochus); as gifts of Hermes: 216 (Hipponax). Zeus raises up and casts down: 114 (Hesiod); the gods overthrow and lift up: 135 (Archilochus); 'glory sent by Zeus': 499 (Pindar). The man who is enjoying good fortune seeks piously to deprecate the 'grudge' of the gods: 459, 476, 500 f. (Pindar). Victory in athletic contests is supposed to be given by the god of the place where the games are held: 497 (Pindar) or by the Dioscuri: 434. Our efforts cannot command success, but it is decided by gods and by fate: 235 f. (Solon); it is one's inborn fate that turns the scale: 482 (Pindar, *Nem.* 5, 40). The power Elithyia (birth) ordains a child for greatness and fame: 482 (Pindar); Tyche, daughter of Zeus, is the bestower of happy dispensations: 439 f. (Pindar); only good luck is necessary for a man: 'pray for good fortune alone': 420 (Theogn. v. 130).

Zeus has once for all laid the burden of labour on man, has exposed him to evils, and given him woman: 116–119 (Hesiod); Zeus created women (or wives) as the worst of all evils: 204 (Semonides).

[5.8–4.] *Deserved ill fortune*. Solon explains Athens' plight as arising not from a divine dispensation, but as deserved by the citizens themselves by folly and anti-social behaviour: 220, 228; the transitoriness of prosperity arises not from divine wilfulness, but is a necessary consequence of men's insatiable desire for gain: 236. According to Pindar many are deprived of prosperity by the hollowness of their pretensions, while others miss the reward ready for them through too much diffidence: 502. On misfortune as a consequence of, or punishment for, evildoing, *see under* [5.6.].

Index B: Greek Words

535

μάρπτειν, 473 n. 9
μένος, 69; 70; 77; 78 f. and n. 8; 80;
306; 361 (fr. 11, 3)
μετάστασις, 304 n. 2
μέτρον, 127; 474 n. 11
μήδεσθαι etc., 79
μυχός, 'inward parts' (not 'corner'),
244 n. 12

ναυσίστονος, 'fighting at sea', 456 n. 24
νέμεσις, νεμεσσάειν, 84; 531 Index A
[5.6–1.1]
νόος, νοεῖν, 78; 82; 134; 135; 306
(v. 581); 310 n. 17; 331 n. 11

παρίστασθαι and προσίστασθαι, 363 n. 36
πάτος, not 'path', 352 n. 10
πείθειν, Πειθώ, 296 n. 15
πελάζειν, 'to bring close', 'to arrive at',
not 'to approach', 355 n. 16
πέρας (πεῖρας), in Parmenides, 356;
361 (fr. 11, 7); 'boundary', or
'threshold' between being and not-
being, 105–107 (Hesiod); ἄπειρος,
262 n. 22; 284 f.
πολύτλας, see τλῆναι
Πόρος, as a universal power in Alcman,
163 f.; 253
πρόσσω καὶ ὀπίσσω, 466 n. 49

ῥαψωδός, not 'stitcher of songs', 17 n. 19;
another misinterpretation, 394 n. 57

σοφός, of one who has practical sagacity, 239; σοφία 322; 329; 407; 415
σύνδικος, 456 with n. 26
συνείδησις, 221 n. 8

Τέκμωρ, as a universal power in Alcman, 164; 253
τέλος, e.g. 'actuality', 210
τιμή, the 'value' in that which is of
value, in Pindar, 486 f.
τλῆναι, τλημοσύνη 87 f.; 530 Index A
[5.5–2(a)]

ὑπέρδικος, 'standing up for the right',
492 n. 15

φίλος, φιλεῖν, 82 f. (epic); ὅττι καλόν, φίλον
ἐστί, 402 (Th.)

χάος, 101 n. 11
χάρις (γλώσσης χάριν in Hesiod), 128 n. 26

ψυχή, 527 f., Index A [5.1–1]

Words denoting 'good luck' in Pindar,
533, Index A [5.8–o]
Words denoting acts of the will, 392 n.
52

Index C. Alphabetical Index

The main references are cited first. A comprehensive coverage has been aimed at for those authors in the surviving literature who have either been translated or explicitly referred to in the text of the book, as well as for the decisive testimonia. Other references have only been included if they lead to information directly relevant to the passage or topic in question, whether by explanation or by referral to a certain context.

Abstract nouns: 482 n. 1

Aeschines 3, 211: 412 n. 26

Aeschylus (numbering of verses after Murray),
Ag. 182 f.: 164 n. 12
Choe. 265–267: 128 n. 26
319 f.: 164 n. 12
Suppl. 1001: 483 n. 5
Prom. Prologue: 100 n. 7
v. 135: 163 n. 10
v. 293–297: 128 n. 26
Elegy on the fallen of Marathon: 318

Acusilaus of Argos (2 *F. Gr. Hist.* Jacoby): 347 f.
T. 6 and F. 1; 4; 5; 6; 13; 14; 22: 347

Alcaeus: 188–199; 219
Fragments (numbered after Lobel-Page)
6: 190
10: 199
34: 194
38: 195
reconstruction of v. 5 and 6: 196 n. 13

39, 7–10: 197
42: 198
44: 198
48, 10: 193 f.
50: 195
63, 7: 193
69: 193
70: 193, 192 n. 6, 223
73: 190, 194 n. 11
74, 6: 460 n. 39
112, 10: 196
115(a): 197
117(b), 27: 405 n. 10
129: 192, 181 n. 30
130: 191
249: 197
283: 197 f.
286: 197
296(b): 197
298: 198
306 (14) and (16): 190
326+208 col. II: 190
327: 199
332: 191, 194 n. 11
335: 194
338: 194, 293 n. 8
341: 197
347: 195, 385 n. 38
348: 192, 223

(Pindar)

Supposed reference to his opponents Simonides and Bacchylides: 458 n. 33

Ideas of Heraclitus: 375 n. 11, 471, 483, 498

Uses the thought of Simonides: 323 n. 38, 436 n. 22, 490 n. 7

Anticipation of Plato: 485–488

Pindar's art: 485–496

Further aspects:

inexhaustible variation of a few typical lines of thought: 496 n. 25

variation of the style: 470 n. 8

peculiarity of the opening words of the poems: 471 n. 1

thoughts echoed from strophe to strophe: 449 n. 20, 494 n. 21

the processional poem *Nem.* 2 was to be sung from beginning to end as often as necessary: 429 n. 6

static images endowed with symbolic power: 431, 445, 446, 469, 495

theatrical stylisation: 446 n. 12

one case of classical stylisation: 502

use of symbols: 437 n. 3, 438, 461 n. 39 ('smoke'): 468, 493

words for values: 486 n. 10

the so-called Priamel as an indicator of values: 459, 459 n. 36, 471, 486–487, 561 (fr. 406)

negative modes of expression: 448 n. 18, 464 n. 44

the 'uncalled one': 448, 458, 476, 500

Pittacus: 191–193, 218, 223, 239

Plato

The Laws

2, 666e: 470 n. 7

12, 957c, 5–7: 391 n. 50

Gorgias 490a: 393 n. 56

Critias 109b: 388 n. 43

Phaedo 60b and 70e: 374 n. 9

71b–c: 373 n. 8

79c and 82a: 390 n. 49

81e: 383 n. 31, 492 n. 14

82e: 383 n. 32

109a: 358 n. 23

Phaedrus 243b: 283 n. 7

Meno 77b ff.: 418 n. 40

Republic 81a–c: 278

VI/VII 506e, 508b, 517b–c: 486 f.

VII (the parable of the cave): 383 n. 28, 383

VIII, 546a: 473 n. 9

Symp. 202a: 335 n. 20

Theaet. 161c: 382 n. 25

Tim. 31b ff. (the twofold proportional equation): 383 n. 28

51a–b: 383 n. 29

70c and 91a: 385 n. 38

Anticipation of Plato in Simonides (the sight of the good): 314 n. 24

in Pindar's idea of values: 485–488

Pliny, *Nat. Hist.* 36, 12: 215 n. 1

Plotinus, *Enn.* 5, 1, 4: 356 n. 17

Plutarch

Mor. 98c: 381 n. 21 and 22

363c: 383 n. 31, 492 n. 14

745c: 164 n. 12

787c: 461 n. 39

957a: 381 n. 21

Pollux 3, 36: 244

3, 42: 173

Polybius 11, 29, 9–11: 228 n. 21

Polyclitus (the 'quadratic' canon): 308 n. 11

Propertius 1, 9, 23 f.: 483 n. 5

1, 15, 12: 228 n. 21

Protagoras

(anticipation of *homo mensura* in Sappho): 187

Pythagoras and the Pythagoreans: 270–279

Pytheas, fr. 7a 1 Mette (in Strabo 2, 4 1): 106 n. 24

Quintilian, *Inst.* 10, 1, 62 (judgement on Stesichorus): 283 n. 6